Forgotten Books takes the uppermost care to preserve the entire content of the original book. However, this book has been generated from a scan of the original, and as such we cannot guarantee that it is free from errors or contains the full content of the original. But we try our best!

Truth may seem, but cannot be:
Beauty brag, but 'tis not she;
Truth and beauty buried be.

To this urn let those repair
That are either true or fair;
For these dead birds sigh a prayer.

Bacon

Hinchliff.

WORKS

OF

APULEIUS

COMPRISING THE

METAMORPHOSES, OR GOLDEN ASS,

THE GOD OF SOCRATES, THE FLORIDA,

AND

HIS DEFENCE, OR A DISCOURSE ON MAGIC.

A NEW TRANSLATION.

TO WHICH ARE ADDED,

A METRICAL VERSION OF CUPID AND PSYCHE,

AND

MRS. TIGHE'S PSYCHE,
A POEM IN SIX CANTOS.

LONDON : GEORGE BELL AND SONS, YORK STREET,
COVENT GARDEN.

BIOGRAPHICAL INTRODUCTION.

The author of the celebrated romance of "The Golden Ass" lived in the early part of the second century, under the Antonines. By most modern biographers he is called *Lucius* Apuleius, or Appuleius, but the authority on which they assign him that prænomen is very questionable. He was a native of Madaura, an inland African town, and he styles himself, in allusion to its position on the borders of two kingdoms, "a half-and-half Numidian and Getulian;" adding that, in that respect, he resembled the elder Cyrus, who was "a Semi-Median and Semi-Persian." Madaura, after having formed part of the kingdom of Syphax, was bestowed by the Romans on their ally Masinissa, and being eventually resumed and peopled by veterans, it obtained the rank and immunities of a "colony," and rose to considerable splendour. The father of Apuleius filled the office of duumvir, the highest magisterial dignity in his native place, and bequeathed at his death the sum of nearly two millions of sesterces to his two sons, one of whom, the subject of our present inquiries, succeeded to his office. These facts we learn from the direct testimony of the son in his Apologia or Defence; but most of the biographers of Apuleius add other particulars, drawn from the assumption that, under the character of Lucius, the imaginary hero of the story of "the Golden Ass," the author has related sundry details of his own personal history. Upon this supposition, we are told that our author's prænomen was Lucius, that his father's name was Theseus, his mother's Salvia, and that she was of a Thessalian family, and descended from the illustrious Plutarch; furthermore, that Apuleius was ignorant of the Latin language until he visited Rome, where he acquired it

without the aid of a master; and that by the time he arrived at
the capital of the empire, he had so completely dissipated his
patrimony, as to be under the necessity of selling his clothes, in
order to defray the cost of his initiation into the mysteries of
Osiris. This latter statement is at variance with the account
which he gives of his fortune in the Apologia, where he says,
merely, that it had been, "modice imminutum," somewhat im-
paired; the other particulars may or may not be true. There
is, no doubt, such a resemblance between Apuleius and Lucius,
both as regards mental characteristics and outward incidents, that
we can hardly suppose it to be fortuitous. It is highly probable
that the author drew his hero from his own likeness; but on the
other hand, it is absurd to look for literal fidelity in such a por-
trait. It is not likely, for instance, that Apuleius would have
deemed it consistent with decorum to speak of himself, his father
and his mother, by their real names, in so frolicsome a work of fiction
as "The Golden Ass," since we find, that when addressing the sons
of a friend in some complimentary verses of a peculiar character,
such as the habits of his day allowed, he thought it his duty to
invent pseudonymes for the objects of his flattery.*

Apuleius received the first rudiments of education at Carthage,
renowned at that time as a school of literature, and there he
adopted the Platonic system of philosophy, in which he perfected
himself by his subsequent studies at Athens. There, too, he
laid the foundations of that copious stock of various and profound
learning, through which he became the most distinguished lite-
rary character of his age. Still thirsting for knowledge, and
impelled, like his own Lucius, by an insatiable curiosity to ex-
plore all that was hidden from the vulgar gaze, he travelled
through Greece, Asia, and Italy, and became a member of
many religious fraternities, and a proficient in their mys-
teries. After his return to Africa, he was about to renew his
travels, and on his way to Alexandria was taken ill at Oëa, a
maritime town, which some geographers have identified with
the modern Tripoli. A young man, named Pontianus, whom

* See Defence, p. 256.

he had known as a fellow-student at Athens, invited the invalid to become the guest of his mother, a wealthy widow, named Pudentilla. In making this hospitable proposal, Pontianus had more in view than the comfort of his friend, and the restoration of his health. Pudentilla was herself also an invalid, being affected with a chronic complaint, which had lasted thirteen years—the duration of her widowhood—and for which her medical advisers all agreed in prescribing marriage as a remedy. The son, seeing his mother prepared to try the effect of that nostrum, was desirous that her new husband should be one of his own choosing. Accordingly, he begged Apuleius would do him the favour to become his stepfather, putting the affair to him, says the latter, in the light of an onerous service, such as one might ask a friend and a philosopher to undertake. The widow was neither young nor handsome, but she was virtuous, fond, and very rich. Apuleius, if not poor, was, at least, reduced in circumstances, in consequence of his long-continued course of study, his protracted residence in foreign countries, and various acts of generosity towards his friends and instructors; moreover, he was a philosopher; so in fine he married the widow.

But this act involved some unpleasant consequences. Before it was accomplished, Pontianus had married the daughter of one Rufinus, who, long eager to secure to his son-in-law as large a share as possible in the fortune of Pudentilla, did all he could to prevent her marriage with Apuleius; and in this he was seconded by Pontianus, over whom he had acquired such an influence, as to make him look with aversion on the success of his own project. But notwithstanding all opposition, Pudentilla persisted in her resolution; and soon after her marriage, Pontianus died. His uncle, Æmilianus, then united with Rufinus in endeavours to ruin Apuleius. They gave out that he had poisoned Pontianus, that he was a magician, and had gained the affections of Pudentilla by witchcraft. They even prosecuted him upon the latter charge, and the cause was tried at Sabrata, before Claudius Maximus, the proconsul of Africa. It was on that occasion he delivered the Defence, a translation of which

will be found in this volume. It is a clever and amusing per·
formance, having nothing of the tragic earnestness of a man who
is pleading for his life ; on the contrary, Apuleius appears, from
first to last, to have felt quite secure as to the issue, and to have
flung himself with great glee into a contest which afforded him
such capital opportunities for displaying his wit, his learning, and
his powers of rhetoric. His adversaries had a bad game to play ;
they played it into his hands, and he made good use of their blun-
ders. The main charge was ridiculous enough, and Apuleius had for
it a ready and sufficient answer : " You are surprised," he said,
" that a woman should have married again after thirteen years of
widowhood ; but the real wonder is, that she should have remained
unmarried so long.   You pretend that magic alone could have
forced a widow of her years to marry a young man ; but that is
just the sort of case in which magic would be quite superfluous."
As if to give the more force to this argument, the prosecutors
were indiscreet enough to lay great stress on the graces and ac-
complishments of the accused, and to press upon the notice of
the court that Apuleius was altogether such a man as was most
likely, in the natural course of things, to find favour in a woman's
eyes ; for he was handsome, and not negligent of his person ; he
used a mirror ; he combed his hair ; he actually cleaned his teeth !
and this handsome man, who cultivated cleanliness as well as phi-
losophy, had a ready wit and a fluent tongue !

After the discomfiture of his wife's relations, it seems probable
that nothing very remarkable occurred to disturb the even tenour
of a life of literary labour to which Apuleius devoted himself.
All that is known of this latter part of his career, is, that he was
a most voluminous writer ; that he frequently declaimed in public
with great applause ; he was a priest of Æsculapius, the pa-
tron god of Carthage ; he had the charge of exhibiting gladi-
atorial shows and wild beast hunts in the province, and statues
were erected in his honour by the senate of Carthage and of other
states.   It was probably in his latter days that he composed his
most celebrated work, " The Metamorphoses, or the Golden Ass ;"
for neither does he allude to it in those passages in which he boasts

of the extent and variety of his literary productions ; nor was any mention made of it upon the occasion of his trial for magic, as would certainly have been done had his prosecutors been aware of the existence of such a book.   This celebrated romance purports to be the autobiography of a certain Lucius of Madaura, whose curiosity with respect to magic has been rewarded by his tranformation into the form of a jackass, in which he undergoes many curious and ludicrous adventures, until he is at last restored to human shape by the interposition of the goddess Isis, to whose service he devotes himself.   Had this amusing story appeared before the trial at Sabrata, it might have been used with formidable effect against its author, whose contemporaries, anticipating the opinions of a subsequent age, might have identified Lucius with Apuleius, and believed the latter to be a great magician.

Lactantius informs us that the early pagan controversialists used to rank Apuleius with Apollonius of Tyana, as a thaumaturgus, and to cite various miracles performed by him as equal, or superior to those of Christ.   A generation later, St. Augustine permitted himself to doubt whether the account given by Lucius, or Apuleius, of his change into an ass was not a true relation : " Aut *indicavit*," says he, " aut finxit."

The Golden Ass, in which many writers, especially Bishop Warburton, have been at pains to discover a profound theological purpose, appears to have been written with a view to little else than the amusement of a profane public.   It is enriched with numerous episodes, of which the best known, and by far the most beautiful, is the story of Cupid and Psyche.   Another forms the second story of the seventh day of the Decameron.   An adventure which befel Lucius, probably suggested to Cervantes the dreadful combat which took place at an inn between Don Quixote and the Wine-skins ; and there is a striking resemblance between the occurrences seen by Lucius at the habitation of robbers, and some of the early incidents in Gil Blas.   Apuleius, who is now comparatively neglected, was familiarly known to all readers of the classics during the three centuries preceding our own ; but it is only through the medium of a translation that Englishmen, at least, are likely to make much acquaintance with him for the future. His Latin is very troublesome to read, and it is not worth reading for its own sake. He is a most amusing writer, with an execrable style, and therefore he is one of the few who ought to gain rather than lose by translation. "No one," says Professor Ramsay, " can peruse a few pages of Apuleius without being at once impressed with his conspicuous excellencies and his glaring defects. We find everywhere an exuberant play of fancy, liveliness, humour, wit, learning, acuteness, and not unfrequently real eloquence. On the other hand, no style can be more vicious. It is in the highest degree unnatural, both in its general tone and in the phraseology employed. The former is disfigured by the constant recurrence of ingenious but forced and learned conceits and studied prettinesses, while the latter is remarkable for the multitude of obsolete words ostentatiously paraded in almost every sentence. The greater number of these are to be found in the extant compositions of the oldest dramatic writers, and in quotations preserved by the grammarians ; and those for which no authority can be produced, were, in all probability, drawn from the same source, and not arbitrarily coined to answer the purpose of the moment, as some critics have imagined. The least faulty perhaps, of all, is the Apologia. Here he spoke from deep feeling ; and although we may in many places detect the inveterate affectation of the rhetorician, yet there is often a bold, manly, straightforward heartiness and truth, which we seek in vain in those compositions where his feelings were less couched."

Of all the voluminous writings of Apuleius there are only six extant of unquestioned authenticity. Two we have already named; the third is a dissertation on the God of Socrates, a work which has been roughly attacked by St. Augustine; the fourth a treatise on the Doctrines of Plato ; the fifth the book entitled *Florida*, which is commonly supposed to be an anthology from the orations of Apuleius, collected either by himself or one of his admirers, but more probably a collection of passages intended as proemia to sundry declamations, or to be introduced, as occasion might serve, into the body of an extemporaneous harangue. The sixth and last is the *De Mundo Liber*, a translation of an anonymous Greek treatise, erroneously ascribed to Aristotle, which we have not thought worth inserting. The treatise on Plato is not included here, as it has already been given in the sixth volume of Mr. Bohn's edition of the entire works of Plato.

The Golden Ass has been several times presented to the English public, but, it is believed, never yet so completely or faithfully. The God of Socrates has once previously been translated, (by Thomas Taylor), but the Florida, and the Apologia or Defence, are now given in English for the first time. The able metrical version of Cupid and Psyche, first published in 1801 anonymously, but attributed to the pen of Hudson Gurney, Esq., and the well-known poem of Psyche by Mrs. Tighe, are adjoined, because of their appropriateness and merit. The latter was highly popular at the time of its first publication, went through several large editions, and was elaborately reviewed and praised in the Quarterly Review of May, 1811.

THE

METAMORPHOSES,

OR GOLDEN* ASS OF APULEIUS.

PREFACE.

In the following Milesian† narrative, I will string together various stories, and regale your listening ears with some merry whispers, if only you will not disdain to look upon this Egyptian papyrus, written with the subtle point of a Nilotic reed; and I will proceed to astonish you with the adventures of men changed into different shapes, and, after various vicissitudes, restored to their original forms. Who I am, I will tell you in a few words:

Hymettus of Attica, the Isthmus of Ephyre,‡ and Tænarus § of Sparta, famous lands, immortalized in books still more famous,

---

* *Golden.*]—The following remarks relative to this epithet are from Dr. Smith's ' Dictionary of Greek and Roman Biography :'—" The epithet ' aureus' is generally supposed to have been bestowed in consequence of the admiration in which this tale was held, for, being considered as the most excellent composition of its kind, it was compared to the most excellent of metals. Warburton, however, ingeniously contends that ' aureus' was the common.epithet bestowed upon all Milesian tales, because they were such as strollers used to rehearse for a piece of money to the rabble in a circle, after the fashion of oriental story-tellers. He founds his conjecture upon an expression in one of Pliny's Epistles (ii. 20), ' Assem para, et accipe auream fabulam,'—' give me a piece of copper, and receive in return a story worth a piece of gold,' or, ' precious as gold,' which brings us back to the old explanation."

† *Milesian.*]—The people of Miletus were famed for their love of merriment and luxury ; hence stories of an amatory or mirthful nature were generally known by the name of ' Milesian stories.'

‡ *Ephyre.*]—The ancient name of Corinth.

§ *Tænarus.*]—This seems a preferable reading to Tenedos.

B

are my old nurseries.* There, in the early studies of my youth, I learned the Attic tongue. Soon after, a stranger in the Latian city, I applied myself to the study of the native language of the Romans; which I acquired with painful labour, without the help of a master.

Behold, then, I preface with asking pardon, should I in any way offend by my unskilful use of a strange and foreign tongue. Indeed this very change of language well befits the description of the transformatory art of magic, of which we purpose here to treat. We will begin, then, a Grecian story :† Reader, attend, you will be delighted.

* *My old nurseries.*]—'Mea vetus prosapia est.' Taylor, following the Delphin interpretation, takes this to mean : 'are the ancient originals of my race.' This version is either expressly warranted or tacitly admitted by all the commentators ; but, however respectable the authorities in its favour, it wants that of common sense. If Lucius, who was a native of Medaura, in Africa, had intended to tell us where his progenitors had lived, why should he have omitted Thessaly, the country of his mother's ancestors ? It is just possible that his father might have traced back his pedigree, through a pair inhabiting one of the places named, to a male and female ancestor belonging severally to the other two ; but would it have followed thence that Lucius should have pursued his early studies in those very three places ? What he desires to make known to the reader is, that Greek was the language of his youth, and Latin a later acquirement, a fact upon which the nationality of two of his remote ancestors could have no bearing whatever. We incline to think that the word 'prosapia,' which literally means, lineage, is here used in a figurative sense, akin to that in which Englishmen speak of their university as their 'alma mater.' Unfortunately we cannot decide the question by references to other authors ; for prosapia, as we learn from Quintilian, is one of those antiquated and obsolete words to the use of which Apuleius and his contemporary Aulus Gellius were inordinately addicted. At all events, 'original seat of a race,' is quite as arbitrary a rendering of 'prosapia' as that which we have ventured to assign to it.—*K.*

† *A Grecian story.*]—This name is probably given to the story, from the scene being laid in Thessaly. It is also not improbable that he calls the work by this epithet in consequence of having derived it from Lucius of Patræ, a Grecian writer, from whom, also, Lucian derived his work, which is somewhat similar, called ονος, 'the ass.'

BOOK THE FIRST.

LUCIUS, JOURNEYING FROM CORINTH TO THESSALY, OVERTAKES
AND CONVERSES WITH TWO TRAVELLERS—FIRST EPISODE: TALE
OF ARISTOMENES, THE COMMERCIAL TRAVELLER—LUCIUS ARRIVES
AT HYPATA—BECOMES THE GUEST OF MILO—MEETS AN OLD AC-
QUAINTANCE IN THE FISH MARKET—A ZEALOUS MAGISTRATE.

I HAD occasion to visit Thessaly on business; for it was there
that our origin on the maternal side was derived, in the first
place, from the celebrated Plutarch,* and afterwards from his
grandson, Sextus, the philosopher, a thing which reflects so
much honour upon us. I had travelled over lofty mountains,
slippery valleys, dewy turf, and thick-clodded plains, being
mounted on a milk-white horse of that country; and as he
was now much fatigued, I jumped upon my feet, in order that
I too might shake off the numbness of my limbs by walking;
then carefully wiped the sweat from my horse with a handful
of leaves,† stroked his ears, threw the reins over his head, and
walked him along at a gentle pace, until the usual functions
of nature had relieved his weariness.

And now, while bending down his head, and cropping the
grass sideways, he was taking his ambulatory breakfast, I made
a third with two persons who were travelling together, and who
happened to be on the road a little before me. While I listened
to hear what was the subject of their conversation, one of them,
bursting into a loud laugh, said to the other, "Do leave off tell-
ing such absurd, such monstrous‡ lies."

Hearing this, I, who am generally athirst after novelty, struck

---

* *Plutarch.*]—Plutarch, the historian, was a native of Bœotia, and his
nephew, Sextus, the preceptor of Marcus Antoninus, in all probability
lived later than the time of Apuleius. It consequently follows either that
Plutarch of Chæronæa is not the person here meant, or that, if he is, the
allusion to Sextus is a mere gloss. There seems no reason to suppose
that Apuleius refers here to his own descent from Plutarch through his
mother, Salvia, though most of the early commentators adopted that notion.

† *A handful of leaves.*]—'Fronde.' Some read 'fronte,' i. e. 'I wiped
the sweat from my horse's forehead.'

‡ *Monstrous.*]—'Immania' seems a preferable reading to 'inania.'

B 2

in, and said, "May I beg you will make me acquainted with
your story; not, indeed, that I would be impertinently inqui-
sitive, but I long to know everything, or at least as much as
I can; besides, some pleasant amusing tales will smooth the
ruggedness of this hill we are just ascending."

"Decidedly," said the first speaker, "this lying story is
about as true as if a person should think fit to assert, that by
magical mutterings rapid rivers can be made to run back-
wards, the ocean be congealed, the winds robbed of breath, the
sun stopped in his course, the moon made to drop her foam,*
the stars plucked from their spheres, the day annihilated, and
the night indefinitely prolonged."

On this, assuming a somewhat confident air, "Do not you,"
said I, "who began the story, repent of having so done, nor
think it a trouble to tell the remainder." And then, turning
to the other: "But as for you," said I, "you reject with dull
ears and stubborn disposition, a statement of things which,
perhaps, are true. Little are you aware, by Hercules! by
what perversity of opinion those things are thought to be lies,
which appear either novel to the hearing, or strange to the
sight, or at least exalted beyond the range of thought; whereas,
if you examine them a little more attentively, you will find
them not only manifest to the senses, but even easy of accom-
plishment. Why, it was only last evening, that, while I was
endeavouring to eat faster than my fellow-guests, and to swallow
too large a mouthful of cheesecake, I was all but choked
through the spongy nature of the glutinous morsel sticking
in my throat, and stopping up my breath at the bottom of my
windpipe. And yet, it was but very lately that at Athens, in
front of the Poecile Portico,† I beheld with these two eyes a
juggler‡ swallow a horseman's two-edged broad-sword, sharp

* *Her foam.*]—It was a common notion with the ancients, that the
moon shed a noxious or poisonous venom or foam, and that sorcerers or
magicians were able to draw her down to the earth by their incantations.
The so-called 'Lunar virus' was a principal ingredient in spells and
magical compositions.

† *Poecile Portico.*]—This portico was so called from the Greek word
ποικίλη—'variegated,' or 'painted.' It was at Athens, and was adorned
with numerous pictures, the works of Polygnotus and Mycon. The battle
of Marathon was there represented.

‡ *A juggler.*]—It is not improbable that the mountebanks and jugglers
of the ancients received their name of 'circulatores' from their exhibit-
ing in a ring of people, like those of the present day.

in the extreme, blade foremost, and afterwards, for a tri-
fling inducement, bury deep in his entrails a hunter's spear,
with that part of it downward which threatens destruction.
And, wondrous to tell! behind the iron head of the spear, at
the part where the handle of the immersed weapon* passed up
the throat,† towards the hinder part of the head, a beautiful
boy mounted up, and wriggled and twisted himself about as
if he had been without sinew or bone in his body, to the ad-
miration of all of us who were present. You would have said
it was the noble serpent, clinging with its slippery coils to the
knotted staff, with half-clipped branches, which the God of
Medicine carries. But you, who began the story, be good
enough to repeat it again, I pray you. I will believe you if
he will not, and will ask you to dinner at the first inn we
come to. This I propose as your remuneration."

"I thankfully decline your offer,"‡ he replied, "but will
begin my story over again. And, in the first place, I will
swear to you by that sun, the all-seeing god, that what I re-
late I know by experience to be true. Nor will you any longer
doubt that such is the fact, when once you come to the next
city of Thessaly, for there the story is in every body's mouth,
as it relates to matters that publicly took place there. But,
that you may first know who I am, and of what country, and
by what pursuits I live, listen to my narrative."

FIRST EPISODE.

TALE OF ARISTOMENES, THE COMMERCIAL TRAVELLER.

"I am a native of Ægina, and I travel to and fro through
Thessaly, Ætolia, and Bœotia, for the purpose of purchasing
honey of Hypata, as also cheese, and other articles of traffic

---

* *Immersed weapon.*]—We follow the Delphin editor, who with mani-
fest propriety substitutes 'immersi' for the common reading, 'inversi.'

† *Up the throat.*]—'Ingluviem' seems a preferable reading to 'inguen.'

‡ *Decline your offer.*]—'Æqui bonique facio,' is a form of thanks which
implies refusal without expressing it, just like the French word 'merci.'
'Æqui bonique consulere,' means, on the contrary, to accept in good part.
Neither Taylor nor Head seem to have been aware of the distinction.
They both make Aristomenes accept the invitation, though the event
shows that Lucius did not understand his reply in that sense.—*K.*

used in cookery.   Having understood that at Hypata,* which
is the principal city of all Thessaly, new cheese of exqui-
site flavour was to be sold ·at a very reasonable price, I made
the best of my way to that place, with the intention of buy-
ing up the whole of it.   But, as generally is the case, start-
ing unluckily with the left foot foremost;† all my hopes of
gain were utterly disappointed.   For a person named Lupus,
a merchant in a large way of business, had bought the whole
of it the day before.

"Weary with my rapid journey, undertaken to so little pur-
pose, I proceeded, early in the evening, to the public baths,
when, to my surprise, I espied an old companion of mine, named
Socrates.   He was sitting on the ground, half covered with a
sorry, tattered cloak, and looked almost another person, he was
so miserably wan and thin; just like those outcasts of Fortune,
who beg alms in the streets.   Consequently, although he had
been my friend and particular acquaintance, I yet accosted
him with feelings of hesitation.

"'How now, friend Socrates,' said I, 'what is the meaning
of this?   Why this appearance?   What crime have you been
guilty of?   Why, you have been lamented at home, and for
some time given up for dead.‡   Guardians have been as-
signed to your children, by decree of the provincial magistrate.
Your wife, having fulfilled what was due to the dead,§ all dis-
figured by grief and long-continued sorrow, and having almost
cried herself blind with excessive weeping, is being worried
by her parents to repair the misfortune of the family by the
joys of a new marriage.   But here you come before our eyes
like some spectral apparition, to our extreme confusion.'

* *Hypata.*]—This was a famous city of Thessaly, situate on the banks
of the river Spercheus.

† *Left foot foremost.*]—To start on a journey by putting the left foot
foremost was considered to be especially significant of ill luck ; so much
so, that the expression came to be generally used to denote a bad omen.

‡ *Given up for dead.*]—'Conclamatus es.'   After a person was dead
it was the custom of the Romans to call on him by name, for the purpose
of recalling him to life, in case he should be only in a trance.   This cere-
mony was called 'conclamatio,' and was generally performed while the
body was being washed, once a day for seven days ; after which period
the body was burnt.

§ *Due to the dead.*]—Ovid, in his Fasti, b. i. l. 36, mentions ten months
as the period assigned by Numa for widows to mourn the loss of their
husbands.

" ' O Aristomenes!' said he, 'it is clear that you are ignorant of the slippery turns, the unstable freaks, and the ever-changing vicissitudes of Fortune.'·

" As he said this, he hid his face, which was crimsoned with shame, in his cobbled covering of tatters, so that he left the rest of his body naked, from the navel downward, as far as the groin. At last, unable to endure the sight of such a miserable spectacle of woe, I took hold of him, and endeavoured to raise him from the ground. But, with his head covered up as it was, he exclaimed, 'Let me alone, let me alone; let Fortune still enjoy the trophy she has erected.'

" However, I prevailed upon him to accompany me: and at the same time pulling off one of my own two garments, I speedily—clothed, or covered him, shall I say? immediately after which, I took him to a bath, and, myself, applied to him the requisite anointing and scrubbing processes, and laboriously rubbed off the coat of filth with which he was defiled. Having paid every attention to him, though tired myself, I supported his enfeebled steps, and with great difficulty brought him to my inn; where I made him rest on a couch, gave him plenty of food, cheered him with wine, and entertained him with the news of the day. And now our conversation took quite a merry turn, we cracked jokes, and grew noisy in our prattle; when, heaving a bitter sigh from the bottom of his ·breast, and violently striking his forehead with his right hand:

" 'Miserable man that I am!' said he; 'to have fallen into these misfortunes while intent on gratifying myself with a famous gladiatorial spectacle. For, as you are very well aware, I went to Macedonia on an affair of business; and after being detained there for the space of ten months, I was on my return homewards, having gained a very pretty sum of money. I had nearly reached Larissa, * which I had included in my route for the purpose of seeing the spectacle I mentioned, when I was attacked by some desperate robbers, in a lonely and rugged valley, and only effected my escape, after being plundered by them of all I possessed. Being thus reduced to extreme distress, I betook myself to a certain woman named Meroë, who kept a tavern, and who, though old, was remarkably engaging; and to her I related the circumstances of my lengthened absence, of my earnest desire to reach home, and of my being

* *Larissa.*]—A city of Thessaly, situated near the river Peneus.

plundered of my property on that day. After I, unfortunate wretch, had related such particulars as I remembered, she treated me with the greatest kindness, supplied me with a good supper, all for nothing, and afterwards, instigated by lust, admitted me to her bed. But from the very moment that I, unhappy man, first lay with her, my mind contracted a lasting malady; and I even made her a present of those garments which the robbers, in their humanity, had left me to cover my nakedness. I likewise presented her with the little earnings I made by working as a cloakmaker while I was yet in good condition of body; until at length this worthy partner, and ill fortune together, reduced me to that state in which you just now saw me.'

" ' By Pollux, then,' said I, ' you deserve to suffer extreme misfortunes, if there is anything still more extreme than that which is most extreme, for having preferred the pleasures of dalliance and a wrinkled harlot, to your home and children.'

" ' Hush! hush!' said he, raising his forefinger to his mouth, and looking round with a terror-stricken countenance to see if he might speak with safety; ' Forbear to revile a woman skilled in celestial matters, lest you do yourself an injury through an intemperate tongue.'

" ' Say you so?' said I. ' What kind of woman is this tavern-keeper, so powerful and queenly?'

" ' She is a sorceress,' he replied, ' and endowed with powers divine; she is able to draw down the heavens, to uplift the earth, to harden the running water, to dissolve mountains, to raise the shades of the dead, to dethrone the Gods, to extinguish the stars, and to illumine the depths of Tartarus itself.'

" 'Come, come,' said I, 'do draw asunder this tragic curtain,* and fold up the theatric drop-scene, and let's hear your story in ordinary parlance.'

" ' Should you like,' said he, ' to hear of one or two, ay, or a

---

* *Tragic curtain.*]—The ' siparium' was a piece of tapestry, stretched on a frame, and, rising before the stage, answered the same purpose as the curtain or drop-scene with us in concealing the stage till the actors appeared. Instead of drawing up this curtain to discover the stage and actors, according to our present practice, it was depressed when the play began, and fell beneath the level of the stage; whence ' aulæa premuntur, meant that the play had commenced. ' Aulæa' seems here to mean the stage-curtain, which divided in the middle and was drawn aside : while the ' siparium ' would more nearly correspond with our drop-scene.

great many of her performances? Why, as for making not
only her fellow-countrymen love her to distraction, but the
Indians even, or the inhabitants of both the Æthiopias,*
and even the Antichthones † themselves; these are only the
leaves, as it were, of her art, and mere trifles. Listen, then,
and hear what she has performed in the presence of many
witnesses. By a single word only, she changed a lover of hers
into a beaver, because he had by force debauched another
woman; since that beast, when in fear of being taken, escapes
from its pursuers by the abscission of its genitals; and she de-
sired that the same might likewise befall him, as a punishment
for having been connected with another woman. She likewise
changed an innkeeper, who was her neighbour, and of whom
she was envious on that account, into a frog; and now the old
fellow, swimming about in a cask of his own wine, or buried
in the dregs, croaks hoarsely to his old customers, quite in the
way of business. She likewise transformed another person, an
advocate of the Forum, into a ram, because he had conducted
a cause against her; and to this very day that ram is always at
loggerheads.‡ Then there was the wife of a lover of hers, whom
she condemned to perpetual pregnancy, when on the point of
increasing her family, by closing her womb against the egress
of the infant, because she had chattered scandal against the
witch; and, for these eight years, according to the general
computation, this poor creature has been swelling with her
burden, as if she were about to be brought to bed of an elephant.§

"After this woman, however, and many other persons, had
been injured by her arts, the public indignation became
aroused against her; and it was determined that on the follow-
ing day a most dire vengeance should be wreaked upon her,
by stoning her to death. But, by the power of her enchant-

* _The Æthiopias._]—The eastern and the western, separated from each
other by the river Nile, which the ancients (as we are informed by Strabo,
Geograph. lib. ii.) considered as the boundary of Asia and Africa.

† _The Antichthones._]—So called from inhabiting τὴν ἐναντίαν χθόνα,
_i.e._ earth contrary to that on which we dwell. Hence they are either the
same with the Antipodes, or, at least, are those who dwell in the inferior
hemisphere which is contrary to ours.

‡ _Is always at loggerheads._]—' Causas agit.' This Sir G. Head cleverly
renders, ' and gives rebutters and surrebutters as he used to do.'

§ _Brought to bed of an elephant._]—Pliny asserts that the elephant goes
with young ten years.

ments, she frustrated this design: and as Medea, having obtained by entreaty from Creon the truce of a single day, prior to her departure, burned his whole palace, his daughter, together with the old man himself, with flames issuing from a garland, so, likewise, did this sorceress, having performed certain deadly incantations in a ditch,* (as she herself lately told me in a fit of drunkenness), confine all the inhabitants of the town, each in his own house, through a secret spell of the dæmons; so that, for two whole days together, neither could the bars be wrenched off, nor the doors be taken off the hinges, nor, in fine, could a breach be made in the walls; until, by mutual consent, the people unanimously cried out, and swore in the most sacred manner, that they would not lift a hand against her, and would, in case any one should think of so doing, afford her timely assistance. Being after this manner appeased, she liberated the whole city.

"In the middle of the night, however, she conveyed the author of this conspiracy, together with all his house, that is to say, with the walls, the very ground, and all the foundations, close shut as it was, into another city, situate at the hundredth milestone hence, and on the summit of a craggy mountain, in consequence of which it is deprived of water. And, as the dwellings of the inhabitants were built so close together, that they did not afford room to this new comer, she threw down the house before the gate of the city, and took her departure."

"'You narrate,' said I, 'marvellous things, my good Socrates, and no less terrible than marvellous. In fine, you have excited in me too, no small anxiety, indeed, I may say, fear, not inoculating me with a mere grain of apprehension, but piercing me with dread as with a spear, lest this old hag, employing in a similar manner the assistance of some dæmon, should come to know this conversation of ours. Let us, therefore, with all speed, betake ourselves to rest, and when we have relieved our weariness by a night's sleep, let us fly hence as far as we possibly can, before daylight.'

"While I was yet advising him thus, the worthy Socrates, overcome by more wine than he had been accustomed to, and by the fatigue of the day, had fallen asleep, and was now

---

* *Incantations in a ditch.*]—Sacrifices to celestial gods were offered on raised altars; those to terrestial gods, on the ground; those to infernal gods, in a pit or ditch.

snoring aloud. Shutting the door, therefore, securing the
bolts, and placing my bed close against the hinges, I tossed it
up well, and lay down upon it. At first, indeed, I lay awake
some time through fear, but closed my eyes at last a little about
the third watch.*

" I had just fallen asleep, when suddenly the door was burst
open with too great violence for one to believe that it was
robbers; nay, the hinges being entirely broken and wrenched
off, it was thrown to the ground. The bedstead, too, which
was but small, wanting one foot, and rotten, was thrown down
with the violence of the shock, and falling upon me, who had
been rolled out and pitched upon the ground, completely covered
and concealed me. Then was I sensible that certain emotions
of the mind are naturally excited by contrary causes. For as
tears very often proceed from joy, so, amid my extreme fear,
I could not refrain from laughing, to see myself turned,
from Aristomenes, into a tortoise.† And so, while prostrate
on the floor, peeping askance to see what was the matter, and
completely covered by the bed, I espied two women, of ad-
vanced age, one of whom carried a lighted lamp, and the other
a sponge and a drawn sword. Thus equipped, they planted
themselves on either side of Socrates, who was fast asleep.

" She who carried the sword then addressed the other, ' This,
sister Panthia, is my dear Endymion,‡ my Ganymede,§ who
by day and by night, hath laughed my youthful age to scorn.
This is he who, despising my passion, not only defames me with
abusive language, but is preparing also for flight—and I, for-
sooth, deserted through the craft of this Ulysses, just like
another Calypso, am to be left to lament in eternal loneliness.'

" Then extending her right hand, and pointing me out to her
friend Panthia; ' And there,' said she, ' is his worthy coun-
sellor Aristomenes, who was the proposer of this flight, and
who now, half dead, is lying flat on the ground beneath
the bedstead, and is looking at all that is going on, while he
fancies that he is to relate disgraceful stories of me with im-

---

* *Third watch.*]—The beginning of this would be midnight.
† *Into a tortoise.*]—From his bed and bedstead being turned over him.
‡ *My dear Endymion.*]—Alluding to the secret of Diana and the shep-
herd Endymion, on Mount Latmus.
§ *My Ganymede.*]—Called ' Catamitus' in the text; by which name he
is also called in the Menæchmi of Plautus.

punity.   I'll take care, however, that some day, ay, and before long too, this very instant in fact, he shall repent of his recent loquacity, and his present inquisitiveness.'

"On hearing this, wretch that I was, I felt myself streaming with cold perspiration, and my vitals began to throb with agitation; so much so, that even the bedstead, shaken by the violence of my palpitations, moved up and down upon my back.

"'Well, sister,' said the worthy Panthia, 'shall we hack him to pieces at once, after the fashion of the Bacchanals, or, shall we bind his limbs and deprive him of virility?'

"To this, Meroë replied—for I perceived from the circumstances, as well as from the narrative of Socrates, how well that name fitted her*—'Rather let him live, if only that he may cover with a little earth the body of this wretched creature.' Then, moving the head of Socrates to one side, she plunged the whole sword into him up to the hilt, through the left side of his throat, carefully receiving the flowing blood into a small leathern bottle, placed under it, so that not a drop of it was anywhere to be seen.   All this did I witness with my own eyes; and, what is more, the worthy Meroë, that she might not, I suppose, omit any due observance in the sacrifice of the victim, thrusting her right hand through the wound, into the very entrails, and groping among them, drew forth the heart of my unhappy companion; while, his windpipe being severed by the thrust of the weapon, he emitted through the wound a voice, or rather I should say, an indistinct gurgling noise, and poured forth his spirit with his bubbling blood.   Panthia then stopped the gaping wound with the sponge, exclaiming, 'Beware, O sea-born sponge, how thou dost pass through a river.'

"When she had thus said, they lifted my bed from the ground, and squatting astride over my face, discharged their bladders, until they had entirely drenched me with their most filthy contents.

---

* *How well that name fitted her.*]—Ausonius, Epigram xix., explains this allusion :

> Et tu sic Meroë: non quod sic atra colore,
>   Ut quæ Niliaca nascitur in Meroë ;
> Infusum sed quod vinum non diluis undis,
>   Potare immixtum sueta merumque merum.

You are named Meroë, not because you are of a swarthy complexion like one born in Meroë, the island of the Nile ; but because you do not dilute your wine with water but are used to drink it unmixed and concentrated.—K.

"Hardly had they passed over the threshold, when the door resumed its former state; the hinges resettled on the pannels; the posts returned to the bars, and the bolts flew back once more to their sockets. But I, left in such a plight, prostrate on the ground, scared, naked, cold, and drenched in chamber-lye, just like some babe that has recently emerged from the womb of its mother, indeed, I may say, half dead, but still surviving myself, and pursuing, as it were, a posthumous train of reflec-tions, or, to say the least, like a candidate for the cross, to which I was surely destined : 'What,' said I, 'will become of me, when this man is found in the morning with his throat cut? Though I tell the truth, who will think my story probable? You ought at least, they will say, to have called for assistance, if you, such a stout man as you are, could not resist a woman. Is a man's throat to be cut before your eyes, and are you to be silent? How was it you were not likewise assassinated? Why did the barbarous wretch spare you, a witness of the murder, and not kill you, if only to put an end to all evidence of the crime? Inasmuch, then, as you have escaped death, now re-turn to it.'

" These remarks I repeated to myself, over and over again, while the night was fast verging towards day.

" It appeared to me, therefore, most advisable to escape by stealth before daylight, and to pursue my journey, though with trembling steps. I took up my bundle, and putting the key in the door, drew back the bolts. But this good and faithful door, which during the night had opened of its own accord, was now to be opened but with the greatest difficulty, after putting in the key a multitude of times.

" 'Hallo! porter,' said I, 'where are you? Open the gates of the inn; I want to be off before break of day.'

"The porter, who was lying on the ground behind the door of the inn, still half asleep, replied, 'Who are you, who would begin your journey at this time of night? Don't you know that the roads are infested by robbers? Ay, ay, though you may have a mind to meet your death, stung by your con-science, belike for some crime you have committed, still, I haven't a head like a pumpkin, that I should die for your sake.'

" 'It isn't very far from day-break,' said I; 'and besides, what can robbers take from a traveller in the greatest po-verty? Are you ignorant, you simpleton, that he who is naked cannot be stripped by ten athletes even?'

"The drowsy porter, turning himself on his other side, made answer, 'And how am I to know that you have not murdered that fellow-traveller of yours, with whom you came hither last night, and are now consulting your safety in flight? And now I recollect that just at that hour I saw the depths of Tartarus* through the yawning earth and in them the dog Cerberus, looking ready to devour me.'

"Then truly I came to the conclusion that the worthy Meroë had not spared my throat through any compassion, but that she had cruelly reserved me for the cross.† Accordingly, on returning to my chamber, I thought about some speedy mode of putting an end to myself: but as Fortune had provided me with no weapon with which to commit self-destruction, except the bedstead alone—' Now, bedstead,' said I, 'most dear to my soul, who hast been partner with me in enduring so many sorrows, who art fully conscious, and a spectator of this night's events, and whom alone, when accused, I can adduce as a witness of my innocence, do thou supply me, who would fain hasten to the shades below, with a welcome instrument of death.'

"Thus saying, I began to undo the rope with which the bed was corded, and throwing one end of it over a small beam which projected above the window, and there fastening it, and making a strong slip-knot at the other end, I mounted upon the bed, and thus elevated for my own destruction, I put my head into the noose. But while with one foot I was kicking away the support on which I rested, so that the noose, being tightened about my throat by the strain of my weight, might stop the functions of my breath; the rope, which was old and rotten, broke asunder, and falling from aloft, I tumbled with great force upon Socrates (for he was lying close by), and rolled with him on to the floor.

"Lo and behold! at the very same instant the porter burst into the room, bawling out, 'Where are you, you who were

* *Saw the depths of Tartarus.*]—Of course in a dream. *Just at that hour:*—He knows all about it, even to the precise time. The promptitude with which the porter decides from the evidence of his dream that the murder had been actually committed, and at the very moment when the dream occurred, is a fine touch of nature.—*K.*

† *For the cross.*]—The cross was the instrument of punishment for slaves and foreigners, especially in cases of murder.

in such monstrous haste to be off at midnight, and now lie snoring, rolled up in the bed-clothes?'

"At these words, whether awakened by my fall, or by the discordant notes of the porter, I know not, Socrates was the first to start up, and exclaim, 'Assuredly, it is not without good reason that all travellers detest these hostlers. For this troublesome fellow, intruding so impertinently, with the intention, no doubt, of stealing something, has roused me out of a sound sleep, by his outrageous bellowing.'

"On hearing him speak, I jumped up briskly, in an ecstasy of unhoped-for joy: 'Faithfullest of porters,' I exclaimed, 'my friend, my own father, and my brother, behold him whom you, in your drunken fit, falsely accused me of having murdered.' So saying, I embraced Socrates, and was for loading him with kisses; but he, being assailed by the stench of the most filthy liquor with which those hags* had drenched me, repulsed me with considerable violence. 'Get out with you,' he cried, 'for you stink like the bottom of a sewer,' and then began jocularly to enquire the cause of this nasty smell. Sorely confused, I trumped up some absurd story on the spur of the moment, to give another turn to the conversation, and, taking him by the right hand, 'Why not be off,' said I, 'and enjoy the freshness of the morning on our journey?' So I took my bundle, and, having paid the innkeeper for our night's lodging, we started on our road.

"We had proceeded some little distance, and now every thing being illumined by the beams of the rising sun, I keenly and attentively examined that part of my companion's neck, into which I had seen the sword plunged. 'Foolish man,' said I to myself, 'buried in your cups, you certainly have had a most absurd dream. Why look, here's Socrates safe, sound, and hearty. Where is the wound? where is the sponge? where, in fine, is the scar of a wound, so deep, and so recent?'

"Addressing myself to him, 'Decidedly,' said I, 'skilful doctors have good reason to be of opinion that it is those who are stuffed out with food and fermented liquors who are troubled with portentous and horrible dreams. My own case is an

---

* *Those hags.*]—'Lamiæ' were enchantresses, who were said to prowl about at midnight to satisfy their lustful propensities, and their fondness for human flesh. They correspond very nearly with the 'Ghouls' mentioned in the Arabian Nights' Entertainments.

instance of this: for having in my evening cups excceded the bounds of temperance, a wretched night has been presenting to me shocking and dreadful visions, so that I still fancy myself besprinkled and defiled with human gore.'

"" 'Tis not gore,' he replied with a smile, ' you are sprinkled with, but chamber-lye; and yet I too, thought, in my sleep, that my throat was cut: some pain, too, I felt in my neck, and I fancied that my very heart was being plucked out: and even now I am quite faint, my knees tremble, I stagger as I go, and feel in want of some food to refresh my spirits.'

"' Look,' cried I, ' here's breakfast all ready for you;' and so saying, I lifted my wallet from off my shoulders, and at once handed him some cheese and bread, saying, ' Let us sit down near that plane-tree.'

" We did so, and I also helped myself to some refreshment. While looking at him somewhat more intently, as he was eating with a voracious appetite, I saw that he was faint, and of a hue like box-wood; his natural colour in fact had so forsaken him, that as I recalled those nocturnal furies to my frightened imagination, the very first piece of bread I put into my mouth, though a very tiny bit, stuck in the middle of my throat, so that it could neither pass downward, nor yet return upward. And then besides, the number of people passing along increased my apprehensions; for who would believe that one of two companions could meet with his death without any harm done by the other?

"Meanwhile, after having devoured a sufficient quantity of food, he began to be impatient for some drink; for he had voraciously eaten a good part of a most excellent cheese; and not very far from the roots of the plane tree, a gentle stream flowed slowly along, just like a placid lake, rivalling silver or glass in its lustre. ' Look,' said I, ' drink your fill of the water of this stream, bright as the Milky Way.'

" He arose, and, wrapping himself in his cloak,* with his knees doubled under him, knelt down upon the shelving bank, and bent greedily towards the water. Scarcely had he touched the dewy surface of the water with the edge of his lips, when the wound in his throat burst wide open, the sponge suddenly rolled out, a few drops of blood accompanying it; and then, his body, bereft of life, would have

* *In his cloak.*]—' Palliolo' seems a preferable reading to ' paululum.'

fallen into the river, had I not laid hold of one of his feet, and dragged it with the utmost difficulty and labour to the top of the bank; where, having, as well as the time permitted, lamented my unfortunate companion, I buried him in the sandy soil that eternally begirt the stream. For my own part, trembling and terror-stricken, I fled through various and unfrequented places; and, as though conscious of the guilt of homicide, abandoning my country and my home, and embracing a voluntary exile, I now dwell in Ætolia, where I have married another wife."

END OF THE FIRST EPISODE.

Here Aristomenes ended his story, but his companion, who from the very first had rejected it with obstinate incredulity, at once exclaimed, " Nothing is there in fable more fabulous than this story, nothing more absurd than these lies." Then turning to me : " And you," said he, " who are a person of liberal education, as your dress and appearance bespeak, do you give credit to this story ?"

I replied, "I consider nothing impossible, but hold that just as the Fates have preordained, so all things happen to mortals. For both to me and to you, and to all men, many things do happen of so wonderful a nature, that they are nigh to not happening at all ; which, nevertheless, if narrated to an ignorant person, would fail to obtain belief. But this story, by Hercules, I do believe, and I return right hearty thanks to the narrator, for having so well entertained us by his pleasant recital, that I have got over a rough and tedious portion of my journey without labour or weariness. With this good service, I fancy that this nag of mine is also much gratified, inasmuch as I have been carried, without fatigue to him, up to the very gate of this city, not on his back, but by my ears."

This was the termination of our conversation and of our journey together ; for both my fellow-travellers turned away to some neighbouring villages on the left ; while I approached the first inn I cast eyes upon, and at once accosted the old woman who kept it : " Is this the city of Hypata ?" said I ; she gave me to understand, by a nod, that it was. " Do you know," said I, " a certain person of the name of Milo, who is

c

one of the first men of the city?" She smiled, and replied, "With good reason is this Milo considered one of the first* men, inasmuch as he dwells beyond the whole city, and in the Pomœrium."† "Joking apart," said I, "tell me, I beg of you, good mother, what kind of man he is, and in what house he lives."

"Do you see," said she, "those last windows which look on this side towards the city, and that gate on the other side, looking upon the blind alley in front? There it is that Milo dwells, a man abounding in money, and extremely opulent; but disgraced by inordinate avarice and shameful sordidness. In short, he entirely devotes himself to usury, taking. pledges of gold and silver. Shut up in a scanty house, and always bending over his pelf, there he dwells with a wife, the partner of his misery. And no one besides does he keep in his house, except one servant girl; and when he goes abroad, he is always dressed like a common beggar."

"Well," said I to myself, with a smile, "my friend Demeas has taken excellent care of me, in giving me a letter of introduction to such a man; while I stay with him I need not be afraid of smoke, or the smell of the kitchen."

Thus saying, and proceeding to a little distance, I came to the gate, which was strongly bolted, and began to hallo and knock.

At length, a damsel came out, and said, "Hallo! you who have been knocking at our door so violently, what is the pledge on which you want to borrow money? Are you the only person that doesn't know that we take in no pledge except it is gold or silver?"

"Meet me with words of better omen," said I, "and rather inform me, whether I have found your master at home?"

"Certainly," she replied; "but what is the cause of your enquiry?"

One of the first.]—The landlady puns on the word ' primus. He may well be called ' the first ' man, as you come to his house first of all on approaching the city.

† *The Pomœrium.*]—The word ' Pomœrium was probably compounded of ' post,' ' behind,' and ' mœrium,' the old name for ' a wall,' and signified a space of ground adjoining the city walls, within which the city auspices were to be taken. The limits of the ' Pomœrium' were marked by stone pillars at certain distances.

"I have brought a letter," said I, "written to him by Demeas, the duumvir of Corinth."*

"Wait here," said she, "while I deliver your message to him." And so saying, she fastened the door again, and returned into the house.

She came back in a few minutes, and, opening the door, said, "My master requests you to come in." I accordingly entered, and found him reclining on a very small couch, and just beginning his dinner. His wife was sitting at his feet,† and a scantily furnished table was before them; pointing at which, he said, "Behold your entertainment."

"'Tis well," said I, and immediately delivered him the letter from Demeas. Having hastily read it, he said, "I thank my friend Demeas for having introduced to me such a worthy guest:" and then he ordered his wife to leave the room,‡ and invited me to sit in her place; at the same time taking hold of my garment, and drawing me towards him, as I still hesitated through bashfulness. "Sit down there," said he, "for through fear of robbers, we cannot provide ourselves with seats, nor even as much other furniture as we have need of." I did so.

"From the genteel appearance of your person," he continued, "and from this maiden bashfulness of yours, I might reasonably conjecture that you are sprung from a good family. Besides, my friend Demeas also asserts the same thing in his letter. I beg, therefore, you will not despise the poverty of our little cottage; and, look you, you will have the little bedchamber adjoining to this room, where you will be very comfortable. Do not, therefore, hesitate to take up your abode with us. For you will magnify our poor house through your condescension, and will, besides, procure for yourself no small

* *Duumvir of Corinth.*]—The 'duum viri' here mentioned were the chief magistrates who presided over the Roman colonies and 'municipia.'

† *Sitting at his feet.*]—His couch was so scanty in dimensions that it would not admit of more than one to recline on it; consequently, his wife had to sit on a chair or stool at his feet. Although, however, this explanation may be admitted in the present instance, as consonant with Milo's stinginess, it was not uncommon for wives among the Greeks to take their seats by the couches as their husbands reclined at meals. We learn from Plautus that parasites were frequently obliged to content themselves with stools or benches, while the other guests were reclining.

‡ *To leave the room.*]—He orders his wife to leave the room, because the dinner was only enough for two.

renown, if, content with a humble dwelling, you emulate the virtues of Theseus, your father's namesake,* who did not disdain the slender hospitality of the aged woman Hecale."†

Then, calling to the maid-servant, "Fotis," said he, "take the baggage of our guest, and put it with care in that bedchamber, and at the same time, bring quickly from the storeroom some oil for anointing, towels for drying, and other needful things useful, and then conduct my guest to the nearest baths; for he must be weary after his very long and toilsome journey."

On hearing these directions, I reflected upon the mode of living, and the parsimonious habits of Milo, and wishing to ingratiate myself with him in a still greater degree—"I do not stand in need of any of these things," said I, "as I generally carry them with me on a journey. And as to the baths, I can easily find my way thither by enquiring where they are. My principal concern is for my horse, who has *so* stoutly carried me hither; do you, therefore, Fotis, take this money, and buy me some hay and barley."

When matters were arranged, and my things had been put into the bedchamber, I went into the provision market on my road towards the baths, that I might first provide us with something in the way of eating. There I saw a splendid supply of fish on sale, and after asking the price of some, and declining it, because the dealer asked a hundred pieces‡ of money, I finally bought it for twenty denars. Just as I was going away from there, I was followed out by one Pytheas, who had been a fellow-student of mine at Athens; who, after having recognised me at last, embraced me in a friendly manner, and exclaimed, "By Gemini, friend Lucius, what a time it is since I last saw you! By Hercules! not since we left our master and quitted the city.§ But what is the cause of this journey of yours?"

* *Your father's namesake.*]—Many of the commentators rush to the conclusion that Theseus was the name of the father of Apuleius; founding the notion upon the present passage.

† *Aged woman Hecale.*]—Hecale was a poor old woman, who received Theseus, on his travels, with marked hospitality; for which that hero established a festival in her honor. She is also mentioned by Callimachus, Ovid, and Plutarch.

‡ *A hundred pieces.*]—The 'nummus' here mentioned was probably a 'didrachm,' the same in value as two 'denarii.'

§ *Quitted the city.*]—'Astu,' 'the city,' was the name by which, in familiar discourse, Athens was generally called among the Greeks.

"You will know," said I, "to-morrow. But what is the meaning of this? I heartily congratulate you; for I perceive attendants and the fasces, and a dress that fully bespeaks the magisterial office."

He replied, "I have the inspection of the markets* and hold the office of ædile, and if it is your wish to buy any provisions, I will take care and accommodate you." I declined his offer, as I had already provided myself with a sufficient quantity of fish for my dinner.

Pytheas, however, having caught sight of my basket, and shaking up the fishes, that he might inspect them the better—"And pray," said he, "what sum may you have given for this rubbish?"

"It was with considerable trouble," said I, "that I could get the fishmonger to take twenty denars for them." On hearing this, he immediately seized me by the right hand, and bringing me back again into the market:

"From which of these men did you buy this worthless stuff?" said he.

I pointed out to him a little old man, who was sitting in one corner; upon which, immediately rebuking him in a most severe tone of voice, in virtue of his authority as ædile, "How now!" said he, "have you no consideration for our friends, not to say for strangers, to sell your pitiful fish at such an exorbitant price, and thus bring this city, the flower of the province of Thessaly, to be as bad as a desert and a rock, through the dearness of provisions? But you shall not escape with impunity. For I will soon make you know how rogues are to be kept in order, as long as I am magistrate."

Then, emptying the basket upon the ground, he ordered one of his officers to jump upon the fish, and trample the whole of them to pieces under his feet. Content with this infliction of moral discipline, my friend Pytheas, recommended me to depart; "for," said he, "my dear Lucius, I have sufficiently disgraced this little old fellow."

Astonished and dumb-foundered, at finding myself deprived of both money and supper, through the clever device of my knowing fellow-student, I betook myself to the baths. After bathing, I returned to the house of Milo, and was going to

Inspection of the markets.]—This officer, whose duties corresponded with those of the Ædile at Rome. was called by the Greeks 'Agoranomus.'

my bedchamber, when the maid-servant, Fotis, said, "Your host invites you to supper."

I, however, who was already aware of the parsimony of Milo, courteously endeavoured to excuse myself by saying, that I thought the fatigue of the journey would be repaired not so much by food, as by sleep. Milo, however, on receiving this message, came himself, and taking me by the right hand, politely tried to lead me in to supper ; and when I hung back, made a little resistance—"I will not quit you," said he, "until you accompany me." At the same time, enforcing his words with an oath, he led me, thus obliged reluctantly to give way to his perseverance, to that same couch of his.

When I was seated—"And how is our friend Demeas?" said he. "Are things going on prosperously with him? How is his wife? Are his children well? What about his servants?" I answered every one of his enquiries. He then minutely questioned me as to the object of my journey; after I had fully informed him, he next asked me, with the most scrupulous inquisitiveness, concerning my country, and the principal people there ; and, lastly, he was enquiring about our prefect, when, on perceiving that, weary from my long journey, as well as from the length of my narration, I nodded, and stopped short in the middle of my sentences, and that, quite knocked up, I was stammering away at different words, so as to render them unintelligible, he at length permitted me to go to rest.

Glad to escape from the prosy and famishing entertainment of the shabby old fellow, overpowered with sleep, and not with good cheer, having made my meal on talk alone : I returned to my chamber, and surrendered myself to the repose I so much longed for.

BOOK THE SECOND.

CURIOSITY OF LUCIUS WITH RESPECT TO WITCHCRAFT—HE MEETS
HIS MOTHER'S FRIEND BYRRHÆNA—THE ATRIUM OF HER HOUSE
DESCRIBED—SHE CAUTIONS HIM AGAINST THE WITCH PAMPHILE,
MILO'S WIFE—HER WARNINGS ONLY INFLAME HIS CURIOSITY—
HE MAKES LOVE TO FOTIS—SUPS WITH MILO AND PAMPHILE—
SECOND EPISODE : DIOPHANES THE CHALDÆAN — LUCIUS SUPS
WITH BYRRHÆNA—THIRD EPISODE : TELEPHRON'S TALE—THE
FESTIVAL OF THE GOD OF LAUGHTER—LUCIUS KILLS THREE
BURGLARS.

So soon as a new sun had dispersed the night, and ushered in
the day, I awoke and jumped out of bed ; being by nature
anxious and, indeed, over-desirous of becoming acquainted with
whatever is rare and admirable, I called to mind that I was
in the very heart of Thessaly,* celebrated, by the unanimous
consent of the whole world, as the land where the incantations
of the magic art are indigenous, and in that very city which
was the scene of the story of my worthy fellow-traveller Aris-
tomenes. Excited in the highest degree by my longing de-
sire and my ardent temperament, I examined everything with
eager curiosity.

Indeed, there was nothing in that city, which on beholding,
I could believe to be what it really was ; but I fancied that
everything was utterly transformed into another shape by
means of some deadly spell, that the stones I kicked against
were petrified men, that the birds I heard singing, were men
transformed and feathered, that the trees which surrounded the
pomœrium, were people in like manner, covered with leaves,
and that the fountains of water flowed forth from the liquefied
human bodies.

I was every instant *expecting* that the statues and pictures
would take to walking, that the walls would speak, that oxen

---

* *Heart of Thessaly.*]—Thessaly is spoken of by many of the ancient
writers as the fruitful source of magic and incantation. Indeed, we find
the name ' Thessala' used by Plautus and Horace to denote a witch or
sorceress.

and cattle of all kinds would utter prophecies,* and that an oracle would issue on a sudden from the rays of the sun in heaven.

Thus bewildered, indeed I may say stupefied with tormenting anxiety, perceiving no likelihood or even trace of the objects of my wishes, I perambulated the whole city. Wandering in this way just like one intoxicated, from door to door, I suddenly, without knowing where I was, found myself in the provision market.

Here, as it happened, quickening my pace, I overtook a lady, who was walking along, attended by a great retinue of domestics. The gold that hung on her cheeks and her embroidered garments, bespoke her to be, beyond a doubt, a woman of the highest rank. Close by her side walked a man considerably advanced in years, who, the moment he saw me, exclaimed, "By Hercules! here is Lucius," and at the same moment embraced me, after which he whispered in the lady's ear something I could not hear.

"And will you not, then," said he, "approach and salute your parent?"†

"I dare not," I replied, "salute a lady whom I do not know;" and immediately the colour rising to my cheeks, I turned away my head and stood stock still; while the lady looked at me with a steady gaze.

"Behold," said she, "the high-born breeding of his most virtuous mother Salvia;‡ and then, his person bears an inexpressible resemblance to hers in every particular; tall, yet not too tall; a slender but well-rounded figure, clear rosy complexion, hair yellow, and arranged without foppery,§ eyes

---

* *Utter prophecies.*]—Lucan, in the Pharsalia, i. 561, mentions as an evil omen, 'the tongues of cattle being adapted to human accents.' Livy and Valerius Maximus inform us that an ox spoke and warned Rome of the disasters which would ensue on Hannibal's arrival in Italy. One of the Scholiasts on Lucan says, that in the civil wars between Cæsar and Pompey, an ass spoke; another informs us that an ox spoke while ploughing, in reproof of his driver, and told him that it was useless to urge him on, for soon there would be no people left in Italy to consume the produce of the fields.

† *Salute your parents.*]—The word 'parens' here is indicative of esteem and veneration, but does not imply relationship in blood.

‡ *Mother Salvia.*]—She recognises him by this resemblance to his mother Salvia. Aptitude to blush was, among the ancients, considered a mark of high birth.

§ *Arranged without foppery.*]—Yellow or flaxen hair much admired by

grey but keen, and glancing in all directions as brightly as an eagle's; in short, he is comely in every point, and his carriage is graceful and unaffected."

Then addressing herself to me, she added, "In these very arms of mine, Lucius, have I nursed you, and, indeed, how could it be otherwise? seeing that I not only participated with your mother in blood, but was brought up along with her. For we are both descended from the family of Plutarch, both of us sucked the breast of the same nurse, and grew up together in the ties of sisterhood; nor is there any other difference between us, except that of rank; for while she contracted a splendid alliance, I married a person in a private station. I am that Byrrhæna, whose name, probably, you may recollect, as having been frequently mentioned among those who brought you up. Come, therefore, with all confidence to our house, or rather, I would say, to your own home."

Having had time to digest my bashfulness while the lady was speaking, I replied, "Far be it from me, my parent, that I should leave my entertainer, Milo, without any just cause of complaint. Nevertheless I will take care not to fail in whatever can be done without a breach of the courtesies of hospitality. And as often as I shall have occasion hereafter to come this way, I will be sure to call upon you."

Conversing in this way, we had proceeded but a few paces, ere we arrived at Byrrhæna's house. The hall* was most beautiful, and had statues of the goddess of Victory,† raised on pillars which stood at the four corners. The wings of the figures were expanded; their dewy feet seemed to brush the surface of a rolling sphere, although it moved not; and they looked, not as if they were attached to it, but hovered in the air. A statue of Diana, in Parian marble, occupied a level space in the middle of the enclosure. The figure was singularly beau-

the ancients, but only fops and debauchees expended their time on curling or dressing the hair. Apuleius inveighs against the practice in his 'Apologia.'

* *The hall.*]—The 'atrium' was not properly the 'hall' of a house in our sense of the word, but was a spacious room beyond the vestibule, lighted from above, and into which the other rooms on the ground floor opened.

† *Goddess of Victory.*]—'Palmaris Deæ.' Literally, the 'palm-holding goddess,' in reference to the branch of palm which the Goddess of Victory was represented as holding in her hand.

tiful; the garments of the goddess were blown back by the wind; she seemed in the act of running directly towards you as you entered, and awed you by the majesty of her godlike form. Dogs supported the goddess on either side, and these, too, were of marble. Their eyes were fierce and threatening, their ears erect, their nostrils open, their jaws agape to devour; and had any barking been heard in the neighbourhood, you would have thought it proceeded from those marble throats. A thing, also, in which the excellent sculptor had given proof of the most consummate art, was this, that the fore feet of the dogs, up-lifted to their chests, were in the act of running, while the hind feet pressed the ground. At the back of the goddess stood a rock, wrought to resemble a grotto, overgrown with moss, grass, leaves, and brushwood; with vines and shrubs here and there; and the reflection of the statue gleamed from the polished marble within the grotto. Over the extreme edge of the rock hung apples and grapes, most exquisitely wrought, and in which art, rivalling nature, had so counterfeited their originals, that you would have thought they might be gathered for eating, when fragrant autumn had breathed upon them the tints of maturity. And if, leaning forward, you had beheld the streamlets, which gently rippled as they ran beneath the feet of the goddess, you would have thought that, like clusters of grapes which hang from the vine, they too resembled real life in the faculty of motion.

In the midst of the foliage was Actæon, carved in marble, peering over his shoulders, and at the very instant changed into the wild form of a stag; and both in the marble and in the reflection of the stream he was seen lying in ambush, await-ing the coming of Diana to bathe.

While I was inspecting these various objects with eager curiosity and delight, " Everything you see," said Byrrhæna, " is yours;" and she then privately ordered all the other per-sons to depart. After they were gone, " I take this goddess* to witness," said she, " my dearest Lucius, how great are the anxious apprehensions I entertain for you, and how earnestly I desire that you, who are as it were my son, should be put upon your guard. Beware, resolutely beware of the wicked arts and nefarious blandishments of that Pamphile, the wife

* *This goddess.*]—Diana.

of Milo, who you say is your host. She is a notorious sor-
ceress, and is believed to be mistress of every kind of necroman-
tic incantation ; so much so, that by merely breathing on twigs,
stones, and such other trifling things, she knows how to sub-
merge all this light of the starry universe beneath the depths
of Tartarus, and into original chaos. Moreover, the instant
she has beheld·any youth of handsome appearance, she is capti-
vated by his good looks, and immediately rivets her eyes and
her affections upon him. She inveigles him with blandish-
ments, takes possession of his heart, and enthrals him in eternal
fetters of profound love ; but as for those who are not suffi-
ciently compliant, she loathes and scorns them, and either
changes them in a moment into stones, cattle, and animals of
every kind,* or utterly annihilates them. I tremble for you,
therefore, and entreat you to be on your guard. For this
woman inflames with a passion that is eternal, and you, with
your youth and your good looks, are exactly fitted for her pur-
pose."

Thus did Byrrhæna counsel me in a most anxious tone.

I, however, who was naturally of an inquisitive turn, as
soon as I heard the name of the magic art, a name that had
ever been the object of my aspirations, was so far from feel-
ing inclined to be on my guard against Pamphile, that, moved
by an irresistible impulse, I even longed to devote myself to
such pursuits, even though it should cost me dear, and to pre-
cipitate myself, with a running leap, into the very abyss *of
magic.*

Wild with excitement, then, I quickly released myself from
the grasp of her hand, as though from some chain, and hastily
bidding her adieu, I flew at the top of my speed to the house
of Milo ; and while I thus scoured along, just like a person
out of his senses, " Now then, Lucius," said I, " look sharp,
and have your wits about you. You have now the long-
wished-for opportunity, and may satiate your mind with mira-
culous stories, as for many a day you have been longing to do.
Away then with puerile apprehensions, grapple with this ad-
venture hand to hand, like a man ; but, at all events, ab-

---

* *Animals of every kind.*]—Homer and Ovid relate the same of Circe,
a Greek sorceress, but evidently of the same stock as the enchantress
queen Labe, whose incantations are so amusingly described in the story
of Beder and Giauhare, in the Arabian Nights.

stain from amorous dalliance with the wife of your host, and religiously respect the conjugal bed of the worthy Milo. But, on the other hand, you may lay siege to the maid-servant Fotis; for she is of charming form, of lively manners, and a pleasant tongue. Yesterday evening too, when you went to rest, she politely escorted you into the bedchamber, helped you attentively into bed, tucked you up very lovingly, and then giving you a kiss, betrayed by her countenance how loth she was to leave you; and lastly, she stood still more than once, and turned round to look at you. Good luck be your speed then!* but come what may, have at this Fotis."

While forming these resolutions, I came to Milo's door, and, as the saying is, entered hot-foot† into the execution of my project. However, I did not find either Milo or his wife at home, but only my charmer Fotis, who was preparing sausages for her master and mistress; she had some minced meat on a platter, ready to mix with gravy, which, as my nostrils augured, was very savoury.

She was neatly dressed in a linen garment, gathered in by a bright red sash, just below her breasts, and as she stirred the saucepan round and round by a circular movement of her rosy hand, her supple form partook in the motion, her loins vibrated, and her flexible spine was thrown into charming undulations.

Entranced by the sight, I stood gazing in admiration; all my passions, which before lay dormant, were aroused. At last I said to her, " With what a graceful, what a delightful twist of your hips, you stir that saucepan, my Fotis ! what honeyed dish are you preparing? Happy, and most surely blessed is he, who is allowed by you to dip his finger therein."

" Begone, unhappy wight," cried the sprightly chatter-box,

---

* *Good luck be your speed then!*]—' Quod bonum, felix et faustum.' This formula, somewhat similar to our, ' I wish you health, happiness, and prosperity,' was made use of by persons about to undertake anything of importance, and was supposed not only to avert an evil omen, but to ensure a good one.

† *Entered hot-foot.*]—This is not the literal translation of the phrase pedibus in sententian vado.' It alludes to the practice of taking divisions in the Roman senate, when those who voted in the affirmative, ' in dextram partem pedibus ibant,' ' arose and took the right side of the house.' The author's meaning is, that Lucius resolutely determined to carry out his project.

"begone as far as you can from my fire; for if but a spark of it touch you, you will be burnt to the vitals; and there will be no one to extinguish your heat but myself, who know equally well how to provide a zest for bed and board." Thus saying, she looked at me and smiled.

I did not leave her, however, till I had carefully surveyed the whole contour of her person. But why speak of other particulars? since it has ever been my sole care, in the first place, to scrutinize the head and the hair in public, and after-wards to enjoy their loveliness in private: and in this I proceed upon sure and fixed principles, first, because these are the most important features of the person, and from their conspicuous position, they are the first to present themselves to our sight; and, secondly, because the natural brilliancy of the hair effects for the head what the cheerful colour of a showy garment effects for the other members of the body.

Besides, most women, in order to display their native charms and loveliness, divest themselves of all neck mufflings, throw open their outer garments, and delight to show their naked beauty; being conscious that they shall please more by the roseate hue of their skin, than by the golden tints of their robes. But, on the other hand, (I shudder to speak of such a thing, and may there never be an instance of a catastrophe so dreadful,) if you deprive the most surpassingly beautiful woman of her hair, and thus strip her face of its native ornaments; though she were begotten by heaven, conceived by the sea, and nurtured amid the waves; though, I say, she were Venus herself, surrounded by all the choir of the Graces, attended by a whole multitude of Cupids, girt with her cestus redolent of cinnamon, and bedewed with balsams—still, if she were bald, she would not find favour even in the eyes of her own Vulcan.

How exquisitely charming is hair of a beautiful hue and rich lustre, when it flashes back the rays of the sun, or shines with milder radiance, and varies its lovely aspect with every change of light! now emitting a brightness like that of gold, now shaded off into the softer hue of honey; raven-black at one moment, at the next reflecting the myriad blossom tints of the pigeon's neck; or, when anointed with Arabian drops,*

* *Arabian drops.*]—Myrrh or spikenard is probably meant.

parted by the slender tooth of the comb, and gathered up be-
hind the head, it presents itself to the eyes of the lover, and
like a mirror reflects his overjoyed features. How beautiful,
when its luxuriant mass is accumulated on the crown of the
head, or suffered to flow down the back in profuse curls. Such,
in short, is the dignity of the hair, that though a woman
should go adorned with jewels of gold, rich garments, precious
stones, and every other kind of ornament, still she could not
possibly seem well dressed, unless she had duly arranged her
hair.

But in my Fotis, not studied artifice, but the neglect of orna-
ment, added graces to her person. For her copious hair, thrown
loosely back and falling adown her neck, rested lightly on the
flexuous fringe of her garment; then, after being gradually
drawn together, the ends were looped up, and fastened by a
knot to the crown of her head. I could no longer sustain the
torturing suspense of such exquisite delight, but bending for-
ward gave her a most luscious kiss, on that part where the hair
was drawn up to the top of the head.

She looked at me over her shoulder, and her eyes lit into my
heart with their sidelong glances: "So then, you school-boy,"
said she, "you have taken a sweet, and at the same time, a
bitter draught. Beware, lest the excessive sweetness of the
honey turn into the lasting bitterness of gall."

"Why do you say so, my charmer?" I replied, "since I am
ready to be laid at full length and roasted upon that fire, so my
pain be soothed by a single kiss." So saying, I clasped her in
my arms, and fell to kissing her.

And now, with responsive desire waxing with mine into
an equality of love, exhaling from her open mouth the odour
of cinnamon, she ravished me with the nectareous touch of her
tongue, so that I exclaimed, "I shall perish, nay, rather, I am
a lost man already, unless you will be propitious."

Smothering me with kisses, she replied, "Be of good cou-
rage, for I am become your bondsmaid through mutual desire,
nor shall our delights be long deferred; but as soon as torches
are lighted, I will come to your chamber. Depart, then, and
hold yourself in readiness, for I will do battle with you all
night long, as bravely as heart can wish." After we had
prattled thus for some time, we parted.

It was just about noon, when Byrrhæna sent me a complimentary present,* consisting of a fat pig, two couple and a half of fowls, and a jar of choice old wine. Calling Fotis, " Look," said I, " Bacchus, the exciter and armour-bearer of Venus, has come here of his own accord. Let us quaff all this wine to-day, in order that it may extinguish in us all bashful hesitation, and stimulate our lusty vigour. For the voyage of Venus stands in need only of such provision as this : that through the whole of the wakeful night, the lamp may be plentifully supplied with oil, and the cup with wine."

The rest of the day I passed in bathing, and at supper : for, being invited by the worthy Milo, I took my place at his epitome of a table, as much as possible out of the view of his wife, as I kept in mind the admonitions of Byrrhæna ; while every now and then, I cast a trembling glance upon her features, as if I was beholding the lake Avernus.† But as I continually followed Fotis, who waited on us, with my eyes, my feelings were refreshed by looking at her.

And now, as the evening had advanced, Pamphile, looking at the lamp, remarked, " We shall have a terrible fall of rain to-morrow."

On her husband asking her how she knew that to be the case, she answered, that the lamp had predicted‡ it to her. At this speech, Milo, bursting into a laugh, exclaimed, " In this lamp, we feed a mighty Sibyl, who looks down from the socket,§ as from a watch-tower, upon all that is going on in the heavens, and even the sun himself."

Mingling in the conversation, I said, " This is only a simple instance of this kind of divination, and, indeed, it ought not to seem wonderful, that this flame, small though it is, and ignited by human hands, should still have a consciousness of

* *A complimentary present.*]—Xeniola. This was the name given to presents sent to strangers at their lodgings, as tokens of hospitality ; which. as in the present case, consisted of the various delicacies of the season.

† *Avernus.*]—Avernus was a lake of Campania, near to Baiæ, and was called as if it was αορνος, *destitute of birds*, because, by its foul exhalations, it destroyed the birds that flew over it. This lake, dedicated to Pluto, was thought to be the entrance to the realms beneath, and is frequently, as in this place of Apuleius, assumed for those realms.

‡ *The lamp had predicted.*]—So in the first Georgic of Virgil, we find that the growth of a fungus on the wick of a burning lamp, is considered to prognosticate rain.

§ *From the socket.*]—The ' candelabra' of the ancients were frequently placed on high, in a recess made for the purpose in the wall.

the greater and celestial fire, as of its parent, and should thus, by divine presage, know and announce to us what the source of its existence is about to effect in the summit of the firmament. For with us, at Corinth, a certain Chaldean stranger is just now disturbing the whole city with his wonderful replies to questions asked him, and is disclosing the secrets of the Fates to the public for payment. Thus, for instance, he would tell the day on which a marriage should be contracted that was destined to last long, or when the foundations of walls should be laid so as to remain for ever; what day would be advantageous to the merchant; or which one would be suited to the traveller, or adapted for setting sail. In fine, when I consulted him as to what would be the result of this journey of mine, he told me many things of a very wonderful and an extremely varied nature. He said, for instance, that I should shortly obtain a very considerable renown, and that I should be the writer of an incredible story, and of sundry books."

"What was the appearance of this Chaldean?" said Milo, with a smile, "and what was his name?"

"He was a tall man," replied I, "of a dark complexion, and his name was Diophanes."

"It is the very same person," said Milo, "and no other, and here also, among us, he made many similar predictions to various persons, and realized thereby no little wealth, indeed, I may say, a considerable sum of money; but at last experienced an inauspicious, or, to speak more truly, a cruel lot."*

SECOND EPISODE.

DIOPHANES THE CHALDEAN.

One day, when, encircled by a great crowd of people, he was dealing out the fates to the bystanders, a certain merchant, Cerdo by name, came to him, desirous to know what day would be suitable for a journey. After Diophanes had named one, Cerdo took out his purse, poured out the money, and counted a hundred denars, which Diophanes was to receive as the price

* *Inauspicious—cruel lot.*]—He puns on the resemblance of the words 'scæva' and 'sæva;' but the play on these words cannot be preserved in English.

of his predictions, when a young man of a noble family, com-
ing softly behind him, pulled him by the garment, and on his
turning round, embraced and kissed him in the most affectionate
manner.

Diophanes having returned the embrace, desired the young
man to take a seat beside him, and, under the surprise of his
unexpected appearance, quite forgot the business with which
he was just then engaged.

"How long is it," said he, "since you, whom I have so
much wished for, arrived in this neighbourhood?"

"I arrived early last evening," replied the other. "But
tell me, brother, in your turn, how it happened that you sailed
so quickly from the island of Euboea to this city, and how
you travelled hither by sea and land."

Then, Diophanes, this egregious Chaldean, taken aback, and
not altogether himself, replied, "May our enemies and evil-
wishers meet with the like cruel, indeed, I may say, Ulyssean
peregrination. For the ship in which we sailed, being shat-
tered by various storms and whirlwinds, after losing both mast
and rudder, was with the utmost difficulty brought to the verge
of the opposite shore, and went down, head foremost; and we,
having lost all our property, with difficulty saved our lives by
swimming. Whatever we could scrape together, either from
the pity of strangers, or the benevolence of our friends, a band
of robbers laid hands on the whole of it; and my only brother,
Arisuatus, resisting their violence, was murdered, poor fellow!
before these eyes."

While Diophanes was dolefully relating these particulars, the
merchant Cerdo, snatching up the money he had paid as the
price of the prediction, instantly took to his heels. Then, in-
deed, Diophanes at length aroused from his fit of abstraction,
perceived the blunder he had made, especially when he saw
all of us who stood around him burst into loud fits of laughter.

END OF THE SECOND EPISODE.

"Nevertheless, master Lucius, I sincerely wish that the
Chaldean may have predicted the truth to you if to no one
else, and that you may be fortunate, and make a prosperous
journey."

While Milo was thus prosing on at interminable length, I

D

groaned inwardly, and was not a little vexed with myself for having voluntarily introduced a series of wearisome stories, and thus losing a good part of the evening, and its delightful enjoyments. At length, therefore, gulping down all my bashfulness, I said to Milo, "Let Diophanes carry his destiny with him, and again expose the plunder of the public to land and sea. But permit me, who am still sore from the fatigues of yesterday, to retire early to rest."

So saying, I rose up and betook myself to my bedchamber; and there I found a very nice assortment of good cheer. The bed of the servant boys was laid on the floor, at a considerable distance outside the door; in order, I suppose, that they might not be within hearing of our chatter in the night. Close by my bed stood a small table, laden with the choice remains of the whole supper, and some fair cups already half filled with wine, only waiting for the admixture of water. Near these, also, was a flagon, with a gradually dilated orifice, for the more convenient pouring forth of the wine; the whole being a whet, as it were, for what was to follow.

I had scarcely laid me down, when, behold! my Fotis (her mistress having now retired to rest) came in throwing a garland of roses upon the bed, and wearing a single rose in full bloom in her bosom. After pressing me close and kissing me, tying a garland round my head, and strewing flowers upon me, she took up a cup, and pouring warm water into it, handed it to me that I might drink a little. Before I had drunk the whole, she gently took it from me, and gradually diminishing with her lips what was left, sipped it sweetly, with her eyes fixed on me all the while. Again and again we pledged each other; until at last, flushed with wine, turbulent in mind and body, and tingling and smarting with desire, I gave my Fotis ocular proof of my amorous impatience:

"Pity me," I said, "and relieve me without delay; for you may perceive how I have been kept on full stretch by the thought of that combat to which you challenged me without the intervention of a herald. Ever since I received the first of cruel Cupid's arrows in my vitals, I have been standing to my arms, and I am greatly afraid my bow-string will be snapped by its excessive tension. But if you would gratify me still more, untie your hair, let it flow freely over your shoulders, and come and give me loving kisses."

In an instant she had snatched away all the eating and drinking apparatus; then, stripping off all her garments, with her hair dishevelled in joyous wantonness, she stood transformed into the image of Venus rising from the sea, her rosy hand shading, with coquettish art rather than through modesty, the beauties it did not conceal. "Fight," she said, "and fight bravely, for I will not give way an inch, nor turn my back. Face to face, come on, if you are a man! Strike home; do your worst, and die! The battle this day is without quarter."

So saying, she jumped into the bed, threw herself upon me, and like an athlete, bending on his haunches over his prostrate but still struggling antagonist, she assailed me with astonishing rapidity of movement and lubricity of spine; till wearied in body and spirit, we lay powerless and gasping for breath in each other's arms. Many times we renewed our wrestling, and so we passed the sleepless night until dawn, refreshing ourselves at intervals with wine, and rekindling our ardour for the pleasant strife. In like manner we passed many other nights.

Cum ego jam vino madens, nec animo tantum verum etiam corpore ipso adlibidinem inquies alioquin et petulans, etiam saucius paulisper inguinum fine, laciniâ remotâ, impatientiam Veneris Fotidi meæ monstrans, Miserere, inquam, et subveni maturius. Nam, ut vides, prælio, quod nobis sine fecialis officio indixeras, jam proximanté vehementer, intentus, ubi primam sagittam sævi cupidinis in ima præcordia mea delapsam excepi, arcum meum en! ipse vigor attendit, et oppido formido, ne nervus rigoris nimietate rumpatur. Sed ut mihi morem plenius gesseris, ineffusum laxa crinem, et capillo fluenter undante, ede complexus amabiles.

Nec mora, cum omnibus illis cibariis vasculis raptim remotis, laciniis cunctis suis renudata, crinibusque dissolutis ad hilarem lasciviam, in speciem Veneris, quæ marinos fluctus subit, pulchre reformata, paulisper etiam glabellum feminale* roseâ palmulâ potius obumbrans de industriâ, quam tegens verecundiâ: Præliare, inquit, et fortiter præliare, nec enim tibi cedam, nec terga vertam. Cominus in aspectum, si vir es,

* *Glabellum feminale*.]—Muliebre pudendum, quod Fotis meretricio more depilaverat.

It happened one day that Byrrhæna pressingly invited me to sup with her; and though I made many excuses, she would not let me off. I, therefore, had to resort to Fotis, and take counsel from her, as from an oracle; and though unwilling that I should depart from her the breadth of a nail, yet she kindly indulged me with a little respite from our amatory warfare.

"But, look you," said she, "take care that you return early from this supper, for a frantic faction of the young nobles has been disturbing the public tranquillity, and you will see murdered men lying here and there in the streets; nor can the forces of the prefect of the province, in consequence of the remoteness of their stations, relieve the city from these outrages. Now, your superior fortune, and contempt for you, as a foreigner, may possibly cause you to be waylaid."

"Do not be under any apprehensions, my Fotis," said I; "for besides that I prefer my own pleasures to the banquets of others, I will return early, in order to remove these fears of yours. However, I shall not go unattended; for girded with my trusty sword, I shall carry a protector of my safety."

Thus equipped I proceeded to the entertainment. There was a numerous assembly of guests, and as Byrrhæna was a woman of rank, it comprised some of the first-rate people of the city. The repast was sumptuous; the couches, framed with polished ivory, were covered with cloth of gold; the cups were capacious, of various graceful designs, and all unique in value. Some were of glass, with figures exquisitely embossed : others of the purest crystal; others, again, of burnished silver, or of

---

dirige, et grassare naviter, et occide moriturus. Hodierna pugna non habet missionem. Hæc simul dicens, inscenso grabbatulo, super me cossim residens, ac crebra subsiliens, lubricisque gestibus mobilem spinam quatiens, pendulæ Veneris fructu me satiavit; usque dum, lassis animis et marcidis artubus defatigati, simul ambo corruimus inter mutuos amplexus, animas anhelantes.

His et hujuscemodi colluctationibus ad confinia lucis usque pervigiles egimus, poculis interdum lassitudinem refoventes, et libidinem incitantes, et voluptatem integrantes. Ad hujus' noctis exemplar similes adstruximus alias plusculas.

glittering gold, or of amber, admirably wrought and hollowed out into beakers. In short, whatever one thought impossible to be made by man, was there.

The carvers* were numerous, and their dresses splendid; the dishes were abundant, damsels waited gracefully at table, while youths with curled locks, and beautifully attired, ever and anon handed to the guests old wine in cups of precious stone.

And now, lights being brought in, the conversation gradually became more convivial; there was abundance of laughter, and good-humoured quips and jokes flew about in every direction, when Byrrhæna thus addressed me : "How do you enjoy yourself in this country of ours? If I am not mistaken, we greatly excel all other cities in temples, baths, and other public works. And then we have an extraordinary abundance of all the commodities of life. Beyond a doubt here one enjoys full liberty, and may live at his ease; for the stranger who is a man of business, there is all the bustle of Rome, while for the new-comer who is of retiring habits, the quiet of a country-house is here to be found. In fine, our city is a place of resort for all the pleasure-seekers of this province."

"What you say is quite true," I replied, "and no where have I felt myself more perfectly at liberty than I am here. But I am sadly frightened at the dark mysteries and irresistible spells of the magic art. For it is said, that here not even the sepulchres of the dead are unmolested, but that certain remnants and cuttings from the dead bodies are sought from the tombs and funeral-piles, to ensure deadly misfortune to the living. I am told also that when foreigners are buried, old hags of sorceresses are in the habit of outstripping the funeral procession, in their speed to ravage the corpse."

"No doubt of it," observed one of the guests; "and what is more, in this place they do not even spare the living. There is a certain person—I don't name him—who suffered from an attack of this nature, and whose face was mutilated and deformed in all manner of ways."

At these remarks, an uncontrollable fit of laughter burst forth from all the guests, and the faces and eyes of all were

---

* *The carvers.*]—'Diribitores.' It was probably the duty of these servants to carry round the viands and distribute them among the guests.

turned towards a person who sat in a corner, apart from the rest of the company. This person, confused by the long-continued merriment, and indignantly muttering between his teeth, was preparing to rise and leave the room, when Byrrhæna addressed him, and said, "Nay, my good Telephron, do not go, but stop a little while, and with your usual good humour, do tell us that adventure of yours over again, that my son, Lucius, here, may also enjoy the pleasure of hearing your entertaining story."

To this the other replied, "You, indeed, madam, always preserve a scrupulous regard for good breeding, but the insolence of some people is such as not to be tolerated."

These words were pronounced by him in a tone of great excitement. Byrrhæna, however, reiterated her request, and conjuring him as he valued her life to tell the story, forced him at last to comply, whether he liked or not. Accordingly, gathering up the coverings of the couch in a heap, resting his elbow thereon, and raising his body a little on the couch, he extended his right hand and arranged his fingers after the manner of *our* orators, closing the last two, and pointing the rest straight forward, with the thumb upturned.* Then, with a courteous smile, he began as follows :—

THIRD EPISODE.

STORY OF TELEPHRON, THE STUDENT.

"While I was yet pursuing my studies, I went from Miletus,† to see the Olympic games; and as I wished also to pay a visit to the chief places of this celebrated province, I travelled over all Thessaly, and arrived under unlucky auspices at Larissa. As the money I had brought with me for my journey had been nearly all got rid of in my rambles, I was put to my shifts to repair my impoverished state. While so doing, I saw a tall

* *With the thumb upturned.*]—Contrary to our practice, the ancients used considerable gesticulation with the thumb, when speaking in public or engaging in a dispute. The upturned thumb was the sign of emphatic and impressive discourse. .

† *Went from Miletus.*]—'Mileto profectus' seems necessarily to have this meaning, though, singularly enough, Taylor and Sir G. Head concur in rendering it, 'went *to* Miletus.'

old man, standing on a stone* in the middle of the forum, and making proclamation in a loud voice : 'If any one will under. take to guard the body of a dead man, he shall be well rewarded for his services.'

"On this, I said to one of the bystanders, 'What am I to understand by this? Are the dead in the habit of running away in this country?'

"'Hold your tongue,' replied he, 'for you are a boy, and a green one too, and a foreigner all over, not to know that you are in Thessaly, where it is a universal practice with witches to tear off pieces from the faces of the dead with their teeth, in order to use them as ingredients in the magic art.'

"'Pray, tell me,' said I, 'in what does this funeral war- denship consist?'

"'In the first place,' he replied, ' ' you must watch inces- santly the livelong night, with eyes fixed steadily on the corpse, wide open and not indulging in a wink ; nor must your gaze ever be turned away to the one side or the other, no, not even may you cast a glance aside it. For these most abominable shifters of their skins, changing, in appearance, into any ani- mal they please, creep upon you unawares, so that they can easily elude the very eyes of Justice and of the Sun. For they assume the forms of birds, dogs, mice, ay, and even of flies ; and thus disguised, they exert their dire incantations, and overwhelm the guardians with sleep. Nor can any person sufficiently describe the extent of the devices which they make use of, for the sake of gratifying their libidinous appetite. And yet, after all, no larger pay than four or six pieces of gold is offered as the reward of such a dangerous service as this. But stop; there is one thing I had almost forgotten : if the person who watches does not on the following morning give up possession of the dead body in an entire state, he is compelled to make good the whole of it with strips cut from his own face, to match whatever has been torn off from that of the corpse.'

"On learning these facts, I summoned up all my courage, and going straightway to the crier, 'Cease from making proclama-

---

* *Standing on a stone.*]—We learn from the Bacchides of Plautus and other works that it was the general custom for the 'præco,' or 'crier,' to mount a stone before making his proclamation.

tion,' said I; 'here is a guardian ready to your hand; tell me what is to be the reward.'

"'A thousand pieces of money will be paid you,' said he. 'But look, young man, you must be very careful to preserve the dead body, which is that of the son of one of the principal persons of this city, from the abominable Harpies.'

"'You are talking nonsense to me,' said I, 'and mere trifles. You behold in me a man of iron nerve, proof against sleep, and, beyond a doubt, more sharp-sighted than Lynceus himself, or Argus; in fact, one who is eyes all over.'

"I had no sooner said this, than he at once led me to a certain house, the main entrance of which being closed, he introduced me through a low back door, and into a darkened bedchamber, with closed window shutters, where there was a lady dressed in black garments, and weeping. Going up to her, the crier said, 'This person has agreed to your terms, and confidently undertakes to watch the body of your husband.'

"On this, the lady, throwing back on each side the hair that hung down over her face, which even in grief was beautiful, and turning towards me, said, 'Take care, I beg of you, to perform vigilantly the duty which you have undertaken.'

"'Never fear,' said I, 'only have in readiness something to throw into the bargain as a present.'

"Assenting to this request, she hastily arose, and bade me follow her into another bedchamber. There, in the presence of seven witnesses who had been introduced into the room, she pointed with her hand to a dead body that was covered with a linen cloth of the purest white; and having wept for a considerable time at the sight of it, she called upon those present to bear testimony, and carefully pointed out to them every particular; while a person made notes on tablets of the parts of the body, which were severally touched for that purpose.

"'Behold,' said she, 'the nose entire, the eyes in a sound condition, the ears safe, the lips untouched, and the chin perfect. Do you, worthy citizens,* bear testimony to this.' Having thus said, and the tablets duly signed and sealed, she was departing, when I said to her,

"'Have the goodness, madam, to order that all things may be furnished to me which are requisite for my use.'

"'And what are they?' said she.

* *Worthy citizens.*]—'Quirites,' more properly 'Roman citizens.'

" 'A good large lamp,' I replied, 'sufficient oil for keeping it alight till daylight, some warm water, with wine vessels and a cup, and a dish furnished with the remains of the dinner.'

" 'Begone, foolish man,' said she, shaking her head, ' do you expect to find in a house of sorrow remains of suppers, in which no smoke whatever has been seen for these many days? Do you think you have come hither for the purpose of eating and drinking? Rather betake yourself to sorrow and tears, as best suited to this place.' Then turning to her maid-servant, she said, 'Myrrhina, give him the lamp and oil directly,' and so saying, she went out, and left the guardian shut up in the bed-chamber.

" Being thus left alone to comfort the corpse, I rubbed my eyes, to fortify them for their duty of watchfulness, and kept up my spirits by singing. And now behold twilight came on, night fell, then night deeper and deeper still, and at last the hour of midnight; then, of a truth, my fears, that had some time been increasing, became redoubled. All of a sudden a weasel, creeping into the apartment, stopped close before me, and fixed its eyes most intently upon me, so much so, that the little creature quite agitated my mind by its unusual confidence. At length, however, I said to it: 'Out with you, nasty little beast! and go hide yourself to the mice that are just like you, before you get a knock-down blow from me. Be off with you, I say!'

" The animal turned tail, and immediately ran out of the chamber: and at the very instant a profound sleep suddenly seized and engulphed me; so that not even the God of Delphi himself could have easily determined which of us two, who there lay prostrate, was the more dead. In fact, I was so insensible, and so much in need of some one else to take care of me, that I might just as well have not been there at all.

" Hardly had the clarion of the crested cohort sounded a truce to the night, when I, at length aroused, and terrified in the extreme, ran up to the dead body; holding the light to it, and uncovering its face, I scrutinized every feature, and found everything in proper order. Presently, the poor widow burst into the room in tears and great distress, with the witnesses of yesterday; and, immediately throwing herself on the body, and kissing it again and again, she began to examine it all over, with the assistance of the lamp. Then turning, she called

Philodespotus,* the steward of her house, and ordered him, without delay, to pay the promised reward to one who had acted as so good a guardian.

"This being given me without delay, 'We thank you sincerely, young man,' said she, 'and, by Hercules! for having so well performed this service, we will henceforth enrol you among the rest of our household.'

"Overjoyed at this unlooked-for piece of good fortune, and enchanted at the sight of the glittering pieces of gold, which every now and then I shook up and down in my hand, 'By all means, madam,' said I, 'consider me one of your servants; and, as often as you stand in need of my services, you may confidently command me.'

"Hardly had I thus spoken, when all the servants, heaping curses upon the dreadful ominousness† of my words, snatched up whatever came to hand, and fell upon me. One began to strike me in the face with his fist, another to dig me in the back and ribs with his elbows, a third to kick me with his feet, a fourth to pull out my hair, a fifth to tear my clothes. Thus, mauled and mangled almost as badly as was Adonis or Orpheus,‡ I was thrust out of doors.

"I stopped to recover myself in the next street, and reflecting too late on my inauspicious and imprudent remark, I could not but acknowledge that I had fully deserved to suffer even still more blows than I had received. By and by the dead person was carried out, accompanied, for the last time, by lamentations and outcries; and, according to the custom of the country, was borne with all the pomp of a public funeral, as being one of the principal men, through the forum. To the side of the corpse there runs up an old man, bathed with

* *Philodespotus.*]—A name, composed of the two Greek words φιλὸς and δἑσπότης, and signifying one who willingly submits to the domination of another; or, in the language of Horace,
——— 'Amicum mancipium domino.'

† *Dreadful ominousness.*]—Omen seems a preferable reading here to omnes.' His expressions certainly were not replete with auspicious omens: as, unwittingly, he anticipated a period when he might have to wait over the corpse of a second dead husband.

‡ *Orpheus*]—In this most corrupt passage, the reading 'Musæi vatis has been adopted. It is possible that Orpheus, the son of the Muse Calliope, may be referred to under that name.

tears, and tearing his venerable white hair; and then, seizing the bier with both his hands, and with a voice raised to the highest pitch, though interrupted with frequent sobs, 'O Romans,' exclaimed he, 'by your faith, and by the public morality, espouse the cause of your murdered fellow-citizen, and wreak your severe vengeance on this abominable and wicked woman, for her most atrocious crime; for she, and no one else, has cut off by poison this unfortunate young man, my sister's son, for the sake of her paramour, and made a prey of the inheritance.'

"After this manner, the old man loudly uttered complaints and lamentations, broken by his sobs. In the meantime, the people began to express their indignation, being impelled to a belief in the charge, on the grounds of its probability alone. They shouted for fire; for stones; they incited the boys to the destruction of the woman; but she, pretending to shed tears, and adjuring all the Divinities, denied most solemnly that she had perpetrated a crime of such great enormity.

"'Well then,' said the old man, 'let us refer the decision of the truth to divine providence. Here is Zachlas, the Egyptian, a first-rate prophet,* who has already agreed with me, for a considerable sum, to recall the soul for a few moments from the realms beneath, to reanimate this body.' Thus saying, he brought forward into the midst of the people a young man, clothed in linen garments,† with his head close shaven, and having on his feet sandals made of palm leaves.‡ After having for some time kissed his hands and embraced his very knees, 'O priest,' said he, 'take pity on me, by the stars of the heavens, by the Gods of the infernal regions, by the elements of nature, by the silence of night, by the Coptic en-

---

* *Prophet.*]—The Egyptians were consummately skilled in astrology and magic; their priests were prophets, and were believed to be divinely wise. Hence Pythagoras, Plato, and the most famous of the Greek philosophers, are said to have associated with them.

† *Linen garments.*]—See book xi., where the linen garments of the priests of Isis are more copiously mentioned. Woollen garments were, according to the doctrine of Orpheus and Pythagoras, profane; but those of linen were considered as most pure.

‡ *Sandals made of palm leaves.*]—'Baxæ,' or 'Baxeæ,' were sandals with wooden soles, made of twigs or fibres. They were worn on the stage by comic actors, and philosophers much affected the use of them. The Egyptians made them of palm leaves or the papyrus.

closures,* by the overflowing of the Nile, by the mysteries of
the Memphis, and by the sistrum of Pharos, I implore you.
Give to this dead body a short enjoyment of the sun, and infuse
a portion of light into eyes that have been buried in eternal
night. We are not offering resistance to fate, nor do we deny
to the earth what is her property; but we only request a short
space of life, that we may have the consolation of avenging
her death.'

"The prophet being thus propitiated, laid a certain herb
three times on the mouth of the corpse, and placed another
on its breast. He then turned towards the east, and silently
prayed to the rising disk of the glorious Sun, whilst an intense
interest was excited among the byestanders, by the sight of
such awful preparations, and the prospect of a miracle. I
mingled with the crowd, and standing on an elevated stone,
close behind the bier, observed every thing with inquisitive
eyes.

"Presently the breast of the corpse began to be inflated, the
artery to throb with pulsation, the body to be filled with breath;
at last the corpse arose, and thus addressed the young man:
' Why, I beseech thee, dost thou bring me back to the duties of
a momentary existence, after having drunk of the Lethæan cup,
and floated upon the Stygian lake? Cease, I beseech thee,
cease and leave me to my repose.' These were the words heard
to proceed from the body.

"On this, the prophet, becoming still more excited, exclaimed,
' Why dost thou not relate to this crowd each particular, and
disclose the mysteries of thy death? Knowest thou not that the
Furies can be summoned by my imprecations to rack thy wearied
limbs?'

"The body looked up from the bier, and with a deep groan
thus addressed the people: ' Cut off through the nefarious arts
of my newly-married wife, and by a poisonous draught, I have
yielded my yet warm bed to her paramour.'

"Then that choice specimen of a wife, arming herself with
audacity, began to contradict the accusation of her husband in
a wrangling and sacrilegious manner. The excited mob took

* *The Coptic enclosures.*]—This probably alludes to certain embank-
ments which were said to be thrown up annually by swallows around an
island near Coptos, which was sacred to Isis. They were said to labour
so hard in thus attempting to preserve the island from the overflowing
of the Nile, that numbers died at the work.

different sides; one party contended that this most iniquitous woman should be immediately buried alive, with the corpse of her husband; the other declared that credit ought not to be given to the lying testimony of the dead body. The subsequent disclosures, however, of the young man put an end to this dispute; for, again heaving a deep groan, 'I will give you,' he said, 'I will give you incontrovertible evidence of the truth of my statements, and will disclose to you what is known to no other person whatever.'

" Then, pointing to me with his finger: 'When that most sagacious guardian of my body,' said he, ' was diligently keeping watch over me, the hags of sorceresses who eagerly hovered over my mortal spoils, and who, to gain possession thereof, had often changed themselves in vain into other forms, on finding that they could not deceive his unwearied vigilance, at length threw over him a cloud of drowsiness, and buried him in a profound sleep; after which, they did not cease to call upon me by my name, till my weakened joints and chilled limbs struggled, with convulsive efforts, to obey the mandates of the magic art. Then this person, who though alive was still dead, so far as sleep goes, happening to be of the same name as myself, unconsciously arose on hearing his name called, and spontaneously walking just like an inanimate shadow, suffered the intended mutilation instead of myself; for although the doors of the bedchamber were carefully bolted, the witches entered through a chink, and cut off his nose first, and then his ears. And, that the rest of the transaction might correspond with their artful doings, they with the greatest exactness fitted on to him wax, fashioned in imitation of his ears that had been cut off, and provided him with a nose of the same substance, just like his own. And here now stands the unfortunate wretch who has obtained the reward dearly earned, not by his vigilance, but by his sore mutilation.'

" Exceedingly terrified on hearing this, I began to test my fortune. Clapping my hand to my nose, I took hold of it, and off it came: I touched my ears, and they fell to the ground. Meanwhile the spectators pointed their fingers at me, nodded their heads, and greeted me with loud roars of laughter, until streaming with cold perspiration I dashed through the surrounding crowd, and effected my escape. Nor, thus mutilated and an object of ridicule, could I return to my native place ;* but, with my hair falling on each side of my face, I concealed the wounds of my ears, and decently covered the disgrace of my nose with this linen cloth, closely applied to it by means of glue."

END OF THE THIRD EPISODE.

As soon as Telephron had ended this story, the guests, elated with wine, again renewed their bursts of laughter. While they were proposing his health,† Byrrhæna thus addressed me: "To-morrow is a day which it has been usual to celebrate from the earliest infancy and very foundation of this city, a day on which we exclusively, among mankind, propitiate the most sacred God of Laughter,‡ with ceremonies of joviality and mirth. Your presence will render the festival still more pleasing to us; and I wish that with your native wit, you would devise something of a right joyous nature in honour of the God, in order that we may the more becomingly and abundantly shew our veneration for so great a Divinity."

"Very well," said I; "what you request shall be done. And, by Hercules! I wish I may invent some piece of merriment with which a god so mighty may be becomingly graced."

By this time, having had my fill of wine, and being warned by my servant it was now night, I immediately arose, and having hastily bid farewell to Byrrhæna, took my way homeward, with unsteady steps. But while we were going through the first street, the light upon which we relied was extin-

* *My native place.*]—Miletus.
† *Proposing his health.*]—'Bibere salutaria' is the reading which has been adopted.
‡ *God of Laughter.*] Pausanias mentions this solemnity, where he speaks of the Hypatensians. Plutarch also. in his life of Cleomenes, mentions a temple which was dedicated to the God of Laughter; and he likewise relates that a statue was erected to this divinity by Lycurgus. Every providential energy of deity, about a sensible nature, was said, by ancient theologists and philosophers, to be the *sport* of divinity. Hence the ancient authors of fables call this peculiarity of the providence of the Gods, energising about the world, *laughter.* So that, as Proclus well observes, (in Plat. Polit.) we must define the laughter of the Gods to be *their exuberant energy in the universe, and the cause of the gladness of all mundane natures.* And, as this energy is never-failing, the laughter of the Gods is very properly said by Homer to be *unextinguished.* The source, therefore, of this exuberant energy and mundane gladness, is the God of Laughter.—*Taylor.*

guished by a sudden gust of wind; so that, with difficulty groping our way through the darkness of the night against which we were so badly provided, and continually knocking our toes against the stones, we were quite wearied before we arrived at home.

When we had now entered our own street, lo and behold, three men, of lusty and stout appearance, were pushing with all their might against our door, and were not in the smallest degree alarmed at our coming up; on the contrary, they kicked at it more and more repeatedly with all their might, so that to us, and to myself especially, they appeared unquestionably to be robbers, and of the most desperate character. Accordingly, I instantly drew forth my sword, which I carried with me concealed under my cloak against such an emergency. Without delay I rushed into the midst of the robbers, and plunged my sword to the hilt into the body of each, as I engaged with him in combat, till at length, pierced with many and deadly wounds, they breathed their last before my very feet.

Awakened by the tumult of this combat, Fotis came and opened the door. I crawled into the house, panting for breath and bathed in perspiration, and immediately threw myself on my bed and fell asleep, as much fatigued with the slaughter of these sturdy robbers, as if I had killed Geryon.*

BOOK THE THIRD.

REFLECTIONS ON THE MORNING AFTER A CAROUSE.—LUCIUS ARRESTED ON A CHARGE OF MURDER.—THE TRIAL.—ITS UNEXPECTED ISSUE.—FESTIVAL OF THE GOD OF LAUGHTER.—REMORSE AND CONFESSION OF FOTIS.—SHE PROMISES TO LET LUCIUS WITNESS PAMPHILE'S MAGIC PERFORMANCES.—HE SEES PAMPHILE TRANSFORM HERSELF INTO AN OWL.—HE ATTEMPTS TO IMITATE HER, AND IS CHANGED INTO A DONKEY.—HE IS ILL-TREATED BY HIS HORSE, AND THRASHED BY HIS SERVANT.—MILO'S HOUSE PLUNDERED BY ROBBERS.—LUCIUS IS LOADED WITH THE BOOTY, AND DRIVEN OFF.

AURORA, with her rosy arm uplifted, had just begun to drive

* *Killed Geryon.*]—The slaying of Geryon, king of Spain, who had three bodies, was one of the twelve celebrated labours of Hercules.

her purple-caparisoned steeds through the heavens; and departing night surrendering me up to day, roused me from placid slumbers. Compunction then seized my mind at the recollection of the deed I had perpetrated on the previous evening. Gathering my feet beneath me, locking my fingers upon my knees, and so sitting up in bed on my haunches, I wept abundantly; picturing to myself, in imagination, now the Forum and the trial, now the condemnation, and lastly, the executioner himself.

"Shall I," said I to myself, "shall I meet with any judge so mild and so considerate as to be able to pronounce me innocent, when here I am, imbrued with the blood of a threefold homicide, and reeking with the gore of so many citizens? Is this the journey so glorious in its results which Diophanes, the Chaldæan, so confidently predicted for me?" While with such reflections ever and anon crossing my mind, I deplored my evil fortune, a violent knocking at the door, and shouting was heard at the gate: without more ado, it was thrown open, and a great multitude rushing into the house, every part of it was filled with the magistrates and their officers, and a miscellaneous gathering of people. Instantly two of the lictors, laying hands upon me, by order of the magistrates, began to drag me along, whilst I offered no resistance. When we had got to the end of the lane,* we were immediately met by such an astonishing multitude, that it seemed as if the whole city was pouring forth. And though I walked sorrowfully along, with my head bowed down towards the ground, or rather, I may say, to the shades below, yet, on casting a glance aside, I saw a thing which caused me the greatest surprise. For among the many thousands of people that surrounded me, there was not a single one who was not ready to split his sides with laughter.

At length, having passed through all the principal streets, and turning corner after corner, like the victim of a lustral sacrifice, led all round the city before it is slain, to expiate the anger of the Gods, I was marched into the Forum, and placed before the judgment seat. And now, the magistrates being seated on an elevated platform, the public crier proclaimed

* *End of the lane.*]—The 'angiportus' here mentioned was probably the lane or blind alley into which the door of the house opened.

silence, when suddenly the people, with one unanimous voice, requested that, in consequence of the multitude of spectators, whose lives were in peril from the enormous pressure, this important trial might take place in the theatre. Forthwith the Forum was evacuated in every direction, the people filled every seat in the body of the theatre* with extraordinary celerity; and in the very entrances also, and over the whole of the roof, they crowded as thick as they could stand. Great numbers clung to the columns; some hung on to the statues; others were only half visible through windows and between the beams of the ceiling; and all, in their ardent desire to witness the sight, paid no attention whatever to their own safety.

The public officers now led me through the proscenium,† just like some victim, and placed me in the midst of the orchestra. The accuser being again summoned by the loud bellowing of the crier, arose, and after water had been poured into a certain vessel,‡ which was finely perforated like a cullender, and through which it flowed drop by drop, for the purpose of regulating the time for speaking, he thus addressed the people :

"A case is now brought before you, most worthy fellow-citizens, which is of no trifling magnitude, but one which especially regards the peace of the whole city, and is likely to prove a momentous example, profitable to future ages. Wherefore, it is the more requisite that each and all of you should have due regard for the public dignity, that so this nefarious homicide, who has murdered so many citizens, may not go unpunished, for having thus cruelly butchered them. And do not suppose that I am actuated by any private grudge, or moved by personal animosity, in making this charge against

* *Body of the theatre.*]—'Caveæ conseptum.' The 'cavea' was the part of the theatre in which the spectators sat. The 'cavea' at Rome was threefold. In the lowest part sat the 'Equites' and Senators; in the uppermost, the lowest of the people; and in the middle, the more respectable classes.

† *The proscenium.*]—The 'proscenium' was the elevated part in front of the stage, on which the actors came forward when speaking.

‡ *Into a certain vessel.*]—He here alludes to the 'clepsydra,' or 'water-clock,' which was used in Greece for the purpose of measuring the time during which persons might speak in courts of justice. Aristotle describes it as being a hollow globe, having a neck at the upper part like that of a bottle, through which the water was poured into it.

him. For I am the prefect of the night-watch : and I fully believe there is not one person who can impeach my vigil·ance and attention. Accordingly, I will faithfully relate the exact circumstances, and the transactions that took place last night.

"When about the third watch,* I had nearly gone my rounds of the whole city, and had examined every corner from door to door with scrupulous attention, I perceived this most blood-thirsty young man laying about him on every side, and slaugh-tering with his drawn sword ; and I saw that three persons, who had just fallen victims to his rage, were laid at his feet, still breathing, and their bodies palpitating amid streams of gore. Then, conscience-stricken, and with good reason, at the commission of such a heinous deed, he immediately took to flight, and having, through the protection of the darkness, es-caped into a certain house, he there lay concealed the whole night. By the providence of the gods, however, which allows no crime to pass unpunished, I took care to arrest him in the morning, and bring him hither for the most august judgment of your venerable tribunal, before he could make his escape clandestinely. You have, therefore, before you a cul-prit defiled with so many murders, a culprit taken in the very fact, a culprit who is a foreigner. Unhesitatingly, then, pass sentence on this stranger, for a crime, for the commission of which you would severely punish one of your own citizens."

My most unsparing accuser having thus spoken, closed his tremendous harangue.

The moment he ceased, the crier ordered me to begin, if I wished to make any reply to what had been said. But as for me, at that moment I could do nothing but weep ; not, by Hercules ! so much on account of the dreadful accusation, as of my own wretched conscience. At last, however, inspired by the gods with some degree of boldness, I thus answered the charge :

"I am far from ignorant how difficult it is for any one, when three corpses of citizens are lying exposed, and he is accused of the murder, to persuade so vast a multitude that he is really innocent, while he speaks the truth, and readily con-fesses that he committed the deed. But if your humanity will allow me a public hearing for a short time, I shall have no

* *Third watch.*]—The night was divided by soldiers into four parts, each of which was called a watch, and consisted of three hours.

difficulty in showing you that I now stand in peril of my life, not through any ill-deserts of my own, but that it is through a fortuitous result of justifiable indignation, that I am innocently subjected to the reproach of so great a crime.

"For, as I was returning from an entertainment, somewhat later than usual, and besides, being in a state bordering on intoxication, which indeed I will not deny was really my crime, I beheld before the door of the place where I reside (for I am staying with your worthy fellow-citizen Milo), I beheld, I say, some most desperate robbers trying to force an entrance, and to wrench the door off its hinges. Already they had with great violence torn away all the bars which had been put up with the greatest care, and at that very moment they were meditating the murder of the inhabitants within. One of them, in fact, who was the most active with his hands, and the largest in bulk, was encouraging the others with these words, ' Come on, my lads, let us fall upon those within while they are asleep, with manly spirits and vigorous hands. Be all hesitation, all sluggishness, banished from your breasts. Let slaughter stalk, sword in hand, from one end of the house to the other. Let him who lies sound asleep be put to death ; let him who endeavours to resist be knocked down. Thus shall we get off in safety, if we don't leave a single person in safety in the house.'

"I confess it, citizens; seeing that I entertained extreme fears both on account of my entertainers and myself, and that I was armed with a sword which I carried with me as a provision against dangers of this kind, I thought it was the duty of a good member of the community, to endeavour to alarm and put to flight these most desperate robbers. But the barbarous and bloodthirsty villains were far from taking to flight; and though they saw that I was armed, they still offered a bold resistance, and stood their ground in battle array. In fact, the leader and standard-bearer, as it were, of the rest, attacking me at once with great impetuosity, seizing me by the hair with both his hands, and bending me backward, tried to smash me with a stone. But while he was crying out for one to be handed to him, making a sure thrust at him, I fortunately laid him prostrate. Presently, I slew another, who was clinging to my legs and biting my feet, piercing him with a well-aimed blow through the middle of his shoulder-blade ; and the third I ran through the breast while rushing upon me off his guard. Thus, the cause of peace being vindicated, and the house of my host, and the safety of the public, being protected, I did suppose that I was not only not liable to punishment, but was even worthy of the public praise : I who have never been accused even of the smallest crime, but have been always highly respected in my own country, and have ever preferred a character without guile to every earthly good. Neither am I able to comprehend why I am now exposed to this accusation for a justifiable feeling of vengeance with which I was incited against these most abominable robbers, since there is not a person who can either prove that prior to this affair there was any private animosity between us, or that these robbers were ever in any way known by me. At all events, let something of which I stripped them be shown, ere it be believed that I perpetrated such a heinous crime through the desire of obtaining booty."

Having thus said, my tears again burst forth, and with hands stretched out in a suppliant attitude, I earnestly invoked first one and then another, appealing to the public commiseration, and the love they bore to their children, pledges of affection. And when I now thought that they were all moved by humanity, and that they were sufficiently affected with commiseration for my tears, calling to witness the eye of Justice and the Sun, and commending to the providence of the gods my present case, I raised my eyes a little, and beheld the entire body of the people ready to burst with laughter, and even Milo, that worthy host of mine, who had professed the affection of a father for me, laughing as immoderately as the rest. Amazed at such a sight, I said to myself, "Alas! where is probity, where is conscience ? Here am I become a homicide, and capitally convicted, in defence of the safety of my host; while he, not content with abstaining from affording me the comfort of his assistance, is grinning besides at my destruction."

In the meantime a certain woman, dressed in black, and carrying an infant at her bosom, came running through the middle of the theatre, crying and lamenting, while behind her followed an aged crone in ragged and dirty apparel, who also testified her grief by similar wailings, while both of them shook branches of olive in their hands. Then, hanging over the bier on which the dead bodies lay covered up, and beating their breasts and howling dismally, they exclaimed, "In the name of public compassion, as you revere the common law of humanity, take pity upon these young men who have been so unworthily slain, and give to our widowed and solitary state the solace of vengeance. At least afford assistance to this unfortunate child, who is left destitute in its infancy, and make a propitiatory sacrifice to your laws and the public well-being with the blood of the cutthroat."

After this appeal, the senior magistrate arose, and thus addressed the people: "That this crime must be visited with a severe punishment, not even he himself, who committed it, is able to deny. Therefore one duty only remains for us, and that of a secondary nature, namely, that we should discover the other persons who were the accomplices in such an atrocious deed. For it is by no means probable, that one solitary individual could have deprived of life three such robust young men as these. The truth, therefore, must be plucked from him by means of torture. For the servant who attended him has secretly taken flight, and the matter is brought to this issue that he must himself be put to the question, and compelled to declare who were his partners in his crime, in order that we may be thoroughly freed from the fear of so dreadful a gang."

Without any delay, the instruments of torture in use among the Greeks, namely, fire and the wheel,* and various sorts of scourges besides, were brought in. Then indeed my misery was infinitely increased, because I was not to be allowed, at least, to die unmutilated. But the old hag, who had aggravated everything by her weeping, exclaimed, "Most worthy citizens, before you fasten to the cross this cutthroat thief, the destroyer of my wretched sons, allow the corpses of the dead to be uncovered, in order that being still more and more incited to a just indignation, by a contemplation of the beauty as well as the youth of the slain, you may vent your rage upon their murderer, with a severity proportioned to the magnitude of his crime."

These words were received with applause, and immediately the magistrate ordered me with my own hands to uncover the dead bodies which were laid on the bier. The lictors used most strenuous efforts to enforce obedience to the command of the magistrates, whilst I resisted and struggled as long as I could,

---

* *Fire and the wheel.*]—Achilles Tatius also mentions the wheel and fire as being used by the Greeks for the purpose of extorting confession.

unwilling to revive, as it were, the crime of the day before by a new display of the victims. At last, however, forcing away my hand from my side, they extended it, to its own destruction, over the dead bodies. Overcome at length by necessity, I yielded; and, though with extreme reluctance, withdrew the pall and exposed the corpses. But, good gods! what a sight was there! what a prodigy! what a sudden change in my fortunes! A moment before, I was the property of Proserpine, and was reckoned one of the family of Orcus, * but now the aspect of affairs was totally changed; and I stood staring like an idiot in mute amazement; nor is it in the power of language to give a fitting description of the sight that now met my eyes.

For these bodies of the murdered men were three inflated wine skins,† pierced in various parts, and, as far as I could call to my recollection my battle of the night before, they were slashed in the very same places in which I had wounded the robbers. Then the laughter which, through the sly management of some persons, had been for a while repressed, burst forth among the people without restraint. Some congratulated me, in the exuberance of their hilarity, others pressed their hands to their stomachs, to relieve their aching; all, indeed, were drowned in floods of mirth as they left the theatre, pausing every now and then to look back at me.

For my own part, from the moment I lifted up that cloth, I stood fixed and ice-cold as a stone, precisely as though I had been one of the statues or columns of the theatre. Nor had I yet emerged from the shades below, when my host, Milo, came up, and taking me by the hand, drew me towards him with gentle force, reluctant as I was to move, and incessantly sobbing with the tears again gushing forth; and then, avoiding the main streets, he led me through certain bye-ways to his house, consoling me all the way with various remarks, for I had not yet got over my grief and trepidation. Nor, indeed, could he by any means assuage my indignation at the insult I had received, which took deep root in my breast. Presently, the magistrates, with their insignia, entered the house, and endeavoured to appease me by addressing me as follows :

* *Family of Orcus.*]—Orcus was one of the names of Plutus.

† *Inflated wine skins.*]—The ' utres,' used for holding wine, were mostly made of goatskins, which were tightly sewed together, and then well pitched over. Sometimes several goat skins were fastened together to make one vessel.

" We are not ignorant, Master Lucius, of your high position, or of your lineage; for the noble name of your illustrious family extends through the whole of this province. Nor was it for the sake of contumely that you were made to suffer that which you take so sorely to heart. Dismiss, therefore, all your present sorrow and anguish of mind. For this festival, which we solemnly celebrate in public as each year returns,* in honor of the most jocund God of Laughter, is always graced with some new invention. This God will every where propitiously and lovingly attend you as his promoter, nor will he ever suffer your mind to be oppressed with grief, but will perpetually exhilarate your brow with a serene cheerfulness. All this city, likewise, has presented you with the highest honors, for the favour which you have conferred on it. For it has enrolled you as its patron, and has passed a vote that your statue shall be erected in brass."

In reply to this address, I said, " To you, and to your most splendid and singularly excellent† city of Thessaly, I return commensurate thanks for such honors. But I would recommend you to keep your statues and images for those who are more worthy and of more advanced years than myself." Having spoken thus modestly, and for a moment smiling with a cheerful countenance, and pretending as much as I possibly could to be more joyful, I courteously saluted the magistrates at their departure.

Just then, a servant came running into the house, and said to me, " Your relation, Byrrhæna, repeats her invitation, and begs to remind you that the hour of the banquet is close at hand, at which you promised last evening to be present."

Full of horror at these words, and shuddering at the very mention of her house, " Tell your mistress," said I, " that I would most willingly obey her commands, if it were possible to do so without violating my promise. But my host, Milo, conjuring me by the deity who presides over this day, has made me pledge myself to sup with him to-day; and he has neither gone out of the house, nor will he suffer me to leave him. On this account, I must put off my engagement to sup with your mistress to another time."

* *As each year returns.*]—If this practice really did prevail with the people of Thessaly, it bore a considerable resemblance to our April Fool Day.

† *Singularly excellent.*]—It is somewhat singular that Solinus, when enumerating the principal cities of Thessaly, does not mention Hypata in the list. It is probably thus called by Apuleius, or rather Lucius, solely by way of compliment.

All this while Milo held me fast by the hand, and when the servant was gone, he took me to the nearest bath, having previously ordered that the bathing utensils* should be sent after us. But I, avoiding the gaze of all men, and shrinking from the laughter of those I met, and of which I was myself the subject, stuck close to his side, and screened myself under its shadow, such was the shame I felt. But how I washed or how I dried myself, or how I got home again, was more than I could tell; so much was I confounded and bereft of my senses on seeing myself pointed out by the eyes, the nods, and the fingers of the people. At last, having hastily despatched a paltry meal with Milo, and excusing myself on the ground of a severe head-ache, occasioned by my long-continued weeping, I readily obtained permission to retire to rest.

Throwing myself upon my bed, I reflected painfully upon all that had happened to me, till at length my Fotis, having put her mistress to bed, came to me, very much changed from her usual appearance; for she did not bring with her a joyous face, nor mirthful prattle, but a gloomy and wrinkled brow. At length, speaking with hesitation and timidly, "I freely confess," said she, "that I have been the cause to you of this day's trouble;" and so saying, she drew forth a kind of lash from her bosom, and offering it to me, thus continued: "Take your revenge, I pray you, upon a perfidious woman; ay, inflict on me any punishment you please. Yet do not, I entreat you, believe that of my own will I have occasioned you this anguish. May the gods be more merciful to me, than that you should suffer even the very smallest annoyance on my account! Nay rather, if any disaster impend over your head, may it be forthwith atoned for with my blood. It is a thing I was ordered to do for quite another reason, that, with a sort of ill luck peculiarly my own, has turned out to your injury."

Urged by my usual curiosity, and longing to have the secret cause of this transaction disclosed, I thus replied: "This most abominable and most audacious of all whips, which you intended for me to beat you with, shall be chopped, and torn to pieces, and utterly destroyed, before it shall touch your

---

* *The bathing utensils.*]—The 'balnearia,' or bathing apparatus, generally taken to the baths, were 'strigils,' or scrapers, 'ampullæ,' or bottles containing oil or pinguents, linen, towels, &c. See the soliloquy of the parasite Gelasinus, in the Stichus of Plautus, act ii. sc 1, where he recounts the requisites for the bath.

downy, milk-white skin. But tell me faithfully, I beseech you, what act of yours is it, that the malignity of fortune has converted to my detriment? I swear by that face of yours, most dear to me, that not any person whatsoever, not even your own self, could make me believe that you harboured a thought that could do me harm. And besides, no adverse results of chance can cause harmless intentions to become culpable."

When I had finished this little speech, with eager thirst and close kisses, I sucked in love from the lips of my Fotis, whose moist and tremulous eyes, half hidden by their drooping lids were dull with the languor of desire. Her spirits being thus revived: "First let me carefully shut the door," she said, "lest I be guilty of a great offence, through the unguarded freedom of the words that may escape me." Thus saying, she bolted and locked the door securely, and then returning to me, and clasping my neck with both her hands, she said, in a low and very subdued tone of voice: "I am terrified, and tremble all over, to disclose the mysteries of this house, and reveal the secret doings of my mistress. But I have too high an opinion of you and your breeding, not to trust you; for besides your high-born dignity, and your own elevated mind, having been initiated into various sacred mysteries, you have fully learned the holy faith of secrecy; whatsoever, therefore, I shall entrust to the inmost depths of this breast of yours, keep it ever religiously concealed, I beseech you, within its recesses, and repay the frankness of my narrative, by the strictest silence. For it is the power of that love by which I am bound to you, that compels me to disclose to you matters which are known to me alone, of all mortals. You will now learn everything that relates to our house; you shall now be made aware of the wondrous secret powers of my mistress, to which the spirits of the dead pay obedience, and by which she disturbs the stars in their course, sways the elements, and enthrals the divinities. Nor does she ever more readily resort to the powers of this art, than when she has cast the eyes of desire upon a good-looking young man, a thing, in fact, that happens to her not unfrequently.

"At the present moment, she is desperately in love with a certain young man of Bœotia, who is extremely handsome, and she is ardently employing the whole power, and every manœuvre of her art. I heard her yesterday evening, with these ears of mine, I heard her, I say, threaten the Sun himself, that she would involve him in a cloud of mist, and interminable darkness, if that Sun did not make haste in his course through the heavens, and speedily give place to the night, that she might the sooner begin to exert her magic spells.

"Yesterday, happening to catch sight of this youth in a barber's shop,* as she was returning from the bath, she secretly gave me orders to bring away the cuttings of his hair, which were lying on the ground. As I was in the act of carefully and stealthily collecting them, the barber caught me; and, because from other circumstances we are publicly notorious as exercising the black art, he laid hold on me, and rudely abused me: 'What, you good-for-nothing jade, you can't leave off pilfering the hair of the good-looking young men every now and then? If you don't, once for all, put an end to this, I will take you without more ado before the magistrates.' Then, suiting the action to the words, thrusting in his hands between my breasts, and groping about them in a rage, he drew out the hair I had previously concealed there. Grievously afflicted by this treatment, and reflecting on the temper of my mistress, who is always excessively enraged, and beats me in the most cruel manner, when she is thwarted in a matter of this nature, I had serious thoughts of running away, but when I thought of you, I instantly abandoned that design. On my way home, sad and empty handed, I espied a man clipping some goat skins with a pair of shears. Seeing them so nicely sewn together, inflated, and standing by themselves, I took up a parcel of the hair from them which lay scattered on the ground, and being of a yellow colour, resembled that of the young Bœotian; and this goat's hair I gave to my mistress, concealing the truth.

"Accordingly, at night-fall, before you returned from the entertainment, Pamphile, my mistress, now in a state of frenzy, went up into a belvedere covered with shingles, which she secretly frequents, as being especially adapted to these pursuits of hers, for it is open on every side to the winds, and commands a prospect of the eastern and all the other points. There she began by arranging in her deadly workshop all the customary implements of her art, such as aromatics of all kinds, plates of metal engraved with talismanic characters, nails from shipwrecked vessels, as also, multitudes of limbs and fragments

* *In a barber's shop.*]—Among the ancients, the 'tonstrinæ,' or barbers' shops, were places devoted to news and gossip; as such, we find them frequently alluded to in the plays of Plautus and Terence.

stolen from graves.   Here, were noses and fingers, thére, the nails by which culprits had been fixed to the cross, and to which portions of flesh adhered; and, in another place, thé blood of murdered persons, bottled up, and mangled skulls of men who had been devoured by wild beasts.

"Next, having pronounced an incantation over entrails still warm and palpitating, she makes a libation with various liquors, first, with water from the spring; next, with the milk of cows; and then, with mountain honey and mead. Then, after plaiting the goats' hairs together, and tying them in a knot, she burns them on live coals, with abundance of perfumes.   That instant, through the irresistible power of the magic art, and through the occult might of the coerced divinities, those same bodies, the hairs of which were smoking and crackling, received human breath, were endowed with understanding, heard, and walked.   Whither the odour of the burning spoils attracted them, thither came they; and instead of that Bœotian youth, it was they who bumped away at the door, endeavouring to effect an entrance.   Just at that moment up came you, well steeped in liquor, and deceived by the darkness of the night, you drew your sword, just like the frantic Ajax, but not like him to slay whole flocks of sheep;* a far more valiant deed was yours, for you deprived of breath three inflated goat skins, so that, having laid your adversaries prostrate, without staining yourelf with a drop of blood, I can now clasp you in my arms, not as a homicide, but as a wine-bagicide."

Responding in the same strain to the jocular remarks of Fotis, I said: "Now, then, I may match this first exploit of my prowess with one of the twelve labours of Hercules, comparing the three wine skins I slaughtered to the three-fold body of Geryon, or to the triple form of Cerberus.   But, that I may forgive you with all my heart for the fault through which you involved me in miseries so extreme, comply with one most earnest request of mine.   Let me have sight of your mistress when she next makes any use of this supernatural power, so that when she is invoking the gods, I may at least see her assume another form.   For I am most ardently desirous of obtaining a nearer acquaintance with the arts of magic; though, by the by, you yourself seem to me to be not altogether a novice in such matters.   This I know, and feel most sensibly;

* *Whole flocks of sheep.*]—In his madness consequent upon his being refused the arms of Achilles, which were awarded to Ulysses.

for whereas I have always been averse to the overtures of
highborn ladies, now by those brilliant eyes of yours, your
rosy lips, your shining hair, your open-lipped kisses, and your
perfumed bosom, you hold me voluntarily enthralled, and sub-
jected to you as much as any slave. In fact, I am neither an-
xious to return home, nor am I making any preparations for that
purpose, and nothing is there which I could prefer to this night."

"How gladly, Lucius, would I accomplish what you desire,"
she replied, "but my mistress is so afraid of the malice and
curiosity of the public, that she always performs her mysterious
ceremonies in the strictest solitude and privacy. Still, I will
consider your gratification more than my own danger, and will
look out for a suitable opportunity to accomplish what you
wish. Do you only, as I admonished you at the beginning,
faithfully preserve silence upon a matter of such importance."

While we thus conversed together, mutual desire seized us;
and inspired with a Bacchanalian frenzy, as it were, we rushed
into each other's arms. At last, after long wakefulness, sleep
fell upon our weary eyes, and detained us in bed till late in the
following day.

After some few nights delightfully passed in this manner,
Fotis came running to me one day in great excitement and
trepidation, and informed me that her mistress, having hitherto
made no proficiency by other means in her present amour, in-
tended to assume feathers like a bird, and so take flight to
the object of her love; and that I must prepare myself with
all due care for the sight of such a wonderful proceeding.
And now, about the first watch of the night, she escorted me,
on tip-toe and with noiseless steps, to that same upper cham-
ber, and bade me to peep through a chink in the door, which
I did accordingly.

In the first place, Pamphile divested herself of all her gar-
ments, and having unlocked a certain cabinet, took out of it
several little boxes. Taking the lid off of one of them, and
pouring some ointment therefrom, she rubbed herself for a con-
siderable time with her hands, smearing herself all over from
the tips of her toes to the crown of her head. Then, after she
had muttered a long while in a low voice over a lamp, she
shook her limbs with tremulous jerks, then gently waved them
to and fro, until soft feathers burst forth, strong wings dis-
played themselves, the nose was hardened and curved into a
beak, the nails were compressed and made crooked. Thus did

Pamphile become an owl.   Then, uttering a querulous scream, she made trial of her powers, leaping little by little from the ground; and presently, raising herself aloft, on full wing, she flies out of doors.   And thus was she, of her own will, changed, by her own magic arts.

But I, though not enchanted by any magic spell, still, rivetted to the spot by astonishment at this performance, seemed to myself to be any thing else rather than Lucius.   Thus deprived of my senses, and astounded, even to insanity, I was in a waking dream, and rubbed my eyes for some time, to ascertain whether or not I was awake at all.   At last, however, returning to consciousness of the reality of things, I took hold of the right hand of Fotis, and putting it to my eyes, "Suffer me," said I, "I beg of you, to enjoy a great and singular proof of your affection, while the opportunity offers, and give me a little ointment from the same box.   Grant this, my sweetest, I entreat you by these breasts of yours, and thus, by conferring on me an obligation that can never be repaid, bind me to you for ever as your slave.   Be you my Venus, and let me stand by you a winged Cupid."

"And are you then, sweetheart, for playing me a fox's trick, and for causing me, of my own accord, to let fall the axe upon my legs?   Must I run such risk of having my Lucius torn from me by the wolves of Thessaly?*   Where am I to look for him when he is changed into a bird?   When shall I see him again?"

"May the celestial powers," said I, "avert from me such a crime!   Though borne aloft on the wings of the eagle itself, soaring through the midst of the heavens, as the trusty messenger, or joyous arm-bearer, of supreme Jove, would I not, after I had obtained this dignity of wing, still fly back every now and then to my nest?   I swear to you, by that lovely little knot of hair, with which you have enchanted my spirit, that I would prefer no other to my Fotis.   And then besides, I bethink me, that as soon as I am rubbed with that ointment, and shall have been changed into a bird of this kind, I shall be bound to keep at a distance from all human habitations; for what a beautiful and agreeable lover will the ladies gain in an owl!   Why! do we not see that these birds of night, when

* *Wolves of Thessaly ?*]—There is some doubt among the Commentators which is meant here by the wolves of Thessaly; but it seems most probable that in her jealousy, Fotis intends to call the damsels of Thessaly by that name.

they have got into any house, are eagerly seized and nailed to
the doors,* in order that they may atone, by their torments,
for the evil destiny which they portend to the family by their
inauspicious flight?   But one thing I had almost forgot to in-
quire : what must I say or do, in order to get rid of my wings,
and return to my own form as Lucius ?"

"Be in no anxiety," she said, "about all that matter ; for my
mistress has made me acquainted with every thing that can
again change such forms into the human shape.   But do not
suppose that this was done through any kind feeling towards
me, but in order that I might assist her with the requisite
remedies when she returns home.   Only think with what
simple and trifling herbs such a mighty result is brought
about : for instance, a little anise, with some leaves of laurel
infused in spring water, and used as a lotion and a draught."

Having assured me of this over and over again, she stole into
her mistress's chamber with the greatest trepidation, and took
a little box out of the casket.   Having first hugged and kissed
it, and offered up a prayer that it would favour me with a
prosperous flight, I hastily divested myself of all my garments,
then greedily dipping my fingers into the box, and taking
thence a considerable quantity of the ointment, I rubbed it all
over my body and limbs.   And now, flapping my arms up and
down, I anxiously awaited my change into a bird.   But no
down, no shooting wings appeared, but my hairs evidently be-
came thickened into bristles, and my tender skin was hardened
into a hide; my hands and feet, too, no longer furnished with
distinct fingers and toes, formed as many massive hoofs, and a
long tail projected from the extremity of my spine.   My face
was now enormous, my mouth wide, my nostrils gaping, and
my lips hanging down.   In like manner my ears grew hairy,
and of immoderate length, and I found in every respect I had
become enlarged.†   Thus, hopelessly surveying all parts of my
body, I beheld myself changed not into a bird, but an ass.

I wished to upbraid Fotis for the deed she had done ; but,
now deprived both of the gesture and voice of man, I could only
expostulate with her silently with my under-lip hanging down,

* *Nailed to the doors.*]—We see the same sort of thing done at the
present day in some parts of England, where owls, hawks, bats, &c., are
nailed in great numbers to the stable doors.

† *Enlarged.*]—The original is : Nec ullum miser reformationis video so-
latium nisi ouod mihi jam nequeunti tenere Fotidem natura crescebat.

and looking sideways at her with tearful eyes. As for her, as soon as she beheld me thus changed, she beat her face with her hands, and cried aloud, " Wretch that I am, I am undone! In my haste and flurry I mistook one box for the other, deceived by their similarity. It is fortunate, however, that a remedy for this transformation is easily to be obtained ; for, by only chewing roses, you will put off the form of an ass, and in an instant will become my Lucius once again. I only wish that I had prepared as usual some garlands of roses for us last evening ; for then you would not have had to suffer the delay even of a single night. But, at the break of dawn, the remedy shall be provided for you."

Thus did she lament; and as for me, though I was a perfect ass, and instead of Lucius, a beast of burden, I still retained human sense : long and deeply, in fact, did I consider with myself, whether I ought not to bite and kick that most wicked woman to death. However, better thoughts recalled me from such rash designs, lest, by inflicting on Fotis the punishment of death, I should at once put an end to all chances of efficient assistance. So, bending my head low, shaking my ear, I silently swallowed my wrongs for a time, and submitting to my most dreadful misfortune, I betook myself to the stable to the good horse which had carried me so well, and there I found another ass also, which belonged to my former host Milo. Now it occurred to me that, if there are in dumb animals any silent and natural ties of sympathy, this horse of mine, being influenced by a certain feeling of recognition and compassion, would afford me room for a lodging, and the rights of hospitality.* But, O Jupiter Hospitalis, and all you the guardian divinities of Faith! this very excellent nag of mine, and the ass, put their heads together, and immediately plotted schemes for my destruction ; and as soon as they beheld me approaching the manger, laying back their ears and quite frantic with rage, they furiously attacked me with their heels, fearing I had design upon their food; consequently I was driven away into the farthest corner from that very barley, which the evening before I had placed, with my own hands, before that most grateful servant of mine.

Thus harshly treated and sent into banishment, I betook my-

---

* *Rights of hospitality.*]—'Lautiæ.' This was properly the name given to the entertainment provided by the Quæstors at Rome, for foreign ambassadors, when maintained at the public expense.

self to a corner of the stable.   And while I reflected on the inso-
lence of my companions, and formed plans of vengeance against
the perfidious steed, for the next day, when I should have be-
come Lucius once more by the aid of the roses, I beheld against
the central square pillar which supported the beams of the
stable, a statue of the goddess Hippona,* standing within a
shrine, and nicely adorned with garlands of roses, and those, too,
recently gathered.   Inspired with hope, the moment I espied
the salutary remedy, I boldly mounted as far as ever my fore
legs could stretch; and then with neck at full length, and ex-
tending my lips as much as I possibly could, I endeavoured to
catch hold of the garlands.   But by a most unlucky chance,
just as I was endeavouring to accomplish this, my servant lad,
who had the constant charge of my horse, suddenly espied me,
sprang to his feet in a great rage, and exclaimed, "How long
are we to put up with this vile hack, which, but a few mo-
ments ago, was for making an attack upon the food of the
cattle, and is now doing the same even to the statues of the
Gods?   But if I don't this very instant cause this sacrilegious
beast to be both sore and crippled"—and searching for some-
thing with which to strike me, he stumbled upon a bundle of
sticks that lay there, and, picking out a knotted cudgel, the
largest he could find among them all, he did not cease to be-
labour my poor sides, until a loud thumping and banging at
the outer gates, and an uproar of the neighbours shouting
thieves! struck him with terror, and he took to his heels.

The next moment the doors were burst open, an armed band
of robbers rushed in, and surrounded the house on all sides;
people ran from all quarters to help the defence, but the rob-
bers beat them off.   Being all furnished with swords and
torches, they illuminated the darkness of the night; and their
swords gleamed like the rays of the rising sun.   Then with
their strong axes they broke open the stout bars and fastenings
of a strong room in the middle of the house, which was filled
with Milo's treasures, and having completely ransacked it,
they hastily divided the booty, and tied it up in separate pack-
ages.   Now the number of packages exceeded that of the men
who were to carry them.   Hence, being brought to extraor-
dinary shifts, through a superabundance of wealth, they led
forth us, the two asses, and my horse, from the stable, loaded

* *The goddess Hippona.*]—This was the guardian goddess of horses and
stables.   'Hippona' seems a preferable reading to 'Epona.'

us with the heaviest burdens they possibly could, and drove us before them from the empty house, flourishing their sticks over us. Leaving one of their companions behind as a spy, to bring them word as to any proceedings taken in consequence of the robbery, they hurried us along through the bye-paths of the mountains, beating us every now and then, so that through the weight of my load, the steepness of the mountain, and the interminable length of the way, I was no better than a dead donkey. At last I very seriously thought of resorting to the aid of the civil power, and liberating myself from so many miseries, by invoking the august name of the Emporor.

Accordingly, when, in broad daylight, we were passing through a certain populous village, which was thronged with people celebrating a fair, I strove, in the midst of that crowd of Greeks, to utter the august name of Cæsar, in the native language, and I cried out O!* distinctly and sonorously ; but that was all, for the name of Cæsar I was not able to pronounce. The robbers abominating my discordant clamour, thumped and gored my miserable hide, and left it hardly fit for a corn sieve.† But at last, that *good* Jupiter‡ bestowed on me an unexpected chance of deliverance. For after we had passed by many small farms and fine country houses, I espied a delightful little garden, in which, besides other sweet flowers, there were virgin roses,§ dripping with the morning dew. With longing desire, and overjoyed by the hope of safety, I moved towards them. But while, with quivering lips, I was preparing to seize them, this very important reflection came across me : if I divested myself of the asinine form, and again became Lucius, while in the hands of the robbers, they would surely kill me, either as a supposed magician, or for fear that I should inform against them. For the present, therefore, as a matter of necessity, I abstained from roses, and putting up with my present misfortune, was fain to champ my bridle under the guise of an ass.

Cried out O !]—He wished to invoke the emperor, in the words ' Oh, Cæsar !' but could not get beyond the interjection. One of the commentators justly remarks, that ' au' would be the sound uttered by him.

† *A corn sieve.*]—Such as, made of sheepskin pierced with holes, are in use in Italy and elsewhere at the present day.—*Head.*

‡ *Good Jupiter.*]—It is well observed by the Delphin editors, that *Jupiter ille* is an emphatic expression, signifying *that Jupiter who providentially attends to all things, and regards the miserable.*—*Taylor.*

§ *Virgin roses.*]—Roses not fully blown.

F

BOOK THE FOURTH.

LUCIUS ENTERS A KITCHEN GARDEN IN SEARCH OF FOOD AND ROSES
—HE IS CAUGHT BY THE GARDENER—HAS TO FIGHT FOR HIS
LIFE, AND ESCAPES, PURSUED BY MEN AND DOGS—HE IS CAUGHT
AND SEVERELY BEATEN, BUT HAS HIS REVENGE—TAKES WARN-
ING FROM THE FATE OF HIS FELLOW ASS—ARRIVES AT THE ROB-
BERS' DEN — THE ROBBERS' CRONE — THEIR CONVERSATION.
FOURTH EPISODE: THE ROBBER'S TALE—THE ROBBERS DEPART
ON AN EXPEDITION—RETURN WITH A CAPTIVE DAMSEL—HER
HISTORY — THE OLD WOMAN ENTERTAINS HER WITH A STORY.
FIFTH EPISODE: TALE OF CUPID AND PSYCHE.

TOWARDS the middle of the day, when everything was scorched
by the burning heat of the sun, we turned aside into a certain
village, to the house of some old men, who were friends and
acquaintances of the robbers; for so their first salutations, their
lengthened conversation, their exchange of embraces, enabled
me, ass as I was, to perceive. They made them presents of
some things which they took off my back; and with secret
whispers seemed to inform them that they had been obtained
by burglary. At length, having lightened us of all our burden,
they turned us into the next meadow, to graze as we pleased.
My sense of conviviality, however, was not sufficient to keep me
in the company of the ass, or of my horse, especially as I was
not habituated to making my dinner upon grass. But as I
was now perishing with hunger, I boldly effected an entrance
into a little garden I caught sight of, behind the stable, and
ate my bellyful of the vegetables, raw as they were. Then
invoking all the gods, I looked about in every quarter to see if
by chance I might any where espy in the neighbouring gar-
dens a rose-tree in full bloom. For the solitude of the spot,
its distance from the public road, and the fruit trees that con-
cealed it, now afforded me great hopes, that if, on taking the
remedy, I should quit the grovelling gait of a four-footed beast
of burden and become erect again, in the shape of a man, I
might do so, unobserved by any body.

Whilst, then, I was fluctuating amid this sea of contempla-
tion, I beheld, a little further on, a dell shaded by a leafy

grove; and among its various plants and delightful foliage, shone the vermilion tint of blooming roses. In my imagination, which was not entirely that of a brute, I pictured this to myself as the grove of Venus and the Graces; among whose shady recesses, the regal splendour of that genial flower was brilliantly glowing. So, invoking Prosperous Event,* I ran with such speed, that, by Hercules! I fancied myself no longer an ass, but an exceedingly swift racer of the circus. Still this remarkable effort of activity was unable to outstrip my evil fortune. For when I had now arrived at the spot, I no longer saw those fresh and charming roses, wet with divine dews and with nectar, which happy brambles and thrice-blessed thorns produce, nor, indeed, any dell whatever, but only the margin of a river's bank, planted with thickset trees. These trees had long leaves like those of the laurel, and bore a sort of inodorous blossom of a cup-like form and red colour. These scentless flowers the ignorant common people call, in their rural vocabulary, rose-laurels, to eat which is sure death to all cattle.

Finding myself ensnared by such a fatality, and casting aside all regard for safety, I determined voluntarily to eat of these envenomed roses. But, while I was hesitatingly approaching in order to pluck them, a young fellow, the very gardener, as I saw, whose vegetables I had so shockingly laid waste, perceiving the loss he had sustained, ran furiously at me with a great stick in his hand, and having caught me, belaboured me so, that I should have been in danger of losing my life, had I not at last had the wisdom to take my own part. For throwing up my rump, I struck out at him rapidly and repeatedly with my hind feet, and having severely punished him, and laid him prostrate against a bank on the mountain's side, sought safety in flight.

Instantly, however, a certain woman, his wife, I suppose, catching sight of him from an elevated spot, as he lay prostrate and half dead, flew towards him, with shrieks and yells, evi-

* *Prosperous Event.*]—*Good Event*, or the cause of prosperity in our undertakings, was adored by the ancients as a God. According to Pliny (lib. xxxv. cap. 6), there was a statue of this divinity, as also of *Good Fortune*, in the Capitol at Rome. This deity is one of the twelve Dii Consentes, from the invocation of whom Varro begins his treatise on Agriculture.—*Taylor*.

F 2

dently on purpose, that by her lamentations she might be the occasion of my instant destruction. For all the villagers, being aroused by her screams, straightway called out their dogs, and from all quarters hounded them on, in order that, exasperated by fury, they might rush upon me and tear me in pieces. I made no doubt whatever but that I was on the brink of death when I saw the dogs, very large ones too, and many in number, and fit to fight with bears and lions, rushing furiously against me from all quarters. Adopting, therefore, what seemed my only chance, I gave up all thoughts of flight, and galloped back to the inn at which we had put up. But the country people keeping off the dogs with much difficulty, seized and bound me with a very stout thong of leather to a staple, and would no doubt have beat me to death, had it not been that my stomach, compressed by the pain of the blows, and disordered by those raw vegetables with which it was stuffed, squirted out its contents, and drove away my persecutors from my aching sides, besprinkling some of them with the most abominable liquid, and choking others with the stench.

Not long afterwards, as the sun was now declining from the meridian, the robbers again led us forth from the stable heavily laden, myself especially, whose burden was far heavier than that of the rest. We had now completed a good part of the journey; I was exhausted by its length and the weight of my burden, sore from the cudgelling I had got, and lame and staggering from my hoofs being quite worn to the quick; so, as I was passing along the winding course of a gently flowing rivulet, I was thinking that I would cunningly seize that excellent opportunity, and lie down, bending my legs under me, fully determined not to rise from the spot, whatever blows might be inflicted on me; ay, ready even, not only to be beaten with a stick, but pierced with a sword, rather than budge. For I imagined that being now fully half dead and exhausted, I should receive an honourable discharge,* on account of bodily infirmity: or, that at least the robbers, irritated at the delay, and desirous of hastening their flight, would divide the load which I carried on my back between the two other beasts of burden, and that, by way of a still more severe revenge, they would leave me a prey to the wolves and vultures.

* *An honourable discharge.*]—' Causariam missionem.' This was a term used in military law to denote a discharge given to a soldier worn out in the service.

My most cruel destiny, however, thwarted the execution of so admirable a plan. For that other ass, divining and anticipating my intention, immediately pretended to be overcome with fatigue, and fell sprawling on the ground with all his baggage, and lying as if he was dead, made no attempt to rise for all their whacking or goading, no, nor even when they tried to pull him up on all sides by the tail, the ears, and the legs. At last the robbers grew tired of the hopeless job, and having conferred together, they resolved that their flight should not be further retarded by wasting time upon an ass that was as good as stone dead. So, having divided his load between me and the horse, and drawing a sword, they cut both his hamstrings; then they dragged him, still breathing, a little out of the public road, and threw him down a very lofty precipice into the valley below. Then, indeed, taking warning by the destiny of my unfortunate comrade, I determined to lay aside all tricks and stratagems, and prove myself to my masters to be a diligent, deserving ass. Besides, I had heard them say to each other, that we should soon come to a stop, and make an end of our journey and our toils, for yonder was the place of their abode.

At length, having passed a little hill of easy ascent, we arrived at the place of our destination. All the things were unpacked and stowed away indoors; and being now relieved from my burden, I took a refreshing roll in the dust in lieu of a bath. The occasion itself, as well as the nature of my story, demands that I should here give a description of the locality and of the cave in which the robbers dwelt. For thus I shall make trial of my own abilities, and at the same time enable you to judge if I was an ass in sense and understanding as well as in form.

It was a rugged mountain, covered with dark forests, and of extraordinary height. Winding athwart its declivity, flanked by steep, inaccessible rocks, ran deep and intricate gullies, choked with brambles, and thus affording a natural defence. A spring burst forth from the summit of the mountain in great bubbling gushes, and rolling its silvery waters down the steeps, parted into a number of rivulets, formed pools in the valleys, and encompassed the base of the mountain with large sheets of standing water. On the rock, over the mouth of the cavern, there was a sort of fort, constructed with strong posts and hur-

dles, enclosing a space well suited for penning sheep. Before
the door there were small shrubs * extending along in place of
a wall, and this enclosure you may fairly denominate, on my
authority, the robbers' receiving room.   There was no other
edifice in the place, except a small hut roughly covered with
reeds; in which sentinels, selected by lot from the band of
robbers, as I afterwards learned, kept watch by night.

Leaving us secured by a stout leather thong before the door,
they crept into the cave, one after another, with their limbs
squeezed together, and bawled angrily to an old woman, who,
though bent with age, seemed to be entrusted with the entire
charge of so many young men.

" What! you old corpse, whom Life is ashamed to own, and
Death scorns, do you mean to make game of us, sitting idly at
home, and not providing a supper to comfort us at this late
hour, after all our toil and peril?   You who do nothing day
and night but swill down wine into that craving stomach of
yours."

"Nay, now," the frightened and trembling old woman
squeaked out, "nay, now, my brave and honourable young
masters, there is plenty of nice stewed meat of all kinds, loaves
in abundance, wine without stint, in polished cups, and warm
water ready as usual for your hasty bath."   When she had
said this, they immediately undressed, and standing naked be-
fore a great fire, sluiced themselves with hot water, anointed
themselves with oil, and then went and reclined at a table
abundantly supplied with dishes.

Hardly had they taken their places, when another and much
more numerous party of young men entered, whom you would
without hesitation have taken to be robbers also; for they, too,
brought with them booty in the shape of gold and silver money,
drinking vessels, and silken garments embroidered with threads
of gold. The new-comers having likewise refreshed themselves
by bathing, joined their comrades; and some who were chosen
by lot waited upon the rest.   They ate and drank in a most
disorderly manner, with meat piled up in heaps, bread in hil-

* *Small shrubs*]—' Exigui ramices,' means very probably what we
should call a ' quick-set hedge.'   This seems a superior reading to that
in Valpy's edition, ' tramites.'   There is a considerable resemblance
between the robber's den and the solitary dwelling of Defoe's hero
Robinson Crusoe.

locks, and tankards ranged in whole platoons upon the board. They were obstreperous in their mirth, sang as loud as they could bawl, exchanged scurrilous jokes, and behaved in all respects like Theban Lapithæ,* or half-brute Centaurs. At last the burliest among them all thus addressed the rest:—

" Right bravely have we ransacked that house of Milo, at Hypata ! And besides the vast booty we gained by our prowess, we have brought back our full number to camp, safe and sound, with an increase, too, of eight feet,† if that is worth mentioning. But you, who have been pillaging the cities of Bœotia, have brought back thinned numbers, having lost that bravest of leaders, Lamachus, whose safety I should certainly have preferred, and with good reason, to all these packages you have brought home. Be that as it may, it was his own excess of bravery that was his destruction, and the memory of so great a hero will be celebrated among illustrious kings and leaders in battle. But as for you, who are very careful robbers, you do a trumpery trade ‡ in petty, dastardly thefts, sneaking timidly about baths, and old women's bits of houses."

To this, one of the new-comers replied, " You don't know, then, what is notorious to everybody, that large houses are much the easiest to sack? For though a great number of servants is kept in them, still each of these has more regard for his own safety than for his master's property. But people who lead a frugal and retired life, vigorously defend their little store, at the hazard of their lives : or else, if it is ample, they keep it, to say the least, pretty carefully concealed. And, in fact, the thing itself will verify what I have asserted."

FOURTH EPISODE.

THE ROBBER'S TALE.

" No sooner had we arrived in the seven-gated city of Thebes, than we diligently made enquiries about the wealth

---

* *Theban Lapithæ.*]—He alludes to the broil between the Centaurs and Lapithæ at the marriage of Pirithous and Hippodamia, which is finely described by Ovid in the Twelfth Book of the Metamorphoses.

† *Eight feet.*]—Viz. the two quadrupeds, Lucius and his horse.

‡ *Do a trumpery trade*]—' Scrutariam facere,' properly means to deal in lumber, rags, or second-hand furniture. It was the custom for thieves to prowl about the baths for the purpose of taking such articles as lay in their way, strigils, for instance, or the clothes of bathers.

of each of the citizens, that being always the first thing to be looked after by men of our profession : and so we came to hear of a certain banker, by name Chryseros, a man who possessed much money, but took great pains to conceal his vast wealth, lest he should be required to serve in public capacities. In fact, content with a small but remarkably well barred and bolted house, he lived there all alone, ragged and dirty, and brooded over his bags of gold.

"Accordingly, we agreed to pay our first visit to him; for, despising the resistance of a single pair of hands, we thought we should, without any difficulty, carry off all his wealth. Without delay, therefore, as soon as it was night, we met together before his gate; but as we did not think it prudent either to take it off its hinges, or force it open, much less to smash it, lest the noise of its two wings* should alarm all the neighbourhood, to our destruction, that magnanimous standard-bearer of ours, Lamachus, confident in his well-tried valour, gradually introduced his arm through an aperture made for the purpose of putting the key inside, and endeavoured to draw back the bolt. But Chryseros, that most villanous of all bipeds, having been on the watch all the time, and aware of all that was going on, crept softly to the door, preserving a profound silence, and with a sudden violent effort, fastened the hand of our leader, with a great nail, to a pannel of the gate. Then, leaving him transfixed, like a wretch on the cross, he ascended to the roof of his hovel, and shouted with all his might to his neighbours, calling to them by their respective names, and advising them to have regard for their common safety, for his house had caught fire unexpectedly. Accordingly, terrified by the proximity of the imminent danger, every one ran anxiously to render assistance.

"In this dilemma, on the point of being overwhelmed by numbers unless we deserted our comrade, we adopted, with his own consent, a desperate remedy, suggested by the circumstances. For we cut off our leader's† arm by a blow right through the joint; and leaving it there, we bound up the

* *Its two wings.*]—The doors of the ancients, whether opening in the street or in the interior of the houses, were generally in the form of folding-doors.

† *Off our leader's.*]—'Antesignani. Properly speaking, the antesignani were picked men, who fought in front of the standard, and mostly in the first line. They were never 'velites,' or skirmishers, but heavy armed troops.

stump with plenty of rags, lest the drops of blood might betray our track, and hastily carried off with us what remained of Lamachus. The whole neighbourhood was now alarmed, and pursued us with loud outcries; and we, in the fear of impending peril, quickened our flight, whilst he could neither keep up with our swift pace, nor yet remain where he was with any safety. Then this most magnanimous and transcendently brave man besought us with all manner of prayers and entreaties, by the right hand of Mars, and by our mutual oaths, to rescue a brave comrade from torture and captivity. 'For how is it possible,' said he, 'that a brave robber can survive the loss of his right hand, with which alone he can plunder and cut throats? It would be happiness for him to meet a voluntary death by the hand of one of his comrades. As, however, he could not persuade any one of us, with all his entreaties, to commit a voluntary act of parricide, he drew his sword with his remaining hand, and after kissing it repeatedly, plunged it with a mighty stroke into the middle of his breast. Filled with veneration for the courage of our magnanimous leader, we carefully wrapped his mutilated dead body in a linen garment, and committed it to the sea,* there to find a place of concealment. And now does our Lamachus† lie entombed, with the whole ocean for his burying-place, after having ended his life in a manner worthy of his heroic deeds.

"And Alcimus likewise, with all his well-concerted enterprises, could not escape the sinister influence of fortune. He had broken into an old woman's cottage while she was asleep, and having ascended into an upper bedchamber, when he ought instantly to have strangled her, he thought proper first to throw all the things down to us, one by one, from the wide window, in order that we might make off with them. Having now cleared the room in a workmanlike manner, he had no mind to spare even the mattress on which the old woman slept;

* *Committed it to the sea.*]—As Thebes was situate many miles from the sea, either Apuleius is caught napping here, or he must have a rather far-fetched meaning assigned to his words, and we must suppose that the body was committed to the river Ismenius, to be carried down to the sea.

† *Our Lamachus.*]—We may here remark, that the several Greek names found in this part of the narration, have their distinct meanings. Lamachus may be rendered 'a champion;' Alcimus, a 'valiant man;' Chryseros, 'a lover of gold;' Demochares, 'beloved by the people;' and Thrasyleon, 'a bold lion.'

so, rolling her out of it, he was preparing to throw the coun-
terpane after the other things, when the abominable old hag
fell on her knees before him, crying: ' Why, my son, I be-
seech you, do you cast the poor and worn-out furniture of a
most wretched old woman to my wealthy neighbours, upon
whose house this window looks out?'

"Alcimus, deceived by these crafty words, and believing what
she said to be true, was afraid that the things he had already
thrown out, and those he was about to send after them, might,
through his mistake, fall not into the hands of his associates,
but into other people's houses; he therefore thrust his body
out of the window, in order that he might make a judicious
survey of the environs, and particularly that he might look
with an eye to future business at that adjoining house she had
mentioned. While, however, he was intent upon this, and
quite careless of his own safety, that old miscreant took him
unawares, as he leaned outwards, with his body balancing un-
steadily, and with a push which, though feeble, was sudden and
unexpected, she pitched him out headlong. Besides falling from
a great height, he dropped upon an enormous great stone
which happened to lie near the house, so that he smashed all
his ribs, and lay vomiting streams of blood, till, after he had
first related* to us what had taken place, death put a speedy
end to his torments Him also we buried in the same manner
as our former leader, and sent him, as a worthy comrade, to
follow Lamachus.

"Having thus suffered a double loss, we now abandoned our
Theban enterprises, and departed for the next city, which is
Plateæ. Here we heard a great deal of talk about a person
named Demochares, who was about to exhibit a spectacle of
gladiators. For, being a man of high birth, and distinguished
for his great wealth and liberality, he catered for the public
amusement with a splendour commensurate with his fortune.
Where is the man with genius and eloquence enough to de-
scribe, in appropriate words, all the various details of the
manifold preparations? There were gladiators famous for
dexterity of hand; hunters of well-tried swiftness of foot; and
criminals who, having forfeited their right to live in safety,
were being fattened as food for wild beasts. There were great

---

* *He had first related.*]—' Primitus' is perhaps a better reading here
than ' imitus.'

wooden stages, with towers formed of planks, like moveable
houses, adorned outside with pictures, and serving as hand-
some receptacles for the performers in the exhibition. And
then what a number, what a diversity of wild beasts! For
he had been at great pains to procure, even from abroad, those
noble living tombs of condemned men.

" Among his other costly preparations, he had procured, in
one way or other, with all the resources of his fortune, a great
number of huge bears. For, besides those captured by his own
servants in the chase, and those which he had bought at much
cost, others had been presented to him by his friends, who vied
with each other in showing him these attentions; and the
whole collection was maintained with great care and cost.
These noble and splendid preparations, however, for the public
amusement, could not escape the evil eye of invidious Fortune.
For these bears, pining and wasting away under their length-
ened confinement, the burning heat of the summer, and the
debilitating effects of want of exercise, were attacked by a
sudden mortality, and reduced to a very inconsiderable num-
ber. Hence, you might everywhere have seen bodies of half-
dead bears lying in the streets, like so many shipwrecked
vessels; and the ignoble mob, whose poverty compelled them
to fill their pinched bellies with any filthy offal, began to flock
about the food that was lying in all directions.

" Prompted by this circumstance, Babulus here and I
thought of the following clever stratagem. We carried the
fattest of these bears to our lodging, as though intending to pre-
pare it for food; and having entirely stripped the skin from the
flesh, carefully preserving all the claws, and leaving the head of
the beast entire, as far as articulation with the neck, we care-
fully scraped the hide, sprinkled it with fine ashes, and exposed
it in the sun to dry. While it was being purified of its oily
juices by the heat of that celestial fire, we gorged ourselves
with its pulpy flesh, and made those of the troop who were pre-
sent take an oath to this effect: that one of our number—one
who surpassed the rest, not so much in stoutness of body as of
heart, and above all, one who should undertake it voluntarily—
being covered with this skin, should assume the form of a bear,
and then, being brought into the house of Demochares, should,
on a seasonable occasion, afford us an easy entrance through
the door, in the dead of night.

"No few of our gallant troop did the cleverness of this scheme encourage to undertake its execution; but Thrasyleon was elected by the suffrages of the band as the fittest to perform the hazardous service. With a serene countenance, he enclosed himself in the hide, which was now rendered soft and pliable; then with fine stitches we drew the edges together, and covered the fine seams with the thick shaggy hair, fitting Thrasyleon's head into the part close by the back of the mouth, where the neck of the beast had been, and leaving small holes for breathing about the nostrils and the eyes. Lastly, we enclosed our most valorous comrade, now changed into a wild beast, within a cage which we had bought for a small sum, into which he sprang with unflinching courage; and having thus completed the preliminaries of the stratagem, we proceeded to the execution of the remainder.

"Having learned, on enquiry, the name of a person called Nicanor, who was sprung from a Thracian family, and between whom and Demochares there were the strongest ties of friendship, we wrote a counterfeit letter, intimating that this kind friend had dedicated the first fruits of his hunting to Demochares, by way of a graceful present. And now, the evening being far advanced, availing ourselves of the favourable darkness, we presented to Demochares the cage in which Thrasyleon was enclosed, together with the counterfeit letter; on which, admiring the huge size of the beast, and overjoyed at the opportune liberality of his friend, he immediately gave orders that ten pieces of gold should be counted out from his coffers to us who had brought him a present that afforded him so much delight. Meanwhile, as novelty always excites the curiosity of men and attracts them to unexpected sights, multitudes flocked together about the brute, admiring its size; but our friend Thrasyleon very cleverly restrained their rather too prying curiosity, by frequently rushing at them in a very alarming way. By the unanimous voice of the citizens, Demochares was pronounced most lucky and fortunate, in that, after so heavy a loss among his wild beasts, he had been able, in some way or other, to repair his losses by this new supply. He ordered the beast, therefore, to be immediately taken to his farm, and that it should be conveyed with the greatest care.

"On this, I interrupted him, and said, 'Be careful, sir, how you suffer this animal, which has suffered severely from the heat of the sun, and the length of the distance, to be trusted among a herd of many others, and those, according to what I hear, not yet recovered. Why not provide some spot in your own house for it, which is open and exposed to the breezes, and, if possible, bordering upon some cool lake? Are you not aware that animals of this kind always couch in shady groves and dripping caverns, on breezy hills, and near pleasant fountains?' Demochares, taking the alarm at these admonitions, and reflecting on the great number of wild beasts he had already lost, assented, without hesitation, to what I said, and readily permitted us to place the cage wherever we pleased. 'Besides,' said I, 'we ourselves are ready to watch here by night, before this cage, in order that we may as carefully as is requisite give the beast its food at the proper time, and its usual drink, as it is distressed by the heat, and the harass it has suffered in being brought hither.' Demochares, however, made answer: 'We do not stand in need of your services; for nearly every one in my household is now, from long custom, well skilled in feeding bears.'

" After this, we bade him farewell; and going out of the gate of the city, we espied a certain monument, standing at a considerable distance from the public road, in a solitary and retired spot. Here we opened some coffins,* which, through rottenness and age, had lost half of their lids, and which were tenanted by dead bodies, that were now nothing but dust and ashes. These we intended to use as so many hiding-places for our anticipated booty. Then having, according to the observance of our craft, watched for that season of a moonless night in which sleep most powerfully invades and overcomes the hearts of mortals with its first impetus, our band drew up, well-armed with swords, before the gates of Demochares, ready to perform our agreement to plunder his house. In like manner, Thrasyleon crept forth from his cage, availing himself of that precise moment of the night which is adapted to theft, and instantly slew with his sword every one of the house guards that lay fast asleep beside his cage, and lastly, the porter himself. Then, taking the key, he opened the folding doors of the

---

* *Some coffins.*]—' Capulus' ordinarily signifies the litter or bier on which the dead body was laid out previous to burial. In this instance, however, it seems to mean a wooden coffin. It was probably much the same as the 'sandapila' used by the lower classes.

gate, and as we immediately rushed in, he pointed out to us
the strong room, where he had sagaciously observed a quantity
of silver plate deposited in the evening. This being instantly
broken open by the combined force of our band, I recommended
each of my comrades to carry away as much gold and silver as
he could, and conceal it in those abodes of the dead, the most
trusty of all people, and then returning with speedy steps, get
ready a second burden, whilst I would remain alone, for our
common good, before the door of the house, and keep a careful
watch, until such time as they should return. Moreover, it
appeared to me that the figure of a bear, running about in the
middle of the house, was adapted to terrify any member of the
family who might happen to be awake. For who, however
brave and intrepid he might naturally be, would not, on behold-
ing the huge form of such an enormous beast, in the night espe-
cially, immediately betake himself to flight, and pulling to the
bolt, shut himself in, terrified and trembling, in his chamber?

"A sinister event, however, thwarted all these judicious ar-
rangements. For while I was waiting, in anxious suspense,
for the return of my comrades, one of the servant lads, happen-
ing, so the Gods ordained, to be awoke by the noise, I suppose,
of the bear, crept gently forward, and seeing the wild beast
running loose, and wandering over the whole house, he silently
retraced his steps, and, as quickly as he could, gave notice to
all of what he had seen; immediately upon which, the whole
house was filled with a numerous assemblage of the domestics.
The darkness was illuminated with torches, lamps, wax tapers,
tallow candles, and other appliances for giving light by night.
And not one was there in the throng without arms of some de-
scription, but all were furnished with clubs, spears, and drawn
swords, with which they guarded the approaches to the house.
And then they hallooed on some of those hunting dogs, with
long ears and shaggy hair, to attack the wild beast.

"Upon this, the tumult still increasing, I made my way
stealthily out of the house, and concealing myself behind the
gate, I saw Thrasyleon defending himself in a wonderful manner
against the dogs. For, though he had now arrived at the very
uttermost goal of life, still, forgetful neither of himself nor of
us, nor his former valour, he struggled, as it were, in the very
jaws of Cerberus. In fact, acting with spirit up to the scenic
character which he had voluntarily assumed, at one moment

flying and at another resisting, with various gestures and con-
tortions of his body, he at length escaped from the house.
Still, though he had gained his liberty, so far as being in the
public road, he was not able to ensure his safety by flight; for
all the dogs belonging to the next lane, and they were very
savage and numerous, joined in whole troops with the hunting
dogs, which had rushed out of the house, in full pursuit of him.
I was then witness of a shocking and frightful spectacle,—our
friend Thrasyleon, surrounded and hemmed in by troops of
raging dogs, and lacerated all over by their teeth.

"At last, unable to endure so shocking a spectacle, I mingled
with the surrounding crowds of people, and this being the
only way in which I could secretly give assistance to my brave
comrade, I thus attempted to divert the promoters of the at-
tack from their purpose, 'Oh what an enormous shame,' said
I, 'thus to destroy such a fine and remarkably valuable beast.'
The artifice failed, however, and all I could say had no in-
fluence in favour of the unfortunate young man. For a tall
strong fellow came running out of the house, and instantly
thrust a spear through the bear's vitals; another followed his
example; and then a great many took courage to assault him
at close quarters, and vied with each other in piercing him
with their swords. But as for Thrasyleon, that distinguished
honor to our band, his heroic life, so worthy of immortality,
being at length vanquished, though not his fortitude, he
did not forfeit the oath he had plighted by any vociferation,
shrieks, or cries. But, lacerated as he was by tooth and steel,
he imitated to the last with all his might the growling and
bellowing of a wild beast, and thus enduring his present cala-
mity with magnanimous fortitude, he kept his glory intact,
while he yielded up his life to fate. Still, so great was the
terror and dismay with which he had struck the crowd, that
until the dawn, ay, even when it was broad day, not one dared
to lay a finger even on the beast, dead as it lay, until at last, a
certain butcher, who was a little bolder than the rest, advanc-
ing slowly and timidly, cut open the belly of the beast, and
stripped the bear's hide off the mighty robber. Thus, then,
was Thrasyleon also lost to us, but not lost to glory.

"And now, immediately collecting those packages which the
trusty dead had taken care of for us, we made all haste to quit
the limits of Plateæ, while ever and anon the reflection came

across our minds, that it is no wonder if fidelity is not to be found among the living, since, abominating their perfidy, it has descended to the dead. In fine, here we are, all of us fatigued with the weight of our loads, as well as the rough roads along which we have travelled ; we have lost three of our comrades, and brought home the booty you see."

END OF THE FOURTH EPISODE.

After the robber had concluded his narrative, they poured out libations of pure wine from golden cups, to the memory of their deceased comrades ; and then, having propitiated the god Mars by some songs, they went to sleep for a short time. Meanwhile, the old woman served out to us fresh barley in such unmeasured abundance, that my horse, in fact, amid such great plenty, and having it all to himself, might have fancied he was supping with the Salii.* But as for me, though I had been in the habit of eating barley, well crushed, and long boiled in broth, having found out a corner in which the remains of the bread, belonging to the whole band, had been stored away, I strenuously exercised my jaws, which ached with long-continued fasting, and began to be covered with spiders' webs.

When the night was far advanced, the robbers arose from sleep, struck their tents, and, being variously equipped, some of them being armed with swords, and others disguised as spectres,† with hasty steps, they sallied forth from their abode. But as for me, not even impending sleep could hinder me from chewing on incessantly and eagerly. And though in former times, when I was Lucius, I could get up from table contented with one or two loaves, yet now, having to fill so capacious a belly, I had nearly eaten up a third basketful of bread, when broad daylight found me still intent upon this employment. At length, however, moved by the modesty of an ass, I quitted my food, but most reluctantly, and slaked my thirst at a rivulet close by.

* *Supping with the Salii.*]—The Salii were priests of Mars, whose duty it was to keep the sacred 'ancilia,' or shields. Like the other priests, they were noted for their fondness of good living and generous wine. Hence, 'Cæna Saliaris,' a dinner fit for a Salian, became a popular saying.

† *Disguised as spectres.*]—'Lemures.' It will be found stated at length by the author, what were the Lemures, in his treatise on the God of Socrates.

Not long after this, the robbers returned, full of anxiety and alarm, bringing with them no booty whatever, not so much as a worthless garment. With all their swords, with all their hands, ay, and with all the force of their band, they brought but a solitary prisoner, a damsel of genteel figure, and, as her style of dress indicated, one of the first rank in those parts; a girl, by Hercules! far from an object of indifference even to me, ass as I was. As soon as they had brought her into the cave, lamenting and tearing her hair and her garments, they addressed her in words intended to alleviate her distress:

"You really are in perfect security, both as to your life and your honor; so have patience for a few days, if only out of regard for our profit, for it is the pinch of necessity that has compelled us to adopt this profession. Of course, your parents, avaricious as they are, will give without delay, out of their great hoards of wealth, a sum of money adequate to the ransom of their own offspring."

The maiden's grief was far from alleviated by such rough comforting as this; and no wonder; on the contrary, she wept immoderately, with her face bent down upon her knees. So they called in the old woman, and ordered her to sit by the damsel, and amuse her as much as possible with soothing conversation; and then they betook themselves to their customary avocations. But not by any words which the little old woman employed could the maiden be made to cease her lamentations; on the contrary, she cried louder than ever, and shook her sides with such unintermitting sobs, that she drew tears from me also.

"Is it possible, that I can cease to weep, or bear to live at all? miserable wretch that I am! torn from such a home, from such friends, from such kind servants, such revered parents; become the prey of nefarious rapine, a captive and a slave, servilely shut up in this rocky prison, and deprived of all those comforts amid which I was born and nurtured; not safe a moment from the butcher's knife; in the power of such a number of outrageous robbers, such a horrible crew of gladiators!" Thus she continued to lament, until, worn out with grief of mind, the spasmodic tension of her throat, and fatigue of body, at last she closed her languid eyes in sleep.

Scarcely, however, had she dozed off, when, suddenly starting up again, as if bereft of her senses, she began to afflict herself much more violently than before, and with cruel hands to beat her bosom and her beautiful face. And although the old woman most urgently enquired the cause of this fresh burst of grief, she only replied with a deep groan:

"Now, alas! beyond a doubt, I am utterly undone, now I renounce all hope of safety. A halter, a sword, or a precipice, that is what I must come to."

On hearing this, the old woman grew a little angry, and bade her, with a severe expression of countenance, say why the plague she was crying so; or why, after having been fast asleep, she thus suddenly renewed her ungovernable lamentations. " It is your design, I suppose," said she, " to defraud my young men of the pretty sum of money which they will get for your ransom. However, if you persist any farther, without caring at all for those tears, of which robbers are in the habit of making little account, I will pretty soon have you burnt alive."

Terrified by this threat, the maiden kissed her hand, and said, " Spare me, my good mother, and, for the sake of humanity, bear a little with my most sad misfortune. Nor, indeed, do I imagine that compassion is entirely extinguished in you, so full of years, so venerable with your gray hairs. In fine then, listen to the story of my misfortune.

" A handsome youth, of the first rank among his fellow-citizens, whom the whole city elected to serve its public offices,* and who besides was my first cousin, only three years older than myself, had been reared along with me from infancy, and was my inseparable companion, dwelling with me in the same house, indeed, sharing the same chamber and couch, and affianced to me by mutual ties and the bonds of holy love. We had long been engaged to each other in marriage, we had even been registered on the tablets,† as wedded by the consent of our parents ; and the youth was engaged in sacrificing victims in the temples and sacred edifices, accompanied by a numerous throng of relatives and neighbours. The whole house was covered with laurel, lighted up with torches, and re-echoed

* *Elected to serve its public offices.*]—Literally, ' had chosen as the son of the public.' This phrase denotes that the youth had become an universal object of interest to his fellow-townsmen, who had made it their care to promote him to the highest offices.

† *On the tablets.*]—The register on which the marriage was entered by the public officers.

with hymeneal song. My unhappy mother, supporting me on
her bosom, had dressed me becomingly in nuptial apparel, and
frequently loading me with honeyed kisses, was now, with
anxious hopes, looking forward to a future line of descendants;—
when, on a sudden, a band of robbers armed like gladiators,
rushed in with swords drawn and glittering, in fierce battle
array. They made no attempt to slay or plunder, but made
straight for our chamber in a compact column ; and without
any struggle, or indeed, any resistance whatever on the part
of our servants, they tore me away, wretched creature, half
dead with fear, from the bosom of my trembling mother.
Thus were our nuptials dissolved, like those of the daughter of
Athrax,* or of Protesilaus.

" And now again is my misery renewed, nay rather, increas-
ed, by a most horrible dream. For I seemed to myself to be vio-
lently dragged away from my home, from my chamber, from
my very bed, and to be hurried through desert wildernesses,
where I called aloud on the name of my most unfortunate
husband ; and he, methought, as soon as he was deprived of
my embraces, still perfumed with essenced ointments, and
adorned with wreaths of flowers, was following my track as
I fled on other feet than my own.† And while with loud
cries he bewailed the loss of his lovely wife, and implored the
assistance of the people, one of the robbers, moved with anger
at his persevering pursuit, snatched up a great stone, and
slew the unfortunate youth, my husband. It was this horrible
sight that aroused me in terror from my dreadful dream."

Sighing in response to her tears, the old woman thus ad-
dressed her : "Be of good cheer, my young mistress, and do
not terrify yourself at the idle fancies of dreams. For not
to mention that dreams dreamt in the daytime are said to be
false, even nightly visions sometimes forebode events quite con-
trary to what really comes to pass. In fact, to dream of weep-
ing, of being beaten, and occasionally, of having our throats

* *Daughter of Athrax.*]—Hippodamia was the daughter of Athrax : on
her marriage with Pirithous, the famous battle of the Centaurs and La-
pithæ took place. It is difficult to say what is the precise allusion made
here to the marriage of Protesilaus ; but it not improbably alludes to his
premature separation from his wife Laodamia, shortly after their marriage,
in the expedition against Troy, where he was slain immediately on landing.

† *Feet than my own.*]—With the feet of robbers, who carried her away
elevated from the ground.

G 2

cut, announce a lucky and prosperous event; while, on the other hand, to laugh, to be stuffing the stomach with sweet-meats, or to dream of amorous enjoyments, predicts that a person is about to be afflicted with sorrow of mind, disease of body, and other evils.* However, I will proceed to divert you, by some pretty stories, and old women's tales."

Accordingly, she thus began:

FIFTH EPISODE.

THE OLD WOMAN'S STORY.—CUPID AND PSYCHE.

"In a certain city there lived a king and queen, who had three daughters of remarkable beauty. The charms of the two elder —and they were very great—were still thought not to exceed all possible measure of praise; but as for the youngest sister, human speech was too poor to express, much less, adequately to extol, her exquisite and surpassing loveliness. In fact, multitudes of the citizens, and of strangers, whom the fame of this extraordinary spectacle gathered to the spot, were struck dumb with astonishment at her unapproachable beauty, and moving their right hand to their lips,† with the forefinger joining the elevated thumb, paid her religious adoration, just as though she were the goddess Venus herself.

"And now the tidings spread through the neighbouring cities and adjacent countries that the goddess whom the azure depths of the ocean had brought forth, and the spray of the foamy billows had nurtured, dwelt in the midst of mortals, and suffered them indiscriminately to behold her divine form; or at least, that once again, impregnated by a new emanation from the starry heavens, not the sea, but the earth, had brought forth another Venus, gifted with the flower of virginity. Thus did her fame travel rapidly every day; thus did the news soon traverse the neighbouring islands, a great part of the con-

---

* *And other evils.*]—Thus also Astrampsychus, in his Oneirocriticon, says:
'If you laugh in your sleep, it indicates to you troublesome events; but if you weep in your sleep, it signifies that you will be perfectly joyful. —*Taylor.* This is in accordance with the popular belief of our own day.

† *To their lips.*]—We learn from Pliny that this was the usual attitude assumed by worshippers when in the act of adoration. The act seems somewhat to have resembled what we call 'kissing the hand.'

tinent, and multitudes of provinces. Many were the mortals who, by long journeys over land, and over the deep sea, flocked from all quarters to behold this glorious specimen of the age. No one set sail for Paphos,* no one for Cnidus, nor even for Cythera, to have sight of the goddess Venus. Her sacred rites were abandoned, her temples suffered to decay, her cushions† trampled under foot, her ceremonies neglected, her statues left without chaplets, and her desolate altars defiled with cold ashes. A young girl was supplicated in her stead, and the divinity of the mighty goddess was worshipped under human features; and the maiden was propitiated in her morning walks with victims and banquets offered her in the name of the absent Venus. And ever, as she passed along the streets, the people crowded round, and adoringly presented her with garlands, and scattered flowers on her path.

"This extraordinary transfer of celestial honors to a mortal maiden, greatly incensed the real Venus; and, unable to suppress her indignation, and shaking her head, in towering wrath, she thus soliloquized: 'Behold how the primal parent of all things, behold how the first source of the elements,‡ behold how I, the genial Venus of the whole world, am treated! The honor belonging to my majesty shared by a mortal girl! My name, that is registered in heaven, profaned by the dross of earth! I must be content, forsooth, with the uncertain homage of a vicarious worship, and with my share in expiations offered to me in common with another! And a mortal girl shall go about in my likeness! It is all for nought that the shepherd Paris, whose justice and good faith the mighty Jupiter approved, preferred me to such mighty Goddesses,§ on account of my unparalleled beauty. But this crea-

* *Set sail for Paphos.*]—Paphos was a city in the isle of Cyprus. Cnidus was a city in Caria. Cythera, now Cerigo, was an island situate to the south of Laconia. These places were all famous for the worship of Venus.

† *Her cushions.*]—The 'pulvinaria' were couches on which the statues of the gods reclined in the temples, with delicate viands placed before them.

‡ *First source of the elements.*]—The ancient philosophers considered Venus to be the first source of all things. See the opening lines of the poem of Lucretius.

§ *Mighty Goddesses.*]—The well-known fable to which this alludes, is thus beautifully unfolded by the Platonic Sallust, in his treatise on

ture, whosoever she be, shall not so joyously usurp my honors; for I will soon cause her to repent of her contraband good looks.'

"Thus saying, the goddess forthwith summons her son; that winged and very malapert boy, who, with his evil manners, sets at nought all ordinary institutions, and, armed with flames and with arrows, runs by night from one man's house to another, and blighting matrimonial happiness on all sides, commits such mighty mischiefs with impunity, and does nothing whatever that is good.

"Mischievous as he was by inborn licentiousness, she incites him to still more evil, by her words: she brings him to that city I mentioned, and points out Psyche to him* (for that was the name of the maiden), and after telling him the whole story about that mortal's rivalry of her own beauty, groaning with rage and indignation, she said,

" ' I conjure you by the ties of maternal love, by the sweet wounds inflicted by your arrow, by the warmth, delightful as honey, of that torch, to afford your parent her revenge, ay, and a full one too, and as you respect myself, severely punish this rebellious beauty: and this one thing, above all, use all your endeavours to effect; let this maiden be seized with the most burning love for the lowest of mankind, one whom fortune has stripped of rank, patrimony, and even of personal safety; one so degraded, that he cannot find his equal in wretchedness throughout the whole world.'

"Having thus said, and long and tenderly kissed her son, she sought the neighbouring margin of the shore on which

the Gods and the World. ' In this fable, which is of the mixed kind, it is said, that Discord, at a banquet of the Gods, threw a golden apple, and that a dispute about it arising among the Goddesses, they were sent by Jupiter to take the judgment of Paris, who, charmed with the beauty of Venus, gave her the apple in preference to the rest. But the banquet denotes the super-mundane powers of the Gods; and on this account they subsist in conjunction with each other. And the golden apple denotes the world, which, on account of its composition from contrary natures, is not improperly said to be thrown by Discord, or strife. Again, however, since different gifts are imparted to the world by different Gods, they appear to contest with each other for the apple. And a soul living according to sense, (for this is Paris), not perceiving other powers in the universe, says, that the beauty of Venus alone is the contended apple.'—*Taylor.*

* *Psyche to him.*]—This was the Greek name for the soul; a moth also was called by the same name.

the waves ebb and flow, and, with rosy feet, brushing along the topmost spray of the dancing waters, behold! she took her seat on the watery surface of the main; where the powers of the deep, the instant that she conceived the wish, appeared at once, as though she had previously commanded their attendance. The daughters of Nereus were present, singing in tuneful harmony; Portunus,* too, rough with his azure-coloured beard, and Salacia,† weighed down with her lapful of fish, with little Palæmon, their charioteer, upon a dolphin, and then troops of Tritons, furrowing the main in all directions. One softly sounded his melodious shell, another, with a silken canopy‡ protected her from the unpleasant heat of the sun, a third held a mirror before the eyes of his mistress, while others, again, swam yoked to her car. Such was the train that attended Venus, as she proceeded to the palace of Oceanus.

"In the meantime, Psyche, with all her exquisite beauty, derived no advantage whatever from her good looks; she was gazed on by all, praised by all, and yet no one, king, noble, or plebeian even, came to woo her for his bride. They admired, no doubt, her divine beauty, but then they all admired it as they would a statue exquisitely wrought. Long before this, her two elder sisters, whose more moderate charms had not been bruited abroad among the nations, had been wooed by kings, and happily wedded to them; but Psyche, forlorn virgin, sat at home, bewailing her lonely condition, faint in body and sick at heart; and hated her own beauty, though it delighted all the rest of the world.

"The wretched father of this most unfortunate daughter, suspecting the enmity of the gods, and dreading their wrath, consulted the very ancient oracle of the Milesian God,§ and sought

* *Portunus.*]—By Portunus here, or Portumnus, who, by the Greeks, was called Palæmon, Neptune is denoted, as the Delphin editor well observes. For Palæmon, who is properly Portunus, is shortly after mentioned as being present.

† *And Salacia.*]—The Goddess Salacia was so called from ' Salum,' the ' salt sea.' She presided over the depths of the ocean.

‡ *With a silken canopy.*]—So in the Fasti of Ovid, b. ii., we find Hercules holding a canopy or umbrella over queen Omphale, to protect her from the rays of the sun.

§ *Milesian God.*]—*i. e.* Of Apollo, who had a temple and oracle at

of that mighty divinity, with prayers and victims, a husband for the maiden whom no one cared to have. But Apollo, though a Grecian and an Ionian, by right of the founder of Miletus, delivered an oracle in Latin verse to the following effect:

> ' Montis in excelsi scopulo desiste puellam
>   Ornatam mundo funerei thalami :
> Nec speres generum mortali stirpe creatum,
>   Sed sævum atque ferum, vipereumque malum ;
> Qui, pinnis volitans super æthera, cuncta fatigat,
>   Flammaque et ferro singula debilitat ;
> Quem tremit ipse Jovis ; quo numina terrificantur ;
>   Flumina quem horrescunt, et Stygiæ tenebræ.'*

"The king, who had led a happy life till then, on hearing the announcement of the sacred oracle, returned home sad and slow, and disclosed to his wife the behests of inauspicious fate. Many days together were passed in grief and tears, and lamentation. But time pressed, and the dire oracle had now to be fulfilled. The procession was formed for the deadly nuptials of the ill-fated maiden; the lighted torch burns ashy, black, and sooty; the strains of Conjugal Juno's pipes are changed for the plaintive Lydian melody; the joyful hymeneal song sinks into a dismal wailing, and the bride wipes away her tears with the nuptial veil† itself. The whole city groaned in sympathy with the sad destiny of the afflicted family, and a public mourning was immediately proclaimed.

"The necessity, however, of complying with the celestial mandates, importunately called the wretched Psyche to her

---

Miletus, a city bordering on Ionia and Caria, and founded by a son of Apollo, whose name it bore.

> * "On some high mountain's craggy summit place
>   The virgin, deck'd for deadly nuptial rites ;
>   Nor hope a son-in-law of mortal race,
>   But a dire mischief, viperous and fierce ;
>   Who flies through æther, and with fire and sword
>   Tires and debilitates whate'er exists,
>   Terrific to the powers that reign on high.
>   E'en mighty Jove the wing'd destroyer dreads,
>   And streams and Stygian shades abhor the pest."—*Taylor.*

† *The nuptial veil.*]—This, which was called 'flammeum,' was of a bright yellow, or flame colour. If the torches that were carried before the bride shed a dim light, or sent forth much smoke, or were extinguished by the wind, it was considered a bad omen.

doom. The solemn preliminaries, therefore, of this direful marriage being completed in extreme sorrow, the funeral procession of the living dead moves on, accompanied by all the people; and the weeping Psyche walks not to her nuptials, but to her obsequies. And while her woe-begone parents, overwhelmed with horror, strove to delay the execution of the abominable deed, the daughter herself thus exhorted them to compliance:

"'Why torment your unfortunate old age with continual weeping? Why waste your breath, which is more dear to me than to you, with repeated lamentations? Why deform your features, to me so venerable, with unavailing tears? Why lacerate my eyes in afflicting your own? Why tear your hoary locks? Why beat your bosoms and those hallowed breasts? Are these to be the glorious results to you of my surpassing beauty? Too late do you perceive that you have been smitten by the deadly shaft of envy. Alas! then should you have wept and lamented, then bewailed me as lost, when tribes and nations celebrated me with divine honors, and when, with one consent, they styled me a new-born Venus. Now do I feel and see that through that name of Venus alone I perish. Lead me away, then, and expose me on the rock to which the oracle has devoted me; I am in haste to encounter these auspicious nuptials; I am in haste to see this noble bridegroom of mine. Why should I delay? Why avoid his approach, who has been born for the destruction of the whole world?'

"The maiden, after these words, said no more, but with unfaltering steps, took her place in the multitudinous procession. They advanced to the destined rock on a lofty mountain, and left the maiden alone on the summit; the nuptial torches, with which they had lighted their way, were now extinguished in their tears, and thrown aside, the ceremony was at an end, and with drooping heads they took their homeward way. As for her wretched parents, sinking under the weight of a calamity so great, they shut themselves up in their darkened palace, and abandoned themselves to perpetual night. Meanwhile, as Psyche lay trembling and weeping in dismay on the summit of the rock, the mild breeze of the gently-blowing Zephyr played round her garments, fluttering and gradually expanding them till they lifted her up, and the god, wafting her with his

tranquil breath adown the lofty mountain side, laid her softly
on the flowery turf in the lap of the valley."*

* *The valley.*]—The translation of this beautiful story would hardly
be complete were we to omit the following remarks on its various ex-
planations, found in Mr. Keightley's valuable and entertaining ' Classical
Mythology.' "This beautiful fiction is evidently a philosophic allegory.
It seems to have been intended by its inventor for a representation of the
mystic union between the divine love and the human soul, and of the trials
and purifications which the latter must undergo, in order to be perfectly
fitted for an enduring union with the Divinity. It is thus explained by
the Christian mythologist Fulgentius : ' The city in which Psyche dwells
is the world ; the king and queen are God and matter : Psyche is the
soul : her sisters are the flesh and the free-will ; she is the youngest, be-
cause the body is before the mind ; and she is the fairest, because the soul
is higher than free-will, more noble than the body. Venus, *i. e.* lust, envies
her, and sends Cupido, *i. e.* desire, to destroy her : but as there is desire
of good as well as of evil, Cupid falls in love with her ; he persuades her
not to see his face, that is, not to learn the joys of desire. At the impul-
sion of her sisters, she put the lamp from under the bushel, that is,
reverted the flame of desire which was hidden in her bosom, and loved it
when she saw how delightful it was : and she is said to have burned it
by the dripping of the lamp, because all sin burns in proportion as it is
loved, and fixes its sinful marks on the flesh. She is, therefore, deprived
of desire and her splendid fortune, is exposed to perils, and driven out of
the palace." This fanciful exposition will probably not prove satisfactory
to all readers. The following one, of a modern writer, may seem to come
nearer the truth. "This fable, it is said, is a representation of the destiny
of the human soul. The soul, which is of Divine origin, is here below
subjected to error in its prison the body. Hence trials and purifications
are set before it, that it may become capable of a higher order of things,
and of true desire. Two loves meet it—the earthly, a deceiver, who draws
it down to earthly things ; the heavenly, who directs its view to the ori-
ginal, fair and divine, and who, gaining the victory over his rival, leads off
the soul as his bride." According to a third expositor, the mythus is a
moral one. It is intended to represent the dangers to which nuptial
fidelity was exposed in such a degenerate country as Greece, and at the
same time to present an image of a fidelity exposed to numerous tempta-
tions, and victorious over them all. We must not omit to observe that
Psyche (Ψυχή) was also a Greek name for the moth. The fondness of this
insect for approaching at night the flame of the lamp or candle, in which
it so frequently finds its death, reminds a mystic philosopher of the fate of
the soul destroyed by the desire of knowledge, or absorbed and losing its
separate existence in the Deity, who dwelt in light, according to the phi-
losophy of the East. But, further, the world presents no illustration so
striking or so beautiful, of the immortality of the soul, as that of the moth
or butterfly, bursting on brilliant wings from the dull grovelling caterpillar
state in which it had previously existed, fluttering in the blaze of day, and
feeding on the most fragrant and sweetest productions of the spring. Hence

BOOK THE FIFTH.

CONTINUATION OF THE FIFTH EPISODE.

CUPID AND PSYCHE.

" PSYCHE, therefore, delightfully reclining in this pleasant and grassy spot, upon a bed of dewy herbage, felt her extreme agitation of mind allayed, and sank into a sweet sleep, from which she awoke refreshed in body, and with a mind more composed.   She then espied a grove, thick planted with vast and lofty trees ; she likewise saw a fountain in the middle of the grove, with water limpid as crystal.   Near the fall of the fountain there was a kingly palace, not raised by human hands, but by divine skill.   You might know, from the very entrance of the palace, that you were looking upon the splendid and delightful abode of some God.   For the lofty ceilings, curiously arched with cedar and ivory, were supported by golden columns.   The walls were encrusted all over with silver carving, with wild beasts and domestic animals of all kinds, presenting themselves to the view of those who entered the palace.   A wonderful man was he, a demigod, nay, surely, a god, who with such exquisite subtlety of art, moulded such vast quantities of silver into various ferine forms.

" The very pavement itself consisted of precious stones cut out and arranged so as to form pictures of divers kinds.   Blessed, thrice blessed, those who can tread gems and bracelets under foot !   The other parts, as well, of this palace of vast extent, were precious beyond all computation ; and the walls being everywhere strengthened with bars of gold, shone with their

it was, in all probability, that the Greeks named the butterfly the *soul*, A correspondent of the *Notes and Queries* remarks of this story (vol. ii. p. 29)—' This is probably an old *Folk-tale*, originally, perhaps an antique philosophical temple-allegory.   Apuleius appears only to have dressed it up in a new shape.   The tale is still current, but in a form *not* derived from him, among the Swedes, Norwegians, Danes, Scots, Germans, French, Wallachians, Italians, and Hindoos.'

own lustre, so that even were the sun to withhold his light, the palace could make for itself a day of its own; so effulgent were the chambers, the porticos, and the doors. The furniture, too, was on a scale commensurate with the majesty of this abode; so that it might well be looked upon as a palace built by mighty Jove, where he might dwell among mankind.

"Invited by the delightful appearance of the place, Pysche approached it, and, gradually taking courage, stepped over the threshold. The beauty of what she beheld lured her on, and everything filled her with admiration. In another part of the palace, she beheld magnificent repositories, stored with immense riches; nothing, in fact, is there which was not there to be found. But besides the admiration which such enormous wealth excited, this was particularly surprising, that this treasury of the universal world was protected by no chain, no bar, no guard.

"Here, while Psyche's gaze was ravished with delight, a bodiless voice thus addressed her; 'Why, lady,' it said, 'are you astonished at such vast riches? All are yours. Betake yourself, therefore, to your chamber, and refresh your wearied limbs on your couch, and, when you think proper, repair to the bath; for we, whose voices you now hear, are your hand-maidens, and will carefully attend to all your commands, and, when we have dressed you, a royal banquet will be placed before you without delay.'

"Psyche was sensible of the goodness of divine providence, and, obedient to the admonitions of the unembodied voices, relieved her fatigue, first with sleep, and afterwards with the bath. After this, perceiving, close at hand, a semicircular dais with a raised seat, and what seemed to be the apparatus for a banquet, intended for her refreshment, she readily took her place; whereupon nectareous wines, and numerous dishes containing various kinds of dainties, were immediately served up, impelled, as it seemed, by some spiritual impulse, for there were no visible attendants. Not one human being could she see, she only heard words that were uttered, and had voices alone for her servants. After an exquisite banquet was served up, some one entered, and sang unseen, while another struck the lyre, which was no more visible than himself. Then, a swell of voices, as of a multitude singing in full chorus, was wafted to her ears, though not one of the vocalists could she descry.

"After these delights had ceased, the evening now persuading to repose, Psyche retired to bed: and when the night was far advanced, a certain gentle, murmuring sound fell upon her ears. Then alarmed for her honor, in consequence of the profound solitude of the place, she trembled and was filled with terror, and dreaded that of which she was ignorant more than any misfortune. And now her unknown bridegroom ascended the couch, made Psyche his wife, and hastily left her before break of day. Immediately the attendant voices of the bedchamber came to aid the wounded modesty of the new-made bride. This course was continued for a length of time; and, as by nature it has been so ordained, the novelty, by its constant repetition, afforded her delight, and the sound of the voices was the solace of her solitude.

"In the meantime, her parents were wasting their old age in sorrow and lamentation; and the report of her fate, becoming more widely extended, her elder sisters had learnt all the particulars; whereupon leaving their homes in deep grief, they hastened to visit and comfort their parents. On that night, did Psyche's husband thus address her—for she could discern his presence with her ears and hands, though not with her eyes:

"'Most charming Psyche, dear wife, cruel fortune now threatens you with a deadly peril, which needs, I think, to be guarded against with the most vigilant attention. For ere long, your sisters, who are alarmed at the report of your death, in their endeavours to discover traces of you, will arrive at yonder rock. If, then, you should chance to hear their lamentations, make them no reply, no, nor even so much as turn your eyes towards them. By doing otherwise, you will cause most grievous sorrow to me, and utter destruction to yourself.'

"Psyche assented, and promised that she would act agreeably to her husband's desire. But when he and the night had departed together, the poor thing consumed the whole day in tears and lamentations, exclaiming over and over again, that she was now utterly lost, since, besides being thus confined in a splendid prison, deprived of human conversation, she was not even allowed to relieve the minds of her sisters, who were sorrowing for her, nor, indeed, so much as to see them. Without having refreshed herself, therefore, with the bath or with food, or, in fact, with any solace whatever, but weeping plenteously, she retired to rest. Shortly afterwards, her husband, coming to her bed earlier than usual, embraced her as she wept, and thus expostulated with her :

" 'Is this, my Psyche, what you promised me? What am I, your husband, henceforth to expect of you? What can I now hope for, when neither by day nor by night, not even in the midst of our conjugal endearments, you cease to be distracted with grief? Very well, then, act now just as you please, and comply with the baneful dictates of your inclination. However, when you begin too late to repent, you will recall to mind my serious admonitions.'

" Upon this, she had recourse to prayers; and threatening that she would put an end to herself if her request were denied, she extorted from her husband a consent that she might see her sisters, to soothe their grief, and enjoy their conversation. This he yielded to the entreaties of his new-made wife, and he gave her permission, besides, to present her sisters with as much gold and as many jewels as she pleased; but he warned her repeatedly and so often as to terrify her, never, on any occasion, to be persuaded by the pernicious advice of her sisters, to make any enquiries concerning the form of her husband; lest by a sacrilegious curiosity, she might cast herself down from such an exalted position of good fortune, and never again feel his embraces.

" She thanked her husband for his indulgence; and now, having quite recovered her spirits, ' Nay,' said she, ' I would suffer death a hundred times rather than be deprived of your most delightful company, for I love you, yes, I doat upon you to desperation, whoever you are, ay, even as I love my own soul, nor would I give you in exchange for Cupid himself. But this also I beseech you to grant to my prayers; bid Zephyr, this servant of yours, convey my sisters to me, in the same manner in which he brought me hither.' Then, pressing his lips with persuasive kisses, murmuring endearing words, and enfolding him with her clinging limbs, she called him coaxingly, ' My sweet, my husband, dear soul of thy Psyche.' Her husband, overcome by the power of love, yielded reluctantly, and promised all she desired. After this, upon the approach of morning, he again vanished from the arms of his wife.

" Meanwhile, the sisters, having inquired the way to the rock on which Psyche was abandoned, hastened thither; and there they wept and beat their breasts till the rocks and crags resounded with their lamentations.   They called to their unfortunate sister, by her own name, until the shrill sound of their shrieks descending the declivities of the mountain, reached the ears of Psyche, who ran out of her palace in delirious trepidation, and exclaimed :

" ' Why do you needlessly afflict yourselves with doleful lamentations ?   Here am I, whom you mourn; cease those dismal accents, and now at last dry up those tears that have so long bedewed your cheeks, since you may now embrace her whom you have been lamenting.'

" Then, summoning Zephyr, she acquaints him with her husband's commands, in obedience to which, instantly wafting them on his gentlest breeze, he safely conveyed them to Psyche. Now do they enjoy mutual embraces, and hurried kisses ; and their tears, that had ceased to flow, return, after a time, summoned forth by joy.   ' Now come,' said *Psyche*, ' enter my dwelling in gladness, and cheer up your afflicted spirits with your Psyche.'   Having thus said, she showed them the vast treasures of her golden palace, made their ears acquainted with the numerous retinue of voices that were obedient to her commands, and sumptuously refreshed them in a most beautiful bath, and with the delicacies of a divine banquet; until, satiated with this copious abundance of celestial riches, they began to nourish envy in the lowest depths of their breasts. One of them, especially, very minute and curious, persisted in making enquiries about the master of this celestial wealth, what kind of person, and what sort of husband he made.

" Psyche, however, would by no means violate her husband's injunctions, or disclose the secrets of her breast; but, devising a tale for the occasion, told them that he was a young man, and very good looking, with cheeks as yet only shaded with soft down, and that he was, for the most part, engaged in rural occupations, and hunting on the mountains.   And lest, by any slip in the course of the protracted conversation, her secret counsels might be betrayed, having loaded them with ornaments of gold and jewelled necklaces, she called Zephyr, and ordered him at once to convey them back again.

" This being immediately executed, these excellent sisters,

as they were returning home, now burning more and more with the rancour of envy, conversed much with each other; at last one of them thus began: " Do but see how blind, cruel, and unjust, Fortune has proved! Were you, my sister, delighted to find that we, born of the same parents, had met with such a different lot? We, indeed, who are the elder, are delivered over as bondmaids* to foreign husbands, and live in banishment from our home, our native land, and our parents; and this, the youngest of us all, the last production of our mother's exhausted powers of parturition, is raised to the enjoyment of such boundless wealth, and has a god for her husband, she who does not even know how to enjoy, in a proper manner, such an abundance of blessings? You saw, sister, what a vast number of necklaces there were in the house, and of what enormous value, what splendid dresses, what brilliant gems, and what heaps of gold she treads upon in every direction. If, besides all this, she possesses a husband so handsome as she asserts him to be, there lives not in the whole world a happier woman than she. Perhaps, however, upon continued acquaintance, and when his affection is strengthened, her husband, who is a god, will make her a goddess as well. By Hercules! it is so already; she comported and demeaned herself just like one: the woman must needs assume a lofty bearing, and give herself the airs of a goddess, who has voices for her attendants, and commands the very winds themselves. But I, wretched creature, am tied to a husband who, in the first place, is older than my father; and who, in the next place, is balder than a pumpkin, and more dwarfish than any boy, and who fastens up every part of his house with bolts and chains.'

" ' But I,' replied the other sister, ' have got to put up with a husband who is tormented and crippled with gout; and who, on this account, seldom honours me with his embraces, while I have to be everlastingly rubbing his distorted and chalky fingers with filthy fomentations, nasty rags, and stinking poultices; scalding these delicate hands, and acting the part not of

---

* *Over as bondmaids.*]—It was a prevalent notion with many of the ancients, that the wife stood towards the husband in relation of a bondmaid. In reference to this notion, Isidore, in his Origines, b. iv. c. 24, informs us, ' One of the ceremonies of marriage anciently was this; the husband and the wife purchased each other, in order that the latter might not be considered as a servant.'

a wife, but of a female doctor.   You, sister, seem to bear all this with a patient, or rather a servile spirit, for I shall speak out fully what I think; but, for my part, I can no longer endure that such a fortunate destiny should have so undeservedly fallen to her lot.   And then, recollect in what a haughty and arrogant manner she behaved towards us, and how, by her boasting and immoderate ostentation, she betrayed a heart swelling with pride, and how reluctantly she threw us a trifling portion of her immense riches; and immediately after, being weary of our company, ordered us to be turned out, and to be puffed and whisked away.   But may I be no woman, nor indeed may I breathe, if I do not hurl her down headlong from such mighty wealth.   And if this contumely offered to us stings you, too, as it ought, let us both join in forming some effective plan. In the first place, then, let us not show these things that we have got, either to our parents or to any one else; in fact, we are to know nothing at all about her safety.   It is quite enough that we ourselves have seen what it vexes us to have seen, without having to spread the report of her good fortune among our parents and all the people; for, in fact, those persons are not wealthy whose riches no one is acquainted with.   She shall know that in us she has got no handmaids, but elder sisters.   For the present, then, let us away to our husbands, and revisit our poor and plain dwellings, that after long and earnest consideration, we may return the better prepared to humble her pride.'

" This wicked project was voted good by the two wicked sisters.   Concealing those choice and sumptuous presents which they had received from Psyche, tearing their hair, and beating their faces, which well deserved such treatment, they redoubled their pretended grief.   In this manner, too, hastily leaving their parents, after having set their sorrows bleeding afresh, they returned to their homes, swelling with malicious rage, and plotting wicked schemes, nay, actual parricide against their innocent sister.

" In the mean time, Psyche's unknown husband once more admonished her thus in their nocturnal conversation: ' Are you aware what a mighty peril Fortune is preparing to launch against you from a distance, one too, which, unless you take strenuous precautions against it, will ere long confront you,*

* *Confront you.*] — ' Velitatur.'   This is a metaphorical expression.

H

hand to hand? Those perfidious she-wolves are planning base stratagems against you with all their might, to the end that they may prevail upon you to view my features, which, as I have often told you, if you once see, you will see no more. If, then, these most abominable vampires* come again, armed with their baneful intentions, and that they will come I know full well, do not hold any converse whatever with them; but if, through your natural frankness and tenderness of disposition, you are not able to do this, at all events, be careful not to listen to or answer any inquiries about your husband. For before long we shall have an increase to our family, and infantine as you are, you are pregnant with another infant, which, if you preserve my secret in silence, will be born divine, but if you profane it, will be mortal.'

"Radiant with joy at this news, Psyche exulted in the glory of this future pledge of love, and in the dignity of a mother's name. Anxiously did she reckon the increasing tale of the days and the elapsing months, and wondered in simple ignorance at the structure of this unknown burden, and how her wealthy womb could have gathered such an increase from a tiny point.

" But now those pests and most dire Furies, breathing viperous virulence, were hastening towards her with the speed of ruthless hate. Then again her husband warned his Psyche to this effect during his brief visit:—'The day of trial, and this most utter calamity, are now at hand. Your own malicious sex, and your own blood, in arms against you, have struck their camp, drawn up their forces in battle array, and sounded the charge. Now are your wicked sisters aiming with the drawn sword at your throat. Alas! darling Psyche, by what mighty dangers are we now surrounded! Take pity on yourself and on me; and by an inviolable silence, rescue your home, your husband, yourself, and that little one of ours, from this impending destruction. Shun those wicked women, whom, after the deadly hatred which they have conceived against you, and having trampled under foot the ties of blood, it were not right to call sisters; neither see, nor

taken from the mode of attack by the ' velites,' or light-armed infantry, who sent their darts and arrows from a distance.

* *Abominable vampires.*]—' Lamiæ.' These witches, or hags, have been referred to in a preceding note.

listen to them, when, like Sirens, hanging over the crag, they shall make the rocks resound with their ill-omened voices.'

" Psyche, in accents interrupted by sobs and tears, thus replied: ' Already, methinks, you have experienced convincing proofs of my fidelity and power of keeping a secret; and the constancy of my mind shall be no less approved of by you in the present instance. Only order Zephyr once again to discharge his duties, and at least grant me a sight of my sisters, by way of compensation for your own hallowed form.' By those aromatic locks, curling on every side! by those cheeks, tender, smooth, and so like my own! by your breast that glows with I know not what a warmth! and by my hopes that in this babe at least I may recognise your features, I beseech you to comply with the affectionate prayers of your anxious suppliant; indulge me with the gratification of embracing my sisters, and refresh with joyousness the soul of Psyche, who is so devoted and so dear to you. Then no longer I shall be anxious to view your features. Henceforth, not even the shades of night will have any effect on me. I clasp you in my arms, and you are my light.'

" Enchanted by these words, and by her honeyed embraces, her husband brushed away her tears with his locks, and assuring her that he would do as she wished, instantly anticipated the light of the dawning day by flight. But the pair of sisters who had engaged in this conspiracy, not having so much as visited their parents, direct their course with precipitate haste straight from the ships towards the rock, and not waiting for the presence of the buoyant breeze, leap into the abyss with ungovernable rashness. Zephyr, however, not forgetful of the royal commands, received them, though reluctantly, in the bosom of the breathing breeze, and laid them on the ground.

" With rapid steps and without a moment's delay, they entered the palace, and deceitfully screening themselves under the name of sister, embraced their prey; then, covering a whole store-house of deeply hidden treachery beneath a joyous countenance, they thus addressed her in flattering terms: ' Psyche, you are not quite so slender as you used to be. Why, you will be a mother before long. Can you fancy what delight you have in store for us in that reticule* of yours?

* In that reticule.]—' Perula.' Her womb.

With what exceeding joy you will gladden our whole house!
O how delighted we shall be to nurse this golden baby, for if
it only equals the beauty of its parents, it will be born a per-
fect Cupid.'

"Thus, by a false appearance of affection, they gradually stole
upon the heart of their sister, while she, after making them sit
awhile to recover from the fatigue of their journey and re-
fresh themselves with warm baths, regaled them in a marvel-
lously splendid manner with innumerable exquisite dainties.
She bade the harp discourse, and its chords were struck; flutes
to play, and they were heard; vocalists to sing in concert, and
they sang; and though invisible, they ravished the souls of
the hearers with the most delicious music.

"But the malice of those wicked women was not softened or
lulled to rest even by the dulcet sweetness of the music; but,
shaping their conversation so as to lead Psyche into the in-
tended snare, they began insidiously to inquire what sort of
a person her husband was, and from what family he was
descended. She, in her extreme simplicity, having forgotten
her former account, invented a new story about her husband,
and said he was a native of the adjoining province; that he
was a merchant, with abundance of money, a man of middle
age, with a few grey hairs sprinkled here and there on his
head. Then, abruptly terminating the conversation, she again
committed them to their windy vehicle, after having loaded
them with costly presents.

"While they were returning homewards, soaring aloft on
the tranquil breath of Zephyrus, they thus interchanged their
thoughts with each other: 'What are we to say, sister, of the
monstrous lies of that silly creature? At one time her hus-
band is a young man, with the down just beginning to show
itself on his chin; at another he is of middle age, and his hair
begins to be silvered with grey. Who can. this be, whom a
short space of time thus suddenly changes into an old man?
You may depend upon it, sister, that this most abominable
woman has either invented this lie to deceive us, or else that
she does not herself know what is the appearance of her hus-
band. But whichever of these is the case, she must as soon as
possible be deprived of these riches. And yet, if she really is
ignorant of the appearance of her husband, she must no doubt
have married a god, and then through this pregnancy of hers.

she will be presenting us with a god. At all events, if she does happen, which heaven forbid! to become the mother of a divine infant, I shall instantly hang myself. Let us therefore in the meantime return to our parents, and let us devise some scheme, as nearly as possible in accordance with the import of our present conversation.'

"The sisters, thus inflamed with passion, called on their parents in a careless and disdainful manner, and after being kept awake all night by the turbulence of their spirits, made all haste at morning to the rock, whence, by the usual assistance of the breeze, they descended swiftly to Psyche, and with tears squeezed out, by rubbing their eyelids, thus craftily addressed her: 'Happy indeed are you, and fortunate in your very ignorance of a misfortune of such magnitude. There you sit, without a thought upon your danger; while we, who watch over your interests with the most vigilant care, are in anguish at your lost condition. For we have learned for a truth, nor can we, as being sharers in your sorrows and misfortunes, conceal it from you, that it is an enormous serpent, gliding along in many folds and coils, with a neck swollen with deadly venom, and prodigious gaping jaws, that secretly sleeps with you by night. Do for a moment recall to mind the Pythian oracle, which declared that you were destined to become the wife of a fierce and truculent animal. Besides, many of the husbandmen, who are in the habit of hunting all round the country, and ever so many of the neighbours, have observed him returning home from his feeding-place in the evening, and swimming across the shoals of the neighbouring stream. All declare, too, that he will not long continue to pamper you with delicacies, but that as soon as ever your pregnancy shall have arrived at maturity, he will devour you, as being in that state a most exquisite morsel. Wherefore, it is now for you to consider whether you shall think fit to listen to us, who are so anxious for your precious safety, and avoiding death, live with us secure from danger, or be buried in the entrails of a most savage monster. But if you are fascinated by the vocal solitude of this country retreat, or the charms of clandestine embraces so filthy and perilous, and the endearments of a poisonous serpent, we have, at all events, done our duty towards you like affectionate sisters.'

"Poor simple, tender-hearted Psyche, was aghast with

norror at this dreadful story; and, quite bereft of her senses, lost all remembrance of her husband's admonitions and of her own promises, and hurled herself headlong into the very abyss of calamity. Trembling, therefore, with pale and livid cheeks, and with an almost lifeless voice, she faltered out these broken words:

" ' Dearest sisters, you have acted towards me as you ought, and with your usual affectionate care; and indeed it appears to me that those who gave you this information, have not invented a falsehood. For, in fact, I have never yet beheld my husband's face, nor do I know at all whence he comes. I only hear him speak in an undertone by night, and have to bear with a husband of an unknown appearance, and one that has an utter aversion to the light of day: I consequently have full reason to be of your opinion, that he may be some monster or other. Besides, he is always terrifying me from attempting to behold him, and threatens some shocking misfortune as the consequence of indulging any curiosity to view his features. Now, therefore, if you are able to give any saving aid to your sister in this perilous emergency, defer it not for a moment.'

" Finding the approaches thus laid open, and their sister's heart exposed all naked to their attacks, these wicked women thought the time was come to sally out from their covered approach, and attack the timorous thoughts of the simple girl with the drawn sword of deceit. Accordingly, one of them thus began: 'Since the ties of blood oblige us to have no fear of peril before our eyes when your safety is to be ensured, we will discover to you the only method which will lead to your preservation, and one which has been considered by us over and over again. On that side of the bed where you are accustomed to lie, secretly conceal a very sharp razor, one that you have whetted to a keen edge by passing it over the palm of your hand; and hide likewise under some covering of the surrounding tapestry* a lamp, well trimmed and full of oil, and shining with a bright light. Make these preparations with the utmost secrecy, and after the monster has glided into the bed as usual, when he is now stretched out at length, fast asleep, and breathing heavily, then slide out of bed, go softly along with bare feet and on tiptoe, free the lamp from its place of concealment in the dark,

* *Surrounding tapestry.*]—' Auleæ' seems a preferable reading here to ' Aululæ.'

and borrow the aid of its light to execute your noble purpose;
then at once, boldly raising your right hand, bring down the
keen weapon with all your might, and cut off the head of the
noxious serpent at the nape of the neck.   Nor shall our assist-
ance be wanting to you; for we will keep anxious watch, and
be with you the very instant you shall have effected your own
safety by his death; and then, immediately bringing you away
with all these things, we will wed you, to your wish, with a
human creature like yourself.

" Having with such pernicious language inflamed the mind
of their sister, and wrought her to a perfect pitch of determi-
nation, they deserted her, fearing exceedingly even to be in the
neighbourhood of such a catastrophe; and, being laid upon the
rock by the wonted impulse of their winged bearer, they im-
mediately hurried thence with impetuous haste, at once got on
board their ships, and sailed away.

" But Psyche, now left alone, except so far as a person who is
agitated by maddening Furies is not alone, fluctuated in sorrow
like a stormy sea; and though her purpose was fixed, and her
heart was resolute when she first began to make preparations
for the impious work, her mind now wavers, and is distracted
with numerous apprehensions at her unhappy fate.   She
hurries, she procrastinates; now she is bold, now tremulous;
now dubious, now agitated by rage; and what is the most
singular thing of all, in the same being she hates the beast,
loves the husband.   Nevertheless, as the evening drew to a
close, she hurriedly prepared the instruments of her ruthless
enterprise.

" The night came, and with it came her husband, and after
their first dalliance was over, he fell into a deep sleep.   Then
Psyche, to whose weak body and spirit the cruel influence of
fate imparted unusual strength, uncovered the lamp, and
seized the knife with masculine courage.   But the instant she
advanced the lamp, and the mysteries of the couch stood re-
vealed, she beheld the very gentlest and sweetest of all wild
creatures, even Cupid himself, the beautiful God of Love, there
fast asleep; at sight of whom, the joyous flame of the lamp
shone with redoubled vigour, and the sacrilegious razor re-
pented the keenness of its edge.

" But as for Psyche, astounded at such a sight, losing the
control of her senses, faint, deadly pale, and trembling all

over, she fell on her knees, and made an attempt to hide the blade in her own bosom; and this no doubt she would have done, had not the blade, dreading the commission of such a crime, glided out of her rash hand. And now, faint and un- nerved as she was, she feels herself refreshed at heart by gazing upon the beauty of those divine features. She looks upon the genial locks of his golden head, teeming with ambrosial perfume, the orbed curls that strayed over his milk-white neck and roseate cheeks, and fell gracefully entangled, some before, some behind; causing the very light of the lamp itself to flicker by their radiant splendour. On the shoulders of the volatile god were dewy wings of brilliant whiteness; and though the pinions were at rest, yet the tender down that fringed the feathers wantoned to and fro in tremulous unceasing play. The rest of his body was smooth and beautiful, and such as Venus could not have repented of giving birth to. At the foot of the bed lay his bow, his quiver, and his arrows, the auspi- cious weapons of the mighty God.

"While with insatiable wonder and curiosity Psyche is ex- amining and admiring her husband's weapons, she draws one of the arrows out of the quiver, and touches the point with the tip of her thumb to try its sharpness; but happening to press too hard, for her hand still trembled, she punctured the skin, so that some tiny drops of rosy blood oozed forth; and thus did Psyche, without knowing it, fall in love with LOVE. Then, burning more and more with desire for Cupid, gazing passion- ately on his face, and fondly kissing him again and again, her only fear was, lest he should wake too soon.

"But while she hung over him bewildered with delight so extreme at heart, the lamp, whether from treachery or baneful envy, or because it longed to touch, and to kiss, as it were, such a beautiful object, spirted a drop of scalding oil from the summit of its flame upon the right shoulder of the god. O rash, audacious lamp! vile minister to love! thus to burn the god of all fire; you whom some lover, doubtless, first invented, that he might prolong even through the night the bliss of beholding the object of his desire! The God, thus scorched, sprang from the bed, and seeing the disgraceful tokens of forfeited fidelity, without a word, was flying away from the eyes and arms of his most unhappy wife. But Psyche, the instant he arose, seized hold of his right leg with both hands, and hung on to him, a wretched appendage to his flight through the regions of the air, till at last her strength failed her, and she fell to the earth.

"Her divine lover, however, not deserting her as she lay on the ground, alighted upon a neighbouring cypress tree, and thus angrily addressed her from its lofty top :—'O simple, simple Psyche, for you I have been unmindful of the commands of my mother Venus; for when she bade me cause you to be infatuated with passion for some base and abject man, I chose rather to fly to you myself as a lover. That in this I acted inconsiderately, I know but too well. I, that redoubtable archer, have wounded myself with my own arrow, and have made you my wife, that I, forsooth, might be thought by you to be a serpent, and that you might cut off my head, which bears those very eyes which have so doated upon you. This was the danger that I told you again and again to be on your guard against, this was what I so benevolently forewarned you of. But as for those choice counsellors of yours, they shall speedily feel my vengeance for giving you such pernicious advice ; but you I will punish only by my flight.' And so saying, he soared aloft, and flew away.

"Meanwhile Psyche lay prostrate on the ground, gazing on the flight of her husband as long as ever he remained in sight, and afflicting her mind with the most bitter lamentations. But when the reiterated movement* of his wings had borne her husband through the immensity of space till she saw him no more, she threw herself headlong from the bank of the adjacent river into its stream. But the gentle river, honouring the God, who is in the habit of imparting his warmth to the waters† themselves, and fearing his power, bore her on the surface of a harmless wave to the bank, and laid her safe on its flowery turf.

"It chanced that just then the rural god Pan was seated on the margin of the river, embracing the goddess Canna,‡ and teaching her to sing all kinds of pleasant ditties. Close by,

* *Reiterated movement.*]—In the original, ' remigio.' ' Remigium alarum,' ' the rowing of the wings,' is a phrase much used by the classical writers.

† *To the waters.*]—That is to say, to the deities and nymphs who inhabit them—not to mention the fish.

‡ *The goddess Canna.*]—This alludes to the well-known fable of Syrinx and Pan. Canna is the Latin for ' cane,' or ' reed.'

some she-goats gambolled as they browsed along the grassy bank. The goat-legged god, aware of Pysche's misfortune, kindly called the fainting, heart-stricken girl to him, and thus comforted her in soothing language:—' Pretty damsel, though I am a countryman and a shepherd, still, through the benefit of a prolonged old age, I have acquired considerable experience; wherefore, if I rightly conjecture—a thing that wise men no doubt consider as good as the power of divination—if I rightly conjecture, from those tottering and repeatedly faltering steps, from the excessive paleness of your countenance, from your frequent sighs, and from the sad expression of your eyes, you are desperately in love. Listen, then, to me; attempt no more to put an end to yourself by leaping from a precipice, or by any kind of self-inflicted death; cease to grieve, lay aside your sorrow, and rather in your prayers worship Cupid, the greatest of the Gods, and as he is a delicate and spoilt stripling, use your best endeavours to please him by soothing attentions.'

" The shepherd God having thus said, Psyche made him no reply, but simply paying her homage to the propitious divinity, departed from the spot. After she had toiled some little way along the road, she came at last to an unknown byepath, and following it, she arrived at a certain city, of which the husband of one of her sisters was king. On learning this circumstance, Psyche requested that her arrival might be announced to her sister. Being immediately conducted to her, when they had mutually embraced, and the forms of salutation were over, on her sister inquiring the cause of her visit, she replied:

" ' Of course you remember the advice you gave me, when you persuaded me to destroy with a sharp razor the beast that lay with me under the assumed name of a husband, before he should swallow me, poor creature, in his voracious maw. I proceeded to do as we had arranged; but as soon as ever I discerned his features by the light of the lamp, I beheld a sight truly wonderful and divine, the very son himself of the goddess Venus, Cupid I say, sunk in tranquil repose. Just, however, as, struck with astonishment at the sight of such a boundless blessing, and in utter ecstasy through an over-abundance of pleasure, I was at a loss how sufficiently to enjoy my fortune, by a most shocking accident, the lamp spirted out some scalding oil upon his right shoulder. Instantly awakened by the

pain, and seeing me armed with the weapon and the light,
'For this shameful conduct,' said he, 'quit my bed this instant,
I divorce you for ever.*   I will at once marry your sister,'—
mentioning you expressly by name,—and then he ordered
Zephyr to waft me beyond the precincts of the palace.'

"Scarcely had Psyche ended her narrative, when the other,
goaded by maddening lust and baneful envy, deceived her hus-
band by a story which she had ready invented, as though she
had heard something about the death of her parents, and im-
mediately embarking, proceeded to the same rock.   When she
arrived there, though another wind was blowing, yet, elated
with blind hope, she exclaimed, 'Receive me, Cupid, a wife
worthy of thee, and thou, Zephyr, acknowledge thy mis-
tress.'   Then with a great bound, she threw herself headlong
from the mountain; but neither alive nor dead was she
able to reach the spot she sought.   For her limbs were
torn in pieces by the crags, and scattered here and there as she
fell, her entrails were rent asunder, just as she deserved; and
so, furnishing a banquet for birds and beasts of prey, she
perished.

"Nor was the other sister's punishment long delayed; for
Psyche's wandering steps led her to another city, in which
that sister dwelt; and she also, deceived by the same tale, and
impiously desirous of supplanting Pysche as a wife, hastened
to the rock, and there met with her death in a similar manner.

"In the meantime, while Psyche wandered through various
nations, anxiously searching for Cupid, he himself, with the
wound from the lamp, lay in his mother's chamber groaning.
A snow-white sea-gull, the bird which skims along the waves
of the sea, flapping them with its wings, dived down into the
bosom of the ocean.   There, approaching Venus, as she bathed
and swam, he informed her that her son was confined to his
bed by a severe burn, was in great pain, and his cure was
doubtful: that all sorts of scandalous reports were flying about
concerning the whole family of Venus; and it was in every-
body's mouth that mother and son had gone off, the one to a
mountain, to carry on an intrigue with a girl; the other to

* *I divorce you for ever.*]—'Tibi tuas res habeto.' Literally, 'take your
things to yourself.' This was the ordinary formula used among the
Romans in cases of divorce, when the husband returned to the wife her
separate property.

amuse herself with swimming in the sea. In consequence
of all this, Pleasure, Grace, and Elegance are no longer to be
found, but everything is rude, rustic, and slovenly; nuptial
ties, social friendships, and love of children, exist no more; but
unbounded disorder, and a bitter loathing of sordid alliances.
Thus did this talkative and very meddling bird chatter in the
ear of Venus, to lower her son in her estimation.

"Venus, exceedingly enraged, instantly exclaimed, ' So then
this hopeful son of mine has already got some mistress or
other.   Come, now, you who are the only one to serve me
with true affection, what is the name of her who has thus de-
coyed the ingenuous and beardless boy? is she one of the tribe
of Nymphs, or of the number of the Hours, or of the choir of
the Muses, or belonging to my own train of Graces?'

" The talkative bird was only too ready to reply, ' I am not
quite sure, mistress.   I think, though, if I remember right, he
is said to have fallen desperately in love with a girl, whose
name is Psyche.

"'What!' exclaimed Venus, in a burst of indignation, ' of
all wenches in the world, is he in love with Psyche, the
usurper of my beauty, and the rival of my fame?   And by
way of additional insult, he takes me for a go-between, through
whose instrumentality he made acquaintance with the girl.'

" Thus exclaiming, she forthwith emerged from the sea, and
hastened to her golden chamber, where finding her son lying
ill, as she had been informed, she bawled out* as loud as ever
she could before she entered the door—'This is pretty conduct,
indeed! and very becoming our dignified birth, and your so-
briety of character.   In the first place, to trample under foot
the commands of your mother, your sovereign mistress, and
refrain from tormenting my enemy with an ignoble love, and
then at your age, a mere boy, to take her to your profligate and
immature embraces, on purpose, I suppose, that I might en-
dure the vexation of having my enemy for my daughter-in-law.
But doubtless you suppose, you scamp, you seducer, you unlove-
able boy, that you are my only high-born son, and that I am
too old to have another.   I would have you know then, that I

* *Bawled out.*]—It is with much concern we find the goddess of grace
and beauty guilty of the unseemly act of bawling, as well as of other ter-
magant behaviour; but it stands so on the record: ' am inde a foribus
quam maxime Loans.'

will have another son, a much better one than you ; nay, what's more, that you may be fully sensible of the disgrace, I will adopt one of the sons of my slaves, and to him will I give those wings and that torch, that bow and those arrows, and all that equipment which I bestowed on you, for purposes very different from these ; for no part whatever of this apparatus was supplied at your father's expense. But from your very childhood, you have been badly inclined, and have always had pugnacious hands. Many a time, too, have you most disrespectfully struck your elders : and even myself, your mother, myself, I say, you parricide, you are everyday exposing before the world. Many a time you have struck me, and you pay no more attention to me than if I were a widow ; you do not even fear your step-father, that most brave and mighty warrior ; quite the contrary, indeed, for you are evermore setting him after wenches, to my torment. But I will make you repent of these tricks of yours, and that you shall find this match a sour and bitter one.'

" ' But now, made a laughing-stock of, what shall I do ? Whither betake myself? How shall I coerce this slippery little lizard? Shall I solicit the assistance of my old foe Sobriety, whom I have so often affronted for sake of this spoiled boy ? Must I have intercourse with that coarse, vulgar being? I shudder at the thought ; and yet the comfort of revenge is not to be despised, come whence it may. I must have recourse then to her, and to her alone ; that she may most soundly chastise this scamp. She shall rifle his quiver, blunt his arrows, unstring his bow, extinguish his torch, aye, and keep his body in order by the sharpest remedies. When I shall have shorn off those golden locks, which these hands have so often sorted, and have clipped off those pinions, which I have dyed in my bosom's nectareous fountain, then, and not till then, I shall believe that atonement has been made for the injury I have received.

" Having thus vented her wrath, she rushed impetuously out of doors, and was immediately accosted by Ceres and Juno, who, observing her angry countenance, asked her why she marred the beauty of her sparkling eyes by such a sullen frown. ' Most opportunely are you come,' she replied, ' to appease* that violence which has taken possession of my

* *To appease.*]—' Perplacatura' seems to be a preferable reading here: to ' perpetraturæ.'

raging bosom. Enquire for me, I beg, with the utmost care and diligence after that runaway vagabond, Psyche; for the infamous stories about my family, and the conduct of my son who does not deserve to be named, cannot be unknown to you.

"The two Goddesses, knowing what had happened, thus endeavoured to mitigate the rage of Venus. 'What mighty offence, good mistress, has your son committed, that you should thwart his pleasures with such stubborn resolution, and be impatient to destroy her with whom he is in love? Is it a crime, if he has freely indulged his liking for a pretty girl? Are you ignorant of his sex, and his youth? Surely, you have forgotten how many years old he is, or is it because he carries his years so prettily, that you would for ever fancy him a boy? Is it possible, that you, who are his mother, and a woman of understanding, can persist in prying inquisitively into the gaieties of your handsome son, finding fault with his indiscretions, taking him to task for his amours, and reproving in him your own arts and voluptuous suggestions? But what God or what man will bear with you, when you are everywhere scattering amorous desires among people, and at the same time would restrain the gallantries of your own house, and shut up the universal magazine of female frailties?'

"Thus did they, through fear of his darts, flatter, and graciously defend Cupid in his absence. But Venus, indignant that her injuries were thus treated with ridicule, turned her back upon them, and with hasty steps again betook herself to the ocean."

BOOK THE SIXTH.

CONCLUSION OF THE FIFTH EPISODE: CUPID AND PSYCHE—LUCIUS ACCOMPANIES THE ROBBERS TO A CAVE WHERE THEY HAVE DEPOSITED BOOTY, AND INCURS THEIR DISPLEASURE—HE ATTEMPTS TO ESCAPE—IS SEIZED BY THE OLD WOMAN; BUT, AIDED BY THE DAMSEL, GALLOPS OFF, WITH HIS ALLY ON HIS BACK—LUCIUS AND THE DAMSEL RETAKEN BY THE ROBBERS—DEATH OF THE OLD WOMAN—LUCIUS AND THE DAMSEL CONDEMNED TO A HORRIBLE LINGERING DEATH.

"In the meantime Psyche wandered about, day and night, restlessly seeking her husband, and the more anxious to find him, because, though she had incurred his anger, she hoped to appease him, if not by the tender endearments of a wife, at least by entreaties as humble as a slave could urge.   Perceiving a temple on the summit of a lofty mountain, ' How can I tell,' said she, ' but yonder may be the residence of my lord?' and immediately she hastened thither, while, wayworn and exhausted as she was, hope and affection quickened her steps, and gave her vigour to climb the highest ridges of the mountain, and enter the temple.   There she saw blades of wheat, some in sheaves, some twisted into chaplets, and ears of barley also.   There were scythes likewise, and all the implements of harvest, but all lying scattered about in confusion, just as such things are usually thrown down, in the heat of summer, from the careless hands of the reapers.

" Psyche began carefully to sort all these things, and arrange them properly in their several places, deeming it her duty not to fail in respect for the temples and ceremonies of any deity, but to implore the benevolent sympathy of all the Gods. Bounteous Ceres found her thus diligently employed in her temple, and cried to her, from a distance : ' Ah, poor unfortunate Psyche ! Venus, full of rage, is eagerly tracking your footsteps, craving to inflict upon you the deadly penalties, and the whole force of her divine vengeance.   And can you then busy yourself with my concerns, and think of anything else but your own safety?'

" Psyche, prostrating herself before the goddess, moistening her feet with abundant tears, and sweeping the ground with her locks, besought her protection with manifold prayers.   ' I implore thee,' said she, ' by thy fruit-bearing right hand, by the joyful ceremonies of harvest, by the mysterious rites of thy cists,* by the winged car of the dragons thy servants, by the furrows of the Sicilian soil, by the chariot of the ravisher,† by the earth that closed upon him, by the dark descent and unlighted nuptials of Proserpine, by the torch-illumined return of thy recovered daughter, and by the other mysteries which Eleusis, the sanctuary of Attica, conceals in silence : succour,

* *Of thy cists.*]—In the processions of Ceres, at Athens, were carried chests or baskets, made of osier, enclosing mystic images of the Deity, which it was not lawful for any uninitiated person to look upon.

† *The chariot of the ravisher.*]—' Per currum rapacem.'   The chariot of Pluto, in which he carried off Proserpine from the plains of Enna, in Sicily, and descended through a chasm of the earth to the shades below.

O succour the life of the wretched Psyche, thy suppliant!
Suffer me, if for a few days only, to conceal myself in that
heap of wheatsheaves, till the raging anger of the mighty
Goddess be mitigated by the lapse of time; or at least until my
bodily powers, weakened by long-continued labour, be renewed
by an interval of rest.'

"'I am touched by your tears and entreaties, Ceres re-
plied, 'and fain would render you assistance; but I cannot
provoke the displeasure of my relative, to whom I am also
united by ties of friendship of old date, and who besides is a
very worthy lady. Begone, therefore, from this temple di-
rectly, and be very thankful that I do not seize and detain
you as a prisoner.'

"Psyche, thus repulsed, contrary to her expectations, and
afflicted with twofold grief, retraced the way she came, and
presently espied in a gloomy grove of the valley below the
mountain, a temple of exquisite structure. Unwilling to omit
any chance of better fortune, though ever so remote, but re-
solving rather to implore the protection of the god, whoever
he might be, she approached the sacred doors. There she be-
held splendid offerings, and garments embroidered with golden
letters, fastened to the branches of trees and to the door-posts
of the temple; upon which was recorded the name of the god-
dess to whom they had been dedicated, and also the particulars
of the favour received.

"Then Psyche fell upon her knees, and with her hands
embracing the yet warm altar, having first wiped away her
tears, she thus offered up a prayer: 'O sister and consort of
mighty Jove! whether thou dost inhabit the ancient temples
of Samos,* which glories in thy birth, thy complaining infancy,
and thy nurture; or whether thou dost frequent the happy
mansions of lofty Carthage, which adores thee as a virgin,
passing through the heavens in a car drawn by lions; or dost
preside over the renowned walls of the Argives, near the banks
of Inachus, where thou art celebrated as the spouse of the Thun-
derer, and the Queen of the Gods; thou whom all the East vene-
rates under the name of Zygia,† and all the West denominates

* *Temples of Samos.*]—The goddess Juno was especially worshipped in
the island of Samos, and the city of Carthage. The Samians boasted that
she was born in that island, near the river Imbrasus, whence she was called
Imbrasia.

† *Name of Zygia.*]—Juno was so called from ζυγος, a 'yoke,' as pre-
siding over the rites of wedlock.

Lucina! be thou, Juno Sospita, a protectress to me in these my overwhelming misfortunes, and deliver me, worn out with long sufferings, from the fear of my impending danger; for I know that thou art accustomed readily to succour pregnant women in time of peril.'

"While Psyche thus prayed, Juno appeared before her, in all the august majesty of her divinity, and said, 'How readily would I lend an ear to your entreaties; but propriety will not permit me to act contrary to the wishes of Venus, my daughter in-law,* whom I have always loved as my own child. Then, besides, the laws forbid † me to receive into my protection any fugitive servant, without the consent of her mistress.'

"Dismayed by this second shipwreck of her fortunes, and being no longer able to make search for her volatile husband, Psyche gave up all hopes of safety, and thus communed with herself. 'What other relief for my sorrows can now be looked for or procured, since even goddesses cannot, though willing, afford me any assistance? In what direction shall I once more bend my wandering steps, entangled, as I am, in snares so inextricable? Concealed in what habitations, in what darkness even, can I escape the ever-vigilant eyes of the mighty Venus? Assume, then, a masculine courage, my soul, boldly renounce vain hopes, voluntarily surrender yourself into the hands of your mistress, and try, though late, to soften her rage by submissive behaviour. Besides, who knows whether you may not perhaps find in his mother's house him whom you have been so long seeking in vain.' Thus prepared for this doubtful experiment of duty, or rather for certain destruction, she considered with herself how she was to preface her entreaties.

"Venus, meanwhile, declining to employ earthly means in pursuing her inquiries after Psyche, returned to heaven. She ordered the chariot to be got ready, which Vulcan had constructed with exquisite skill, and presented to her before the celebration of her marriage. The nuptial gift was of burnished gold, and was even the more precious through the diminution of its material by the file.‡ Four white doves, out of the many

* *My daughter-in-law.*]—Venus being the wife of Vulcan, the son of Juno.

† *The laws forbid.*]—Probably by this expression reference is made to the Fabian law, entitled 'De Plagiariis.'

‡ *More precious through the diminution, &c*]—That is to say, the loss

I

that nestled about the chamber of their mistress, advanced with joyous flutterings, and bending their painted necks to the jewelled yoke, flew forward with the chariot that contained the goddess. Around it wantoned chattering sparrows, and other birds of sweet note, which announced the approach of Venus in melodious strains.

"And now the clouds dispersed, heaven unfolded itself before its daughter, and the lofty æther received the goddess with joy; nor did the tuneful retinue of Venus dread the attack of eagles, or rapacious hawks. She went straightway to the royal citadel of Jove, and with a haughty air demanded, as especially necessary, the services of the crier god; nor did the azure brow of Jupiter refuse its assent. Exulting Venus, accompanied by Mercury, immediately descended from heaven, and thus anxiously addressed him: 'My Arcadian brother, you well know that your sister, Venus, never did anything without the presence of Mercury, nor are you ignorant how long I have been unable to find my absconded female slave. Nothing remains, therefore, to be done, but for you to proclaim her in public, and announce a reward to him who shall find her. Take care, therefore, that my commands are speedily executed, and clearly describe the marks by which she may be recognized; that no one may excuse himself on the plea of ignorance, if he incurs the crime of unlawfully concealing her.'

" So saying, she gave him a little book, in which were written Psyche's name, and sundry particulars. This done, she immediately returned home. Nor did Mercury neglect her commands; for going about among all nations, he thus performed his duties as crier: ' If any one can seize in her flight, and bring back, a fugitive daughter of a king, a handmaid of Venus, and by name Psyche, or discover where she has concealed herself, let such person repair to Mercury, the crier, behind the boundaries of Murtia,* and receive, by way of re-

of the precious material was more than compensated by the value of the workmanship. Materiam superabat opus.

* *The boundaries of Murtia.*]—The spot here mentioned was at the back of the temple of Venus Murtia, or guardian of the myrtle, which was built on Mount Aventine, at Rome. In the first idyl of Moschus, Venus thus proclaims the reward for her fugitive child:

' On him who the haunts of my Cupid can show,
A kiss of the tenderest stamp I'll bestow;
But he who can bring me the wanderer here,
Shall have something more rapturous, something more dear.'

This ' something more' is the quicquid post oscula dulce of Secundus

ward, for the discovery, seven sweet kisses from Venus herself, and one exquisitely delicious touch of her charming tongue.'

"Mercury having thus made proclamation, the desire of obtaining such a reward excited the emulous endeavours of all mankind, and this circumstance it was that quite put an end to all Psyche's hesitation. She was already near her mistress's gates, when she was met by one of the retinue of Venus, whose name was HABIT, and who immediately cried out, as loud as she could bawl, ' So, you most good-for-nothing wench, have you at last begun to discover that you have a mistress? And do you pretend, too, in your abundant assurance, that you don't know what immense trouble we have had in endeavouring to find you out? But it is well that you have fallen into my hands, of all others, and have got within the very jaws of Orcus, to receive, without delay, the penalty of such obstinate contumacy.'

" So saying, she instantly twisted her hands in Psyche's hair, and dragged the unresisting captive along. But Venus, the moment she was dragged into her presence, burst into a loud laugh, such as people laugh who are furiously angry; and shaking her head and scratching her right ear.* 'At length,' said she, 'have you deigned to pay your respects to your mother-in-law? Or rather, are you come to see your sick husband, who is yet dangerously ill from the wound you gave him? But make yourself easy; for I shall at once give you a reception such as a good mother-in-law ought to give. Where,' she cried, ' are those servants of mine, ANXIETY and SORROW?' These attending, at her call, she delivered her to them to be tormented. Thereupon, in obedience to the commands of their mistress, they scourged and inflicted other torments on the wretched Psyche, and after they had tortured her, brought her back again into the presence of Venus.

" ' Just look at her,' said Venus, again setting up a laugh; ' her interesting state quite moves my compassion, since it is through that, forsooth, that she is to make me a happy grandmother. Fortunate, indeed, am I, who, in the very flower of my age, am to be called a grandmother! And the son of a vile handmaid is to hear himself called the grandson of Venus! And yet I talk nonsense in calling him my grandson; for ill-assorted marriages, contracted, too, in a country place, without

* *Scratching her right ear.*]—According to Pliny, the throne of Nemesis, the goddess of revenge, is behind the right ear.

any witnesses, and without the father's consent, cannot possibly be deemed legitimate; consequently this child will be a bastard, even if I do suffer you to bring it into the light at all.'

"Having thus said, she flew upon her, tore her clothes in a great many places, pulled out her hair, shook her by the head, and grievously maltreated her. Then, taking wheat, barley, millet, poppy, vetches, lentils, and beans, and, mixing them all together in one heap, she said to her: ' You seem to me, such an ugly slave as you now are, to be likely to gain lovers in no other way than by diligent drudgery. I will, therefore, myself, for once, make trial of your industrious habits. Take and separate this promiscuous mass of seeds, and having properly placed each grain in its place, and so sorted the whole, give me a proof of your expedition, by finishing the task before evening.' Then having delivered over to her the vast heap of seeds, she at once took her departure for a nuptial banquet.

"But Psyche astounded at the stupendous task, sat silent and stupified, and did not move a hand to the confused and inextricable mass. Just then, a tiny little ant, one of the inhabitants of the fields, became aware of this prodigious difficulty; and pitying the distress of the partner of the mighty god, and execrating the mother-in-law's cruelty, it ran busily about, and summoned together the whole tribe of ants in the neighbourhood, crying to them, 'Take pity on her, ye active children of the all-producing earth! Take pity, and make haste to help the wife of Love, a pretty damsel, who is now in a perilous situation.'

"Immediately the six-footed people came rushing in whole waves one upon another, and with the greatest diligence separated the whole heap, grain by grain; then, having assorted the various kinds into different heaps, they vanished forthwith.

"At nightfall, Venus returned home from the nuptial banquet, exhilarated with wine, fragrant with balsams, and having her waist encircled with blooming roses. As soon as she saw with what marvellous expedition the task had been executed, 'This is no work of your hands, wicked creature,' she said, 'but his whom you have charmed, to your own sorrow and his;' and throwing her a piece of coarse bread, she went to bed.

"Meanwhile, Cupid was closely confined in his chamber, partly that he might not inflame his wound by froward indulgence, and partly lest he should associate with his beloved. The lovers, thus separated from each other under one roof,

passed a miserable night.   But as soon as Aurora had ushered
in the morning, Venus called Psyche, and thus addressed her:
' Do you see yonder grove, stretching along the margin of a
river, whose deep eddies receive the waters of a neighbouring
fountain ?   There shining sheep of a golden colour wander
about, feeding without a shepherd.   I desire that you bring
me immediately a flock of that precious wool, get it how you
may.'

" Psyche willingly set out, not with any intention of exe-
cuting this command, but to procure rest from her misfortunes,
by hurling herself headlong from the rock into the river.   But
when she came to the brink, a green reed, the nurse of sweet
music,* divinely inspired by a gentle breath of air, thus pro-
phetically murmured : ' Psyche ! exercised in mighty sorrows,
neither pollute my sacred waters by your most miserable death,
nor venture yet to approach the formidable sheep on the oppo-
site bank.   While heated by the burning radiance of the sun,
they are transported with savage rage, and are the destruction
of mortals, either by their sharp horns, their stony foreheads,
or their venomous bites.   Therefore until the sun has declined
from the meridian, and the serene spirit of the flood has
lulled the animals to rest, you may hide yourself under yonder
lofty plane tree, which drinks of the same river with myself;
and as soon as the sheep have mitigated their fury, if you shake
the branches of the neighbouring grove, you will find the woolly
gold every where sticking to them.'   Thus the artless and
humane reed taught the wretched Psyche how to accomplish
this dangerous enterprise with safety.

" Psyche, therefore, observing all the directions, found her
obedience was not in vain, but returned to Venus with her
bosom full† of the delicate golden fleece.   Yet she was not able
to win the approbation of her mistress by this her second peri-
lous labour.   But Venus, smiling bitterly with knitted brows,
thus addressed her : ' I do not fail to perceive another's hand
in the performance of this task also ; but I will now try whe-
ther you are endowed with a courageous mind and singular
prudence.   Do you see the summit of yonder lofty mountain ?
From that peak fall the dusky waters of a black fountain, which.

---

* *Nurse of sweet music.*]—So called because the pipe of Pan was
formed of reeds joined together.

† *Her bosom full.*]—The ancients used the part of the robe that
covered the bosom, as a pocket.

after being confined in the neighbouring valley, irrigate the Stygian marshes, and supply the hoarse streams of Cocytus? Bring me immediately in this little urn, ice-cold water drawn from the very midst of the lofty fountain.' Thus speaking, she gave her a vessel of polished crystal, and at the same time threatened her more severely than before.

" But Psyche started off with the utmost celerity to reach the very summit of the mountain, presuming that there, at least, she would find the period of her most miserable life. However, when she arrived at its confines, she saw the deadly difficulty of the stupendous undertaking. For a rock, enormously lofty, and inaccessibly rugged, vomits from its middle the horrid waters of the fountain, which, immediately falling headlong, are carried unseen through a deep, narrow, and covered channel into the neighbouring valley. On the right and left hand they creep through hollow rocks, over which fierce dragons stretch out their long necks, and keep a perpetual watch with unwinking vigilance. And the vocal waters exclaim ever and anon as they roll along, ' Begone; what are you about? Mind what you do; take care; fly; you will perish.'

" Psyche, therefore, petrified through the impossibility of accomplishing the task, though she was present in body was absent in mind, and being perfectly overwhelmed by the inextricable danger, was even deprived of the benefit of tears, the last solace of the wretched. But the sorrow of the innocent soul is not concealed from the penetrating eyes of Providence. The rapacious eagle, Jove's royal bird, on a sudden flew to her with expanded wings, remembering his ancient obligations to Cupid, who enabled him to carry the Phrygian cup-bearer up to Jove; therefore, in gratitude to the young god, the eagle deserted the lofty paths of Jupiter, and bringing seasonable assistance to Cupid's wife in her distress, he thus addressed her: ' Can you, simple as you are, and inexperienced in attempts of this kind, ever hope to steal one drop of this most holy and no less terrible fountain? Have you not heard, at least, that these Stygian waters are formidable even to Jupiter himself, and that as you swear by the divinity of the gods, so they are accustomed to swear by the majesty of Styx? But give me that little urn.' Snatching it in haste, he sailed away on his strong wings, steering his course to the right and to the left, between the rows of raging teeth, and the three-

forked vibrating tongues of the dragons until he reached and
drew the reluctant waters, which warned him to begone while he
might in safety. But he pretended that Venus herself wanted
some of the water, and had ordered him to procure it; and on
this account his access to the fountain was somewhat facilitated.

"Psyche, therefore, joyfully receiving the full urn, returned
with all speed to Venus. Yet not even by the accomplishment of
this dangerous enterprise, could she appease the anger of the
raging goddess. For designing to expose her to still more outra-
geous trials, Venus thus addressed her, a smile, the harbinger of
ruin, accompanying her words: 'You appear to me to be a pro-
found and malevolent sorceress, or you never could with so
much dexterity have performed my commands: but there is
one task more, my dear, which you must perform. Take this
box,' she said, delivering it to her, 'and direct your course to
the infernal regions and the deadly palace of Pluto. Then pre-
senting the box to Proserpine, say, Venus requests you to send
her a small portion of your beauty, at least as much as may be
sufficient for one short day; for she has consumed all the
beauty she possessed, through the attention which she pays to
her sick son. But return with the utmost expedition; for I
must adorn myself with this beauty of Proserpine, before I go
to the theatre of the gods.'

"Psyche was now truly sensible that she was arrived at the
extremity of her evil fortune; and clearly perceived that she
was openly and undisguisedly impelled to immediate destruc-
tion, since she was forced to direct her steps to Tartarus and
the shades below. Without any further delay, therefore, she
proceeded towards a lofty tower, that she might thence hurl
herself headlong; for she considered that she should thus
descend by a straight and easy road to the infernal regions.
But she was no sooner arrived there, than the tower suddenly
addressed her in the following words:

"'Why, O miserable creature, dost thou seek to destroy thy-
self by falling headlong hence? And why dost thou rashly
sink under this thy last danger and endurance? For as soon
as thy breath shall thus be separated from thy body, thou wilt
indeed descend to profound Tartarus, but canst not by any
means return thence. Listen, therefore, to me. Lacedæmon,
a noble city of Achaia, is not far from hence. Near this city,
concealed in devious places, is Tenarus, which you must seek;
for there you will find a cavity, which is Pluto's breathing

hole, and an untraversed road presents itself to the view through the yawning gap. As soon as you have passed the threshold of this cavity, you will proceed in a direct path to the palace of Pluto. You ought not, however, to pass through those shades with empty hands, but should take a sop of barley bread, soaked in hydromel, in each hand, and in your mouth two pieces of money. And when you have accomplished a good part of your deadly journey, you will meet a lame ass laden with wood, with a driver as lame as himself, who will ask you to reach him certain cords to fasten the burden which has fallen from the ass: but be careful that you pass by him in silence. Then, without any delay, proceed till you arrive at the dead river, where Charon, immediately demanding his fee, ferries the passengers over in his patched boat to the farthest shore.

"'Avarice, it appears, lives among the dead; nor does Charon himself, nor the father Pluto, though so great a god, do any thing gratuitously. The poor man dying, ought to prepare his viaticum; but if he has no money at hand, will no one suffer him to expire? To this squalid old man give one of the pieces of money which you carry with you; yet in such a manner, that he may take it with his own hand from your mouth. While you are passing over the sluggish river, a certain dead old man, floating on its surface, and raising his putrid hand, will entreat you to take him into the boat. Beware, however, of yielding to any impulse of unlawful pity. Having passed over the river, and proceeded to a little distance beyond it, you will see certain old women, weaving a web, who will request you to lend them a helping hand; but it is not lawful for you to touch the web. For all these, and many other particulars, are snares prepared for you by Venus, that you may drop one of the sops out of your hands. But do not suppose that this would be a trifling loss; since the want of only one of these sops, would prevent your return to light. For a huge dog, with three large, fierce, and formidable necks and heads, barking with his thundering jaws, terrifies in vain the dead, whom he cannot injure; and always watching before the threshold and black palace of Proserpine, guards the void Plutonian mansion. Having appeased this dog with one of your sops, you may easily pass by him, and then you will immediately enter the presence of Proserpine herself, who will receive you in a very courteous and benignant manner, desire you to repose on a soft seat, and persuade you to partake of a sumptuous banquet. But seat yourself on the ground, ask for a piece of common bread, and eat it; then deliver your message, and having received what you came for, bribe the cruel dog with the remaining sop. Afterwards, having given to the avaricious ferryman the piece of money which you have reserved, and having passed his river, you will return by the way you came to the choir of the celestial stars. But, above all things, I warn you, be particularly cautious not to open or look on the box which you carry, or explore that concealed treasury of divine beauty.' In this manner, the propitious tower delivered its prophetic admonitions.

" Psyche, therefore, without delay, proceeded to Tenarus, and duly taking her pieces of money and her sops, ran down the infernal avenue. Here, having passed by the lame ass in silence, given the ferryman his fee, neglected the entreaties of the floating corpse, despised the fraudulent prayers of the spinsters, and lulled the rage of the horrid dog with a sop, she entered the palace of Proserpine. Nor did she accept the delicate seat, or delicious banquet; but humbly sat at the feet of Proserpine, and contented with a piece of common bread, delivered her embassy from Venus. Immediately after this, she received the box secretly filled and shut; and having stopped the barking mouth of the dog with the remaining sop, and given the ferryman the other piece of money, she returned from the infernal regions much more vigorous than before.

" Having again beheld and adored the fair light of day, though she was in haste to finish her errand, she was seized with a rash curiosity : ' Behold,' said she, ' what a foolish bearer am I of divine beauty, who do not even take the least portion of it, that I may by this means appear pleasing in the eyes of my beautiful lover.' As she ended this soliloquy, she opened the box; but it contained no beauty, nor indeed anything but an infernal and truly Stygian sleep, which being freed from its confinement, immediately seizes her, suffuses all her members with a dense cloud of somnolence, and holds her prostrate on the very spot where she opened the box; so that she lay motionless, and nothing else than a sleeping corpse.

" But Cupid, being now recovered of his wound, and unable to endure the long absence of his Psyche, glided through the narrow window of the bedchamber in which he was confined.

His wings, invigorated by repose, flew far more swiftly than before; he hastened to his Psyche, and carefully brushing off the cloud of sleep, and shutting it up again in its old receptacle, the box, he roused Psyche with an innoxious touch of one of his arrows. 'Behold,' said he, 'unhappy girl, again you have all but perished, a victim to curiosity. Now, however, strenuously perform the task imposed upon you by my mother, and I myself will take care of the rest.' Having thus spoken, the lover soared aloft on his wings, and Psyche immediately carried the present of Proserpine to Venus.

"In the meantime, Cupid, wasting away through excess of love, and dreading his mother's sudden prudery, betakes himself to his usual weapons of craft, and having with rapid wings penetrated the summit of heaven, supplicates the mighty Jupiter, and defends his cause. Then Jupiter, stroking the little cheeks of Cupid, and kissing his hand, thus addressed him :—
'Though you, my masterful son, never pay me that reverence which has been decreed me by the synod of the Gods, but perpetually wound this breast of mine, by which the laws of the elements and the revolutions of the stars are governed, and frequently defile it with earthly intrigues, contrary to the laws, the Julian edict,* and public discipline, injuring my reputation and fame by base adulteries, and sordidly changing my serene countenance into serpents, fire, wild beasts, birds, and cattle; nevertheless, remembering my own moderation, and that you have been nursed in these hands of mine, I will accomplish all that you desire. At the same time you must be sensible that you ought to guard against rivals, and to recompense me for this service, by presenting me with any girl of transcendent beauty that may now happen to be upon the earth.'

"Having thus spoken, he ordered Mercury immediately to summon an assembly of all the Gods; and at the same time to proclaim, that if any one of the celestials absented himself, he should be fined ten thousand pieces of money. The fear of such a penalty caused the celestial theatre to be filled immediately; whereupon lofty Jupiter, sitting on his sublime throne, thus addressed the assembly of Gods:—'Ye conscript Gods, whose names are registered in the white roll of

* *The Julian edict.*]—Alluding to the law against adultery, instituted by Augustus Cæsar.

the Muses, you are all well acquainted with that youth whom I have reared with my own hands, and the impetuous fire of whose juvenile years I deem it necessary to restrain by some bridle or other. It is sufficient that he is every day defamed in conversation, for the adulteries and all manner of corruption of which he is the cause. Every occasion of this must be taken away, and his youthful libertinism must be bound in nuptial fetters. He has made choice of a girl, and deprived her of her virginity. Let him, therefore, hold her, let him possess her, and embracing Psyche, always enjoy the object of his love.' Then turning his face to Venus, ' Nor do you, my daughter,' said he, ' be sorrowful on this occasion, nor fearful that your pedigree and rank will be disgraced by a mortal marriage; for I will now cause the nuptials not to be unequal, but legitimate, and agreeable to the civil law.' Immediately after this, he ordered Mercury to bring Psyche to heaven; and as soon as she arrived, extending to her a cup of ambrosia, ' Take this,' said he, ' Psyche, and be immortal; nor shall Cupid ever depart from your embrace, but these nuptials of yours shall be perpetual.'

" Then, without delay, a sumptuous wedding supper was served up. The husband, reclining at the upper end of the table, embraced Psyche in his bosom; in like manner, Jupiter was seated with Juno, and after them, the other gods and goddesses in their proper order. Then Jupiter was presented with a bowl of nectar, the wine of the Gods, by the rustic youth Ganymede, his cup-bearer; but Bacchus supplied the rest. Vulcan dressed the supper; the Hours empurpled everything with roses and other fragrant flowers; the Graces scattered balsam; the Muses sang melodiously; Apollo accompanied the lyre with his voice; and beautiful Venus danced with steps in unison with the delightful music. The order, too, of the entertainment was, that the Muses should sing the chorus, Satyrus play on the flute, and Peniscus* on the pipe. Thus Psyche came lawfully into the hands of Cupid; and at length, from a mature pregnancy, a daughter was born to them, whom we denominate PLEASURE."†

END OF THE FIFTH EPISODE.

---

* *Peniscus.*]—One of the satyrs of the wood.
† The following explanation of this beautiful fable is, for the most part,

Such was the tale told to the captive damsel by that delirious
and tipsy old woman; but I, who stood not far from her,

extracted from the Introduction to a translation of it, formerly made by
me, and published in the year 1795.

This fable, which was designed to represent the lapse of the soul from
the intelligible world to the earth, was certainly not invented by Apuleius;
for, as it will appear in the course of this note, it is *evidently* alluded to by
Synesius, in his book on Dreams, and *obscurely* by Plato and Plotinus. It
is clear, therefore, that Plato could not derive his allusion from Apuleius;
and as to Plotinus and Synesius, those who are at all acquainted with the
writings of the Greek philosophers, well know that they never borrowed
from Latin authors, from a just conviction that they had the sources of
perfection among themselves.

I have said, that this fable represented the lapse of the human soul; of
the truth of which, the philosophical reader will be convinced by the fol-
lowing observations. In the first place, the Gods, as I have elsewhere
shown, are super-essential natures, from their profound union with the
first cause, who is super-essential without any addition. But though the
Gods, through their summits or unities, transcend essence, yet their unities
are participated either by intellect alone, or by intellect and soul, or by
intellect, soul, and body; from which participations the various orders of
the Gods are deduced. When, therefore, intellect, soul, and body, are in
conjunction, suspended from the super-essential unity, which is the centre,
flower, or blossom, of a divine nature, then the God from whom they are
suspended is called a mundane God. In the next place, the common pa-
rents of the human soul are the intellect and soul of the world: but its
proximate parents are the intellect and soul of the particular star about
which it was originally distributed, and from which it first descends. In
the third place, those powers of every mundane God, which are partici-
pated by the body suspended from his nature, are called mundane; but
those who are participated by his intellect, are called super-mundane; and
the soul, while subsisting in union with these super-mundane powers, is
said to be in the intelligible world; but when she wholly directs her at-
tention to the mundane powers of her God, she is said to descend from
the intelligible world, even while subsisting in the heavens.

Thus much being premised, let us proceed to the explanation of the
fable. Psyche, then, or soul, is described as transcendently beautiful, and
this is indeed true of every human soul, before it profoundly merges itself
in the defiling folds of dark matter. In the next place, when Psyche is
represented as descending from the summit of a lofty mountain, into a
beautiful valley, this signifies the descent of the soul from the intelligible
world into a mundane condition of being, but yet without abandoning its
establishment in the heavens. Hence, the palace which Psyche beholds
in the valley, is, with great propriety, said to be ' a royal house, which
was not raised by human, but by divine hands and art.' The gems, too,
on which Psyche is said to have trod in every part of this palace, are
evidently symbolical of the stars. Of this mundane, yet celestial condi-

lamented, by Hercules, that I had not the means of committing to writing such a beautiful fable.

And now the robbers returned laden with booty, having

tion of being, the incorporeal voices which attended upon Psyche, are likewise symbolical: for outward discourse is the last image of intellectual energy, according to which the soul alone operates in the intelligible world. As voices, therefore, they signify an establishment subordinate to that which is intelligible, but so far as denuded of body, they also signify a condition of being superior to a terrene allotment.

Psyche, in this delightful situation, is married to an invisible being, whom she alone recognises by her ears and hands. This invisible husband proves afterwards to be Cupid, or Love; that is to say, the soul, while established in the heavens, is united to love of the purest kind, *i. e.* to intellectual love, or, in other words, is not fascinated with outward form. But in this beautiful palace she is attacked by the machinations of her two sisters, who endeavour to persuade her to explore the form of her unknown husband. The sisters, therefore, signify those two powers of the irrational part of the soul, *anger* and *desire*, the latter of which powers is well defined by the Pythagoreans to be a certain tendency, impulse, and appetite of the soul, in order to be filled with something, or to enjoy something present, or to be disposed according to some sensitive energy; just as *reason* or the rational soul is signified by Psyche. The stratagems of these sisters at length take effect, and Psyche beholds and falls in love with Love; that is to say, the rational part, through the incentives of anger and desire, becomes enamoured of, and captivated with, outward form; in consequence of which Cupid, or intellectual love, flies away, and Psyche, or the rational soul, is precipitated to earth. It is remarkable that Psyche, after falling to the ground, is represented as having '*a stumbling and often reeling gait;*' for Plato, in the Phædo, says, that the soul is drawn into body with a *staggering* motion.

After this, commence the wanderings of Psyche in search of Cupid, or intellectual love, from whose embraces she is unhappily torn away. In the course of her journey, she arrives at the temples of Ceres and Juno, whose aid she suppliantly implores. Her conduct, indeed, in this respect, is highly becoming. For Ceres comprehends in her essence Juno, who is the fountain of souls; and the safety of the soul arises from converting herself to the divine sources of her being.

In the next place, Venus is represented desiring Mercury to proclaim Psyche through all lands, as one of her female slaves, that had fled from her service. It is likewise said that she gave him a small volume, in which the name of Psyche was written, and every other particular respecting her. Now, I think, it cannot be doubted that Synesius alludes to this part of the fable, in the following passage from his treatise on Dreams: ' When the soul descends spontaneously to its former life, with mercenary views, it receives servitude as the reward of its mercenary labours. But this is the intention of descent, that the soul may accomplish a certain servitude to the nature of the universe, prescribed by the

apparently fought a severe battle. Nevertheless, some of the more active spirits among them leaving the wounded at home

laws of Adrastia, or inevitable fate. Hence, when the soul is fascinated with material endowments, she is affected in a manner similar to those who, though born free, are, for a certain time, hired to employments, and, in this condition, captivated by the beauty of some female servant, determine to act in a menial capacity, under the master of their beloved object. Thus, in a similar manner, when we are profoundly delighted with external and corporeal good, we confess that the nature of matter is beautiful, who marks our assent in her secret book ; *and if, considering ourselves as free, we at any time determine to depart, she proclaims us deserters, and endeavours to bring us back, and, openly presenting her mystic volume to the view, apprehends us, as fugitives from our mistress.* Then, indeed, the soul particularly requires fortitude and divine assistance, as it is no trifling contest to abrogate the confession and compact which she has made. Besides, in this case force will be employed ; for the material inflicters of punishments will then be roused to revenge, by the decrees of fate, against the rebels to her laws.'

Venus, however, must not be considered here as the nature of matter ; for though she is not the celestial Venus, but the offspring of Dione, yet, according to Proclus in Cratylum, she is that divine power which governs all the co-ordinations in the celestial world and in the earth, binds them to each other, and perfects their generative progressions, through a kindred conjunction. As the celestial Venus, therefore, separates the pure soul from generation, or the regions of sense, so she that proceeds from Dione binds the impure soul, as her legitimate slave, to a corporeal life.

After this, follows an account of the difficult tasks which Psyche is obliged to execute, by the commands of Venus ; all which are images of the mighty toils and anxious cares which the soul must necessarily endure after her lapse, in order to atone for her guilt, and recover her ancient residence in the intelligible world. In accomplishing the last of these labours, she is represented as forced to descend even to the dark regions of Hades, which indicates that the soul, through being enslaved to a corporeal life, becomes situated in obscurity, and is deprived of the light of day, *i. e.* of the splendour of truth and reality; agreeably to which, Empedocles sings,

> I fled from deity and heavenly light,
> To serve mad discord in the realms of night.'

But Psyche, in returning from Hades, is oppressed with a profound sleep, through indiscreetly opening the box given her by Proserpine, in which she expected to find a portion of divine beauty, but met with nothing but an infernal Stygian sleep. This obscurely signifies, that the soul, by expecting to find that which is truly beautiful in a corporeal and terrene life, passes into a profoundly dormant state ; and it appears to me, that both Plato and Plotinus allude to this part of the fable, in the following

to be cured, proposed to go and bring away the other bundles of plunder, which, as they said, they had concealed in a certain cave. So having hastily devoured their dinner, they turned me and my horse into the road, intending to load us with those bundles; and striking us with staves, they marched us over many ups and downs, and through many windings, until we arrived, towards evening, very weary, at a certain cavern, from whence they quickly brought us back, heavily loaded, without having allowed us a moment's rest. Such was their haste and trepidation, that they drove me by their blows against a stone which lay in the road, and caused me to fall down; and then the blows fell thicker and faster to compel me to rise, which I could hardly do being severely hurt in my off leg and near hoof. "How long," cried one of them, "shall we waste food on this worn-out ass, and who is now gone lame too?" "He has brought us ill-luck," said another; "and ever since we had him we have gained little else than blows, and the loss of our brave comrades." "Decidedly,"

passages, the originals of which may be seen in p. 10 of my Dissertation on the Eleusinian and Bacchic Mysteries. In the first place, then Plato in book vii. of his Republic observes, ' that he who is not able, by the exercise of his reason, to define the idea of *the good*, separating it from all others, and piercing, as in a battle, through every kind of argument; eagerly striving to confute, not according to opinion, but according to essence, and in all these, marching forward with undeviating reason,— such a one knows nothing of *the good itself*, nor of any good whatever; but if he has attained to any image of *the good*, we must say he has attained to it by opinion, not by science; that in the present life he is sleeping, and conversant with dreams, and that, before he is roused, *he will descend to Hades, and there be profoundly and perfectly laid asleep.* And Plotinus, in Ennead. I. lib. viii. p. 80, says, ' The death of the soul is for it, while merged, as it were, in the present body, to descend into matter, and be filled with its impurity, and, after departing from this body, to lie absorbed in its filth, till it returns to a superior condition, and elevates its eye from the overwhelming mire. *For to be plunged into matter, is to descend to Hades, and fall asleep.'*

Cupid, however, or *intellectual love*, at length recovering his pristine vigour, rouses Psyche, or *the rational part of the soul*, from her deadly lethargy. In consequence of this, having accomplished her destined toils, she ascends to her native heaven, becomes lawfully united to Cupid, (for, while descending, her union with him might be called illegitimate), lives the life of the immortals, and the natural result of this union is pleasure or delight. And thus much for an explanation of the fable of Cupid and Psyche.—*Taylor.*

said a third, " as soon as he has brought home this burden,
which he carries so unwillingly, I will immediately hurl him
down a precipice as dainty food for vultures."

While those mildest of men were debating with each other
about the death I was to die, we had now reached our home ;
for fear had made wings of my hoofs. Then having hastily
removed our burdens, and paying no attention to our wants,
nor even thinking of my death, they took their wounded com-
rades with them and started off again, to make up, as they say,
for the time lost through my sluggishness.

Meanwhile, I was made not a little uneasy by thoughts of
the death with which I was threatened ; and I said to myself:
" Why do you stand still, Lucius?   Why do you tamely await
the last calamity that can befall you?   Death, and that of the
most cruel kind, is decreed for you by the robbers, nor is the
execution of the sentence a thing to cause them any great diffi-
culty.   You see those neighbouring precipices, and those sharp
rocks projecting from their sides, which, fall wherever you
may, will penetrate your body and tear you limb from limb.
For that illustrious magic you were so fond of has given
you only the form and the labours of an ass, but has invested
you not with the thick hide of that animal, but with the deli-
cate skin of a horse-leech. Why do you not, therefore, assume
a masculine spirit, and consult your safety while yet you
may?   You have an excellent opportunity for flight while the
robbers are away.   Are you afraid of a half-dead old woman,
whom you may finish with one blow of your lame foot?   But
whither on earth shall I fly, or who will receive me under his
roof?   Nay, that is a stupid, and perfectly asinine reflection;
for where is the traveller who would not gladly ride off upon
a beast that fell in his way?"   And with that I made a strong
effort, broke the thong by which I was tied, and was off as
fast as my four legs could carry me.

Yet I could not escape the hawk's eyes of the crafty old
woman; for, as soon as she saw me free, she laid hold of the
thong, with a boldness above her sex and age, and strove to
lead me back again.   I, however, bearing in mind the deadly
purpose of the robbers, was moved by no pity, but immedi-
ately knocked her down with a stroke of my hind feet.   But
even when sprawling on the ground, she held on to the thong
with a tenacious gripe, so that for a while I dragged her along,

in my gallop. She immediately began, too, with clamorous howl-ings, to implore the assistance of a stronger hand; but all the noise she made was of no use; for there was no one but the captive virgin that could afford her aid; and she, startled by the uproar, ran out of the cave, and saw, by Hercules, a most remarkable scene, the old woman, like another Dirce, only hanging not to a bull, but to an ass.* Then did the virgin, with virile daring, perform an admirable exploit. For, wrest-ing the thong from the hands of the old woman, she checked my speed with bland words, mounted cleverly on my back, and again incited me to hasten away. Besides my own spon-taneous desire to escape, I was now impelled by a wish to liberate the virgin, and further urged by the blows with which she frequently admonished me; so that my four feet beat the ground at the rate of a courser's gallop; and all the while I endeavoured to reply by my braying to the sweet words of the virgin. Sometimes, also, turning my neck, and pretending to scratch my back, I kissed her beautiful feet.

' At last, sighing deeply, and looking anxiously to heaven, " O ye Gods," she said, " give me your aid, now or never, in my extreme danger; and thou, O cruel Fortune, now cease thy rage. Thou hast surely been sufficiently appeased by these my miserable torments. And you (addressing her-self to me), in whom I rely for liberty and life, if you bring me home safe, and restore me to my parents and my beautiful lover, what thanks shall I not give you, what honours shall I not bestow upon you, and what food shall I not afford you? In the first place, I will comb that mane of yours nicely, and adorn it with my virgin hands; next, I will grace-fully part and curl the hairs that hang over your forehead; and then I will, with all diligence, comb out and disentangle the rough and matted bristles of your long-neglected tail. I will stud you all over, my preserver, with many golden or-naments, which will make you as resplendent as the stars of heaven; I will lead you along in triumph, while the people joyfully follow; and I will daily fatten you, bringing to you nuts and tit-bits in my silken apron.

* *To an ass.*]—Apuleius here alludes to the story of Dirce, the wife of Lycus, king of Thebes, whom he married after he had divorced Antiope. Zethus and Amphion tied her to the tail of an untamed bull, and turned the animal loose; but the Gods compassionately changed her into a foun-tain.

K

"But think not that amidst that delicate food, complete leisure, and tho blessedness of your whole life, a glorious dignity shall be wanting to you. For I will leave a perpetual monument of my present fortune, and of divine providence; and will dedicate, in the vestibule of my house, an image of my present flight, depicted on a tablet. This history, also, though rude, shall be narrated in fables, and delivered to posterity in the writings of the learned; viz. THE HISTORY OF A ROYAL VIRGIN FLYING FROM CAPTIVITY ON THE BACK OF AN ASS. You shall likewise be numbered among the miracles of antiquity. For, from the example of your true history, we shall believe that Phryxus crossed the sea on the back of a ram, that Arion piloted a dolphin, and that Europa sat on a bull. And, truly, if Jupiter lowed under the form of a bull, something human or divine may be concealed in my ass."

While the virgin ran on in this way, mingling frequent sighs with her ebullitions of hope, we came to a certain place where three roads met; and there, seizing me by the headstall, she strove hard to turn me into the road on the right hand, because it led to the abode of her parents. But I, who knew that the robbers had taken that path, in order to bring away the remainder of their spoil, strenuously resisted, and thus silently, in my own mind, expostulated with her: "What are you doing, O unhappy virgin? What are you about? Why will you hasten to Hades? What sort of use is this you want to make of my feet? You will be the cause not only of your own destruction, but of mine likewise."

While we were thus at variance about the road we should take, and were contending like coheirs in a law-suit about the lordship of the ground and the division of the path, the robbers, laden with their plunder, perceived us, and recognizing us at a considerable distance, by the light of the moon, saluted us with a malignant laugh; and one of their number thus addressed us: "Whither away so fast by moonlight? Do you not fear the shades and ghosts that roam by night? Are you hastening, most dutiful maiden, to pay a clandestine visit to your parents? Well, you shall not travel all alone, we will escort you, and show you a shorter way to your friends." And with that, he laid hold on my rein, and turned me round, at the same time beating me unmercifully with the knotted staff he carried in his hand. Then I, returning full loth to prompt destruction, recollected the pain of my hoof, and began to walk lame, with my head bobbing up and down; upon which, said the robber who had turned me back: "So, then, you stumble and stagger again. Your rotten feet are able to gallop away, but cannot walk. Yet, just now, you surpassed the winged speed of Pegasus."

While my kind conductor thus jeered me, whacking me at the same time with his staff, we had now arrived at the outward enclosure of the robbers' abode. And there, behold, we found the old woman, with a rope tied about her neck, suspended from a branch of a lofty cypress tree. The robbers took her down, and dragging her along by her own rope, pitched her over the brink of a precipice. Then, having put the virgin in chains, they fell savagely upon the supper which the unhappy old woman had prepared for them, with posthumous diligence, as it were. And now, while they were devouring everything with greedy voracity, they began to discuss the question of our punishment, and their own revenge, and the opinions expressed on the subject were various, as is usually the case in a turbulent crowd. One proposed that the virgin should be burnt alive; a second was for exposing her to wild beasts; a third was of opinion that she should be crucified; and a fourth, that she should be mangled by various torments. At all events, she was condemned to die, in one way or other, by the suffrage of all.

At last one of them, having prevailed on the rest to cease the tumult, addressed them thus, in a mild and placid tone: "It does not accord with the ordinances of our association, nor with the clemency of each of us, nor indeed with my own moderation, to suffer you to inflict punishment which exceeds the magnitude of the crime; nor that you should employ for this purpose wild beasts, or the cross, or fire, or torments, or invoke the hasty darkness of a rapid death. Hearken, then, to my counsel, and grant life to the maiden, but such life as she deserves. You have not, of course, forgotten what you some time ago decreed respecting that ass, who was always sluggish, indeed, but a prodigious eater, and who now also has counterfeited lameness, and has made himself the instrument and servant of the virgin's flight. It will be well, therefore, to cut his throat to-morrow, and, having taken out all his intestines, to sew up the virgin, naked, in the belly

of the ass, who has preferred her to us; so that, her face
alone may project and be visible, and the rest of her body
may be confined in the beastly embrace of his belly.   Then
let the ass, with the virgin thus sewn up in him, be exposed, on
some stony cliff, to the heat of the burning sun.   Thus both of
them will suffer everything which you have rightly decreed.
For the ass will be put to death, as he has long ago deserved; while
she will endure the bites of creatures of prey, when her limbs
are gnawed by worms; the scorching heat of fire, when the
blazing sun shall have burnt up the belly of the ass; and the
torment of the cross, when dogs and vultures tear out her en-
trails.   Reckon up, too, her other miseries and torments.   In
the first place, she will remain alive in the belly of a dead
beast; in the next place, her nostrils will be filled with a
most fetid vapour; and, in the third place, she will waste
away with protracted hunger, and will not have her hands at
liberty to end her agonies by death."

After he had spoken to this effect, the robbers agreed to his
proposal, which they relished to their very heart's content.
On hearing their decision with my long ears, what could I do
but bewail my poor body that was to be a dead carcase next
morning?

BOOK THE SEVENTH.

ARRIVAL OF THE SPY WHOM THE ROBBERS HAD LEFT AT HYPATA—
HE REPORTS THAT THE ROBBERY OF MILO'S HOUSE IS UNIVER-
VERSALLY IMPUTED TO LUCIUS—THE ROBBERS ARE JOINED BY
A NEW RECRUIT.   SIXTH EPISODE: THE RECRUIT'S STORY—
HE IS CHOSEN LEADER OF THE BAND—HE DISSUADES THEM FROM
KILLING THEIR CAPTIVE—A GRAND FESTIVAL—LUCIUS SHOCKED
BY THE DAMSEL'S HEARTLESS LEVITY—THE PRETENDED ROBBER
REVEALS HIMSELF—ESCAPE OF THE DAMSEL, TLEPOLEMUS AND
CHARITE—THEIR TRIUMPHAL ENTRY INTO THE NATIVE CITY OF
THE LOVERS—DESTRUCTION OF THE WHOLE BAND OF ROBBERS
—LUCIUS IS PETTED, BUT UNHAPPY—HE IS SENT TO PASTURE,
AND AGAIN DISAPPOINTED—MADE TO TURN A MILL—ILL-USED
BY THE HORSES—MADE TO FETCH WOOD FROM THE FOREST—
CRUELLY TREATED BY HIS DRIVER—IS ABOUT TO BE CASTRATED

—DEATH OF HIS DRIVER—LUCIUS SEIZED BY A STRANGER—
THE STRANGER AND LUCIUS TAKEN BY HIS MASTER'S SERVANTS
—LUCIUS BEATEN AND TORTURED BY HIS DRIVER'S MOTHER.

As soon as darkness gave place to the fair light of day, and
all things were illuminated by the splendid chariot of the sun,
a certain person, one of the robbers' comrades, arrived; for so
he appeared to be, by their mutual salutations. This man sat
down at the entrance of the cavern, and after he had reco-
vered his breath, and was able to speak, he made the following
narration to his companions:—

" With respect to the house of Milo, of Hypata, which we
lately plundered, we may now be quite at our ease, and fear
nothing. For after you, brave men, had returned to our cave,
carrying off with you all Milo's property, I mingled with the
crowd of the citizens, and assuming the appearance of one who
was grieved and indignant at what had happened, observed
what course was taken for an investigation of the affair, and
whether, and to what extent, they would inquire after the
robbers; in order that I might relate to you every particular,
conformably to your injunctions. Now one Lucius, whoever
he may be, was accused, by the unanimous voice of all the mul-
titude, as the manifest author of the robbery, and this not upon
dubious surmises, but upon convincing evidence. This Lucius,
not long before, by false commendatory letters, passing himself
off for a respectable man, strongly ingratiated himself with
Milo, so that he was hospitably received by him, and ranked
among his intimate friends. And when he had remained there
not a few days, having ensnared the mind of a maid servant of
Milo with false love, he diligently explored the bolts and bars
of the house, and curiously surveyed those parts of it in which
all the property was usually deposited. This, also, was con-
sidered as no small indication of his guilt, that he fled on the
very same night, and at the very moment the robbery was
committed, and has not been heard of since. He had ready
means of flight too, whereby he could rapidly elude his pur-
suers, and get farther and farther away from their search; for he
rode away on his own white horse. Moreover, his servant was
found in the same house, and, being accused as accessary to the
felony and escape of his master, was, by order of the magis-
trates, committed to the common gaol, and subjected on the fol-
lowing day to many torments. But though tortured till he

was almost dead, he confessed, after all, nothing of the kind.
Nevertheless, many persons were sent to the country of tha*
Lucius in search of him, in order that he might undergo the
punishment of his crime."

While he was narrating these things, my vitals were wrung
with grief at the comparison they suggested between my an-
cient fortune and my present calamity, between that once
happy Lucius and a miserable jackass. It also occurred to me,
that not without reason had ancient sages pronounced Fortune
to be blind, and entirely deprived of eyes; since she always
bestows her riches on the unworthy and the wicked, and never
judiciously makes any mortal the object of her regard; but
indeed attaches herself for the most part to men from whom,
if she could see, she ought to fly far away. And what is worst
of all, she causes opinions to be entertained of us that are at
variance with our real character, or even contrary to it; so as
to enable the bad man to exult in the renown of the good man,
and, on the other hand, to cause the most innocent to suffer
such punishment as befits the most guilty. Here, methought,
am I, to whom she has done her worst in changing me into a
beast, and a quadruped of the vilest condition, I, whose mis-
fortune would strike the most hardened reprobate as worthy to
be lamented and commiserated, I am here accused of the crime of
burglary, committed upon my most dear host; a crime for which
burglary is too mild a name, and which one may more rightly
denominate parricide. Yet I was not permitted to defend
myself, or to utter so much as one word in denial of the charge.
Now, however, when it was made in my presence, lest my
silence should be mistaken for the acquiescence of a guilty
conscience, I was racked with impatience to speak, were it
only to say, *Non feci*, I did not do that deed. The former
word, indeed, [*non*] I roared out again and again, but the
other [*feci*] I could by no means pronounce, but I continued
to vociferate *non non;* and no more could I get out, though I
made my pendulous lips vibrate with excessive rotundity.

Why, however, do I prolixly complain of the spitefulness of
Fortune, since she was not ashamed to make me a fellow-
servant and yoke-mate with my own horse. While these
thoughts were floating through my mind, a concern of a more
important nature engaged my attention, viz., the recollection
that I was destined by the decree of the robbers to be a victim

to the manes of the virgin; and frequently casting a look at my belly, I seemed to myself to have the unhappy damsel enclosed within it.

The robber who had just brought the news of that false accusation against me, having drawn out a thousand pieces of gold coin, which he had sewn up and concealed in his garment, and which he had taken, as he said, from different travellers, and had conscientiously brought to the common treasury, began to inquire anxiously concerning the welfare of his comrades. Finding that some of them, and indeed all the bravest, had perished by various deaths, but all with great gallantry, he advised them to leave the highways at peace for some time, and rather apply themselves to searching after other associates, and to supplying the deficiency of their warlike band by the election of new hands from among the youths of the country. For, he observed, those that were unwilling might be compelled by fear, and the willing be incited by reward; and not a few would gladly abandon an abject and servile life, and unite themselves to an association which possessed a power like that of royalty. For his own part, he had some time since met with a certain man of a lofty stature, young, of vast bodily dimensions, and of great strength; and after much argument had at length persuaded him to make better use of his hands, which had become torpid through long idleness; to enjoy while he might the advantages of a prosperous condition of body; and instead of holding out his powerful hand for alms, to exert it rather in helping himself to gold. All present assented to what he said, and decreed to receive the man he had spoken of, as he appeared to be a tried man, and also to search after others who might supply the places of those they had lost.

He went out, and returning shortly after, brought with him, as he had promised, a certain tall young man, with whom I do not think any one present could have stood a comparison; for, besides the great bulk of his body, he surpassed all the rest in height by a whole head, and yet the down had but just begun to overspread his cheeks. He was only half clothed, with odds and ends of cloth, cobbled together, through the joinings of which his brawny breast and belly seemed ready to burst forth. Thus entering, " All hail," said he, " ye, who are under the protection of the most powerful God Mars, and who are now become my trusty comrades; receive willingly a willing recruit, a man of magnanimous spirit, who more cheerfully receives wounds in his body than gold in his hand, and who despises death, which others dread. And think not that I am a needy or abject man, nor judge of my merits from these rags; for I have been the leader of a most powerful band, and have, in fact, plundered all Macedonia. I am that famous robber Hæmus the Thracian, whose name whole provinces dread; and am the offspring of Thero, who was an equally illustrious robber; nourished in human blood; educated among bands of men of this description, and the heir and imitator of my father's valour. But I lost in a short space of time all my old band, all my brave comrades, and, all the great wealth we had amassed. For passing by Oratum,* I attacked one of Cæsar's commissaries, who had been high in office, but was afterwards deprived of his employment through the malignity of fortune. I will, however, relate the whole affair in order that you may understand it the better.

SIXTH EPISODE.

THE RECRUIT'S STORY.

" There was a certain person honourably distinguished by the many offices he held in the palace of Cæsar, and who was also well esteemed by Cæsar himself. Malignant envy, and the crafty accusations of certain persons, hurled him into exile. But his wife, Plotina, a woman of rare fidelity and singular chastity, who had given stability to the family of her husband by the birth of ten children, spurned and despised the pleasures of city luxury, and became the companion of her husband's flight, and a partaker of his misfortune. For this purpose she cut off her hair, changed her dress, so that she might appear like a man; and begirt with necklaces of the greatest value and with zones of gold coin, she moved intrepidly amidst the drawn swords of the soldiers that guarded her husband, a partaker of all his dangers, maintaining an everwakeful care for his safety, and enduring continual labours with the fortitude of a man. And now having vanquished the greater part of the difficulties of the journey, and the dangers of the sea, she went with her husband to Zacynthus,† which

---

* *Oratum.*]—The precise situation of Oratum has not been determined.
† *Zacynthus.*]—Now the island of Zante.

their fatal destiny had decreed to be their temporary habitation. As soon, however, as they had arrived on the shores of Actium, where we were then roving about on our return from Macedonia, they went late at night to a certain cottage which was near the shore and their ship, and there they slept in order to avoid the tossing of the sea. In this cottage we attacked and plundered them of every thing. Yet we did not depart without great danger. For as soon as the mistress of the house heard the first noise of the gate, she ran into the bedchamber, and disturbed all that were in the house by her tumultuous clamours. She likewise called on her servants by name, and on all her neighbours; but it so happened that we escaped with impunity through the general fear, each concealing himself out of regard to his own safety.

" This excellent woman, however, (for the truth must be spoken), who was a pattern of fidelity and was beloved for her virtues, immediately pouring forth her prayers to the majesty of Cæsar, obtained both a speedy return for her husband, and a complete revenge of the assault. In short, Cæsar was unwilling that the band of the robber Hæmus should any longer exist, and it was forthwith immediately destroyed. So much can the mere wish of a great prince effect. At length, when, by the pertinacious pursuit of the emperor's army, all our band was destroyed, I scarcely saved myself, and escaped from the midst of the jaws of hell, after the following manner. I clothed myself in the florid vestment of a woman, with numerous flowing folds, covered my head with a small woven mitre, and put on my feet those white and thin shoes which are worn by women; and thus, as it were, implanted and concealed in the other sex, I passed through the midst of the troops of hostile soldiers, riding on an ass laden with sheaves of barley. For, believing me to be a female ass-driver, they let me pass free; because at that time my beardless cheeks were still soft and smooth as a boy's. Yet I have not degenerated from my paternal glory, or forgotten my fortitude, though somewhat fearful in consequence of being placed in the midst of martial blades; but protected by the disguise of a dress foreign to my sex, and attacking villas or towns, single handed, I have procured for myself this small viaticum by plunder."

END OF THE SIXTH EPISODE.

Ripping open his rags as he spoke, he poured forth into the midst of them two thousand pieces of gold coin. "There," said he, "I willingly offer to your band this contribution, and myself also (if you do not reject my offer), as a most faithful leader, who, in a short space of time, will make this your habitation to be no longer rocky, but golden." The robbers, without hesitation, unanimously elected him their leader. They also brought forth a tolerably fair garment, which he put on, throwing away his rich rags. And having thus changed his attire, and embraced each of them, he was placed on the couch at the head of the table, and his leadership was inaugurated by a supper, and copious bowls.

In the conversation that ensued, the robber was made aware of the flight of the damsel, of my carrying her, and of the monstrous death to which each of us was destined. He asked where the virgin was, and being taken to her, and seeing her laden with chains, he turned away from her, with a contemptuous curl of his nose, and said : " I am not indeed so stupid, or at least so rash, as to oppose your decree; but I should have to endure the reproaches of my own conscience, if I dissembled what appears to me to be for your benefit. But, in the first place, suffer me, who am solicitous for your sake, to speak boldly, especially since, if my views are not acceptable to you, you may fall back on what you have decreed concerning the virgin and the ass. Now, I think that those robbers who are truly wise ought to prefer nothing to their own gain, not even vengeance itself, which is often detrimental to those who inflict it as well as to others. If, then, you destroy the virgin in the body of the ass, you will gratify nothing but your indignation, without any profit to yourselves. It is my opinion that she should rather be taken to some city, and there sold; for a virgin of her age may be sold for no small price. I myself, some time ago, knew certain bawds, one of whom might, as I think, give a great sum of money for this virgin, and place her in a brothel, suitable to her birth, and from which she will not be likely to run away again. She will also have afforded you some revenge, when she has passed into bondage at a brothel. I have sincerely offered this counsel to you, as conducive to your advantage; but you are the masters of your own judgments and acts." Thus it was that this advocate of the robbers' exchequer, and no less excellent saviour of the virgin and ass, pleaded our cause.

The rest of the robbers, after tormenting my entrails and my miserable spirit by their tedious deliberations, at length cordially acceded to the opinion of the new robber, and immediately freed the virgin from her bonds. But as for her, from the moment she beheld that young man, and heard him mention a brothel and a bawd, she began to be elated, and to smile most joyfully, so that I felt inclined, with good reason, to vituperate the whole sex, when I saw a virgin, who pretended that she was enamoured of a young lover, and was desirous of a chaste marriage, now suddenly delighted with the name of a vile and filthy brothel. It was a case in which the character of the whole female sex was in question, and the verdict depended on the judgment of an ass. The young man, however, resuming his discourse, said : " Why do we not proceed to supplicate Mars to be propitious to us in selling the virgin, and searching for other associates ? But, as far as I see, we have not any beast for sacrifice, nor sufficient wine for drinking largely. Send with me, therefore, ten of our comrades, with whom I may go to the next town, and bring you thence meat and drink fit for priests." Accordingly, he departed, attended by ten of the robbers, and the rest prepared a great fire, and raised an altar of green turf to the god Mars.

The foragers soon returned, bringing with them skins full of wine, and driving before them a great number of cattle; from among which they selected a large he-goat, old and shaggy, and sacrificed it to Mars the Secutor* and Associate. A sumptuous supper was immediately prepared. Then the stranger said : " You must consider me as a strenuous leader not only of your plundering expeditions, but also of your pleasures." And with that he went cleverly to work, and performed every thing that was requisite with admirable dexterity. He swept the floor, made the couches smooth, cooked the meat, seasoned the dishes, and served them up handsomely ; but especially he plied each of them, and that frequently, with large bowls of wine. Nevertheless, under pretence of fetching what he wanted from time to time, he often went to the virgin, and gaily presented her with fragments which he had secretly taken away, and cups of wine, of which he had previously tasted. And she most willingly received what he brought her, and sometimes, when he wished to kiss her, she readily responded to his wish, and kissed him quite lovingly

* ɪ. The gladiator, or sword-player.

These things greatly displeased me; and I said to myself:
Shame upon you, girl, do you forget your faithful lover and
your nuptials?   Do you prefer this foreign and cruel homicide
to that young man, whoever he be, to whom your parents have
betrothed you?   Does not your conscience prick you, that you
thus trample on affection, and are pleased to act libidinously
among gleaming spears and swords?   What if the other rob-
bers, likewise, should, by some means or other, perceive what
you are doing, would you not again return to the ass, and again
procure my destruction?   Really you are playing your game
at the risk of another's skin.

Whilst I was thus cogitating in great indignation, and falsely
accusing the virgin in my own mind, I gathered from certain
words of theirs, which though dubious, were not obscure to an
intelligent ass, that the young man was not the famous robber
Hæmus, but Tlepolemus, the bridegroom of the virgin.   For,
in the course of their conference, caring nothing for my pre-
sence, he said somewhat more distinctly: " Be of good cheer,
dearest Charite; for you shall presently have all these your
enemies in captivity."   And I observed that while he himself
refrained from drinking immoderately, he never ceased to ply
the robbers more and more with wine, now unmingled with
water, and moderately heated, so that they began to be over-
come with intoxication.   And, by Hercules, I suspect that
he had mingled in their cups a certain soporiferous drug.   At
last, when they all, without a single exception, lay dead drunk
on the floor, then Tlepolemus, having without any difficulty
bound them strongly with ropes, and tied them together as he
thought proper, placed the damsel on my back, and directed
his steps to his own home.

As soon as we arrived there, the whole city turned out at
the wished-for sight.   Parents, kindred, retainers, bondmen,
and servants, joyfully ran out to meet us.   You might see a
procession of every age and sex, and, by Hercules, a new and
memorable spectacle, a virgin riding in triumph on an ass.*   As
for myself, rejoicing with all my might, and not choosing to
be at variance with the present display, as if I had no concern
in it, I brayed strenuously, with erect ears and expanded nos-
trils, or rather, I trumpeted with a noise like thunder.

* *Riding in triumph on an ass.*]—It has been conjectured that the
pagan Apuleius intends by this a covert sneer at Christ's entry into
Jerusalem.

The damsel having now retired to her chamber, where her parents cherished and caressed her, Tlepolemus immediately took me back to the cave, accompanied by a great number of beasts of burden, and a multitude of his fellow-citizens. Nor did I return unwillingly; for, curious at all times, I was then particularly desirous to be a spectator of the captivity of the robbers, whom we found still fast bound, with wine even more than with ropes. Having, therefore, ransacked the cave, and brought out every thing that was in it, and we, and all the rest being loaded with gold and silver, Tlepolemus and his attendants rolled some of the robbers, bound as they were, over the neighbouring cliffs, and others they beheaded with their own swords. Then we returned to the city, exulting and rejoicing in so complete a revenge. The robbers' wealth was deposited in the public treasury; but the damsel, who had been recovered by Tlepolemus, was given to him according to law.

Then that noble woman paid the greatest attention to me, whom she called her saviour; and, on the very day of her nuptials, ordered my manger to be completely filled with barley, and as much hay to be given me as would be enough for a Bactrian camel. But what sufficiently dire execrations could I imprecate on Fotis, who had transformed me not into a dog, but an ass, when I saw all the dogs stuffed and crammed with the relics of the most abundant supper, and with the food they had pillaged? After the first night, the bride did not cease to tell her parents and her husband how greatly she was indebted to me, till they promised that they would confer on me the highest honours. Convoking, therefore, their most intimate friends, they held a consultation as to how I might most worthily be rewarded. One was of opinion that I should be shut up in the house, and there, leading an idle life, be fattened with choice barley, beans, and vetches. But the opinion of another prevailed, who regarded my liberty, and persuaded them rather to give me the run of the plains and meadows, where I might take my pleasure among the herds of horses, and procreate many mules, for the masters of the mares. The keeper of the horses was accordingly summoned, and I was delivered over to him, with many injunctions that he should take care of me. And right gaily did I trot along by his side, rejoicing at the thought that I was now to have nothing more to do with packs and bags, and so forth, and that having obtained my liberty, I should doubtless find some roses in the meadows, when they began to blossom in spring. Frequently, too, it occurred to me, that since such great marks of gratitude and so many honours were conferred on me when but an ass, so much the greater would be the respect and favour shown me when I had recovered the human form.

But when the keeper of the horses had taken me to the country, I found there none of the pleasure or the liberty I expected. For his wife, an avaricious, bad woman, immediately yoked me to the mill, and frequently striking me with a green stick, prepared bread for herself and her family at the expense of my hide. And not content to make me drudge for her own food only, she also ground corn for her neighbours, and so made money by my toil. Nor, after all my weary labours, did she even afford me the food which had been ordered for me; for she sold my barley to the neighbouring husbandmen, after it had been bruised and ground in that very mill, by my own roundabout drudgery; but to me, who had worked during the whole of the day at that laborious machine, she only gave, towards evening, some dirty, unsifted, and very gritty bran. I was brought low enough by these miseries; but cruel Fortune exposed me to fresh torments, in order, I suppose, that I might boast of my brave deeds, both in peace and war, as the saying is. For that excellent equerry, complying, rather late, indeed, with his master's orders, for a short time permitted me to associate with the herds of horses.

At length a free ass, I capered for joy, and softly ambling up to the mares, chose out such as I thought would be the fittest for my concubines. But here my joyful hopes gave place to extreme danger. For the stallions, who had been fed high for the sake of copulating with the mares, and who, independently of this, were terribly strong creatures, more than a match for any ass, regarding me with suspicion, and anxious to preserve the purity of their race, furiously pursued me as their rival, without respect for the laws of hospitable Jupiter. One of them, with his head and neck and ample chest aloft, struck at me like a pugilist with his forefeet; another, turning his brawny back, let fly at me with his hind feet; and another, with a vicious neigh, his ears thrown back, and showing his white teeth, sharp as spears, bit me all over. It was like what I have read in history of the King of

Thrace,* who exposed his unhappy guests to be lacerated and devoured by wild horses. For so sparing was that powerful tyrant of his barley, that he appeased the hunger of his voracious horses by casting human bodies to them for food. In fact, I was so worried and distracted by the continual attacks of the horses, that I wished myself back again at the mill round.

Fortune, however, who could not be satiated with my torments, soon after visited me with another calamity. For I was employed to bring home wood from a mountain, and a boy, the most villanous of all boys, was appointed to drive me. It was not only that I was wearied by toiling up and down the steep and lofty mountain, nor that I wore away my hoofs by running on sharp stones, but I was cudgelled without end, so that all my bones ached to the very marrow. Moreover, by continually striking me on the off-haunch, and always in the same place, till the skin was broken, he occasioned a great ulcerous cavity, gaping like a trench or a window; yet he never ceased to hit me on the raw. He likewise laid such a load of wood on my back, that you might have thought it was a burden prepared for an elephant, and not for a jackass. And whenever the ill-balanced load inclined to one side, instead of taking away some of the faggots from the heavier side, and thus easing me by somewhat lightening, or at least equalizing the pressure, he always remedied the inequality of the weight by the addition of stones. Nor yet, after so many miseries which I had endured, was he content with the immoderate weight of my burden; but when it happened that we had to pass over a river, he would leap on my back in order to keep his feet dry, as if his weight was but a trifling addition to the heavy mass. And if by any accident I happened to fall, through the weight of my burden, and the slipperiness of the muddy bank, instead of giving me a helping hand as he ought to have done, and pulling me up by the headstall, or by my tail, or removing a part of my load, till at least I had got up again; this paragon of ass-drivers gave me no help at all, however weary I might be, but beginning from my head, or rather from my ears, he thrashed all the hair off my hide with a huge stick, till the blows stirred me up and served me instead of a stimulating medicament.

* Diomede, Vid. Hygin, Fab. 30, et Ovid. in Ibin. v. 381.

Another piece of cruelty he practised on me, was this. He twisted together a bundle of the sharpest and most venomous thorns, and tied them to my tail as a pendulous torment; so that, jerking against me when I walked, they pricked and stabbed me intolerably. Hence, I was in a sore dilemma. For when I ran away from him, to escape his unmerciful drubbings, I was hurt by the more vehement pricking of the thorns; and if I stood still for a short time, in order to avoid that pain, I was compelled by blows to go on. In fact, the rascally boy seemed to think of nothing else than how he might be the death of me by some means or other; and that he sometimes threatened with oaths to accomplish. And, indeed, there happened a thing by which his detestable malice was stimulated to more baneful efforts; for on a certain day, when his excessive insolence had overcome my patience, I lifted up my powerful heels against him; and for this he retaliated by the following atrocity. He brought me into the road heavily laden with a bundle of coarse flax, securely bound together with cords, and placed in the middle of the burden a burning coal, which he had stolen from the neighbouring village. Presently the fire spread through the slender fibres, flames burst forth, and I was all over in a blaze. There appeared no refuge from immediate destruction, no hope of safety, and such a conflagration did not admit of delay, or afford time for deliberation. Fortune, however, shone upon me in these cruel circumstances; perhaps for the purpose of reserving me for future dangers, but, at all events, liberating me from present and decreed death.

For by chance perceiving a neighbouring pool muddy with the rain of the preceding day, I threw myself headlong into it; and the flame being immediately extinguished, I came out, lightened of my burden, and liberated from destruction. But that audacious young rascal threw the blame of this most wicked deed of his on me, and affirmed to all the shepherds, that as I was passing near the neighbours' fires, I stumbled on purpose, and set my load in a blaze; and he added, laughing at me, "How long shall we waste food on this fiery monster?"

A few days after this, he had recourse to still worse artifices against me. After having sold my load of wood at the nearest cabin, he led me home unladen, declaring that he could not manage so vicious a brute, and that he renounced the miserable office of being my driver. "Look at that lazy, crawling, out-and-out jackass," said he. "Besides all his other miss-deeds, he is now worrying me with new ones that put me in mortal fear. For whenever he sees a traveller, be it a comely woman, or a marriageable girl, or a tender youth, he imme-diately makes at them as if he was mad, upsetting his burden, and sometimes pitching off his very pack-saddle, and throws them down with abominable intentions, makes up his great ugly mouth as if to kiss them, and bites and tramples them most indecently. All this occasions us no small strife and quarrels, and will perhaps bring us into trouble with the ma-gistrates. Just now, espying a decent young woman, this frolicksome gallant ran at her, scattering all his wood, threw her down in the mud, and wanted to have his wicked will of her there and then. Had not her shrieks brought some people to her help, who were passing that way, and who snatched her half dead from under his hoofs, she must have died a horrible death, and left us to suffer the last penalty of the law."

With these and other such lies, which hurt my modesty the more because I could not reply to them, he desperately incensed the herdsmen against me. At last said one of them, "Why do we not immolate as he deserves this public paramour, this universal adulterer? Hark ye, boy; cut off his head, throw his entrails to the dogs, and keep his flesh to feed the work-people; then we will carry his skin, well rubbed with ashes and dried, to our master, and easily make up a story of his having been killed by a wolf.

Without delay my villanous accuser prepared joyfully to execute the herdsman's sentence with his own hand, and began to sharpen his knife on a whetstone, mocking my woe, and maliciously calling to mind the kick I had given him, and which, by Hercules! I wished had finished him. But one of the rustics exclaimed that it was a shame to slaughter so fine an ass. "Why lose the services of so useful a beast," he said, "merely because he is too lustful? Only geld him, and he can no how play his pranks any more; we shall be safe from danger on his account, and besides, he will grow stouter and fatter than ever. I have known many an animal, not asses merely, but even high-spirited horses, that were so hot after mares, as to be quite furious and unmanageable, and which, after being cut, became quiet and fit to carry loads or do any-

thing else that was required of them. So if you have no ob-
jection to what I say, after I have been to the market, which
will not detain me long, I will fetch the implements from home,
and immediately come back and geld this terrible rude gallant,
and make him gentler than any wether."

Snatched by this proposal from the very clutches of death,
but reserved for a most cruel punishment, I grieved as though
I were about to perish wholly in losing an appendage to my
body, and thought of destroying myself by continual fasting,
or by leaping down a precipice: in that way I should die
none the less, but I should die entire. Whilst I was pondering
my choice of deaths, morning came again, and that boy, who
was my tormentor, led me as usual up the mountain, where
fastening me to a branch of great oak, he went a little way off,
and began to cut down a load of wood with his axe. Just
then, I saw a horrid bear lift up its great head, and creep out
of a cave close by. Appalled at the sudden sight, I started
back, sinking down with all my might upon my haunches,
while my head and neck were held up by the thong, until it
broke ; whereupon I dashed down the mountains, not on my feet
only, but projecting myself bodily, reached the plains beneath,
and scoured across them, running with all my might from the
dreadful bear, and the boy that was worse than the bear.

A man who was passing that way, seeing me roam at large,
caught me, got on my back, and thumping me with a stick,
turned me into a side road unknown to me. I carried him
along with good will, thinking I was running away from that
cruel operation, and caring little about the blows I received,
for I was used to that sort of thing. But Fortune, with her
inveterate malice, anticipated so opportune a chance of escape,
and gave me over to fresh sufferings. For my master's herds-
men having gone out in all directions to look for a stray heifer,
nappened to fall in with us, and seizing me by the head stall,
which they readily identified, they began to lead me away.
My rider, however, making a bold resistance, called gods and
men to witness against them. " Why do you pull me about in
this violent way ?" he said, " Why do you lay hands on me ?"

" Do we behave unjustly to you," said the herdsmen,
" when we find you making off with our ass ? Tell us where
you have hid the body of his driver, whom you have killed, no
doubt." So saying, they knocked him to the ground, and

kicked and pummelled him with their fists, he swearing all the while that he had seen no one with the ass, but had found it running away, alone, and had caught it, that he might restore it to its owner, and be rewarded for his trouble.

"Would to heaven!" he cried, "that I had never seen this ass, or that he could speak with a human voice, and bear testimony to my innocence. You would surely be ashamed of the way in which you treat me."

But all his protestations were of no avail, for the angry herdsmen marched him along, with a rope round his neck, to the forest on the mountain, where the boy used to fetch wood. He was no where to be found; but at last they discovered what were plainly the remains of his body, torn to pieces and strewed here and there. I knew well it was the bear's teeth had done this, and I would certainly have said so, had I possessed the faculty of speech. All I could do was to rejoice silently at seeing myself revenged at last.

After they had with much pains collected the scattered fragments of the body, they buried them on the spot, and marched my Belerophon* to their cottages, there to remain tied fast, as a thief taken in the fact, and a bloody assassin, until they delivered him up next morning, for condign punishment, into the hands of the magistrates. Meanwhile, in the midst of the lamentations raised by the parents of the dead boy, up came that rustic who had promised to perform the operation upon me, and who now proposed to keep his word. "Our present loss is not of his causing," said one of the byestanders; "nevertheless you may cut what you please to-morrow from this villanous jackass—his head if you have a mind, and you shall not want for help."

Thus it came to pass that my calamity was postponed for another day, and I gave thanks to that kind boy, whose death, at all events, procured me one little day's respite from the knife. But I was not allowed even that short space of time to be grateful to him or to enjoy repose; for his mother rushed into my stable, weeping and bewailing her son's premature death, dressed in a black robe, tearing out her white hair, bestrewed with ashes, and vehemently beating her breasts.

* *My Belerophon.*]—Lucius jocularly compares his rider to Belerophon, and himself, by implication, to the winged steed Pegasus, which that here bestrode.

"Look at him," she screamed, "how easily he takes it, that cursed ass, with his head stuck in the manger, indulging his gluttony, and for ever stuffing his insatiable belly. He has no pity for my affliction, nor does he bestow a thought upon the horrible fate of his deceased driver; no, he despises my age and weakness, and thinks that he shall get off with impunity after his enormous crime; perhaps he has the audacity to suppose he shall be thought innocent; for it is the nature of the worst criminals to expect impunity, even in spite of the reproaches of their own guilty conscience. Now, in the name of all the Gods, most infamous of quadrupeds, though you could borrow the use of speech for a while, do you think you could persuade any one, aye the veriest fool, that you were without fault in that horrid disaster, when you could have fought for my poor boy, and defended him with heels and teeth? You could often lift your heels against himself; why could you not use them with the same alacrity in his defence? You should have galloped off with him on your back, and saved him from the bloody hands of the robber; above all, you should not have fled alone, after throwing and deserting your fellow-servant, your conductor, your comrade, the friend who fed you. Do you not know that those who refuse help to persons in mortal peril are punished, because therein they offend against all good principles? But you shall no longer rejoice over my calamities, murderer that you are; I will let you know what strength there is in violent grief."

So saying, she took off her girdle, and tied my feet separately, and as tightly as she could, so as to deprive me of the means of revenging myself. Then snatching up a great stake, which was used to bar the stable door, she never ceased whacking me with it until her strength was quite spent, and it fell from her wearied hands. Then complaining of the too speedy exhaustion of her arms, she ran back into the house, fetched a live coal from the hearth, and thrust it between my thighs; until, employing the only means of defence left me, I squirted a volley of liquid ordure into her face and eyes, and thus putting her to the rout, blinded and stinking, I saved myself from destruction; otherwise the ass would have perished like another Meleager by the brand of this raving Althea.*

* *Meleager—Althea.*]—When Althea was delivered of Meleager, she saw the three Fates sitting by the fire, and heard them say, "The child

BOOK THE EIGHTH.

ARRIVAL OF A SERVANT OF CHARITE—SIXTH EPISODE: DEATH OF
CHARITE AND TLEPOLEMUS—FLIGHT OF THE KEEPERS OF THE
HORSES WITH LUCIUS AND OTHER ANIMALS—ALARM OF WOLVES
—THE PARTY ATTACKED BY DOGS—A MARVELLOUS AND SHOCKING
ADVENTURE—SEVENTH EPISODE: SINGULAR PUNISHMENT OF A
CRIMINAL—LUCIUS OFFERED FOR SALE AT A FAIR—IS BOUGHT
BY AN ITINERANT PRIEST—THE FRAUDS OF THE PRIESTS OF THE
SYRIAN GODDESS—THEIR EXPOSURE—LUCIUS IN GREAT PERIL
OF HIS LIFE.

AT that time of the night when the cocks crow, a young man
came from the next city, who, as I perceived, was one of the
servants of that virgin Charite, who had endured equal sorrows
with myself among the robbers.   Sitting near the fire, in the
company of his fellow-servants, he related, as follows, the
wonderful and execrable particulars of her death, and the de-
struction of her whole house.   "Grooms, shepherds, and
cow-herds, we have lost our unfortunate mistress, Charite, and
by a most grievous catastrophe.   Yet she did not depart to the
shades alone.   But, that all of you may know the particulars,
I will narrate to you from the beginning what happened, and
which deserves to be committed to writing, in the form of a
history, by more learned men, on whom Fortune has conferred
the ability of writing with facility and elegance.

SIXTH EPISODE.

DEATH OF CHARITE AND TLEPOLEMUS.

" There was a young man in the next city, whose name was
Thrasyllus, of noble birth, of knightly rank, and very rich;
but he was a man addicted to the luxury of taverns, and to
harlots, and potations by day.   On this account he iniquitously

will live as long as this brand lasts." As soon as they were gone, Althea
rose, took the brand off the fire, extinguished it, and put it carefully
away. When Meleager was grown up, he slew the famous boar that ra
vaged all the country of Calydonia, and presented its head to Atalanta
Althea's two brothers wanted the head, and quarrelled for it with Meleager,
who killed them both.   To revenge their death, Althea slowly burned the
fatal brand, and so caused her son to die in lingering torture.

associated with a factious band of robbers, and his hands were
dyed with human blood.   Such was the man, and such was
the report concerning him.   Now, as soon as Charite was mar-
riageable, he was among her principal suitors, and most ar-
dently endeavoured to obtain her in wedlock.   And, though
he surpassed in nobility all the rest of her lovers, and solicited
her parents with splendid gifts, yet he was rejected by them,
on account of his morals, and suffered the disgrace of a repulse.
When, therefore, Charite, my master's daughter, came into the
hands of the worthy Tlepolemus, Thrasyllus, though disap-
pointed in his hopes, yet firmly cherishing his love, and adding
to his passion the rage he felt on account of his rejected suit,
sought for an opportunity of perpetrating a bloody deed.   At
length, a seasonable occasion presenting itself, he prepared to
execute the wickedness which had for a long time been the
subjects of his thoughts.   On the day on which the virgin had
been liberated, by the cunning and fortitude of her spouse,
from the deadly swords of the robbers, he mingled with the
crowd of those that congratulated her, and made himself re-
markable by the exulting joy he professed in the present safety
of the new married pair, and in the hopes of their future off-
spring.   Hence, being received into our house, among the
principal guests, as the nobility of his race demanded, and con-
cealing his wicked designs, he falsely personated the character
of a most faithful friend.

"And now, gradually ingratiating himself more and more
by his assiduity, by frequent conversation, and sometimes also
by sitting as a guest at the young couple's table, he fell, by
imperceptible degrees, into deeper love than ever.   Nor is this
wonderful, since the flame of love, small at first, delights with
a gentle glow; but, when fanned by continued familiar inter-
course, it waxes fierce, and burns a man up wholly.   Thra-
syllus for a long time pondered how he might find an oppor-
tune place for clandestine conference.   He perceived that he
was more and more excluded from the avenues to an adulterous
intercourse by the multitude of observers, and that the strong
bonds of a new and increasing affection could not be severed;
and, further, that even if Charite were willing to comply with
his desires, which she never would be, her ignorance of the
art of deceiving a husband would hinder such a purpose.   Yet,
in spite of all these obstacles, he was bent with desperate ob-

stinacy on the accomplishment of what was impossible, as
though it had not been so.　Things which seem difficult in the
beginning of love, appear easy when it has been strengthened
by time.　Hear now, and carefully note, I pray you, to what
deed he was driven by the violence of his furious lust.

"One day Tlepolemus, accompanied by Thrasyllus, went to
hunt wild beasts, if, indeed, the roe comes under that denomi-
nation; for Charite would not allow her husband to pursue
beasts armed with tusk or horn.　The toils were spread round
a hill thickly covered with trees, and the high-bred hounds
were turned in to rouse the beasts from their lairs.　Their good
training was immediately seen, for they spread abroad so as to
enclose every avenue.　For a while they followed the scent in
silence, till at last one gave tongue, and then they all burst out
with impetuous, dissonant yells, that made everything ring
again.　But it was not a roebuck, nor a timid doe, nor a hind,
the gentlest of all wild creatures, that was started, but an enor-
mous boar, the like of which was never seen—a brawny, thick-
hided, filthy brute, with bristles standing upright on his back,
foaming and gnashing his teeth, with eyes that darted fire, and
rushing along like a thunderbolt.　The keenest of the hounds
that pressed upon his flanks were ripped up by his tusks, and
flung here and there; then he broke through the toils at the
first charge, and got clear off.　We, meanwhile, were terror-
stricken, having been used only to such hunting as was without
danger, and being, besides, without weapons or means of de-
fence; so we hid ourselves the best way we could under thick
foliage and behind trees.

"Thrasyllus now seeing a favourable opportunity for accom-
plishing his intended treachery, said insidiously to Tlepolemus:
'Why do we remain stupified with surprise, or even dismayed,
like these low-souled slaves, and trembling like women, whilst
we suffer such a fine prey to escape us?　Why not mount and
pursue?　You take a javelin, and I will take a lance.'

"Without more said, they jumped at once on their horses,
and made after the brute with all speed.　But the boar, confi-
dent in its strength, wheeled round, and looking horribly fero-
cious as it gnashed its teeth, stood glaring at them uncertain
which to attack first.　Tlepolemus hurled his javelin, and
lodged it in the animal's back; but Thrasyllus, leaving the boar
alone, charged the horse Tlepolemus rode with his lance, and

cut its hamstrings. The quadruped, sinking down in a pool of its own blood, rolled over on its back, and involuntarily threw its master, whom the boar immediately rushed at in fury, and after tearing his clothes, rent his body in many places as he was endeavouring to rise. Meanwhile, his good friend felt no remorse for the infamous deed he had begun, nor was his cruelty yet satisfied; for whilst Tlepolemus was striving to defend his gored legs, and was piteously calling to him for help, he pierced him through the middle of the right thigh with his lance; which he did the more boldly, because he judged that the wound would resemble those made by the brute's tusks. Afterwards he ran the boar through and through without difficulty.

"After the young man was thus slain, we were all called out from our hiding-places, and ran to him in great grief. But Thrasyllus, though he had accomplished his purpose, and rejoiced in having slain him whom he looked on as his enemy, yet concealed his joy under a countenance that simulated sorrow; and ardently embracing the corpse that he himself had made, he cleverly counterfeited all the signs of mourning, only his tears refused to flow. Thus imitating us who lamented truly, he falsely cast upon the boar the odium of the deed his own hand had done.

"The news of this crime spread quickly, and first of all reached the family of Tlepolemus, and smote the ears of his unhappy wife. The moment she heard it—she will never hear news more—she lost her senses, and ran like a frantic bacchanal through the crowded streets, and away over the fields, screaming out her husband's name, and bewailing his fate. The compassionate citizens flocked after her; all who met her followed her, sympathizing in her grief; and the whole city was emptied to see the sad spectacle. At last, she reached the spot where lay the body of her husband; there, swooning away, she fell prostrate on his corpse, and all but yielded up on the spot the soul that was devoted to him; but her friends with difficulty forced her away, and she remained unwillingly alive.

"At last, the body was carried to the tomb, the whole city joining in the funeral procession. Then did Thrasyllus cry, and roar, and beat his breast, and even weep, for the tears which he had been unable to shed in his first feigned sorrow, were now supplied him by his augmented joy. He concealed his real feelings with all sorts of affectionate words, calling piteously to the deceased by name, as his friend, his playmate in boyhood, his comrade, his brother. And every now and then he would take hold of Charite's hands to hinder her from beating her bosom; would try to mitigate her grief and wailing with words expressive of the liveliest sympathy, and with various examples of the uncertainty of life. And amidst all these false shows of humanity and friendship, he took every opportunity of touching the person of the bereaved woman, and nourishing his own odious passion by that stolen pleasure.

" The funeral being ended, the widow was now impatient to join her husband, and thought over all means to that end. At last, she chose one that was gentle, cost no effort, needed no weapon, and was like quietly falling asleep. She abstained from food, neglected her person, and would have passed away from daylight to the darkness of the grave, but for the urgent pertinacity of Thrasyllus, who, partly by his own efforts, partly through those of her friends and her parents, prevailed on her to refresh her disfigured and almost perishing body with the bath and with food.

" Charite, who revered her parents, yielded against her will to a religious sense of duty, and with a somewhat more serene countenance did what was necessary for the preservation of her life ; but still her inmost soul was consumed with grief. She spent all her days and nights in pining remembrance, and in paying divine honours to an image of the deceased, which she had caused to be made in the costume of the god Bacchus, so that she tortured herself, even by that kind of consolation. Meanwhile, the reckless, headlong Thrasyllus, without waiting until the tears she shed had satisfied her grief, nor till the commotion of her spirits had partly subsided, and time had gradually blunted the keenness of her sorrow, did not forbear to speak to her of marriage while she was still weeping for her husband, rending her garments, and tearing her hair, and to reveal to her by his indecent importunity the secret of his breast and his ineffable treachery.

" Charite was seized with horror and loathing at the abominable proposal, which came upon her like a clap of thunder, or a blast from some malignant star, and she fell senseless as if smitten by lightning. Recovering after a while, with wild shrieks, she called to mind what had passed between her and the villain Thrasyllus, and postponed her reply to his suit until she should have maturely considered it.

"During that delay, the shade of the cruelly-slain Tlepolemus, lifting up its ghastly, gory face, thus addressed her as she slept: 'My own wife, a name which none else shall call you, if my memory dwells in your heart—if my cruel death has broken the bonds of affection that united us, contract a happier marriage with whom you will, only give yourself not into the sacrilegious hands of Thrasyllus: neither talk with him, nor sit at the same board, nor share the same bed with him. Shun the blood-stained hand of my murderer; begin not your marriage with parricide.* Those gory wounds which you have washed with your tears were not all inflicted by the tusks of the boar; but the lance of the wicked Thrasyllus has parted me from you.' And then he told her all the circumstances, and set before her the whole scene of the crime.

"When Charite had first laid her head upon her pillow, her tears flowed over her beautiful cheeks even while she slept; but roused by the vision of her restless sleep as by the wrench of the rack, she broke out again into loud and long wailing, tore her night-dress, and beat her lovely arms with merciless hands. Yet she imparted to no one the story of the apparition she had seen; but concealing altogether the knowledge she had obtained of the crime, she secretly resolved to punish the nefarious murderer, and to deliver herself from the intolerable burthen of life.

"Again the odious and importunate suitor assailed her obdurate ears with proposals of marriage; but she gently declined them, and dissembling her purpose with admirable artifice, she thus replied to his urgent supplications: 'The sweet face of your brother, my beloved husband, is still before my eyes; the cinnamon odour of his ambrosial body is still in my nostrils; the beautiful Tlepolemus still lives in my bosom. You will do best then if you allow a most wretched woman the necessary time for mourning, and let the remaining months of the year be spent in that legitimate duty. What I ask concerns not only my own reputation, but your safety also, lest by a premature marriage we provoke the just indignation of my husband's ghost to your destruction'

* *With parricide.*]—The crime of Thrasyllus was a sort of parricide, since he had murdered his friend; and Charite would have been in a manner its accomplice. if she had married him.

"Unchecked in his importunity by these arguments, and even by the promise that accompanied them, Thrasyllus persisted in molesting her ears with his vile addresses, until, apparently overcome, Charite said to him: 'One thing at least, Thrasyllus, you must grant to my earnest entreaties, and that is that our cohabitation be quite secret and unknown to any of my family until the year is out.' Thrasyllus was completely duped by her feigned compliance with his suit; he consented with alacrity to the clandestine intercourse, and passionately longed for the return of night and darkness, caring for nothing in comparison with the possession of Charite. 'But mind,' said Charite, 'come well muffled up, without any attendant, and approach my door in silence at the first watch. Only whistle once, and wait for my nurse, who will be on the watch behind the door, and will instantly open it for you, and conduct you in the dark to my chamber.'

"Thrasyllus, suspecting nothing, was delighted with the scheme of those funereal nuptials, and was only troubled with impatience at the length of the day and the slow approach of evening. At last, when daylight had disappeared, dressed as Charite had directed, he was admitted by the watchful nurse, and stole full of hope to the nuptial chamber. There the old woman, treating him with obsequious attention by her mistress's orders, noiselessly produced cups and a flagon containing wine mixed with a soporiferous drug. Then excusing her mistress's delay on the pretext that she was with her father, who was ill, she plied him with the beverage, which he drank freely, and without suspicion, until he fell fast asleep.

"As soon as he lay stretched on his back in that helpless state, Charite was summoned, and rushing in with dire determination, stood quivering with rage over the murderer, 'Behold,' she cried, 'this faithful companion of my husband! Behold this gallant hunter! Behold this dear bridegroom! This is the hand that shed my blood; this is the breast that conceived treacherous plots for my undoing: those are the eyes that to my sorrow I delighted, but that now anticipate their coming punishment, wrapped in the darkness that will cover them perpetually. Sleep securely; dream of delight; I will not smite you with sword or spear. Far be it from me to put you on an equality with my husband in the manner of your death. Your eyes shall die in your living head, and you shall never see more but in dreams. I will make you think your enemy's death happier than your own life. Never shall you see the light; you shall need to be led by the hand; you shall not clasp Charite; you shall not enjoy your promised nuptials; you shall know neither the repose of death nor the pleasure of life; but you shall wander like an erring phantom between the infernal regions and the sun; and you shall long seek the hand that has blinded you, and, what is the most miserable thing in calamity, you shall not know whom to complain of. I will make a libation of the blood of your eyes at the tomb of my Tlepolemus, and sacrifice those eyes to his sacred shade. But why do I suffer you to have a respite from your deserved torture, while you are dreaming perhaps of embracing me, who am your bane? Wake from the darkness of sleep to a worse darkness; lift up your sightless face; recognize my vengeance; comprehend your misfortune; compute the sum of your miseries. Thus have your eyes charmed your modest bride; thus have the nuptial torches lighted your chamber; you shall have the Furies for bridesmaids, and blindness and the perpetual stings of conscience for companions.'

"Having poured out these words like one inspired, Charite drew out the pin from her hair, and plunged it over and over again into the eyes of Thrasyllus; then leaving him to awake in pain and blindness from his lethargic sleep, she caught up the naked sword which Tlepolemus used to wear, and rushed frantically through the city towards her husband's tomb, manifestly bent on some desperate deed. All of us, servants, and the whole population, anxiously pursued her, crying out to each other to wrest the weapon from her insane hands. But Charite standing by the coffin of Tlepolemus, kept everybody off with the glittering blade; and when all around her were weeping and lamenting, she cried: 'Away with these importunate tears! Away with this wailing, which ill accords with my fortitude. I have taken vengeance upon the bloody murderer of my husband. I have punished the accursed destroyer of my nuptials; it is now time that with this sword I make my way straight to my Tlepolemus.'

"Then having related all that her husband had told her in the dream, and the artifice by which she had inveigled Thrasyllus, she plunged the sword beneath her right breast, fell bathed in blood, murmured a few broken' words, and breathed out her magnanimous spirit. The friends of the unfortunate Charite immediately washed her body with care, and depositing it by the side of Tlepolemus, re-united her for ever to the husband she loved.

" When Thrasyllus was aware of all this, he thought he could not inflict on himself a death commensurate with the calamities he had caused, and that the sword could not suffice to expiate his guilt; therefore he had himself carried to the tomb of Tlepolemus and Charite, where, crying out repeatedly, ' Behold, O ye injured manes, here is your voluntary victim,' he caused the doors to be firmly closed upon him ; and there he suffered the doom pronounced by himself, and perished by starvation."

END OF THE SEVENTH EPISODE.

Such was the story, interrupted with many sighs and tears, which the servant told to the sorrowing rustics, who fearing a change of master, and deeply commiserating the misfortune of the house to which they had belonged, determined to run away. The master of the stud, the same to whom I had been given in charge with such impressive orders to be kind to me, plundered the cottage of everything valuable in it, and loading me and other beasts of burden with the spoil, deserted his old abode. We carried women and children, cocks and hens, geese, kids, whelps ; in short, whatever was unable to keep up with our pace, was made to walk with our feet. But enormous as my load was, I did not care for it, so glad was I of the flight that saved me from the knife of that abominable gelder.

Having crossed a steep mountain covered with a forest, and descended to the plain on the other side, we arrived, just as evening was throwing its shadows on our road, at a certain populous and thriving town, whence the inhabitants would not allow us to proceed by night, nor even in the morning. The reason of this was, that the whole district was infested by multitudes of fierce wolves of enormous bulk and strength, that even beset the roads and fell like highway robbers on those who travelled by them. Nay, sometimes impelled by the rage of hunger, they stormed the neighbouring farms, and the men were no more safe from their fury than their defenceless flocks. They told us too, that the road we should have to travel was strewn with half-eaten human bodies, and whitened with fleshless bones; and therefore, that we ought to proceed with extreme caution, and be especially careful to travel only in broad day-light, while the sun was high in the heavens, since its light checks the fury of those dreadful creatures; 'and that we should move, not stragglingly, but in close compact order, through those dangerous places.

But our rascally fugitive conductors, in blind haste to escape the risk of pursuit, despised these salutary warnings, and without waiting for day-light, loaded and drove us forward. Then I, aware of the danger, took all possible care to keep between the other beasts in the very middle of the throng, so as to save my buttocks from the fangs of the wolves; and all our conductors were much surprised to see me beat the horses in speed. But this was not the result of my natural quickness of limb, but of my fear; and I thought within myself that it was nothing else than fright which had given such agility to the renowned Pegasus, and that the reason why he had been styled winged, was, doubtless, because he had skipped and bounded up to the very sky, in his dread of being bitten by the fire-breath-ing Chimæra.

Meanwhile the herdsmen who drove us had armed themselves as if for battle. This one carried a lance, that one a hunting spear, another a bundle of javelins, another a club; and some had provided themselves with stones, which the rough road supplied in abundance. A few carried sharpened stakes, and a great number waved blazing torches to frighten the beasts; and nothing but the trumpet was wanting to give our troop the appearance of an army in battle array. But after having terribly frightened ourselves, we escaped the threatened danger only to fall into a worse one. For, whether scared by the shouting of so large a body of men, and by the glare of the torches, or being engaged elsewhere, the wolves never approached us, nor did one of them come in sight even at a distance. But the labourers on the farm which we were then passing, taking us for a gang of robbers, and letting slip enormous dogs, which had been carefully trained for their masters' defence, and were fiercer than any wolves or bears, urged them against us with all sorts of shouts and cries. With their natural ferocity thus encouraged and exasperated, the dogs rushed at us, attacked us on all sides, men and cattle without distinction, and after mauling them a long time, laid many of them low. It was certainly a remarkable, and still more a pitiable spectacle, to see all those dogs seizing those that fled, ravening at those who stood their ground, mounting upon the bodies of those who were down, and overrunning our whole troop, biting all that came before them.

This was terrible indeed, but worse was added to it; for the peasants poured down showers of stones upon us from the roofs of their cottages and from an adjacent hill, so that we were quite at a loss to know which we should most avoid, the dogs that attacked us at close quarters, or the stones that were launched at us from a distance. One of the latter fell upon the head of a woman who was seated on my back, and who, smarting from the blow, immediately began to scream and roar for her husband to come to her aid. Wiping the blood from her wound, the herdsman cried out, " In the name of all the gods, why do you so cruelly assault and maltreat poor hard-working travellers ? Have we offered to rob you ? What harm have we ever done you ? You do not live in dens like wild beasts, or in caves like savages, that you should take delight in shedding human blood."

As soon as he had said this, the shower of stones ceased, the ferocious dogs were called off, and one of the peasants cried out from the top of a cypress tree on which he was perched : " And we too, are no robbers, and do not want to plunder you; we only fight to protect ourselves from suffering the like at your hands, so now you may go your ways in peace and safety." Therefore we continued our journey, but wounded in all manner of ways, some with stones, others by the teeth of the dogs, but all more or less hurt.

Having gone a little way further, we reached a grove of tall trees, with pleasant green glades, where our leaders thought good to rest and take some refreshment, and dress the wounds of their bruised and mangled bodies. So they threw them-selves on the ground in all directions, and after lying awhile to recover from their fatigue, they began to apply various re-medies to their wounds, washing the blood from them in the running stream ; applying wet sponges to their contusions, and tying up their gaping wounds with bandages. In this way each did the best he could for himself. Meanwhile, an old man was descried on the top of a hill, with goats feeding round him, and plainly showing that he was a goat-herd. One of our people called out, and asked him had he any milk or new cheese to sell. But he, shaking his head a long while, replied : "And are you thinking of food or drink, or of any refreshment at all? Do you not know what sort of a place you are in?" So saying, he turned his back upon us, and went off with his flock.

His words, and the manner of his departure, struck our people with no small fear; and while they were all anxious to ascertain the nature of the spot where they lay, but could find no one to tell them, another old man made his appearance. He was a tall man, bent with age, and dragged his feet slowly and wearily along, leaning heavily on his staff, and weeping profusely. When he came up with our men, he threw himself on his knees before them, and embracing them one after the other, thus besought in most piteous accents : "By your fortunes, by your genii,* and as you hope to live strong and hearty till you reach my age, help an unfortunate old man, who has lost his only hope, and save my little boy from the jaws of death. My grandson, the sweet companion of my journey, tried to catch a sparrow chirping on a hedge, and he fell into a ditch close by here, that was hidden with low shrubs, and there he lies in extreme peril of his life. I know indeed, by his cries to me for help, that he is still alive. But being so weak in body, as you see, I cannot succour him. But you, who enjoy youth and strength, can easily aid an unhappy old man, and save for him this child, the last and only scion of my stock."

As the old man made these entreaties and tore his white hair, we were all moved with pity; and one of the party, the youngest, boldest and strongest of them all, who besides, was the only one that had come off unwounded from the late conflict, sprang to his feet, and enquiring where it was the boy had fallen, went with the old man towards some rough bushes which the latter pointed out a little way off. Meanwhile, after the cattle had done feeding, and their drivers had finished their meal and the dressing of their wounds, each of them packed up his baggage again, and made ready for another start. They called loudly to the young man who had gone away with the old stranger, and afterwards, surprised by his long delay, they sent one of their number to look for him, and tell him it

* *Your genii.*]—The Romans believed that to every human being belonged a special protecting deity, who lived and died with his protégé, as the hamadryad did with her oak. These personal gods were called the Genius, or the Juno, according as they belonged to a man or a woman.

was time to be off. The messenger came back soon, trembling, and ghastly pale, and brought strange news of his fellow-servant. He had seen him, he said, lying on his back, half eaten, and a monstrous dragon squatting over him; whilst the unfortunate old man was not to be seen at all.

Considering this matter, and comparing it with the .words of the shepherd on the hill, which had doubtless been intended to warn them against that terrible inhabitant of the neighbourhood, our men hurried away as fast as they could from the deadly spot, drubbing us briskly with their sticks. After getting over a long stage at a very quick rate, we arrived at a village where we halted for the night, and there I learned a very extraordinary occurrence which I will relate.

EIGHTH EPISODE.

SINGULAR PUNISHMENT OF A CRIMINAL.

THERE was a servant to whom his master had committed the management of all his affairs, and who was bailiff of that large farm where we had taken up our quarters. He had married one of his fellow-servants, but fell in love with a free woman who was not of the household. Enraged by his adultery, his wife burned all his account books, and all the contents of his store-room. And not content with having thus avenged the wrongs of her bed, but turning her fury against her own flesh and blood, she put a rope round her neck, fastened to it also an infant she had borne to her husband, and threw herself into a deep well along with her little one. Her master was exceedingly incensed at her loss, and seizing the servant who had provoked his own wife to the commission of such a dreadful deed, had him stripped naked, smeared all over with honey, and bound fast to a fig-tree, the rotten trunk of which was filled with the nests of a prodigious multitude of ants, that were continually running to and from all directions. As soon as these ants smelt the honey with which the bailiff's body was smeared, they fastened upon him, and with minute, but innumerable and incessant bites, gradually consumed his flesh and his entrails; and after the miserable man had been thus tortured a long while, his bones were at last picked clean; and so they were still to be seen, quite dry and white, attached to the fatal tree.

END OF THE EIGHTH EPISODE.

Quitting this detestable dwelling, and leaving the rustics in great sorrow, we proceeded on our journey. After travelling all day over a level country, we came much fatigued to a handsome populous town. There our men resolved to stop and take up their permanent abode, both because the place offered them every convenience for hiding from those who might come from a distance in pursuit of them, and because the town was abundantly blessed with provisions. Myself and the other beasts were allowed three days' rest to improve our condition, and then we were led out for sale. The crier proclaimed the price of each of us with a loud voice, and all were bought by wealthy persons, except myself, whom all the purchasers passed by with contempt. I lost patience at the manner in which I was handled, and my teeth examined to ascertain my age; there was one man especially, who was always poking his nasty dirty fingers against my gums; but at last, I caught his hand between my teeth, and nearly crushed it. That deterred every one from buying me, as a ferociously vicious brute. Then the crier, bawling till his throat was almost split, cracked all sorts of ridiculous jokes upon me. " What is the use," said he, " of offering for sale this old screw of a jackass, with his foundered hoofs, his ugly colour, his sluggishness in everything but vice, and a hide that is nothing but a ready-made sieve? Let us even make a present of him, if we can find any one who will not be loth to throw away hay upon the brute." In this way the crier kept the byestanders in roars of laughter.

But my merciless fortune, which I had been unable to leave behind me, far as I had fled, or to appease by all my past sufferings, again cast its evil eye upon me, and for a wonder, produced a purchaser, the fittest of all men to prolong my hard sufferings. He was an old eunuch, partly bald, with what grizzled hair he had left hanging in long curls, one of those lowest dregs of the rabble who compel the Syrian goddess to beg, hawking her about the highways and the towns, and playing on cymbals and castanets. This man having a great mind to buy me, asked the crier of what country I was. The latter replied that I was Cappadocian,* and a fine strong

---

* *Cappadocian.*]—Part of the crier's fun consists in talking of the ass as if he was a human slave. Hence his mention of Cappadocia, which had no particular reputation for its breed of asses, but which surpassed all the other provinces of the empire in the number and value of the slaves it supplied to Rome.

animal. Again, the other asked my age. "The mathematician who cast his nativity," replied the joking crier, "calculated that he was five years old; but no doubt he is better informed on this point than any one else, from the register of his birth. Now though I make myself liable to the penalties of the Cornelian law if I knowingly sell you a Roman citizen for a slave, what should hinder you from buying a good and useful servant, who will do your pleasure at home and abroad?"

The odious purchaser went on asking questions without end, and at last came to the important point, was I gentle? "Gentle?" said the crier; "it is not an ass, but a wether you see before you, such a quiet thing you may do what you will with him; none of your biters or kickers; but altogether such an animal that you might suppose there was a decent, honest man under his ass's hide. You may convince yourself of the fact without difficulty; only stick your face between his thighs, and you will see how patient he will be."

Thus did the crier make fun of the old vagabond; but the latter perceived that the other was mocking, and cried out in a passion: "What, you deaf and dumb carcase, you crazy crier, may the omnipotent and all-procreant Syrian goddess, and blessed Sabazius, and Bellona, and the Idœan mother, and our mistress Venus, with her Adonis, strike you blind, you that have been flinging your scurrilous jokes at me this ever so long. Do you think me such a fool as to put the goddess on the back of a vicious brute, that he might pitch the divine image to the ground, and that I should have to run about with my hair streaming, to look for some one to lift my goddess from the ground, and repair her hurts?"

When I heard him talk in this strain, I thought of prancing suddenly, like mad, that seeing how very wild I was, he might give up the thought of buying me. But the anxious purchaser anticipated my intention by at once paying down the price, seventeen denars, which my master promptly took up, to his own satisfaction and my vexation, and immediately delivered me to my new owner, Philebus, with a rush halter round my neck. Philebus took me home with him, and cried out the moment he reached the door: "Hallo, girls! here is a handsome servant I have bought for you." Now these girls were a set of eunuchs, who immediately broke out into screams of joy, with broken, hoarse, effeminate voices, thinking it was

a slave fit to render them good service. But when they per-
ceived the substitution, not of a stag for a virgin,* but of a
jackass for a man, they turned up their noses, and jeered at
their leader, saying he had not brought a servant for them,
but a husband for himself. "Mind," said they, "you don't
keep this pretty dear all to yourself, but let us too, your doves,
have the use of him sometimes." Thus babbling, they took
and tied me to the manger.

There was among them a strapping young fellow, who played
extremely well on the horn, and whom they had bought at
the slave mart, with the money they had collected here and
there. Abroad he used to play before them when they led the
goddess in procession, and at home they employed him in other
ways. As soon as he witnessed my arrival, he was greatly
delighted, and gave me plenty of fodder, joyfully exclaiming:
"You are come at last to relieve me in my terrible labours;
long may you live, and be a pleasure to your masters, and give
me a chance to recruit my exhausted strength." Hearing him
talk thus, I pondered on the new troubles that were before me.

Next day they went out, all dressed in various colours,
hideously bedizened, their faces and eyelids daubed with paint,
with small mitres on their heads, and wearing saffron-coloured
linen and silk vestments. Some of them had white tunics,
covered with narrow purple stripes in all directions; and they
all wore girdles and yellow shoes. They laid the goddess,
covered with a silk mantle, on my back; and brandishing
enormous swords and axes, with their arms bared to the shoul-
der, they danced and bounded like maniacs to the sound of the
flute. After going about a good many cottages, they came to
a rich man's villa, and setting up their yells at the very gate,
they rushed frantically in. Bending down their heads, they
rolled their necks about, making their long hair stand out in a
circle; from time to time they bit their flesh with their teeth,
and lastly, they cut their arms with the sharp weapon which
each of them carried. There was one of them who was trans-
ported with a more ecstatic fury than the rest, and heaving his
breath rapidly from the bottom of his chest, as if filled with
the divine spirit, he pretended to be stark mad; as if the pre-
sence of the gods did not do men good, but weakened or disor-
dered them. But you shall see how by divine providence they

* *The substitution, not of a stag for a virgin.*]—As happened when
Iphigenia, the daughter of Agamemnon, was about to be sacrificed at Aulis.

received their due reward.   The fellow began by delivering a trumped-up story of his own guilt, and crying out aloud, in the tone of a prophet, that he had committed some offence against the holy laws of religion ; and then he called upon his hands to inflict on him the chastisement due to his crime.   At the same time he took up one of the whips usually carried by those half men, with several long lashes of twisted wool, strung with knuckle-bones of sheep, and gave himself a severe flogging, the pain of which he endured with astonishing firmness. You might see the ground wet with the blood that flowed from the gashes of the sword and the strokes of the whip.   Now the sight of all this blood and wounds caused me no slight uneasiness, lest perchance the stomach of the foreign goddess might crave for ass's blood, as some men's for ass's milk.

When at last they were tired, or thought they had scarified themselves sufficiently, they left off their butchery.   Then the byestanders vied with each other in dropping money, not only brass, but silver too, into the open bosom of their robes.   They received, besides, a barrel of wine, milk, cheese, barley, and wheaten meal, besides barley for myself, the bearer of the goddess.   All these things they stuffed into bags provided for the receipt of such doles, and laid them on my back ; so that being doubly laden, I was at once a walking temple and a walking granary.   Roaming about in that manner, they plundered the whole region.

One day, being highly pleased with an unusually large collection they made in a certain town, they resolved to regale themselves and be merry.   They begged a very fat ram from a farmer, whom they cajoled with a lying prophecy, and told him they would sacrifice it to appease the hunger of the Syrian goddess.   Having made all their preparations for the banquet, they went to the baths, and on their return they brought a remarkably vigorous peasant home with them to supper.   They had only tasted a few morsels of the first course, when they started up from table, and gathering round the young man, began to assail him with execrable solicitations.

Unable to endure the abominable spectacle, I tried to shout, O CITIZENS ! but could not get beyond the O, which I uttered in a fine sonorous tone, well becoming a jackass, but very unluckily timed.   For several young men, who were looking for an ass that had been stolen the night before, and who were closely examining all the inns to see if the animal was not in one of them, happening to hear me bray, and thinking it might be their own ass that was hidden in the house, rushed in unexpectedly, and caught these miscreants in the very midst of their detestable turpitudes. Instantly calling in the neighbours from all quarters, they made them aware of the horrible discovery, bestowing at the same time sarcastic compliments on the sanctimonious purity of those priests. Struck with consternation at this disclosure of their infamy, which spread rapidly among the people, and made them objects of universal abhorrence, my masters packed up every thing, and secretly quitted the town about midnight.

After getting over a good deal of ground before dawn, and arrived by daylight in an unfrequented spot, they held a long consultation, which ended in their proceeding to punish me unmercifully. They lifted the goddess off my back, and laid her on the ground, stripped off all my trappings, tied me to a tree, and flogged me with their whip strung with sheep's bones until I was all but dead. There was one who proposed to hamstring me with an axe, because I had so foully scandalised his modesty; but the others voted for leaving me alone, not from any good will to me, but in consideration of the image that lay on the ground.

They replaced my load therefore on my back, and drove me before them with blows of the flat of their swords, till we arrived at a great town. One of its principal inhabitants, a very religious man, who had a great reverence for the gods, hearing the tinkling of the cymbals, the beating of the timbrels, and the soft Phrygian music, came to meet us, and offer his devout hospitality to the goddess. He lodged us all within his fine spacious mansion, and sought to win the divine favour by the most profound veneration and the finest victims

Here it was that my life was exposed to the greatest danger I ever remember to have incurred. A certain person in the country had sent as a present to our host, who was his landlord, the haunch of a very large and fat stag he had killed in the chase. It had been carelessly hung rather low behind the kitchen door, where a hound seized it, and carried it off. When the cook discovered his loss, which he imputed to his own negligence, his lamentation was extreme, and for a long time he shed unavailing tears, thinking that his master would presently call for his supper. Terrified at last at the punishment that awaited him, he tenderly kissed his little son, snatched up a rope, and set about hanging himself.   But his affectionate wife became opportunely aware of his desperate case, and seizing the fatal noose in both hands with all her might, " What," she cried, " has this accident frightened you out of your senses ? Do you not see the remedy which the providence of the gods has offered to your hands ?   If you have any sense left in this whirlwind of disaster, rouse it up and listen to me.   Take that ass, that was brought here to-day, to some out-of-the-way place, and cut his throat ; then take from the carcase a haunch just like that which is lost, cook it nicely, dress it with the most savoury sauce you can make, and serve it up before your master, instead of the venison."

The rascally cook was delighted at the thought of saving his own life at the cost of mine ; and highly extolling his wife's sagacity, he set about sharpening his knives, to execute the butchery she had recommended.

BOOK THE NINTH.

THUS did that cursed butcher arm his nefarious hands against

me.   There was no time to be lost; the danger was too urgent
to allow of long cogitation; I resolved to escape by flight from
the knife that was so near my throat, and instantly breaking
the halter with which I was tied, I galloped away as fast as
my legs could carry me, flinging out my heels as I ran for the
greater safety.   Having quickly shot across the first portico, I
dashed without hesitation into the dining-room, where the
master of the house was feasting with the priests of the god-
dess on the sacrificial meats; and I upset and smashed great
part of the supper things, and even the tables.   The master of
the house, greatly annoyed by such unseemly havoc, ordered
one of his servants to take away "the troublesome, frisky
brute," as he called me, and gave the man strict injunctions
to shut me up in some safe place, that I might not again dis-
turb the quiet of his guests by such pranks.   For my part,
having saved myself from the knife by this clever feat, I was
very glad to enjoy the security of my prison.

But certainly it is not for mortal man to prosper against the
will of fortune, nor can all the contrivances of human wisdom
overthrow or alter the fatal disposition of divine providence.*
That very device of mine, which seemed to have afforded me
a momentary deliverance, brought upon me another peril,
which went near to cause my instant destruction; for one of
the servants, as I afterwards learned from what passed between
his fellows, rushed in great agitation into the supper-room,
and told his master that a mad dog had just before run into
the house through a back door, opening on a lane; that he had
fallen furiously on the hounds; then made for the stables,
where he had wreaked his rage on the horses; and lastly, that
he had not spared the men either, for he had bitten Myrtilus,
the muleteer, Hephæstion, the cook, Hypatius, the chamber-

---

* *The fatal disposition of divine providence.*]—In the original, *divinæ
providentiæ fatalis dispositio,* which the Delphin editors erroneously in-
terpret, *ordo immutabilis providentiæ divinæ.*   For Providence, according
to the Platonic philosophy, (and Apuleius was a Platonist), is superior to
Fate; and in consequence of this, whatever is produced by Fate is also
produced by Providence; but not *vice versa.*   Apuleius, therefore, rightly
ascribes the *fatal disposition* of things to Divine Providence, because this
disposition or order proceeds primarily from Providence, but secondarily
from Fate; but the *fatal* is not the same with the *immutable* order of
things: for the latter pertains to Providence alone, but the former to
Providence in conjunction with Fate.—*Taylor.*

lain, and Apollonius, the physician, besides a great many other servants who had endeavoured to drive him out; and some of the animals he had bitten, already showed undoubted symptoms of rabidness.

The whole party was struck with dismay at this intelligence, and guessing from my wild behaviour, that I was infected with the same malady, they caught up such weapons as lay at hand, and exhorted each other to despatch me for their common safety, though, in fact, it was they themselves who were mad, and not I. They would doubtless have cut me to pieces with the lances, spears, and even axes, with which the servants readily supplied them, had I not run before the storm, and burst into the bed-chamber of the priests, my masters. My pursuers then fastened the door upon me, and kept me besieged, that the deadly virus might do its work, and destroy me, without their running the risk of coming in contact with me. Finding, therefore, that I was left alone and free to do as I pleased, I profited by the opportunity which fortune offered me, lay down on a bed, and enjoyed what I had so long foregone, a good sleep in human fashion.

Having slept off my fatigue on that good bed, I awoke when it was already broad daylight, and jumped up fresh and hearty. Then I heard the people who had kept watch all night outside the door, thus debating with one another about me. "Is it likely that this unfortunate ass can go on raging everlastingly? Surely not. It is rather to be presumed that the virus has spent itself, and his fit is over." As their opinions differed on this question, they agreed to have a look at me; and peeping through a chink in the door, they saw me standing at my ease, apparently as quiet and as well as ever. Thereupon, they ventured to open the door and examine my state more fully; and one of them, who was sent from heaven to be my saviour, proposed to the rest a means of knowing whether I was mad or not. This was to put a vessel full of fresh water before me; if I drank it without hesitation, in my usual way, this would be a sure proof that I was quite free from all distemper; on the contrary, if I shunned the water with manifest horror at the sight of it, it would be a clear case that the dreadful malady had still fast hold of me; for so it was laid down in ancient books, and confirmed by frequent experience.

This advice being voted good, they forthwith fetched a large vessel full of fine clear water from the nearest fountain, and placed it before me, still keeping on their guard. I went up to it at once, being very thirsty, and plunging my head into the vessel, drank up the water, which truly did me much good in every way. Then I quietly suffered them to pat me with their hands, rub my ears, lead me by the headstall, and do whatever else they pleased by way of trying me, until they were all convinced of my gentleness, and of their own mistake in supposing me to be mad.

Having thus preserved myself from two great dangers, I was again loaded next day with the divine baggage, and marched away to the sound of cymbals and castanets, to continue our mendicant rounds. After visiting a great number of hamlets and towns, we arrived at a village built on the ruins of a town that had formerly been very opulent, as the inhabitants reported. We entered the first inn we came to, and there we heard a pleasant story of the way in which the wife of a poor man cuckolded her husband: and you shall hear it too.

NINTH EPISODE.

WHAT THE POOR MAN GOT FOR HIS TUB.

There was a poor man who had nothing to subsist on but his scanty earnings as a journeyman carpenter. He had a wife who was also very poor, but notorious for her lasciviousness. One day, when the man had gone out betimes to his work, an impudent gallant immediately stepped into his house. But whilst he and the wife were warmly engaged, and thinking themselves secure, the husband, who had no suspicion of such doings, returned quite unexpectedly. The door being locked and bolted, for which he mentally extolled his well-conducted wife, he knocked and whistled to announce his presence. Then his cunning wife, who was quite expert in such matters, released the man from her close embraces, and hid him quickly in an old empty butt, that was sunk half-way in the ground, in a corner of the room. Then she opened the door, and began to scold her husband the moment he entered. "So you are come home empty-handed, are you?" said she, "to sit here with your arms folded, doing nothing, instead of going on with your regular work, to get us a living and buy us a bit of food; while I, poor soul, must work my fingers out of joint, spinning wool day and night, to have at least as much as will keep a lamp burning in our bit of a room.   Ah, how much better off is my neighbour Daphne, that has her fill of meat and drink from daylight to dark, and enjoys herself with her lovers."

"What need of all this fuss?" replied the abused husband; "for though our foreman has given us a holiday, having business of his own in the forum, I have nevertheless provided for our supper to-night.   You see that useless butt, that takes up so much room, and is only an incumbrance to our little place; I sold it for five denars to a man who will be here presently to pay for it and take it away.   So lend me a hand for a moment, till I get it out to deliver it to the buyer."

Ready at once with a scheme to fit the occasion, the woman burst into an insolent laugh: "Truly I have got a fine fellow for a husband; a capital hand at a bargain, surely, to go and sell at such a price a thing which I, who am but a woman, had already sold for seven denars, without even quitting the house."

Delighted at what he heard, "And who is he," said the husband, "who has bought it so dear?"

"He has been down in the cask ever so long, you booby," she replied, "examining it all over to see if it is sound."

The gallant failed not to take his cue from the woman, and promptly rising up out of the butt, "Shall I tell you the truth, good woman?" he said; "your tub is very old, and cracked in I don't know how many places."   Then turning to the husband, without appearing to know him: "Why don't you bring me a light, my tight little fellow, whoever you are, that I may scrape off the dirt from the inside, and see whether or not the tub is fit for use, unless you think I don't come honestly by my money?"

That pattern of all quick-witted husbands, suspecting nothing, immediately lighted a lamp, and said, "Come out, brother, and leave me to make it all right for you."   So saying, he stripped, and taking the lamp with him into the tub, went to work to scrape off the old hardened dirt.   And while he was polishing the inside, the charming gallant polished off the carpenter's wife, laying her on her belly on the outside, she meanwhile amusing herself, like a harlot as she was, with

making fun of her husband, poking her head into the tub, and
pointing out this place and that to be cleaned, and then another,
and another; until both jobs being finished, the unfortunate
carpenter received his seven denars, and had to carry the butt
on his back to the adulterer's house.

END OF THE NINTH EPISODE.

After staying a few days in this town, where they were
pampered by the bounty of the public, and made a great deal
by their soothsaying, these pious priests bethought them of a
new device for getting money. They composed a single
oracular response, which would fit a variety of cases, and thus
they gulled a great number of persons who came to consult
them upon all sorts of subjects. The oracle was as follows:

> The steers are yoked, and till the ground,
> That crops may rise, and joys abound.*

Suppose now that a person consulted the oracle with regard
to his marrying: to him it said plainly that he should take
upon him the yoke of matrimony, and raise a fine crop of chil-
dren. Suppose it was one who had a mind to buy land: the
yoked oxen and the abundant harvests were quite to the point.
If the applicant was anxious about a journey he had to take:
the meekest of quadrupeds were ready yoked, and the produce
of the soil signified a lucrative result. If he was one who had
to go into battle, or to pursue a gang of robbers: the priests
declared that the oracle promised him victory, and that he
should bring the necks of his enemies under the yoke, and reap
a rich harvest of booty

My masters had gained no little money by this cheating
method of divination; but exhausted at last by perpetual in-
terrogations for which they had but one answer, they again
departed by a road much worse than that which we had tra-
velled the preceding night. The greater part of it was broken
up into deep ruts and holes full of water, and the rest was co-
vered with thick mud and very slippery. At last, greatly
fatigued, and with my legs bruised by continually slipping and

* *The Steers, &c.*]—In the Latin:
> Ideo conjuncti terram proscendunt boves,
> Ut in futurum lætæ germinent sata.

falling, I had just reached a smooth bit of ground, when sud-
denly a body of armed men on horseback galloped down upon
us, and after pulling up with difficulty, seized Philebus and
his companions by the throat, and beat them with their fists,
calling them sacrilegious, obscene villains. Then they hand-
cuffed them all, and bellowed to them to produce the golden
bowl they had stolen. "Produce," they shouted, "that proof
of your crime, which you filched from the very shrine of the
Mother of the Gods, when you shut yourselves up in her tem-
ple, under pretence of solemnizing secret rites; and then you
quitted the town before daylight without saying a word to any
one, as if you thought you could escape punishment for such
abominable guilt." Meanwhile, one of them searching the
goddess I carried on my back, found the gold cup in her bosom,
and drew it forth in the sight of all present. But even that
palpable evidence could not abash or dismay those nefarious
wretches, but affecting to laugh, and to turn the affair into a
joke, they exclaimed: "What an untoward accident! How
often the innocent are put in jeopardy! Here are ministers of
religion put in peril of their lives only for a cup which the
Mother of the Gods made a present to her sister, the Syrian
Goddess, as a pledge of hospitality." But in spite of all such
frivolous excuses, the rustics marched them back, and lodged
them in prison; and the cup and the image I had carried
having been solemnly deposited in the temple, I was brought
forth on the following day, and again offered for sale by the
voice of the crier. A certain baker from the next town bought
me for seven denars more than Philebus had given for me;
and putting on my back a good load of corn he had just bought,
he took me to his mill by a very rough road, full of stones and
roots of trees.

There were a good many beasts employed there, in turning
several millstones, and that not only by day, but all night long
too, for the mill was always kept going. Lest I should be
disgusted with the beginning of my servitude, my new master
treated me with all the honours due to a stranger of consider-
ation, and I had a holiday, and a manger abundantly supplied;
but the beatitude of having nothing to do and plenty to eat did
not last beyond the first day. On the following day, I was
fastened up to turn what seemed to me the largest mill-
stone of all, and with my head covered I was put into a little

hollow path in the form of a circle, in which I was to go round and round perpetually.   But I had not so far forgotten my old cunning as to fall in easily with this new discipline; and though when I was a man I had often seen machines of that kind revolve, yet, as if I was quite a novice at the work, and did not know what to do, I stood stock still, pretending stupefaction. I imagined that when they saw I was not fit for the work, they would put me to something else that was less fatiguing, or that they would let me eat and do nothing.   But my craft, instead of doing me good, only brought me into trouble.   For several men armed with sticks came round me while I suspected nothing, for my head was covered and I could not see ; and at a given signal they all shouted out together, and let fall upon me a storm of blows.   I was so terrified by the uproar, that, abandoning all thoughts of trickery, and pulling at the trace with all my might, I paced the ring nimbly, and excited a general burst of laughter by my sudden change of behaviour.

The day was near its end, I was very tired, when they loosed the rush ropes that fastened me to the mill, and let me go to the manger.   Though exhausted with fatigue and hunger, and in great need of having my strength recruited, yet prompted by my natural curiosity, I neglected the food that was before me to observe with a sort of pleasure the economy of our detestable work-place.   O gods ! what a set of stunted men I saw there !   Their skins were seamed all over with marks of the lash ; their scarred backs were shaded rather than covered with tattered frocks ; some had only aprons ; and all were so clothed, that their skin was visible through the rents in their rags.   Their foreheads were branded with letters ; their heads were half shaved ; they had irons on their legs ; they were hideously sallow ; their eyes were bleared, and sore and raw from the smoke of the ovens ;* and they were covered with flour, as athletes are with dust when they contend in the arena.

But how shall I describe my brute companions ?   What worn-out old mules and geldings !   How they hung their heads at the manger as they chewed the heaps of straw !   Their necks were covered with putrid sores ; they coughed incessantly, and panted through their gaping nostrils ; their chests were raw from the friction of the rush breast rope ; their flanks laid

* *The smoke of the ovens.*]—The miller's and the baker's trade were generally combined in those days.

open to the bone with continual cudgelling; their hoofs lengthened to an extraordinary degree by dint of walking in the mill round; and their hides were rough all over with mange. Beholding the wretched plight of those animals, whom I myself might be brought to resemble, and recollecting my own happy fortune when I was Lucius, I hung my head and sorrowed over the deep degradation into which I had fallen. The only consolation I had was in the pleasure of indulging my inborn curiosity, by observing all that was said and done around me without reserve, for no one took any account of my presence.   Truly, it was with good reason that the divine author of the ancient Greek epos, wishing to depict a man of consummate wisdom and prudence, sang of one who had visited many cities and become acquainted with many peoples.*   I myself hold my asinine days in grateful remembrance, be-cause, being hidden under that form, I went through a great number of adventures, which made me acquainted with many things, if they have not rendered me wiser.   Thus I picked up an excellent story, which particularly interested me, and which you shall hear.

The baker who had bought me was a worthy, well-conducted man, but suffered the most cruel domestic affliction in conse-quence of having to wife the wickedest of all women; inso-much, that even I often groaned in secret over his sad lot. There was not one vice from which that nefarious woman was free; but every kind of iniquity had flowed into her soul, as into a cesspool for the reception of all uncleanness.   She was mischievous, malignant, addicted to men and to wine, froward and stubborn, vilely rapacious, unbounded in profusion, a foe to faith and chastity.   Moreover, despising and trampling under foot the majesty of heaven, instead of the true religion, she affected to entertain some fantastic and sacrilegious notion of a God whom she declared to be the only one,† and under

With many peoples.]—He alludes to Homer's account of Ulysses, in the Odyssey.

† *A God whom she declared to be the only one.*]—Having to depict a woman of the most flagitious character, Apuleius thought to give likelihood to a portrait that might otherwise have seemed overcharged and unna-tural, by making this paragon of wickedness a Christian.   Nothing was too bad to be believed on trust of that decried sect in those days.   But such virulent prejudice was not peculiar to pagan times.

pretence of certain frivolous observances with which she im-
posed upon the public and beguiled her unfortunate husband,
she got drunk in the morning, and prostituted her body at all
hours.

This woman persecuted me with amazing rancour. For
before the dawn of morning, as she lay still in bed, she used
to call out and bid them yoke the new ass to the mill; as soon
as she was up she used to order me to be drubbed without
stint in her presence; and when the cattle were unyoked at
breakfast-time, she would order me to be kept from the manger
long after the rest. These cruelties greatly whetted my natu-
ral curiosity to scrutinize her behaviour. I perceived that a
certain young fellow was continually going into her room, and
I greatly longed to catch sight of his face, if the covering put
on my head had only allowed me the use of my eyes; in that
case I should not have wanted sagacity enough to discover in
some way or other the criminal proceedings of the abandoned
woman.

A certain old woman, who was her confidante, and the go-
between in her intrigues, was with her every day from morn-
ing to night. After breakfasting together, they used to sit and
drink neat wine as if for a wager, all the while devising schemes
to cheat the unfortunate husband. Now, though I was greatly
vexed at the blunder committed by Fotis, who had made an
ass of me when intending to change me into a bird, yet I had
at least this comfort in my lamentable deformity, that being
furnished with very long ears, I could hear what was said
even at a great distance. One day, for example, I heard the
squeaking old woman talk as follows :

"Make up your mind, mistress, what you will do with that
pluckless acquaintance you chose without consulting me, a
coward that shudders at the grim frown of your sour and
odious husband, and torments you by the laggard weakness of
his love, that corresponds so ill with your own warmth. What a
different man is Philesietæros! young, handsome, generous, met-
tlesome, and more than a match for all the useless vigilance of
husbands. By Hercules! he is the only man that deserves to
enjoy the embraces of all the ladies of quality, he alone de-
serves to be crowned with gold, if it was only for that capital
trick he lately played on a jealous husband. Listen, now, and
see the difference between such a man and your lover. You

know one Barbarus, the decurion* of our town, whom the people nickname Scorpion, on account of his peevish, spiteful disposition. He has a wife of a good family, and surpassing beauty, whom he keeps shut up at home with all the caution imaginable."

"To be sure," said the miller's wife, "I know her very well. You mean my schoolfellow, Arete?"

"Then you know the whole story about Philesietærus?" rejoined the old woman.

"Not at all," replied the other; "but I long to hear it, so tell it all, mother, from beginning to end." Accordingly, the old woman, who was an interminable chatterer, began as follows:

TENTH EPISODE.

THE JEALOUS HUSBAND OUTWITTED

"This Barbarus, being obliged to go a journey which he could not avoid, and wishing to take all possible measures to keep his dear wife faithful to him, secretly communicated his intentions to his slave Myrmex, the one in whom he had most confidence, and ordered him to watch over the conduct of his mistress, threatening him with chains, and prison, and starvation, and a torturing death to end all, if any man so much as touched her with the tip of his finger as he passed her in the street; and all these threats he confirmed with the most solemn oaths. Having thus left Myrmex terribly frightened and disposed to keep a most vigilant watch over his wife, Barbarus set out on his journey without fear of bad consequences.

"Intensely anxious about his charge, Myrmex would never let his mistress go out alone. He kept her shut up all day spinning wool, always under his own eye; and when it was necessary for her to go in the evening to the public baths, he went with her, sticking like glue to her side, and holding the skirt of her robe in his hand, so wonderfully awake was he to all the duties of his trust.

"But the beauty of the lady could not escape one who was so keen-sighted in matters of gallantry as was Philesietærus; but what piqued and incited him above all things, was the repute of her impregnable virtue, and the extraordinary care with which it was guarded. He resolved, then, to lay siege

* *Decurion.*] — The 'decuriones' were the senators of the Roman ' municipia,' or free towns.

with all his might to the house in which she was immured, and to make his way in at all costs and hazards, in spite of its commander's vigorous discipline. And knowing well the frailty of human nature, and that gold can smooth down all difficulties, and break open adamantine gates, he addressed himself to Myrmex, whom he fortunately met alone, told him of his love for his mistress, and conjured him to afford some remedy for his torments; assuring him that his speedy death was certain, if his desires were not quickly fulfilled. 'Besides,' said he, 'you have nothing to fear in so easy a matter as that which I ask of you; since no more is required than that I should steal into your house alone, under cover of darkness, and remain there only a moment.' These insinuating arguments he followed by the application of a wedge that was well adapted to cleave asunder the stubborn toughness of the servant's resolution; for holding out a handful of shining gold coin fresh from the mint, he told him that twenty of them were for the lady, and that ten of them should be freely at his own service.

"Terrified at the stupendous proposal, Myrmex took to his heels at once, without listening to another word. But he could not get the lustre of the yellow gold out of his sight; and though he had left it behind, and had never stopped running till he got home, he still seemed to behold the beautiful coin, and clutched it in imagination. Miserably was the poor fellow distracted between opposite feelings: he thought of the fidelity he owed his master, and then of his own gain; the fear of horrible punishment made him hang back; the bewitching thought of that money lured him on. At last the gold prevailed over the fear of death, and time by no means allayed his longing for that lovely coin; it clung to him like a pestilence even through the anxious night; so that while his master's threats would have detained him at home, yet the gold irresistibly summoned him abroad. Gulping down all shame, therefore, he went straightway to his mistress, and delivered his message from Philesietærus; and she, a wanton born, at once sold her virtue for cursed metal. So Myrmex, deluged with joy at the wreck of his fidelity, and eager to finger the gold which it was his ill fate to have seen, went in quest of Philesietærus, and told him that at last, with great difficulty, he had effected his wishes. Then he asked on the spot for the promised recompense, and suddenly found himself possessed of a handful of gold coin, he who had never in his life been master of a copper.

"When night was come, he conducted the bold gallant, alone and with his face well muffled, to the house, and into his mistress's chamber. But just as the pair were paying their first adorations to Love, just as the naked recruits in the warfare of Venus were performing their first service, the husband, who had chosen that time of night on purpose, arrived suddenly at the moment when he was least expected. He knocked, he called, he pounded at the door with a stone, and growing more and more suspicious in consequence of the delay, he threatened terrible vengeance against Myrmex, who was so bewildered by the sudden calamity that he knew not what to do, and could only excuse himself by saying that the darkness of the night had hindered him from finding the key, which he had hidden with great care. Meanwhile, Philesietærus, alarmed by the noise, hastily put on his clothes, and ran out of the bedroom, but forgot in his confusion to thrust his feet into his shoes.

"Then Myrmex put the key in the lock and let in his master, who was still bawling and swearing with all his might; and whilst the latter hurried to his chamber, Myrmex let Philesietærus slip out unperceived, shut the door behind him, and went back to his bed with his mind quite at ease. But when Barbarus got up in the morning, he saw a strange pair of shoes under the bed; and instantly suspecting what had happened, but saying not a word to his wife or any of the servants, he took up the shoes unobserved and hid them in his bosom; then ordering Myrmex to be bound and marched off to the forum, he went thither himself, groaning inwardly, and assuring himself he should trace out the adulterer by means of the shoes.

"As Barbarus walked along the street with lowering brows and a face swollen with rage, Myrmex followed him in chains. He had not, indeed, been taken in the fact, but overwhelmed by a guilty conscience, he cried and lamented, so as to excite the useless compassion of the beholders. Philesietærus happened very opportunely to pass that way, and though he had business which called him elsewhere, yet being forcibly struck, but not dismayed, by the spectacle that suddenly came before him, he recollected the mistake he had made in his haste, and immediately inferring all the consequences, he acted on the spot with his usual cleverness and presence of mind. Pushing aside the other servants, he rushed upon Myrmex, bawling at him with all his might, and hitting him on the face with his fists, but so as not to hurt him much : 'Villain and liar !' he cried, 'may your master and all the gods, by whose names you forswear yourself, punish you as such a rascal deserves! You that stole my shoes yesterday from the bath. You deserve, by Hercules, to have those chains upon you until they are worn out, and to be shut up for ever in the darkness of a dungeon.'

"Completely duped and befooled by the ready-witted stratagem of the bold youth, Barbarus went back to his house, called Myrmex before him, and putting the shoes into his hands, forgave him with all his heart, and advised him to return them to their owner from whom he had stolen them."

END OF THE TENTH EPISODE.

No sooner had the old woman ended her story, than the baker's wife cried out : "Happy is the woman who has such a stout-hearted lover as that ; while I, poor thing, have got one that trembles at the mere sound of the mill, and even at the hoodwinked face of that mangy ass."

"Never mind," said the old woman. "I will engage to bring you this brisk lad presently, well inclined, and in good courage." Then, having arranged to return in the evening, she went away.

The chaste wife forthwith set about preparing a banquet fit for priests. She filtered choice wine, made fresh savoury ragouts, and furnished out an abundant table. In short, she made ready for her paramour's arrival as for that of some god; for it happened conveniently for her, that her husband supped abroad with his neighbour the fuller. The hour of noon having arrived, I was released from the mill, and let go to feed; but what pleased me most was, not that I had a respite from drudgery, but that having my head uncovered and the free use of my eyes, I could watch all the doings of that wicked woman. At last, when the sun had sunk beneath the ocean to illuminate the inferior zones of the earth, in came the bold gallant alongside of the wicked old hag. He was quite young, with smooth blooming cheeks, and very handsome. The miller's wife received him with all sorts of caresses, and the supper being ready, she made him take his place at the table.

But scarcely had he put his lips to the preparatory potion, taken by way of a whet, when the husband was heard returning much sooner than he had been expected. Thereupon, his exemplary wife, heaping all sorts of curses upon him, and wishing he had broken his legs, hid the pale and trembling youth under a bin for sifting corn which happened to be at hand; then, with a face of perfect composure, she asked her husband why he had so soon quitted the entertainment of his crony, and returned home.

The miller, who seemed greatly distressed, replied, with a sigh: "I hurried away because I could not endure the abominable guilt of his abandoned wife. Good gods! what a faithful, well-conducted matron she seemed, and how infamously she has disgraced herself! I swear by yonder sacred Ceres, that even yet I can hardly believe the evidence of my own eyes against such a woman."

The miller's impudent wife hearing her husband talk thus, and being curious to hear the whole story, pressed him to relate all that had happened; and never ceased importuning him until he yielded, and began to relate to her the disgrace of his neighbour's house, while he yet knew not of his own.

ELEVENTH EPISODE.

THE FULLER'S WIFE.

"THE wife of my old comrade, the fuller," said he, "who appeared a very honest woman, and bore the best character, and seemed to manage her husband's house with great propriety, fell in love with a certain man, and as they saw each other frequently in secret, it happened that when the fuller and I returned from the baths to supper, the pair were then in the very act.

"Startled and confused by our sudden arrival, the woman could do no better on the instant than hide her paramour under a very high wicker cage, hung round with cloths, which were exposed there to the bleaching fumes of sulphur burned beneath them. Having thus concealed him, quite safely as she thought, she came and sat down with us to supper. Meanwhile, the young man was obliged to breathe the suffocating vapour of the sulphur; and, according to the usual effect of that acrid and penetrating mineral, he was forced to sneeze repeatedly. The husband, who was opposite his wife at table, hearing the sound that came from behind her, thought it was herself that sneezed, and said, 'Jove save you!' as usual on such occasions. This happened a second, a third, and many more times in succession; till at last, surprised at these endless sneezings, he began to suspect the real state of the case, and pushing aside the table, he upset the cage, and discovered the man, who lay panting for breath, and almost suffocated.

"Transported with rage at the outrage done him, he shouted for his sword, and would have cut the throat of the half-dead wretch, had I not, with great difficulty, restrained him from an act which would have been perilous to us all, by assuring him that his enemy would soon die from the effect of the sulphurous fumes, without our making ourselves guilty of his death. Yielding not so much to my persuasions as to the necessity of the case, he dragged the half-lifeless young man into the next lane; and then I pressed his wife, and at last prevailed upon her, to quit the house and take refuge with some of her friends, until time should have somewhat cooled her husband's boiling rage; for I made no doubt but that, in the furious exasperation he then exhibited, he would proceed to some desperate extremity against her and himself too. I had now had more than enough of my friend's entertainment, and so I returned home."

END OF THE ELEVENTH EPISODE.

Whilst the miller was telling this story, his wife, with unparalleled effrontery, broke out from time to time with invectives and curses upon the fuller's wife, calling her a perfidious wretch, a shameless strumpet, an opprobrium to her whole sex, to fling aside all sense of honour and decency; to trample on the obligations of the marriage-bed; to turn her husband's house into an infamous brothel; to have abandoned the dignity of a married woman, and earned for herself the name of a prostitute. Such women, she said, ought to be burnt alive.

Conscious, however, of her own secret guilt, she pressed her husband to go to bed early, that she might the sooner relieve her gallant from the misery of his confinement; but the miller having been disappointed of his supper at the fuller's, and having returned home hungry, requested her to have the table laid. She quickly served him up, but with anything but good will, the supper she had provided for another. Meanwhile, my very entrails were racked when I thought of the late doings and present effrontery of that abominable woman; and I pondered anxiously in my mind whether I could not find some means of doing a service to my master by disclosing her treachery; and whether I could not expose the young fellow to the eyes of every body, by upsetting the bin under which he was squatting like a tortoise.

Whilst I was thus distracted by the thought of the outrage done my master, the providence of the gods came to my aid. For a lame old man, who had charge of the horses and other beasts of burthen, seeing it was the time to give us water, came to drive us all to the next pond. This afforded me a most favourable opportunity for vengeance. I noticed, as I passed, that the young gallant's fingers projected beyond the edge of the bin, and pressing the point of my hoof on them I squeezed them flat, so that yelling with the intolerable pain, and throwing off his cover, he stood manifest to every eye, and unmasked the falsehood of that libidinous woman.

The miller did not seem greatly shocked by the disclosure of his wife's debauchery, but began with a mild and quiet countenance to reassure the lad, who trembled all over, and was pale as death. "Don't be afraid, my boy," he said; "I am not a barbarian, or a man of rough and savage ways. I will not smoke you to death with sulphur; nor will I put such a pretty boy as you into the hands of justice, to suffer the severe penalties of the law against adultery. But I will come to an arrangement with my wife, not, however, for a division of property; no, I will rather make a partnership affair of it, so that, without any dispute or disagreement, we three may make ourselves comfortable in one bed. I have always lived with my wife on such harmonious terms, that, as became discreet people, what the one liked the other liked also. But common justice demands that the wife should not have more authority than the husband."

After quietly joking in this way, he made the unwilling youth go with him to his chamber, and shutting out his modest wife, he exacted what he thought a pleasant sort of vengeance for the wrong done to his bed. But when the sun had risen next morning, he called for two of the strongest of his workpeople, who hoisted the lad, while the miller himself flogged his buttocks with a rod. "What!" said he, "you, who are so soft and tender, a mere boy, you hanker after women, do you? And nothing will suit you but women of free condition, that have got husbands; you have such a precocious longing for the reputation of an adulterer." After reprimanding him in this sort of way, and giving him a right good flogging, he thrust him out of doors. And thus did that most enterprising of all gallants escape far better than he had hoped for, but in woful plight and with aching buttocks.

The baker, moreover, divorced his wife, and made her quit his house forthwith. Thereupon the woman's natural malignity being exasperated by this affront, however well deserved, she had recourse to her familiar weapons, and to the customary devices of women. She sought out with diligence a certain nefarious woman, who was believed to be able to do whatever she pleased by means of her enchantments and drugs; her she loaded with presents, and importunately besought her to do one of two things: either to soften the heart of her husband, that he might be reconciled to her; or if that could not be done, to send at least some ghost, or some dire demoniacal power, to take away his life by violent means. Upon this, the witch, who was capable of exercising an influence upon the gods, employed at first only the milder resources of her wicked art, and endeavoured to influence the feelings of the husband that had been so seriously offended, and lead them back to their former affection. When, however, the result turned out to be quite different from what she had anticipated, being incensed with the gods, for the contempt with which they had treated her, as well as by the loss of the gain which was to have been hers, if she succeeded, she now began to level her attacks against the life of the unfortunate husband, and to stimulate to his destruction the ghost of a certain woman, who had met with a violent death.

Perhaps, however, O scrupulous reader, you will carp at my story, and will reason as follows: "How is it possible, you silly ass, that you could know, as you say you did, what was done by women in secret, when at the very moment you were pent up within a bakehouse?" Hear, then, how I, an inquisitive man, wearing the shape of a beast of burden, came to know all that was transacted with a view to the destruction of my master, the baker.

About midday there suddenly appeared in the bakehouse a

woman of a hideous aspect, marked by guilt and extreme sorrow; she was half clad in a patched mourning mantle, her feet were naked, and her haggard face was sallow as boxwood. Her grizzly, dishevelled hair, defiled with ashes, hung over her forehead, and concealed the greater part of her face. This strange-looking woman, taking the baker gently by the hand, led him aside into his chamber, as if she had something to say to him in secret, and having shut the door, remained there a very long time.

However, when all the wheat was ground which had been delivered out to the workmen, and it became necessary to get more, the servants went to the door of the chamber, and calling to their master, asked for more wheat for the mill. But as no master answered them, though they shouted to him again and again, they began to knock more loudly at the door. Finding, too, that it had been carefully bolted, they suspected something tragical had occurred, and making a violent effort, they tore the door off the hinges, and rushed in. The woman, however, was no where to be found, but they saw their master hanging lifeless from a beam. Loosening the rope from his neck, they took him down, and with great lamentations and weeping, bestowed upon the corpse the last ablution. Finally, having performed the customary offices for the dead, they committed him to the tomb, a great crowd attending the funeral.

On the following day, his daughter came running from the neighbouring village, where she had lately been married, full of sorrow, shaking her dishevelled hair, and ever and anon beating her breasts with her hands. For she had discovered all that happened, although no one living had related to her the misfortune that had befallen the family; but the piteous form of her father had presented itself to her in her sleep, his neck still bound with the halter, and disclosed to her all the wickedness of her stepmother, her infidelity, the enchantment, and how he had been strangled by a ghost, and had descended to the realms below. After she had given way to long-continued lamentations, at last, being prevailed upon by the united entreaties of her friends and acquaintances, she put an end to her wailings. And now, the funeral solemnities being in the usual manner completed at the tomb, on the ninth day, she had the slaves, the furniture, and all the beasts of burden, brought forth to be sold by auction, for the benefit of

the heiress.   Then did capricious fortune, by the chance results
of a sale, disperse in various ways the property of one house.

A poor gardener made purchase of me for fifty pieces of
money, which he said was a great price; but he paid it in order
that he might procure subsistence for himself by our common
labour.   The occasion appears to me to require that I shoul l
explain the nature of these services of mine.   Every morning,
my master was in the habit of leading me to the next city,
with a heavy load of vegetables; and after he had sold them
to the general dealers there, he returned to his garden, sitting
on my back.   Then, while he was digging and watering, and
was busied with other laborious employments, I was left to
take my ease, and refresh myself with silence and rest.   But,
lo! the revolving year had now, after the autumn delights of
the vintage, descended to the wintry frosts of Capricorn;*
and then I was perished with continual cold, through the
constant rains and the nightly dews, being exposed to the open
air in a stable without a roof.   For my master, in consequence
of his extreme poverty, could not purchase even for himself,
much less for me, any straw, or bed-clothes, his only protec-
tion from the cold being the thatch of his little cottage.
Besides this, in the morning I had to endure great fatigue,
in walking with unshod feet on clay that was quite frozen,
and pieces of very sharp ice; and I never even got a bellyful
of food.   For both my master and myself had meals alike in
quality and quantity, and very meagre they were; since they
consisted of old and unsavoury lettuces, which had run to seed,
looked just like so many brooms, and were full of a clammy,
bitter juice, that smelt disgustingly.

One night, a householder who lived in the next village,
having lost his way through the darkness of a moonless night,
and got drenched to the skin with rain, turned with his wea-
ried horse into our garden; and being as courteously received
as circumstances would allow of, and being invited to take
there a night's repose, which, if not surrounded by many re-
finements, was at all events very welcome, he desired to make a
present to his hospitable entertainer, and promised that he
would give him from his farm some corn and oil, and two casks
of wine.   My master therefore proceeded, without delay, to

* *Capricorn.*]—The sun enters the sign Capricorn at the beginning of
winter.

the farm of the householder, which was distant from his garden sixty stadia,* seated on my bare back, and carrying with him a little sack, and some empty wineskins.

The journey accomplished, we arrived at the farm, and there the kind host immediately asked my master to partake of a sumptuous entertainment. But while they were drinking jovially, a most astonishing prodigy took place. One of the hens in the poultry-yard, running through the middle of the yard, kept up a continual cackling, as if she wanted to lay. On this her master, looking at her, said, "Notable servant that you are, and remarkably prolific, for this long time you have treated us with your daily productions. And now, too, I see, you are thinking about helping us to a dainty morsel. Boy!" said he, speaking to one of his servants, " get the basket that the hens lay in, and place it in the corner as usual." When the boy had done as he was desired, the hen, refusing to go to her nest as usual, produced before the very feet of her master a premature offspring, and one of a singularly ominous nature. For she did not bring forth an egg, as we usually see hens do, but a chicken, perfectly formed, with feathers and claws, eyes and voice; which immediately began to follow its mother about.

Another prodigy also occurred, of a far more astonishing nature than the former, and at which all men might with great reason be terrified. For, under the very table which held the remnants of the entertainment, the earth opened with a yawning chasm from its inmost depths, and a copious fountain of blood gushed forth; while numerous drops, as they splashed about, sprinkled the table with gore. At that very instant also, while every one was struck with astonishment and dismay at these divine presages, one of the servants came running from the wine cellar, and announced that all the wine, that had long ago been racked off, was boiling up in all the vessels, with a heat as if a large fire had been put under it. In the meantime also, some weasels were observed, outside of the house, dragging into it a dead serpent. Then, too, out of the mouth of the sheep-dog jumped a small green frog; and a ram that stood near him rushing on the same dog, strangled him at a single grip. These numerous portents, and others of like nature, filled the minds of the master of the house and

* *Sixty stadia.*]—Seven miles and a half.

all his family with intense amazement and terror; what was to be done first or what last; what they ought especially to do, and what they ought not to do to appease the anger of the Gods; with how many and what sort of victims they should make atonement, they were quite at a loss to decide.

While all were stupefied with expectation of some dreadful catastrophe, a servant came running in, and announced to the master of the house a great and fearful visitation.

TWELFTH EPISODE.

THE RURAL TYRANT.

THIS good man was the proud father of three sons, now grown up, well educated, and remarkable for their good conduct.

Between these young men and a poor man, the owner of a small cottage, there had been an intimacy of long standing. Now, close adjoining to the humble cottage lay the extensive and fertile domain of a wealthy and powerful young man, who made but bad use of the influence derived from his high birth. As he was powerful from the number of his dependents, and did what he pleased in the city, he behaved in a very unceremonious manner to his poor neighbour, killing his sheep, driving away his oxen, and trampling down his corn before it was ripe. Already he had deprived him of all hopes of a harvest, and now he wanted to expel him from the possession even of his land. To this end, raising a frivolous question about the boundaries of the fields, he laid claim to the whole of the land as his own.

Upon this, the countryman, who was otherwise a mild, harmless man, seeing himself plundered, through the avarice of his rich neighbour, collected together a considerable number of his friends, for the purpose of ascertaining what were the actual boundaries of his land, in order that, at all events, he might keep enough of his paternal land to dig himself a grave. Among others, the three brothers were present, to give such small assistance as best they might, in their friend's extreme need. Still, the mad oppressor was not in the least daunted, or even moved, by the presence of many citizens, and was so far from being disposed to abstain from acts of rapine, that he would not even confine himself to civil language. For, when they mildly expostulated with him, and endeavoured to pacify his boisterous disposition by soothing words, he swore in the most solemn manner by his own life and that of his dearest relatives, that he cared but little for the interference of so many arbitrators; and that, in fact, he would forthwith order his servants to take that neighbour of his by the ears, and drag him far away from his cottage, and banish him altogether.

His words aroused the greatest indignation in the minds of all who heard him; and one of the three brothers answered, without hesitation, and told him plainly, that it was in vain, that trusting to his riches, he made such arrogant threats, since the poor even can obtain redress against the insolence of the wealthy, through the liberal protection of the laws. What oil is to flame, what sulphur is to a conflagration, what the whip is in the Fury's hand, such was the fuel afforded by these words to the furious disposition of this man. Roused to a perfect frenzy, and bidding them all, and their laws too, go and be hanged, he ordered the shepherds' dogs to be let loose, as well as those upon the farm, savage and blood-thirsty creatures, accustomed to prey upon the dead carcases that were thrown into the fields, and to bite and mangle the passing traveller. Accordingly, incited by the well-known hallooing of the shepherds, the dogs rushed upon the men, barking horribly, and tore the flesh off their bones. Nor even when the men fled did they spare them; but pursued them with so much the more ferocity.

In this scene of havoc and slaughter of the confused multitude, the youngest of the three brothers stumbled against a stone, and was thrown to the ground, where he was devoured by those ferocious dogs. The moment his brothers recognized his dying shrieks, they ran to help him, and wrapping their cloaks around their left hands, used every effort to protect their brother, and to drive off the dogs, by volleys of stones. But they were unable to quell their ferocity; and the unfortunate youth was torn in pieces, and died, entreating with his breath, that they would avenge the death of their youngest brother on that most villanous purse-proud man. Then the two remaining surviving brothers, not, by Hercules, so much despairing of, as spontaneously disregarding their own safety, made an attack upon the rich man, and with furious impetuosity hurled a shower of stones against him. Then the blood-thirsty wretch, who, before this, had been trained by practice in many similar deeds of outrage, hurled a lance, and pierced one of the two brothers through the middle of the breast. And yet, though mortally wounded, the young man did not fall to the ground. For the lance, which had pierced him, and the greater part of which had come out at his back, was by the force of the blow fixed in the earth, and kept his body suspended by the firmness of the handle, as it stood quivering in the ground. In addition to this, one of the assassin's servants, a tall robust fellow, violently hurled a stone from a distance, and tried to hit the third brother on the right arm; but the stone, passing just by the tips of his fingers, and so expending its force in vain, fell to the ground without inflicting any injury, contrary to the expectation of all who were present. Now as the youth was endowed with singular presence of mind, this fortunate circumstance afforded him some hope of revenge. For, pretending that his hand was disabled, he thus addressed his most savage antagonist :— "Exult in the destruction of our whole family, glut your insatiable vengeance with the blood of three brothers, and complete your glorious triumph over your prostrate fellow-citizens; only remember, that after you have deprived this poor man of his lands, extend and extend as you may, you will still always have some neighbour or other. But this right hand of mine, which should undoubtedly have struck off your head, hangs powerless, smitten by the iniquitous decree of fate." The furious cutthroat, exasperated by these words, seizing a sword, rushed eagerly on the wretched youth, with the intention of slaying him with his own hand. However, he had provoked one who was not inferior to himself. For the youth, quite contrary to his anticipation, seized hold of his right hand with a most powerful grasp; and then brandishing his sword, with repeated blows dismissed the impure soul of the rich man from his body; and lastly, to free himself from the hands of the attendants who were running to give assistance, he cut his own throat with the sword that was still reeking with the blood of his enemy.

END OF THE TWELFTH EPISODE.

These were the events which the astounding prodigies had
foreshown; and these were the events which were related to
the most unfortunate master.   The old man, overwhelmed by
so many misfortunes, could not so much as utter a single word,
or even shed a tear, but seizing the knife with which he had
just before been helping his guests to cheese and other viands,
he pierced his own throat with numerous gashes, thus following
the example of his most unhappy son; so that falling with his
face on the table, he washed away, with a river of flowing
blood, the stains of that portentous gore which had before
fallen upon it.   The gardener, commiserating the fate of this
house, which had thus come to destruction in the shortest space
of time, and deploring his own mischance, made a return for
his meal with his tears, and ever and anon clasping together
his empty hands, immediately mounted on my back, and re-
turned the way we came.

His return, however, was by no means free from accident.
For a certain tall fellow, who was a soldier belonging to one
of the legions,* as his dress and appearance seemed to indicate,
met us on the road, and asked the gardener, in a haughty and
insolent tone, whither he was leading that unladen ass?   My
master, who was still full of grief, and was ignorant, besides,
of the Latin language, passed on without making any reply.
Upon this, the soldier could not control the insolence that was
so natural to him; but considering his silence as a mark of
contempt, thrust him from my back, at the same time striking
him with a vine-stick,† which he carried in his hand.   The
gardener humbly declared that he did not understand what the
soldier said, being ignorant of the language in which he spoke.
The soldier, therefore, demanded in Greek, "Whither are you
leading that ass?"   The gardener replied, that he was going
to the next town.   "But I am in want of it," said the soldier;

* *One of the legions.*]—The Roman armies were composed of two
orders of soldiers, legionaries and auxiliaries; the former were properly
Romans, the latter were drawn from nations allied to Rome.   The legion-
aries were treated with much more consideration than the auxiliaries.

† *A vine-stick.*]—This shows either that the soldier was a centurion
or that he assumed that rank to impose on the peasant; for it was pecu-
liar to the centurions to carry vines, with which they chastised the soldiers
under their command.   Hence, in Latin, a vine is metonymically used by
poets for the office of a centurion.

"it must help, with other beasts, to carry from the neighbouring village the baggage of our commanding officer." With that, laying hold of the rope by which I was led along, he began to pull me away. The gardener, however, wiping away the blood that trickled down his face from the blow he had just received, again entreated the soldier to act more civilly and humanely, and supplicated him to do so, by all his hopes of future good fortune. "This ass," said he, "is very lazy, and then besides, he has that abominable complaint, the falling sickness; it is as much as he can do to carry a few bundles of vegetables from my garden close by; it quite blows him; so he is not a likely beast for the carriage of larger burdens."

When, however, he found that the soldier could not be softened by entreaties, but was still more and more savagely bent on plundering him, and that now he had shifted his hold of the vine-stick, and was preparing to fracture his skull with the large knob at the end, he had recourse to his last chance. Feigning that he would embrace the soldier, in order to excite his compassion, he bent down, and pulling both legs from under him, dashed him violently to the ground; then instantly throwing himself upon his sprawling antagonist, he bit him, and thumped him, and jobbed him all over, face, arms, and ribs, with his fists, his elbows, and with a stone which he picked up in the road. As for the soldier, he could neither resist nor at all defend himself, from the very moment that he was laid prostrate on the ground; but could only threaten from time to time that the moment he got up he would cut him to pieces with his sword. The gardener, taking warning by this hint, snatched the sword from his side, and throwing it far away, again pummelled him harder than ever, so that the soldier, stretched on his back and disabled with wounds and bruises, had to counterfeit death, as the only means of saving his life. The gardener, then taking the sword away with him, mounted my back, and made off at my utmost speed straight towards the town; and, not caring to visit his own garden, at all events for the present, he directed his steps towards the house of an intimate friend of his. After relating all the circumstances, he begged and entreated his friend to stand by him in his present dangerous position, and to conceal him and his ass there for a short time, so that by keeping out of the way two or three days, he might escape the penalty of the capital offence he had committed. This man, not being forgetful of their former friendship, he readily received him, and having dragged me with my legs tied together up stairs into an attic, the gardener crept into a chest that was in the warehouse below, and covering himself with the lid, there lay concealed.

Meanwhile the soldier, as I afterwards learned, like one recovering from a violent fit of intoxication, made his way to the town, staggering and tottering, sore with the pain of so many wounds, and with difficulty supporting himself on his stick. Ashamed to mention to any of the citizens the particulars of his own violence and his ignominious defeat, he silently digested the affront he had received, until meeting at last with some of his fellow-soldiers, he told them of his misfortune. They were of opinion, that he should conceal himself for some time in the barracks; (for, besides the disgrace to himself, he feared also the military oath sworn by the Genius,* on account of the loss of his sword), while they, noting down the description he gave of us, would make the most zealous endeavours for our discovery, and the gratification of their own vengeance. Nor was a perfidious neighbour wanting to tell them very speedily where we were concealed.

Thereupon, the soldier's comrades applied to the magistrates, and falsely asserted that they had lost on the road a silver cup of considerable value, that belonged to their commanding officer, and that a certain gardener had found it, and would not give it up, but was now lying concealed in the house of a friend. The magistrates, on being made acquainted with the loss, and the name of the commanding officer, came to the door of our dwelling, and with a loud voice, gave notice to our host that it would be better for him to deliver us up, who were beyond a doubt concealed in his premises, than to render himself liable to capital punishment. But our friend, not being in the least daunted, and resolute to save the guest

---

* *Military oath sworn by the Genius.*]—*i. e.* The Genius of the emperor, by whom the Roman soldiers solemnly swore never to desert, &c. This oath they deemed more sacred, as Tertullian remarks, than if they had sworn by all the gods put together. The loss of the sword, the buckler, or any other of their principal accoutrements, was punished as equivalent to desertion.

he had taken under his protection, declared that he knew no-
thing about us, and that he had not seen that gardener for
several days.   On the other hand, the soldiers, swearing by
the Genius of the emperor, maintained that he was concealed
there, and nowhere else.

At length the magistrates were determined, by making a
strict search, to confute him in this his obstinate denial.   Ac-
cordingly, sending the lictors and other public officers into the
house, they ordered them carefully to search every hole and
corner.   But, after all their search, the officers reported that
no human being, nor yet any ass, was to be found within the
threshold.   The dispute now grew very warm on both sides;
the soldiers swore by Cæsar that they knew for certain we were
there, while the master of the house swore as stoutly by all
the gods in denial of the assertion.   On hearing this conten-
tion and clamour, I, who was in general an ass of an inqui-
sitive and restless disposition, stretched my neck out of a little
window, and tried to see what all the noise was about; but
one of the soldiers, by chance turning his eyes in the direction
of my shadow, instantly called out to all of them to observe it;
whereupon they instantly raised a loud shout, and rushing up
the steps, some of them seized hold of me, and led me prisoner
from my place of concealment.   And now, without more de-
lay, they narrowly examined every corner, and opening the
chest, they found the wretched gardener, dragged him out, and
carried him before the magistrates, and finally to the public
gaol, in order that he might suffer capital punishment.   Nor
could they ever have done joking and laughing at the notion
of my looking out of the window.   From this circumstance,
also, the well-known proverb originated, about the peeping
ass and his shadow.[*]

* *Peeping ass and his shadow.*]—This proverb, which Apuleius jocu-
larly says originated from the above-mentioned circumstance, is of much
greater antiquity.   Lucian has only ἐξ ὀνοῦ παρακυψεὼς, *from the peep-
ing of an ass.*   There is also another Greek proverb, mentioned by Me-
nander, Plato, and many others, ὑπὲρ ὀνοῦ σκιᾶς, *concerning the shadow
of an ass*, which is said of those who are anxious to know things futile,
frivolous, and entirely useless.   These two proverbs Apuleius has mingled
into one.

BOOK THE TENTH.

LUCIUS DEPARTS WITH HIS NEW MASTER, THE SOLDIER — THIR-
TEENTH EPISODE : THE WICKED STEPMOTHER—LUCIUS SOLD TO
TWO BROTHERS, COOK AND CONFECTIONER TO A MAN OF HIGH
STATION — DEPREDATIONS OF LUCIUS IN THE LARDER — HIS
FONDNESS FOR HUMAN FOOD DISCOVERED—HIS BEHAVIOUR AT
THE SUPPER-TABLE OF THE GREAT MAN WHO BUYS HIM—LUCIUS
IS PAMPERED AND PETTED, AND EXCITES PUBLIC CURIOSITY
AND ADMIRATION—CARRIES HIS MASTER TO CORINTH—A LADY
OF QUALITY FALLS IN LOVE WITH HIM—HIS MASTER PROPOSES
TO MAKE LUCIUS PERFORM STRANGE THINGS IN THE AMPHI-
THEATRE—FOURTEENTH EPISODE : HISTORY OF A WOMAN CON-
DEMNED TO BE THROWN TO WILD BEASTS—DRAMATIC EXHIBITION
IN THE AMPHITHEATRE—LUCIUS MAKES HIS ESCAPE, AND GAL-
LOPS TO CENCHREÆ.

WHAT became of my master, the gardener, on the following day, I know not. But the soldier, who had been so hand-somely thrashed for his overbearing conduct, untied me from my manger and took me away, there being no one to hinder him. Then going to his barracks, as it appeared to me, he led me into the public road, laden with his baggage, and equipped quite in military style. For he put on my back a glittering helmet, of remarkable brightness, a shield still more splendid, and a long gleaming lance. The latter he took care to place conspicuously on the top of the pole, which he had arranged in the form of a trophy, not so much in compliance with the regu-lations, as for the purpose of terrifying unfortunate travellers. Having passed over a level country by an easy road, we came to a little town, but we did not put up at an inn, but at the house of a certain decurion. After having delivered me to the care of a servant, the soldier repaired without delay to the presence of his officer, who had the command of a thousand men.

I remember that a few days after our arrival, a most wicked and dreadful crime was perpetrated in that town. I will re-cord it in my book, that you also may read it.

o 2

THIRTEENTH EPISODE.

THE WICKED STEPMOTHER.

THE master of the house had a son, a young man of great literary attainments, and consequently remarkable for his piety and modesty; so that any one would have wished to have just such a son. The mother of this young man having been dead many years, his father contracted a second marriage, and his second wife had borne him another son, who had now just passed his twelfth year. But the stepmother, who held supreme sway in her husband's house, rather in consequence of her good looks than her good morals, regarded her stepson with lustful eyes, whether it was that she was naturally vicious, or was impelled by Fate to such extreme criminality. Know, therefore, excellent reader, that you are about to peruse a tragic, and not a comic tale, and that you will have to ascend from the sock* to the buskin.

Now as long as the little Cupid was in its infancy, this woman easily repressed her rising blushes, and concealed them in silence. But when love, raging without control, wrapped her whole soul in flame, she then succumbed to the cruel God; and, feigning illness, concealed the disease of the mind under the pretence of bodily ailment. Now every one knows that all the morbid changes in the bodily condition and appearance are quite alike in those who are sick and those who are in love; such, for instance, as an unsightly paleness, languor of the eyes, restless sleep, and sighs the more deep from the slowness of the torment. You might have supposed that she was only afflicted by fitful attacks of fever, had it not been that she wept. Alas! for the unskilful impressions of her doctors! what meant the hurried pulse, the sudden flush, the oppressed respiration, the frequent tossings and turnings from side to side. Good Gods! how easy is it even for one who is no doctor, but is acquainted with the symptoms of love and passion, to comprehend the true nature of the case, when he sees a person burning without bodily heat?

Unable any longer to control her raging passion, she at length broke her long silence, and sent for her son to be called to her, a name she wished he had never borne or might bear no more,

---

* *The sock, &c.*]—*i. e.* From comedy to tragedy; the sock was worn by actors in comedy, the buskin in tragedy.

that she might not, by using it, be reminded of her shame. The young man obeyed without delay the command of his love-sick parent, and with a forehead wrinkled with sorrow, like that of an old man, he went into the chamber of her who was the wife of his father and the mother of his brother, paying that obedience to her which, to a certain degree, was her due. As for her, fast aground, as it were, upon the shoals of doubt, and long unable to break a silence that tortured her, she again rejects every word which she had at first conceived to be most adapted to the present interview, and even still in a state of indecision, through shame, she cannot tell how to begin. The young man, however, suspecting nothing wrong, with a downcast countenance, spontaneously asked her what was the cause of her present malady. Upon this, availing herself of the pernicious opportunity afforded her, she took courage to falter out these few words, while she wept profusely, and hid her face with her garment:

"You yourself are the sole cause and origin of my malady, and you are the remedy too, and the only chance of life now left me. For those eyes of yours, penetrating through my own into the inmost core of my heart, have kindled there a most vehement fire. Take pity, therefore, on me, who am perishing for your sake; and let no scruples on your father's account have the least weight with you, for, by complying with my wishes, you will preserve for him a wife, who is otherwise doomed to die. It is with reason that I love you, since in your face I recognize his features. We are alone; you have nothing to fear; you have full opportunity for this act, so necessary to my existence—a thing that no one knows."

The young man being in utter confusion at this unexpected misfortune, although he recoiled from the mere thought of such an abominable deed, yet did not think it right to exasperate her by too abrupt a refusal of a denial, but rather that he ought to appease her by a delusive promise. He promised, therefore, without reserve, and earnestly persuaded her to keep up her spirits, restore her strength by nutriment, and pay attention to her health, till his father should go on some journey or other, and leave them free to enjoy their pleasures. He then withdrew from the baneful presence of his stepmother, and conceiving likewise that this calamity with which his house was threatened called for the deepest consideration, he immediately related the affair to an aged man of well-tried prudence, who had been his tutor. After long deliberation, nothing seemed to be so advisable as to escape this storm, let loose by adverse fortune, by instant flight.

The woman, however, impatient at even the smallest delay, invented some pretext or other, and found means cunningly to persuade her husband to take a journey, with all speed, to some small farms of his, which were situate at a very considerable distance. This being done, in a state of frantic eagerness for the fulfilment of her hopes, she solicited her stepson to perform his promise. The young man, however, now pretending this thing, now that, as an excuse, avoids her execrable presence, till at last, clearly perceiving, from the varying nature of his messages, that he refused to fulfil his promise, her nefarious love became suddenly changed into hatred far more intense. Immediately summoning a most villanous slave of hers, who had formed a portion of the dowry she brought her husband, and who was ready for the perpetration of any crime, she communicated to him her perfidious designs, and there was no course that seemed to them preferable to depriving the unfortunate youth of life. Accordingly, this villain was sent immediately to buy a poison of the most deadly quality, and, having carefully mixed it in wine, she prepared it for the destruction of her guiltless son-in-law.

As it so happened, while the wicked pair were deliberating about a suitable opportunity for giving him the poison, the younger boy, this most abandoned woman's own son, returning home after his morning studies, and feeling thirsty from his breakfast, found the cup of wine which contained the poison, and swallowed at a draught the contents; but no sooner had he drunk the deadly potion which had been prepared for his brother, than he fell lifeless on the ground. His tutor, horrified at his sudden death, alarmed the mother and the whole family with his cries. And now, when the cause was ascertained to have been the noxious draught, opinions varied as to who were the authors of the crime. But this wicked woman, a singular specimen of a stepmother's malice, not at all moved by the shocking death of her son, nor by the consciousness of having murdered him, nor by the misfortune of her house, nor by the grief her husband would feel for the loss of his son, seized upon the destruction of her own offspring as a ready means of vengeance. She immediately sent a messenger to inform her husband, who was on his journey, of the calamity which had befallen his house; and when he returned home with all possible haste, she, with enormous effrontery, pretended that her son had been destroyed by poison, administered to him by her stepson. And in this she did not altogether speak falsely, because the boy really had met with the death which had been intended for the young man. She, however, pretended that the younger brother had been put an end to through the wickedness of her stepson, because she would not comply with the licentious proposals the latter had made to her. Nor was she contented with lies of such enormity, but even added, that he had likewise threatened her with a sword, in consequence of her detection of his wickedness.

Grievously was the unhappy man afflicted at the death of both his sons; for he saw his younger son buried before his face, and he knew that his other son would certainly be condemned to death for incest and fratricide; and then, besides, he was impelled to extreme hatred of this son by the feigned lamentations of a wife whom he held too dear. No sooner, therefore, had the funeral rites of the unfortunate boy been arranged, than the unhappy old man hastened straight from the pile to the forum, with the tears still wet upon his cheeks, and tearing his white hairs, begrimed with ashes; and there, giving loose to his passionate feelings, he used every endeavour to procure the destruction of his remaining son, by tears and by entreaties, even embracing the very knees of the decurions; and never imagining the treachery of his most infamous wife, he exclaimed that his son was an incestuous wretch, who had attempted to violate his father's bed; that he was a fratricide, and had threatened to kill his stepmother. In fine, by his lamentations, he aroused not only the senate but the people, to such a degree of pity and indignation, that, impatient of the tedious formality of a judicial process, and waiving incontestable proofs in support of the accusation, and the studied subterfuges of pleaders, they shouted out with one consent, that a public crime ought to be punished by the public, and that the author of it ought to be stoned to death. In the meantime, the magistrates, apprehensive, on their own account, lest the growing excitement should lead to results destructive of all order and of the civic weal, began, partly by expostulating

with the decurions, and partly by soothing the feelings of the
public, to induce them that the trial might proceed in due
order, and in conformity with the customs of their ancestors,
the allegations on both sides being duly weighed, and the sen-
tence pronounced in a legal manner.   They added, that no one
ought to be condemned without a hearing, after the manner of
fierce barbarians or lawless tyrants, since, by so doing, they
would leave, in those times of profound peace, a dreadful pre-
cedent for posterity.

This sound advice prevailed; and immediately the crier
proclaimed aloud that the senators were to assemble in the
senate-house.   These having immediately taken their accus-
tomed places, according to their rank and dignity, the crier
again made proclamation aloud, and the accuser first came
forward; then the prisoner was called and brought into
court, and, lastly, the crier, in conformity with the law of
Athens and the process of the Areopagus, announced to the
advocates on both sides that they were to plead without pre-
amble, and to avoid all appeals for the purpose of exciting com-
miseration.   That this was the manner of proceeding I learned
from overhearing the remarks of many people, as they were
talking with one another.   But as I was not present at the
trial, but tied up to a manger, I shall only commit here to
writing what I ascertained to be exactly the truth.

As soon as the harangues of the orators were concluded, the
senators determined that the truth of the charges should be
established by certain proofs, and that a question of such great
consequence should not be left to suspicion and conjecture.
They, likewise, thought it requisite that the servant, who was
said to be the only person who knew the facts of the case,
should be brought forward.   Nor was that candidate for the
gallows in the least dismayed, either by the doubtful result of
so serious an investigation, or by the view of the thronged
senate house, or even by his own guilty conscience, but began
to state and affirm as true a number of things which he him-
self had invented.   He said, that the young man, being indig-
nant at the repulse received from his step-mother, had sum-
moned him; that, in order to avenge the affront, he had or-
dered him to destroy her son; that he had promised him a
great reward to ensure his secrecy; that on his refusal to do
what he wished, he had threatened to put him to death; that

he had delivered to him the poison mixed with his own hand,
to be given to his brother; and that the young man, suspecting
he had forborne to administer the potion, and had reserved it,
to produce as evidence of the crime, at last gave it to the boy
with his own hand."

When this villanous knave had, with an affected agitation,
uttered these egregious lies, which bore a most plausible re-
semblance to truth, the trial was brought to a conclusion, and
not one was there among the senators so favourably disposed
towards the young man, as not to pronounce him clearly guilty,
and condemn him to be sewed up in the leathern sack.   The
verdicts, in which they all agreed, were about to be com-
mitted to writing, according to custom, and to be placed in
the brazen urn; after which, the die being cast, no change
could lawfully be made, but the life of the criminal was placed
in the hands of the executioner.   Just then, an aged physician,
a member of the senate, and a person of approved integrity,
and of remarkable influence, covering with his hand the mouth
of the urn, that no one might rashly put his billet into it, thus
addressed the court:

"I rejoice that, long as I have lived, I have ever enjoyed
your approbation; and I will not suffer a manifest act of homi-
cide to be perpetrated, by condemning a man to death on a
false accusation; nor you to violate your oath, as judges, for
the lying testimony of a slave.   I myself will not cheat my
own conscience, and trample on the reverence which is due to
the gods, by pronouncing an unjust sentence.   Learn, there-
fore, from me, the real circumstances of the case.   This vil-
lanous fellow came to me some time ago, and offered me a
hundred golden solidi for a prompt and deadly poison, telling
me he wanted it for a person who, being grievously afflicted
with an incurable disease, wished to rid himself from the tor-
ment of life.   Noticing the confusion and incoherence of the
rascal's story, and feeling sure that he was about to perpetrate
some crime, I certainly gave him the potion, but as a precaution,
in case the affair should be looked into at some future time, I
did not immediately take the money that was agreed upon,
but said to him, 'Lest by chance any of these golden coins
which you offer me should be found to be light or spurious,
put them in this bag, and seal it with your own seal, till they
are to-morrow examined in the presence of a money-changer.'

He complied, and sealed up the money; as soon, therefore, as he was brought into court to give evidence, I ordered one of my servants to go with all haste and fetch the bag from my shop, and here I now produce it before you. Let him look at it, and examine the impression of his own seal. Now how can the brother be accused of having procured the poison which this fellow bought?"

On the instant, a violent fit of trembling seized the villain; his natural hue gave place to a deadly paleness; and a cold perspiration suffused all his limbs. He began to shift about his feet with irregular movements; to scratch now this, now that side of his head; and, with his mouth half open, stammering and stuttering, to utter I know not what silly nonsense, insomuch that not a single person could reasonably suppose him to be innocent of the crime. Recovering, however, his craftiness once again, he unceasingly denied the charge, and accused the physician of lying. On this, the physician, independently of his being bound by oath to give a just judgment, when he saw that his honour was openly impeached, made redoubled efforts to confute this villain; till at last the public officers, by order of the magistrates, seizing the slave's hand, found the iron ring, and compared it with the impression on the bag. As the result corroborated the suspicion previously entertained, the rack and the wooden horse were put in operation, according to the Greek custom. Being upheld, however, by a wonderful amount of boldness, he was proof against all blows, and even fire itself.

At last, the physician exclaimed, "I will not suffer, by Hercules! I will not suffer, either that this innocent young man shall receive a punishment at your hands contrary to justice, or that this fellow shall stultify our judgment and escape the punishment due to his crimes. I will give you an evident proof on this matter under consideration. When this most abandoned man was anxious to obtain the deadly poison, I was of opinion that it ill accorded with my art to furnish any one with the means of producing death, being sensible that medicine was sought not for the destruction, but for the preservation of mankind; yet I feared that if I should refuse to give it him, I should thereby prompt him to another method of perpetrating the crime, and that he would accomplish the criminal purpose upon which he had resolved, either by buying a deadly potion

BOOK X.   THE CRUEL STEPMOTHER BANISHED.   203

from some other person, or, at all events, by the sword, or some such weapon ; fearing this, I gave him indeed a drug, but it was a preparation of the soporiferous plant called mandrake, remarkable for the torpor which it is known to occasion, and which produces a sleep exactly resembling death. Nor is it to be wondered at, that this most desperate knave, being certain of undergoing, if convicted, the utmost penalty that can be inflicted on him, conformably to the customs of our ancestors, should be ready to endure these tortures, as being lighter evils. But if the boy has really taken the potion which was mixed by my hands, he is still alive, in a torpid state, and asleep : and immediately his drowsy slumbers are shaken off, he will return to the light of day. But if he is really dead, you may look for some other way of accounting for his decease."

The old man having addressed them to this effect, they assented to what he said ; and immediately proceeded in great haste to the pile on which the body of the boy was laid. Not a member was there of the senate, nor a person of the first rank, who did not run thither, impelled by curiosity. And behold, the father himself, having with his own hands removed the lid of the coffin, found his son rising that moment from the dead, the deathlike sleep shaken off ; and most ardently embracing him, and unable in words to express his present joy, he led him forth into the presence of the people, and the boy was brought into court, just as he was, swathed and bound in the grave-clothes.

And now the naked truth was obvious to every one, the wickedness of the nefarious slave, and of the still more abandoned woman, being clearly exposed. Accordingly, the stepmother was condemned to perpetual banishment, the slave was crucified ; and by the consent of all, the golden solidi were presented to the worthy physician, as a reward for the trance he had produced with such happy results. Thus did the singular and romantic fortune of the old decurion come to a termination worthy of Divine providence ; since, in a passing moment, indeed an instant of time, he suddenly became the father of two young men, after he had been in danger of losing both.

END OF THE THIRTEENTH EPISODE.

As for myself, you shall hear what changes of fortune I experienced at that time.

The soldier who had made me his own without paying for me, being about to carry letters to the great prince at Rome, in obedience to the commands of his tribune, sold me for eleven denars to two brothers, servants of a very wealthy personage in the neighbourhood. One of them was a confectioner, who made bread and sweetmeats; the other was a cook, and dressed rich stews seasoned with the relishing juices of pounded herbs and aromatics. These two, dwelling together and living in common, bought me for the purpose of carrying the numerous vessels which were required for their master's use, when he was travelling through different countries. I was admitted, therefore, as a third companion with these two brothers; and never, at any time, during my transformation, did I experience a fortune so marked with good luck. For, in the evening, after the supper, which was always on a magnificent scale, my masters were in the habit of bringing home to their little room numerous fragments that were left; the one brought ample remains of roast pig, chickens, fish, and delicate dishes of that kind; while the other brought bread, pastry, sugar-plums, hook cakes, lizard cakes, and many kinds of honied sweetmeats. Accordingly, after they had fastened the door of their chamber, and had gone to the baths for the purpose of refreshing themselves, I used to cram myself with the dainties that fell in my way through the favour of the Gods. For I was not so much a fool, nor so truly an ass, as to neglect this most delicious fare, and feed upon coarse hay. My thievish manoeuvres for a long time succeeded most beautifully, because, as yet, I pilfered cautiously and sparingly, only a few articles out of a great number, and they had no suspicion of such tricks being played by an ass. But when, becoming still more fearless of detection, I devoured all the nicest bits, and, rejecting all that was stale, began to lick up the more choice morsels, the brothers were not a little surprized and perplexed. And though even then they did not believe such a thing of me, still they made diligent enquiry as to who was the author of their daily losses. At length, indeed, they even went so far as to accuse each other of this most base act of theft; and they began to keep sharper watch, and to count all they put by.

At length, throwing off all hesitation and reserve, one of them thus addressed the other: "Why, really now, this is neither fair nor like a man, for you every day to be diminishing what has been put by, and to be purloining the choicest parts, and then to go and sell them, so as slily to increase your own stock, and then cry halves of the remainder. If, in fact, you are tired of our partnership, we may still live as brothers in all other respects, and yet give up this partnership concern of ours. For I see that when dissatisfaction at the loss has increased to a very considerable extent, it will create very great discord between us."

To this the other rejoined, "I do, by Hercules! admire this effrontery of yours, after you have secretly been pilfering the articles, to forestall my complaints, which, in silence and sorrow, I have kept to myself, being determined to put up with it as long as ever I could, rather than accuse my brother of shabby theft. But it is well, that having spoken upon the matter on both sides, we are put upon seeking a remedy for our loss, lest our misunderstanding, gathering strength by silence, should produce between us a strife like that of Eteocles and his brother."

Bandying these and similar reproaches against one another, they both of them solemnly declared that they had been guilty of no fraud whatever, nor of the slightest purloining; but agreed, that they ought by every possible contrivance try to discover the thief who was the author of their common loss. It was not possible, they said, that the ass, which was the only being there, could take a fancy to such kind of food: and still, every day the choicest portions were nowhere to be found; and certainly no flies found their way into their room, that were as large as were the harpies of old, who robbed Phineas of his dainties.

In the meantime, I, being bountifully crammed with dainty morsels, and well stuffed with human food, found my body plumped up, my hide softened with rich juices, and my coat grown sleek and shining. But that same comeliness was the cause of a great shock to my feelings. For being roused to suspicion by the uncommon breadth of my back, and perceiving that my hay remained every day quite untouched, they now directed all their attention to me. Accordingly, having shut the door at the accustomed hour as usual, as though they

were going to the bath, they peeped at me through a little
crevice, as I was intent upon eating the fragments which were
exposed in various directions.   And now, forgetting all con-
sideration for their loss, they burst into a violent fit of laughter
at the monstrous epicurism of an ass; and then calling toge-
ther a number of their fellow-servants, they pointed out to
them the incredible appetite of an animal like me.   Then
laughter so loud and so continued seized them all, that the
master, who happened to be passing by, asked what fun was
going on to make his servants laugh so excessively.   Being
told what it was, he came himself and peeped through the
same cranny.   Then he too laughed until his stomach ached,
and opening the door of the room, he came nearer to me, and
observed me very attentively.   But as for me, seeing that for-
tune was inclined to smile more propitiously upon me, I went
on eating quite at my ease, the merriment of those present in-
spiring me with additional confidence; till at last the master
of the house, enchanted by the novelty of the sight, ordered me
to be led to the supper-room; or rather he led me to it with
his own hands; and the table being laid, he directed every
kind of substantial food to be placed before me, and dishes
that had not been tasted.   Now, though I was well stuffed
already, yet desiring to render myself more agreeable, and
more pleasing to him, I ate of the food placed before me as if
I had been quite hungry.   But they, prompted by extreme
curiosity, thinking of every thing which an ass would be most
likely to loathe, offered it to me, for the purpose of testing my
politeness; such as meat seasoned with assafœtida, fowls
sprinkled over with pepper, and fish soused in foreign pickle.
In the meantime, the banquet room resounded with roars of
laughter.

At last, a bit of a buffoon who was present, said, " Give a
little wine to our comrade."   " Well said, rogue," cried the
master; " I dare say our friend would have no objection to a
cup of honied wine."   " Here, lad," said he, " wash well that
golden cup, fill it with honied wine, and offer it to my guest;
and at the same time, tell him that I have drunk his good
health."   All the guests now awaited the result in a state of
intense curiosity; the huge cup was handed to me, and without
more ado, I emptied it at a single draught quite deliberately, and
with a very jovial air, screwing up the extremities of my lips,

in resemblance of a tongue. Then a shout of applause arose, and all, with one accord, drank my health.

In the end, the master, being excessively pleased, after calling the servants who had bought me, ordered that four times the price they had paid for me should be given to them; thereupon he delivered me into the charge of a certain person, a freedman of his, to whom he was much attached, and who was very well off, and desired him to take all possible care of me. This person treated me in a very humane and kind manner; and that he might still more deserve the esteem of his patron, most studiously consulted his amusement by teaching me clever tricks. In the first place, he taught me to recline at table, leaning on my elbow; next, to wrestle and to dance even, raising my fore feet; and—a thing that won especial admiration—to use signs instead of words, so as to indicate what I disapproved of by throwing back, and what I approved of by bowing my head. He also taught me, when I was thirsty, to look towards the cup-bearer, and by winking first one eyelid then another, to show that I wanted something to drink. In all these matters I showed myself very ready and obedient; as I could have done them all, though no one had shown me how. But I was afraid, lest, if I should happen to perform them, in imitation of human beings, without the aid of a master, most people would think that it portended sinister events, and that I, as a monster and prodigy, might have to part with my head, and be given as fat provender to the vultures.

And now my renown was spread abroad in all directions, so that I rendered my master quite famous and illustrious, in consequence of my wonderful accomplishments. " This," said the people, " is the man who has an ass for his guest and companion; an ass that wrestles, an ass that dances, and understands the language of men, and expresses what he means by signs." It is proper, however, that I should now, at all events, inform you, though I ought to have done so in the beginning, who this Thyasus was, and whence he came; for such was the name of my master. The country which gave him birth was Corinth, a city which ranks as the chief of all the province of Achaia. And, as he had gradually attained all the honours which his pedigree and dignity demanded, he had now been nominated to the office of quinquennial magis-

trate.   Accordingly, in order that he might act conformably
to the splendour of that office, he had promised to exhibit a
show of gladiators for the space of three days; thus extending
his liberality to the greatest possible degree.   In fact, it was
his desire of receiving the public applause that had now
brought him to Thessaly, in order to procure from thence the
most noble wild beasts and some celebrated gladiators.

And now, having made all his arrangements and completed
all his purchases quite to his satisfaction, he was preparing to
return home.   Disdaining, however, his own splendid chariots,
which, some covered and some open, were drawn along in the
rear of the cavalcade; regardless also of his Thessalian horses,
and his other beasts of Gallic breed, whose generous pedigree
bore testimony to their rarity and value; despising and neglect-
ing all these, he rode most lovingly on me, who was decked out
with golden trappings, a coloured saddle, purple cloths, a silver
bit, an embroidered girth, and some little bells that tinkled as
I went along, and sometimes he addressed me in the kindest
of words.   Among many other expressions too which he made
use of, he declared how extremely delighted he was at pos-
sessing in me, at one and the same time, a companion and a
bearer.

And now, having finished our journey, partly by land and
partly by sea, we arrived at Corinth, where vast numbers of
the citizens came out to meet us, not so much as it seemed to
me for the purpose of doing honour to Thyasus, as from a
desire of seeing me.   For so great a rumour had pervaded that
city about me, that I was a source of no small emolument to
my keeper.   For perceiving that many were eagerly desirous
to see my pastimes, he had the doors shut, and admitted them
one by one, charging each a good price for admission.   By
this means he managed every day to pick up no small sums.

Among the number of spectators, there was a lady of rank
and fortune, who having purchased a sight of me, was quite
enchanted with my manifold tricks, and at last conceived a
wonderful desire of being more intimate with me.   In short,
her passion grew to such a height, that, like an asinine Pasi-
phäe, she prevailed on my keeper, for a considerable sum of
money, to let her have my company for a single night: and
the good-for-nothing fellow consented, regardless of all con-
siderations save only his own gain.

Jam denique cœnati e tridinio domini decesseramus; et jamdudum præstitantem cubiculo meo matronam offendimus. Dii boni! qualis ille, quamque præclarus apparatus! Quatuor eunuchi confestim, pulvillis compluribus ventose tumentibus plumâ delicatâ, terrestrem nobis cubitum præstruunt; sed et stragulâ veste, auro ac murice Tyrio depicta, probe consternunt; ac desuper, brevibus admodum, set satis copiosis pulvillis, aliis nimis modicis, quibus maxillas et cervices delicatæ mulieres suffulcire consueverunt, superstruunt. Nec dominæ voluptates diutinâ sua præsentiâ morati, clausis cubiculi foribus, facessunt. At intus cerei præclarâ micantes luce, nocturnas nobis tenebras inalbabant.

Tunc ipsa cuncto prorsus spoliata tegmine, tæniâ, quoque, quâ decoras devinxerat papillas, lumen prope assistens, de stanneo vasculo, multo sese perungit oleo balsamo, meque indidem largissime perfricat; sed multo tanto impensius crura etiam natesque perfundit meas. Tunc exosculata pressule, non qualia in lupanari solent basiola jactari, vel meretricum poscinummia vel adventorum negotinummia, sed pura atque sincera instruit, et blandissimós affatus. "Amo, et cupio, et te solum diligo, et, sine te jam vivere nequeo; et cætera quîs mulieres et alios inducunt, et suas testantur affectiones. Capistroque me prehensum, more quo didiceram, declinat facile. Quippe cum nil novi, nihilque difficile facturus mihi viderer; præsertim post tantum temporis, tam formosæ mulieris cupientis amplexus obiturus. Nam et vino pulcherrimo atque copioso memet madefeceram; et unguento fragrantissimo proluvium libidinis suscitaram. Sed angebar plane non exili metu, reputans, quemadmodem tantis, tamque magnis cruribus possem delicatam matronam inscendere; vel tam lucida, tamque tenera, et lacte ac melle confecta membra, duris ungulis complecti: labiasque modicas ambrosio rore purpurantes, tam amplo ore tamque enormi, et saxeis dentibus deformis saviari; novissime, quo pacto quanquam ex unguiculis perpruriscens, mulier tam vastum genitale susciperet. Heu me qui dirupta nobili fæminâ, bestiis objectus, munus instructurus sim mei domini? Molles interdum voculas, et assidua savia, et dulces gannitus, commorsicantibus oculis, iterabat illa. Et in summa, " Teneo te," inquit, " teneo meum palumbulum, meum passerum." Et cum dicto, vanas fuisse cogitationes meas, ineptumque monstrat metum. Arctissime namque complexa totum

P

me, prorsus sed totum recepit.   Illa vero, quotiens ei parcens,
nates recellebam, accedens totiens nisu rabido, et spinam pre-
hendens meam, appliciore nexu inhærebat : ut, Hercules, etiam
deesse mihi aliquid ad supplendum ejus libidinem crederem ;
nec Minotauri matrem, frustra delectatam putarem adultero
mugiente.

And now, the laborious and wakeful night being finished,
the woman, to avoid being seen, withdrew from my embraces
before day-light, at the same time making a contract with my
keeper for some future night, at the same price.   He was
willing enough to gratify her, partly for the large sum he re-
ceived from her, and partly for the opportunity afforded him
of displaying such a novel spectacle to his lord; to whom,
without delay, he unfolded the whole scene of our lust.   There-
upon Thyasus, having liberally rewarded his freed man, des-
tined me to be shown in public.   And, because that egregious
wife of mine could not be publicly connected with me, being
a person of quality, nor any other volunteer could be found for
the same purpose, a certain vile woman, who had been sen-
tenced by the prefect to be devoured by wild beasts, was pro-
cured, for a great sum of money, to have connexion with me
in the theatre, in the sight of all the spectators.   Of this wo-
man I have heard the following history :—

FOURTEENTH EPISODE.

THE JEALOUS WIFE.

She had a husband, whose father, when setting out on a
journey, had given directions to his wife, the young man's
mother, whom he left in a state of pregnancy, that if she
brought forth an infant of the weaker sex, she should imme-
diately have it put to death.   Now she, having brought forth
a girl during her husband's absence, and being moved by the
natural affection of a mother, disobeyed the commands of her
husband, and delivered it to her neighbours to be brought up.
On her husband's return, she informed him that she had been
delivered of a daughter, who had been destroyed.   When now
the bloom of age called for the maiden's nuptial day, as she
could not give her daughter a portion suitable to her parentage,
without the knowledge of her husband, the only way she could

do was to disclose the secret to her son. Besides, she was very much afraid lest he, by some accident, might in the ardour of youth inadvertently make some attempt on the chastity of his sister, who was also ignorant that he was her brother.

The young man, who was remarkable for his affectionate disposition, religiously obeyed the commands of his mother, behaved like a good brother, and kept the family secret so well, that to all appearance he entertained for his sister only an ordinary degree of good will. But he undertook to perform a brother's duties by receiving her into his own house, as if she had been some orphan girl of the neighbourhood, who had been deprived of the guardian care of her parents; and he proposed to marry her, ere long, to a most dear companion of his, with whom he was united by the closest ties of friendship, and to bestow on her most liberally a dowry at his own expense.

But these excellent and innocent arrangements could not escape the deadly malevolence of Fortune, who caused a dire jealousy to spring up in the young man's house, and drove the wife to those crimes for which she was now condemned to be thrown to the wild beasts. She began by suspecting the girl to be a rival, who supplanted her in her husband's affections; then she hated her, and finally she resolved to put her to death in the most inhuman manner.

Accordingly, she had recourse to the following wicked stratagem: having stolen her husband's ring, she went to a farm of theirs in the country, and from there sent a servant, who, though faithful to her, was an utter villain, and told him to inform the girl that the young man had come to the farm and desired to see her, adding, that she was to come alone, with all possible speed. And, lest any doubt might happen to arise in her mind about the propriety of coming, she delivered to him the ring which she had stolen from her husband, to show as a token that his message was authentic. On this, in compliance with the injunctions of her brother, for she was the only one who knew that he was her brother, and having also taken notice of his seal, which was shown to her, she promptly did as she was desired. As soon, however, as, through this most base stratagem, she had fallen into the snares which were prepared for her, the wicked wife, goaded to madness by her jealous fury, stripped the girl naked, and had her flogged until she was nearly dead. It was in vain that the poor girl confessed the truth, which was wrung from her by the lash, and declared that she was wrongfully accused; in vain she cried out again and again that the young man was her brother. Her sister-in-law treated her story as a falsehood, and thrusting a burning brand between her thighs, made her suffer a hideous death.

Immediately upon this, her brother and her husband being informed of her cruel death, hastened to her, and in sore affliction committed her to the tomb. Nor was the young man able patiently to endure the miserable fate of his sister, by the hands of her, too, by whom, least of all, it ought to have been occasioned; but, being racked with grief and choler, he fell into a burning fever, so that he seemed in urgent need of medical aid. On this his wife, who had long since forfeited her claim to that title, went to a certain physician, notorious for his perfidy, who, being famous for his victories in many a mortal struggle, could enumerate the mighty trophies which his right hand had gained. To him she immediately offered fifty thousand sesterces, if he would sell her poison so efficacious as to destroy in an instant, that so she might purchase the death of her husband.

This done, she and the physician pretended that the most excellent potion which they had brought, and which the learned call sacred, was necessary for mitigating pains of the viscera, and carrying off the bile; but, in its stead, was substituted another potion, sacred to the interests of Proserpine.* And now, in the presence of the sick man's household, and some of his relations and friends, the physician, with his own hand, after having well stirred the contents, offered the cup. But that audacious woman, in order that she might at the same moment remove the accomplice in her crime, and save the money which she had promised, held back the cup in the presence of them all, and said, "Most worthy of doctors, you must not give this draught to my dearest husband till you have swallowed a good portion of it yourself. For how am I to know but that there may be some deadly poison in it? And this ought by no means to offend you, who are a man so prudent and so learned, if I, as an affectionate wife, am anxious for

* *Proserpine.*]—The goddess of death.

the safety of my husband, and so perform a necessary act of duty." The physician, quite confounded by the desperate assurance of the bloodthirsty woman, and having no time to think of any subterfuge, could not help drinking largely of the potion, lest he should excite suspicion of his guilt if he showed any hesitation or fear. Then the young man, confidently following his example, took the cup from his hand, and drank what was left.

The matter being for the present finished, the physician was preparing to return home as quickly as possible, in order that he might counteract the deadly effects of the poison he had taken, by a timely antidote. But the barbarous woman, bent on completing her infernal work, would not suffer him to depart from her a hair's breadth till, as she said, the potion should have been digested and its effect determined by actual proof. However, after much importunate entreaty, she at length reluctantly allowed him to go. In the meantime, the virulence of the fatal poison had spread through all his inside, and made havoc in his vitals. Stupified, and in excruciating pain, it was with the utmost difficulty he reached home, where he had barely time to relate what had happened, and give injunctions to his wife, at all events, to demand the promised reward for thus ensuring the death of two persons. Thus cut off by a violent death, did this very celebrated doctor breathe his last.

Nor did the young man live much longer, but perished by the same kind of death, amid the feigned tears of his false wife. After he had been committed to the tomb, and a few days had intervened, during which funeral obsequies were performed for the dead, the widow of the physician came and demanded the money which was due for the double homicide. But the other widow, always consistent with herself, put on a very unreal appearance of good faith, and replied with great suavity, assuring the applicant that she would promptly pay her the stipulated sum, only she wished she would give her a little of the same mixture, for the purpose of completing the business she had begun.

Completely duped by her insidious perfidy, the doctor's widow readily consented to do as she was requested; and that she might ingratiate herself the more with this wealthy woman, she hastened home, and immediately brought her the whole box of poison. Having, therefore, obtained that powerful instrument of crime, the wretch now prepared to indulge her murderous propensities without stint.

She had an infant daughter, by the husband whom she had lately murdered; and she felt extremely galled that the laws would give to this little child the inheritance of her father, as being his next of kin. Coveting the whole patrimony of the daughter, she waited only for an opportunity of depriving her of life. Making sure, therefore, that wicked mothers come in for the reversion of the inheritances of their deceased children, she showed herself to be just such a parent as she had been a wife. Accordingly, preparing a breakfast, she seized her opportunity, and with the same poison destroyed both the widow of the physician and her own daughter. As for the child, the baneful venom instantly stopped her breathing, and consumed her tender life. But as for the doctor's widow, when she felt the virus of the detestable drug creeping through her lungs, she at once suspected the truth; the increasing difficulty of her breathing converted her suspicion into a certainty, and she hastened at once to the house of the governor of the province, clamorous for justice, and declaring she had enormous crimes to reveal. A great concourse of people gathered round her, and the governor immediately gave her a hearing. After she had unfolded to him from first to last all the atrocities of that horrible woman, she was seized with a fit; her mouth, that was open in the act of speaking, closed convulsively; she ground her teeth violently together, and fell dead at the governor's feet. That able and energetic functionary would not allow the manifold crimes of this execrable poisoner to lose their terrors by delay, but immediately ordered her chambermaids to be brought before him, and extracted the truth from them by means of torture. On their deposition he sentenced the culprit to a punishment which was no doubt less than she deserved, but as no other torment could be devised so well adapted to the enormity of her guilt, he ordered that she should be thrown to wild beasts.

END OF THE FOURTEENTH EPISODE.

With such a woman as this it was determined that I should be publicly connected, as if I had been lawfully married to her. It was with extreme anguish, therefore, that I looked forward to the day of the spectacle; being frequently tempted rather to destroy myself with my own hand, than be defiled by contact with such an abandoned woman, or be disgraced by the infamy of such a public spectacle.   But, as I was destitute of human hands and of fingers, I had no means of drawing a sword with my round and stumpy hoof.   However, I consoled myself, as well as I could, in my extreme anguish, with a slender hope; for the spring now beginning to appear, would deck all the country with flowering buds, and clothe the meadows with a purple glow; the roses would burst forth from their thorny cells, exhaling aromatic odours, and these would restore me to my former shape as Lucius.

And now behold, the day destined for the show came; and amid shouts of applause, a long train escorting me, I was led to the amphitheatre.   During the first part of the performance, which was devoted to the joyous choral dances of the players, I was placed outside the gate, and was glad to crop some very fresh grass which grew just at the entrance; while I every now and then delighted my curious eyes with a most agreeable view of the spectacle through the open gate.

Beautiful boys and maidens, in the bloom of youth, splendidly dressed, moved with great elegance of gesture through the graceful evolutions of the Greek Pyrrhic dance.   Now they revolved in a circle; now they deployed into an oblique line, with hands joined; at times they formed a wedge-like figure enclosing an open square; then they parted into two troops, and went through a variety of intricate movements, till they ceased at the sound of the trumpet.   Then the screen was lowered, the hangings were drawn aside, and a dramatic scene was exhibited.

There was a wooden structure formed in imitation of that celebrated mountain, Ida, of which the poet Homer has sung. It was a fabric of considerable height, covered over with turf and with growing trees up to the very top, whence, by the contrivance of the artist, a fountain was made to flow and pour down a stream of water.   A few goats cropped the grass, and a young man, handsomely arrayed in flowing Barbaric vestments, and having his head covered with a golden tiara, in resemblance of Paris, the Phrygian shepherd, appeared to be employed in pastoral pursuits.   A beautiful boy then came forward, his only garment being the mantle generally worn by striplings, which covered his left shoulder. His beautiful yellow hair flowed loosely, and from the midst of it issued a pair of little golden wings; these and the caduceus he carried showed him to be Mercury. He danced forward, holding in his hand a golden apple, which he presented to the performer who personated Paris, made known to him by signs what Jove commanded, and gracefully retired. A girl then made her appearance, of noble features, representing the goddess Juno : for her head was surrounded with a white diadem, and she bore a sceptre in her hand. Another then entered, who was easy to be recognized as Minerva, having on her head a shining helmet, encircled with a wreath of olive. She raised her shield aloft, and brandished her spear, like that goddess when engaged in battle. After these came another female, of surpassing beauty; the loveliness of her divine complexion declared her to be Venus, and Venus such as she was while yet a virgin. Her perfect form was naked, all but some charms imperfectly concealed by a gauze scarf, which the wind played with amorously, sometimes uncovering the beauties beneath it, sometimes pressing it against the limbs, and displaying their delicious contour. The goddess appeared in two different colours; her body was dazzlingly white, because she had descended from the heavens, while her silken garment was azure, because she had emerged from the sea.

The virgins who represented the goddesses were accompanied by their respective attendants : Juno by two young players, representing Castor and Pollux, whose heads were covered with helmets of semi-oval form, graced with a cluster of stars. She advanced with a calm and unaffected air to the warbling of the flute, and promised the shepherd, with modest gestures, that she would bestow on him the empire of all Asia, if he adjudged to her the prize of beauty.

She who personated Minerva was attended by two armed youths, Terror and Fear, who danced before her with drawn swords. Behind her a piper played a martial air, mingling shrill and deep-braying tones, and excited the agility of the dancers as with the blast of the trumpet. With restless head and threatening glances, Pallas bounded forward, and with animated gesture signified to Paris that if he pronounced her victorious in the contest of beauty, she would render him illustrious for his valour, and his achievements in war.

Greeted with vast applause from the spectators, Venus advanced with a sweet smile, and stood still in a graceful attitude in the middle of the stage, surrounded by a throng of merry little boys, such plump, round-limbed, fair-skinned little fellows, you would have sworn they were real Cupids, who had just flown from heaven or from the sea ; for they had little wings, and arrows, and all other accoutrements conformable ; and they carried gleaming torches before their mistress, as if to light her way to a nuptial banquet.   She had also in her train a lovely choir of virgins, the charming Graces and the Hours, who strewed the path of their goddess with loose flowers and bouquets, and propitiated the queen of pleasure with the pleasant offerings of the spring.

Presently the flutes began to breathe soft Lydian airs, that thrilled the audience with delight ; but greater still was their delight, when Venus began to move in concert with the music, and with slow lingering steps, and gentle sinuous flexure of the spine and head, and graceful movements of the arms, to respond to the soft modulations of the flutes ; while now her eyes swam with voluptuous languor, now flashed with the ardour of passion, and sometimes she seemed, as it were, to dance with her eyes alone.   As soon as she had approached close to the judge, she was understood to promise, by the movements of her arms, that if she was preferred to the other goddesses, she would bestow on Paris a wife surpassing all women in beauty, in a word, one like herself.   Gladly, then, did the young Phrygian deliver to her the golden apple he held in his hand, as a token of her victory.

What wonder is it, then, you vilest of people, forensic cattle rather, vultures clad in gowns, if all judges now sell their decisions for a price ?   Even in the early ages of the world, favour was able to corrupt judgment in a question agitated between Gods and men, and a young man, a rustic and a shepherd, elected judge by the counsels of mighty Jupiter, bartered the first judicial decision for the lucre of lust, ensuring thereby the destruction of all his race.   Ay, by Hercules, and another such judgment was given in later times, by the illustrious leaders of the Greeks, when Palamedes, renowned for wisdom and learning, was condemned on false accusations as a traitor ; as also when the mendicant Ulysses was preferred to the mighty Ajax, who excelled in military prowess.   And what sort of judgment was that given by those renowned lawgivers, the Athenians, those clever people, and masters of all the sciences? Was not that divinely wise old man, whom the Delphic god pronounced superior in wisdom to all men, circumvented by the treachery and envy of a most infamous faction, as a declared corrupter of youth, though he restrained their excesses as with a bridle? Was he not cut off by the deadly juice of a pestilential herb, leaving to his fellow-citizens the stain of indelible ignominy? For even at this day the most excellent philosophers make choice of his most holy sect before all others, and swear by his name, in their highest aspirations for consummate happiness.

Lest, however, any one blame this outburst of indignation, and say to himself, Look ye now, are we to suffer an ass to philosophize to us? I shall again return to the point in the narrative from which I digressed. After that judgment of Paris was finished, Juno and Minerva retired from the stage in sorrow and anger, and showed by their gestures the indignation they felt at being rejected; but Venus, full of joy and merriment, testified her gladness by dancing with all her choir. Then wine, mixed with saffron, burst forth on high from the summit of the mountain, through a pipe that lay concealed, and flowing in scattered streams, besprinkled as it fell, with an odoriferous shower, the goats that fed around, and changed their native whiteness for a more beautiful yellow tint. And now, the whole theatre exhaling a sweet odour, a chasm of the earth absorbed the wooden mountain.

One of the soldiers now ran down the street, to fulfil the demands of the people, and bring from the public prison the woman before-mentioned, who, as I have stated, was condemned to the wild beasts, on account of her manifold crimes, and destined to be my illustrious bride. What was intended also to be our genial bed was already prepared. It was brilliantly adorned with the Indian tortoise-shell, swelling with feathery heaps, and decorated with a silken coverlet. As for me, besides the shame of being thus publicly exhibited, and besides the contact of that wicked and polluted woman, I was also in the highest degree tormented with the fear of death; for it struck me that if, while we were performing our prescribed part in the exhibition, any wild beast should be let in on purpose to destroy the woman, it would not be so remarkably well trained or sagacious, or so temperate and abstemious, as to tear the woman to pieces who was at my side, and spare me, as being uncondemned, and guilty of no crime.

Being therefore alarmed, not on grounds of delicacy alone, but on account of my life, while my master was intent on preparing for the representation, and all his servants were partly engaged in getting ready for the spectacle of hunting, and partly in gazing at the grandeur of the show : and as no one thought that so tame an ass required to be so very attentively watched, and I was free to follow my own devices, accordingly little by little I stole away softly and quietly. When I reached the nearest gate, I hurried along at a most rapid pace. And after I had travelled a hot gallop of six miles, I arrived at Cenchreæ; a city which has the reputation of being the most noble colony of the Corinthians, and is washed by the Ægean and Saronic sea. Here, also, there is a port, which is a most safe harbour for ships, and frequented by a vast concourse of people.

Avoiding, therefore, the crowds, and choosing a sequestered spot on the sea-shore, close to the spray of the waves, I stretched my weary body on the soft bosom of the sand. The chariot of the sun had sped onward to the end of its course; and I resigned myself to repose, and was soon wrapped in sweet sleep.

BOOK THE ELEVENTH.

LUCIUS ON THE SEA-SHORE AT NIGHT—HIS PRAYER TO THE GOD-
DESS ISIS—THE GODDESS RESPONDS IN PERSON—PROCESSION OF
THE GODDESS—LUCIUS RECOVERS HIS PROPER SHAPE—ADDRESS
OF THE PRIEST OF ISIS TO LUCIUS—DEDICATION OF A SHIP TO
THE GODDESS—RELIGIOUS CEREMONY IN THE TEMPLE—LUCIUS
RECOVERS HIS WHITE HORSE—LUCIUS INITIATED AS A PRIEST
OF ISIS—HE SAILS FROM CENCHREÆ, AND ARRIVES AT ROME—
INITIATION INTO THE MYSTERIES OF OSIRIS AND SERAPIS—LUCIUS
ADMITTED INTO THE COLLEGE OF THE PASTOPHORI.

AWAKING in sudden alarm about the first watch of the
night, I beheld the full orb of the moon shining with re-
markable brightness, and just then emerging from the waves
of the sea. Availing myself, therefore, of the silence and soli-
tude of night, as I was also well aware that the great primal
goddess possessed a transcendent majesty, and that human
affairs are entirely governed by her providence; and that not
only cattle and wild beasts, but likewise things inanimate, are
invigorated by the divine influence of her light; that the bodies
likewise which are on the earth, in the heavens, and in the
sea, at one time increase with her increments, and at another
lessen duly with her wanings; being well assured of this, I
determined to implore the august image of the goddess then
present, Fate, as I supposed, being now satiated with my many
and great calamities, and holding out to me at last some pro-
spect of relief.

Shaking off all drowsiness, therefore, I rose with alacrity,
and directly, with the intention of purifying myself, began
bathing in the sea. Having dipped my head seven times in
the waves, because, according to the divine Pythagoras, that
number is especially adapted to religious purposes, I joyously
and with alacrity thus supplicated with a tearful countenance
the transcendently powerful Goddess:—

" Queen of heaven, whether thou art the genial Ceres, the
prime parent of fruits, who, joyous at the discovery of thy
daughter, didst banish the savage nutriment of the ancient

acorn, and pointing out a better food, dost now till the Eleusi‥ nian soil ; or whether thou art celestial Venus, who, in the first origin of things, didst associate the different sexes, through the creation of mutual love, and having propagated an eternal offspring in the human race, art now worshipped in the sea-girt shrine of Paphos ; or whether thou art the sister of Phœbus, who, by relieving the pangs of women in travail by soothing remedies, hast brought into the world multitudes so innumerable, and art now venerated, in the far-famed shrines of Ephesus ; or whether thou art Proserpine, terrific, with midnight howlings, with triple features checking the attack of the ghosts, closing the recesses of the earth, and who wandering over many a grove, art propitiated by various modes of worship ; with that feminine brightness of thine, illuminating the walls of every city, and with thy vaporous beams nurturing the joyous seeds of plants, and for the revolutions of the sun ministering thy fitful gleams : by whatever name, by whatever ceremonies, and under whatever form* it is lawful

---

* *Whatever form.*]—The Moon, being the last of the celestial divinities, receives in herself, according to the Orphic theology, processions from all the orders of Gods superior to, and also contains in herself casually all the divinities inferior to her. Hence, from what is asserted here, and farther on, this Goddess is celebrated as containing all the female deities, just as Osiris contains all those of a male character. In short, according to this theology, each of the Gods is in all, and all are in each, being ineffably united to each other and the highest God, because, each being a superessential unity, their conjunction with each other is a union of unities. And hence it is by no means wonderful that each is celebrated as all. But another and a still more appropriate cause may be assigned of the Moon being called by the appellations of so many female deities, which is this, that, according to the Orphic theology, each of the planets is fixed in a luminous etherial sphere called an ολοτης, or *wholeness,*† because it is a part with a *total* subsistence, and is analogous to the sphere of the fixed stars. In consequence of this analogy, each of these planetary spheres contains a multitude of Gods, who are the satellites of the leading divinity of the sphere, and subsist conformably to his characteristics. This doctrine, which, as I have elsewhere observed, is one of the grand keys to the mythology and theology of the ancients, is not clearly delivered by any other ancient writer than Proclus, and has not, I believe, been noticed by any other modern author than myself. The following are the passages in which this theory is unfolded by Proclus, in his admirable commentaries

---

† Each of these spheres is called a *wholeness,* because it contains a multitude of *partial* animals co-ordinate with it.

to invoke thee; do thou graciously succour me in this my extreme distress, support my fallen fortune, and grant me rest

on the Timæus of Plato. ' In each of the celestial spheres, the whole sphere has the relation of a monad, but the cosmocrators [or planets] are the leaders of the multitude in each. For in each a number analogous to the choir of the fixed stars, subsists with appropriate circulations.' And in another part of the same book (p. 280), ' There are other divine animals following the circulations of the planets, the leaders of which are the seven planets; all which Plato comprehends in what is here said. For these also revolve and have a wandering of such a kind as that which he a little before mentioned of the seven planets. For they revolve in conjunction with and make their apocatastases together with their principals, just as the fixed stars are governed by the whole circulation of the [inerratic sphere].' And still more fully in p. 281; " Each of the planets is a whole world, comprehending in itself many divine genera invisible to us. Of all these, however, the visible star has the government. And in this the fixed stars differ from those in the planetary spheres, that the former have one monad [viz., the inerratic sphere], which is the wholeness of them; but that in each of the latter there are invisible stars, which revolve together with their spheres; so that in each there is both the wholeness and a leader, which is allotted an exempt transcendency. For the planets being secondary to the fixed stars, require a twofold prefecture, the one more total, but the other more partial. But that in each of these there is a multitude co-ordinate with each, you may infer from the extremes. For if the inerratic sphere has a multitude co-ordinate with itself, and earth is the wholeness of terrestrial, in the same manner as the inerratic sphere is of celestial animals, it is necessary that each intermediate wholeness should entirely possess certain partial animals co-ordinate with itself; through which, also, they are said to be wholenesses. The intermediate natures, however, are concealed from our sense, the extremes being manifest: one of them through its transcendently luminous essence, and the other through its alliance to us. If, likewise, partial souls [such as ours] are disseminated about them, some about the sun, others about the moon, and others about each of the rest, and prior to souls, dæmons give completion to the herds of which they are the leaders, it is evidently well said, that each of the spheres is a world; theologists also teaching us these things when they say that there are Gods in each prior to dæmons, some of which are under the government of others. Thus, for instance, they assert, concerning our mistress the Moon, that the Goddess Hecate is contained in her, and also Diana. Thus, too, in speaking of the sovereign Sun, and the Gods that are there, they celebrate Bacchus as being there—

> " The sun's assessor, who with watchful eye
> Surveys the sacred pole."

They likewise celebrate the Jupiter who is there, Osiris, the solar Pan, and *others of which the looks of theologists and theurgists* are full;

and peace, after the endurance of so many sad calamities. Let there be an end of my sufferings, let there be an end of my perils. Remove from me the dire form of a quadruped, restore me to the sight of my kindred, restore me to Lucius, my former self. But if any offended deity pursues me with inexorable cruelty, may it at least be allowed me to die, if it is not allowed me to live."

from all which it is evident, that each of the planets is truly said to be the leader of many Gods, who give completion to its peculiar circulation.'

From this extraordinary passage, we may perceive at once why the Sun in the Orphic hymns is called Jupiter, why Apollo is called Pan, and Bacchus the Sun; why the Moon seems to be the same with Rhea, Ceres, Proserpine, Juno, Venus, &c., and in short, why any one divinity is celebrated with the names and epithets of so many of the rest. For from this sublime theory it follows that every sphere contains a Jupiter, Neptune, Vulcan, Vesta, Minerva, Mars, Ceres, Juno, Diana, Mercury, Venus, Apollo, and in short, every deity, each sphere at the same time conferring on these Gods the peculiar characteristic of its nature; so that, for instance, in the Sun they all possess a solar property, in the Moon a lunar one, and so of the rest. From this theory, too, we may perceive the truth of that divine saying of the ancients, that all things are full of Gods; for more particular orders proceed from such as are more general, the mundane from the super-mundane, and the sublunary from the celestial; while earth becomes the general receptacle of the illuminations of all the Gods. 'Hence,' as Proclus shortly after observes, 'there is a terrestrial Ceres, Vesta, and Isis, as likewise a terrestrial Jupiter and a terrestrial Hermes, established about the one divinity of the earth, just as a multitude of celestial Gods proceeds about the one divinity of the heavens. For there are progressions of all the celestial Gods into the Earth: and Earth contains all things, in an earthly manner, which Heaven comprehends celestially. Hence, we speak of a terrestrial Bacchus and a terrestrial Apollo, who bestows the all-various streams of water with which the earth abounds, and openings prophetic of futurity.' And if to all this we only add, that all the other mundane Gods subsist in the twelve above-mentioned, and in short, all the mundane in the super-mundane Gods, and that the first triad of these is *demiurgic* or *fabricative*, viz. Jupiter, Neptune, Vulcan; the second, Vesta, Minerva, Mars, *defensive;* the third, Ceres, Juno, Diana, *vivific;* and the fourth, Mercury, Venus, Apollo, *elevating* and *harmonic;* I say, if we unite this with the preceding theory, there is nothing in the ancient theology that will not appear admirably sublime and beautifully connected, accurate in all its parts, scientific and divine.

The Delphin editor, having no conception of this theory, and being unable to assign the reason why the Moon is here said to be *Deorum Dearumque facies uniformis*, thinks with Elmenhorstius, that the word Deorum' should be obliterated. — *Taylor.*

Having after this manner poured forth my prayers and
added bitter lamentations, sleep again overpowered my stricken
feelings on the same bed. Scarcely had I closed my eyes,
when behold! a divine form emerged from the middle of the
sea, and disclosed features that even the gods themselves might
venerate. After this, by degrees, the vision, resplendent
throughout the whole body, seemed gradually to take its stand
before me, rising above the surface of the sea. I will even
make an attempt to describe to you its wondrous appearance,
if, indeed, the poverty of human language will afford me the
power of appropriately setting it forth; or, if the Divinity
herself will supply me with a sufficient stock of eloquent
diction.

In the first place, then, her hair, long and hanging in tapered
ringlets, fell luxuriantly on her divine neck; a crown of varied
form encircled the summit of her head, with a diversity of
flowers, and in the middle of it, just over her forehead, there
was a flat circlet, which resembled a mirror, or rather emitted
a white refulgent light, thus indicating that she was the
moon. Vipers rising from furrows of the earth, supported
this on the right hand and on the left, while ears of corn pro-
jected on either side. Her garment was of many colours,
woven of fine flax; in one part it was resplendent with a clear
white colour, in another it was yellow like the blooming
crocus, and in another flaming with a rosy redness. And
then, what rivetted my gaze far more than all, was her
mantle of the deepest black, that shone with a glossy lustre.
It was wrapped around her, and passing from below her right
side over the left shoulder, was fastened in a knot that resem-
bled the boss of a shield, while a part of the robe fell down in
many folds, and gracefully floated with its little knots of fringe
that edged its extremities. Glittering stars were dispersed
along the embroidered extremities of the robe, and over its
whole surface; and in the middle of them a moon of two
weeks old breathed forth its flaming fires. Besides this, a
garland, wholly consisting of flowers and fruits of every kind,
adhered naturally to the border of this beautiful mantle, in
whatever direction it was wafted by the breeze.

The objects which she carried in her hands were of a diffe-
rent description. In her right hand she bore a brazen sistrum,*

*Brazen sistrum.]—This *rattle* (in the original *crepitaculum*) of Isis

through the narrow rim of which, winding just like a girdle
for the body, passed a few little rods, producing a sharp shrill
sound, while her arm imparted motion to the triple chords.
An oblong vessel, made of gold, in the shape of a boat, hung

is the same with the celebrated *sistrum* of that Goddess, as is evident from
what is asserted of the latter by Martial, Propertius, and Plutarch.

The following is a translation of what Plutarch says concerning this
sistrum in his treatise of Isis and Osiris, and is remarkably interesting
both to the antiquarian and philosopher: 'The sistrum likewise indicates
that it is necessary that beings should be agitated, and never cease to rest
from their local motion, but should be excited and shaken, when they
become drowsy and marcid. For they say that Typhon is deterred and
repelled by the sistra; manifesting by this, that as corruption binds and
stops [the course of things], so generation again resolves nature, and
excites it through motion. But as the upper part of the sistrum is convex,
so the concavity of it comprehends the four things that are agitated. For
the generable and corruptible portion of the world is comprehended indeed
by the lunar sphere; but all things are moved and changed in this sphere,
through the four elements of fire and earth, water and air. And on the
summit of the concavity of the sistrum they carved a cat having a human
face; and on the under part, below the rattling rods, they placed on one
side the face of Isis, and on the other that of Nephthys, obscurely signify-
ing by these faces generation and death [or corruption]: for these are the
mutations and motions of the elements. But by the cat they indicated
the moon, on account of the diversity of colours, operation by night, and
fecundity of this animal. For it is said, that she brings forth one, after-
wards two, three, four, and five kittens, and so adds till she has brought
forth seven; so that she brings forth twenty-eight in all, which is the
number of the illuminations of the moon. This, therefore, is perhaps
more mythologically asserted. The pupils, however, in the eyes of the
cat, are seen to become full and to be dilated when the moon is full, and
to be diminished and deprived of light during the decrease of this star.'

In this extract, Baxter, in his translation, makes the rods of the sistrum
to be four. For he translates υπο τα σειομενα, 'below the four jingling
things,' which I have translated, *below the rattling rods*. The sistrum,
however, according to all the representations of it that are extant, contained
but three rods. Baxter was doubtless led thus to translate τα σειομενα,
because Plutarch had observed a little before that '*the concavity of the
sistrum comprehends the four things that are agitated,*' *i. e.* the four ele-
ments. But as there is no sphere of fire, as there is of each of the other
elements; for sublunary fire is an efflux of the celestial fire, and subsists
in the cavities of the other elements; hence, the three rods indicate the
three elements, air, water, and earth, and the concavity of the arch of the
sistrum will represent the summit of the air, which imitates the purity of
the vivific and unburning fire of the heavens. For true fire is in the heavens;
but of sublunary fire the purest is ether, and the most gross is in the inte-
rior parts of the earth.— *Taylor.*

down from her left hand, on the handle of which, in that part in which it met the eye, was an asp raising its head erect, and with its throat puffed out on either side. Shoes, too, woven from the palm, the emblem of victory, covered her ambrosial feet.

Such was the appearance of the mighty goddess, as, breathing forth the fragrant perfumes of Arabia the happy, she deigned with her divine voice thus to address me: "Behold me, Lucius; moved by thy prayers, I appear to thee; I, who am Nature, the parent of all things, the mistress of all the elements, the primordial offspring of time, the supreme among Divinities, the queen of departed spirits, the first of the celestials, and the uniform manifestation of the Gods and Goddesses; who govern by my nod the luminous heights of heaven, the salubrious breezes of the ocean, and the anguished silent realms of the shades below: whose one sole divinity the whole orb of the earth venerates under a manifold form, with different rites, and under a variety of appellations. Hence the Phrygians, that primæval race, call me Pessinuntica, the Mother of the Gods; the Aborigines of Attica, Cecropian Minerva; the Cyprians, in their sea-girt isle, Paphian Venus; the arrow-bearing Cretans, Diana Dictynna;* the three-tongued Sicilians,† Stygian Proserpine; and the Eleusinians, the ancient Goddess Ceres. Some call me Juno, others Bellona, others Hecate, and others Rhamnusia. But those who are illumined by the earliest rays of that divinity, the Sun, when he rises, the Æthopians, the Arii, and the Egyptians, so skilled in ancient learning, worshipping me with ceremonies quite appropriate, call me by my true name, Queen Isis. Behold then, commiserating your calamities, I am come to thy assistance; favouring and propitious I am come. Away, then, with tears; leave your lamentations; cast off all sorrow. Soon, through my providence, shall the day of deliverance shine upon you. Listen, therefore, attentively to these my instructions.

"Eternal religion has consecrated to me the day which will be born from this night; to-morrow my priests offer to me the

---

* *Dictynna.*]—The invention of nets is ascribed to Diana, which in Greek are called δίκτυα, *dictyna*.

† *The three-tongued Sicilians.*]—For they first spoke in the Sicilian, afterwards in the Grecian, and at last in the Latin tongue.

first fruits of the opened navigation, and dedicate to me a new ship, for that the wintry tempests are now appeased, and the stormy waves of the ocean lulled, and the sea itself has become navigable. That sacred ceremonial you must await, with a mind neither full of anxiety, nor intent upon subjects that are profane. For the priest, at my command, will carry in the procession a crown of roses, attached to the sistrum in his right hand. Without delay, then, pushing the crowd aside, join my procession, and put your trust in my gracious disposition ; then, having approached close, as though to kiss the hand of the priest, gently pluck the roses, and at once divest yourself of the hide of that abominable beast, which I have long looked upon with detestation.

" Nor hold in dread any thing pertaining to my concerns as difficult. For even at this very same instant* of time in which I appear to you here present, I am giving orders also to my priest how to bring about the things that are to take place hereafter. By my command, the dense crowds of people shall give way before you. Neither, amid the joyous rites and festive scenes, will any one view with abhorrence the unsightliness of the figure which you bear, or malignantly accuse you, by putting a sinister interpretation on the sudden change of your form. Only remember, and always keep it fast in the very depths of your heart, that the remaining period of your life must be dedicated to me, even to the moment of your latest breath. Nor is it unjust that you should devote your whole life to that goddess, by whose assistance you will have been restored to human form. But under my protection you will live happy, you will live glorious : and when, having passed through the allotted period of your life, you shall descend to the realms beneath, there, also, in the subterranean hemisphere, you, dwelling in the Elysian fields, shall frequently adore me whom you now behold thus propitious to you, and shall there see me shining amidst the darkness of Acheron, and reigning in the Stygian realms. And further, if you shall be found to deserve the protection of my divinity by sedulous obedience, religious devotion, and inviolable chastity, you shall be sensible that it is possible for me, and me alone, to extend your life beyond the limits that have been appointed to it by your destiny.''

* *At this very same instant.*]—For a divine nature is at one and the same time present every where.— *Taylor.*

The venerable oracle having thus concluded, the invincible divinity dissolved into herself. Instantly shaking off sleep, I arose, in a state of fear and joy, and bathed in perspiration. Astonished in the highest degree at so evident a manifestation of the powerful goddess, having sprinkled myself with the spray of the sea, and intent on her high commands, I tried to recall to mind the successive particulars of her injunctions. Soon after this, the golden sun arose, and put to flight the clouds of dark night: and now, behold, a crowd of people filled all the streets with a religious procession, conducted in a style of triumph. All things likewise, independently of my own delight, seemed to me to be affected with the greatest hilarity, insomuch that I thought even the cattle of all kinds, every house, and the day itself, wore an aspect of gladness and serenity; for a sunny and placid day had suddenly succeeded to the frost of the previous one; so that, allured by the warmth of the spring, the tuneful little birds sang sweetly, and with their merry warbling soothed Her who was the mother of the stars, the parent of the seasons, and the mistress of the whole universe. And then the trees, too, both those prolific and those which only yielded a shade, unbound from their wintry sleep by the warm southern breezes, and embellished with young foliage, sent forth a sweet rustling sound from their branches. The waves of the sea, no longer heaving turbidly to the roaring blast of the tempest, gently washed the shore; the dark clouds were dispersed, and the heavens shone with the serene splendour of their native light.

And now, behold, the prelude to the grand procession came gradually into action. The persons who composed it were all finely caparisoned in various ways, each according to his own taste and inclination. This man, being girded with a belt, represented a soldier; another was equipped as a hunter, with a short scarf, a hunting-knife, and javelin. Another, wearing gilded sandals, a silken garment, and precious female ornaments, and with false hair on his head, personated a woman by his appearance and his gait. Another, with his boots, his shield, his helmet, and his sword, appeared as though he had come straight from the school of the gladiators. There was one who played the part of a magistrate, with the fasces and the purple robe; another that of a philosopher, with his cloak, his staff, his wooden-clogged shoes, and his goatish beard; two persons, with dissimilar reeds, represented, the one a fowler with bird-lime, and the other a fisherman with his hook. I also saw a tame she-bear, wearing the dress of a woman, and carried in a chair; an ape, too, with a plaited straw hat on its head, and clothed with a Phrygian garment of saffron colour, carrying in its hand a golden cup, and representing the shepherd Ganymede; likewise an ass, on which wings were glued, and which walked near a feeble old man ; so that you would certainly have said that the one was Bellerophon, and the other Pegasus; but still you would have enjoyed your laugh at both.

Amid this merry masquerade of the swarming people, the procession proper of the guardian Goddess now advanced. Females, splendidly arrayed in white garments, expressing their joy by various gestures, and adorned with vernal chaplets, scattered flowers on the ground from their bosoms, along the path of the sacred procession. Others, again, with mirrors placed upon their backs, showed all who followed to the Goddess, with their faces towards her as if they were coming to meet her. Others, carrying ivory combs, imitated the combing and bedecking of her regal hair, with the motion of their arms, and the twisting of their fingers. There were others, too, who sprinkled the streets with drops of genial balsam, and other kinds of perfume. In addition to all this, there was a great multitude of men and women, who propitiated the Goddess, offspring of the celestial stars, by bearing lamps, torches, wax-tapers, and other kinds of artificial light. Next came musicians, playing sweetly on pipes and flutes. A graceful choir of chosen youths, in snow-white garments, followed them, repeating a beautiful song, which an excellent poet had composed under favour of the Muses, the words of which explained the first origin of the votive procession. Pipers also, consecrated to the great Serapis, played an air appropriate to the worship of the god, on pipes with transverse mouth-pieces, and tubes held obliquely towards their right ears. There were, also, a number of persons, whose office it was to give notice that room should be left for the sacred procession to pass. Then came a multitude of those who had been initiated into the sacred rites of the goddess, consisting of men and women of all classes and ages, resplendent with the pure whiteness of their linen garments. The women had their anointed hair enveloped in a transparent covering; but the men had shaven and shining

pates ; earthly stars were these of extreme sanctity, who kept
up a shrill and incessant tinkling upon brazen, silver, and even
gold sistra.   But the chief ministers of the sacred rites, clothed
in garments of white linen, drawn close over the breast, and
hanging down to their feet, carried the insignia of the mighty
Gods, exposed full to view.   The first held aloft a brilliant
lamp, not by any means resembling those lamps of ours which
illumine banquets at night ; but it was of gold, of a boat-like
form, and emitted a flame of considerable magnitude, from an
aperture in the middle.   The second was arrayed in a similar
manner, but carried in both his hands models of altars,* to
which the auxiliary providence of the supreme goddess gave
the appropriate name of "auxjlia."   The third bore a palm
tree, the leaves of which were beautifully wrought in gold, as
also the caduceus of Mercury.   The fourth displayed the sym-
bol of Equity, a left hand, fashioned with the palm expanded ;
which seems to be more adapted to administering Equity than
the right, from its natural inertness, and its being endowed
with no craft and no subtlety.   The same person also carried a
golden vessel, which was rounded in the shape of the female
breast, and from which he poured forth milk on the ground.
The fifth bore a golden corn-fan, made with thickset branches
of gold ; while another carried an amphora.

In the next place, appeared the gods that deigned to walk
with the feet of men.   Here, dreadful to view, was the mes-
senger of the gods above, and of those of the realms beneath,
standing erect, with a face partly black, and partly of a golden
hue, bearing in his left hand a caduceus, and shaking in his
right a green branch of palm ; close upon whose footsteps fol-
lowed a cow, in an erect position ; this cow being the prolific
resemblance of the all-parent goddess, and seated on the shoul-
ders of one of the blessed devotees of this divinity, who acted
gesticulatingly as he walked.   Another carried a chest, con-
taining the secret utensils of this stupendous mystery.   Another
bore in his beatified bosom a venerable effigy of his supreme
Divinity, bearing no resemblance to any bird or beast, wild or
tame, or even to man ; but worthy of all veneration for the
exquisite art with which it was wrought, as also for its very

* *Models of altars*]—These *altars* (*altaria*) were symbols of the aid
afforded by Isis ; and hence Apuleius says, they were called *auxilia.*—
Taylor.

originality, and an ineffable symbol of a sublime religion, the mysteries of which were ever to be kept in deep silence. It was of burnished gold, after the following manner: there was a small urn, hollowed out in a most artistic manner, with a bottom quite round, and which outside was covered with the wonderful hieroglyphics of the Egyptians. The spout of this urn was very long, not much elevated; a handle was attached to the other side, and projected from the urn with a wide sweep. On this lay an asp, uplifting its scaly, wrinkled, and swollen throat, and embraced it with its winding folds.

At last the moment was at hand, when I was to experience the blessing promised me by the most potent goddess; and the priest, attired just as she had described, approached with the means of my deliverance. In his right hand he carried the sistrum of the goddess, and a crown of roses ; and by Hercules, a crown it was for me ; since by the providence of the mighty goddess, after having endured so many hardships, and escaped so many dangers, I should now achieve a victory over my cruel enemy, Fortune.

Still, however, though agitated by a sudden burst of joy, I did not rush forward at once, lest the tranquil order of the sacred procession should be disturbed by the impetuosity of a quadruped ; but passed through the crowd with a quiet and altogether human step, and a sidelong movement of my body, and as the people gave way, through the interference, no doubt, of the goddess, I gradually crept nearer and nearer. But the priest, as I could plainly perceive, recollecting the nocturnal oracle, and struck with wonder at the coincidence with the duty which he had been commanded to perform, instantly stood still, and extending his right hand of his own accord, presented the chaplet to my very mouth. Trembling, and with a great beating of my heart, I seized the bright rosy chaplet, and greedily, most greedily devoured it.

Nor did the celestial promise deceive me; for immediately my unsightly and brutal figure left me. First of all, my rough hair fell off, and next my thick skin became thin; my big belly shrank in; my hoofs spread out into feet and toes ; my hands were no longer feet, but ready for the duties of their elevated position. My long neck was shortened ; my face and my head became round ; my enormous ears were restored to their former small dimensions; my stony teeth returned to the diminutive size of those of men; and the tail, which before especially annoyed me, was no where to be seen. The people were astonished, and the religious adored the power of the supreme Divinity, so manifested in the facility of my restoration, which resembled the visions of a dream. Extending their hands towards the heavens, they attested, with a loud and unanimous voice, the favour of the goddess thus signally displayed.

As for me, I stood riveted to the spot in excessive astonishment, my mind being unable to contain a delight so sudden and so great, quite at a loss what first and in especial to say, how to make a commencement with a new voice, how most auspiciously to prepare my address, my tongue being now born again, and in what words sufficiently to express my thanks to a Goddess so great. The priest, however, who through the divine admonition knew all my misfortunes from the beginning, though he himself also was in a state of utter astonishment at this remarkable miracle, at once signified his wish by nodding his head, and ordered that a linen garment should be given me, for the purpose of covering my nakedness. For, the very instant that the ass had laid aside his abominable covering, I carefully shaded myself with a natural screen, as much as it was possible for a naked person to do, by closely compressing my thighs, and applying my hands. Upon this one of the throng of devotees promptly throwing me his upper tunic, covered me therewith; which being done, the priest with a benign countenance, and, by Hercules, astonished at my perfectly human appearance, thus addressed me:—

" At last, Lucius, you have arrived at the haven of peace and the altar of mercy, after the many and various hardships you have undergone, and all the buffetings of stormy Fortune. Neither the nobility of your descent, nor your dignified position, nor even the learning in which you excel, have benefited you in the slightest degree; but falling into the slavery of pleasure, in the wantonness of buxom youth, you have reaped the inauspicious reward of your ill-fated curiosity. Nevertheless, blind Fortune, while harassing you with the worst of dangers, has conducted you, in her short-sighted malice, to this state of religious beatitude. Let her go now, and rage with all her fury, and let her seek some other object for her cruelty;* for direful calamity has no power over those

* *Let her go now, &c.*]—This passage—' Eat nunc, et summo furore

whose lives the majesty of our Goddess has claimed for
her own service. What advantage has unscrupulous For-
tune derived from the robbers, from the wild beasts, from the
servitude, from the long toils on rugged roads, and from the
fear of death to which you were daily exposed? You are
now received under the guardianship of Fortune, but of a For-
tune who can see, and who even illuminates the other Deities
with the splendour of her light. Assume henceforth a more
joyous countenance, such as befits that white garment which
you wear. Follow the train of the Goddess your deliverer with
triumphant steps. Let the irreligious see, let them see and ac-
knowledge their error. Behold now, Lucius, rejoicing in the
providence of great Isis, and freed from his former miseries,
triumphs over his destiny. Nevertheless, that you may be
more secure and better protected, enrol your name in this holy
militia, which you will hereafter rejoice to belong to; dedicate
yourself to the service of our religion, and voluntarily bend
your neck to the yoke of this ministry; for when you have
once begun to serve the Goddess, you will then in a still higher
degree enjoy the fruit of your liberty."

The worthy priest having uttered these words, while his
breath heaved with inspiration, concluded his address, and I
mingling with the throng of devotees, accompanied the pro-
cession; an object of curiosity to the whole city. All pointed
at me with their fingers and heads, and said, "This day
has the august power of all mighty God restored that person to
the human form. Happy, by Hercules! and thrice blessed he,
to have merited, by the innocence and probity of his past life,
such special patronage of heaven; in that, being after a manner
born again, he is immediately affianced to the service of the
sacred ministry."

sæviat, et crudelitati suæ materiam quærat aliam,' is alone sufficient to
show that Lesage, when he composed Gil Blas, had in view the Metamor-
phoses of Apuleius. In addition to the coincidence of the case of the
robbers, the robbers' narrative, Dame Leonarda, the captive damsel, and
her escape with the hero of the tale, being persons and events introduced
into both compositions, the above apostrophe to Fortune is rendered
almost literally in Latin verse by Lesage. The lines inscribed by G..
Blas, about to devote himself to a life of rural retirement, over the door of
his house, are—

> ' Inveni portum, spes et fortuna valete,
>   Sat me lusistis; ludite nunc alios.'—*Head.*

While these remarks were being made, and amid the tumult of their noisy congratulations, moving slowly on, we now approached the sea-shore, and came to that very place where, on the preceding day, I, while yet an ass, had laid me down. The images of the Gods being there arranged in proper order, the chief priest dedicated and consecrated to the Goddess a very skilfully built ship, pictured all over with the curious hieroglyphics of the Egyptians, after having most carefully purified it with a lighted torch, an egg, and sulphur, while at the same time his chaste lips poured forth solemn prayers. The shining white sail of this auspicious bark bore an inscription in large characters, which was a repetition of a vow that had been made on shore for the prosperity of the convoy at this season of the recommencement of navigation. Now the mast was raised, which was a rounded pine tree, tall and well polished, and conspicuous for the beauteous appearance of its head. The prow also was turned in imitation of a goose's neck,* and covered with gold leaf, the bark shone resplendently, while the whole of the highly polished keel consisted of shining citron wood. All the people, religious and profane,† vied with each other in heaping together corn-fans laden with aromatics and other sacrificial offerings, and poured upon the waves a libation of milk mixed with other ingredients; until the ship, freighted with abundant gifts and auspicious prayers, and let slip from the ropes that held the anchor, put to sea with a serene breeze, which seemed to have sprung up for her sake alone. And after she had proceeded so far on her course that she could no longer be distinguished by us, the bearers of the sacred things again took what each had brought, and began joyfully to return to the temple, in an orderly manner, and in the same form of procession in which they had come.

Now as soon as we arrived at the temple, the chief priest and those who carried the sacred images, and those who had already been initiated into the venerable mysteries, being admitted into the sanctuary of the Goddess, deposited in the accustomed form the breathing effigies.‡ Then, one of these, whom all of them

---

A goose's neck.]—The goose is sacred to Isis.—*Taylor.*

† *Religious and profane.*]—The words are used in a sense nearly analogous to clergy and laity. ' Profane,' means primitively nothing worse than an ' outsider,' with regard to the service of the temple.

‡ *Breathing effigies.*]—These *breathing* effigies were statues of the

called the scribe, standing before the doors, whilst the company
of the Pastophori,* which is the name of the brotherhood of this
sacred college, convoked together as to a council, uttered from a
high pulpit auspicious wishes, from a book in which was written:
—"To the great Prince, to the Senate, to the Equestrian order,
in naval matters and in ships, and all those who are subject to
our dominion;" and then he pronounced in the Greek language,
and according to the Greek custom, the Λαοις ἄφεσις, [the people
may depart,] to which the people responded with a clamour
which testified their general satisfaction. Then every one went
home, full of joy, carrying branches of olive, sweet herbs, and
garlands of flowers, and after kissing the feet of a silver image
of the Goddess, which stood on the steps of the temple. But my
feelings would not allow me to move so much as a nail's breadth
from that place; but with my eyes intently fastened on the image
of the Goddess, I recalled to memory my past misfortunes.

Fleeting Fame, however, had not in the meantime let her
wings remain idle, but had immediately circulated in all direc-
tions in my native country the adorable bounty of the provident
Goddess, and my own memorable adventures. Accordingly, my
domestics and servants, and those who were nearest to me
by blood, laying aside the sorrow with which they had been
afflicted at the false intelligence of my death, and elated with
this sudden joy, hastened forthwith to see me, who had been
divinely saved and brought back, as it were, from the shades
below, and they presented me with gifts of various kinds.
I, too, was delighted to see them, and returned them many
thanks for their handsome presents, and the more especially,
as my domestics had providently taken care to bring me what
would be abundantly sufficient in the way of clothes and
money. Having, therefore, spoken to each of them in such
manner as I was in duty bound to do, and related to them my
former sorrows and my present joyous prospects, I again re-
turned to what was to me the greatest subject of delight, 'the
contemplation of the Goddess, and procured for myself a tem-
porary habitation within the enclosure of the temple, constantly
taking part in the private services of the Goddess, and being
inseparable from the brotherhood of the priests, and a constant

Gods, fabricated by *telestæ*, or *mystic operators*, so as to become animated,
illuminated by divinity, and capable of delivering oracles.—*Taylor.*

* *The Pastophori.*]—The priests that carried the shrines of the Gods.

adorer of the great Divinity. Nor did I pass a single night or
ever close my eyes without some vision from this Divinity, in
which she commanded me to be now initiated in her sacred
mysteries, to which I had long since been destined. As for
me, though prompted by eager inclination, I was still restrained
by religious fear. For after diligent enquiry, I had found that
the requirements of a religious life were full of difficulties;
that the chastity required was a very difficult thing to observe,
and that it needed extreme circumspection to preserve such a
habit of life from casual defilements. Frequently pondering
over these things, I somehow or other delayed being initiated,
although hastening to that conclusion.

One night I had a dream, in which I thought that the chief
priest made his appearance, and presented to me his lap full of
various things, and on my asking what they were, he answered
me, that the things had been sent to me from Thessaly; for
that a servant of mine, whose name was Candidus, had arrived
from that province. When I awoke, I revolved in my mind
over and over again what the vision portended, especially as I
was certain that I never had any servant who was called by
that name. Still, however, I believed that some profitable
result was undoubtedly signified by the priest offering me the
things. Thus, in a state of anxious and bewildered eagerness,
I awaited the opening of the temple in the morning. The white
curtains having been drawn aside, we prayed to the venerable
presence of the Goddess; and the priest going round the altars,
performed the sacred ceremonial with solemn supplications,
and poured forth libations from a chalice of water drawn from
a fountain in the precincts of the sanctuary. The sacred rites
therefore, being now duly performed, the devotees, saluting
the breaking dawn, in a loud voice announced the first hour of
the day.

And now, behold! some servants arrived from my country
whom I had left there at the time when Fotis, by her unfortu-
nate mistake, had fitted me for a halter; so recognizing them as
my own servants, and finding that they had brought back that
horse of mine, after it had been sold from place to place, and
which I identified by a mark on its back; I was then especially
struck with admiration at the fitness of my dream, because not
only had it come true with respect to the gain it had promised,
but it had also predicted to me the recovery of my horse, which

was of a white colour, under the designation of my servant Candidus.

I continued to apply myself wholly to attendance on the worship of the Goddess, perceiving that the hopes which I had conceived of future good were now confirmed by present benefits. And besides, my desire of receiving initiation in the sacred duties, increased daily more and more. Accordingly, I frequently went to the chief priest, and most earnestly entreated him to initiate me into the mysteries of the holy night; but he, who was a man of a grave disposition, and remarkable for his strict observance of that abstemious religion, checked my urgent importunity in a mild and gentle manner, and in the way in which parents are in the habit of moderating the inconsiderate requests of their children, while at the same time he soothed me with hopes for the better. For he said, that the day on which each aspirant might be initiated was indicated by tokens from the Goddess, and that by her providence the priest was selected who was to perform the sacred rites; and that in like manner by her mandate the expense necessary for the ceremonial was ordained. All these circumstances, he was of opinion, ought to be awaited with obsequious patience, since we ought, on every consideration, to avoid precipitation and contumacy, and neither be dilatory when called, nor precipitate when not called. Nor, indeed, was there a single one of their number who was so lost to a sense of propriety, or rather so bent on his own destruction, as to dare rashly and sacrilegiously to undertake the ministry of the Goddess, and so bring upon himself a deadly mischance, unless she especially ordered him so to do; for the gates of the realms beneath, and the guardianship of life, are placed in the hands of the Goddess, and the initiation into her mysteries is celebrated as bearing a close resemblance to a voluntary death, with a precarious chance of recovery. Wherefore the divine will of the Goddess has been accustomed to choose for this purpose men who, having arrived at a great age, are now standing at the very utmost limit of life, to whom, however, the mighty secrets of her religion may be safely entrusted,* and whom, through her providence, being after a manner born again, she restores

---

To whom, however, &c.]—That is to say, who are not yet so infirm and imbecile as to be incapable of preserving secrecy.

to the career of a new existence. Therefore it was requisite
that I should await the celestial mandate, although by the clear
and manifest favour of the great Deity I had already been
marked and destined for her blessed ministry; and I ought
thenceforth to abstain from profane and forbidden food, in com-
mon with the other devotees, in order that I might with the
most scrupulous strictness proceed on my course to the secret
mysteries of the most pure religion.

Thus did the priest express himself, nor was my compliance
interrupted by feelings of impatience; but I attentively per-
formed the daily duties of the sacred ministry, intent upon
maintaining a calm demeanour and laudable silence.   Nor did
the salutary benevolence of the powerful goddess disappoint
me, or torment me with a long delay; but she clearly admo-
nished me by no obscure mandates in the darksome night,
that the day was now arrived that had always been the object
of my desire, and in which she would put me in possession of
my extreme wishes.   She also stated what sum of money
would be requisite for the expenses of the ceremonial, and at
the same time appointed for me, as the dispenser of the rites,
the same Mithras, her own high priest, who, she said, was
united to me by a certain conjunction of the stars.

Refreshed in mind by these and other benevolent precepts
of the supreme Goddess, and shaking off slumber, though it
was not yet clear day, I hastened at once to the dwelling of the
priest, and saluted him just as he was coming out of his bed-
chamber.   I had now determined to request more earnestly
than ever initiation into the sacred rites, as being a thing that
was due to me.   He, however, the instant that he saw me,
was the first to speak: "O my Lucius, how happy and blessed
are you, whom the august divinity has thus greatly honoured
by her propitious will!   And why," said he, " do you now
stand idle, or make any delay?   The day you so earnestly
prayed for has now arrived, in which you will be initiated into
the most holy mysteries by these hands of mine, in obedience
to the divine mandates of the many-titled Goddess."

And the old man, taking me by the right hand, led me im-
mediately to the doors of the vast temple; and having performed
the office of opening them in the accustomed solemn way, and
celebrated the morning sacrifice, he drew forth from the secret
recesses of the shrine certain books, written in unknown cha-

racters, partly representing in compendious form the words expressive of their meaning by figures of animals of every kind, and partly fortified against the inquisitive perusal of the profane, by characters wreathed like knots, and twisting round in shape of a wheel, and with extremities twining one with another, like the tendrils of a vine. From these books he informed me what was necessary to be provided by me for the purpose of initiation.

Immediately, therefore, I diligently set about purchasing and procuring requisites, and even on a more liberal scale than I was ordered to do, partly at my own expense, and partly through my friends. And when, now the time, as the priest said, required it, he led me to the nearest bath, accompanied by a crowd of devotees; and after I had taken the customary bath, he himself washed and sprinkled me with the purest water, having first implored the pardon of the Gods. Then, again, he brought me back to the temple, and there placed me at the very feet of the Goddess, two-thirds of the day having now elapsed; and giving certain secret instructions, which are too holy to be uttered, he distinctly ordered, before all who were present, that I should abstain from luxurious food for the ten succeeding days, and that I should eat the flesh of no animal, and should abstain from wine.

These ten days having been duly passed by me in reverential abstinence, the day had now arrived for pledging myself to the sacred ministry, and the sun descending, was ushering in the evening. Then, behold, there was a concourse of the people flocking from every side, every one honouring me with various gifts, according to the ancient custom of these sacred rites. After this, the priest, all the profane being removed to a distance, taking hold of me by the hand, brought me into the inner recesses of the sanctuary itself, clothed in a new linen garment. Perhaps, curious reader, you may be eager to know what was then said and done? I would tell you, were it lawful for me to tell you; you should know it, if it were lawful for you to hear. But both the ears that heard these things, and the tongue that told them, would reap the evil results of their rashness. Still, however, kept in suspense as you probably are with religious longing, I will not torment you with long-protracted anxiety. Hear, therefore, but believe what is the truth. I approached the confines of death, and having trod on the threshold of Proserpine, I returned therefrom, being borne through all the elements. At midnight I saw the sun shining with its brilliant light; and I approached the presence of the Gods beneath, and the Gods of heaven, and stood near, and worshipped them. Behold, I have related to you things of which, though heard of by you, you must necessarily remain ignorant. I will therefore only relate that which may be enunciated to the understanding of the un-initiated without a crime.

The morning came, and, the solemnities being performed, I came forth consecrated by being dressed in twelve stoles, an habiliment no doubt of most religious character, but of which I am not forbidden by any obligation to speak, because it was seen by many who were present on the occasion. For, by order of the priest, I ascended a wooden pulpit, which was in the very middle of the sacred dwelling, and placed before the image of the Goddess, 'full in view, in a garment which was of linen, but elegantly coloured. A precious scarf also descended from my shoulders behind my back down to my ankles, and to whatever part of me you directed your view, you would have seen something to arrest your attention in the animals which were painted round my vestment in various colours. Here were Indian serpents, there Hyperborean griffins, which the other hemisphere generates in the form of a bird wearing wings. The persons devoted to the service of the divinity call this the Olympic stole. Then, in my right hand I carried a burning torch; while a graceful chaplet encircled my head, the shining leaves of the palm tree projecting from it like rays of light. Thus arrayed like the sun, and placed so as to resemble a statue, on a sudden, the curtains being drawn aside, I was ex-posed to the gaze of the multitude. After this, I celebrated the most joyful day of my initiation, as my natal day, and there was a joyous banquet and mirthful conversation. The third day also was celebrated with the like rites and cere-monies, and was accompanied by a religious breakfast, and the due termination of the ceremonial. After this, having stayed for some days in that place, I enjoyed the inexplicable pleasure of viewing the holy image, being indebted to it for a benefit which can never be sufficiently rewarded. At length, how-ever, through the admonition of the Goddess, having suppli-antly given her thanks, not such as she deserved, but still, to the best of my ability, I prepared myself, though very slowly, to return home.

With difficulty did I rend asunder the ties of my most ardent affection. At last I prostrated myself in the presence of the Goddess, and having for a long time watered her feet with my tears, interrupting my words by frequent sobs, and, as it were, half swallowing my voice, I thus addressed her:—" Thou, O holy and perpetual preserver of the human race, always munificent in cherishing mortals, dost bestow the sweet affection of a mother on the misfortunes of the wretched. Nor is there any day or night, nor so much as the minutest particle of time, which passes unattended by thy bounties. Thou dost protect men both by sea and land, and, dispersing the storms of life, dost extend thy health-giving right hand, by which thou dost unravel the inextricably entangled threads of the Fates, and dost assuage the tempests of fortune, and restrain the malignant influences of the stars. The gods of heaven adore thee, those in the shades below do homage unto thee; thou dost roll the sphere of the universe round the steady poles, thou dost illuminate the sun, thou dost govern the universe, thou dost tread the realms of Tartarus. The stars move responsive to thy command, the Gods rejoice in thy divinity, the seasons return by thy appointment, and the elements are thy servants. At thy nod the breezes blow, the clouds are nurtured, the seeds germinate, and the blossoms increase. The birds as they hover through the air, the wild beasts as they roam on the mountains, the serpents that hide in the earth, and the monsters that swim in the sea, are terrified at the majesty of thy presence. But I, so weak in capacity for celebrating thy praises, and possessing such slender means for offering sacrifices, have far from eloquence sufficient to express all that I conceive of thy majesty; not a thousand mouths, and tongues as many, not an eternal flow of unwearied speech, would be equal to the task. I will, therefore, use my utmost endeavours to do what, poor as I am, still one truly religious may do—I will figure to myself thy divine countenance, and will ever preserve this most holy divinity locked up in the deepest recesses of my breast."

After this manner, having offered up my prayer to the supreme Goddess, I embraced the priest Mithras, who was now my parent, and hanging on his neck, and giving him many

R

kisses, I begged him to forgive me, that I could not remunerate
him in a manner adequate to such mighty benefits. At length,
after having been long engaged in giving him thanks, I de-
parted, and prepared to journey directly to my paternal abode,
in order to revisit it after an absence so prolonged. A few
days after, having hastily tied up my packages, through the
admonition of the powerful Goddess, embarking on board a
ship, I set sail for Rome. Being sure of a favourable wind
during my voyage, I very speedily entered into port, and tra-
velling by chariot* with the greatest rapidity, arrived at the
holy city,† on the day before the Ides of December in the
evening. Thenceforward no study was there of such primary
importance with me, as that of daily supplicating the supreme
divinity of Queen Isis; who is there propitiated with the
greatest veneration under the name of Campensis,‡ which ap-
pellation she derives from the situation of her temple. In fine,
I became a constant worshipper, a foreigner indeed as to her
temple, but indigenous as to her religion.§

Behold the mighty sun, having passed through the sign-
bearing circle of the zodiac, had completed the year, when the
vigilant care of the beneficent Goddess again interrupted my
sleep, and again reminded me of initiation and sacred rites.
On this I wondered what object she had in view, and what future
event she announced. For how could I do otherwise? as I
considered myself to have been most fully initiated already.

While, therefore, I revolved my religious doubts in my own

By chariot.]—There are instances among the ancients of extraor-
dinary celerity in travelling. Alexander, to suppress the rebellion of the
Arici, travelled with his army six hundred stadia in two days, *i. e.* each day
seventy-two miles. Julius Cæsar used to travel commonly one hundred
Roman miles in a day, as we are informed by Suetonius. Curio, according
to Appian, travelled with Cæsar's letters three thousand three hundred
stadia in three days, *i. e.* three hundred and seventy-seven English miles.
And Tiberius Nero, as we are informed by Pliny, travelled with three
chaises in one day and one night, a journey of two hundred miles to see
his brother when he was sick.—*Taylor.*

† *The holy city.*]—Rome, which was considered to be the seat of the
Gods, and the true name of which it was not lawful to enunciate even in
the performance of sacred rites.—*Taylor.*

‡ *Campensis.*]—The temple of Isis was in the Campus Martius,
whence she was called Campensis.—*Taylor.*

§ *Religion.*]—Because he had been initiated in the mysteries of Isis at
Corinth.—*Taylor.*

mind, and availed myself of the counsels of the priest, I ascertained a thing that was novel and quite wonderful to me ; that I was only inititated into the mysteries of the goddess, but that I had not yet been admitted to the knowledge of the rites of the great God, and supreme parent of the Gods, the invincible Osiris. For though the essence of their divine nature and religion is connected, or rather, is transcendently united, nevertheless, there is a very considerable difference in the initiations into their mysteries. Hence, it was for me to know that I was called upon by the great God to become one of his servants. Nor did the matter long remain ambiguous. For on the following night, I saw in a dream one of the devotees, who, clothed in linen garments, and bearing in his hands thyrsi and ivy, and certain other things which I am not permitted to mention, placed them before my household Gods, and then seating himself in my chair, announced to me that I must prepare a plentiful religious banquet. He also walked gently with a hesitating step, the ancle of his left foot being slightly bent, in order no doubt that he might afford me some sign, by which I might recognize him. All the mists of ambiguity were therefore removed, after such a manifest declaration of the will of the gods.

Accordingly, the instant I had performed the morning salutations to the goddess, I made a most careful examination of each, to see whether there was any one of the priests resembling him whom I had seen in the dream. Nor was he wanting. For I immediately beheld one of the Pastophori, exactly corresponding with the nocturnal vision, not only with regard to the mark of his foot, but also in his stature and general appearance ; whose name I afterwards learnt to be Asinius Marcellus, an appellation not without some degree of reference* to my transformation. Without delay, therefore, I addressed this priest, who was himself very far from ignorant of what I intended to say, because he had already been admonished by a similar mandate, that he should initiate me into the mysteries of Osiris. For on the preceding night, while he was placing chaplets on the statue of the great God, he imagined that he had also heard from that mouth of his by which he pronounces the destinies of all things, that he should send to him a native

---

* *Some reference.*]—For between *Asinus*, an ass, into which he had been changed, and *Asinius*, there is a great resemblance.

of Madaura, to whom, though he was very poor, he must immediately impart the sacred mysteries. That, through his providence, glory would accrue to that person from his religious exercises, and great profit for himself.

After this manner, being affianced to the sacred mysteries, I was retarded, contrary to my inclination, by reason of the slenderness of my means. For the expense to which I had been put in my journey had frittered away the small substance of my property; and the sums I was obliged to expend in the city, exceeded those which had been disbursed in the provinces. Rigid poverty, consequently, greatly interfering with my wishes, I was much afflicted, being placed, as the old proverb says, between the altar and the stone.* Nor yet was I less urged from time to time by the present mandates of the God. At last, after being repeatedly reminded, and finally commanded, not without considerable perturbation, taking off my back my garment, small as it was, I scraped together a sufficient sum. And this very thing I had been expressly commanded to do. For the God said to me, " Would you hesitate in the least to part with your garments, if you were attempting to procure any thing which might administer to your pleasures? and are you now, when you are going to enter upon so great a ceremonial, doubtful whether you shall commit yourself to a poverty of which you will never have to repent?"

All things, therefore, being abundantly prepared, again being satisfied for ten days with other than animal food, and besides this, being also admitted to the nocturnal orgies of Serapis, a god of the first rank, I now applied myself to the service of the god, full of that confidence which my knowledge of a kindred ritual produced. This event afforded me the greatest consolation for my sojourn in a foreign country, and at the same time supplied me more plentifully with the means of subsistence. For, under favour of the deity of Good Event, I supported myself on a little gain which I made in the forum by pleading causes in the Latin tongue.

A short time after, I was again addressed by the unexpected

* *Between the altar and the stone.*]—Equivalent to the modern phrase, ' between the hammer and the anvil.' The proverb is derived from the ancient manner of ratifying a covenant, in which the priest killed a pig with a blow of a stone, exclaiming, ' May Jupiter smite him who breaks this covenant, as I smite this pig.'

and perfectly miraculous mandates of the gods, and was compelled to undergo a third initiation.* This caused me no slight anxiety, and much was I perplexed to know what could be the meaning of this new and unusual expression of the will of the gods; and what could still remain to be added by way of supplement to an initiation that had been already twice repeated. Surely, thought I, both the priests have advised me either wrongly or less fully than they ought to have done. And, by Hercules, I now began even to entertain a bad opinion of their fidelity. While, however, I was thus fluctuating amid a stormy tide of thought, and agitated to the verge of insanity, the benevolent figure of the divinity instructed me by a nocturnal vision. "There is no reason," said he, "that you should be terrified by the repeated series of religious rites, as if any thing had been previously omitted; but you ought rather exceedingly to rejoice on account of these reiterated marks of favour on the part of the divinities, and to exult that you will thrice obtain that which is scarcely even once granted to others. And you may confidently believe from that number that you will always be blessed. Besides, you will find that this ceremonial is most necessary for you, if you will only now consider with yourself, that the stole of the goddess with which you were invested in the province, still remains deposited in the same spot, and that you cannot so much as supplicate at Rome on solemn days in a garment of this kind, or be ennobled by that auspicious apparel, when you are commanded to assume it. In order, then, that you may enjoy health, happiness, and prosperity, once again with joyous feelings be initiated in the sacred mysteries, the mighty gods being your advisers."

Thus far did the persuasive majesty of the hallowed vision announce to me what was requisite to be done. Nor did I, after this, neglect the matter, or defer it; but immediately relating what I had seen to my priest, I forthwith submitted to the yoke of abstinence from animal food, and having of my own accord extended my abstinence beyond those ten days prescribed by a perpetual law, I bought what was requisite for my initiation, spending more largely from pious zeal than with reference to the measure of the things provided. Nor, by Hercules, did I at all repent of my trouble and expense.

* *A third initiation.*]—This third initiation was into the mysteries of the Roman Isis, as the first was into those of the Achaian Isis.—*Taylor.*

And why should I? for by the bounteous providence of the gods, I was sufficiently enriched ·by my forensic emoluments. At length, after a very few days had elapsed, the God Osiris, who is the chief of the great gods, the highest among the greatest, the greatest among the highest, and the ruler of the greatest, not now veiling himself under some figure other than his own, but deigning to address me in his own person, and in his own divine words, seemed in my sleep to declare, that I should forthwith become renowned through my pleading causes in the forum, and that I should not fear the slanders of the malevolent, to which the learning I had acquired by laborious study had rendered me liable.

Besides this, in order that I might minister to his sacred rites, mingling with the throng of devotees, he chose me to be a member of the college of his Pastophori, and still more, to be one of the quinquennial Decurions. Finally, therefore, my hair being closely shaved off, I joyfully fulfilled the duties of that most ancient college, which had been established in the days of Sylla, not shading or covering my baldness, but freely exposing it to the public gaze, whithersoever I went.

END OF THE GOLDEN ASS.

THE DEFENCE OF APULEIUS.

A DISCOURSE ON MAGIC.

(SEE BIOGRAPHICAL INTRODUCTION.)

MAXIMUS CLAUDIUS, and you who are sitting here in judgment,* I felt fully assured, that Sicinius Æmilianus,† an old man, notorious for audacity, would, for want of substantial charges, fill up with nothing but abuse the accusation he undertook to make against me, before he had well considered the matter. Now any innocent person may be accused, but no one can be proved guilty unless he is so. Relying especially on this consideration, by the Gods of heaven! I do rejoice that, with you for my judge, the power and the opportunity have fallen to my lot, of exculpating Philosophy in the eyes of the ignorant, and defending myself.

And yet these charges—serious-looking charges at first view—were made with a suddenness that tended to embarrass my defence. For, as you remember, five or six days ago, when I was beginning to plead the cause of my wife,‡ Pudentilla, against the Granii, the advocates of this Æmilianus, by a concerted plan, and at a moment when I least expected it, assailed me with abuse, and accused me of magical practices, and even of the death of my step-son Pontianus. As I saw that these were not so much charges brought forward for judicial enquiry, as imputations for the mere purpose of abuse, I challenged them of my own accord, urgently and repeatedly, to

---

* *In judgment.*]—As assessors to Maximus Claudius, the proconsul of Africa.

† *Æmilianus.*]—The brother of Sicinius Clarus, the first husband of Pudentilla, the wife of Apuleius.

‡ *Cause of my wife.*]—It is not known to what he refers: but it is not improbable that he alludes to some question as to her rights of dower as the widow of Sicinius Clarus.

prefer their accusation.   But then Æmilianus, seeing that you
too, Maximus, were considerably moved, and that a judicial
affair had arisen out of his words, began, in distrust of his
cause, to look about for some subterfuge from the consequences
of his temerity.

Accordingly, when he, who shortly before had been crying
out that Pontianus, his brother's son, had been murdered by
me, was compelled to sign his name to the accusation, he in-
stantly forgot all about the death of his young kinsman, and all
of a sudden was mute as to the specification of a crime of such
extreme atrocity.   Still, that he might not seem altogether
to have abandoned his charges, he selected this accusation
of magical practices—an accusation more easily made than
proved—as the only one in which he should persist.   And even
that he did not dare do openly; but, on the day after, he
gave in an indictment, in the name of my son-in-law, Sicinius
Pudens, a mere boy, and annexed his own name thereto as his
supporter; thus adopting a new fashion of making an attack
in another's name; no doubt, in order that, by putting for-
ward one so young, he himself might be screened from due
punishment for his false accusation.   When you, with great
sagacity, perceived this to be the case, and thereupon com-
manded him again to support in his own name the accusation
he had originally made, he promised that he would; but after
all, he could not be prevailed upon to do so.   While you are
urging him to come to close action with me, he, in his contu-
macy, shoots his calumnious missiles even against yourself.
Thus ever shunning the danger of making an open accusation,
he persevered in the safe course of seconding it.

Accordingly, before the trial had even commenced, it was
easy for any one to understand what would be the nature of the
prosecution, the framer and contriver of which feared to under-
take its responsibility.   This was more especially the case,
since the person in question was Sicinius Æmilianus; who,
if he had ascertained anything substantial against me, would
certainly never have manifested any such hesitation in im-
peaching one who was a stranger to himself, of crimes so
numerous and so heinous—he who, well knowing that his
uncle's will was genuine, denounced it as a forgery; and with
such obstinacy, that when Lollius Urbicus, the pro-consul, with
men of consular dignity sitting as his assessors, had pronounced

that it was proved genuine, and ought to be held valid, still that madman persisted, with his voice raised to the loudest pitch, in swearing that the will was a forgery; so that Lollius Urbicus hardly refrained from visiting him with capital punishment. Relying on your justice and my own innocence, I trust that on this trial also he will have occasion to burst forth into exclamations of a similar nature. For he knowingly accuses one who is innocent; and does so, no doubt, with the greater readiness, because, as I have said, he has already, on a trial of the greatest importance, been convicted of uttering falsehoods before the Prætor of the city.

For, as after having once committed a fault, every good man is the more careful to avoid it; so one who is evil-disposed repeats his offence with increased audacity; and, from that time forward, the more frequently he offends, the more undisguisedly he does so. For it is with shame as with a garment—the more it is worn, the less it is cared for.

For this reason, then, I deem it necessary, in order to maintain the integrity of my character, to refute all his malevolent aspersions before I come to the main charge. For I am undertaking not only my own defence, but that of philosophy also, whose high character spurns the least slur as though it were the weightiest of charges; for as much as the advocates of Æmilianus have been just now babbling forth with their mercenary loquacity, many things trumped up against myself individually, and many others that are commonly uttered by the ignorant against philosophers in general. Now, although it may be manifest that these charges are gabbled by them, in order to gain their fees, and to earn a premium for their impudence, according to a sort of usage now universally established among pettifogging pleaders of this sort—a race who are in the habit of letting out the venom of their viperous tongues to give pain to others—still, even for my own sake, they must be briefly rebutted; lest I, who am exerting all my energies, that I may not appear to admit of any stain or any blemish upon my character, might seem to some, in case I should pass by any of these frivolous charges, rather to have admitted them than to have held them in contempt.

For, according to my way of thinking, it is the part of a modest and honorable spirit to be incensed even by a false accusation; seeing that even those who are conscious to them-

selves of the commission of any offence, are still greatly
excited and angered by reproach; although from the very
moment that they began to do wrong, they may have been
accustomed to hear themselves ill-spoken of. Nay, even if
silence is observed by others, they are still fully conscious
that they may with justice be censured. On the other hand,
every man who is virtuous and without guile, whose ears are
utterly unused to the language of obloquy, and who, from re-
peatedly hearing himself praised, is unprepared for reproach, is
the more grieved at heart on hearing those things said un-
deservedly against him, which he could with truth allege
against others. If then, perchance, I shall appear disposed to
defend myself against charges that are absurd and utterly
frivolous, that circumstance ought, in fairness, to be imputed
as a fault to those who are disgraced by having even uttered
them against me; and no blame ought to attach to me, in
whom it will be becoming to have refuted even such things.

You heard, then, a short time since, at the commencement
of the accusation, words to the following effect: "We accuse
before you a handsome philosopher, and a man of distinguished
eloquence,"—oh, monstrous!—"both in the Greek and in the
Latin tongues." For, unless I am mistaken, it was in these
self-same words that Tannonius Pudens, a man most certainly
not of distinguished eloquence, commenced his harangue against
me. How I wish he had good grounds for making such
weighty charges against me—of being possessed of good looks
and of eloquence—I should have had no difficulty in answer-
ing him, as Paris does Hector, in Homer :*

> " Man may not reject
> The glorious bounty by the Gods bestowed,
> Nor follows their beneficence our choice."

Such would have been my answer to the charge of good
looks: and I would have told him besides, that it has been
deemed allowable even for philosophers to be of graceful ap-
pearance; I would have shown that Pythagoras, who was the
first to call himself a philosopher, was the handsomest person of
his age; that Zeno, of ancient times, the native of Elea, he
who was the first of all, with truly critical skill, to divide
speech into two departments,† that this same Zeno, too, was,

* *In Homer.*]—Iliad, III. 65, 66.
† *Into two departments.*]—Rhetoric and dialectics, or logic.

as Plato affirms, most remarkable for the graces of his person. I would also have told him that many other philosophers have been handed down to memory as most remarkable for the beauty of their features, and who have set off the graces of their persons by the virtues of their lives.

This mode of defence, however, as I have already observed, but ill becomes me; for, whereas naturally I had but small pretensions to good looks, unremitting application to learned labours has effaced from me all comeliness, has made me thin, dried up my natural juices, expunged my healthy colour, and impaired my vigour. This hair, which they, with falsehood so manifest, affirmed that I had allowed to grow to such a length, in order to add to the allurements of my beauty—you see how far it is from being handsome and neatly arranged—all clogged and matted together, like a rope of twisted tow, shaggy and uneven, lumped and felted; its knots inextricable through prolonged neglect, not only of combing, but even of disentangling and separating it. The charge, then, as to my hair, which they have made as it were a capital count in the indictment, has, I fancy, been sufficiently refuted.

And then, as to eloquence, if I had been possessed of any, it ought not to appear surprising, or a ground for envy, if, after devoting myself, with all my energies, from my earliest years up to the present moment, to the cultivation of literature alone, in contempt of all other pleasures, I had succeeded in acquiring it, after expending upon it an amount of labour, by night and by day, exceeding, probably, that employed by any other man, and at the cost of a total disregard and sacrifice of my health. However, let them stand in no fear of my eloquence, an accomplishment which I am rather in hopes of acquiring, than able to display at present, if, indeed, I have made any progress at all.

And yet, if the words are true which Statius Cæcilius is said to have written in his poems, that "Innocence is eloquence," then, on that principle, I am ready to admit, and I do boldly assert, that in eloquence I will yield the palm to no man whatever. For, taking this view, what man living is there more eloquent than myself, who have never so much as entertained a thought to which I did not dare give utterance?*

---

* *Give utterance ?*]—He plays upon the resemblance of the words

I affirm, that I am most truly eloquent, for all guiltiness I
have ever esteemed as a thing not to be named; I affirm that
I am most ready in argument, for no deed or saying of mine
is there which I am not able, before all the world, by argu-
ment to support. For instance, I will now take up the argu-
ment with reference to the lines, which they put forward as
compositions of mine, of which I ought to be ashamed; when
you saw me smiling at them in scorn, because they delivered
them in so uncouth and illiterate a manner.

In the first place, then, they read out of my book of jokes,*
a short letter, the subject of which was dentifrices; this was
written in verse, to one Calpurnianus, who, no doubt, when he
produced that letter against me, did not perceive, in his eager-
ness to injure me, that if there was anything criminal in it,
he himself was affected thereby in an equal degree with me.
Now, that he had asked me for something to be used for the
purpose of cleaning his teeth, the lines themselves bear wit-
ness—

> " In hurried verse, I bid Calpurnian hail.
> I've sent, as you required, the dentifrice,
> Arabian produce, brightener of the mouth,
> A fine choice powder, a rare whitener,
> A soother of the swollen tender gums,
> A cleaner-out of scraps of yesterday;
> That no unsightly blemish may be seen,
> If you should chance with opened lips to laugh."

And now, pray, what do these lines contain, in meaning or
in language, that I should at all be ashamed of? What is there
that a philosopher should be at all unwilling to acknowledge
as his own composition? Unless, perchance, I was deserving of
reprehension for sending to Calpurnianus a powder made of
Arabian drugs, seeing that he was a person who might have
with much more propriety, after the filthy manner of the Ibe-
rians,

> " With his own water washed his teeth and rusty gums,"

as Catullus says.

' eloquens ' and ' eloquor,' ' facundus ' and ' nefas,' ' disertus ' and ' dis-
sero:' but his meaning cannot be easily expressed in English.

* *Book of jokes.*]—Called ' Ludicra.' This book is lost, with the
exception of one line, besides those found here. It probably consisted of
jests and amatory stories.

I perceived just now some who could hardly controul his laughter, when the orator inveighed with such asperity against cleaning of the teeth, and pronounced the word "dentifrice" with more indignation than any body else would speak of poison. And why should he not? No doubt it is a crime not to be overlooked in a philosopher, if he is particular in his precautions against dirt; if he allows no part of his body that is exposed to view to be unclean and filthy, the mouth especially, which man makes frequent use of openly and conspicuously: whether he kisses another, or discourses on any subject, or lectures before an audience, or repeats his prayers in a temple. For so it is that words precede every act of mankind; words which, as the first of poets says, issue forth from "the hedge* of the teeth." If you could at the present day produce any one gifted with powers of utterance so grand as those with which he was endowed, he would declare in his usual manner, that from him above all men who has any care for the art of speaking, the mouth requires more sedulous attention than all the rest of the body, seeing that it is the vestibule of the mind, the gateway of speech, and the outer court of the thoughts.

At all events, according to my way of thinking, I should say that nothing so ill becomes a man who is of free birth and liberal education as inattention to the appearance of the mouth. For this portion of the person is elevated in position, exposed full in view, and in continual use. On the other hand, with wild beasts and cattle the mouth is low-seated, and brought down on a level with the legs; it lies close to the feet and to the grass on which they feed, and is scarcely ever to be seen but when they are dead, or in a state of exasperation and ready to bite; whereas you look upon no feature before this in a man while he is silent,—no one more frequently while he is in the act of speaking. I only wish, now, that my censor, Æmilianus, would answer me this question: whether he is ever in the habit of washing his feet, or whether, if he does not deny the fact, he would contend that greater care ought to be bestowed upon the cleanliness of the feet than of the teeth? If, indeed, a person, like yourself, Æmilianus, will hardly ever open his mouth except to utter

* *The hedge.*]—He alludes to the expression ἕρκος ὀδόντων, frequently found in Homer.

calumnies and revilings, I am clearly of opinion that he ought
to bestow no attention whatever on his mouth, nor to clean
his teeth with powders brought from abroad, when he might
much more appropriately rub them with charcoal snatched from
the funeral pile; and that he ought not so much as to rinse
them with common water.

On the contrary, let his malignant tongue, the caterer of
falsehoods and of bitter abuse, for ever lie amid the stench
and foulness which so well become it. For how, in the name
of misfortune, is it consistent with reason that one should have
a clean and purified tongue, and at the same time a loath-
some and offensive voice? that he should, like the viper, instil
black venom from teeth white as snow? On the other hand,
in the case of him who knows he is going to utter language*
that is neither inappropriate nor unpleasing, it is with good
reason that his mouth is washed beforehand, just like a cup
when it is prepared for containing a pleasant draught.

But why enlarge any further upon this topic, with regard to
mankind? That huge beast, the crocodile, which is produced
in the Nile, even it, as I am informed, opens wide its jaws,
and, without inflicting injury, allows its teeth to be cleansed.
For as it has an immense mouth and no tongue, and generally
lies concealed beneath the water, numbers of leeches fasten
about its teeth; wherefore it repairs to the banks of the river,
and opens its mouth, and one of the river birds, a friend
to it, thrusts in her beak and picks its teeth, without in-
curring any risk.

No more of this. I now come to the rest of these love verses,
as they style them; but which they read in such harsh and
uncouth tones, as rather to provoke hatred.

But really, what has it to do with magical practices, if I
did celebrate in verse the children of my friend Scribonius?
Am I of necessity a magician, because I am a poet? Who
ever heard tell of a suspicion like this, a conjecture so happy,
an argument so convincing? "Apuleius has composed verses;"
if they were bad ones, it is a fault, no doubt, but then it is not
the fault of the philosopher, but of the poet. If, on the other
hand, they were good ones, on what grounds do you accuse
him? "But then," say you, "he composed verses of a jocu-

* *Utter language.*]—'Orationem' seems a preferable reading to 'rati-
onem.'

lar and amorous character." Is this, then, your charge against me, and did you make a mistake in the name, when you accused me of practising magic? And yet other persons have done the same: among the Greeks (if you are not aware of the fact), a Teian, a Lacedæmonian, a Ceian,* and innumerable others; a woman, too, a native of Lesbos,† wrote in wanton numbers, and with such gracefulness, as to reconcile us to the strangeness of her dialect by the sweetness of her lines; then, among ourselves, Ædituus, and Portius, and Catullus, and others without number.

"But these were not philosophers," you say. Will you go so far, pray, as to deny that Solon was a man of serious habits and a philosopher? and yet he was the composer of that most wanton line,

> "Desirous of her thighs and honeyed mouth."

Now what is there in all my verses put together, to be compared in lasciviousness of expression with this one line? not to say a word about the writings of Diogenes, the cynic, and of Zeno, the founder of the sect of the Stoics? I will now read some of my lines over again, that they may understand that I am not ashamed of them.

> " Thou, Critias, art my bosom's joy;
> Charinus too, my sun-bright boy,
> Thy portion in my love's the same;
> I burn for both with equal flame.
> And fear ye not—this double fire
> I'll bear, to win my soul's desire.
> Let me by both be·looked upon
> As by himself is each dear one;
> Look on me thus, and you shall be
> As precious as two eyes to me."

And now I will read the other ones, which they read the last of all, as though they were of surpassing indecency.

> " Garlands and song I weave for thy sweet sake;
> This for thyself; those let thy Genius take:
> Song, to extol the happy day that brings
> Fulfilment of my Critias' fourteen springs;

---

* *A Ceian, &c.*]—He alludes to Anacreon, of Teos, a city of Ionia, and Simonides, of Ceos, an island in the Ægean Sea. It is not known to whom he alludes as the native of Lacedæmon.

† *Native of Lesbos.*]—Sappho, the poetess. She wrote in the Æolic dialect.

> Garlands, to crown thy brows in this glad time,
> And deck with blooming flowers thy blooming prime.
> For flowers of spring, give thy own spring to me,
> And shame my gifts, repaid thus bounteously;
> For garlands twined, with twining arms caress me;
> For roses, with thy roseate kisses press me;
> And for my song, wake thy own vocal reed,
> Gifts, song, and all will be surpassed indeed."

Here, then, Maximus, you have the charge against me founded upon garlands and songs, just as though I were some wanton reveller. You also observed, that this, too, was made a charge against me, that whereas the youths are called by other names, I have given them those of Charinus and Critias. Why, upon similar grounds, they might accuse Catullus, for calling Clodia Lesbia; and just in the same way, Ticida, because he wrote Pærilla, whereas the lady's name was Metella; Propertius too, who speaks of Cynthia, but means Hostia; and Tibullus, who had Plania in his thoughts, while Delia was named in his lines. For my own part, although C. Lucilius was a poet who wrote Iambic lines, I should still consider him worthy of censure, because he openly defamed the youths Gentilis and Macedo in his lines under their own names. How much more beseemingly does Virgil, the poet of Mantua, act, who, just as I have done, when praising the son of his friend Pollio, in his sportive Bucolics, refrains from making mention of names, and calls himself Corydon, and the youth Alexis.*

But Æmilianus, more of a clownish churl than any of the shepherds and herdsmen of Virgil, a man who will ever be a bumpkin and a barbarian, while he flatters himself that he is of more rigid morals than your Serrani, Curii, or Fabricii avers that this kind of composition does not befit a Platonic philosopher. And will you still persist in affirming this, Æmilianus, if I shew that these lines have been composed after a precedent afforded us by Plato himself, of whose composition there are no verses in existence, except some elegiac lines on Love; for all his other poems, I suppose because they were not so elegant, he committed to the flames. Hear, then, the verses of Plato the philosopher, to the boy Aster, if indeed, at your time of life, you are still able to learn anything in the way of literature.

* *The youth Alexis.*]—He alludes to the Second Eclogue of Virgil. The name of the youth is supposed to have been Alexander.

> Why dost thou gaze upon the sky ?
>> Oh, that I were yon spangled sphere,
> And every star should be an eye
>> To wander o'er thy beauties here.
>
> In life thou wert my morning star ;
>> And now that death hath stol'n thy light,
> Alas, thou shinest dim and far,
>> Like the pale beam that weeps at night."*

Hear, also, the lines addressed by the same writer, Plato, to the boys Alexis and Phædrus, where he addresses them in a joint poem.

> " Although I nothing said but this—' How fair
> Alexis is,' all turn and gaze on thee.
> My soul, why show to dogs a bone, and then
> Torment them ? did we not lose Phœdrus thus ?"

And, again, not to quote any more lines than these, I will just repeat his last distich on Dion of Syracuse, and then make an end.

> " Thou sleep'st in honour on thy country's breast,
> Dion, beloved of my extatic soul ! "

But really am I not acting absurdly, even to mention these things in court? and are you not rather acting the part of calumniators, even to produce these matters as the grounds of your accusation against me? just as though, forsooth, it were any proof of a man's mode of life, that he writes wanton lines. Have you not read Catullus, where he thus replies to the malevolent?

> " 'Tis fit the worthy poet should be chaste—
> There's no need that his verses should be so."

The divine Adrian, when he honoured the tomb of his friend the poet Voconius with his verse, wrote to this effect :—

> " Wanton thou wast in verse, but chaste in mind:"

a thing he never would have said, if verses somewhat sprightly were to be considered as indicative of pruriency of thought. I recollect, too, having read many verses of a similar character by the divine Adrian himself. Assert then, if you dare, Æmilianus, that it is evil to do that which the divine Adrian, our emperor and censor, has done, and has handed down to memory as having been done by him. Besides, do you suppose that

---

* *Weeps at night.*]—Translated by Thomas Moore.

Maximus is likely to censure anything that he knows I have done after the example of Plato? whose lines, which I just now quoted, are the more chaste for being undisguised, the more modest for their plainness of expression. For, to dissemble and to conceal these and all such matters, is the part of an offender, while, to discourse of them openly and without disguise, is the part of him who speaks but in jest; for so it is, that by nature the power of utterance has been given to innocence, while silence has been allotted to criminality.

But I will forbear to enlarge upon those deep and holy mysteries of the Platonic philosophy, which, while they are revealed to but few of the pious, are totally unknown to all the profane; how, that Venus is a twofold goddess, each of the pair producing a peculiar passion, and in different kinds of lovers   One of them is the "Vulgar," who is prompted by the ordinary passion of love, to stimulate not only the human feelings, but even those of cattle and wild beasts, to lust, and commit the enslaved bodies of beings thus smitten by her to immoderate and furious embraces. The other is the "Heavenly" Venus, who presides over the purest love, who cares for men alone and but few of them, and who influences her devotees by no stimulants or allurements to base desire. For the love that is engendered by her is not a wanton or lascivious love, but, on the contrary, it is serious and unadorned, and allures its votaries to virtue by its own intrinsic beauty; and if at any time she does commend a graceful form, she scrupulously protects it against all cause for reproach. Nor, indeed, is there anything else in the beauty of the person deserving of love, beyond the fact that it recalls to the mind which took its origin in Deity, that beauty which in all its truth and purity it once beheld among the gods. Hence it is, that Afranius, with his usual eloquence, has left this line :—

" Where wise men love, all others will desire."

However, Æmilianus, if you wish to hear the truth, or if you can ever arrive at a perception of the fact, the wise man does not so much love, as recall to mind.* Do pardon, then, the philosopher Plato, for his verses on love, that I may not

---

* *Recall to mind.*]—The beauty of which it was sensible, when in a former state. The mind was, according to the Platonic philosophy, a part of Deity.

feel myself necessitated, contrary to the maxim of Neoptolemus in Ennius,* to "philosophize in detail;" or, at all events, if you decline to do so, I will readily submit, with reference to verses of this nature, to be censured in company with Plato. And to you, Maximus, I return abundant thanks, for having so attentively listened to these appendages to my defence, which I have deemed necessary, inasmuch as they are put forward in answer to charges brought against me; and for the same reason I request that you will listen as readily and as attentively as you have hitherto done, to what I have to say, before I come to the main charges.

For next follows the lengthy and cutting attack about the looking-glass, upon which, Pudens, screaming aloud, commensurately with the atrocity of the offence, almost burst himself, crying, "a philosopher has a looking-glass!—a philosopher possesses a looking-glass!" Let me then confess that I have one, lest you should flatter yourself that you had hit me hard if I denied it; but it is by no means a necessary inference, that I am in the habit of dressing too before a looking-glass. For suppose I were in possession of a theatrical wardrobe, would you argue thence that I was in the habit of using the long train of the tragedian, the saffron-coloured dress of the comedian, or the little mantle of the mimic, as at the triennial orgies of Bacchus? You would not, I think. And on the other hand, there is many a thing of which I am not possessed, but of which I still enjoy the use.

If, then, the possession of a thing is no proof of the use of it, or the non-possession of the non-use of it, and if not so much the possession of a looking-glass is censured by you, as the looking into it, it then necessarily follows, that you must shew when and in whose presence I looked into the glass; for, according to the present state of the case, you make it a greater offence for a philosopher to look into a looking-glass, than for one of the uninitiated to pry into† the mysteries of Ceres.

* *In Ennius.*]—We learn from Aulus Gellius, that the maxim here alluded to was, ' we ought to philosophize concisely, for to do so in detail is not pleasant.' Ennius was one of the oldest of the Latin poets.

† *To pry into.*—He alludes to the baskets or boxes which were carried by the Canephori in the processions of Ceres, and were supposed to contain images of the goddess with other articles of a mystic nature.

Come now, even if I should confess that I have looked into it, pray what crime is it to be acquainted with one's own features, and to have their image not put up* in one fixed spot, but to carry it about in a little mirror, ready to be surveyed wherever you please? Are you ignorant that there is nothing more deserving to be viewed by a man than his own features? For my part, I know that those sons are the most beloved who bear the strongest resemblance to the parents and that a man's own statue is erected at the public expense in his honour as the reward of merit, in order that he may look upon the same; else what is the use of statues and images thus framed with the varied resources of art? unless, perchance, we admit that the very same thing that is worthy of admiration when produced by artistic skill, is to be deemed culpable when presented by nature; whereas, on the contrary, the readiness and exactness of nature are even still more deserving of our admiration. For in tracing all likenesses by the hand, a considerable time is consumed in the work, and yet, after all, no resemblance is to be seen comparable with that to be viewed in a mirror; for clay is deficient in vigour, stone in colour, painting in firmness, while all are devoid of the power of motion, which brings the likeness before us in the highest degree.

For in the mirror is to be seen the image wonderfully reflected, not only with the resemblance traced out, but endowed, too, with motion, and obedient to every gesture of the person whom it represents. Then, besides, it is always of the same age with the beholder, from the earliest boyhood down to the very close of old age: so many aspects of life does it assume, of such varied conditions of the body does it partake, such numerous changes of the same features, whether influenced by joy or by grief, does it imitate. But, on the other hand, the resemblance that is moulded from clay, formed of molten brass, hewn out of stone, impressed by heat on wax, laid on a surface with paint, or represented by any other resource of human art, after no long interval of time becomes quite unlike the original; and besides, it always preserves the same rigid unmoved features, just like a corpse. To such a degree then, does the highly-wrought smoothness of its po-

* *Not put up.*]—That is to say, in a portrait.

lished surface, and artificial brightness of the mirror, surpass all art in reflecting the likeness of the person.

Either, then, we are bound to adhere to the opinion of Agesilaus the Lacedæmonian, who having but a poor opinion of his own appearance, would never allow himself to be represented in painting or sculpture, or else, if the usages of all the rest of mankind appear worthy to be retained, and statues and images are not to be eschewed, what reason have you to be of opinion that each man ought to see his likeness rather in stone than in silver, rather in a picture than in a mirror? Do you think it a disgrace for a man carefully to survey his own figure? Is it not said of the philosopher Socrates, that he even advised his disciples to view themselves repeatedly in a mirror, so that he among them who was smitten with his own good looks, might be the more scrupulously careful not to disgrace the beauty of his person by bad manners; while, on the other hand, he who thought himself not so highly gifted in appearance, might carefully use his best endeavours to screen his ugliness by his virtues. And thus did a man, who was wiser than all others, make use of the mirror for the purpose even of improving moral cultivation.

Then too, who knows not how Demosthenes, that most excellent master in the art of oratory, always got up his causes before a mirror, just as though in presence of a master? So that most excellent orator, after he had learned eloquence from the philosopher Plato, and the art of reasoning from Eubulides the logician, endeavoured to obtain the extreme perfection of the art of oratory by the assistance of the mirror.

Which, then, do you think ought to pay the greater attention to grace in the impressive delivery of his language, the wrangling rhetorician or the warning philosopher? the one who for a few moments disputes before certain judges who are chosen by lot, or the one who is continually discussing questions in the presence of all mankind; he who wrangles about the limits of fields, or he who defines the limits of good and evil? Why, if it was only for this purpose, ought not a philosopher to look into a mirror? For it is often incumbent upon him not only to view his own likeness, but to consider too the manner in which that likeness is so reflected; whether it is that, as Epicurus says, images which emanate from our bodies in a perpetual flow, being a kind of slough, as it were, as soon as they strike against any smooth and solid surface, are thrown back again, and so turned the contrary way; or whether it is that, as other philosophers argue, our rays of vision, (whether flowing from the middle of the eyes, and mingling and uniting with the external light as Plato thinks, or whether only proceeding from the eyes without any foreign admixture whatever, as Archytas supposes, or whether being broken by the tension of the atmosphere, as the Stoics imagine), when they have struck upon any body that is dense, smooth, and shining, rebound and return to the features at the same angles of incidence at which they have struck that body, and so represent in the mirror that which they touch and behold externally to it. Does it not seem to you to be a matter of duty that philosophers should investigate all these subjects and duly enquire into them, and that they ought to be the only persons to look into mirrors of all kinds, whether with a watery surface or with a dry? For their province it is, besides what I have already mentioned, to enter upon that other enquiry, why in mirrors with a plain surface images generally appear alike, while in mirrors which are spherical and convex in surface, all objects appear diminished, and, on the other hand, in those which are concave they are magnified; at what distance and for what reason before a concave mirror the left hand takes the place of the right; in what cases it is that the image at one moment withdraws within, and at another, seems to be stepping out* of the same mirror; why it is that a concave mirror, if it is held facing the sun ignites fuel placed close to it: how it happens that distinct rainbows are seen in the clouds, and that two suns exactly similar are to be beheld: besides numerous other questions of a similar nature, which are discussed in the ample volume of Archimedes the Syracusan, a man endowed far beyond all other men with a wonderful degree of skill in all geometrical subjects; though I am not quite sure but he is worthy of especial note for the fact that he consulted the mirror often and carefully. If you had only been acquainted with his book, Æmilianus, and had applied yourself not only to your fields and your clods, but to the geometrician's board and fine sand, believe me, when I say it,

---

* *Stepping out.*]—He alludes to the appearance, on advancing the finger or other portion of the body towards and withdrawing it from a convex mirror.

that although your extremely ugly features differ but very little from those of the Thyestes of tragedy, there is no doubt but you would have looked into the mirror with the object of learning something new, and would at last have given up the plough, in the intensity of your admiration of the numerous furrows and wrinkles to be seen in your own face.

Now, I should not wonder if you took it in very good part that I make mention of those most distorted features of yours, but am silent as to your manners, which are far more repulsive. The fact is, that whereas I am not naturally of a quarrelsome disposition, I was, moreover, quite willing until the last few days, to remain in ignorance whether you were a white or a black man, and even now, by Hercules! I am far from certain on that point. This arises from the fact, that while you have been buried in the obscurity of a country life, I have been busied with my studies. So, while the shade thrown around you by your ignoble condition has stood between yourself and an observer, I have never made it my object to learn the misdeeds of any person, but have always, in preference, studied how to veil my own failings rather than pry into those of others. I am just in the same position, then, with reference to you, as the man who chances to be standing in a place upon which a bright ligh is thrown, while another, concealed in deep shade, is looking at him. For just in a similar manner, while you can easily observe, in your obscurity, what I am doing in the open daylight and before all the world, you yourself, being concealed by your ignoble station, and shunning the light, cannot in your turn be distinguished by me.

Hence it is, that whether you have slaves to till your lands, or whether you make exchange of labour with your neighbours, turn and turn about, I neither know nor am I anxious to know ; but you know very well that in one day I manumitted three slaves at Œa,* and this your advocate, among other points upon which he had been instructed by you, made an objection against me; although but very shortly before, he had asserted that I had come to Œa with but a single servant as my attendant. Now I wish you would answer me this: out of one servant how could I manumit three, unless

* *At Œa.*]—A city of Africa, between the greater and the lesser Syrtes.

this, too, is to be set down to the account of magic? Am I to suppose that such is your blindness in lying, or such the inveteracy of that habit in you? "Apuleius came to Œa with a single servant," and then, after babbling out a few words, "Apuleius manumitted three slaves at Œa in one day." Why, not even would your story have been credible, had you said that I had come attended by three servants, and had liberated them all; and yet if I had done so, why should you look upon the possession of but three servants as a mark of poverty, rather than the manumission of three as a proof of opulence? You know not, most decidedly you know not, Æmilianus, how to bring a charge against a philosopher, when you throw in my teeth the scantiness of my retinue, a thing that I ought rather, for the sake of my own credit, to have feigned, had it been necessary so to do, inasmuch as I was well aware that not only the philosophers, of whom I profess to be a disciple, but even emperors of the Roman people have gloried in the small number of their servants.

And have not your advocates, pray, read to the same effect? How that M. Antonius, a man of consular dignity, had but eight servants in his house, and how that Carbo, who attained the highest honours, had one less? And then, again, how Manius Curius, who was rendered so illustrious by his numerous victories, for three times did he enter at the same gate in triumph, how that Manius Caius, I say, employed but two camp servants in his expeditions? So likewise the man who triumphed over the Sabines, the Samnites, and Pyrrhus, had fewer servants in number than the triumphs he enjoyed. Then, again, Marcus Cato, little expecting that others would mention it of him, has left it written in a speech of his, that when he set out as consul for Spain, he took with him from the city but three attendants, and no more; when he arrived, however, at the public villa,* these seemed too few for his requirements, whereupon he ordered two youths to be purchased in the forum at the slaves' platform,† and these five he took

---

* *Public villa.*]—The 'publica villa' was a house of reception used by the Roman people for the entertainment of foreign ambassadors, taking the census, and other public purposes.

† *Slaves' platform.*]—' De mensa.' The 'mensa' here alluded to was a stone or platform on which the slaves stood when put up for sale by the præco' or 'auctioneer.'

with him to Spain. If Pudens had read all this, according to my way of thinking he would either have entirely spared this invective, or else in three servants he would have seen cause rather to censure the multitude of a philosopher's attendants, than the scantiness of his retinue.

He has even gone so far as to reproach me with my poverty, a charge truly acceptable to a philosopher, and one to which I readily plead guilty. For Poverty has long been the hand-maid of Philosophy, frugal, temperate, contented with little, eager for praise, averse from the things sought by wealth, safe in her ways, simple in her requirements, in her counsels a promoter of what is right. No one has she ever puffed up with pride, no one has she corrupted by the enjoyment of power, no one has she maddened with tyrannical ambition; for no pampering of the appetite or of the passions does she sigh, nor can she indulge it.

But it is your fosterlings of wealth who are in the habit of perpetrating these disgraceful excesses and others of a kindred nature. If you review all the greatest enormities that have been committed in the memory of mankind, you will not find a single poor man among the perpetrators: whilst, on the other hand, in the number of illustrious men, hardly any of the rich are to be found; poverty has nurtured from his very cradle every individual in whom we find anything to admire and commend. Poverty, I say, she who in former ages was the foundress of all cities, the inventress of all arts, she who is guiltless of all offence, who is lavish of all glory, who has been honoured with every praise among all nations. For this same Poverty it was that among the Greeks showed herself just in Aristides, humane in Phocion, resolute in Epaminondas, wise in Socrates, and eloquent in Homer. It was this same Poverty, too, that for the Roman people laid the very earliest foundations of their sway, and that offers sacrifice to the immortal Gods in their behalf with the ladle and the dish of clay, even to this day.

If there were now sitting as judges at this trial, C. Fabricius, Cneius Scipio, and Manius Curius, whose daughters, by reason of their poverty, went home to their husbands portioned at the public expense, carrying with them the glories of their family and the money of the public, if Publicola, the expeller of the kings, and [Menenius] Agrippa, the reconciler of the people, the expense of whose funerals was, in consequence of their limited fortunes, defrayed by the Roman people, by contributions of the smallest coins;* if Attilius Regulus, whose little field was, in consequence of a like poverty, cultivated at the public expense; if, in fine, all those ancient families, ennobled by consulships, censorships, and triumphs, could obtain a short respite, and return to light and take part in this trial, would you then have dared to reproach a philosopher for his poverty, in the presence of so many consuls distinguished for theirs?

Or is it that Claudius Maximus appears to you to be a suitable listener, while you are deriding poverty, because he happens to be the owner of an ample estate? You are mistaken, Æmilianus, and little are you acquainted with his feelings, if you form your estimate of him according to the indulgence of Fortune, and not according to the strict rules of philosophy; if you suppose that a man of such rigid morals and so long used to warfare, is not better disposed towards circumscribed moderation than fastidious opulence; if you suppose that he does not approve of wealth on the same principles that he does a garment, rather when it suits the person than when it is remarkable for its length. For wealth, too, if it is not conveniently carried, becomes an impediment to us, and trips us up, no less than a draggling garment. Indeed, in all matters which are needed for the requirements of life, every thing that steps beyond becoming moderation is superfluous, and is rather a burden to us than useful. Hence it is, that immoderate wealth, just like a large and disproportioned rudder, is more apt to sink than to guide, for in such a case people have a useless abundance, a pernicious superfluity.

I see, besides, that among the most opulent persons, those are especially commended who make no bustle, no immoderate show; who live without thrusting their wealth into public view, who manage their vast resources without ostentation and without pride, and who imitate the poor in the appearance of limited means. If, then, the rich even seek a certain appearance—a colour of poverty—in order to put on the semblance of limited means, why should those who are poorer be ashamed of it, when they have to endure a poverty not affected, but real?

* *Smallest coins.*]—'Sextantibus.' The 'sextans' was the sixth part of an 'as.'

I could, indeed, raise an argument with you about the very name itself, and I could show that none of us are poor who do not wish for superfluities, and who possess the things that are necessary, which, by nature, are but few indeed. For he has the most who desires the least: he who wants but little, is most likely to have as much as he wants. For this reason it is that riches are not better estimated according to lands and income than according to a man's own mind; for if a man is craving through avarice, and always greedy of gain, not even by mountains of gold will he be satisfied, but he will be always begging for something, that he may increase his store. And this is the real exposition of poverty. For all desire of acquiring, arises from the opinion which each man entertains as to what is poverty. And it matters not how great is the amount of which you are in want—Philus had not so great an estate as Lælius, Lælius as Scipio, Scipio as Crassus the Rich, nor even Crassus the Rich as he wished. So that, although he surpassed all in wealth, he himself was surpassed by his own avarice, and seemed to be rich in the eyes of all others rather than in his own. But, on the other hand, those philosophers of whom I have made mention, wishing for no more than they could obtain, and actuated by desires commensurate with their means, were rightfully and deservedly rich and opulent. For you become poor through the want of acquisition, and rich through having no wants to satisfy; inasmuch as a state of poverty is ascertained from the manifestation of desire, opulence from the fact of being satisfied. Therefore, Æmilianus, if you wish me to be accounted poor, you must of necessity first show that I am avaricious. For if, in my mind, there is nothing wanting, I care not what external things may be wanting; for in the abundance of these consists no praise, in the want of them no blame.

Suppose, however, that it is otherwise, and that I really am poor, because Fortune has denied me riches; suppose that, as often is the case, either my guardian has made away with them, an enemy robbed me of them, or my father failed to leave me any; is a man, then, to be censured for a thing which is imputed as a fault to no one of the animals. neither the eagle, nor the bull, nor the lion? If a horse has good qualities, and is an easy trotter, and swift in his gallop, no one censures him for being in want of fodder; and will you

impute it as a fault to me, not that I have said or done
anything that is bad, but that I live contented with my
humble means, that I have but few servants, that I eat
sparingly, that I am lightly clad, and that I cater but
meagrely? And yet, on the other hand, small as you think my
means in all these respects, I both think them abundant, and
more than sufficient, and I desire to restrict myself to still
fewer necessities, being fully assured that I shall be the more
happy, the more circumscribed my wants. For it is with the
mind just as with the body; in a healthy state it is lightly
clad, but in sickness it is wrapped in cumbrous clothing
and it is a sure sign of infirmity to have many wants. It is
with life just as with swimming; that man is the most ex-
pert who is the most disengaged from all encumbrances. Just
the same way, amid the stormy tempests of human life, that
which is light tends to our buoyancy, that which is heavy, to
sink us.

For my part, I have learned that in this especially the Gods
surpass mankind, that they have to satisfy no necessities. Hence
it is, that him among us who has the fewest possible necessities,
I consider most strongly to resemble a God. I was very well
pleased, therefore, when you said, intending it as a reproach,
that my property consisted of a staff and a wallet. And I only
wish that I had such perfect control over my mind, that I
required nothing whatever beyond those articles, and be-
comingly submitted to the same equipment which Crates,
throwing all riches aside, spontaneously desired. This Crates,
if you will take my word for it, Æmilianus, was a man of the
higher class of Thebes, rich, and ennobled in his city through
his love of that very state which you impute to me as a fault.
He presented his large and ample property to the people, and
putting away his numerous retinue of servants, made choice of
a life of solitude; his trees, numerous and fruitful as they
were, he scorned in comparison with a single staff; his most
elegant villas he changed for a single scrip; the praises of
which he afterwards even sang in verse, on experience of
its utility, adapting to the purpose those lines of Homer in
which he celebrates the Isle of Crete. I will mention the
words with which he commences, that you may not suppose I
have only invented this for the purpose of my defence—

" Scrip is a city's name,* which 'mid dense smoke
Lies fair and flourishing."

And then follow lines so admirable, that, if you were to read them, you would be much more inclined to envy me my wallet than the hand of Pudentilla. Do you censure philosophers for their scrip and staff? By the same reasoning, you ought to censure horsemen for their trappings, foot-soldiers for their bucklers, standard-bearers for their ensigns, and those, in fine, who enjoy a triumph for their white steeds, and their robes embroidered with sprigs of palm.

These, however, are not the equipments of the Platonic sect, but they are the insignia of the class of Cynics. Still, the scrip and the staff were the same to Diogenes and to Antisthenes, as the diadem to kings, the martial cloak to generals, the rounded hat to priests, and the crooked staff to augurs. Indeed, Diogenes the Cynic, when disputing with Alexander the Great as to who was the true king, boasted of his staff as serving him in the stead of a sceptre. Even the invincible Hercules himself—(you will, no doubt, feel a perfect contempt for those others, as a set of mendicants) — Hercules himself, I say, the traveller over the whole earth, the cleanser thereof from wild beasts, the subduer of nations, when he was travelling through the earth, and shortly before he was summoned to heaven for his virtues, had no better clothing than a single hide, although he was a God, and no other attendants than a single staff.

If, however, you think nothing at all of these instances, and have summoned me not to plead a cause, but to discourse upon my income, that you may not be in ignorance about any of my affairs, if, indeed, you are ignorant, I admit that my father left me and my brother a little under twenty hundred thousand sesterces, and that that sum has been a little diminished by me, in consequence of prolonged travel, close study, and frequent donations. For I have given assistance to most of my friends, paid their fees to numbers of instructors, and have given dowries even to the daughters of some : nor indeed, for my own part, should I have hesitated to spend even the whole of my patrimony, in order to acquire, what to me is of far greater value, a contempt for all wealth.

* *Scrip is a city's name.*]—He puts Πήρη, a ' scrip,' or ' wallet,' in place of the name of Crete, used by Homer.

You, on the other hand, Æmilianus, and men like you, un-polished and uncouth, are to be valued, no doubt, just according to what you possess ; just as a barren and unproductive tree, which bears no fruit, is to be estimated in value according to the amount of timber to be found in its trunk.   Nevertheless, forbear, Æmilianus, from this time forward, to throw his poverty in the teeth of any man, seeing that, up to a very re-cent date, you used to plough for three days single-handed the one little field at Zaratha, which your father left you, with the assistance of a solitary ass to get it ready before the usual wet season.   Nor is it such a very long time since the nume-rous deaths of relatives came to your support, by giving you the possession of property that you little deserved ; a circum-stance from which, still more than from that most ugly face of yours, you have obtained the name of Charon.

And now as to my native country, and your shewing that it is situate on the confines of Numidia and of Getulia, from writings of mine, in which I confessed, when I was lecturing before that most illustrious man, Lollianus Avitus, that I was a Semi-Numidian and a Semi-Getulian ; I do not see what I have to be ashamed of in that respect, any more than the elder Cyrus, because he was of mingled parentage, being a Semi-Median and a Semi-Persian.   For the proper subject of enquiry is not where a man is born, but what are his man-ners; not in what country, but upon what principle he began life is the thing to be considered.   It is with good reason allowed the gardener and the vintner to recommend vege-tables and wine according to the nobleness of the soil ; the wine of Thasos,* for instance, and the vegetables of Phlius.   For it is a fact, that those productions of the earth are much im-proved in flavour by the natural fertility of the district, the rain of the heavens, the mildness of the breezes, the brightness of the sun, and the richness of the soil.

But, on the other hand, while the mind of man is sojourning in the abode of the body which is foreign to it, how can any of these particulars in any way add to or subtract from its merits or its demerits ?   When was it not the case that in every

* *Of Thasos.*]—Thasos, an island in the Ægean sea, was famous for the excellence of its wines.   The vicinity of the city of Phlino, near Ar-gos, was equally famous for its growth of vegetables.

nation various dispositions were to be found? and this, although some of them seem to be peculiarly distinguished for stupidity, others for talent. Among the Scythians, a people most remarkable for their stupidity, was born the wise Anacharsis; among the clever Athenians, the fool Melitides. Nor do I say this because I am in any way ashamed of my country, even though ours had still been the city of Syphax:* we, however, were conquered, on which we were presented as a gift of the Roman people to king Masinissa, and after that, on a new allotment of land being made among the veteran soldiers, we rose to be what we now are, a most famous colony. In this colony it was, that my father, a man of the highest rank, a duumvir, enjoyed every honour; whose position I have occupied in the same community, from the time I was admitted to the rank of decurion, having in no way degenerated from him, and, I both hope and think, enjoying the same amount of honor and of estimation.

Why do I mention these particulars? In order that you, Æmilianus, may have the fewer pretences for levelling your invectives against me in future; and that you may be the more inclined to pardon me, if, in my negligence, I did omit to make choice of that Attic Zarath† of yours, to be born in. Are you not ashamed of yourselves, thus perseveringly, in the presence of such a man, to prefer such accusations as these? To bring forward matters so frivolous, and at the same time of so conflicting a nature, and yet to charge me as being guilty of them all? Have you not accused me on contradictory grounds? on those of the wallet and the staff, because of my rigidness of life; on those of the verses and the looking-glass, on account of my frivolity; of having but one servant, as being penurious; of having three freedmen, as being a spendthrift; and then, besides, of being in eloquence a Greek, by birth a barbarian. Why do you not rouse up your senses, and recollect that you are pleading your cause before Claudius Maximus, before a man of serious habits, and one engaged with the affairs of this entire province? Why not

* *City of Syphax.*]—Who, contrary to his promise, sided with Hannibal against the Romans, and was afterwards captured by Musinissa, and delivered to the Romans, who starved him to death in prison.

† *Attic Zarath.*]—He says this ironically, and in allusion to the barbarism of the city of Zarath in Mauritania.

away with these vain reproaches? Why not prove, what you have accused me of, heinous crimes, lawless misdeeds, and wicked artifices? Why is your speech thus weak in argu ments, thus mighty in outcry?

I now come to the charge itself of magic, that blazing brand which you lighted up against me with such immense clamour, but which has disappointed the expectation of all, dying out into I know not what old woman's stories. Have you not, Maximus, sometimes beheld a fire that has broken out amid stubble? how loud its crackling, how large its blaze, how rapid its growth, and yet, after all, how slight the fuel on which it feeds, how short-lived the flame, that leaves after it no remains! In that flame behold this accusation, which began in abuse, which has been fanned by assertions, which has failed in its proofs, and which, after your sentence shall have been pronounced, is destined to survive in not a single remnant of this false charge: a charge which has been entirely centred by Æmilianus in the proof of this one point, that I am a magician; for which reason I may be allowed to enquire of these most learned advocates of his, what a magician is.

For if, as I have read in many authors, a magician* means, in the language of the Persians, the same thing that the word "priest" does in ours, what is the crime, pray, in being a magician? what is the crime in properly knowing, and understanding, and being versed in the laws of ceremonials, the solemn order of sacred rites, and religious ordinances? What if, indeed, that is magic, which Plato calls "the service of the Gods," when he relates with what careful training the Persians bring up a youth who is destined for the throne. I recollect the very words of that divine man, and do you, Maximus, recall them to your memory with me: "When he is fourteen years of age, those persons take charge of the boy, whom they call 'the royal tutors.' These are four persons, whom they select from the highest classes of the Persians, and who are ap proved of for their age. One of these is the most wise, another the most just, another the most prudent, and the fourth the most valiant man. Of these, one instructs him in the magic of Zoroaster and of Oromazes, which is the service of the Gods. He also teaches him the art of governing."

* *A magician.*]—Magus.

Do you not hear then, you who are so rash as to accuse me of it, that magic is an art acceptable to the Gods, one that most correctly teaches us how to worship and to venerate them ; one that is consequently consistent with piety, and skilled in all divine matters; one that has been ennobled from the very times of Zoroaster and of Oromazes, its inventors, as being the handmaid of the inhabitants of heaven? For among the very rudiments of the royal training this art is taught : nor is any one of the Persians rashly allowed to be a magician, any more than he is to be a king.

The same Plato, in another discourse of his, when speaking of a certain Zamolxis, a Thracian by birth, but a man skilled in the same art, has left a passage in his writings to the following effect :—" But he said, O happy man, that the soul is healed by certain incantations ; and that these incantations are soothing words." And if this is the fact, what reason is there why I should not be allowed to understand either the soothing words of Zamolxis, or the priestly duties enjoined by Zoroaster? But if, after the common usage, these people imagine that a magician is properly a person who, from communication and discourse with the immortal Gods, is able, by a certain incredible power centred in his incantations, to do everything he pleases, then I greatly wonder, why they have not been afraid to accuse me, when they admit that I am possessed of such mighty powers. For you cannot take precautions against a power that is of a nature so mysterious and so divine, in the same way that other influences may be guarded against. He who summons an assassin before the judge, comes there attended by others ; he who accuses a poisoner, uses every precaution in taking his food ; he who charges a man with theft, keeps watch over his property.

But here, on the other hand, he who puts a magician, such as they speak of, on trial for his life, by means of what attendants, what precautions, what guards, is he to ward off a destruction that is as unforeseen as it is inevitable? Most assuredly, by none : hence a charge of this kind is not likely to be preferred by one who believes in its truth. But these accusations, by a kind of error universally prevalent among the ignorant, are generally made against philosophers; thus, for instance, such of them as make enquiry into the pure and primary causes of matter, they look upon as irreligious, and, on

T

that account, assert that they deny the existence of Gods;
such as Anaxagoras, Leucippus, Democritus, Epicurus, and
other advocates of natural causes; others, again, who, with more
than ordinary curiosity, enquire into the governance of the
world, and with the greatest earnestness venerate the Gods,
to these, too, do the vulgar give the name of magicians; sup-
posing that they know how to bring about those operations
which they know to take place : such, for instance, were in
former days, Epimenides, Orpheus, Pythagoras, and Ostanes.*
In like manner, the Purifications of Empedocles, the Dæmon
of Socrates, and the abstract " Good" of Plato, became similar
objects of suspicion.   Consequently, I congratulate myself,
when I find myself added to this long list of great men.

Still, I am afraid that the frivolous, silly, and trifling things
that they have alleged against me in support of their charge,
you will consider to make against me, if only on the ground
that they have been so alleged. " Why," said he, " have
you been enquiring after certain kinds of fishes?" Just as
though a philosopher were not at liberty to do that, in the
cause of knowledge, which an epicure may do to satisfy his
gluttony. " Why has a free-born woman married you after
she has passed fourteen years in a state of widowhood?" Just
as though it were not a greater cause for wonderment that she
remained unmarried so many years. " Why, before she was
married to you, did she write I know not what thoughts of
hers in a certain letter?" Just as though any one were bound
to tell another the reasons for his thoughts. " Then, besides,
she, a person advanced in years, did not hesitate to marry a
young man." Why, that very fact, affords a proof that there
was no need of magic to prompt a woman to marry a man, a
widow a bachelor, one advanced in years, her junior; and then
come these other points of a similar nature—" Apuleius has
got something at home which he worships in secret." Just as
though it would not rather be a ground for crimination not to
have some object to worship. " A boy fell down in the pre-
sence of Apuleius." And what if a young man, what if an
old man even had fallen to the ground while I was standing
by, whether he happened to be attacked by some bodily malady,

* *Ostanes.*]—There were two Persian philosophers of this name. One
accompanied the expedition of Xerxes against Greece; the other was
patronized by Alexander the Great.

or lost his balance through the slippery nature of the ground? Is it on these proofs you would convict me of magical practices—the tumbling down of a boy, the marriage of a woman, and the purchase of some fish?

For my own part, I certainly could, with entire safety to myself, be content, after saying even thus much, to come to a conclusion. Still as, in proportion to the lengthiness of the speech made for the prosecution, the water [in the clepsydra] shows that there is abundance of time left, let us, if you think proper, consider things in detail. And, for my part, all the charges that have been brought against me, whether they are true or false, I shall not deny, but will admit them, just as though they really were the fact; so that all this vast multitude, which has flocked together from every quarter to hear this trial, may fully understand, that not only nothing can be truthfully alleged against philosophers, but that nothing even can be falsely devised against them, which they would not prefer to rebut, although they could deny it, in full reliance on their innocence. First, then, I will meet their arguments, and will prove that they bear no relation whatever to the practice of magic; and, after that, I will show that, even if I had been a magician of first-rate ability, still, no cause or opportunity has existed for them to detect me in any malpractice whatever. I will at the same time discuss more fully their unfounded envy, their shameful conduct in reading the letters of this lady, and their still more disgraceful interpretation put upon those letters, with all the circumstances of the marriage between myself and Pudentilla: and I will show that I entered into that alliance more from a sense of duty than for gain. And, really, what a mighty cause of torment and uneasiness has this marriage of ours proved to Æmilianus! Hence all that anger, and rage, and absolute frenzy, which have found a vent in the present prosecution. And if I shall succeed in proving all these points clearly and distinctly, then I shall call upon you, Claudius Maximus, and all you who are here present, to bear witness that this youth, Sicinius Pudens, my son-in-law, in whose name and by whose wish I am accused by his uncle, has but just now been removed from my charge, since his brother Pontianus, his senior in years, and his superior in character, departed this life; and I will show that he has been thus nefariously worked upon against myself and his mother, through

no fault of mine ; and that, having forsaken the pursuits of
literature, and abandoned all studies, he is likely, if we may
form a judgment from the wicked plans betrayed in this accu-
sation, to turn out much more like his uncle Æmilianus than
his brother Pontianus.

I will now proceed, as I originally purposed, to all the frantic
conceptions of Æmilianus here, and I will begin with that
one which you heard him state at the outset as affording the
strongest grounds for suspecting me of the practice of magic—
the fact, I mean, that I have purchased various kinds of fish of
some fishermen. Which, now, of these circumstances is it
that is to lead to a suspicion of magic ? Is it the fact that
fishermen have endeavoured to procure these fish for me ? I
suppose, then, this task ought to have been entrusted to some
dyers or carpenters; and that, on the same principle, the pur-
suit of every art ought to have changed hands, so that the
carpenter should have netted fish for me, and the fisherman
have planed wood. · Or, is it that you feel satisfied that fishes
must be sought for unlawful practices, because they are sought
on the terms of purchase ? If I had wanted them to set on
table, I should have tried to get them for nothing, no doubt.
Why, then, do you not accuse me in like manner on many other
points ? For many a time have I, for money, purchased wine,
vegetables, fruit, and bread. Why, if you carry out this prin-
ciple, you prescribe starvation to all purveyors of dainties. For
who will dare to make purchase of them, if it is looked upon
as a matter of course, that all eatables that are procured with
money are wanted, not for food, but for the purposes of magic ?

But if there is no suspicion whatever existing, either in con-
sequence of the fact of fishermen being induced, for a sum of
money, to do that which they are in the general habit of do-
ing, namely, catching fish—(they have taken care, however,
to summon none of these fishermen as witnesses, for the best
of reasons, because none such there were)—nor yet of the fact
of a price being given for a marketable commodity—(the
amount of which price, however, they have taken care not to
state, for fear lest, if they had named a moderate price, their
story might have met with contempt, and, if an exorbitant
one, it might not have been believed) ; if, on these points, I
say, no ground for suspicion exists, then let Æmilianus answer
me, on what evident grounds was he induced to make this

charge of magical practices? "You endeavoured to procure some fish," says he. I do not wish to deny the fact. But tell me, I beg of you, is he who endeavours to procure some fish a magician? For my own part, I don't think he is a bit the more so than if he were in search of hares, or boars, or fowl. Or is it that fishes alone are in possession of certain properties that are hidden from other people, but known to magicians? If you know what this property is, then it is clear that you yourself are a magician; but if you do not know it, then you must, of necessity, confess that you are accusing a person of a thing about which you know nothing whatever.

Are you, then, so unversed in all literature, nay, in all the stories of the vulgar, that you cannot so much as coin these fictions of yours with some air of probability? For how should a lumpish and chilly fish, or anything that is found in the sea, be able to kindle the flames of desire? But perhaps you were induced to frame this falsehood from the circumstance that Venus is said to have arisen from the sea. Take note, if you please, Tannonius Pudens, of how much you were ignorant, when you undertook to prove the practice of magic from the procuring of fish. Had you been a reader of Virgil, you certainly would have known that other things are usually sought for such purposes. For, so far as I recollect, that poet enumerates fillets of soft wool, unctuous vervain, male frankincense, and threads of various colours; besides crackling laurel, clay that hardens, and wax that liquefies, as well as some other things, which he has described in his more serious work.*

> " She sprinkles round,
> With feign'd Avernian drops, the hallow'd ground,
> Culls hoary simples, found by Phœbe's light,
> With brazen sickles reap'd at noon of night;
> Then mixes baleful juices in a bowl,
> And cuts the forehead of a newborn foal,
> Robbing the mother's love."

But you, libeller of the fishes, attribute far different appli-

* _Serious work._]—He alludes to the Æneid. The quotation is from the Fourth Book, translated by Dryden.

† _The forehead, &c._]—The 'hippomanes' was a substance said to grow on the forehead of the foal, and to be eagerly swallowed by the dam at the moment of its birth. It was much employed in philtres and incantations.

ances to magicians; substances not to be torn off from tender foreheads, but to be cut away from scaly backs; not to be dug up from the ground, but to be drawn up from the sea; not to be cropped with the sickle, but to be hooked up with the fisher's barb. In fine, for the purpose of incantations, he makes mention of poisons, you of dainties, he of herbs and suckers, you of scales and bones; he culls from the meadow, you ransack the deep. I could also have quoted to you similar passages from Theocritus, others, again, from Homer, and a great number from Orpheus, and I could have repeated a multitude of lines from the Greek comedies and tragedies, as well as from the historians, had I not already observed that you were unable to read the letter of Pudentilla, because it was written in Greek. I will therefore just dip into one more Latin poet: here are the lines, which those will easily recognise who have read Lævius : *

> " Look for your antidote ;† on every side
> They snatch up charms of all sorts, whirling rhombs,
> Of magic potency; wing tails, and threads
> Of varied colours, and entwined; with roots
> And herbs and suckers; from the neighing colt
> Torn is the stimulant ‡ of fierce desire."

If you had had any acquaintance with literature, you would have framed your fictions with much more probability, if you had stated that I had sought for these and other things; for perhaps, in consequence of the stories so universally spread about them, some credit would have then attached to your mention of these particulars. But when a fish is caught, what is it good for except to be cooked and served up at table? but for magic it is of no avail.

I will state to you my reasons for thinking so. Many have supposed that Pythagoras was a follower of Zoroaster, and was, like him, skilled in magic, and have informed us in their writings, that when in the vicinity of Metapontum, on the shores of his own part of Italy which he had made a kind of second Greece,§ he saw a seine drawn up by certain fisher-

---

* *Lævius.*]—It is a matter of doubt whether the reading here is ' Lævius' or ' Læltius.' Of neither of these poets is anything known.

† *Antidote.*]—Pliny tells us that the ' Antipathes' was a black stone, which was valued as being proof against the operations of witchcraft.

‡ *The stimulant.*]—The hippomanes.

§ *Second Greece.*]—He alludes to the south of Italy, which was called

men, whereupon he purchased the chances of the haul; and that after he had paid the money, he immediately gave orders that the fish which had been caught should be released from the nets, and returned to the deep. Now, I suppose, he would not have let them go out of his hands, if he had found in them anything useful for magical purposes. For this man, so well versed in all learning, and so close an imitator of the ancients, remembered full well that Homer, a poet gifted with universal knowledge, had, in his writings, attributed all the power of drugs to the earth, and not to the sea; for when speaking of a certain enchantress, he writes thus:

> " These drugs, so friendly to the joys of life,
> Bright Helen learned from Thone's imperial wife,
> Who swayed the sceptre, where prolific Nile
> With various simples clothes the fatten'd soil;
> With wholesome herbage mix'd, the direful bane
> Of vegetable venom taints the plain."*

And so likewise in another passage:

> " Thus while he spoke, the sovereign plant he drew,
> Where on th' all-bearing earth unmark'd it grew."†

While, on the other hand, you will never find in his writings either that Proteus drugged his changing figure with any marine and fishy substance, or Ulysses the trench,‡ Æolus the bag, Helen the goblet, Circe the cup, or Venus her girdle. Why, you are the only people to be found in the memory of man who, forming, as it were, a kind of hodge-podge of the productions of nature, make nothing of transferring the virtues of herbs, and roots, and suckers, and pebbles from the tops of mountains to the depths of the sea, and there sewing them up in the bellies of fishes. Hence, just as Mercury, the conveyer of incantations, Venus, the charmer of the soul, Luna,

Magna Græcia. Here Pythagoras set up a school of philosophy at the city of Crotona.

* *The plain.*]—Odyssey Book IV. l. 227. Pope's Translation.

† *It grew.*]—Odyssey Book X. l. 302.

‡ *The trench.*]—He alludes to various passages found in the works of Homer; the transformations of Proteus, Book IV.: the trench dug by Ulysses when sacrificing to Pluto, Book X.; the bag in which Æolus enclosed the winds for Ulysses, Book X.; the goblets in which Helen mingled wine and drugs, to banish grief and tears, Book IV.; the cup in which Circe mingled the drugs, by means of which she changed the companions of Ulysses into swine, Book X.; and the girdle of Venus, the wondrous virtues of which are mentioned in the Iliad, Book XIV.

the looker-on in the night, and Trivia, the mistress of the
shades, used to be summoned to the ceremonies of the magi-
cians; so, according to your account, henceforth Neptune, in
company with Salacia, and Portumnus, and the whole throng
of the Nereids, will have been transferred from the surging agi-
tations of the waves to the agitations of passionate desire.

I have now stated why, in my opinion, there is nothing in
common between magicians and fishes. But now, if you think
proper, let us believe, Æmilianus, that fishes really are in the
habit of promoting magical influences. Does it, then, follow,
as a necessary consequence, that whoever seeks for a fish is a
magician? By the same rule, the person who tries to procure
a light cutter is a pirate, he who looks for a crow-bar is a
housebreaker, and he who seeks a sword is a cut-throat.
Nothing of ever so harmless a nature can you mention, but
may possibly be used to man's disadvantage; and nothing, of
ever so pleasing a tendency, but may be taken in bad part.
Yet it is not, for all that, a necessary consequence that all
things should obtain an utterly bad reputation; as, for instance,
that you should suppose that frankincense, and cassia, and
myrrh, and such other aromatics, are only bought for the pur-
pose of being used at funerals, seeing that they are also used
in medical preparations, and in sacrifices.

But, according to this mode of reasoning about fish, you
would suppose that the companions of Menelaüs, too, were
magicians, inasmuch as the greatest of poets says that at the
island of Pharos they banished hunger by using curved hooks.
In the same class, too, you will have to place sea-gulls, dol-
phins, and cray-fish; and then all epicures, too, who pur-
chase largely of fishermen; and even the fishermen them-
selves, who, in pursuit of their calling, seek for all kinds of
fish. "Why, then," say you, "do you try to procure them?"
Really I do not choose, nor do I deem it necessary, to tell
you; but show me, I beg of you, if you possibly can, that I
have tried to procure fish for those purposes you state. Sup-
pose I had bought hellebore, hemlock, or the juice of poppies,
and other things, the use of which, in moderation, is conducive
to health, but which, when mixed or taken in large quan-
tities, are dangerous; who could with common patience have
endured it, if you had accused me of poisoning, because by
means of these things a man may lose his life?

Let us see, however, what were the different kinds of fishes which were so necessary for me to possess, and so rarely to be met with, as to deserve to be sought for on the promise of a reward. Three only have they named; in one they were mistaken, while the other two they invented. They were mistaken in saying that the fish was a sea-hare, for it was quite a different kind of fish altogether; one which my servant Themiso, a person by no means ignorant of the medical art, as you have heard from his own lips, brought to me quite unasked, for me to look at; for the fact is, that he has not even yet managed to find a sea-hare. Still, I am ready to admit that I have been in search of other kinds besides, and that I have given a commission not only to fishermen, but to my friends also, wherever a person meets with a fish of any unusual kind, either to describe to me the form of it, or else to show it me alive, or, if he cannot do so, dead. Why I have done this, I will presently proceed to inform you.

But these accusers of mine, so extremely clever, as they fancy themselves to be, were guilty of a falsehood, when, towards the end of their charge, they invented the story that I had been in search of two marine productions with indelicate names. Those productions, Tannonius here, though he wished the genitals of both sexes to be understood, could not, all-accomplished pleader as he is, think of mentioning for very bashfulness; and, at last, after much stammering and bungling, he called the fish he meant, by a vile paraphrasis, "the marine virile member."* But as for the fish called "feminal,"† finding himself unable, in any way whatever, to mention it with common decency, he betook himself to my writings, and, because he had read a passage from a book of mine, to this effect—"May cover the 'interfeminium' both by crossing the thighs and shading it with the hand," in due conformity‡ with the gravity of his own character, he imputed it as a fault to me, that I was not ashamed to speak decently of shameful things.

Why, on the contrary, I might, with much more justice,

* *The marine virile member.*]—The fish was the Veretilla, a name synonymous with the male organs of generation.
† *Feminal.*]—A Latin name for the female organs; the name also of a kind of shell-fish.
‡ *In due conformity.*]—This is said ironically.

have censured him, who, whilst he publicly professes the art
of eloquence, babbles shamefully even about things that are
proper to be mentioned, and often, when speaking about sub-
jects that present not the slightest difficulty, either hems and
haws, or comes to a dead stop altogether.   Now, tell me, if I
had said nothing at all about that statue of Venus,* and had
never mentioned the word "interfeminium," pray, in what
words would you have accused me on this matter, so suited
alike to your stupidity and to your tongue?   Can there be
anything more silly, than from a similarity of names to infer
a similarity of meaning in things?   And yet, perhaps, you
thought that you had shown great acuteness in this dis-
covery of yours.   Why, then, you should have invented in
your charge that I had been in search of these two marine
productions, the "veretilla" and the "virginal,"† for ma-
gical purposes ; for I must teach you the Latin names of things,
and I therefore give you their various appellations, that you
may be instructed another time in what language to make your
charges against me.   Bear this in mind, however, that it would
be as ridiculous an argument to hold, that marine productions
with obscene names are required for venereal purposes, as it
would be to say that sea-combs or scallops are sought for the
purpose of combing the hair, or that the hawk-fish is taken
for the purpose of catching birds that fly, the boar-fish for
hunting boars, or sea-skulls with the object of raising the dead.
I make answer, then, to this position of yours, devised, as it is,
no less foolishly than absurdly, that I neither obtained these
marine trifles and gimcracks at any cost whatever, nor yet
gratuitously.

And this answer I give you furthermore, that you did not
know what it was you were pretending I had been in search
of.   For these trifles which you have mentioned, are generally
found lying in abundance on the sea-shores of all countries,
and, without labour on the part of any one, are spontaneously
thrown up by the tide, however gentle the ripple of the waves.
Why, then, do you not assert that, just in the same way, pay-
ing a heavy price for them, I have employed numbers of

* *Statue of Venus.*]—In describing which, he made use of the word
'interfeminium.'

† '*Virginal.*'—This word seems here to have the same meaning as
'feminal,' previously alluded to.

fishermen to collect on the sea-shore streaked mussels, lumpish shells, and smooth pebbles? Why not add the claws of crabs, the shells of sea-urchins, the feelers of cuttle-fish, and bits of chips, old stumps, scraps of rope, and worm-pierced oyster-shells?* Why not, in fine, moss and sea-weed, and other things which are thrown up by the sea, which are drifted by the winds in all quarters upon the shore, cast up on the surface with the scum, tossed in the tempests to and fro, and stranded in the calm?

And not a jot the less, in the case of the matters which I have mentioned, may similar suspicions be broached, in accordance with their respective names. You affirm that things gathered from the sea, and that bear the names of the male and female organs, are efficacious in venereal matters, because of the similitude of the names; how, then, can it possibly be other than the fact, that the calculus or smooth pebble that is picked up from the same sea-shore bears some reference to the bladder, the shell known to us as "testa"† to a testamentary devise, the cancer to a cancerous ulcer, the "alga," or sea-weed, to ague?‡

Assuredly, Claudius Maximus, you are a most forbearing man, and one endowed with the greatest humanity, for having, by Hercules! so long tolerated these arguments of theirs. For my own part, when these things were stated by them as being matters serious and unanswerable, I laughed at their folly, and was surprised at your powers of endurance. But as Æmilianus is so very anxious about my affairs, he must be made acquainted why it is that I have examined so many fishes of late, and why I did not wish to remain unacquainted with any of them. Although he is well-stricken in years, and in the decline of life, still, if he chooses, let him receive some instruction, however late, and in a manner posthumous. Let him read the records of the ancient philosophers, that at last he may understand, that I was not the first to make these researches; but that, long before me, my predecessors Aristotle, Theophrastus, Eudemus, Lycon, and others after the time

---

* *Oyster-shells.*]—The word 'pergami' is not translated, as it is pretty clear that it is out of place here.

† '*Testa.*']—The name of a shell-fish, the present denomination of which is unknown.

‡ *To ague.*]—Which is attended with shivering fits.

of Plato, enquired into these matters; and let him know that they have left many books which treat of the generation of animals, their diet, their formation, and all their classifications.

It is fortunate, Maximus, that this cause is tried before you, who, learned as you are, have no doubt read the numerous volumes of Aristotle "On the Generation of Animals," "On the Anatomy of Animals," "On the History of Animals;" besides innumerable problems of the same writer, as well as works written by others of the same sect, in which various matters of the same nature are treated of.

If it was honorable and praiseworthy in them to write on these particulars which had been investigated with such scrupulous care, why should it be disgraceful for me to try to do the same? And the more especially, when I am making it my object to write on the same subjects, both in the Greek and Latin languages, with an improved arrangement, and in more concise terms, and to ascertain what has been omitted on each point, or else to supply what is defective? Permit, if you have the leisure, some of my magical compositions to be read, in order that Æmilianus may learn that I have made more careful researches and enquiries than he imagines. Produce* one of my Greek books, which perhaps my friends have brought here with them, and which treats on researches into nature, and that one, in especial, in which are set forth a great number of facts relative to the class of fishes.

In the meantime, while he is looking for it, I will just mention an instance appropriate to the present occasion. Sophocles, the poet who was the rival of Euripides, and his survivor (for he lived to a very advanced age), was accused by his own son of madness, as having, through extreme old age, fallen into a state of dotage. On this, it is said he produced his Œdipus Coloneus, the most excellent of his Tragedies, and which he happened just then to be writing, and having read it to the judges, he added not a word in his defence, except that he requested them, without hesitation, to pronounce him mad if the lines written by him in his old age should show him to be so. On that occasion, I find that all the judges arose to pay all due respect to a great poet, and wondrously extolled

* *Produce.*]—He says this to one of the scribes or clerks of court, in whose hands the documents had been deposited connected with the prosecution.

him, both for the skill displayed in his plot, and the tragic elegance of his composition; and it all but turned out that, on the contrary, they pronounced the accuser mad.

Have you found the book? I am much obliged to you. Come now, let us make trial, whether my literary productions too will stand my friends in a court of justice? Read a few lines at the beginning, and then something on the subject of fishes. And do you, while he is reading it, take care and keep the water from dropping.* [*The officers read some passages from the speaker's physical works, which are now lost.*] You have heard here, Maximus, much that no doubt you have read in the writings of the ancient philosophers; bear in mind, too, that these volumes were written by me on the subject of fishes alone; in them you will find it stated, which of them are produced from copulation, which are generated from mud, how often, and at what time of the year, the females and the males of each kind are bent on coupling; in what parts, and from what causes, nature has produced a difference between such of them as are viviparous, and such as are oviparous; for by those names I denote those which the Greeks call ζωοτόκα and ᾠοτόκα.

And, not to be at the trouble of going through all the genera of animals, I will next request a few passages to be read from my Latin compositions, which likewise treat of the same kind of knowledge, both with reference to their classifications, their food, their members, their ages, and numerous other particulars, which, necessary as they are to be known, have but little to do with a court of justice; in these, you will find, however, facts that are known to but very few, as well as some names that are even unknown by the Romans, and are not used, as far as I know, up to the present day; they are names, however, which by means of my labour and study have been so derived from the Greek, as still to bear upon them the stamp of the current Latin coinage. If such is not the fact, then, Æmilianus, let your advocates inform us where they have read these names set forth as being Latin words. I will only touch upon aquatic animals, and no other class, except in

* *Water from dropping.*]—He says this to the officer whose charge it is to watch the clepsydra. The time taken up in reading quotations or documents was not deemed part of that allowed for the speech in defence.

those cases where there are differences of genera in common with them and others.

Listen now to what I am going to say. You will presently cry out, that I am repeating a string of magical terms after the Egyptian or Babylonian custom—these are the classes— σελάχεια, μαλάκια, μαλακόστρακα, χονδράκανθα, ὀστρακόδερμα, καρχαροδοντα, ἀμφίβια, λεπιδωτὰ, φολιδωτὰ, δερμόπτερα, πεζὰ, ἰέποδα, μονήρη, συναγελαστικὰ.—I could still go on, but it is not worth while to consume the day on these subjects, in order that I may have time to proceed to other points. In the meantime, as to the few that I have mentioned, run over the names I have given them in Latin. [*The Latin names for the same genera of fishes are lost.*]

Which, then, do you think, in case of a philosopher, not one, rude and untaught, in accordance with the impudence of the cynics, but one who bears in mind that he belongs to the school of Plato, which do you think is the more disgraceful to him, to know these matters, or to be ignorant of them? to neglect or to attend to them? To come to a perception how fully, even in these objects, the workings of providence are displayed, or merely to take your father's and mother's word as regards belief in the immortal gods?

Q. Ennius, in his work called "Hedyphagetica,"* which he has written in verse, enumerates the almost numberless genera of fish which he had, no doubt curiously, examined. I remember a few of his lines, which I will repeat.

> " The best of eel-pouts are at Clypea found ;
> At Ænus sea-loche.   From Abydos come
> Oysters in plenty.   Mitylene sends
> Her scallops.   From Ambracia's rocky shores
> We fetch the sea-goat.   Good thy sarges† are,
> Brundusium ; if they're large, make sure and buy.
> Know that Tarentum sends of boar-like fish‡
> The best.   Buy sword-fish at Surrentum, buy
> Blue fish at Cumæ.   But why fail to name

* ' *Hedyphagetica.*']—This seems likely to be the most correct reading. The meaning will be 'a treatise on good eating.' The following lines are in a most corrupt state.

† *Sarges.*]—It is not known what fish was called ' sargus.'

‡ *Boar-like fish.*]—' Apriculum.'—It is not known what fish was thus called by the diminutive of ' aper,' a ' boar.'

> The scarus, equal to the brain of Jove!
> In Nestor's land 'tis found, both fine and good;
> The black-tail, sea-thrush, whiting, an l the swift
> Sea-shadow,* the Corcyrean polypus;
> Atarna's skull-fish fat, the purpura,
> Murex, muriculus; sweet urchins, too."

Others, besides, he has celebrated in many of his lines, and has shown in what countries each of them is to be found, and whether it has the finest flavour when boiled or pickled; and yet, for all this, he is not censured by the learned. Let me not be censured then, when I set forth in the Latin tongue, under elegant and appropriate names, matters which, having been hitherto treated of in Greek, are known to but very few indeed.

As I have spoken at sufficient length on this subject, next hear me on another. Now what can they say against it, pray, if, being neither unacquainted with the medical art, nor unskilled in it, I seek for certain antidotes in fishes? for as very many such are mingled and implanted in all other objects by the bounty of nature, so too there are some, no doubt, to be found in fishes. Do you suppose that to understand the nature of antidotes, and to search for them, is the province rather of a magician, than of a physician, or a philosopher even? One who is going to use them not for his own profit, but for the purpose of benefiting others? Why, the ancient physicians were even acquainted with certain charms by way of remedy for wounds, as Homer, that most trustworthy author of all antiquity, informs us, when he represents the blood that flowed from the wound of Ulysses, as being staunched by means of a charm.† Nothing that is done for the purpose of ensuring health can be criminal in itself.

"But then," says he, "for what purpose but a bad one did you cut up the fish which your servant Themiso brought you?" As though, indeed, I did not say, a short time since, that I have written on the parts of all animals, their position, their number, and their purposes; and that I make it my study to examine and to enlarge the' works written by Aristotle "On Dissections." And, indeed, I am surprised that you should only know that one little fish has been examined by me,

---

* _Sea-shadow._] — 'Umbra marina,' or 'sea-shadow,' so called from its swarthy colour.

† _Of a charm._ — See the Odyssey, Book XIX., _et seq._ l. 456.

when I have in the same manner, on previous occasions,
examined vast numbers of them, whenever they have been
brought to me; especially, seeing that I do nothing in secret,
but everything openly, and any one, a stranger even, may
come and be present as a spectator.   Herein I act according to
the customs and usages of my masters, who say, that a man
of ingenuous birth and high spirit, ought, if he can, to carry
his mind pourtrayed in the very front of his forehead.

Now this little fish, which you call a sea-hare, I showed to
a great number of persons who were present, and I can not
yet make up my mind what it shall be called, until I shall
have made a more careful examination of it; for among the
ancient philosophers, I find no account of the properties of
this fish, although it is the rarest of all kinds, and, by Her-
cules! one that well deserves to be described.   For this is the
only fish, so far as I know, that, being without bones in other
parts, has certain bones, twelve in number in the belly, con-
nected and united one with another, much like the pastern
bones of a pig in appearance.   If Aristotle had been aware
of this fact, he certainly never would have omitted to commit
it to writing, since he has mentioned, as a remarkable fact,
that there is a little heart found in the middle of the belly of
the codfish, and of that fish alone.

"You cut up the fish," says he.   Who can endure that being
a crime in a philosopher, which would not have been so in a
butcher or a cook?   "You cut up the fish!"   Is it because
it was raw, that you censure me for so doing?   If I had ex-
amined the belly, after boiling the fish, and had dug out the
entrails, just as this stripling, Sicinius Pudens, has learned
to do at your house,* with fish bought with his own pocket-
money; would you not have deemed that a fitting ground
for accusing me?   But know that it is a greater crime for a
philosopher to eat fishes than to examine them.   Shall sooth-
sayers, then, be allowed to inspect the entrails, and shall a
philosopher be forbidden to observe them, when he knows
that he is the diviner, who gathers omens from all animals;

* *At your house.*]—In this passage, he accuses Æmilianus of neglect-
ing the duties of an uncle towards Pudens; while he censures the latter
for inordinate epicurism; as, among nice eaters, the entrails of fish were
generally esteemed the most dainty bits.   He seems also to hint, that
Pudens was not over-well fed at the house of Æmilianus.

that he is the priest of all the Gods? Do you censure in me, the very thing that Maximus and I agree in admiring in Aristotle? whose books unless you banish from the libraries, and tear them from the hands of the studious, you can bring no accusation against me.

But on this point I have almost said more than I ought. Now, only see to what an extent these people confute themselves. They say, that a woman was captivated by me through magic arts and charms derived from the sea; this, too, at a time at which they will not deny that I was far inland among the mountains of Gætulia, where may be found fishes left by Deucalion's flood. I really congratulate myself that they were not aware that I have also read the tract of Theophrastus, "On animals that bite and are venomous," as well as the book on antidotes written by Nicander. For in such case, they would have accused me of poisoning too, though I have only pursued these studies in imitation of Aristotle, whose works I have carefully read, my own Plato, in some measure, encouraging me thereto, when he says, that he who investigates these matters, "knows things that are godlike and immortal, if he hits upon the truth."

Now that their fish story has been sufficiently exposed, listen to another invention of theirs, quite its equal in folly, but far more absurd and dishonest. They knew, themselves, that their fish argument would turn out utterly futile and worthless, and ridiculous for its singularity. For who ever heard of fishes being wont to be scaled and boned for magical malpractices? On the contrary, they ought rather to have concocted something with reference to matters more universally known, and that have already obtained credit.

For this reason it is, that they have trumped up a tale quite in accordance with prescribed notions and common report, how that,—all overlookers being removed—in a secret spot, with lamp and little altar, I bewitched a certain boy by my incantations—and how that, a few witnesses being privy thereto, after he had been enchanted, he fell to the ground, and afterwards awoke in a fit of utter bewilderment. No further, however, than this, did they dare to proceed in their fiction; but still, that the story might be rendered complete, it was found necessary to add, that the same boy had, in a spirit of prophecy, foretold many events, for such, we generally hear, is

U

the result of employing incantations. And not only by the universally received notions of the vulgar, but even by the authority of learned men, is this miraculous power of boys con-firmed.

I remember, that in the works of Varro the philosopher, a man who was most intimately acquainted with all learning and knowledge, I read the following relation among others of a similar nature :—When the people of Tralles were consult-ing the magical art, as to what would be the result of the Mithridatic war ; a boy,* while looking upon the reflection of a statue of Mercury in the water, uttered a prophecy of a hun-dred and sixty lines, setting forth what was about to come to pass. Furthermore, that Fabius, having lost five hundred denars, came to Nigidius,† to consult him; on which, certain boys, who had been inspired by him by means of charms, pointed out in what place the purse had been buried, together with some part of the money; how the rest had been distri-buted, and how that even M. Cato the philosopher was in possession of one of the pieces; upon which, M. Cato con-fessed that he had received that very coin at the hands of an attendant of his for the contribution to Apollo.‡

These, and other statements, about boys being employed for magical purposes, I certainly have read in many authors; but I am doubtful whether to say that such things are possible, or to deny it. Still, I do think with Plato, that there are

* *A boy.*]—We learn from Mr. Lane, and other travellers in Egypt, that it is supposed that boys have, in certain cases, the gift of prophecy or omniscience, and that they can see events passing in other parts of the world, reflected in a drop of black ink on the finger nail, or palm of the hand.

† *To Nigidius.*]—Nigidius Figulus was a Roman philosopher, famous for his extraordinary learning. He was noted for his mathematical and physical investigations, and followed the secrets of the Pythagorean school of philosophy. He was also famed as an astrologer, and in the Eusebian Chronicle is called a magician. A letter of Cicero to him is still extant, in the Epistles, Ad Familiares, Book IV., ep. 13. He is said to have re-ceived the name of ' Figulus,' which means a ' potter,' from the circum-stance of having promulgated, on his return from Greece, that the globe whirled round with the rapidity of the potter's wheel.

‡ *To Apollo.*]—It was not considered seemly for the upper classes, among the Romans, to carry money in the streets. Consequently, the ' pedissequi,' or ' footmen,' by whom they were attended, usually carried their purses for them.

certain divine powers which are intermediate both in nature
and locality, between the Gods and mankind, and that these
powers preside over all divinations and miracles of magicians.
And I am further of opinion, that the human mind, and espe-
cially the uncontaminated mind of a boy, may be lulled to
sleep, and so estranged from the body, as to become oblivious
of the present, being either summoned away from it by the
agency of charms, or else enticed by the allurements of sweet
odours ; and that so, all remembrance of what is done in the
body having been banished for a time, it may be restored and
brought back to its original nature, which no doubt is divine
and immortal, and thus, being in a kind of trance, as it were,
may presage future events.*

But be this as it may, if any credit is to be given to these
matters, whatever boy is to prophesy, ought, so far as I can
understand, to be of graceful features and of unblemished
body, of quick wit, and fluent in speech ; that so, either the
Divine power may take up its abode in him, as in a beseeming
habitation, (if, indeed, it can, under any circumstances, be
becomingly enclosed in the body of a boy ;) or else, his mind,
on being released from the body, may quickly return to its
power of divination ; and that such power being readily within
its reach, and not blemished or impeded by obliviousness, may
be the more easily resumed. For, as Pythagoras used to say,
" It is not out of every log of wood that a Mercury can be
carved."

If, then, such is the fact, mention the name of this boy, of
sound mind, good health, quick wits, and singular beauty,
whom I have thought proper to initiate in these arts, through
my incantations. As for this Thallus, whom you have named,
he stands more in need of a physician than of a magician.
For he, poor creature! is so affected with epilepsy, that fre-
quently, as many as three or four times in a day, he falls to
the ground without any incantations whatever, and injures
all his limbs with the blows so received : he has a face, too,
full of ulcers ; his head, both before and behind, is covered

* *Future events.*]—This notion is very similar to that of the mesmer-
ists of the present day. This similarity has been recently remarked by
an ingenious correspondent in ' Notes and Queries,' vol. vi., p. 8. The
divine nature and origin of the human mind or soul, will be found fully
discussed in the treatise, ' On the God of Socrates.'

all over with bruises; his sight is dim, his nostrils are ex-
panded, and he is quite shaky in the legs.   He would be
the greatest magician of all, in whose presence Thallus could
stand up for any length of time together; so frequently does
he stagger and fall down under the influence of his disease,
just as though he were fast asleep.   And yet you have thought
proper to assert, that he has been made to fall down through
my incantations, because he happened to fall on one occasion
when I was present.   Many of his fellow-servants are here,
whom you gave notice to produce.   They can tell you, all
of them, why they shun the society of Thallus; why it is that
no one ventures to eat with him from the same dish, to drink
with him from the same cup.

   But why speak of the servants?   Deny it yourselves, if you
dare, that Thallus, long, long before I came to Oëa, was in
the habit of falling down when suffering from attacks of this
disease, and had been repeatedly in the hands of the physicians.
Can his fellow-servants, who are in your own service, deny
that?   I will confess myself guilty on all the charges, if he
has not, this long time past, been banished to a farm at a great
distance in the country, lest he might infect the whole house-
hold.   That this is the fact, not even they themselves can
deny.   This, too, has been the reason, why he could not be
produced by us to-day.   For, just in accordance with the pre-
cipitate and hurried manner in which this accusation was
preferred, it was only the day before yesterday, that Æmilianus
gave us notice to produce our fifteen servants before you.   The
fourteen who were in the city are present.   Thallus, as I
mentioned, is the only one that has been sent away into the
country, almost a hundred miles out of our sight.   Thallus is
the only one absent; but still we have sent a person, post haste,
for the purpose of bringing him hither.   Enquire, Maximus,
of these fourteen servants, whom we produce, where the boy
Thallus is, and in what state of health; enquire of the servants
of my accusers.   They will not deny the fact, that this most
unsightly lad has a body rotten and diseased, that he is liable
to falling fits, is uncouth, and a mere clod.

   A handsome youth, indeed, you have chosen, for any person
to employ in the sacred rites, to touch his head, [in initiating
him], to clothe him with a pure garment, and to expect him
to give responses!   By Hercules! I only wish he had been

here, I would have handed him over to you, Æmilianus, to take hold of him, and question him yourself. Why, in the very middle of your examination of him, here, in this same spot, and before the very tribunal, he would have fixed his staring eyes upon you, slobbered and spit in your face, clenched his hands, dropped his head, and, at last, fallen right upon your breast. The fourteen servants, whom you demanded, I have brought; why don't you make use of them for examination? One lad, and that one a poor epileptic creature, you ask for, when you know, as well as I do, that he has long since left this place. How can there be a more manifest calumny than this? At your demand, fourteen servants. are here—of them you take no notice—one young boy is absent, about him you attack me.

After all, what is it you want? Suppose Thallus to be present, do you wish to prove that in my presence he fell to the ground? I am quite ready to admit it. Do you say that this was effected through incantations? About that, the lad knows nothing at all: I will prove that such was not the fact. Now that the lad was suffering from epilepsy, not even you yourself will dare to deny. Why, then, ought his falling down to be attributed to incantations rather than to disease? Could it not possibly happen that he should be seized with an attack in my presence, just as he has often been seized on other occasions, while many other persons were present? If I had considered it a matter of great importance to make an epileptic person fall down, what necessity was there for me to use incantations, when the stone called "agate," after being subjected to the action of fire, as I read in the writers on Physics, readily and easily tests the presence of this malady? It is by means of the smell of this, too, that trial is usually made in the slave-markets of the soundness or unsoundness of the slaves. Then besides, the wheel, when whirled round by the potter, readily affects with vertigo a person suffering from this malady, so much does the sight of the rotatory motion affect his debilitated spirits; so that a potter is much better able than a magician to cause the epileptic to fall prostrate.

You have asked, and for no purpose, that I should produce the servants; I ask, and not for no purpose, that you will mention by name the witnesses who were present at these nefarious rites, when I thus brought to the ground the already tottering Thallus. Only one young lad, after all, do you name, this Sicinius Pudens here, in whose name you accuse me; he declares that he was present; but even if his boyhood did not in the slightest degree detract from his credibility with the court, still his position as accuser would impair the value of his testimony. It would have been much easier, Æmilianus, and would have carried much greater weight, if you had said you yourself were present, and that in consequence of these rites you were first attacked with insanity, rather than entrust all this business, as though it were a mere joke, to boys. A boy fell down,—a boy saw him fall down,—and may not some boy have acted the enchanter too? Tannonius Pudens here, craftily enough, when he perceived that this lying fiction also fell cold and harmless, and that it was all but hissed outright, asserted that he would produce some other boys who had also been enchanted by me, that thus at least, by raising your expectations, he might lull the suspicions of some among you; and then he passed on to another head of his argument.

Now, although I might very well have taken no notice of this, still, as I have challenged him to proof on all other points, so I volunteer to do on this. For I long for these boys to be produced, who, I hear, have been encouraged to give false evidence against me, through hopes held out to them that they shall thereby gain their liberty. However, no more do I say than this: Let them produce them; I demand, Tannonius Pudens, and insist that you will fulfil the promise you have made. Produce these boys, in whom you have put such confidence; inform us what are their names; a portion of the time that has been allotted for my own speech I give you leave to employ for the purpose. Tell us, I say, Tannonius— why are you silent? why do you hesitate? why cast your eyes on the ground? If he does not know what it is he has said, or if he has forgotten the names, then do you, Æmilianus, step this way; say what were the instructions you gave to your counsel; bring forward the boys; what makes you turn so pale? why thus silent? Is this the way to bring an accusation of such magnitude? to make a laughing-stock of Claudius Maximus, a man of such exalted station, and to persecute me with your calumnious charges?

But if, perchance, your advocate did make a slip, and if you have no such boys to produce, at all events employ, for some purpose or other, the fourteen servants whom I have brought here; or else why was it that you required such a large household to be brought into court? Accusing me of magic, you have given me notice to produce fifteen servants. If you had accused me of acts of violence, how many servants, pray, would you have demanded? Is it, then, that the fifteen servants know all about it, and yet it is a secret? or is it no secret at all, and yet an affair of magic? One of these two things you must necessarily confess; either that what I did was not unlawful, since I did not fear to allow so many persons to be privy to it, or else that if it was unlawful, so many witnesses ought not to have been privy to it. This magic, from all I can learn, is a thing denounced by the laws, and from the remotest times forbidden by the Twelve Tables, in consequence of the incredible blasting of standing corn by means of incantations. Consequently, it is a thing no less secret in its practices than foul and abominable; it is generally carried on by night, hidden in deep gloom, removed from all observation, and effected by whispered spells: a process at which few, not to say slaves, but even free men, are allowed to be present.

Do you want to make out that fifteen servants were present as spectators? Was it a wedding, then, or some other ceremonial, or an afternoon carousal? Fifteen servants are here taking part in these magic rites, just like so many Quindecemvirs,* elected for the performance of sacred duties. But to what end should I have employed so large a number, if the privity of but one is far more than is requisite? Fifteen free men! why, that makes a whole borough.† That amount of servants! 'tis a whole household; the same number, if placed in chains, would fill a whole gaol;‡ or was it that such a multitude as this was necessary to hold the victims for sacrifice? But all the while you have mentioned no victims except hens.

* *Quindecemvirs.*]—These were persons whose especial duty it was to preserve the Sibylline books at Rome. As the text informs us, they were fifteen in number.

† *Whole borough.*]—Fifteen free men, with their households, constituted a Roman 'pagus,' or Athenian 'demus.'

‡ *A whole gaol.*]—'Ergastulum.' This was a place on estates in the country, to which refractory slaves were sent from the town residences of the Romans, to work in chains.

Or were they required to count the grains of frankincense?
or to knock down Thallus?

You stated, besides, that a free-born woman had been
brought to my house, afflicted with the same malady as
Thallus; that I promised to cure her, and that she, too, fell to
the ground enchanted by me. So far as I can see, you have
come here to charge me with being a wrestler, and not a
magician, seeing that you assert in this fashion that all who
have come near me have been levelled with the ground. How-
ever, upon being questioned by you, Maximus, Themiso, the
doctor, by whom the woman was brought for me to examine,
denied that anything whatever happened to her, except that
I put the question, whether there was a ringing in her ears,
and if so, in which of them in the greatest degree? upon
which she made answer, that her right ear was very much dis-
turbed by it, and immediately after took her departure.

And here, Maximus, although at the present moment I am
careful to refrain from praising you, that I may not appear
to flatter you with a view to this trial, still I cannot forbear
from praising your acuteness in cross-examination. For just
now, when these matters were discussed, and they asserted that
the woman was enchanted, whilst the doctor, who was present,
denied it, you very sagaciously enquired, what I was to gain
by thus bewitching her; on which they answered, that the
woman should fall to the ground. " Well, what then?" you
asked, " did she die?" They said no. " How then," say you,
" what advantage would it have been to Apuleius if she
fell?" For to this effect did you fairly and perseveringly
put the question to them as many as three several times, be-
cause you well knew that the motives for all actions ought
most carefully to be enquired into, and that often, when facts
are admitted, the causes of them become subjects for enquiry;
and you were aware that for this very reason the advocates of
persons engaged in suits at law have the name given to them
of " causidici," because it is their province to explain the causes
for which each thing has been done. But, on the other hand,
to deny that a thing has been done is an easy matter, and
needs the services of no advocate whatever; while to show
that it has been done rightfully or wrongfully is a most
arduous and difficult task. It is useless, then, to enquire
whether a thing has been done, which has had no evil cause

to prompt its being done. Hence it is, that he who is accused before a conscientious judge of having done a thing, is free from all fears of enquiry, if he has had no reason for doing what was wrong.

Now, since they have neither proved that the woman was enchanted, nor yet that she was thrown to the ground, and as I do not deny that, at the request of a medical man, she was examined by me, I will tell you, Maximus, why I did make the enquiry about the ringing in the ears ; and I shall do so, not so much for the sake of exculpating myself in this affair, which you have already pronounced to have nothing in it of faultiness or criminality, as because I would not wish to be silent on any matter that is suited to your ears and your learning. I will state it, then, as succinctly as possible, seeing that you are to be put in mind only, not instructed by me.

The philosopher Plato, in that most celebrated dialogue of his, entitled "Timæus," after having, with a sort of celestial eloquence, explained the structure of the entire universe, most ingeniously discussed the threefold powers of our mind, and aptly shown why our several parts were formed by the Divine Providence, proceeds to range the causes of all maladies under three heads. The first cause he attributes to the elements of our bodies, in cases where the qualities of those elements, being the moist and the cold, and the two qualities that are their opposites, do not agree the one with the other ; and this takes place when any one of them has exceeded its limits, or has shifted from its proper locality. The next cause of maladies exists in the corruption of those parts which are formed by a coalition of simple elements, united so as to form a single substance ; these are, for instance, blood, flesh, bones, and marrow ; and then those parts, which are formed from a mixture of these several substances. In the third place, there are in the body collections of various coloured bile, and of restless and flatulent wind, and gross humours, all which are most frequent causes of diseases.

In the number of these last is especially to be found the primary cause of the falling-sickness, about which I purposed to speak. For the flesh, through a noxious degree of heat, sometimes deliquesces into a moist state, that is, dense and cloggy, and a certain flatulency rises therefrom, in consequence of the heat of the compressed air, and a corrupt matter of

whitish and frothy appearance flows from it. Now, this cor-
rupt matter, if it can find a vent to ooze forth from the body,
is ejected with more unseemliness than danger. For it marks
the exterior of the skin with leprosy, and variegates it with
all kinds of spots; the person, however, to whom this happens
is never afterwards attacked by epilepsy; and thus it is that
a most afflicting malady of the mind is compensated by a slight
disfigurement of the body.

But, on the other hand, if these pernicious secretions are
held in check, and become united with the black bile, these,
raging at large, penetrate through all the vessels; and when
they have done this, making their way towards the crown of
the head, they mingle their destructive humours with the
brain; and instantly affect that regal portion of the under-
standing which, all-important as it is in the reasoning facul-
ties, has fixed its seat in the head of man as its citadel and its
palace. For its divers passages and its paths that lead to wis-
dom, these humours clog up and overwhelm; this, however,
they do with less work during the hours of sleep, as at such
times the patient, being filled with food and drink, only
suffers from a slight attack of impeded respiration, which is
a symptom of epilepsy. But if the humours increase to such
a degree as even to attack the head while the patient is awake,
then, a cloud suddenly comes across the spirit, he becomes
torpid, the breath ceases, and the body falls to the ground,
like that of a dead person.

This our forefathers styled, not only the "major" and the
"comitial," but also the "divine" disease; just as the Greeks,
with good reason, have styled it ιερα νοσὸς, inasmuch as it
attacks especially the reasoning parts of the mind, which are
by far its most holy portion. You see, then, Maximus, what
is the theory of Plato, which I have explained as perspicuously
as I could, considering the time allowed me; and as I believe
with him, that the Divine disease [or epilepsy] proceeds from
these bad humours mounting to the head, it is clear I had
good reason to make the enquiry, did this woman's head ache,
was her neck torpid and stiff, and was there a throbbing in
her temples, and a tingling in her ears? And, what is still
more, inasmuch as she admitted that she had a repeated ring-
ing in the right ear, that was a clear sign that the malady had

taken a deep root. For as the right side of the body is the strongest, the less hope of recovery is there left, when even that gives way to disease. Aristotle has also left it written in his Problems, that, in the case especially of those who are epileptic, and are attacked by the disease on the right side, the cure will be most difficult. It would take a long time if I were to repeat the opinions stated by Theophrastus also with reference to the same malady; but there is in existence an excellent book of his, written on the subject of epilepsy. Persons afflicted with this disease, are told in another book which he has written "On animals that envy," that the sloughs· of newts (which those animals, like the rest of the serpent tribe, cast aside at stated periods, like a sort of old age,) are' very useful as a remedy ; but if you do not quickly take them` away, these animals will instantly turn round and devour them, whether it is that they act through a malignant pre- sage [of their possible usefulness], or through a natural appetite.

These matters I have mentioned, and have been careful to name both the points discussed and the books written by these celebrated philosophers, while, at the same time, I have not thought of giving any of the physicians or poets, in order that these people may cease to wonder, if philosophers, by the aid of those studies which are peculiar to themselves, gain some knowledge of the causes and remedies of diseases. Ad· mitted, then, that an afflicted woman was brought to me to examine for the purpose of effecting a cure, and that, by the confession of the medical man who brought her, I acted rightly, then I think, they must either come to the conclusion that it is the part of a magician, and of a man guilty of malpractices, to heal diseases, or else, if they do not dare to make such an assertion, they must confess that, in the case of the boy and the woman afflicted with epilepsy, they have uttered frivolous and abortive calumnies.

Nay, if you wish to hear the truth, Æmilianus, you yourself are much afflicted with the falling-sickness, having fallen flat so often in attempts to calumniate me. For it is not a more grievous thing to fail in body than in spirit, to be found giving way rather in the feet than in the mind, and to be defiled with spittle in a private chamber, than to be execrated in this most illustrious assembly. However, you fancy, perhaps, that you

are sane in mind, because you are not confined at home, but
follow your mad fit just where it may chance to lead you.
Still, if you compare your own madness with that of Thallus,
you will find that there is no such great difference between
them, except that Thallus attacks himself, while you go so far
as to attack others.   Besides, Thallus distorts his eyes, you
the truth ; Thallus screws his hands, you your advocates ;
Thallus falls flat on the pavement, you before the tribunal.   In
fine, whatever he does, he does through infirmity ; he offends
in ignorance, while you, wretched man, knowingly and advi-
sedly, are guilty.

So extreme is the violence of the disease that holds its sway
over you, that you accuse me of what is false as though it were
the truth; a thing that was never done, you charge me with
doing ; one whom you know, beyond a doubt, to be innocent,
you still accuse as though he were guilty.   I have omitted,
besides, to say that there are some things of which you con-
fess yourself ignorant, and yet persist in charging me with,
just as though you were fully acquainted with them.   For you
assert that I kept something wrapped up in a napkin in the
same room with the Lares of Pontianus.   What these things
were, thus wrapped up, and what was their nature, you con-
fess you know not, and you admit there is no one who has
seen them; and yet, at the same time, you assert that they
were appliances of magic.

. Let no one flatter you, Æmilianus.   This is no proof of
your skill in framing an accusation, nor of your effrontery
even; so don't you suppose that it is.   What is it then ?   It
is the unhappy frenzy of an embittered spirit, the wretched
insanity of a soured old age.   For, almost in these very words
did you plead before a judge so distinguished for his gravity
and his shrewdness : "Apuleius kept certain articles wrapped
up in a linen cloth in the same room with the Lares of Pon-
tianus.   As I do not know what these articles were, I assert
that they were for magical purposes ; believe me, therefore,
in what I assert, because I am asserting what I know no-
thing about."   An excellent argument, and one that so con-
vincingly proves my guilt !   "Such and such it was, because
I know not what it was."   You are the only person that has
ever yet been found, Æmilianus, to know even those very
things that you do not know.   To such a degree as this have

you been exalted above all in folly! While, on the one hand, the ablest and most sagacious of philosophers have asserted that we must not so much as place confidence in those things even which we see; you, on the other hand, go so far as to assert the existence of things that you have never so much as seen or heard of. If Pontianus were alive, and you were to ask him what was within that cover, he would tell you he did not know. The freed man, too, who has kept the keys of that place up to this very day, and is one of your supporters, declares that he never looked into it, although, as being the keeper of the books which were put away there, he opened and shut the place nearly every day. Many a time has he gone into the room with me, and much more frequently alone, and has seen a linen cloth lying upon the table, without any seal, without any fastening upon it. And why so? Magical implements were concealed in it—that was the reason why I kept them in such a careless manner. Still more, I needlessly exposed them for him to pry into and examine, and even, if he had thought fit, to take them away; I entrusted them to the care of another person, I left them at the mercy of another.

What, then, is it that you now want to be believed? That a thing about which Pontianus, who lived on terms of inseparable intimacy with me, knew nothing at all, you are fully acquainted with, you, whom, before I met you in this court of justice, I never in my life set eyes upon? Or is it that, when a freedman was there at all times and seasons, and had every opportunity of examining, you, who never went there, saw a thing which that same freedman never saw? In short, do you wish it to be believed that a thing which you never saw, is just what you affirm it to have been? But, you blockhead, if you, this very day, had gained possession of that same napkin, whatever you might have produced therefrom, I could have denied that it was ever employed for magical purposes.

However, I give you full permission; invent whatever you please, plan, devise anything that may possibly appear applicable to magical practices, I could still dispute the question with you; I could either say that it had been surreptitiously placed there, or that it was employed as a remedy, or that it had been entrusted to me for the performance of sacred rites, or had been recommended to me in a dream. There are a

thousand other means by which I could, after the most ordi-
nary methods in use, truthfully rebut your assertions. Now,
this is what you require, that the very thing which, if made
known and discovered, would not prejudice me before an up-
right judge, may, while it remains undiscovered and un-
known, lead to my condemnation, upon an idle suspicion.
I don't know whether you will again say, as usual with
you,—"What was it, then, that you kept covered up with
a linen cloth, and so carefully put away in the same room with
the Lares?" Is it so, Æmilianus? You make your accusations
in such a way that you gain all your information from the
person accused, while you yourself bring forward nothing
that is known for certain. "For what purpose did you try to
procure the fishes?" "Why did you examine the sick woman?"
"What was it you kept in the napkin?" Which of the two have
you come here to do, to accuse or to interrogate me? If to
accuse me, prove yourself the assertions you make; if to in-
terrogate me, do not prejudge the fact, since the very reason
that makes it necessary for you to interrogate me, is that you
are ignorant of the fact.

But really, according to this mode of proceeding, all men
will have accusations brought against them, if there is to be
no necessity for one who makes a charge against another to
prove his case, but, on the contrary, he may enjoy every possible
facility for making enquiries. For in such case, charges of
magical practices may be made against any body, and every
thing he may chance to have done, will be brought forward
against him. "You placed your vow in writing upon the
thigh of some statue, therefore you are a magician; if not,
why did you so place it?" "You silently put up prayers
to the Gods in a temple, therefore you are a magician, or else
why did you so express your wishes?" On the other hand,
"You omitted to pray in the temple, therefore you are a
magician, else why did you not address your supplications to
the Gods?" Just the same may happen, whether you present
some donation, offer up a sacrifice, or take home some of the
sacred herbs.

The day would not suffice for me, if I were to attempt to
enumerate all the matters on which a calumnious accuser
will thus call for an explanation. In especial, what is put
away in one's house, what is placed under seal, what is

shut up, and kept there; all these things, by the same line of reasoning, will be said to be of a magical nature, or else will have to be transferred from the store-room to the forum, and into a court of justice. For my own part, Maximus, I could discuss at very considerable length the value to be set upon such points as these, what their character is, how large a field for calumnious charges is opened by this course adopted by Æmilianus, and what an enormous amount of trouble* and vexation has been caused to innocent persons by this one single napkin. I will do, however, as I originally purposed, even where there is no necessity that I should do so; I will give him the benefit of an admission, and, as I have been interrogated by Æmilianus, I will give him an answer.

You ask, Æmilianus, what it was I had in the napkin. Now, although I might utterly deny that any napkin belonging to me was ever placed in the library of Pontianus, I will grant, by all means, that such was the case, as it still remains in my power to say, that nothing whatever was wrapped up in that napkin. And if I do say so, by the testimony of no one, by no proof can I be refuted. For there is not a person who ever touched it, and only a single freed man, according to your own story, who saw it. Still I tell you, so far as I am concerned, I am quite ready to admit that it was stuffed full of something; think so, if you like, just as in days of yore the companions of Ulysses fancied that they had found a treasure when they fingered the leather bag that was blown out with the winds.† Would you like me to tell you what the things were, thus wrapped up in the napkin which I entrusted to the charge of the Lares of Pontianus? You shall be indulged. I have been initiated into most of the sacred rites of Greece. Certain of their tokens and insignia, which have been given to me by the priests, I carefully keep as reminiscences. Of nothing unusual, nothing unheard-of am I speaking. You, too, brother members of the college of that single God, father Bacchus, who are here present, you,

* *Amount of trouble.*]—He puns upon 'sudor,' 'sweat,' and 'sudariolum,' a 'sweat cloth,' meaning a napkin or 'handkerchief.' Literally, the passage would be, 'and how much sweat has been caused to innocent persons by this one sweat cloth?'

† *With the winds.*]—He alludes to the bag mentioned in the tenth book of the Odyssey, as having been given by Æolus to Ulysses, filled with winds that would ensure his safe return.

I say, know full well what it is you keep so carefully trea-
sured up at home, and what it is that, after excluding the
uninitiated, you venerate in silence.   Well, then, I, as I was
saying, in my eagerness for truth and in performance of my
duty towards the Gods, have become acquainted with mani-
fold rites, usages, and ceremonials.   I do not invent this to
suit the present occasion; for nearly three years since, when,
at the very earliest period after my arrival at Oëa, I was de-
livering a public lecture on the majestic attributes of Æscu-
lapius, I mentioned the very same thing with reference to my-
self, and reckoned up the number of sacred mysteries with
which I was acquainted.   That lecture of mine is very well
known; every body reads it; it is in the hands of all; being
recommended to the religious of Oëa, not so much by my own
eloquence, as by its mention of Æsculapius.*   Repeat some
of you, if there are any who happen to remember it, the be-
ginning of that discourse.   [*It is repeated.*]   Do you hear,
Maximus, how many are able to quote it?   Nay, more, only
look; the book is handed to me.   I will request that those
same passages be read; for judging by the very kind expres-
sion of your countenance, I am fully assured that you will
not object to hear them read.   [*The passages so read are want-
ing.*]   Can it, then, seem wonderful to any man who has any
thought or regard whatever for religion, that a person who has
been initiated into so many sacred mysteries of the Gods, keeps
in his house certain tokens connected with those sacred rites,
and that he wraps them up in woven linen, a substance that
forms the purest of all coverings for things of a holy nature?

For wool, being an excrement of a most inert body, and
taken from an animal's back, has ever been held to be an im-
pure covering, in conformity with the dicta of Orpheus and
Pythagoras; while, on the other hand, flax, the purest pro-
duction of the earth, and one that springs up from the ground
among the choicest of its fruits, is employed by the most holy
of the priests of the Ægyptians, not only for their dress, but
also for the purpose of covering things of a sacred nature.
Still, I am quite aware that there are some, and Æmilianus
here especially, who make a joke of sacred matters, and laugh
them to scorn.   For, from what I can learn from some of the

Æsculapius.]—This God was the patron deity of Oëa, where he had
a fine temple.

people of Oëa, who are acquainted with him, up to this pre-
sent advanced period of life, he has offered his supplications
to no deity, crossed the threshold of no temple. If he chances
to pass by any holy place, he holds it an abomination to
move his hand to his lips for the purpose of shewing venera-
tion. Not even to the Gods of husbandry, who feed him and
clothe him, does this man offer any first-fruits of his crops, or
his vines, or his flocks: no shrine is there built on his estate,
no consecrated spot or grove is there to be found. But why
do I talk about groves and shrines? Those who have been
there, declare that they never so much as saw a single anointed
stone within the boundaries of his estate, or one branch
crowned with garlands. Hence it is, that two nicknames
have been given him, Charon, as I have mentioned already,
in consequence of the unseemliness of his features and his dis-
position ; and another, which he likes better, and which is
given him on account of his contempt for the Gods, namely,
that of Mezentius.* For this reason, I can very easily un-
derstand that these initiations into so many sacred rites will
appear to him to be mere nonsense; and perhaps, in his con-
tempt for things divine, he will persuade himself not to be-
lieve me, when I say that I most religiously preserve these
tokens and reminiscences of so many sacred ceremonials.

But what Mezentius may choose to think of me, not one
snap of a finger do I care. To the rest, however, who are
around me, in my loudest voice I give notice, that if any
one happens to be present who has been initiated into the same
rites as myself, if he will give me the sign, he shall then be at
liberty to hear what it is I keep with such care. For, so far
as I am concerned, by no peril will I ever be compelled to dis-
close to the uninitiated the things that I have had entrusted to
me on condition of silence. I have now then, Maximus, to
my thinking, fully satisfied the mind of any man, even the
most unreasonable ; and, so far as the napkin is concerned,
have wiped away every stain of suspicion; and I believe I may
now pass on in perfect security from the suspicions of Æmili-
anus to the testimony of Crassus, which, next to the preceding
matters, they adduced as of the greatest importance.

You heard read in the information, the testimony of a cer-

* *Mezentius.*]—This contemner of the Gods is mentioned in the Æneid,
as one of the allies of Turnus against Æneas.

tain glutton and desperate debauchee, Junius Crassus by name, who stated that I had been in the habit of performing sacred rites at night in his house, together with my friend Appius Quintianus, who had paid a sum for the hire of that house. This Crassus affirms, too, that although at that very time he was at Alexandria, he still knows this for a fact, from the smoke left by the torches and from the feathers of birds which were found there.   I suppose he means to say, that while he was celebrating his orgies at Alexandria, (for this, you must know, is that same Crassus who delights to creep at midday into his dens of brothels,) he caught, amid the steams of the kitchen, the feathers that had been wafted thither all the way from his abode, and that he recognized the smoke of his own house, as it curled afar from his paternal roof.   If he really did manage to see it with his eyes, he certainly is blessed with a power of sight that far transcends the wishes and aspirations of Ulysses himself.   Ulysses, for many a year, looked out in the distance from the sea-shore, and longed in vain to espy the smoke as it ascended from his native land.* Crassus, in the few months during which he was absent, without the slightest trouble, espied that smoke while seated in a wineshop.

And if, too, he managed to snuff up with his nostrils the fumes that arose from his house, why, then, he outdoes even dogs and vultures in the keenness of his scent.   For by what dog, by what vulture, under the Alexandrian sky, can anything possibly be smelt all the way from the confines of Oëa? No doubt this Crassus is an inordinate glutton, and far from unskilled in all kinds of fumes; but really, considering his fondness for drinking, the only thing for which he has become distinguished, it would be much more easy for the fumes of wine, than the smell of smoke to reach him at Alexandria. Even he himself was sensible that this would not be easily believed.   For the report is, that before the second hour of the day, with an empty stomach, and before he had taken a drop of wine, he made sale of this same testimony of his; upon which, he wrote down that he had made this discovery in the following manner.

---

* *His native land.*]—He alludes to the passage in the first book of the Odyssey, in reference to which, Horace says, that Ulysses ' preferred to behold the smoke rising from his native land, to gaining immortality.'

Upon his return from Alexandria, he straightway repaired to his own house, which Quintianus had just quitted: in the vestibule of it he found a great many feathers of birds, and perceived that the walls were black with soot. On enquiring of his servant, whom he had left at Oëa, what was the reason of this, the servant informed him of the nocturnal rites celebrated by me and Quintianus. How very cleverly invented! What a very likely story, that, if I had wanted to do anything of that kind, I should not have done it at my own house in preference. That Quintianus here, who is now standing by me, (whose name, in consideration of the strictest ties of friendship which exist between him and me, of his extraordinary learning and his most consummate eloquence, I here mention for the purpose of honouring and extolling him,) that this same Quintianus, I say, if he was going to have any fowls for his dinner, or if, as they say, he required them to be killed for magical purposes, could find no servant to pluck the feathers and throw them away! Moreover, that the smoke was in such volumes, that it quite blackened the walls! and that Quintianus was willing to put up with this dirty appearance in his room, all the time that he was residing there!

You make no answer to this, Æmilianus; it is not likely you would; but perhaps Crassus, on his return, did not direct his steps to the chamber, but, consistently with his usual practice, made straight for the kitchen-stove. But on what ground did the servant of Crassus form this suspicion of his, that the walls got blackened in the night time precisely? or why, that it was smoke with which they were discoloured? It is, I suppose, because smoke that escapes by night, is blacker than the smoke of the daytime, and so differs from it in its effect! And then, why should a servant, so full of his suspicions, and so notable a person, allow Quintianus to leave, without having the house cleaned out? Why did those feathers, just like so many lumps of lead, lie there all that time, even till Crassus had returned? Ought not Crassus to scold his servant for this? No, he has preferred to trump up this falsehood about the soot and the feathers, because, even in giving his evidence, he cannot tear himself from the kitchen.

And then, why did you read his evidence from the record? Where is Crassus himself? Has he got tired of his house, and returned to Alexandria? Is he busily engaged in cleaning down those walls of his? Or, what is much more likely, is that gormandizer at this moment laid up with a fit of indigestion? For I, my own self, Æmilianus, saw him no longer ago than yesterday, here at Sabrata,* publicly enough, hiccupping away to you, in the middle of the market-place. Make enquiry then, Maximus, of your clerks of court, although, no doubt, he is better known to cookshop-keepers than to clerks of court; still, ask them, I say, whether they have seen here Junius Crassus, a native of Oëa; they will not say no. Therefore, let Æmilianus bring before us this most worthy youth, in whose testimony he places such confidence. You see what time of the day it is. I am ready to affirm, that long before this hour, Crassus has been snoring away dead drunk, or else, that he is at this moment taking his second bath, and sweating off his wine, that he may be ready for a second drinking bout after dinner. This fellow, though he is quite close at hand, speaks through the record: not but that he is so utterly void of shame, that if even he were in your presence, he would lie, without changing colour in the slightest; but very probably, from his drunken habits, he has not been able to exercise even such a slight degree of control over himself, as to keep sober and await this hour. Or else it is, that Æmilianus has done this designedly, in order that he might not have to place him before such scrutinizing eyes as yours; his object being that you might not, from his appearance, form a bad opinion of the brute, with his lank jaws, and his sinister aspect; when you saw his head despoiled of beard and hair, though he is still a young man, his eyes distilling rheum, his eyelids swollen, his lips bedewed with slaver, his voice quite cracked, his hands shaking, as he grins† and belches by turns. All his patrimony he has long ago devoured, and nothing of his family possessions is there now left, except one solitary house, for the purpose of affording him an opportunity of making sale of his false evidence; and which he has never let at a more remunerating rate, than in affording this bit of testimony. For this drunken fabrication of his, he has bartered to

* *At Sabrata.*]—This was a city near Oëa. There is considerable doubt, however, as to the correct reading of the passage.

† *As he grins.*]—This passage is incomplete in the text: though both the words, 'rictum' and 'ructu,' make their appearance.

Æmilianus for three thousand pieces of money, a fact of which there is not a person in Oëa who is ignorant. Before the bargain was concluded, we all knew of it, and by giving timely information, I might have put a stop to it, if I had not been well aware that so silly a lie would do far more harm to Æmilianus, who was making purchase of it to no purpose, than to myself, who could well afford to hold it in contempt. I was willing that Æmilianus should have to suffer a loss, and that Crassus should be exposed for the disgraceful character of his evidence.

Why, it is no longer ago than the day before yesterday, that, without the slightest attempt at concealment, the transaction was concluded, at the house of one Rufinus, of whom I shall just now have to make mention, the said Rufinus and Calpurnianus acting as the go-betweens and promoters of the transaction. And this part Rufinus was the more ready to act, because he felt very sure that Crassus would bring by no means the smallest part of his bribe to his own wife, at whose intrigues he purposely connives. I perceived you too, Maximus, the very moment that the information was produced, showing, by your looks, that you regarded the whole matter with contempt; for, with your usual wisdom, you suspected their plot, and saw that it was a conspiracy got up against me. And yet, after all, possessed though they are of unbridled audacity and insolent effrontery, not even they have dared to read through the evidence of Crassus, for they saw that it stunk in your nostrils, nor have they ventured to place any reliance upon it.

Now this is why I have mentioned these things, not that with you for my judge, I was frightened by their feathers and their smoke stains, but that Crassus might not escape unpunished for his offence in selling smoke* to a country clown like Æmilianus.

Then there was a charge made by them, when they read the letters of Pudentilla. It was about a certain little image, which they say I ordered to be secretly made, of the most costly wood, for purposes of magic. They assert, too, that, although it was the figure of a skeleton, something quite shocking and horrible, I was in the habit of paying the

* *Selling smoke.*]—A proverbial expression, signifying to 'take in' a person.

greatest veneration to it, and calling it by the Greek name of βασιλευς, or "king." If I am not mistaken, I am following their steps in regular order, and unravelling the whole texture of their calumnies piecemeal. How can the fabrication of the image have possibly been secret, as you allege, when you know so well who was the maker of it, that you have given him notice to appear? Look, here is Cornelius Saturninus, the carver, a man praised among his fellow-citizens for his skill and esteemed for his character; the same person, Maximus, who, a short time since, when you carefully enquired into all the circumstances of the transaction, recounted them with the strictest fidelity and veracity. He stated that, after I had seen at his house a number of geometrical figures made of box-wood, in a very clever and workmanlike manner, I was induced by his skill to request him to make for me some mechanical implements, and at the same time gave him a commission to carve for me the figure of any god he might think fit, and out of any material, so long as it was wood, that I might address my prayers to it, after my usual practice. Accordingly, he tried boxwood first. He also stated that, in the meantime, while I was in the country, my son-in-law, Sicinius Pontianus, who made it his study how to gratify me, having obtained from a most respectable lady, Capitolina by name, some boxes made of ebony, brought them to him, and requested him to make the implements of that material in preference, as being rarer and more durable; remarking that I should be especially gratified by such a present. In conformity with my son-in-law's request, he made the articles, as far as the wood of the boxes sufficed, and was able to complete besides a small figure of Mercury, by putting the layers of ivory piece by piece one upon another, in order to give it the requisite thickness.

As I say, all these particulars you heard from him: added to which, on examining the son of Capitolina, a most worthy young man, who is now present, you were told to the same effect; how that Pontianus asked for the boxes, and how that Pontianus took them to the artist, Saturninus. The fact, too, is not denied, that Pontianus received the image when completed from Saturninus, and afterwards made a present of it to me. All these matters being clearly and distinctly proved, what remains after all this, in which any ground for suspicion of magical practices can lurk? Or rather, what is there in the whole matter that does not convict you of a manifest lie ? You declared that the image was made secretly, while the fact is, that Pontianus, an illustrious knight, had it made ; and that Saturninus, a man of respectability and of high character among his fellow-citizens, seated in his own workshop, carved it openly and without concealment ; while a lady of the highest reputation aided the work by the present she made ; numbers, too, both of my own servants and of my friends, who were in the habit of visiting me, knew that it was about to be made, and that it was made.

Were you not ashamed to invent such a lie, and to assert that I had gone all the city over in search of the wood, and that I had taken the greatest trouble in so doing, whereas you knew full well that at that very time I was absent, and had given orders, as was fully proved, that it was to be made of any kind of material ? Your third lie was, that the figure was made to resemble a frightful corpse, all lean, or rather fleshless, quite horrible and spectre-like. Now, if you were aware of the existence of such an evident proof of magic, why did you not give me notice to produce it ? Was it that you might be at liberty to lie as you pleased about a thing that was not before the court ? Thanks, however, to a certain habit of mine, you cannot make this falsehood pass. For it is my custom, wherever I go, to carry with me the image of some god or other stowed away among my books, and to address my prayers to it on festive days, together with offerings of frankincense and wine, and sometimes victims. Accordingly, when I heard just now that most impudent fabrication of yours about a skeleton, I requested a person to go, post haste, and fetch from my lodgings the little image of Mercury which Saturninus had made for me at Oëa.

Come, let them see it ; handle it, examine it. There it is before you—the thing that this scoundrel has called a skeleton. Do you not hear the expressions of displeasure so loudly uttered by all present ? Do you not hear their condemnation of your falsehood ? Are you not at last utterly ashamed of so many calumnious charges ? Is this a skeleton? Is this the figure of a spectre ? Is this a thing that you will persist in calling a demon ? Is this an image adapted to magical practices, or is it one of the usual and ordinary kind ? Take it, pray, Maximus, and look at it : to hands so pure and so holy as yours a sacred thing is well entrusted. There, now, just look at it; how beauteous its figure, and how replete with stalwart vigour; how smiling are the features of the god; how becomingly does the first growth of down overspread the cheeks, and how gracefully do the crisped locks peep forth upon the head from beneath the shelving brim of the cap! How charmingly do the wings shoot forth above his temples! How smartly, too, is the garment laid down in plaits about the shoulders! Any one who dares to call this a skeleton, it is clear that he never sees an image of the Gods; or if he does, he passes them all in heedless contempt. Any one who takes this to be the figure of a spectre, is a spectre-stricken being himself.

In return, Æmilianus, for this lie of yours, may this Divinity, who visits the Deities above and the shades below, bring upon you the enmity of the Gods who dwell in either realm, and may he thrust upon your vision phantoms of the dead, all the shades of hell, all the Lemurs, all the Manes, all the hobgoblins, all the apparitions of the night, all the spectres of the sepulchres, all the terrors of the tombs—from making a more intimate acquaintance with which, you are not very far distant, both in age and in deserts. But as for us, the disciples of Plato, of nothing do we know, except that which is festive and joyous, consistent with propriety, divine and heavenly. Nay, more, in its aspirations for what is exalted, this sect has even explored things loftier than the very heavens, and has taken up its abode on the convex side* of the firmament. Maximus knows that I speak the truth, for he has attentively read in the Phædrus of "the place" which Plato mentions as "being above the heavens, and upon the back thereof." Maximus, too, understands full well (to answer you in relation to the name†) who it is that was called first of all, not by me but by Plato, by the title of "Basileus," the first cause, and reason, and primitive origin of universal nature, the supreme father of the mind, the eternal preserver of animated beings, the ever-watchful artificer of his universe. And, indeed, he is an artificer who knows not labour, a preserver devoid of anxiety, a father without generation, one compre-

---

* *Convex side.*]—Literally, 'the back of the universe.'

† *To the name.*]—Of 'Basileus,' or 'king:' said to have been given by him to the image.

hended by no space, by no time, by no name, and therefore to be conceived by few, to be expressed by none. See, then, I volunteer to add to your suspicions of my magical pursuits. I do not answer you, Æmilianus, as to who it is I worship under the name of "Basileus." Nay, more, even if the proconsul himself were to ask me who my God is, I should be silent. With reference to the name, for the present I have said enough; as for the rest, I am not unaware that some who stand around me are anxious to hear why I wished the image to be made not of silver or gold, but of wood especially; and this I believe they desire to know, not so much for the purpose of ensuring my acquittal as of gaining information, so that they may have their minds set at ease even upon this little matter, when they have seen every ground for suspicion abundantly confuted.

Listen, then, you who wish to know; listen with the closest attention, as though you heard the very words of the sage Plato, which are found in his last book, "On the Laws." "It is right that a moderate man should present offerings in moderation to the Gods. But as the earth, like the domestic hearth, is sacred to all the Gods, let no one dedicate that a second time to the Gods." He gives this prohibition in order that no private person may presume to erect a temple on his own property. For he thinks that public temples are sufficient for the citizens for the purpose of immolating victims. He then subjoins, "For gold and silver, both in other cities and in our own, employed in temples, is an odious thing. Ivory, too, as proceeding from a body deprived of life, is not a becoming offering. Again, iron and copper are instruments of warfare. But of wood, let each person consecrate as much as he pleases, so long as it is of a single kind, and the same as to stone, in the temples that are common to all."

The expressions of assent on all sides, and yours especially who sit here in judgment, show that I have most fortunately employed Plato not only as the guide of my life, but as my advocate in this trial, whose directions you see me so ready to obey.

It is now time* to turn to the letters of Pudentilla, or, in-

* *It is now time.*]—In many editions this begins what is called the 'Second Apology' or 'Defence of Apuleius.' It is clear, however, from internal evidence, that the whole speech was delivered on the same occasion.

deed, to go a little further back, and retrace all these events, in order that it may be palpable to all, that if I, who, they persist in saying, effected an entrance into the house of Puden- tilla from motives of cupidity, had thought of any thing like gain, I ought rather to have always shunned that house, and an alliance that in other respects has turned out for me so far from fortunate. It is one, indeed, that would have proved disastrous to me, had it not been that my wife in herself, by her many virtues, makes ample amends for disadvantages so numerous; for really nothing can you find but disappointed envy as the prompter of this accusation, and the source of many previous perils to which I have been exposed.

But why, even if he really had found me to be a magician, should Æmilianus have been moved to indignation, when not only has he never been injured by any act, but not by the slightest word even of mine, so as to give him a pretext for taking umbrage and entertaining a desire for revenge? Nor yet is it for the sake of renown that he accuses me; the ruling motive when M. Antonius accused Cneius Carbo; C. Mutius, A. Albertius; P. Sulpitius, Cneius Norbanus; C. Furius, M. Aquilius; C. Cario, Q. Metellus. For all these persons, men of the greatest learning and in the prime of life, made these their first efforts in the forensic art for the sake of gaining re- nown; and their object was, that by engaging in some cele- brated cause they might become known to their fellow-citizens. But this custom, which, among those of former times, was allowable in rising young men, for the purpose of showing off the vigour of their intellect, has long since gone out of usage; and even if at the present day it were in use, it ought to have been resorted to by him the last of all. For neither would the boasts of eloquence have become a person so rude and so unlearned, the desire of glory one so clownish and so uncouth, nor the practice of pleading causes an aged man with one foot in the grave; unless it is, perchance, that Æmilianus, in ac- cordance with his severity of manners, has wished to set an example, and from the very hostility that he entertains to vice itself, has, in conformity with the unblemished character of his morals, taken upon himself to make this charge. But this I could hardly have believed even of Æmilianus, not this African one, but him who was called Africanus* Numantinus,

* *Africanus.*]—He puns upon the resemblance of the names 'Afer,' an

and who had held, too, the office of censor; much less can I entertain the notion that in this stick here there is any hatred of crimes, or even so much as a comprehension of what they are.

What is the reason, then? To any one it is as clear as day that it is nothing else but envy that has instigated him and his prompter, Herennius Rufinus (of whom I shall have to speak presently), and the rest of my enemies, to frame these calumnious charges of magical practices.

There are five points, then, which it is incumbent upon me to discuss; for so many, if I remember aright, have they objected against me in relation to Pudentilla. Now, the first point is, their assertion that after her first husband's decease she would never have married again, had she not been forced by my incantations; the second concerns her letters, which they consider to be an admission of magical practices; then, in the third and fourth places, they have made the objection that in the sixtieth year of her age she was married to gratify lustful propensities, and that the marriage contract was signed not in town, but at her country house. The last and the most odious charge is that which bears reference to her fortune. Into that they have with all their might discharged their whole venom; upon that point they were most especially anxious, and this is what they have alleged; they say that immediately after we were married, at her country house, remote from all witnesses, I extorted from my fond wife this large fortune of hers. All these assertions I will prove to be so false, so worthless, so unfounded, and will so easily and beyond all question refute them, that truly, Maximus, and you councillors, I do very much fear you will think that the accuser has been engaged and suborned by me, to give me an opportunity publicly to extinguish the rancorous hatred with which I have been pursued. Believe me when I say it, and the event will prove my words true, that I shall have to take all possible pains that you may not suppose rather that I have in my craftiness devised, than that they have in their folly undertaken so frivolous a prosecution.

Now, while I briefly recount the circumstances of the case in their order, and force Æmilianus himself to own on what false grounds he has been induced to hate me, and that he has wan-

African by birth, and 'Africanus,' the surname given to P. Cornelius Scipio Æmilianus, the conqueror of Carthage.

dered far indeed from the truth, I beg that you will as carefully as you have already done, or even more so, if possible, consider the very origin and foundation of this trial.

Æmilia Pudentilla, who is now my wife, had, by one Sicinius Amicus, to whom she was previously married, two sons, Pontianus and Pudens. These children were left orphans, and under care of their paternal grandfather (for it so happened that Amicus died, leaving his father surviving him), on which she manifested the most exemplary affection, and brought them up with the greatest care for a period of fourteen years. Still, however, it was by no inclination of hers that, in the flower of her age, she remained so long in a state of widowhood; but the grandfather of the children used all his endeavours to unite her, much against her wish, to Sicinius Clarus, another son of his, and for that reason he kept all other suitors at a distance, while at the same time he threatened that if she should marry a stranger, he would by his will leave no portion of their paternal property to her sons. Being a woman endowed with prudence and of exemplary affection, and seeing this match so perseveringly proposed to her, she complied, and executed a marriage contract with Sicinius Clarus, that she might not, through any conduct of hers, be the cause of detriment to her children. However, by resorting to various pretexts, she put off the nuptials until such time as the grandfather of the children had departed this life, leaving her sons his heirs, and upon the understanding that Pontianus, who was the elder, should be the guardian of his brother.

On being thus set free from this state of perplexity, she was sought in marriage by men of the highest rank, and she accordingly made up her mind no longer to remain in a state of widowhood; for, although she might have been able to endure the tediousness of celibacy, she was quite unable to bear up against bodily ailment. A woman of inviolable chastity, who had lived so many years in a state of widowhood, without a blemish, without an aspersion on her character, with her system torpid from her prolonged disuse of the married state, afflicted with a protracted inactivity of the vital parts, the interior of her womb disordered—she was often brought by her sufferings to extreme peril of her life. Both doctors and midwives agreed that the disease had taken its rise through disuse of the married state, that the malady would gain strength every day, and her weakness become still greater; and they strongly suggested that while some hopes of life were still remaining, recourse ought to be had to marriage.

Other persons, too, approved of this advice, Æmilianus here, in especial, the very man who, a short time since, asserted with most audacious falsehood, that Pudentilla never entertained a thought about marriage, until she was coerced by me through magical practices; and that I was the only one found to violate the flower of her widowhood, a kind of virginity, as it were, by means of my charms and drugs. I have many a time heard it said, with very good reason too, that "A liar ought to have a good memory." Now, did it not occur to your recollection, Æmilianus, that before I even came to Oëa, you had gone so far as to write a letter to her son, Pontianus, who was then grown up, and residing at Rome, in which you recommended that she should marry? Give me the letter, will you, or rather hand it to him; let him read it; by his own voice and by his own words let him convict himself. [*He reads the beginning of the letter.*] Is not that your own writing? Why do you turn pale? for blush you decidedly cannot. Is not this your signature? Read it, I beg, and aloud, too, so that all may understand what a vast difference there is between this man's tongue and his hand, and how much less he disagrees with me than with himself. [*The clerk of court reads the rest of the letter.*]

Were you not the writer, Æmilianus, of these words which have been read? "I know that she wishes and ought to marry; but whom she may choose, I do not know." Quite right, no doubt you did not know. For Pudentilla, being well aware of your spiteful malignity, only thought proper to inform you of the fact, but said nothing at all about a suitor. You, however, deluded by vain hopes that she would marry your brother Clarus, even went so far as to advise her son Pontianus to consent to her marriage. Consequently, if she had made choice of Clarus, a clownish and decrepit old man, you would have been ready to assert that, quite spontaneously, and without any magical practices whatever, she had long been anxious to marry; but as she has made choice of such a youth as you talk of, you affirm that it was by compulsion she did so, and that, otherwise she always entertained an aversion to marriage. You little thought, dishonest man, that your letter on this matter had been preserved; you little thought that you were going to be convicted on your own testimony. Pudentilla, however, knowing full well how fickle and changeable you were, and how untruthful and shameless to boot, thought it better to keep this letter than to part with it, as an evidence of your own wishes on the subject.

Besides, she herself wrote to her son, Pontianus, while he was at Rome, on the same subject, and entered very fully too upon the causes that prompted her to take this resolution. She mentioned to him all the matters connected with her health, that besides there was no reason why she should persist any longer in remaining unmarried; she reminded him, how that, disregarding her own welfare, she had, by her prolonged state of widowhood, obtained for them their grandfather's property, and had with the most scrupulous carefulness increased the same; that, thanks to the Gods, he himself was now of marriageable estate, and his brother ready to assume the manly gown:* that they ought now at last to allow her to find some alleviation for her state of solitude and sickliness: that they need be under no apprehension as to the constancy of her affection, and her remembering them in her last will: that such as she had shown herself towards them while a widow, she would still prove when a wife. I will request the copy of this letter to be read, which she sent to her son. [*The copy of the letter of Pudentilla to her son Pontianus is read.*]

I think that from this letter it may be quite manifest to any one that it was not by any incantations of mine that Pudentilla was prevailed upon to abandon her prolonged state of widowhood, but that having been for a long time not averse to marriage, she perchance preferred me to the rest. And I really do not see why this choice made by a woman of such respectability, ought to be imputed to me as a crime, rather than an honor. But I do wonder that Æmilianus and Rufinus take amiss this decision of the lady, when those persons who aspired to the hand of Pudentilla bear with resignation the fact that I was preferred to them. Besides, in so doing, she rather consulted her son's wishes, than her own feelings on the subject. That such was the fact, not even Æmilianus can deny.

* *The manly gown.*]—The 'toga virilis,' assumed by youths at the age of seventeen.

For Pontianus, on receiving his mother's letter, instantly
flew hither with all haste from Rome, being greatly afraid,
if she should take some greedy fellow for a husband, she would
be carrying off everything, as too frequently is the case, to her
husband's house. This anxiety influenced his feelings in no
slight degree : for all the hopes of himself and of his brother
were centred in possessing the property of their mother.
Their grandfather had left a small property, their mother's
possessions amounted in value to four millions of sesterces.
Out of this sum she did, no doubt, owe some money to her
sons, which she had borrowed from them without giving any
vouchers, but simply on her own credit. These apprehensions
of his he kept secret; for he did not dare openly to offer op-
position, lest he should seem to distrust her. While mat-
ters were in this state, the mother being wooed, and the son
racked with apprehensions, whether it was by chance, or by a
kind of fatality, I happened to arrive there, being on my road
to Alexandria. " By Hercules, I only wish it had never so
happened," I might add, if respect for my wife did not pre-
vent me. It was the winter season. Fatigued by the journey,
I made a stay of several days at the house of the Appii, old
friends of mine, whose names I mention to testify for them
my honor and my esteem. • While I was staying there, Pon-
tianus called upon me; for, some few years before, he had
been introduced to me at Athens, by some common friends of
ours, and had been subsequently united to me by ties of the
strictest intimacy. He was in everything sedulous to testify
his respect for me, to promote my welfare, and dexterously to
prompt my affections. For he thought that in me he had now
found a very suitable husband for his mother, and one to whom
he might, without any risk, entrust the welfare of the family.

He began to sound my inclination by hints, and as he per-
ceived that I was intent upon pursuing my travels, and averse
to wedlock, he begged that I would at least make a short stay.
He said that it was his wish to accompany me, that it was un-
advisable then to proceed on account of the burning heat of
[the sands of] the Syrtis, and the wild beasts that infested
it, and that as my bad state of health had deprived me of the
present winter, it would be as well to wait for the next. By
force of entreaties, he withdrew me from the house of my
friends, the Appii, to transfer me to his mother's abode, as

likely to prove a more healthy place of residence for me; besides, I should be able from her house to enjoy a very extensive view of the sea, a thing that for me has especial charms. He urged these considerations with great earnestness, and introduced to me his mother and his brother, this same youth. They received some assistance from me in their common studies, and the intimacy increased apace.   In the meantime I recovered my health, and at the request of my friends I gave a public lecture.   All who were present in the thronged basilica,* the place appointed for its delivery, cried out with one accord, requesting that I would remain there, and become a citizen of Oëa.   When the audience had departed, Pontianus addressed me, and began by saying that he interpreted this accordance in the public voice as an omen from heaven.   Then he disclosed to me that it was his own wish, if I had no objection, to unite me to his mother, whom a great many persons were eager to obtain ; seeing that, as he said, I was the only person in whom he placed entire trust and confidence.   Would I take upon me that incumbrance? for it was no pretty maiden he offered me, but a woman, the mother of children, and of homely features. If, on thinking over these things, I should reserve myself for some other match, with the view of gaining beauty or riches, he would neither take me for a friend nor a true philosopher.

My speech would be far too long, were I to relate what I stated to him in answer; at what length, and how frequently the subject was discussed by us; with what repeated and earnest entreaties he plied me; and how he never ceased till he had finally gained his point.   Not but that having now lived in the same house with her a whole year, I had become thoroughly acquainted with Pudentilla's character, and had discovered her virtuous endowments; still, as I was anxious to travel, I declined for some time to marry, as being likely to prove an impediment to my design.   Before very long, however, I was no more disinclined to take such a woman for my wife, than if I had sought her of my own accord.

Pontianus, too, had prevailed upon his mother to choose me in preference to all others, and showed incredible anxiety to bring it about as soon as possible.   It was with difficulty we obtained of him even a short respite, until such time as he

* *Basilica.*]—The ' basilica' was a large building, where public meetings were held, and the magistrates sat in judgment.

himself should have married, and his brother have assumed the manly gown; after which we agreed to be united in marriage. I wish, by Hercules! it were possible, without the greatest injury to my cause, to pass over the matters which I am obliged next to mention, that I might not appear now to accuse Pontianus of fickleness, whom I forgave freely and without reserve, when he asked forgiveness for his error. For I am ready to confess a thing that has been brought forward as a charge against me, that, after he was married, he was guilty of a breach of that fidelity which he had pledged to me, and that, suddenly changing his mind, he endeavoured with equal pertinacity to prevent that which he had before endeavoured with the greatest zeal to promote—that, in fact, he was ready to submit to anything, to do anything, in order that our marriage might not take place. And still, all this unbecoming change of mind on his part, and this ill-will against his mother, ought not to be imputed as a fault to him, but rather to his father-in-law, who stands there, Herennius Rufinus, a man who has left not one individual upon the face of the earth more vile, more dishonest, or more iniquitous than himself.

In a very few words, as I am necessitated so to do, I will describe the man, but still in language as moderate as I possibly can; lest, if I should be altogether silent about him, he should have lost his pains, in using his utmost endeavours to create for me all this trouble. For it is he who is the instigator of this stripling; it is he who is the prompter of this prosecution; it is he who is the hirer of these advocates; it is he who is the suborner of these witnesses; it is he who is the furnace wherein this calumny has been annealed; it is he who acts as the torch and the goad of Æmilianus here; while in the presence of all, he boasts most immoderately that it is through his machinations that I have been accused. And, no doubt, he has in these matters very good grounds for congratulating himself. For he is the base contractor of all litigation, the inventor of all falsehoods, the framer of all pretences, the hot-bed of all mischiefs; he, too, is a very haunt, a den, a brothel for lusts and debaucheries; from his very earliest age he has been universally notorious for his disgraceful vices. Formerly, in his boyhood, before he was disfigured by that baldness of his, he was subservient to his corruptors in the perpetration of every infamous crime; after that, in his youth, as a dancer on the

Y

stage, he was so pliant in body as to seem to be utterly without bones and nerves ; but, from what I hear, he was remarkable for a coarse and uncouth effeminacy. Indeed, he is said to have had nothing whatever of the actor, except the immodesty. At his present age, too, the years at which he has now arrived—may the Gods confound him!—high commendations these to be uttered in his hearing—his whole house is a brothel, his entire household a mass of corruption, himself devoid of all shame, his wife a prostitute, his sons just like himself. His door, a sport, day and night, for the young men of the place, is battered by their heels, his windows serenaded by their ditties, his dining-room kept in an uproar by revellers, and his bed-chamber a common thoroughfare for adulterers ; nor, in fact, has any one the least fear to enter it, with the exception of him who has brought no admission-fee to the husband. In this way is the dishonor of his bed a source of income to him. Formerly he used to earn money by his own person ; now he earns it by letting out the person of his wife.

With this same man, many a one—I am telling no falsehood —with this same man, I say, many a one has bargained for a night with his wife. Hence, then, that collusion which is so notorious between the husband and the wife. When people have brought a handsome compliment for the woman, no one takes any notice of them, and they take their departure at their own time and pleasure. But as for those who have come not so well supplied, on a signal given, they are seized as adulterers ; and, as though they had come for the purpose of learning a lesson, they do not get away before they have done a little writing.*

But really what was the wretched man to do when he had lost a very handsome fortune—one, however, which he had quite unexpectedly picked up through his father's fraudulent proceedings ? This father of his, being eaten up by usurious debts due to a great number of creditors, preferred to save his money rather than his honor. For when he was dunned on all sides on his bonds, and clutched hold of by all who met him, just as though he had been a madman—"Have patience," he exclaimed; and then he declared it was not in

* *A little writing.*]—They are forced, under fear of maltreatment, to give a promissory-note, or a cheque upon their bankers.

his power to pay his debts; laid aside his gold rings and all the insignia of his rank, and made a composition with his creditors. But, by a most artful fraud, he managed to transfer the greater part of his property into the name of his wife; and so, himself in want, and stripped naked, though covered with his ignominy, he left to Rufinus here—I am telling no falsehood in so saying—three millions of sesterces for him to devour. For fully that sum came to him as his mother's property, free and unencumbered, besides all that his wife has earned for him by her marriage-portions* from day to day. All these sums, however, this gluttonous wretch has so carefully stowed away in his paunch, and squandered upon his orgies of all kinds, that you would really suppose he was afraid lest it might be said that he retained possession of anything that was the result of his father's frauds. This man, so just and so pure in his morals, used his utmost endeavours that what was so badly gotten should be as badly lost; and, from being the possessor of this enormous fortune, he has nothing left, except a wretched ambition and an insatiate appetite.

As for his wife, being now an old woman and nearly worn out, she has at last given up her disgraceful courses. And then, as for his daughter, after having, to no purpose, at the instigation of her mother, gone the round of all the rich young men, and after having been lent even to some of her suitors for them to make trial of her, if she had not fallen in with the good-natured, easy tempered Pontianus, she would perhaps have been still sitting at home a widow before she was a wife. Although we most strongly dissuaded him from doing so, Pontianus conferred on her the false and misplaced name of wife, not being unaware that, shortly before he married her, she had been deserted by a young man of the highest respectability, who had become tired of her, and to whom she had been previously engaged.

Accordingly, his new-married wife came home to him full of assurance, and unabashed, with her chastity rifled, her virginity lost, her nuptial veil all sullied; after her so recent repudiation, a virgin once more, but bringing with her rather the name than the unblemished character of a maid. In a litter supported by eight persons was she borne along. You

---

* *Her marriage-portions.*]—That is to say, the presents received by her from her paramours.

saw, no doubt, you who were present, how shamelessly she
stared about her at the young men, how immodestly she ex-
posed herself. Who was there that did not recognize the mo-
ther's training, when, in the daughter, he beheld the face be-
plastered with cosmetics, the rouged cheeks, and the ogling
eyes? The very day before, her entire fortune was swept
away by a creditor, to the utmost farthing, and certainly a
larger one than a house impoverished and full of children
would bespeak.*

However, this fellow, whose circumstances are as limited as
his hopes are inordinate, his avarice being commensurate with
his neediness, had in his vain anticipations gulped up the whole
four million sesterces belonging to Pudentilla; and therefore,
as he thought that I ought to be got out of the way, in order
that he might more easily practise upon the pliable disposition
of Pontianus and the solitary state of Pudentilla, he began to
rate his son-in-law for having engaged his mother to me;
prompted him, while yet he had the opportunity, as speedily
as possible, to extricate her foot from such great peril; told
him that he himself ought to possess his mother's property,
rather than purposely hand it over to a stranger; and in case he
should decline to do so, this crafty knave alarmed the ena-
moured youth by threatening that he would take home his
daughter. Why enlarge upon the subject? At his own will
he led the simple-minded youth, entangled in the allure-
ments of his new-made bride, quite away from his original
design. Carrying with him the words of Rufinus, he goes
straight to his mother. However, after trying in vain to
shake her constancy, after taking upon himself to censure her
for levity and fickleness, he had to carry back no pleasing re-
port to his father-in-law: that, contrary to her extremely
mild and imperturbable disposition, his mother had been
roused to anger by his expostulations, which served in no
slight degree to support her in her obstinate determination:
that, finally, she declared she was by no means unaware
that it was through the advice of Rufinus he expostulated
with her, for which reason she should be all the more in-

---

* *Would bespeak.*]—'Postulabat.' This seems to be the meaning of
the passage; and the speaker would almost appear to hint that the *in-
tended* fortune of the daughter of Rufinus was a very large one, but only
—*upon paper.*

clined to obtain the protection of a husband against his desperate avarice.

On hearing these words, this pander to his wife so swelled with anger, so blazed with rage, that in the presence of her own son he said things against this lady, a woman of most chaste and modest character, which would have been far more befitting his own chamber, and shouted out that she was a love-sick creature, and I was a magician and sorcerer; and this in the hearing of many persons, whom, if you desire it, I will name; and declared that with his own hand he would put an end to me. Hardly, by Hercules! can I moderate my anger, so great is the indignation which rises in my mind. What, you, you most effeminate wretch! do you threaten death to be dealt with your hand to any man? With what hand, pray? Is it the hand of Philomela? or of Medea? or of Clytemnestra? whom, when you personate in the dance, such is the effeminacy of your disposition, such is your dread of steel, that you are afraid to dance with the mimic sword.*

But, not to digress any further, when Pudentilla saw that her son was corrupted contrary to her expectations, she went into the country, and there wrote to him that famous letter of hers, in which, as they said, she admitted that she had been bereft of her senses and induced to love me through my magical practices. And yet this very letter, by your order, Maximus, I copied at length the day before yesterday, in presence of the public registrar, and before witnesses, Æmilianus taking a copy at the same time; and in every point it is found to tell in my favour, and against their accusations. For even if she had distinctly called me a magician, it might seem that in excusing herself to her son, she preferred to do so rather on the ground of my irresistibleness than of her own inclination. Is Phædra the only woman that ever wrote an untrue letter on the subject of love? Is not this a common artifice with all females, to try and make it appear that they act by compulsion, when they have once set their minds upon any thing of this nature?

And even if she did in her own mind think that I was a magician, am I any the more a magician, because Pudentilla

* *Mimic sword.*]—'Cludine.' The 'cluden' was a sword or dagger used on the stage, and so contrived that, in seeming to penetrate the body, the blade fell into the hilt.

has written to that effect? You, by your numerous arguments, your multitude of witnesses, your lengthy oration, fail to prove that I am a magician; was she by a single expression of hers to prove it? And yet of how much greater weight ought a charge to be considered which is undertaken to be proved in a court of justice, than an assertion merely made in a letter? But why do you not convict me by my own actions, and not by the words of another person? Henceforth, on the same principle, many will be accused of all sorts of offences, if things are to be held as true which anybody, influenced by love or by hatred of another, has written in a letter. Pudentilla has written that you are a magician, therefore you are a magician. Suppose she had written that I was a consul, would it follow that I really am a consul? And what if a painter, what if a physician? what, in fine, if she had said I was innocent? would you have believed her in any one of these assertions, merely because she said so? In none of them, no doubt. Well, but it is most unjust to give credit for evil to one to whom you would decline to give the same credit for good; to allow his letters to have power to injure, and yet not to have power to save. "But her feelings were racked with anxiety," you say; "she loved you to distraction." For the moment, I will grant it. Is it the fact, then, that all who are beloved are magicians, if the person who loves happens to write to that effect? You must admit, now, that at this period Pudentilla did not love me, inasmuch as she wrote that to others which was destined to be to my prejudice before the public. In fine, which do you wish to assert, that she was sane, or that she was insane, when she wrote the letter? Sane, do you say? then she has suffered nothing from my magical practices. Insane, will you answer? then she did not know what it was she wrote, and therefore we must put no faith in her assertion.

And then, besides, if she had been insane, she would not have known that she was insane. For in the same way that the person acts absurdly who says that he is silent, because in the very act of saying that he is silent, he is not silent, and by his very affirmation he contradicts what he affirms: so, even more self-contradictory is the expression, "I am insane," because it is not true, unless he who says it knows what it is to be insane. But he who knows what insanity is, is sane; whereas insanity can no more be sensible of its own existence, than blindness can see itself. Consequently, Pudentilla, if she fancied that she was not in her senses, was quite in her senses. I could, if I chose, enlarge upon the subject, but I will now have done with logic. I will have the letter itself read, which cries aloud to a far different effect, and which seems as though it had been prepared and framed for the very purpose of this trial. Take it and read on until I interrupt you. [*Part of the letter of Pudentilla is read.*] Cease reading for a moment, for we have now arrived at the turning point in this matter.

Thus far, Maximus, from all that I can perceive, this lady has no where mentioned the name of magic, but has recounted the very same train of circumstances that I did a short time since, as to her long widowhood, the cause of her bad state of health, her wish to marry, my own good qualities, of which she had heard an account from Pontianus, and his recommendation that she should marry me in preference to any one else. Thus far has now been read; there remains the other portion of the letter, which, though written in like manner in my favour, has been made to turn its horns against me, and which, while it was sent for the very purpose of removing from me all suspicion of magical practices, has, to the transcendent glory of Rufus, changed sides, and gone so far as to gain for me a quite opposite character in the eyes of certain persons in Oëa, as though I really were a magician. Much in the interchange of conversation, Maximus, you have heard, still more in reading you have learned, and no little knowledge by experience you have gained; but still, you must declare that treachery so insidious, and contrived with such astounding wickedness, you never heard of. What Palamedes, what Sisyphus, what Eurybates, in fine, what Phrynondas* could have thought of such a thing? All those whom I have named, and any besides who have been famed for their cunning, if put in comparison with this single device of Rufinus, would seem to be utter fools and blockheads. O wondrous invention! O subtlety, worthy of the prison and the dungeon cell! who would have believed that it could come to pass that what was a defence, could possibly, while the characters still

---

* *Phrynondas.*]—Eurybates and Phrynondas were persons, probably magicians, whose names among the Greeks had become proverbial for craft and duplicity.

remained the same, be transformed into an accusation? By Hercules! it transcends all belief!

But how this thing, which so transcends belief, was brought about, I will now explain to you. It was the rebuke of a mother to her son, because, at the dictation of Rufinus, he was now declaring, that I, a man whom he had so highly extolled to her, was a magician. The words themselves were to this effect: [*in Greek.*] "Apuleius is a magician, and I have been enchanted by him! I certainly do love him. Come then to me, until such time as I shall have recovered my senses." Now these words, which I have read in Greek, picked out by themselves, and separated from their proper context, Rufinus showed to everybody, as a confession made by the lady, at the same time leading Pontianus with him as he hawked them about the forum.

He allowed the letter which she wrote to be read, just as far as I have quoted; what was written before and after he used to conceal, saying, it was of too disgraceful a nature to be shewn, and that it was enough to know that the lady had made confession of magical practices. What could be wanted more? It appeared a very probable story to all. The very words that had been written for the purpose of exculpating me, stirred up intense hatred against me, among those who did not understand the matter. This abominable fellow, raving in the midst of the forum, like a very bacchanal, collected crowds together; ever and anon opening the letter, he would appeal to the citizens, and exclaiming, "Apuleius is a magician, what she feels and suffers she herself declares; what more would you have?" There was no one to take my part, and thus to answer him, "Have the goodness to give me the whole of the letter. Allow me to see every part of it, and to read it from beginning to end. There are many things, which when produced in an unconnected form, may seem amenable to accusation. Any person's language may afford ground for a charge, if words which are connected with preceding ones are to be curtailed of their beginning; if certain parts in the current order of what has been written are to be suppressed at pleasure; if what has been asserted ironically, is to be read rather in the tone of a person who admits, than of one who indignantly expostulates."

How justly these and other such remarks might have been

made on those occasions, the tenor itself of the letter will show. Now tell us, Æmilianus, whether you did not, in the presence of witnesses, copy these words at the same time as myself. [*In Greek.*] "For when I was desirous, for the reasons I mentioned, to marry, you yourself persuaded me to choose him in preference to all others, because you admired the man, and greatly wished, through my means, to make him a connection of ours. But now, when wicked and evil-minded men prompt you, all on a sudden, Apuleius is a magician, and I have been enchanted by him. I certainly do love him. Come then to me, until such time as I shall have recovered my senses." I ask you, Maximus, if letters, some of which are called vocals [*vowels*], could indeed find a voice, if words were winged, as poets say, would they not, the instant Rufinus, with such bad faith, made these extracts from this letter, and read a few words only, while he purposely withheld the greater and better part,—would not the rest of the letters have shouted aloud, that they were being wickedly suppressed? Would not the words so suppressed, have taken flight from the hands of Rufinus? Would they not have filled the whole forum with their outcries? Would they not have declared that they, too, were sent by Pudentilla, that they, too, had a message to speak? Would they not have said this, in order that people might not listen to a dishonest and wicked man attempting to establish a falsehood by means of the letter of another person, but listen in preference to their own declaration, that Apuleius was not accused by Pudentilla of the practice of magic, but when accused by Rufinus, was acquitted by her of the fact. All these things, although not then expressed, are now made clearer than daylight, at a time when they are of still greater service to me. Your artifices, Rufinus, are exposed; your frauds are detected; your falsehoods are set forth to view. The truth, before suppressed by you, now raises itself erect, and emerges as it were from the deep pit of calumny. You challenged me to abide by the letter of Pudentilla; by that letter do I conquer; and if you choose to hear the latter portion of it also, I will not prevent it. Read the words with which this spell-bound, insane, demented, and love-stricken woman closes her epistle: "I have not been enchanted at all; that I am in love, is the work of Fate."

What more than this do you require? Pudentilla contra-

dicts you, and, by proclamation as it were, defends her sanity
from your calumnious charges.   For the cause or necessity of
her marrying, she ascribes to fate, from whose operations
magic is far removed indeed, nay, utterly estranged.   For
what virtue is there left in spells and enchantments, if the
fate of each individual thing, like a torrent of most impetuous
violence, can neither be restrained, nor yet accelerated in its
course? Why, in this sentence of hers, Pudentilla has not only
denied that I am a magician, but even that such a thing as
magic exists.

It is fortunate that Pontianus, according to his usual cus-
tom, kept his mother's correspondence safe; it is fortunate
that the speedy hearing of this cause has precluded you from
finding leisure to make any alteration in this letter.   This ad-
vantage is owing to you, Maximus, and to your foresight; be-
cause, seeing from the very first into the calumnious nature of
these charges, you hurried on the hearing of them, in order that
they might not gain strength by lapse of time; and so, by
granting them no respite, you have nipped their growth.

Suppose, now, that in a letter written in confidence, the mo-
ther had, as often is the case, made some confession to her son
with reference to love, would it have been right, Rufinus, not
to say duteous or manly even, for the contents of such a letter
to be divulged and published, and that above all, on the infor-
mation of her son?   But I am a simpleton to expect that
you should be observant of the fair name of another, seeing
that you have lost your own.   But why do I complain of what
is past, when the present is no less distressing?   That this
boy should be so utterly corrupted by you, as to read aloud
the letters of his own mother, which he takes to be of an
amatory character! and that he should, before the tribunal
of a proconsul, before Claudius Maximus, a man of the strictest
virtue, in presence of these statues of the emperor Pius,* ac-
cuse his own mother of shameless incontinence! Who is there
so meek as not to be incensed at this? What! make it your
business to pry into your parent's thoughts in such matters;
to watch her eyes; count her sighs; scrutinize her feelings;
intercept her letters; accuse her of amorousness.   What! spy

* *Emperor Pius.*]—Antoninus Pius. It was considered criminal and
impious to use any gross expression, or to make any offensive or calum-
nious charge, in presence of the statue of a Roman emperor.

out what is done in the retirement of the chamber, not to say by your own mother when in love, but by any lady whatsoever! Is it possible you can imagine that she was inspired by any other than the affectionate feelings of a parent?

Alas! unhappy was thy womb, Pudentilla! Oh, barrenness, how far preferable to progeny! Oh, ten months* productive of what unhappiness! Oh, fourteen years of widowhood thus ill repaid! The viper, I have heard say, eats through the womb of its mother, and crawls forth to light, and so owes its birth to parricide. But upon thee, while living, are inflicted wounds still deeper, those, too, by a son who has already arrived at years of maturity. Thy state of solitude is lacerated, thy fair name is mangled, thy breast is stabbed, thy inmost vitals are torn away!

Is this the way that, like a good son, you make return to your mother for having given you life—for acquiring an inheritance for you—for providing for your support during fourteen long years? Or has your uncle trained you in a course like this, in order that you might feel convinced that your sons would turn out like yourself, and so might not venture to marry? There is a line of a poet† which is not uncommonly quoted:

" I hate precocious wisdom in young boys."

But, still more, who would not hate and detest precocious wickedness in a boy? when he beholds him, like a sort of monster, full grown up in crime before he is mature in years, venomous before he is come to his strength, green in boyhood, in villany hoary, and even more baneful because he is sure of impunity, and while he is abundantly able to inflict injuries, he is not liable‡ to pains and penalties. Injuries, did I say? Nay, crimes rather, and those against a parent; crimes infamous, enormous, astounding! Why, the Athenians, in consideration of the common rights of humanity, when the intercepted letters of Philip of Macedon, their enemy, were read in public, forbade one to be published which had been written by Philip to his wife, Olympias. They chose rather to spare an enemy than to divulge the secrets which had been entrusted

* *Ten months.*]—Of gestation.
† *Of a poet.*]—It is not known what poet is here referred to.
‡ *Not liable.*]—Not having arrived at man's estate, he was not liable to capital punishment.

by a husband to his wife, being of opinion that universal right ought to be regarded rather than private vengeance.

Such did enemies shew themselves towards an enemy; what sort of a son have you shewn yourself towards your mother? Do you see how extremely similar are the cases I compare? And yet you, a son, read letters written by your own mother, on amorous subjects, as you allege, in the presence of this numerous assemblage, before whom, if you had been requested to read some wanton poet, you assuredly would not have ventured to do so, but would have been prevented by some sense of shame; indeed, if you had ever touched upon letters in general, you would never have touched letters* written by your own mother. But what an epistle of your own was it that you ventured to give to be read! the letter which, most disrespectfully, most insultingly, and most basely, you wrote about your mother, and secretly sent to Pontianus, at the very time that you were still nurtured in her bosom! in order, I suppose, that you might not have sinned once only, and that such reputable conduct as yours might not be buried in oblivion. Wretched youth! you do not perceive that your uncle allowed this to be done, in order that he might exculpate himself in the sight of men, when it should become known from your own letter, that even before you betook yourself to him, even when you were still fawning upon your mother, even then you were acting a fox-like and unnatural part. Besides, I cannot bring myself to believe that Æmilianus is so simple as to suppose that the letter of a boy, and that boy my accuser, could do me any injury.

Then, there was that counterfeit letter, which was neither written by my hand, nor even forged with any likelihood, by which they wished to make it appear that this lady had been plied by me with blandishments. Why should I need to resort to blandishments, if I relied on my magical powers? Besides, by what means, too, was a letter to come into their hands, which was, no doubt, sent to Pudentilla by the hands of some trusty messenger, as usual in matters of this nature? And why should I write in expressions so ungrammatical, in language so barbarous, when they assert that I am far from unacquainted with the Greek language? Why, too, should I solicit

---

* *Touched letters.*]—This pun exists in the original.

her with compliments so absurd, so pot-house like,* when they say that I am able to express myself elegantly in the wanton numbers of amatory verse? The truth, no doubt, is this: to every one it is self-evident:—he who was not able to read the letter of Pudentilla, because it was expressed in purer Greek, could read this more easily, and find himself more at home in descanting upon it, because the composition was his own.

But now, I shall consider that I have said sufficient on the subject of these letters, when I shall have added this single fact, that Pudentilla, after having written by way of irony and joke, "Come until such time as I shall have come to my senses," after the date of that very letter invited to her house her sons and her daughter-in-law, and lived there with them for a period of nearly two months. Let this dutiful son declare what, during that period, he saw his mother either do or say that was unbecoming, in consequence of this insanity of hers. Let him deny that she did, in the most intelligent manner, audit and sign the accounts of the bailiffs, and the shepherds, and the grooms; let him deny that his brother Pontianus was seriously warned by her to be on his guard against the insidious designs of Rufinus; let him deny that he was justly censured for having everywhere carried about the letter which she had written to him, and yet not having read it faithfully; let him deny that, after all this, his mother was married to me at her country-house, the place previously agreed on between us.

For we had thought it better for us to be united at her country-house in the suburbs, in order that the people of the city might not again flock to us for largesses; as it was not very long since Pudentilla had expended fifty thousand pieces of money, her own property, upon the public, on the day on which Pontianus was married, and this boy was invested with the manly gown. Another reason, was our wish to escape numerous invitations and annoyances which newly-married people generally have to submit to. Here, Æmilianus, you have the entire cause why the marriage contract between me and Pudentilla was signed, not in town, but at the country-house, that she might not have again to expend fifty thousand pieces of money, and that we might not be obliged to feast in your company, or at your house.

* *So pot-house like.*]—' Tamque tabernariis

Was not the cause, then, a reasonable one? Still I am surprised that you, who generally live in the country, have such a remarkable aversion to a country-house. The Julian law, at all events, in its ordinances for the regulation of marriages, nowhere contains any prohibition to this effect—"Marry not a wife at a country-house." Nay, to say the truth, a wife is married under much better auspices, so far as relates to progeny, at a country-house, than in a town—upon a fruitful soil, than in a sterile spot—upon the glebe of the field, than upon the stones of the Forum. She who is destined to be a mother, ought to enter upon the marriage state in the very bosom of her mother, among the ripening ears of corn, and upon the fertile sod; or else she should recline beneath the wedded elm, on the lap of her mother earth, amid the offspring of the grass, the progeny of the vines, and the offshoots of the trees. Closely in accordance with this is that line,* so frequently quoted in the comic writers—

"Children in fields are lawfully begot."

To the Romans of ancient times, the Quintii,† the Serrani, and many others like them, not only wives, but consulships even, and dictatorships, were presented in the country. I will check, myself, however, in a field of such ample range, that I may not gratify you [a rustic] by lavishing praises upon a country-house.

And now, as to the age of Pudentilla, about which, after these other matters, you uttered falsehoods with such great assurance, as even to assert that she was sixty years of age when she married, I will say a few words; for, on a matter so self evident, it is not necessary to descant at any great length. Her father, at her birth, made the usual declaration, that she was his daughter. Her register is preserved, one part in the public registry, the counterpart at home, and the latter is now presented before your face. Hand that register to Æmilianus. Let him see the fastenings,‡ examine the impression of the seal, read the names of the consuls, and count the years. Of the sixty years

---

* *That line.*]—The author of this line is now unknown.

† *The Quintii.*]—In allusion to Q. Cincinnatus. See Livy, Book iii. c. 28.

‡ *The fastenings.*] — Public documents were preserved in tablets, through which a string was run, which was fastened on the outside, and covered with wax stamped with the impression of a seal.

that he gave to this lady, let him prove as much as five and fifty. By a whole lustrum* has he deviated from the truth. But that is not enough : I will deal with him still more liberally. For he has made a present of a great number of years to Pudentilla; I shall, therefore, have to give them back to him by way of return. Like Ulysses, Mezentius† has gone astray ten whole years; let him prove, at least, that this lady is fifty years of age. But why use many words? To deal with him as I would with a four-fold informer,‡ I will double the five years twice over, and at once strike off twenty. Order the consuls to be reckoned, Maximus : if I am not mistaken, you will find that Pudentilla is not now much beyond her fortieth year. Oh, audacious and outrageous lie, that ought to be visited with an exile of twenty years! Do you dare, Æmilianus, to amplify your lies, by thus adding to them one half as much again? If it had been thirty years§ that you stated instead of ten, you might possibly have appeared to have made a mistake in the position of your fingers in counting, and, where you ought to have contracted the fingers in a circle,‖ to have opened them too wide.¶ But when the number forty, which is denoted more easily than any of the others, by opening out the palm of the hand, when this number forty you increase by half as much again, you can have made no such mistake in the position of your fingers ; unless, perhaps, you took the years of Pudentilla to be thirty, and accidentally added together the two consuls for each year.

* *Whole lustrum.*]—A period of five years, or, more properly, four years and a fraction of a fifth.

† *Mezentius.*]—He has previously called Æmilianus by this nickname, in consequence of his contempt of the worship of the gods.

‡ *Four-fold informer.*]—'Quadruplator.'—This name, signifying 'four-folder,' was first given as a name of infamy to the informers at Rome, who practised their calling for the purpose of obtaining the four-fold penalty on conviction.

§ *Thirty years.*]—The ancients, in counting with the fingers, denoted ten by touching the joint of the thumb with the forefinger of the same hand, while thirty was signified by touching the top of the thumb with the forefinger. Forty was denoted by opening the hand wide. He says that in counting, it would not have been impossible to mistake the notation of ten for thirty, and thus to have made an error of twenty years: but that in the act of signifying forty years, the palm being wide open, no such mistake could possibly arise.

‖ *In a circle.*]—When denoting ten.

¶ *Opened them too wide.*]—By denoting thirty.

All these matters I pass by: I now come to the very root of
this accusation, to the very cause of the alleged magic.   Let
Æmilianus and Rufinus make answer for what profit, even if
I had been the greatest of magicians, I should by charms and
by drugs have enticed Pudentilla to marry me.   And yet I am
well aware, that many a person has been accused of a crime,
where certain motives for the commission of it could be proved
to exist, and still, has most successfully defended himself by
shewing that his whole course of life has been utterly averse
to misdeeds of such a nature; and that it ought not to prove
to his detriment if there seemed to exist some inducements
for the perpetration of the crime.   For not every thing which
possibly may have happened, ought to be considered as really
having happened.   There are various fluctuations in human
affairs; but the disposition of each person affords a sure evi-
dence, for, as it is always affected with the same tendency to-
wards virtue or towards vice, it affords an unerring proof of the
readiness to embrace criminality or to reject it.

Although I might, with the greatest justice, make use of
these arguments, still, I spare you them; nor do I deem it
enough to have abundantly proved my innocence on all the
points on which you accuse me, and to have never allowed
the slightest suspicion even of the practice of magic to attach
to me.   Only consider what a degree of confidence in my own
innocence I display, and what supreme contempt of you [my
accusers], when I say that if even the slightest ground shall
appear why I should have coveted this match with Pudentilla
for the sake of any advantage to myself, if you shall prove the
most trifling gain to me thereby, then may I be held to be a
Phrynondas, a Damigeron,* a Moses, a Jannes, an Apollonius,
or even Dardanus himself, or any one else, who, since the

* *Damigeron.*]—He is mentioned by Tertullian as a famous magician:
Dardanus was also celebrated for his skill in the same art.   Phrynondas,
Apollonius of Tyana, Zoroaster, and Ostanes have been previously al-
luded to.   Moses, the law-giver of the Hebrews, was universally looked
upon among the heathens as a magician, and is mentioned as such by
Strabo, Pliny, and Tacitus.   Jannes, and his brother Jambres, are sup-
posed to have been two of the chief magicians who opposed Moses in the
court of Pharaoh.   They are also mentioned in the Second Epistle to
Timothy, iii. 8.   Jannes is also mentioned, together with Moses, by
Pliny, and he and Jambres are spoken of by Numenius and Palladius as
most skilful magicians.

days of Zoroaster and Ostanes, has been celebrated among magicians.

Do see, Maximus, I beg of you, what an uproar they raise, merely because I have enumerated a few of the magicians by name. What am I to do with men so ignorant, so barbarous? Am I to tell them over again, that these and very many other names I have read in public libraries, in the works of authors of the highest reputation? Or am I to discuss the point, that it is one thing to be acquainted with their names, but quite another to have been initiated into the art itself, and that the appliances of learning, and the recollections of erudition, are not to be held to be a confession of criminality? Or shall I do better, and rely, Claudius Maximus, on your learning, and extensive information, and not think it worth my while to make answer on these matters to foolish and illiterate men? I will adopt that course. What they may think of it, I care not a nutshell. I will proceed to prove what I stated: that I had no reason whatever for using incantations to induce Pudentilla to form an alliance with me.

They took it upon themselves to disparage the looks and the age of this lady, and then they imputed it to me as a crime, that I desired to gain such a wife, in order to satisfy my avarice, and that for that reason, at the very earliest moment after our union, I wrested from her a large and ample fortune. It is not my intention to fatigue you, Maximus, by a lengthened speech in reply to this. There is no need of words, when the documents themselves speak so much more eloquently; documents by which you will find that I have acted throughout, both as regarded present arrangements, and provisions for the future, in a manner quite at variance with what they surmised of me, in conformity with their own rapacious dispositions. In the first place, then, the amount put in settlement by this lady of such vast wealth, you will find to have been but small, and that amount not a sum paid down, but only secured in remainder. Besides this, you will find that the union took place upon these terms; in case she should depart this life without issue by me, the entire sum so settled was to go to her sons, Pontianus and Pudens; but, if she should die, leaving one such son or one daughter surviving her, then, in such case, one half of the sum was to go to the last born son, and the residue to the older ones. This, I say, I will

z

prove, from the instrument itself. It may possibly happen, that not even then, Æmilianus will believe that only three hundred thousand pieces of money were so settled, and that by arrangement they were to go in reversion to the sons of Pudentilla.

Take this document in your own hands, [Æmilianus], and give it to your prompter, Rufinus, for him to read. Let him be ashamed of his swelling aspirations, and his ambitious mendicity; for he himself, though in utter want, and stripped naked, gave, as a marriage portion to his daughter, four hundred thousand pieces of money taken from a creditor; Pudentilla, on the other hand, a wealthy woman, has contented herself with a settlement of three hundred thousand pieces, and has a husband, too, who, after having many a time rejected settlements of ample sums, rests contented with the empty name of such a trifling sum as this, for he reckons all other things, except his wife, as nothing at all, and centres all his possessions and all his wealth in the concord of the marriage state, and in mutual attachment.

And yet, who, of all men that had the slightest knowledge even of the world, would have presumed to censure her, if a woman, who was a widow and of average good looks, but beyond mid age, being desirous to marry, had by offering an ample settlement and handsome terms, held out a temptation to a young man who was by no means to be despised either for his looks, his intellect, or his fortune? A beauteous virgin, even though she may chance to be utterly destitute, is still provided with an ample marriage portion; for she brings to her new husband the winning nature of her disposition, the charms of her beauty, the first fruits of her maidenhood. The very recommendation itself of virginity is rightly and deservedly most highly esteemed by all husbands. For whatever else you gain by way of portion, you may, whenever you please, return the whole of it, so as to remain under no obligation whatever. Money you may repay in full, slaves you may restore, a house you may quit, an estate you may leave. Virginity alone, when once it has been bestowed, can never be returned; of the things that form a marriage portion, that alone must of necessity remain with the husband.

A widow, on the other hand, on a divorce taking place, departs just as she came on marriage; nothing does she bring that she may not reclaim; but she comes to you deflowered by another; to say the least, very far from being an apt scholar in carrying out your wishes; holding her new abode in no less suspicion than that in which, by reason of her separation from her former husband, she herself deserves to be held; whether it is that she has lost that husband by death, in which case, as being a woman of unlucky omen, and unfortunate in wedlock, she ought to be avoided; or whether it is, that she has been separated from him by divorce, in which latter case a woman must have one or the other of these two faults; she must have been either so unbearable as to have been repudiated, or else so froward as to have divorced herself. For these and other reasons it is, that widows generally invite suitors by more ample settlements; a thing that Pudentilla, even, might have done in the case of another husband, if she had not met with a philosopher who held all settlements in contempt.

Well, now, if I had desired to gain this lady in order to satisfy my avarice, what plan would there have been more feasible by which to gain possession of her house, than to sow discord between the mother and her sons? to erase from her feelings all affection for her children, in order that I might the more freely and the more certainly, on being left without rivals, gain full possession of the desolate woman? Was not this the part of a robber such as you pretend that I am? and yet I, the author, promoter, and supporter of peace, and concord, and affection, not only did not sow new dissensions, but even utterly eradicated those which previously existed. I prompted my wife, the whole of whose property they assert I had already made away with, I prompted her, I say, and at last succeeded in persuading her, on her sons demanding repayment of their money, as I have already mentioned, to repay them without delay, and that in lands valued at a low figure, and at whatever price they themselves pleased. Besides this, out of her own private-property, I persuaded her to give them some of the most fertile of her farms, a fine house, too, fitted up in a most costly manner, with a great quantity of wheat, barley, wine, oil, and other products of the soil; slaves, too, no less than four hundred in number, and cattle not a few, and of no small value; and all this, that she might set them at ease as to that portion of her property which she thus gave them, and encourage them to be of good hopes as to the remainder. All this I obtained with great difficulty, and by urgent entreaties, from the angry and reluctant Pudentilla—for as such was the fact, she will not object to my saying so. I reconciled the mother to her sons; I enriched my step-sons, (who in this first expe-rienced the benefit of having a step-father,) with a large sum of money. Throughout the whole city this fact was well known. All vented execrations against Rufinus, and lavished commend-ations upon me. Pontianus came to us, together with this bro-ther of his, so unlike him in disposition, before his mother would consent to make this gift; and, throwing himself at our feet, asked us to forget and forgive all that had passed, weeping and kissing our hands, and saying how much he repented that he had listened to Rufinus and those like him.

After that, he suppliantly entreated me to excuse him to Lollianus Avitus,* that most illustrious man, to whom, shortly before, he had been recommended by me at the outset of his professional career;† for he had become aware that a few days previously I had written and informed Avitus of every thing that had taken place. This, too, he prevailed upon me to do. Accordingly, furnished with a letter by me, he set out for Carthage, where, Maximus, the period of his proconsulship being now nearly expired, Lollianus Avitus was awaiting your arrival. After reading my letter, in conformity with his usual extreme kindness of disposition, he commended Pontianus for having so readily made amends for his error, and wrote back to me, by him, good Gods! what a letter! what a style, what wit, what grace and sweetness of expression! He wrote, in fact, just as a good man, and one skilled in the arts of elo-quence, ought to write. I am sure, Maximus, that you will hear his letter with pleasure; and if I do read it, it shall be with my own lips. Hand me the letter of Avitus, that so, what has ever been an ornament to me, may now prove my safety too. You, in the meantime, may suffer the water [of the Clepsydra] to run on; for were I to read over the letter of that most excellent man three or four times, I would not think it lost time. [*He reads the letter of Lollianus Avitus, which is now lost.*]

I am not unaware that I ought, after that letter of Avitus, to come to a close. For whom can I produce to speak more

---

* *Lollianus Avitus.*]—The proconsul of Africa before Claudius Maximus.
† *Professional career.*]—That of a pleader or advocate.

abundantly in my commendation? what witness to my charac-
ter more worthy of all confidence? what more eloquent advo
cate? Many eloquent men who bore the Roman name have I
known and studied during my life, but never did I admire any
one so much as him. There is not an individual at this day,
in my opinion, of any name, of any promise in the arts of elo-
quence, but would greatly prefer to be Avitus, if, all envy
laid aside, he would think proper to institute a comparison be-
tween Avitus and himself. For in this one man are united
all the various gifts of eloquence, even those that are almost
opposite in their nature. Whatever the speech Avitus may
compose, so perfect and finished will it be in all its parts, that
in it Cato would not fail to find his own gravity, Lælius his
smoothness, Gracchus his vehemence, Cæsar his vigorous
subtlety, Hortensius his perspicuity, Calvus his wit, Sallust his
terseness, nor Cicero his richness of expression; once, for all,
I say, not to review each particular, if you were to hear Avitus,
you would wish nothing added, nothing withdrawn, nothing
changed. I see, Maximus, with what pleasure you hear those
characteristics described, which you recognize as distinguishing
your friend Avitus. It is your kindness that has induced me
to say even this little of him. But I will not so far indulge
your sympathy as to allow myself, nearly exhausted as I now
am, and my defence drawing to its close, to begin at this late
hour to descant on his exemplary virtues; but I will, in pre-
ference, reserve these topics for my recruited strength and a
leisure opportunity.

For now, to my disgust, my discourse must be turned from
the praises of a man of such eminent worth, to these pestilent
wretches. And would you dare then, Æmilianus, to set your-
self in comparison with Avitus? Him whom he pronounces to
be a good man; him whose manner of life Avitus so abundantly
commends in his letter, will you pursue with your charges of
magic and criminality? Is it for you to be more annoyed at
my thrusting myself into the house of Pudentilla and plunder-
ing her of her property, than was Pontianus, who, even in
my absence, made full amends to me before Avitus, for the en-
mity of a few days into which he had been led by your insti-
gation; and who expressed his gratitude to me in presence of a
man of such eminence?

Suppose, now, I had stated what took place before Avitus,

but had not read his letter, what would you, or what would any one, have found to censure in this matter? Pontianus himself declared that it was by my bounty he had received what had been presented to him by his mother; from his inmost heart Pontianus congratulated himself that it had fallen to his lot to have me for a step-father, and would that he had returned in safety from Carthage! or, since it was thus decreed by Fate, would that you, Rufinus, had not obstructed the carrying out of his latest intentions! What grateful thanks would he have expressed to me, either personally or in his last will! Still the letters which he sent to me from Carthage, as well as while on the road home—those written while in robust health, the others when reduced by sickness, but both replete with commendations of me, both filled with expressions of affection—these, Maximus, I beg you will allow, for a moment, to be read, in order that his brother, my accuser, may know how different in every respect is the career which he is running from that of his brother, a man of most blessed memory. [*The letters of Pontianus are read.*]

Did you hear the epithets which your brother, Pontianus, bestowed on me; how, both repeatedly on other occasions, as also at his latest moments, he called me his parent, his master, his instructor? I could also produce letters of yours to the like effect, if I thought it worth while to waste a moment upon them. I would prefer, rather, that your brother's last will, unfinished as it is, should be produced, in which he makes most affectionate and most honorable mention of me. That will, however, Rufinus would not allow to be seen, nor even to be completed, through his vexation at losing the property; a property which he had valued at the large price of the nights of a few months during which he was the father-in-law of Pontianus. Besides this, he had consulted some Chaldæan astrologers or others, in what way he might dispose of his daughter with profit to himself. They, as I hear, and I only wish that they had not in this given a true answer, replied that her first husband would die in the course of a few months. But the rest of their answer, as to his property, they framed, as is generally the case, just in conformity with the wishes of the person who consulted them. However, the Gods so willed it, that just like some blind beast, he opened wide his jaws, but got nothing at all. For Pontianus, on detecting her guilt, not only did not make the daughter of Rufinus his heir, but did not so much as leave her a decent legacy; but ordered that, as a mark of disgrace, linen cloth,* of about two hundred denars in value, should be presented to her, in order that it might be understood that he had disinherited her, prompted by a feeling of indignation, and had not omitted her through forgetfulness.

For in this will, as well as in a former one which was read, he made his mother and his brother his heirs; the latter of whom, though still a mere boy, as you see, Rufinus is plying with this same daughter of his, as his engine of attack, throwing her in his way, and thrusting upon this wretched youth a woman greatly his senior in age, and but recently the wife of his own brother. As for him, being captivated and enthralled by the allurements of the harlot of a daughter and the wiles of the pimp of a father, the moment that his brother breathed his last, he left his mother, and betook himself to his uncle, in order that, being at a distance from us, his designs might be the better put into execution. For Rufinus is a favourite with Æmilianus, who wishes him success in his plans. Good! it is well that you have reminded me :† his own expectations, too, this worthy uncle, cherishes and promotes, by adopting this course, as he well knows that he is more likely‡ to be the legal heir of the boy if he dies intestate, than his appointed heir under a will. By Hercules! I should have been sorry if that notion had originated with me. It is not in accordance with my moderation openly to give vent to what are the secret suspicions of all: it was wrong on your part to suggest it.

At all events, Æmilianus, if you would have the truth, many persons are surprised at this affection of yours for this boy, which has so suddenly sprung up since the death of his brother Pontianus; whereas, before that, you were so much a stranger to him, that, many a time when you met him, you

* *Linen cloth.*]—Isidorus, in his ' Origines,' informs us that linen garments were in especial worn by courtezans, and that matrons taken in adultery were clad in garments of this material. This custom may perhaps be here covertly alluded to.

† *Reminded me.*]—Some of his friends in court have suggested this to him as the possible design of Æmilianus.

‡ *He is more likely.*]—And therefore pampers the boy with indulgences, that he may have neither leisure nor inclination to think of making a will.

did not know by face the son of your own brother. Now, however, you show yourself so considerate of him, so spoil him by indulgence, are so careful not to thwart him in anything, as, by this course, to produce a confirmation of such suspicions. You received him from us a stripling; you instantly invested him with the privileges of puberty.   As long as he was under our management, he was in the habit of attending masters; now, taking a wide flight from them, he makes for the brothel; his friends of steady demeanour he shuns, while, at his tender age, this young boy passes his life with young men of the most abandoned character, amid courtesans and cups.   It is he who is the ruler in your house, it is he who is the head of your family, it is he who is the master of your banquets.   At the gladiatorial exhibitions, too, he is a constant attendant, and, like a lad of gentility, he is instructed by his fencing-master in the names of the gladiators, their combats, and their wounds.

He never speaks but in the Punic tongue, or any little smattering of Greek he may still retain, after learning it from his mother.   But in Latin he has neither the will nor the inclination to speak.   You heard, Maximus, a short time ago, my step-son, the brother of Pontianus, a young man who was distinguished for his eloquence—shame and disgrace to him!— stammering out with the greatest difficulty a few syllables, at the time when you enquired of him whether his mother had presented to them the property which I asserted she had at my prompting so presented.   I therefore call you to witness, Claudius Maximus, and you who are sitting here in judgment, and you also who aid me with your presence on this my trial, that these corruptions, and scandals in his life, ought to be attributed to his uncle here, and to this candidate for the honor of being his father-in-law; and I protest that I shall, from this time forward, congratulate myself that such a step-son as this has shaken off from his neck the yoke of my guardianship, and shall no more think of entreating his mother in his behalf.

For,—I had all but forgotten to mention it—very recently, and since the death of her son Pontianus, Pudentilla, being then in bad health, was making her will, on which I had a struggle with her of considerable duration in order to prevent her from disinheriting him, in return for insults so glaring, for injuries

so numerous. With earnest entreaties I begged her to strike
out [of the will] a most severe character of him, the whole of
which, I solemnly declare, she had already written. In fine,
I threatened to separate from her, if I did not prevail in my
request. I entreated her to grant me this favour, to conquer
her wicked son by kindness, and so release me from all chance
of incurring hatred. Nor did I cease until she had complied
with my request

I am vexed that I have thus removed this ground of anxiety
from Æmilianus, that I have pointed out to him a path so
entirely unexpected. Do look, I beg of you, Maximus, how,
on hearing this, he has suddenly become quite bewildered, how
he has riveted his eyes upon the ground. For he had fancied,
and not without reason, that the fact was far otherwise. He
knew that this lady was offended at the insults offered by her
son, and was strongly influenced by my attentions to her. As
regarded me, too, he had good grounds for apprehension. For
any person, even though he had been as much a despiser of
wealth as I am, might still not have declined to take his re-
venge on a step-son who had shown himself so undutiful. It was
this anxiety, above all, that urged them to bring this accusa-
tion against me. Arguing from a knowledge of their own
avarice, they have wrongly conjectured that the whole of her
property has been left to me. As regards the past time, I will
release you from that fear ; for neither the opportunity of gain-
ing property, nor yet revenge, were able to shake my mind in
the position which it had taken. I, the step-father, struggled
with his offended mother in behalf of a wicked step-son, just
as though I had been a father striving with a step-mother
in favour of his best of sons ; nor was I content unless I
checked, far more than I ought to have done, the abundant
generosity of an affectionate wife, which was ready to be shown
in my own favour.

Hand me the will which has been made by the mother
since her son has been at enmity with her, and of which
I, whom these people call a robber, prefaced each word with
my entreaties. Order, Maximus, that document to be opened ;
you will find her son named as her heir, while to myself, as a
mark of regard, there is left some trifling legacy or other ; in
order that, if anything should happen to her, I, the husband,
might not find my name altogether omitted in the will of my

own wife. Take that will, written by your mother, a will which is truly forgetful of the ties of duty. For why? In it she has disinherited a most attentive husband, while she has named as her heir a most vindictive son, or rather, I may say, not her son, but the hopes of Æmilianus, and the match designed by Rufinus, as well as that besotted crew, your parasites.

Take it, I say, best of sons, and lay aside for a moment the amatory epistles of your mother, and read her will in preference. If she has written anything when labouring under a kind of insanity, as it were, here you will find it, ay, and from the very beginning—"Let Sicinius Pudens, my son, be my heir." He who reads that, I admit, will take her to be insane. "Is this son [he will say] appointed your heir, who, on the occasion of the very funeral of his brother, having called together a band of most abandoned youths, attempted to exclude you from the house which you yourself had presented to him? A youth who was vexed and annoyed that you had been left by his brother joint-heir with himself? Who, amid your sorrow and mourning, instantly abandoned you, and fled from your bosom to Rufinus and Æmilianus? Who afterwards, before your very face, gave utterance to numerous insults, and, with the assistance of his uncle, was guilty of perpetrating others? Who bandied your name about before tribunals? Who attempted publicly to cast a stain upon your fair name, by producing your own letters against you? Who brought a capital charge against the husband of whom you had made choice, a husband whom, as he himself objected against you, you loved to distraction?" Open, worthy youth, open the will, I beg; by so doing you will the more easily prove your mother's insanity. Why do you decline? Why refuse?—that, too, after you have had all anxiety removed as to the inheritance of your mother's property. I will, however, Maximus, place this document here, in this spot, before your feet, and I protest that, from henceforth, I shall take much less interest in what it is Pudentilla inserts in her will. Let him, from this time forward, entreat his mother, as he pleases; to me he has left no grounds for supplicating any more in his behalf. Henceforth let him, as he is his own master, and addresses most virulent letters to his mother, take upon himself to assuage her wrath. He who could undertake a prosecution, will be able to plead his own cause.

It is quite enough for me, if I have not only most abundantly disproved the crimes laid to my charge, but have even utterly uprooted the grounds for bringing me to trial—I mean the envy on account of the property supposed to have been sought by me. That I may omit no one of all these things, I will prove, before I come to a conclusion, that this, too, has been falsely laid to my charge. You have asserted that with a large sum of money belonging to this lady, I have made purchase in my own name of a very fine estate. I say, in answer, that it was a small property, worth but sixty thousand pieces of money; and that I was not the purchaser, but Pudentilla, who bought the estate in her own name; that the name of Pudentilla is in the purchase-deed, and that it is in the name of Pudentilla that the taxes are paid for this farm. The public quæstor is here present, to whom they have been paid, Corvinus Celer, a man of the highest character. There is also here the guardian* and adviser of the lady, a man of the greatest respectability and of the most unblemished name, one who deserves to be mentioned by me with all honor and respect, Cassius Longinus, I mean. Ask him, Maximus, as in making this purchase he acted as her adviser, at what a trifling price it was that a lady so wealthy purchased this farm of hers. [*Cassius Longinus and Corvinus Celer being questioned, gave their evidence.*] Is it not as I said? Does my name anywhere appear in this purchase? Is the price paid for this little property any ground for complaint? Or, at all events, has it been transferred to me?

What is there still remaining, Æmilianus, that I have not, in your judgment, refuted? What reward of my magical practices have you discovered? Why should I work upon the feelings of Pudentilla by incantations? To gain what advantages from her? Was it that she might make a trifling settlement upon me in preference to a large one? O charms of surpassing excellence! Or was it that she might enter into a new engagement, and settle her fortune in reversion upon her sons, rather than leave it to me? What else is there that can possibly be added to such a magic as this? Is it the fact that, at my entreaty, she presented the greater portion of her property to her sons, when, before she was married

---

* *The guardian*]—His duties were somewhat similar to those of the next friend,' as he is now called, in our courts of law.

to me, she had given them nothing at all—this, too, while she bestowed nothing whatever upon myself? Oh atrocious crime, shall I say, or rather, oh kindness ill repaid? Or is it rather the fact that, in the will which she made when angered against her son, she left that very son with whom she was offended her heir, rather than myself, to whom she was so much attached? This I certainly did, after employing many spells,* with the greatest difficulty obtain.

Suppose, now, that this cause is being tried, not before Claudius Maximus, a man of equity and scrupulous justice, but substitute some other judge, a dishonest and cruel man, one who is an encourager of accusations, and anxious to condemn; give him some point upon which to fasten, supply him with ever so slight a ground, wearing the semblance of probability, on which he may be enabled to pronounce in your favour. At least, invent, devise something to say by way of answer, when he invites you so to do. And, as it is a matter of necessity that some cause or other should precede every effect, state, you who say that Apuleius influenced the mind of Pudentilla by magic spells, what it was he wanted of her, and why he did so. Was it her beauty he was anxious to gain? You say no. At all events, was it her riches that he coveted? The marriage-contract, the deed of gift, the will, say "no" to that, in all of which he is shown not only not to have grasped at with greediness, but even to have harshly repulsed, the liberality of his wife.

What other ground then is there? Why are you mute? Why do you not speak? Where is that fierce commencement of your charge, drawn up in the name of my step-son? "Him, my lord Maximus, I have determined to accuse before you."— Why did you not add, then, "to accuse my instructor, to accuse my step-father, to accuse my mediator?" But what comes next?—"of numerous offences, and those most evident." Of these so "numerous," produce but a single one; of these offences "most evident," produce but one which is even so much as dubious, one which can even sustain a moment's question.

To each of your innumerable charges I answer in a couple

* *Many spells*]— There is a pun here in the original upon the word 'cantamina,' or 'carmina,' which means, 'spells,' or charms, as also 're-peated entreaties.'

of words.* "You clean your teeth"—Pardon my cleanliness. "You look in a mirror"—A philosopher ought. "You compose verses"—'Tis not unlawful to do so. "You examine fishes"—Aristotle teaches me. "You make Gods of wood"—Plato advises it. "You marry a wife"—The laws enjoin it. "She is older than you"—No uncommon thing. "You have sought to advantage yourself"—Take up the deed of settlement, recollect the gifts you have received, read over her will.

If I have abundantly rebutted all these charges; if I have refuted all these calumnies; if, amid not only all the accusations, but even all the aspersions uttered against me by these persons, I have kept philosophy aloof from censure; if I have in no way blemished the honour of philosophy, which is dearer to me than my own well-being, nay, rather, if I have kept it most carefully shielded on every side; if, in each of these respects, what I say is found to be the truth, then I may more securely afford to respect your good opinion than to dread your power; seeing, I deem it less grievous and less to be dreaded by me, to be condemned by a proconsul, than to incur the censure of a man so good and so virtuous as yourself.

* *In a couple of words.*]—It must be remembered, that in the English language his answers cannot be expressed in two words only.

END OF THE DEFENCE OF APULEIUS.

APULEIUS

ON THE

GOD* OF SOCRATES.

PLATO has made a triple division of all nature, and especially of that part of it which comprises animated beings; and he

* *God.*]—In many places, Plato calls the participants of the divinities, Gods. Thus, in the Laws a divine soul is called 'a God;' and in the Phædrus, it is said, 'That all the horses and charioteers of the Gods are good, and consist of things that are good.' And when he says this, he is speaking of divine souls. After this, also, in the same dialogue, he still more clearly says, 'And this is the life of the Gods.' What, however, is still more remarkable is this, that he denominates those beings Gods, who are always united to the Gods, and who, together with them, give completion to one series. For in the Phædrus, Timæus, and other dialogues, he extends the appellation of the Gods as far as to dæmons, though the latter are essentially posterior to, and subsist about the Gods. But what is still more paradoxical, he does not refuse to call certain men Gods : for in the 'Sophista,' he thus denominates the Elean guest or stranger.

According to Plato therefore, one thing is a God simply, another on account of union, another through participation, another through contact, and another through similitude. For of super-essential natures, each is primarily a God : of intellectual natures, each is a God according to union; and of divine souls, each is a God according to participation. But divine dæmons are Gods, according to contact with the Gods; and the souls of men are allotted this appellation through similitude.

As the dæmon of Socrates, therefore, was doubtless one of the highest order, as may be inferred from the intellectual superiority of Socrates to most other men, Apuleius is justified in calling this dæmon a God. And that the dæmon of Socrates indeed was divine, is evident from the testimony of Socrates himself in the First Alcibiades : for in the course of that dialogue he clearly says, 'I have long been of opinion that *the God* did not as yet direct me to hold any conversation with you.' And in the Apology, he most unequivocally evinces that this dæmon is allotted a divine transcendency, considered as ranking in the order of dæmons.

Ignorance of this distinction has been the source of infinite confusion and absurd hypotheses, to the modern writers on the mythology and theology of the Greeks.—*Taylor.*

is of opinion, that there are Gods of the highest, the middle, and the lowest station. Understand, however, that this division is based not only upon local separation, but also upon comparative dignity of nature, which is itself distinguished not in one or two, but in many modes. It was the clearer way, however, to begin with the distinction of locality;* for this has assigned the heavens to the immortal Gods, conformably to what their majesty demands. And of these celestial Gods, some we form a notion of by sight, while others we endeavour to comprehend by the intellect.

> ——You, refulgent ministers of light,
> Who through the heavens conduct the gliding year.†

We do not, however, perceive by the eyes, those principal Gods only, the Sun the maker of the day, the Moon the rival of the Sun, and the glory of night; whether she is horned or divided,‡ whether gibbous or full; exhibiting a varying brightness in her light; being more largely illuminated the farther she departs from the Sun; and, by an equal increase both of her path and her light, defining the month by means of her increments, and afterwards by means of her decrements in like degree: whether it is, as the Chaldeans think, that she possesses a proper or§ permanent light of her own, and is on one side gifted with light, but destitute of brightness on the other, and so changes her appearance by manifold revolutions of her various coloured face; or whether it is that being wholly void of brightness of her own, and standing in need of foreign light, with an opaque body, or with a body polished like a

* *Distinction of locality.*]—It is here requisite to observe, that divine natures are not in bodies, but externally rule over them. Hence they impart from themselves to bodies every good they are able to receive, but they themselves receive nothing from bodies; so that neither will they derive from them certain peculiarities. By no means, therefore, must it be admitted (as Iamblichus well observes,) that the cause of the distinction of the divine genera is an arrangement with reference to bodies; as of Gods to ethereal bodies, of dæmons to aërial bodies, and of souls to such as are terrene.— *Taylor.*

† *The gliding year.*]—These lines are taken from Book I. of the Georgics of Virgil.

‡ *Divided.*]—In the original, *dividua;* and the moon is *dividua* when she is a quarter old.

§ *Or.*]—'Ceu' is no doubt the correct reading here, meaning the 'or' explicative, and not the 'or' alternative.

mirror, she receives either obliquely or direct the rays of the Sun, and, to use the words of Lucretius, Book IV.—

" ——Throws from her orb a spurious light."

Whichever of these opinions is true, (for that I shall afterwards consider,) there is not any Greek, or any barbarian, who will not easily conclude that the Sun and Moon are Gods; and not these only, as I have observed, but also the five stars, which are commonly styled " erratic," *or "planets,"* by the unlearned, though, in their undeviating, certain, and established course, they perform, by their divine changes, movements most orderly and eternal; movements which are indeed various in appearance, but which are made with a celerity that is always equable, and represent with wonderful alternation, at one time progressions, and at another retrogressions, according to the position, ellipticity, and inclination of their orbits, with which he is well acquainted who understands the risings and settings of the stars.

You who are of the same opinion with Plato, must also rank in the same number of visible Gods those other stars,

The rainy Hyades, Arcturus, both the Bears : *

and likewise the other radiant Gods, by whom we perceive, in a serene sky, the celestial choir bedecked and crowned, when the nights are painted with a severe grace and a stern beauty; beholding, as Ennius says, in this most "perfect shield of the universe," engravings wrought with surprising brilliancy.

There is another species of Gods, which nature has denied to our sight; and still we may contemplate them with admiration through intellect, acutely surveying them with the eye of the mind. In the number of these are those twelve Gods† who are included by Ennius, with a metrical arrangement of their names, in two verses:

Juno, Vesta, Minerva, Ceres, Diana, Venus, Mars,
Mercurius, Jovi,‡ Neptunus, Vulcanus, Apollo;

and others of the like kind, whose names, indeed, have been long known to our ears, but whose powers are conjectured by

* This verse is taken from Book III. of the Æneid.
† *Twelve Gods.*]—These Gods form, in the Platonic theology, the super-celestial, or 'liberated' order, being immediately proximate to the mundane order of Gods.
‡ *Jovi.*]—The old nominative used instead of Jupiter.

our minds, our attention being called to them through the various benefits which they impart to us in the affairs of life in those things over which they severally preside. The crowd, however, of the ignorant, who are rejected by Philosophy as uninitiated, whose notions of holiness are misplaced, who are deprived of genuine reason, who are destitute of religion, and incapable of grasping the truth, dishonour the Gods, either by a worship most over acted, or a most insolent disdain of them ; one part being always in alarm through superstition, while the other is always swelling with contempt. Very many there are who venerate all these Gods, established in the lofty heights of the firmament, and far removed from human contagion : but not in such manner as they ought : all fear them, but through ignorance ; a few deny their existence, but in a spirit of impiety. Plato thought these Gods to be incorporeal* and animated natures without an end or beginning, but eternal both with reference to time past and time to come ; spontaneously separated from the contact of the body by the nature peculiar to themselves ; through perfection of intellect possessing supreme beatitude ; good, not through participation in any extraneous good, but of themselves ; and able to procure for themselves every thing requisite, with a facility which is prompt, simple, unrestrained, and absolute.

But of the parent of these, who is the lord and author of all things, and who is free from all obligations to act or to suffer, not being bound by any necessity to the performance of any duties, why should I now begin to speak ? For Plato, who was endowed with a heavenly eloquence, discoursing in language worthy of the immortal Gods, frequently proclaims that on account of the incredible and ineffable transcendency of his majesty, he cannot possibly be even in the slightest degree comprehended, under any definition, through the poverty of human language ; and that the intellectual apprehension of this God can hardly flash upon wise men, when they have separated them-

---

* *To be incorporeal.*]—The Delphin editor of this treatise, who appears to have been perfectly ignorant of the philosophy of Plato, says, that Plato is of an opinion contrary to what is here asserted by Apuleius, in the Epinomis and in the Timæus, because, in the former dialogue, he gives to the celestial Gods a *most beautiful*, and in the latter an *igneous* body. But if rational souls are incorporeal, according to Plato, though connected with bodies, much more this must be the case with the Gods.

selves from body, as much as possible, through the vigour of the intellect; and that sometimes this knowledge does blaze forth with a most instantaneous flash, like a dazzling light amid the most profound darkness.*   I will therefore omit the discussion of this theme, for which all words adequate to the amplitude of the subject are not only wanting to me, but could not even be found by my master Plato.   Hence I shall at once sound a retreat, as to things which very far surpass my humble powers, and at length bring down my discourse from heaven to earth, in which we men are the principal animated things, though most of us, through the neglect of training, are so depraved, and are so imbued with all errors and the most atrocious crimes, and have become so utterly ferocious, through having nearly quite abandoned the mildness of our nature, that it may seem there is not an animal on the earth more vile than man.   But at present our object is not to discuss feelings, but to treat of the natural distribution of things.

Men, therefore, dwell on the earth, possessing the gift of speech, having immortal souls, but mortal members, with frivolous and anxious minds, with bodies brutish and infirm, of dissimilar manners, but similar errors, of presumptuous audacity, long-lived hope, labouring in vain, with variable fortunes, severally mortal, but taken altogether in their whole species, eternal, quitting the scene in regular succession, and leaving offspring to supply their place, fleeting in their time, tardy at gaining wisdom, speedy in meeting with death, and dissatisfied in life.   You have, then, in the meantime, two kinds of animated beings, Gods entirely differing from men, in the sublimity of their abode, in the eternity of their existence, in the perfection of their nature, and having no proximate communication with them;† since those that are supreme are

---

* *Profound darkness.*]—This is a very remarkable passage, but is not to be found in any of the writings of Plato that are now extant.   Something similar to this is said by Plato, in his seventh epistle, respecting the intuition of *idea*, or *intellectual form;* viz. " that from long converse with the thing itself, accompanied by a life in conformity with it, on a sudden, a light, as if from a leaping fire, will be enkindled in the soul, and will there itself nourish itself."

† *Proximate communication with them.*]—A divine nature is *immediately* present with all things, but all things are not immediately present with it; because aptitude in the participant is here requisite to a union with that which is participable

separated from the lowest habitations by such a vast interval of distance; and life is there eternal and never-failing, but here decaying and interrupted, and the natures are there sublimated to beatitude, while those below are depressed to wretchedness. What then? Has rature connected itself by no bond, but allowed itself to be separated into the divine and human parts, and to be thus split and crippled, as it were? For, as the same Plato remarks, "No God mingles with men." But this is the principal mark of their sublime nature, that they are not contaminated by any contact with us.* One part of them only is to be seen by us with our blunted vision; as the stars, about whose magnitude and colour men are still in doubt, while the rest are only known to our understandings, and that by no prompt perception. This, however, ought by no means to be wondered at with reference to the immortal Gods, since even among men, who are raised to opulence by the favour of Fortune, and are elevated to the tottering throne and the unsteady tribunal of a kingdom, access is rare, all beholders being kept at a distance, and they enjoy their dignity in retirement; familiarity breeds contempt,† but privacy gains admiration.

"What, then, shall I do," some person may object, "after this very celestial, but almost inhuman decision of yours? if, so it is, that men are entirely removed from the immortal Gods, and are so exiled in these Tartarean realms of earth that all communication whatever with the heavenly Gods is denied them, and not one of the celestials occasionally visits them, as a shepherd visits his flocks of sheep, a groom his horses, or a herdsman his lowing cattle, in order that he may curb the more vicious, heal the diseased, and assist those which are in want? No God, you say, interferes in human affairs. To whom, then, shall I address my prayers? To whom shall I make my vows? To whom shall I immolate victims? Whom shall I invoke throughout my whole life, as the helper of the unfortunate, the favourer of the good, and the adversary of the wicked? And whom, in fine, (a thing for which necessity most frequently

---

* *Contact with us.*]—*i.e.* By any habitude or alliance to our nature.

† *Breeds contempt.*]—'Parit conversatio contemptum,' one of the most hacknied phrases now in existence.

occurs,) shall I adduce as a witness to my oath? Am I to say, like Virgil's Ascanius,*

> "Now by this head I swear, by which before
> My father used to swear?"

Why, no doubt, Iulus, your father might use this oath among Trojans, who were allied to him by birth, and also perhaps among Greeks, who were known to him in battle; but among the Rutuli, who were but recently known by you, if no one believed in this head, what God would you have to be surety for you? Would you have your right hand and your dart, like the ferocious Mezentius? For these only, by which he defended himself, did he adjure:

> "For me my right hand and the missile dart,
> Which now well-poised I hurl, are each a God."†

Away, I beseech you, with such sanguinary Gods; a right hand weary with slaughter, and a dart rusted with gore. Neither of these is a fit object for you to adjure, nor that you should swear by them, for this is an honor that is peculiar to the highest of the Gods. For a solemn oath, as Ennius says, is also called *Jovisjurandum.* What, then, is your opinion? Am I to swear by Jupiter, in the shape of a stone, after the most ancient custom of the Romans? Why, if the opinion of Plato is true, that God never mingles with men, a stone will hear me more easily than Jupiter."

Such is not the fact: for Plato shall answer for his opinion in my words. "I do not affirm," says he, "that the Gods are so far separated and alienated from us, that not even our prayers can reach them; for I have not removed them from attention to the affairs of mankind, but only from contact with them."

Besides, there are certain divine powers of a middle nature, situate in this interval of the air, between the highest ether and the earth below, through whom our aspirations and our deserts are conveyed to the Gods. These the Greeks call by name "dæmons," and, being placed as messengers between the inhabitants of earth and those of heaven, they carry from the one to the other, prayers and bounties, supplications and assistance, being a kind of interpreters and message carriers for

* *Ascanius.*]—See Book XI. of the Æneid.
† See Book X. of the Æneid.

both. Through these same demons, as Plato says in his Symposium, all revelations, the various miracles of magicians, and all kinds of presages, are carried on. For specially appointed individuals of this number, administer everything according to the province assigned to each; either by framing dreams, or causing ominous fissures in entrails, or governing the flights of some birds, or instructing others in song, or inspiring prophets, or by launching thunders, or causing the lightning to flash in the clouds, or other things to take place by means of which we obtain a knowledge of future events. And we have reason to believe that all these particulars are by the will, the power, and the authority of the celestial Gods, but through the obedience, aid, and services of demons; for it was through the employment, the services, and the care of these, that dreams forewarned Hannibal of the loss of one of his eyes; that inspection of the entrails foretold to Flaminius a perilous carnage; and that auguries assured to Attius Navius the miracle of the whetstone. Just in the same manner, tokens of future empire are imparted beforehand to certain persons; as, for instance, an eagle hovered over the cap on the head of Tarquinius Priscus, and a flame shone from the head of Servius Tullius. And lastly, to these are owing all the presages of diviners, the expiatory sacrifices of the Etrurians, the sacrificial enclosure of places struck by lightning, and the verses of the Sibyls; all which, as I have said, are effected by certain influences that carry on the communication between men and Gods.

Nor, indeed, would it be conformable to the majesty of the celestial Gods, that any one of them should either frame a dream for Hannibal, or withdraw the victim from Flaminius, or direct the flight of the bird for Attius Navius, or form in verse the predictions of the Sibyl, or be willing to snatch the hat from the head of Tarquin, and restore it, or place a splendid flame upon the head of Servius, but so as not to burn him. It is not becoming that the Gods of heaven should condescend to things of this nature. This is the province of the intermediate Gods, who dwell in the regions of the air, which are adjacent to the earth, and on the confines of the heavens, just as in each part of the world there are animals peculiarly adapted to it, those which fly living in the air, and those which walk, on the earth. For since there are four elements universally known, nature being as it were divided into four grand portions, and there are animals peculiar to earth, water, and flame; (for Aristotle informs us that certain animals peculiar thereto, and furnished with wings, fly about in burning furnaces, and pass the whole period of their existence in fire,* come to life therein, and with it die), and besides this, since, as we have already observed, so many stars are beheld floating above in æther, that is to say, in the very brightest heat of fire,†—*since this is the case*, why should nature suffer this fourth element, the air, which is so widely extended, to be the only one void of every thing, and destitute of its own inhabitants? Why should not animated beings be generated in this air in the same manner as animals that exist in flame are generated in fire, animals that float, in water, and those of an earthly nature, on earth? For you have every reason to pronounce his opinion false who assigns the birds to the air; for not one of them raises itself above the summit of Mount Olympus, which, though it is said to be the highest of all mountains, yet if you measure its height in a straight line, the distance to its summit is not equal, according to the opinions of geometricians, to ten stadia; whereas the immense mass of air extends as far as the nearest portion of the cycle of the moon, beyond which æther takes its rise in an upward direction. What, then, are we to say of such a vast body of air, which ranges in extent from the nearest part of the revolutions of the moon as far as the highest summit of Mount Olympus? Will that, pray, be destitute of its own appropriate animated beings, and will this part of nature be without life, and impotent? Moreover, if you attentively consider the matter, birds themselves may, with greater propriety, be said to be terrestrial than aërial animals; for their whole living is always on the earth; there they procure food, and there they rest; and they only make a passage through that part of the air in flying which lies nearest to the earth. But, when they are wearied by the rowing motion of their wings, the earth is to them as a harbour. If, therefore, reason evidently requires that its appropriate animals must also be admitted to exist in

* *In fire.*]—This is asserted by Aristotle, in Book V. chap. xix. of his History of Animals.

† *Heat of fire.*]—It must be observed, however, that the fire of which æther consists, and also the stars, for the most part, are, according to Plato, vivific and unburning.

the air, it remains for us to consider what they are, and what is their nature.

They are then by no means animals of an earthly nature, for such have a downward tendency, through their gravity. But neither are they of a fiery nature, lest they should be carried aloft by their heat. A certain middle nature, therefore, must be conceived by us, in conformity to the middle position of their locality, that so the nature of the inhabitants may be conformable to the nature of the region. Well, then, let us form in our mind and generate in our ideas bodies so constituted as neither to be so sluggish as terrestrial, nor so light as ethereal, but in a certain measure distinct from both, or else composed of a mixture of both, either removed from, or modified by, a participation of both. They will, however, be more easlly conceived, if admitted to be a mixture of both, than if they assumed to be mingled with neither. The bodies of these demons, therefore, must have some little weight, in order that they may not be carried aloft; and they must also have some lightness, in order that they may not be precipitated to the realms below. However, that I may not appear to you to be devising things that are incredible, after the manner of the poets, I will just give you an example of this equipoised middle nature. We see the clouds unite in a way not much different from this tenuity of body; but if these were equally light as those bodies which are entirely devoid of weight, they would never cap the heights of a lofty mountain with, as it were, certain wreathed chains, depressed beneath its ridges, as we frequently perceive they do. On the other hand, if they were naturally so dense and so ponderous that no union with a more active levity could elevate them, they would certainly strike against the earth, of their own tendency, just like a mass of lead and stone. As it is, however, being pendulous and moveable, they are guided in this direction and in that by the winds amid the sea of air, in the same manner as ships, shifting sometimes in proximity and remoteness; for, if they are teeming with the moisture of water, they are depressed downward, as though for the purpose of bringing forth. And on this account it is that clouds that are more moist descend lower, in dusky masses, and with a slower motion, while those that are serene ascend higher, and are impelled like fleeces of wool, in white masses, and with a more rapid flight. Have

you not heard how Lucretius most eloquently expresses himself
concerning thunder in his Sixth Book?

> " The azure heavens with dreadful thunders shake.
> Because th' ethereal clouds, ascending high,
> Dash on each other, driven by adverse winds."

But if the clouds fly aloft, all of which originate from the
earth, and again flow downward to it, pray what should you
conclude as to the bodies of demons, which are so much more
attenuated in their composition? For they are not heaped
up from feculent vapours and dense mists, as is the nature of
clouds, but they are formed of the most pure liquid and serene
element of air, and on this account they are not visible on
every occasion to the human eye, but only when by divine
command they allow themselves to be seen. For in them no
earthly density occupies the place of light, so as to encounter
our perception, and necessarily to arrest our visual ray by that
solidity; but the lineaments of the bodies which they have
are rare, shining, and attenuated, to such a degree, that
they allow all the rays of our vision to pass through them
in consequence of their rarity, refract them by their bright-
ness, and baffle them by their subtlety. Hence that de-
scription of Minerva, in Homer, presenting herself in the
midst of the assembly of the Greeks, for the purpose of check-
ing the wrath of Achilles. If you will wait a moment I will
give you the Greek line in Latin, and here it is on the spur of
the moment. Minerva, then, as I said, by the command of
Juno came, in order to moderate the wrath of Achilles,

> " Seen by him only, by the rest unseen."*

Hence, also, Virgil's Juturna, when in the midst of many thou-
sands of men, for the purpose of aiding her brother,

> " With soldiers mingled, though by none perceived," †

fully accomplishing that which the captain in Plautus boasted
of having effected by his shield,

> " Which dazzled by its light the vision of his foes."

And not to discuss prolixly the rest of the instances, the poets,
from this multitude of demons, are accustomed, in a way by

---

* *Unseen.*]—Soli perspicua est, aliorum nemo tuetur. Iliad. lib. i. v. 198.
† Æneid, lib. xii.

no means remote from the truth, to feign the Gods to be haters and lovers of certain men, and to give prosperity and promotion to some, and to oppose and afflict others. Hence, they are influenced by pity, moved by indignation, racked with vexation, elated with joy, and are subject to all the affections of the human mind; and are agitated by all the fluctuations of human thought, with similar commotions of the spirit and agitations of the feelings.* All which storms and tempests are far alien from the tranquil state of the celestial Gods. For all the celestials always enjoy the same state of mind, with an eternal equanimity, which in them is never driven from its own fixed state either in the direction of pleasure or of pain; nor is it moved by any thing from its own everlasting rule, towards any sudden line of conduct; neither by any external force, because there is nothing more powerful than deity; nor of their own impulse, because nothing is more perfect than deity.

And furthermore, how can he appear to have been perfect, who moves from a former condition of being to another condition which is better? And this the more especially, as no one spontaneously embraces any thing new, unless he is tired of what he had before; for a new mode of proceeding cannot be adopted, without disapproving the preceding modes. Hence, it follows, that a God ought not to be employed in any temporal functions either of beneficence or love; and, therefore, is neither to be influenced by indignation nor by pity, nor to be disquieted by any anxiety, nor elated by any hilarity; but he is free from all the passions of the mind, so as never either to grieve or to rejoice, nor on sudden impulse to will or unwill.†

But all these, and other qualities of the like kind, properly

* *Agitations of the feelings.*]—According to the ancient theology, the lowest order of those powers that are the perpetual attendants of the Gods, preserve the characteristics of their leaders, though in a partia manner, and are called by their names. Hence, the passions of the sub-jects of their government are, in fables, proximately referred to these.

† *Will or unwill.*]—"Divinity," says Sallust (in chap. xiv. of his treatise on the Gods and the World), "neither rejoices; for that which rejoices is also influenced by sorrow; nor is angry; for anger is passion: nor is appeased by gifts; for then he would be influenced by delight. Nor s it lawful that a divine nature should be well or ill affected from human

accord with the middle nature of demons.* For they are in-
termediate between us and the Gods, both in the place of their
habitation, and in their nature ; having immortality in common
with the Gods of heaven, and passions in common with sub-
ordinate beings. For they are capable, just as we are, of being
affected by all that soothes as well as all that moves the mind; so
as to be stimulated by anger, influenced by pity, allured by gifts,
appeased by prayers, exasperated by affronts, soothed by ho-
nours, and swayed by all other circumstances, just in the same
way that we are. For, to embrace the nature of them in a de-
finition, demons are as to genus animated beings, as to mind
rational, as to feelings passive, as to body aërial, as to duration
eternal. Of these five characteristics which I have mentioned,
the three first are the same as those which we possess, the
fourth is peculiar to themselves, and the last they possess in
common with the immortal Gods, from whom they differ in
being subject to passion. Hence, according to my idea, I have
not absurdly called demons passive, because they are subject to
the same perturbations as we are : and on this account it is
that we may place some confidence in the different observances
of religions, and the various propitiatory offerings made in sacred
rites. There are likewise some among this number of Gods who
rejoice in victims, or ceremonies, or observances, nocturnal or
diurnal, public or performed in secret, replete with the greatest
joy or marked with extreme sadness. Thus, the Egyptian deities
are almost all of them delighted with lamentations, the Grecian in
general with dances, and those of the Barbarians with the sound
produced by cymbals, tambourines, and pipes. So, in like
manner, other points relating to sacred rites present consider-
able diversities, according to different regions ; as, for instance,
the crowds that swell the sacred processions, the mysteries,
the duties performed by the priests, and the observances per-

concerns : for the divinities are perpetually good and profitable, but are
never noxious, and ever subsist in the same uniform mode of being. But
we, when we are virtuous, are conjoined with the Gods through similitude :
but when vicious, we are separated from them through dissimilitude.
And while we live according to virtue, we partake of the Gods, but when
we become evil, we cause them to become our enemies ; not that they are
angry, but because guile prevents us from receiving the illuminations of
the Gods, and subjects us to the power of avenging demons."
    * Of demons.]—This, however, applies only to the lowest order of
demons.

formed by the devotees: and then, again, the images of the Gods, and their insignia, the rites performed in, and the situations of, their temples, and the variety of blood and colour in their victims. All these particulars are regulated and set forth in the accustomed form peculiar to the usage of each place, so much so that we have frequently ascertained by means of dreams, oracles and prophecies especially, that the Divinities have been indignant, if anything in their sacred rites has been neglected through slothfulness or contumacy; of which circumstances I have an abundance of examples. They are, however, so universally mentioned, and so generally known, that no one could attempt to recount them, without omitting a great number more than he mentioned. On this account, I shall desist for the present from expending words upon these particulars, which if they have not obtained assured credit with all men, still, at least, are universally within the knowledge of all. It will be more advisable, therefore, to discuss this point in the Latin tongue, that there are kinds of demons enumerated by the philosophers, in order that you may more clearly and more fully come to an understanding on the presage of Socrates, and his familiar demon.

Now, according to a certain signification, the human soul, even when it is still situate in the body, is called a demon.

> " O say, Euryalus, do Gods inspire
> In minds this ardour, or does fierce desire
> Rule as a God in its possessor's breast ?"*

If, then, this is the case, a longing of the soul that is of gooo tendency is a good demon. Hence it is that some think, as we have already observed, that the blessed are called ἐυδαίμονες, _eudæmones_, the _demon_ of whom is good, that is, whose mind is perfect in virtue. You may call this demon in our language, according to my mode of interpretation, by the name of " Genius," whether quite correctly I am not altogether sure, but at all events, at any risk you may so call it; because this God, who is the mind of every one,† though immortal, is never-

---

* These verses are taken from Book IX. of the Æneid.

† _Every one._]—" The soul," says Proclus, in his Commentary on the First Alcibiades, " that, through its similitude to the demoniacal genus, produces energies more wonderful than those which belong to human nature, and which suspends the whole of its life from demons, is a demon according to habitude' (_i. e._ proximity or alliance). But an _essential_ de-

theless, after a certain manner, generated with man; so that those prayers in which we implore the Genius, and which we employ when we embrace the knees [genua] of those whom we supplicate, seem to me to testify this connexion and union, since they comprehend in two words the body and the mind, through the communion and conjunction of which we exist.

There is also another species of demons, according to a second signification, and this is the human soul, after it has performed its duties in the present life, and quitted the body: I find that this is called in the ancient Latin language by the name of Lemur. Now, of these Lemures, the one who, undertaking the guardianship of his posterity, dwells in a house with propitious and tranquil influence, is called the "familiar" Lar. But those who, having no fixed habitation of their own, are punished with vague wandering, as with a kind of exile, on account of the evil deeds of their life, are usually called "Larvæ," thus becoming a vain terror to the good, but a source of punishment to the bad. But when it is uncertain what is the allotted condition of any one of these, and whether it is Lar or Larva, it is called a God Manes; the name of God being added for the sake of honor. For those only are called Gods, who being of the number of the Lemures, and having regulated the course of their life justly and prudently, have afterwards been celebrated by men as divinities, and are universally worshipped with temples, and religious rites; such, for instance, as Amphiaraus in Bœotia, Mopsus in Africa, Osiris in Egypt, and others in other nations, but Esculapius everywhere. All this distribution, however, has been made of those demons, who once existed in a human body.

But there is another species of demons, more exalted and august, not fewer in number, but far superior in dignity, who, being for ever liberated from the bonds and conjunction of the body, preside over certain powers. In the number of these are Sleep and Love, who possess powers of a different nature; Love, of exciting to wakefulness, Sleep of lulling to rest.

mon is neither called a demon through habitude to secondary natures, nor through an assimilation to something different from himself; but is allotted this peculiarity from himself, and is defined by a certain summit, or flower of essence, by appropriate powers, and by different modes of energies."

From this more elevated order of demons, Plato is of opinion that a peculiar demon is allotted to every man, to be a witness and a guardian* of his conduct in life, who, without being visible to any one, is always present, and is an overseer not only of his actions, but even of his thoughts. But when life is finished, and THE SOUL has to return *to its judges*, then the demon who has presided over it immediately seizes, and leads it as his charge to judgment, and is there present with it while it pleads its cause; and censures it if it is guilty of any untruthfulness; corroborates what it says, if it asserts what is true; and conformably to its testimony, sentence is passed. All you, therefore, who hear this divine opinion of Plato, as explained by me, so adapt your minds to whatever you may have to do, or to whatever may be the subject of your meditation, as men who know that there is nothing concealed from those guardians either within the mind or external to it; but that the demon scrupulously takes part in all these matters, sees all things, understands all things, and dwells in the most profound recesses of the mind, in the place of conscience.†

* *A guardian.*]—According to Plato, our guardian demons belong to that order of demons which is arranged under the Gods that preside over the ascent and descent of souls. Olympiodorus, in his Commentary on the Phædo of Plato, observes, " that there is one demon who leads the soul to its judges from the present life; another who is ministrant to the judges, giving completion, as it were, to the sentence which is passed; and a third, who is again allotted the guardianship of life."

† *Of conscience.*]—In the original, *in ipsis peritissimis mentibus vice conscientiæ diversetur.* This is a most remarkable passage, since it perfectly accords with what Olympiodorus says of our allotted demon, in his Scholia on the First Alcibiades of Plato, and contains a dogma concerning this demon, which is only to be found explicitly maintained in these Scholia. The words of Olympiodorus are as follows:—" This is what is said by the interpreters [of Plato] concerning demons, and those which are allotted to us. We, however, shall endeavour to discuss these particulars in such a way as to reconcile them with what is at present said by Plato; for Socrates was condemned to take poison, in consequence of introducing to young men novel demoniacal powers, and for thinking those to be Gods which were not admitted to be so by the city. It must be said, therefore, that the allotted demon is *conscience*, which is *the supreme flower of the soul*, is guiltless in us, is an inflexible judge, and a witness to Minos and Rhadamanthus of the transactions of the present life. This also becomes the cause to us of our salvation, as always remaining in us without guilt, and not assenting to the errors of the soul, but disdaining them, and converting the soul to what is proper. You will not err, there-

He of whom I speak is entirely our guardian, our individual
keeper, our watcher at home, our own proper regulator, a

fore, in calling the allotted demon conscience. But it is requisite to know
that, of conscience, one kind pertains to our gnostic powers, and which
is denominated *conscience* (*co-intelligence*), homonymously with the genus."
In this passage, as Creuzer, the editor of these Scholia, well observes,
something is wanting at the end; and a part of what is deficient, I con-
ceive to be the words, τὸ δὲ ἐπὶ ταῖς ζωτίκαις, *i. e. but another kind to
our vital powers;* for the great division of the powers of the soul is into
the gnostic and vital.

The singularity in this dogma of Olympiodorus, respecting our *allotted
demon*, is, that in making it to be the same with conscience, if conscience
is admitted to be a part of the soul, the dogma of Plotinus must also be
admitted, " that the whole of our soul does not enter into the body, but
that something belonging to it always abides in the intelligible world."
But this dogma appears to have been opposed by all the Platonists pos-
terior to Plotinus; and Proclus has confuted it in the last proposition of
his Elements of Theology; for he there demonstrates, " that every par-
tial soul, in descending into generation [or the sublunary realms], descends
wholly; nor does one part of it remain on high, and another part de-
scend." But his demonstration of this is as follows :—" For if something
pertaining to the soul remain on high, in the intelligible world, it will
always perceive intellectually, without transition, or transitively. But if
without transition, it will be intellect, and not a part of the soul, and
this partial soul will proximately participate of intellect [*i. e.* not through
the medium of demoniacal and divine souls]. This, however, is impos-
sible. But if it perceives intellectually with transition, from that which
always, and from that which sometimes, energizes intellectually, one
essence will be formed. This, however, is also impossible; for these
always differ, as has been demonstrated. To which may be added, the
absurdity resulting from supposing that the summit of the soul is always
perfect, and yet does not rule over the other powers, and cause them to
be perfect. Every partial soul, therefore, wholly descends." Hence, if
Olympiodorus was likewise hostile to this dogma of Plotinus, it must
follow, according to him, that *conscience* is not a part of the soul, but
something superior to it, and dwelling in its summit. Perhaps, therefore,
Olympiodorus on this account calls the allotted demon *the supreme
flower of the soul.* For the summit, or *the one* of the soul, is frequently
called by Platonic writers, τὸ ἄνθος, *the flower*, but not ἄκρον ἄνθος,
the supreme flower; so that the addition of *supreme* will distinguish the
presiding dæmon from the summit of the soul. The place in which this
dogma of Plotinus is to be found, is at the end of his treatise *on the
Descent of the Soul.*

I only add, that the celebrated poet Menander appears to have been
the source of this dogma, that conscience is our allotted demon; for one
of the Excerptæ from his fragments is, " To every mortal conscience is
a God."—*Taylor.*

searcher into our inmost fibres, our constant observer, our inseparable witness, a reprover of our evil actions, an approver of our good ones; if he is becomingly attended to, sedulously examined and devoutly worshipped, in the way in which he was worshipped by Socrates in justice and in innocence; he is our forewarner in uncertainty, our monitor in matters of doubt, our defender in danger, and our assistant in need. He is able also by dreams, and by tokens, and perhaps even openly, when necessity demands it, to avert from you evil, to increase your blessings, to aid you when depressed, to support you when falling, to lighten your darkness, to regulate your prosperity, and modify your adversity.

What wonder, then, if Socrates, who was a man perfect in the highest degree, and wise even by the testimony of Apollo, should know and venerate this his God; and that hence, this Lar, his keeper, and nearly, as I may say, his co-mate and his domestic associate, should repel from him everything which ought to be repelled, foresee what ought to be foreseen, and forewarn him of what he ought to be forewarned of, if at any time, the functions of wisdom falling short, he stood in need, not of counsel, but foreknowledge; in order that when he was vacillating through doubt, he might take a firm stand through being forewarned. For there are many things respecting which even wise men have recourse to diviners and oracles. Do you not very clearly perceive in Homer, as in a kind of large mirror, these two properties of divination and of wisdom separated widely from each other? For when those two pillars of the whole expedition disagreed, Agamemnon potent in sway, and Achilles powerful in battle, and a man famed for his eloquence and renowned for his skill, was wanting, who might allay the pride of the son of Atreus, and curb the anger of the son of Peleus, command the attention of both by the weight of his character, admonish them by examples, and soothe them by his words; who, then, on such an occasion undertook to speak? Why, *Nestor*, the Pylian orator, who was so bland in his eloquence, wary through experience, and venerable for his age; who was known by all to have a body weakened by years, but a mind vigorous in counsel, and words flowing with honeyed sweetness.

In like manner, when in dubious and adverse circumstances, spies are to be chosen, to penetrate into the camp of the enemy at midnight, are not Ulysses and Diomedes selected for that purpose, as counsel and aid, mind and hand, spirit and sword? But, on the other hand, when the Greeks are detained in Aulis, kept back by the winds, and through weariness are shrinking from the difficulties of the war; when the means of proceeding, the tranquillity of the sea, and the clemency of the winds, have to be ascertained by means of the indications of the entrails, the courses taken by birds, and the food devoured by serpents;* then were those two supreme summits of the Grecian wisdom, the Ithacan and the Pylian, both of them silent; but Calchas, who was far more skilful in divining, as soon as he had surveyed the birds, and the altars, and the tree, immediately through his divination appeased the tempests, brought the fleet out to the sea, and foretold a war which should last ten years. Just so in the Trojan army also, when affairs required the aid of divination, that wise senate is silent, nor does either Hicetaon, Lampus, or Clytius, presume to give any opinion; but all of them listen in silence, either to the distasteful auguries of Helenus, or to the discredited predictions of Cassandra. After the same manner, Socrates too, if at any time advice not within the province of wisdom was requisite, was then governed by the prophetic power of his dmeon; and he was sedulously attentive to his admonitions, and on that account was acceptable in a far higher degree to his God.

The reason also, has been in some measure already stated, why the demon of Socrates was generally in the habit of forbidding him to do certain things, but never exhorted him to the performance of any act. For Socrates, being of himself a man exceedingly perfect, and prompt to the performance of all requisite duties, never stood in need of any one to exhort him; though sometimes he required one to forbid him, if danger happened to lurk in any of his undertakings; in order that, being admonished, he might use due precaution, and desist for the present from his attempt, either to resume it more safely

---

* *Devoured by serpents.*] —Apuleius here alludes to the serpent which, in the presence of the Greeks at Aulis, ascended into a plane tree, and devoured eight little sparrows, together with their mother. Whence Calchas prophesied that the Trojan war would last nine years, but that the city would be captured in the tenth year. See the Iliad, lib. ii. v. 300.

THE GOD OF SOCRATES.

at a future period, or enter upon it in some other way. On occasions of this kind, he used to say, " That he heard a certain voice, which proceeded from the divinity." For so it is asserted by Plato ; and let no one suppose that he was in the habit of deriving omens from the ordinary conversation of men. Once, for example, when he was with Phædrus, beyond the precincts of the city, under the covering of a shady tree, and at a distance from all overlookers, he perceived a sign which announced to him that he must not pass over the small stream of the river Ilissus, until he had appeased Love, who was indignant at his censure of him, by a recantation.* And then, besides, if he had been an observer of omens, he would sometimes also have received positive encouragement from them, as we see frequently the case with many of those, who, through a too superstitious observance of omens, are not directed by their own minds, but by the words of others; and who creeping about the lanes, gather counsel from the remarks of strangers, and, if I may use the expression, do not think with the understanding, but with the ears.

But be this as it may, it is certain that those who hear the words of soothsayers, generally receive a voice with their ears, concerning the nature of which they have no doubt, and which they know to proceed from the human mouth. But Socrates did not simply say that he heard a voice, but a " certain voice," transmitted to him : by which addition, you must certainly understand, that neither an ordinary nor a human voice is signified ; for had it been so, it would have been no use to say a " certain" voice, but rather " a voice," " or the voice of some one," as the courtesan in Terence says,

" I thought just now I heard the captain's voice."†

But he who says that he heard a certain voice, is either ignorant whence that voice originated, or is in some doubt concerning it, or shows that it had something unusual and mysterious about it, as Socrates did of that voice, which he said was transmitted to him opportunely and from a divine source. And, indeed, I think that he used to perceive indications of his demon, not only with his ears, but even with his eyes; for he

* *Recantation.*]—See the Phædrus of Plato.

† *Voice.*]—'Audire vocem visa sum modo militis.' This verse is from the Eunuch of Terence.

very frequently declared that not a voice, but a divine sign, had been presented to him. This sign too might have been the form of his demon, which Socrates alone beheld, just as, in Homer, Achilles beheld Minerva.

I suppose that most of you will with difficulty believe what I have just said, and will greatly wonder what was the form of the demon Socrates was in the habit of seeing. Aristotle, however, who is a pretty good authority, I think, informs us that it was usual with the Pythagoreans to express great surprise if any one denied that he had ever seen a demon. If, therefore, the power of beholding a divine form may be possessed by any one, why might it not, in an especial degree, fall to the lot of Socrates, whom the dignity of wisdom rendered equal to the very highest divinity? For nothing is more similar and more acceptable to Deity, than a man intellectually good in a perfect degree, for he as much excels other men as he himself is surpassed by the immortal Gods. Do we not, then, ourselves feel elevated by the example and mention of Socrates? And ought we not to devote ourselves to the felicitous study of a like philosophy, and stand in awe of like Divinities? A study from which we allow ourselves to be drawn away, for what reason I know not. And nothing is there which excites in me so much surprise, as that all men should desire to live most happily, and should know that they cannot so live in any other way than by cultivating the mind, and yet leave their minds uncultivated. Just so, if any one wishes to see clearly, it is requisite that he should pay attention to his eyes by which he sees; if he desires to run swiftly, attention must be paid to the feet by which he runs; and so, too, if you wish to be a stout pugilist, your arms must be strengthened with which you engage in that exercise. So it is with all the other members; the care of each must be made your study. And, as all men may easily see that this is true, I cannot sufficiently account to myself, and wonder to the extent that the thing deserves, why they do not, with the aid of reason, cultivate their minds. For this art of living is equally necessary for all; whereas the same is not the case with the art of painting, nor with the art of singing, which any worthy man may despise, without any censure upon his understanding, without baseness, and without disgrace. I know not how to play on the flute like Ismenias, still I fee!

no shame that I am not a player on the flute : I know not how to paint in colours like Apelles, nor to carve like Lysippus, still I am not ashamed that I am not an artist; and the same as to other arts, not to recount them all individually; you are at liberty to be ignorant of them, and yet not to feel ashamed. But, on the other hand, be good enough to say, I know not how to live aright as Socrates, as Plato, and as Pythagoras lived, and I feel no shame that I know not how to live aright. This you will never dare to say.

It is, however, especially to be wondered at, that people should still neglect to learn those things of which they by no means wish to appear ignorant, and shun at one and the same moment, both acquaintance with and ignorance of the same art. Hence, if you examine their daily outlay, you will find that they are prodigally profuse in their ordinary expenditure, but bestow nothing on themselves; I mean on proper attention to their demon, which proper attention is nothing else than the secret obligations of philosophy. They build sumptuous villas, no doubt, richly decorate their houses, and collect a numerous household; but in all these, and amidst such vast affluence, there is nothing to be ashamed of but the master himself, and with good reason; for they have an accumulation of things which they have collected with exquisite care, while they themselves wander about among them, rude, uncultivated, and ignorant.

Accordingly, you will find the things on which they have lavished their patrimony, to be most pleasing to the view, and most exquisitely built; villas raised that rival cities, houses decorated like temples, most numerous retinues of servants, with carefully curled locks, costly furniture, every thing betokening affluence, every thing bespeaking opulence, every thing bearing marks of refinement, except the master himself; who alone, just like Tantalus, needy, poor, and in want in the midst of his riches, though he does not snatch at retreating fruit, nor endeavour to quench his thirst with shifting water, still hungers and thirsts for want of true beatitude, that is to say, a genuine life,* and a happy and discreet existence. For he does not perceive that it is usual to look upon rich men in the same way that we do horses when we buy them; for in

* *Genuine life.*]—In the common text, ' secundæ vitæ;' but we read, with the Roman edition, ' sinceræ vitæ.'

BB 2

purchasing horses we do not look to the trappings, nor the decorations of the belt, nor do we contemplate the riches of the neck with all its ornaments, and examine whether chains of various patterns, and made of silver, gold, or gems, are hanging from it ; whether elaborate baubles surround the head and neck; whether the bits are embossed, the saddle painted, and the girths gilt; but all this outside show being removed, we survey the bare horse itself, and direct our attention only to his body and his temper, in order to ascertain whether he is of handsome form, vigorous for the race, and strong for purposes of carriage. In the first place, we consider whether there is in his body

> "A head that's slender, and a belly small,
> A back obese, and animated breast,
> In brawny flesh luxuriant."*

And besides, whether a twofold spine passes along his loins; for I would have him not only to carry me swiftly, but to afford me an easy seat.

In a similar manner, therefore, in examining men, do not take into account these foreign particulars, but closely consider the man himself, and look upon him in a state of poverty, as was my Socrates. But I call those things foreign which our parents have produced, and which Fortune has bestowed, none of which do I mingle with the praises of my Socrates ; no nobility of birth, no high pedigree, no long line of ancestors, no envied riches, for all these, I say, are foreign. It is glory sufficient derived from Protaonius, if he was such a man that he was not a disgrace to his grandson. In like manner, may you enumerate every thing of a foreign nature. Is he of noble birth? You praise his parents. Is he rich? I put no trust in Fortune ; nor do I admire these things a bit the more. Is he strong? He will be weakened by sickness. Is he swift in the race? He will fall into old age. Is he beautiful? Wait a little, and he will be so no longer. But is he well instructed, and extremely learned in the pursuits of philosophy, and wise, and skilled in the knowledge of good, as much as it is possible for man to be? Now, then, at last you praise the man himself. For this is neither an hereditary possession from his father, nor depending on chance, nor yet on the suffrages of the people, nor subject to bodily decay, nor mutable

* These lines are taken from Book III. of the Georgics of Virgil.

through age. All these my Socrates possessed, and therefore cared not for the possession of other things. Why, then, do not you apply yourself to the study of wisdom, or, at least, strive that you may hear nothing of an alien nature in your praises? but that he who wishes to compliment you, may praise you in the same manner as Accius praises Ulysses, in his Philoctetes, where he says, at the beginning of that tragedy

> " Fam'd hero, in a little island born,
> Of celebrated name and powerful mind,
> Once to the Grecian ships war's leading light,
> And to the Dardan race th' avenger dire,
> Son of Laertes."

He mentions his father last of all. But you have heard all the praises of that man; Laertes, Anticlea, and Acrisius, claim no share of it. The whole of the praises are, as you see, a possession belonging to Ulysses alone. Nor does Homer teach you anything else with regard to the same Ulysses, in always representing Wisdom as his companion, whom he poetically calls Minerva. Hence, attended by her, he encounters all terrific dangers, and rises superior to all adverse circumstances. For, assisted by her, he entered the cavern of the Cyclops, but escaped from it; saw the oxen of the Sun, but abstained from them, and descended to the realms beneath, but emerged from them. With the same Wisdom for his companion, he passed by Scylla, and was not seized by her; he was surrounded by Charybdis, and was not retained by her; he drank the cup of Circe, and was not transformed; he came to the Lotophagi, yet did not remain with them; he heard the Sirens, yet did not approach them.*

* *Approach them.*]—The concluding part of this treatise on the God of Socrates has a great resemblance to the conclusion of the dissertation of Maximus Tyrius, entitled, *Whether there is a Sect in Philosophy, according to Homer?* and which is as follows: " And with respect to Ulysses himself, do you not see how virtue, and the confidence which he acquires through her aid, preserve him, while he opposes art to all-various calamities? This is the *moly* in the island of Circe, this is the fillet in the sea, this delivered him from the hands of Polyphemus, this led him from Hades, this constructed for him a raft, this persuaded Alcinous, this enabled him to endure the blows of the suitors, the wrestling with Irus, and the insolence of Melanthius. This liberated his palace, this avenged the injuries of his wife, this made the man a descendant of Jupiter, like the Gods, and such a one as the happy man is according to Plato."

END OF APULEIUS ON THE GOD OF SOCRATES.

FLORIDA OF APULEIUS.

I.

It is a common custom with religious travellers, when they come upon some grove or sacred place, to beseech favour, offer up prayers, and sit down a while; in like manner, now that I have entered this most hallowed city, though I am in great haste, I must entreat favour, make oration, and check my hurry. For the traveller can find no fitter motives for a religious pause in an altar decked with flowers, or a dell shaded with foliage, or an oak loaded with horns, or a beech festooned with skins, or even a consecrated and enclosed hillock, or a trunk chiselled into the form of an image, or a turf redolent of libation, or a stone bedewed with ointment. These are small things indeed, and though adored by the few who scrutinise them, are passed unnoticed by those who are not aware of them.

II.

But not so my predecessor, Socrates, who, when he had looked for some time upon a handsome but silent youth, exclaimed: "Say something, that I may see you." Socrates saw not a silent man; for he thought that men were to be considered not with the eyes, but with the rays of the intellect and the gaze of the soul. In this he differed in opinion with the soldier in Plautus, who says: "One eye-witness is worth more than ten ear-witnesses." Nay, he held the converse of this verse with regard to the examination of men: "One ear-witness is worth more than ten eye-witnesses." But if the judgments formed by the eyes were more valued than those of the mind, the palm of wisdom would be due to the eagle. For we men can neither discern things far away nor very near us, but are all in a measure blind; and if you consider us only with regard to our eyes, and our earthly and dull vision, truly the great poet has well said that there is a mist, as it were, before our eyes, and that we cannot see clearly beyond a stone's throw. But the eagle when he has soared aloft as high as the clouds, sweeping with his wings all that space in which it rains and snows, a height beyond which there is no place for the thunder or lightning, on the very base of the ether and summit of the tempest, so to speak; the eagle when he has soared thither, glides along bodily, with a gentle inclination left or right, turning his sail-spread wings in whatever direction he pleases, using his tail as a small helm. Looking down thence on all below him, with unwearied rowing of his wings, and with his flight stayed awhile, he remains at gaze suspended nearly in the same spot, and considers in what direction he shall swoop down on his prey like a thunderbolt; seeing at one glance, himself unseen in the heavens, cattle in the fields, wild beasts on the mountains, and men in the towns, he considers where he may pierce with his beak or hook with his talons a heedless lamb or timid hare, or any living thing that chance may offer him to tear and devour.

III.

Hyagnis, as we have heard say, was the father and teacher of Marsyas the flute-player, and surpassed all in his performance in an age as yet uncultivated in music; not that he played, indeed, with such soul-subduing tone as later musicians, or with such manifold modulations, or on a pipe of so many holes; for the art had been but recently invented, and was then in its infancy. Nothing can be perfect in the beginning, but in almost all cases some rudiment of the promised thing precedes its consummation. Before Hyagnis appeared then, most people could do no more than, like the shepherd or neatherd in Virgil,

" Grate on their scrannel pipes of wretched straw."*

And if there was any one who appeared to have made somewhat more progress in the art, even he too, followed the common practice of playing only on one pipe, just as on one trumpet. Hyagnis was the first who separated the hands in playing; the first who gave breath to two pipes; the first who mingled a

* *Grate, &c.*]—This line, from Milton's *Lycidas*, is a pretty close translation of one from Virgil's third eclogue.

shrill and a grave tone in musical concert, by means of left and right apertures. His son Marsyas, when he had acquired the paternal art of minstrelsy—a Phrygian and a barbarian he was, a rough brutish-looking fellow, hirsute, with a dirty beard, covered with bristles and hairs,—is said (oh monstrous!) to have contended with Apollo: a Thersites with a beautiful youth, a clown with a scholar, a brute with a god! The Muses with Minerva sat as judges by way of a joke, to laugh at the barbarity of that monster, and no less to punish his stupidity. But Marsyas, not perceiving that he was made a laughing stock, which is the greatest proof of folly, before he began to play, sputtered out some barbarous nonsense about himself and Apollo, praising himself because he had short crisp hair, a squalid beard, a shaggy breast, was in art a flute-player, and in fortune needy; on the other hand, ridiculous to relate, he decried the opposite merits as so many faults in Apollo, saying: that Apollo had unshorn locks, a handsome face, and a smooth body; that he was of manifold proficiency in art, and opulent in fortune. In the first place, said he, his locks flow freely, those in front being drawn forward, those behind tossed back; his whole form is beautiful; his limbs are smooth and fair; his tongue is prophetic, and endowed with equal eloquence in prose and verse. What! his garment is fine in texture, soft to the touch, and glowing with purple. What! his lyre is ruddy with gold, white with ivory, and variegated with gems. What! he trills most skilfully and most sweetly. "All these prettinesses," he says, "are by no means becoming to virtue, but adapted to luxury, whereas the native quality of my own person exhibits the greatest comeliness." The Muses laughed when they heard things like these, which a wise man might well desire, charged as crimes against Apollo; and when the flute-player had been beaten in the contest, they left him, like a two-footed bear, stripped of his skin, with his flesh naked and torn. Thus Marsyas played for punishment and suffered it. But Apollo was ashamed of so low a victory.

IV.

Antigenidas was a certain flute-player, a honeyed modulator of every tone, and a skilled performer in every mode, whether it were the simple Æolian, the varied Asian, the plaintive Lydian, the religious Phrygian, or the warlike Dorian. Being thus a most distinguished flutist, he used to say, that nothing so vexed and fretted his mind, as, that the horn-players at funerals were called flutists. But he would have patiently endured this community of names if he had seen mimes. Then he would have seen some commanding, others suffering blows, and all dressed nearly alike in purple. So also if he saw our games : for there too he would see a man preside, a man fight. He would see the toga employed both for the registering of a vow and for a funeral. Likewise he would see corpses covered, and philosophers clad with a pallium.

V

For you have assembled in the theatre with good will, as knowing that the place does not detract from the weight of what is delivered there ; but that the chief thing to be considered is, what you find in the theatre. For if it is a mime, you may laugh ; if it is a rope-dancer, you may be alarmed ; if it is a comedy, you may applaud ; if it is a philosopher, you may learn.

VI.

The Indians are a populous nation of vast extent of territory, situated far from us to the East, near the reflux of the ocean and the rising of the sun, under the first beams of the stars, and at the extreme verge of the earth, beyond the learned Egyptians, and the superstitious Jews, and the mercantile Nabathæans, and the flowing robed Arsacidæ, and the Ityræans, poor in crops, and the Arabians rich in perfumes. Now I do not so much admire the heaps of ivory of these Indians, their harvests of pepper, their bales of cinnamon, their tempered steel, their mines of silver, and their golden streams ; nor that among them the Ganges, the greatest of all rivers,

> Rolls like a monarch on his course, and pours
> His eastern waters through a hundred streams,
> Mingling with ocean by a hundred mouths ;

nor that those Indians, though situated at the dawn of day, are yet of the colour of night ; nor that among them immense dragons fight with enormous elephants, with parity of danger, to their mutual destruction ; for they hold them enwrapped in their slippery folds, so that when the elephants cannot disengage their legs, or in any way extricate themselves from the scaly bonds of the tenacious dragons, they are forced to seek revenge from the fall of their own bulk, and to crush their captors by the mass of their bodies.   There are among them also various kinds of inhabitants.   I will rather speak of the marvellous things of men than of those of nature.   There is among them a race who know nothing but how to tend cattle ; whence they are called neatherds.   There are races clever in trafficking with merchandise, and others stout in fight, whether with arrows or hand-to-hand with swords.   There is also among them a pre-eminent race called Gymnosophists.   These I exceedingly admire, for they are men skilled not in propagating the vine, nor in grafting trees, nor in tilling the ground.   They know not how to cultivate the fields, or to wash gold, or to break horses, or to tame bulls, or to shear or feed sheep or goats.   What is it then ? They know one thing instead of all these.   They cultivate wisdom, both the aged professors and the young students.   Nothing do I so much applaud in them as that they hate torpor of mind and sloth.   Accordingly, when the table is laid, before the meal is served up, all the young men assemble round it from their several places and occupations, and the masters enquire what good thing each has done that day since sunrise.   Thereupon one relates that having been chosen arbitrator between two, he has allayed their quarrel, restored good will, cleared up suspicion, and changed them from enemies to friends.   Another states that he has obeyed some command or another of his parents; and another, that he has found out something by his own reflection, or from another's teaching.   In short, all tell their tale.   He who has no cause to offer why he should dine, is turned out of doors, and sent about his business without a dinner.

VII.

It was the will of Alexander, that most excellent of all kings, who received the surname of the Great for his achievements, that he who had attained that singular glory, should never be named without praise.   For he alone, since the beginning of time, as far as human memory extends, having possessed himself invincibly of the dominion of the world, was greater than his fortune, and both induced its vast successes by his valour, and equalled them by his merits, and surpassed them by his superior greatness.   He alone was so illustrious

beyond all rivalry, that no one can dare to hope for his excel-
lence or covet his fortune. You would be wearied with ad-
miring the lofty deeds of that great Alexander, whether those
which he achieved in war, or those which he wisely accom-
plished in peace; all which, my Clemens, the most learned
and sweetest of poets, has undertaken to illustrate in a very
beautiful poem. Now this is a most signal fact respecting
Alexander, that in order to have his image descend the more
authentically to posterity, he would not allow it to be vulgar-
ised by many artists, but commanded throughout all his em-
pire, that no one should presumptuously make the king's like-
ness in brass, or in painting, or with the graver; but that
Polycletus alone should mould it in brass, Apelles alone deli-
neate it in colours, Pyrgoteles alone should elaborate it with
the graver. Besides these three artists, far the most eminent
in their several kinds, if any other was found to have put his
hands to the king's most sacred image, he should be punished
just as one who had committed sacrilege. The consequence
of that fear imposed on all was, that Alexander was presented
with singular excellence in all his likenesses; so that in all
statues, pictures, and engraved gems, he appears with the
same vigorous aspect of a most intrepid warrior, the same
genius of a mighty hero, the same beauty and freshness of
youth, the same noble expansion of forehead. Now I would
that in like manner, it were a valid decree of philosophy that
no one should presumptuously attempt its likeness; that a few
good artists, and those soundly instructed, should consider the
study of philosophy in every way, and that no rude, squalid,
ignorant pretenders should imitate philosophers as far as re-
gards their garb, and should disgrace that royal science which
was devised both for speaking well and living well, by talk-
ing ill and living no better. Both which things are indeed
very easy; for what can be easier than rabidness of tongue and
baseness of conduct, the former from contempt of others, the
latter from self contempt? For to conduct oneself basely is
self-contempt; to vilify others barbarously, is insolence to-
wards one's hearers. Does he not insult you in the highest
degree who supposes you to delight in slanders against any
good man; who thinks you do not understand bad and vicious
words, or that if you understand, you like them? Where is
the clown, the porter, or the pothouse sot, so silly that if

he had a mind to put on the pallium, he could rail in better terms ?

VIII.

For he owes more to you than to his dignity, although that is not common to him with others. For out of countless men there are but few senators, and of senators few are of noble birth ; and of those consular men few are good, and of those good, moreover, few are learned. But to speak only of his dignity, its insignia are not to be lightly assumed either in the garments or the foot-dress.

IX.

If perchance in this fair assembly sits any malicious person of the number of those my enemies—since in a great city that kind of men is also found who like rather to rail at their betters than to imitate them, and who affect enmity towards those whom they cannot hope to resemble ; men whose own names being obscure, wish to become known through mine ; if, then, any of those croakers has come hither to be a blot upon this brilliant assembly, I should like him to run his eyes for a while over this incredible concourse ; and having contemplated such a crowd as never before my time was seen gathered together to listen to a philosopher, let him compute in his own mind, how great a risk of sustaining his reputation is here encountered, by one who has not been used to be contemned ; since it is an arduous and very difficult thing to satisfy even the moderate expectations of a few, especially for me, whom my acquired reputation, and your favourable predisposition towards me, suffer not to utter any thing negligently, and without deep reflection. For which of you would forgive me a single solecism ? Which of you would absolve me for one syllable of barbarous pronunciation ? Which of you would permit me to jabber, like crazy people, any unauthorised and corrupt words that come uppermost? Yet these faults you easily and very justly pardon in others. But every phrase of mine you scrutinise keenly, weigh it carefully, test it by the file and the rule, and again compare it with the lathe and the buskin.* Lowliness is as much excused as dignity is difficult to sus-

---

* *The lathe and the buskin.*]—That is, you require it to be as smooth as if turned in the lathe, and to have the sentitious gravity of tragedy (the buskin).

tain. I acknowledge then my difficulty, and do not desire
you to think otherwise of it. Nor let a paltry and spurious
similitude mislead you, since, as I have often said, certain
cloaked lies* walk about. The crier ascends the tribunal with
the proconsul, and he too is seen there dressed in the toga ;
and indeed he stands there a long while, or he walks about,
or he bawls often with all his might; but the proconsol him-
self speaks in a moderate tone, rarely, and in a sitting pos-
ture, and he generally reads from a tablet. For the crier's
garrulous voice is the function of his office; but the tablet
is the proconsol's sentence, which when once read, cannot be
lengthened or shortened by a single letter, but as soon as it is
pronounced, it is inserted in the registry of the province. I,
in my degree, suffer something like this in my studies. For
whatever I have delivered to you is immediately taken up and
recited, nor is it free to me to recall any part of it, or to
change or correct it in any respect. Wherefore, I must be
the more scrupulous in speaking, and that too not in one kind
of matter only. For there are extant more works of mine in
the Muses than of Hippias in art. What that means, give me
your attention, and I will diligently and accurately set forth.

This Hippias was one of the sophists, superior to all in the
number of the arts he knew, inferior to none in eloquence.
He was contemporary with Socrates, a native of Elis, of what
family is not known. His glory was great, his fortune small;
but his genius was great, his memory excellent, his studies
various, his rivals many. This Hippias came once to Pisa to
the Olympic games, where he was not less remarkable for the
ornaments he wore than for the fact that he had wrought
them himself. Of all those things he had with him he had
purchased not one, but had made them with his own hands;
the garments in which he was clad, the shoes on his feet, and
everything he carried on his person. For clothing he had an
inner tunic of very fine texture, of triple thread, and double
purple dye. He had wrought it single-handed at home. He
was girt with a belt adorned with a sort of Babylonian pic-
ture of admirable colours. Nor had any one helped him in
that work. His outer covering was a white cloak, which
also is known to have been his own handiwork. Also he

* *Cloaked lies.*]—Impostors who are bearded and cloaked like philo-
sophers.

had put together the soles of his own foot gear; and as for the gold ring on his left hand, bearing a most skilfully cut seal which he often exhibited, he himself had rounded the ring, and had closed the pallet, and engraved the gem. I have not yet told all he did. For I shall not be loth to relate what he was not ashamed to display, who asserted in a large assembly that he had also made himself an oil flask which he carried about him, of a lenticular form, of a rounded outline and small convexity; and with it a neat little scraper to be used in the bath, with a convenient handle and tubulated face, so that it might be held steadily in the hand, and that the sweat might flow out of it in a stream. Who will not extol a man skilled in so many arts; illustrious for such manifold knowledge; a Dædalus in the use of so many tools? Certainly, I admire Hippias, but I would rather rival the fecundity of his genius in matters of learning, than in multitudinous appliances for personal use.

I confess, indeed, that I am not expert in handicraft arts; that I buy my garments at the clothier's—these shoes at the shoe-maker's; that I wear no ring, and hold gems and gold of no more account than lead and pebbles; that I buy a scraper, a flask, and other bath utensils at the shops. I am far from denying that I do not know how to use the loom, or the awl, or the file, or the lathe, or any such implements; instead of these, I confess I prefer to compose with a writing reed, poems of all kinds adapted to the laurel branch,* the lyre, the sock, the buskin; likewise satires and enigmas; likewise various histories; as, also, orations praised by the eloquent, and dialogues praised by philosophers; and to compose these and such like works, both in Greek and Latin, with two-fold study, with equal diligence and in similar style. These things I would, indeed, Proconsul, excellent man, that I could lay before you not singly and piece-meal, but collectively in one heap, and enjoy your honourable testimony regarding all my literary labours. It is not, indeed, from penury of fame that I desire this, for fame has long subsisted for me, bright and unbroken among all your predecessors,` down to yourself; but because by no one am I more desirous of being esteemed than

* *The laurel branch.*] Those who recited poems in public or at private entertainments, carried a branch of laurel or myrtle in their hands, whence they were called by the Greeks ῥαβδωδοὶ and ιιχωδοι.

by him which I justly esteem above all others. For it is a law of nature that whom you praise, him you also love; and moreover, whom you love, by him you would wish to be praised. Now I profess myself one who prizes you dearly, being bound to you by no private, but by all manner of public favours. I have, indeed, obtained nothing from you, for nothing have I asked. But philosophy has taught me to love not only kindness but injury, and rather to do homage to reason than to seek my own advantage, and to prefer public expediency to my own. Hence, whilst the majority love the beneficial effects of your goodness, I love its principle. And this I have begun to do whilst considering your conduct in the affairs of the inhabitants of this province, for which they ought to love you intensely : such of them as have felt it in their own persons, for sake of the benefit they have received; such as have not personally experienced it for sake of the example. For you have benefited many individually, and all by your example. For who does not delight to learn from you by what adjustment may be acquired that pleasant gravity of yours, that mild austerity, that placid firmness, that gracious vigour of mind. Never, to my knowledge, did the province of Africa ever revere more, and fear less any proconsul; in no year of administration but yours, had shame more power than fear towards restraining offences. No one but you has used the like power so often to serve, so seldom to terrify. No one has brought with him a son more resembling himself in virtue. Hence, no proconsul has remained longer in Carthage. For at the time you made a tour of the province, while Honorinus remained with us, we did not feel your absence so much as rather to wish you back. There is in the son the equity of the father, in the youth the prudence of the old man, in the legate the personal weight of the consul. So thoroughly does he copy and reflect all your good qualities, that truly, such excellence would be more worthy of admiration in the young man than in you, were it not that you had imparted it to him. Would that we might always enjoy it! What to us are these changes of proconsuls? What these brief years and rapid months? O swift days of good men! O quickly lapsing tenure of the best governors! Our whole province, Severianus, now grieves to lose you. But Honorinus is called by his own worth to the prætorship, and the favour of the Cæsars is preparing

him for the consulship; our love beholds him, at present; and
the hope of Carthage promises for the future, relying on the
sole consolation of your example, that he who leaves us a
legate, soon returns to us as proconsul.

X.

> " Sun, who with burnished car and rushing steeds
>   Display'st thy radiant flames and glowing fire." *

Likewise the Moon, imitatress of his light, and the five other
powers of the planets, power beneficent in Jupiter, voluptu-
ous in Venus, swift in Mercury, pernicious in Saturn, fiery in
Mars.   There are also other intermediate powers of gods,
which we can feel, but which it is not given us to see; as of
Love and the like, whose form is unseen, their force known;
that power, likewise, which in one part of the earth reared
the lofty peaks of mountains, and elsewhere levelled the ex-
panse of plains, as the design of Providence required; like-
wise, that which everywhere defined the courses of rivers, the
green vigour of the meadows, and gave flight to birds, gliding
folds to serpents, swift feet to wild beasts, and upright gait
to men.

XI.

For just as those who have the misfortune to cultivate a
sterile farm, and a stony field, mere rocks and brambles,
since there is no produce in their unkindly ground, and they
see in it no other growth, but

> " Unlucky darnel and unfruitful straw," †

lacking harvest of their own, go and thieve from others, and
pluck their neighbours' flowers, to mingle them forsooth with
their own thistles; just so does he who has no virtue of his
own.

XII.

The parrot is a bird of India, in form a little less than the
dove; but its colour is not that of the dove, for it is not
white, nor blackish, or yellowish on either side, or variegated;
but the parrot's colour is green both in its inner down and
its outer feathers, except that it is varied in the neck alone.

* *Sun, &c.*]—From the Phœnissæ of L. Attius or Accius.
† *Unl: ty darnel, &c.*]—From Virgil, Eclogue V.

For its neck is encompassed and girded with a red circle, like a gold necklace, and of equal splendour. Its beak is hard in the highest degree. When it swoops down from its highest flight upon a rock, it lights there upon its beak, and fixes itself as with an anchor. Its head too, is as hard as its beak. When it is compelled to imitate our speech, its head is beaten with a little iron rod, to make it attend to the commands of its master. This is the ferula beneath which it learns. Its schooling begins when it is but a chick, and continues until its second year, as long as its mouth is easy to mould, and its tongue is pliable. If taken old, it is indocile and forgetful. But that kind of parrot is apter to learn human speech which feeds on nuts, and which has feet with five toes like man ; for all parrots have not that characteristic ; but it is common to them all to have the tongue broader than that of other birds, whereby they more easily articulate human words, as having a more expanded plectrum and palate. But what it has learned it sings, or rather speaks, like us, so that if you heard it, you would suppose it was the voice of a man ; but if you saw it, you would say it was not speaking, but trying to do so. Now both the crow and the parrot pronounce only what they have been taught. If you teach a parrot ribaldry, he will be a ribald, screaming scurrility day and night. This is its song ; this it considers warbling. When it has run through all the scurrilous phrases it has learned, it begins the same strain over again. If you would be free from its ribaldry, you must cut out its tongue, or at once send it back to its woods.

XIII.

For philosophy has not bestowed on me that kind of speech, as nature has endowed some birds with a brief and periodical song, a morning song to swallows, a mid-day to cicalas, an afternoon to buzzards, an evening to screech owls, a nocturnal to horned owls, a peep of day song to cocks. All these creatures differ from each other in the period and the manner of their song ; the cocks sing with an awakening strain, the horned owls moan, the screech owls are querulous, the buzzards have inflected notes, the cicalas are obstreperous, the swallows twitter shrilly. But the discourse of the philosopher is practised at all seasons, and is reverend to hear, useful to understand, and omnisonant in compass.

XIV

Crates, the follower of Diogenes, who was adored like a domestic Lar by the Athenians of his time, was one against whom no door was ever shut; nor had any father of a family a secret so profound as not to admit the seasonable interposition of Crates, the analyser and arbitrator of all disputes and altercations between relations. As the poets relate that Hercules formerly quelled by his valour horrid monsters, both human and brute, so was that philosopher a Hercules against anger and envy, avarice and lust, and other monsters and enormities of the human mind. All these pests he drove out from the minds of men, purged families of them, and quelled malevolence. He, too, was half naked, and notable for his club; he was likewise a native of Thebes, whence Hercules is known to have derived his birth. Before he became downright Crates, he was numbered among the nobles of Thebes: his family was one of the best, his household numerous, his dwelling adorned with an ample vestibule. He himself was well dressed, and well endowed with lands. Afterwards he came to understand that no security was bequeathed him with his wealth that he should enjoy it all his life; that all things are unstable and insecure; that all the riches under the sky avail nothing towards a happy life. When Crates learned these and similar truths, partly from Diogenes and partly from his own reflection, he at last went out into the forum, and threw down his wealth like a load of dung, more fatiguing than useful. Then when a great crowd had assembled, he cried out, "Crates manumits Crates." Thenceforth he lived happily all his days, not only without servants, but also bare and disencumbered of every thing. And so much was he sought after, that a noble virgin, scorning younger wooers, voluntarily chose him for her own. And when Crates uncovered his shoulders and showed how he was hunchbacked, and laid his wallet and staff and his cloak on the ground, telling her that these were his worldly gear, and that such as she had seen was his beauty, and bidding her therefore ponder carefully, that she might not find reason to complain afterwards, Hipparche still accepted the proposed conditions. She replied that she had already sufficiently considered the matter; that she could nowhere in the world find a richer or a handsomer husband; and he might therefore take her where he pleased. The cynic led her to the portico, and there lay with her in a frequented spot, publicly in broad daylight; and he would have deflowered her in all men's sight, prepared as she was to bear it with equal indifference, had not Zeno concealed his master from the gaze of the surrounding throng, by hanging his tattered cloak before him.

XV.

Samos is an island of moderate extent in the Icarian Sea, opposite Miletus, situated to the westward of it, and separated from it by no great breadth of sea. Passing with easy sail from one to the other, the second day puts you in port. The soil of the island is inapt for corn, unfit for the plough, more productive of olives, nor is it dug by the vinegrower or the gardener. Its whole cultivation consists in hoeing and planting rows of olives, from the produce of which the island is more fructiferous than frugiferous.* Furthermore, it abounds in inhabitants, and is much frequented by strangers. It has a town by no means corresponding to its reputation; but that it was once large is shown by the ruins of walls in many places. There stands the most celebrated temple of Juno. It stands near the sea-shore, at a distance, if I remember rightly, of not more than twenty stadia from the town. It contains a most opulent shrine of the goddess, and a vast quantity of silver in platters, mirrors, cups, and such like utensils. There is also a great amount of bronze, in various figures, of very ancient and handsome workmanship. For instance, there is before the altar a statue of Bathyllus, dedicated by the tyrant Polycrates, than which I do not think I have seen anything more exquisite. Some erroneously suppose it to be the statue of Pythagoras. It is a youth of remarkable beauty, with hair parted on the forehead, and falling evenly on the cheeks; but behind the hair is longer, and covers the neck, which shines through them as far as the verge of the shoulders. The neck is plump, the cheeks round and beardless, and there is a little dimple in the chin; the costume is exactly that of a harper; he looks towards the goddess like one who is singing; he

---

* *Fructiferous than frugiferous.*]—It abounds more in fruit (*fructus*) than in corn and garden stuff (*fruges*). This is an example of that jingling of words in which Apuleius so inordinately delights.

wears a figured and coloured tunic, flowing down to his feet, with a zone in the Greek fashion; and a chlamys covering both arms to the wrists. The other histrionic ornaments hang upon the figure. The lyre is suspended from a short engraved baldrick. The hands are delicate; the left is stretched out, and touches the strings with its spread fingers; the right applies the plectrum to the lyre, as if ready to strike the chords when the voice has paused in singing. Meanwhile he seems to pour out his song from his rounded mouth, with lips intentionally half opened. Now this is the statue of a certain youth beloved by Polycrates, the tyrant, whom Anacreon, the Teian, celebrates in song for friendship's sake. But it is far from being the statue of Pythagoras, the philosopher.

The latter was by birth a Samian, most remarkable for beauty, deeply versed in minstrelsy and all kinds of music, and he lived about the time when Polycrates ruled in Samos. But the philosopher was by no means a favourite with the tyrant. Just after the latter had began to rule, Pythagoras fled privily from the island, having lately lost his father Mnesarchus, whom I find to have been an artist, and to have acquired reputation rather than wealth, by very cleverly engraving gems. Some say that Pythagoras was at that time conveyed to Egypt among the captives of king Cambyses, and that he had for teachers the Persian magi, and especially Zoroaster, the adept in every divine mystery; and that he was afterwards received by a certain Gillus, a leading man among the inhabitants of Crotona. But the more generally received story is, that he went of his own accord to acquire the learning of Egypt, and that he was there taught by the priests the incredible powers of ceremonies, the wonderful commutations of numbers, and the most ingenious figures of geometry; but that not satisfied with these mental accomplishments, he afterwards visited the Chaldæans and the Brahmins, and among the latter the Gymnosophists. The Chaldæans taught him the stars, the definite orbits of the planets, and the various effects of both kinds of stars upon the nativity of men; as also, for much money, the remedies for human use derived from the earth, and the air, and the sea. But the Brahmins taught him the greater part of his philosophy: what are the rules and principles of the understanding; what the functions of the body; how many are the faculties of the soul, how many the mutations of life; what torments or rewards devolve upon the souls of the dead according to their respec.ive deserts. Moreover, there was Pherecydes, a native of the island of Syros, who was the first who ventured to reject the fetters of verse, and to write in prose: him, too, Pythagoras waited on as another master, and when turned into a scab of creeping things by the corruption of a most horrible disease, he buried him religiously. He is said also to have discussed natural science under Anaximander, the Milesian; to have followed for instruction Epimenides, of Crete, the illustrious seer and poet; and likewise Leodamas, the disciple of Creophylus, which latter is said to have been the host of the poet Homer, and his imitator in song.

Instructed by so many masters, having drunk of so many various fountains of knowledge all over the world, this man of surpassingly mighty genius, and of more than human grandeur of soul, the first namer and founder of philosophy, taught his disciples nothing in the first place but to be silent. With him the first study imposed upon the future sage was to hold his tongue altogether, and as for the words which poets call winged, to pluck their plumes and shut them up within the walls of his white teeth. This was, I say, absolutely the first rudiment of wisdom, to learn to think, and unlearn to prate. But they did not abstain from speaking all their lives long, nor did all follow their master in silence during an equally long period; but silence observed during a short space of time was thought enough for men of graver disposition, whilst the more talkative were punished by a silence of five years, their voice being sent, as it were, into exile. Now our master, Plato, imitates Pythagoras, differing in little or no degree from his sect. I, too, among a great many men, having been admitted into his sect by my teachers, have learned both these things in academic meditations: to speak with all my might when speech is required; and when silence is required, to hold my tongue willingly. Through this moderation I think I have obtained credit from all your predecessors, not less for my opportune silence, than for my timely speaking.

XVI.

Before I begin, noblemen of Africa, to thank you for the statue which you did me the honour to propose during my presence here, and which you kindly decreed to erect to me during my absence, I wish first to acquaint you with the reason why I have not been seen by this assembly for a good many days, having betaken myself to the Persian waters, so pleasant to healthy bathers, and so curative to the sick. For I have made it my resolution thus to submit the whole course of my time to your approval, to whom I have perpetually dedicated myself. Never will I do anything, great or small, of which I will not make you cognizant and judges. That you may know, therefore, why I suddenly disappeared from the sight of this your illustrious assemblage, I will relate an almost parallel case of the comic writer, Philemon, as an example of what unforeseen dangers suddenly befal men. You who know enough of his genius, hear a few words about his death. Do you wish me to say a few words also about his genius? This Philemon was a poet, and a writer of the middle comedy. He produced pieces for the stage along with Menander, and contended with him, being perhaps inferior to him, but at all events his rival. For that he was often victorious over him is a shameful thing to tell. Nevertheless, we find in him much wit; plots ingeniously involved; recognitions clearly made out; personages suited to the matter; phrases appropriate to each character; gaieties not beneath the sock; gravities not quite up to the buskin. Impurities are rare in his works, and amours are admitted as errors. Nevertheless, you find in him the perjured pimp, the hot lover, the cunning slave, the wheedling mistress, the peremptory wife, the indulgent mother, the scolding uncle, the helpful friend, and the fighting soldier, together with various parasites, and stingy parents, and wanton harlots.

Distinguished by these merits as a comic writer, it happened that he recited part of a play he had recently composed. When he had come to the third act, and was exciting those pleasant emotions which comedy delights in, a sudden shower of rain coming on, as very lately happened to myself when speaking before you, compelled him to dismiss his audience and suspend his reading. But many persons calling for the remainder, he promised that he would deliver it on the following day without interruption. Next day, accordingly, a great concourse assembled, extremely eager for what was to come, and every one took the nearest seat he could find opposite the reader's place. The late comer nodded to his friends, who found sitting room for him. The whole theatre being crammed, the pressure was great, and they began to complain of each other. All those who were so late as to be excluded from the benches were pitied. Those who had not been present at the first day's reading enquired what had then been delivered; those who had been present recalled to mind what they had heard, and knowing all that had gone before, began to look for what was to come. Meanwhile the day was passing away, and Philemon did not keep his appointment. Some murmured at the poet's delay, many defended him. But when the audience had waited an unreasonable time and no Philemon appeared, some of the readiest were sent to fetch him, and found him dead in his bed. He had just stiffened after giving up the ghost, and lay resting on his elbow on the bed as if thinking. His hand was still inserted in the scroll; his face was turned toward the book which he held straight before him; but he was already senseless, unconscious of the book, and regardless of his audience. Those who had entered stood still awhile, struck with wonder at so unexpected an event, so beautiful a death. They then returned and announced to the people that Philemon, who was expected to finish his fictitious plot in the theatre, had concluded the real comedy at home. He had said to human affairs, " Farewell and applaud," but to his friends, lament and wail; that shower of yesterday had boded him tears; his comedy had arrived sooner at the funeral than the nuptial torch. And since this excellent poet had made his exit from life, it was meet that the audience should proceed straightway to his obsequies; that his bones should now be collected, and by and by his poems.

I learned long ago, that these facts occurred as I have related; but I have been reminded of them to-day by my own mischance. For, as you remember, when my recitation was interrupted by the rain, I postponed it at your desire to the following day; and certainly after Philemon's example; for the very same day I so violently sprained my ankle in the palæstra, that I all but broke off the joint from the leg. It was put out of place, however, and is still infirm from the dislocation; and when I reduced it at first with great force, I sweated profusely and had long rigors. Then I suffered acute pain of the intestines, which hardly ceased until its vio-

lence had destroyed me, and compelled me, after the manner
of Philemon, to be dead before I had read; to finish what was
written for me in the book of fate sooner than what I had
written; to end my life sooner than my history.   As soon,
then, as I had recovered the power of walking at the Persian
waters, by their mild temperature and their no less useful
than soothing warmth, not, indeed, so as to be able to tread
firmly, but as much as seemed to me sufficient for my haste to
return to you, I came to perform what I had promised; whilst
you in the meantime had, by your kindness, not only taken
away my lameness, but even added speed to my feet.

Had I not good cause to hasten, that I might return you
many thanks for that honour for which I had not petitioned
you?   Not but that the grandeur of Carthage is worthy that
even a philosopher should sue to it for honours; but that your
kindness should be whole and unimpaired, if no solicitation of
mine detracted from its spontaneous grace.   For neither does
he who prays buy the object of his prayers for a cheap consi-
deration, nor does he who is solicited accept a small price, so
that you would rather buy all kinds of commodities than beg
for them.   This, I think, is especially to be considered a
matter of honour: he who obtains with much pains and solici-
tation on his own part, owes one debt of gratitude to himself
for as much as he has succeeded in his suit; but he who has
received it without the trouble of a canvass, owes a double
debt of gratitude to the grantors; both because he has not
sought, and he has obtained.   I therefore owe you twofold
thanks, nay, manifold thanks, as I shall always and every-
where declare.   But now for the present time I will publicly
profess it, as is my wont, in this book composed by me, on ac-
count of this honour.   For there is a certain method in which
a philosopher ought to return thanks for a statue publicly de-
creed to him: from that method that book will diverge little
which the distinguished honour of Strabo Æmilianus demands,
a book which I think I can suitably compose, if you will join
in extolling him to-day with me.   For he so excels in studies,
that he is much more illustrious by his own genius than by
his father's consulship.

In what words, Æmilianus Strabo, of all men who have
been, or are, or will be in Numantia, most illustrious amongst
the best, and best among the most illustrious, and most learned

among both; in what words shall I return thanks in my discourse for this disposition of yours towards me? In what worthy manner I can extol your honourable good-will, with what remuneration of speech I can match the high praise of this act of yours, by Hercules! I am yet at a loss to know; but I will diligently seek and strive to discover,

" Whilst conscious of myself, whilt spirit rules this frame." *

For at present, I will not deny it, joy overpowers my eloquence, and thought is hindered by pleasure, and my mind, engrossed with delight, is at present more inclined to exult than to extol. What shall I do? I wish to appear grateful, but joy will not leave me free to express gratitude. Let no one, let no one of those morose censors vituperate me because I do not less deserve than I appreciate this honour; because I exult in so great an honour conferred on me by a most illustrious and erudite man. A consular man, to whom it is a high honour to be merely known, has borne testimony for me in the equally illustrious and most benign senate of Carthage. He has also been in a manner my panegyrist before the chief men of Africa. For as I learn, in a memorial he sent in the day before yesterday, in which he asked for a frequented site for the erection of my statue, he mentioned in the first place the rights of friendship honestly cemented between us through our companionship in study under the same masters; and then he enumerated all my vows for his successive advancement in public honours. That is in itself a first kindness, that he records his having been my fellow-student. And this is another, that a man of his eminence declares that he is beloved reciprocally by me. Moreover, he has mentioned that statues and other honours have been decreed to me in other countries and cities. What can be added to these encomiums by a man of consular dignity? Nay, he proved from the priesthood I have taken upon me, that the highest honour in Carthage was before me. This is a capital service he has conferred on me, and far excelling the rest, that he, a most influential witness, commends me to you even by his own suffrage. Finally, he has promised that he will erect a statue to me in Carthage at his own expense, he to whom all provinces delight every where to erect equestrian statues, with chariots of four

* *Whilst conscious, &c.*]—A line from Virgil, Æneid, Book iv.

and of six horses. What more, then, is wanting to the base and summit of my honour, to the culmination of my glory? Nay, what more is there behind? Æmilianus Strabo, a consular man, soon by universal consent to be proconsul, pronounced his opinion concerning the honours to be paid to me in the senate of the Carthaginians: all followed his lead. Does not this seem to you tantamount to a decree of the senate? What? that all the Carthaginians who were present in that most august senate, so willingly appointed a place for my statue as to make it apparent, as I hope, that they only postponed to the next senate a motion for another statue to me, in order that, saving the veneration and reverence due to their consular member, they might seem not to have rivalled but followed his act: that is to say, that a public testimonial should be conferred on me on a fresh day. Moreover, those excellent magistrates and most obliging nobles remembered that what they desired was prescribed to them by you. Could I be ignorant of this? Should I fail to vaunt it? I should be ungrateful. Truly, I feel and profess the greatest possible thanks to your whole order for your exceeding kindness to me, you who have dignified me with the most flattering acclamations in that senate-house, in which to be named merely is the highest honour. So, then, what was hard to do, and what I thought truly arduous, to be pleasing to the people, acceptable to the order, and approved by the magistrates and chief men; this—fascination apart*—has some how befallen me. What, then, remains that I should enjoy the honour of a statue, but the price of the bronze and the pay of the artist? things which never failed me even in small cities, not to speak of Carthage, where the most illustrious order is wont rather to decree than to compute the cost even in greater affairs. But of these things I will speak more when you shall have done more. Also to you, noble senators, famous citizens, worthy friends, I will express my thanks more at large in the book I

---

* *Fascination apart.*] — *Præfiscine dixerim.* This was a common form of speech for averting the ill luck which was supposed to be imminent where a man was excessively praised by himself or others. This superstition still lingers in parts of the old Roman empire. In Corsica, for instance, an affectionate father, fondling his child, will call it ugly names, and bid it go be cursed—by way of cheating the devil, who is always on the watch to bring about the very reverse of what men desire.

will presently compose for the dedication of my statue; and I will incontinently bid that book go through all the provinces, and publish abroad the praises of your bounty throughout the whole world, in all time to come, among all nations, throughout all years.

XVII.

Let those who are in the habit of obtruding themselves upon the leisure moments of governors, consider how they promote the fame of their genius by the immoderate volubility of their tongue, and glorify themselves in a pretended appearance of your friendship. Both these faults are far alien from me, Scipio Orfitus. For whatever be my little genius, it is already in its degree too well known to the world to need new commendation; and I desire more than I boast of your good-will and that of men like you; since no one can desire a thing unless he thinks it really desirable; but any one may boast falsely. Moreover, I have always thus studiously applied myself to good morals from the outset of my life; and you yourself are a most sufficient witness that I have sought such a character as to my life and pursuits both in your province and in Rome with your friends; so that my friendship is not less worthy of your acceptance than yours of being sought by me. For not readily to forgive one who makes his visits scarce, argues a desire that one should come often; and it is a great proof of friendship to delight in the frequent presence of friends, to be angry with them when they stay away, to praise him who is constant in his attendance, to feel the loss of him who stays away; for it is certain that he must be liked whose absence gives pain. But a voice bound down to perpetual silence, would be of no more use than nostrils stuffed with rheum, ears closed by wind, eyes veiled by cataract. What if the hands be manacled? What if the feet be fettered? or our guide, the mind, be relaxed in sleep, or drowned in wine, or buried in disease? Truly as the sword is brightened by use, and rusts when laid by; so the voice sheathed in silence loses power by long torpor. Disuse makes every one slow, and sloth causes lethargy. Unless tragedians declaim daily, their throats lose clearness of voice; therefore they clear off their huskiness by vociferating again and again. In other respects it is lost labour to exercise the human voice, fo

it is surpassed in a great many ways, since the trumpet brays*
more grimly than the voice of man, the lyre is of more varied
compass, the flute more sweetly plaintive, the pipe warbles
more agreeably, and the horn is heard to a greater distance.
I say nothing of the inarticulate voices of many animals, which
are to be admired for distinct qualities: such as the deep
lowing of the bull, the shrill howl of the wolf, the melancholy
bray of the elephant, the cheerful neigh of the horse; then
there are the songs of excited birds, the angry roar of the lion,
and other voices of animals, both fierce and gentle, as they
are called forth by vehement rage or pleasure. Instead of
these, the gods have given man a voice of less volume, in-
deed; but it affords more of utility to the mind than of delight
to the ear. Wherefore it should be the more cultivated by
frequent use, and that nowhere else than in the public assem-
bly, under the presidency of so great a man, in this excellent
concourse of many learned, many gracious men. Certainly
though I were a first-rate performer on the lute, I would seek
only crowded audiences. In solitude

"Orpheus in woods, Arion harped mid dolphins."†

Now, if legends are to be believed, Orpheus was made a soli-
tary by exile, Arion was thrown overboard from a ship. The
one was a soother of savage beasts, the other was a delighter
of compassionate brutes; both were very unfortunate min-
strels, for they played not spontaneously for praise, but of ne-
cessity for safety. I would admire them more if they had
delighted men rather than brutes. Such sequestered places
were certainly better suited to birds, such as thrushes, night-
ingales, and swans. Thrushes sing in lonely spots; nightingales
warble their song of youth in the African desert; swans mo-
dulate their song of age in unfrequented streams. But whoso
has a song to sing that is good for youth, and adults, and
seniors, let him sing in the midst of thousands of men. Such
is this song of mine concerning the virtues of Orfitus; late,
perhaps, indeed, but serious; and not less pleasing than pro-
fitable to the youths, and adults, and seniors of the Cartha-
ginians, whom this worthiest of all proconsuls has relieved by

---

* *The trumpet brays.*]—The Delphin edition read *vox, tubâ, lyrâ,* &c.,
which are manifestly quite the reverse of the author's meaning.

† *Orpheus in woods, &c.*]—Virgil, Eclogue 8.

his indulgence; and has, by the moderation of his desires and his temperate treatment, given plenty to youth, joyfulness to adults, serenity to seniors. I fear, indeed, Scipio, since I have touched upon your praises, lest I be curbed at present either by your generous modesty or my ingenuous bashfulness. But I cannot forbear, out of very many things which are most deservedly admired in you, I cannot forbear from touching upon at least a very few of these very many. Citizens preserved by him, tell these over with me.

XVIII.

You have come in such a multitude to hear me, that I must rather congratulate Carthage that it counts in it so many friends of learning, than apologize because as a philosopher I have not refused to lecture. For the audience collected is proportioned to the greatness of the city, and the place selected is proportioned to the magnitude of the audience. Moreover, in an assembly of this sort, what is to be considered is not the marble of the floor, nor the painting of the proscenium, nor the columns of the stage; nor yet the height of the roof, nor the brilliancy of the cornices, nor the extent of the benches; nor that here at other times the mime foots it, the comedian speaks, the tragedian declaims, the rope-dancer incurs danger, the juggler filches, the pantomimist gesticulates, and all the other players exhibit their several performances to the people; but setting aside all these things, nothing else ought to be considered but the understanding of the audience and the language of the speaker. Wherefore, as the poets are wont to represent various cities on this spot, like that tragic writer who makes the player say in the theatre,

" Bacchus, who in this grand Cithæron dwellest ;"

or that comic writer,* who says—

" Of all your pleasant city's ample space,
How small the part which Plautus asks, whereon
He may place Athens without architects ;"

in like manner let it be allowed me, too, to set here before you no distant or transmarine city, but the very senate-house, the very library of Carthage itself. Therefore, if I utter words

* *That comic writer.*]—Plautus, prologue to Truculentus.

worthy of the senate, think of them as though you heard me in the senate itself; if the things I deliver are learned, accept them as though they were read in the library.   I would that I had ready a long oration corresponding to the magnitude of my audience, and that my speech did not halt here where I should wish to be most eloquent.   But the common saying is a true one: "Nothing has been granted to man by the gods so fortunate but that some difficulty is nevertheless attached to it;" so that in every greatest delight there lurks at least some little grievance, by a certain combination of honey and gall.   Where there is a breast of milk there is a tuberosity. This I have experienced at other times, and now especially, for the more suffrages I seem to have among you in my favour, the more timid I am in addressing you, from the exceeding respect I bear you.   I, who many a time disputed with the greatest readiness among foreigners, now hesitate among my own countrymen, and, strange to say, I am deterred by what should allure, curbed by what should spur me, restrained by what should incite me.   Have I not many encouragements among you, I who am neither alien to you by birth, nor unseen by you in boyhood, who have had masters among you, whose sect is not unknown to you, whose voice has not been unheard, nor my books unread or disapproved by you?   Thus, my country is within the bounds of Africa, my boyhood has been spent among you, and you were my masters; and my philosophy, though confirmed in Attic Athens, was begun here; and my voice has been for more than six years familiar to your ears in both languages.   My books, too, nowhere receive a higher honour than that they are approved by your judgment.   These great and manifold common inducements no less invite you to hear than they check me from haranguing; and I could more easily celebrate your praises anywhere else than among yourselves: thus, a man's modesty stands in his way among his own people, but before foreigners truth is free.   Accordingly, I extol you always and every where as my parents and first masters, and I pay you your due remuneration: not that which Protagoras, the sophist, bargained for and did not receive, but that which Thales the wise did not bargain for, but received.   I see what you desire.   I will tell both stories.

Protagoras was a sophist of very varied knowledge, and extremely eloquent, as being one of the first inventors of rhetoric. He was the fellow-citizen and contemporary of Democritus, the physical philosopher, from whom he derived his knowledge. They say that this Protagoras stipulated with his disciple, Euathlus, for an inordinate payment upon a whimsical condition, namely, that he should pay him the stated sum if he was successful in the first cause he pleaded before the judges, and not otherwise. Euathlus, then, who was of a shrewd and cunning turn of mind, having easily learned all the artifices for softening judges and deceiving adversaries, and all the tricks of pleaders, and knowing to his full content what he had desired, began to be unwilling to pay what he had promised, and to cheat his teacher with cunningly-devised excuses, and for a long time would neither refuse outright nor pay. At last, Protagoras summoned him before the judges, and stating the condition on which he had undertaken to teach him, propounded this dilemma:—"If I gain the cause, you will have to pay the price as cast in judgment; or, if you gain, you will nevertheless have to pay, as bound by your bargain. Thus, if you beat me, you fall under the force of the condition; if you are beaten, you will lie under the decree of the court. What more would you have?" The conclusion appeared to the judges to be cogently and unanswerably made out. But Euathlus, as a most finished disciple of so subtle a teacher, turned his own dilemma against him. "If the thing is so," said he, "in neither way do I owe what you demand. For either I gain the cause, and am cleared by the decree of the court, or I am beaten, and then I am discharged by our bargain, according to which, I owe you no payment if I shall have been beaten in this first cause I plead before the judges. Thus, I am acquitted in every way; by the verdict if I beat you, by our condition if I am beaten."

Do not these sophisms, turned against each other, seem to you like burs rolled together by the wind, which stick each other alike by their prickles? Let us leave then this thorny pay of Protagoras to the crafty and the avaricious; far better is that other pay which Thales is said to have demanded. Thales, the Milesian, was decidedly the foremost of the celebrated seven wise men: for he was the first discoverer of geometry among the Greeks, a sure explorer of nature, and a skilful observer of the stars; by means of small lines he discovered vast things, the circuits of the seasons, the courses of the winds, the paths of the stars, the sonorous marvels of the thunder, the oblique courses of the constellations, the annual revolution of the sun; likewise, the increase of the new moon, the waning of the old, and the obstacles that cause her light to fail. He also, when advanced in years, excogitated a divine theory, respecting the sun, which I have not only learned but confirmed by experience, namely, by what multiple of its diameter the sun measures its own orbit. Thales is related to have demonstrated this recent discovery of his, to Mandraytus the Prienensian, who being intensely delighted with that new and unexpected observation, bade him name whatever reward he desired for so great a communication. "I shall be sufficiently paid," said Thales the Wise, "if, when you have begun to unfold to others what you have learned from me, you do not attribute it to yourself, but declare that it was I, and no one else, who discovered it." A handsome payment truly, worthy of such a man, and perpetual! For at this day, and in all time to come, that tribute will be paid to Thales by all of us who are truly acquainted with his celestial studies. This is the kind of payment I everywhere make on your account, Carthaginians, for the education I received among you in my boyhood, For I everywhere declare myself a nursling of your city; everywhere I extol you in all manner of ways; I diligently cultivate your literature; I boast of your wealth; and I religiously venerate your gods.

Now, too, I will take for the most auspicious subject of my exordium, your god, Æsculapius, who propitiously regards your citadel of Carthage with his indubitable divinity. I will here sing to you a hymn in honour of that god, which I have composed in Greek and Latin. For I am his not unknown priest, nor recent worshipper, nor unfavoured minister; and I have already paid him reverence in prose and verse, in like manner as I shall now sing his hymn in both languages. I have prefaced it with a dialogue likewise in Greek and Latin, the speakers being Sabidius Severus and Julius Persius, men who, with good reason, are the warmest friends to each other, and to you, and to the public weal, and are equals in learning, eloquence, and good feeling; and of whom it is a question whether they are more distinguished by their placid moderation, their prompt ingenuity, or their eminent honours. Thoroughly at concord as they are, there is yet between them this sole emulation, this sole contest, which of them more loves Carthage, and on this point they both contend with all their might, but neither yields the victory. Thinking that a discourse between them would be most pleasing to you, a congenial subject of composition to me, and worthy of being dedicated to the service of religion, I introduce in the beginning of my work, one of my fellow students at Athens inquiring of Persius, in Greek, what I had delivered the day before in the temple of Æsculapius; and presently I add to them Severus, whom meanwhile I have made speak Latin. For though Persius is perfectly acquainted with Latin, he will to-day speak for you and me in the Attic tongue.

XIX.

Asclepiades, one of the first of physicians, and superior to all, Hippocrates alone excepted, was the first who used wine as a remedy for the sick; but with this precaution, that he gave it in good time, a point which he was very sagacious in determining, being a most diligent observer of the inordinate or depraved pulsation of the arteries. Once, when he returned to the city from his country house, he saw a great funeral pile in the outskirts of the town, and around it a vast multitude, who had followed the funeral, all in great grief and soiled garments. He went up to the spot, as is the nature of the human mind, that he might know who it was, since no one answered his enquiries. Or, rather, he went that he might notice something in the deceased by means of his art. At all events, he took away death from that man who was stretched on the bier and nearly consigned to the tomb. The unfortunate man's body was already all bedewed with perfumes, and his face was anointed with odorous ointment. Having carefully contemplated the man thus anointed and made ready for the funeral banquet, he noticed in him certain signs, handled the body again and again, and found life latent in it. Instantly he cried out that the man was alive, that they should take away the torches, put out the fire, pull down the pile, and carry back the funeral banquet from the tomb to the table. Meanwhile, a murmur arose, some saying that the physician should be believed, others making a mock of medicine. Finally, against the will of all the relations, whether it was that they were disappointed of the inheritance, or that they did not

believe him, Asclepiades, with great difficulty, obtained a brief
respite for the defunct, and so, in the end, he took him back
to his house, snatched from the hands of the undertakers, and
as it were from the infernal regions, and immediately revived
his spirits, and called forth, by some medicine, the vital breath
that was lurking in the recesses of his body.

XX.

There is a celebrated saying of a wise man concerning the
table. The first cup is for thirst, the second for mirth, the
third for delight, the fourth for madness. The goblet of the
Muses, on the contrary, the oftener it is drained and the more
unmixed it is, the more it conduces to soundness of mind.
The first cup, that of the reading master, takes away igno-
rance; the second, of the grammarian, instructs in science;
the third, the rhetorician's, arms with eloquence. Thus far
most people drink. But I have drunk other cups at Athens;
the cup of poetry, the inventive; of geometry, the limpid;
of music, the sweet; of dialectics, the roughish; and of uni-
versal philosophy, the never-satiating nectareous cup. For
Empedocles gives us verses; Plato, dialogues; Socrates,
hymns; Epicharmus, modulations; Xenophon, histories;
Xenocrates, satires: your Apuleius all these together; and he
has cultivated the nine Muses with equal assiduity, that is to
say, with more good-will than capacity. Perhaps he is the
more to be praised for this, since in all good things the at-
tempt is laudable, the effect contingent; whilst, conversely in
evil things, crimes that are but designed, not accomplished,
are punished; the mind being blood-stained, the hands pure.
Therefore, just as it suffices for the incurring of punishment
to have meditated things that deserve punishment, so it is a
sufficient cause of praise to attempt laudable things. But
what greater or surer source of praise is there than to speak
well at Carthage, where all your citizens are most learned:
among whom, boys learn all they know, adults exhibit it, and
old men teach it? Carthage, the venerable mistress of our
province; Carthage, the celestial Muse of Africa; Carthage,
the Camœna of those who wear the toga.

XXI.

Even necessary haste sometimes admits of proper delay, so

that you may often be pleased at the interruption of your pur-
pose. So it is with those who have occasion to travel fast, so
that they would rather ride on horseback than sit in a car, on
account of the annoyance of baggage, the weight of vehicles,
the clogging of wheels, the roughness of the track, the heaps
of stones, the projecting roots of trees, the streams on the
plain, and the declivities of hills. Wishing, then, to avoid all
these retardations, they select a riding-horse of enduring powers
and lively speed, strong to bear and a good goer,

> " That sweeps at equal pace o'er hill and dale,"

as Lucilius says. Then, when they are riding at the horse's
speed along the way, if they espy any man of high station, of
great influence, and well known, in spite of their haste they
check their speed and stop their horse; they jump down, and
pass the rod they carry for beating the horse into their left hand.
With their right hand thus at liberty, they go up and salute
him; and if he asks questions at some length, they walk for
some time, and chat with him. In short, they willingly sub-
mit to any delay, as a matter of courtesy.

XXII.

As we see a good ship, well built, stoutly put together
within, elegantly painted without, having a helm that moves
freely, strong rigging, a tall mast, a fine mast top, shining sails,
and, in short, found in everything requisite for use, and fair to
see; but if the helmsman does not steer that ship, either it is
driven before the tempest, or the deeps engulf, or the rocks
shatter it with all its excellent gear. Again, when physicians
enter a house to visit a sick man, none of them ever bids the
patient be of good cheer, because they see in the house hand-
some bookcases, gilded cornices, and crowds of boys and youths
of comely form waiting in the chamber round the bed. But
when the physician has sat down by the patient, he takes his
hand, feels it, notes the pulse and the force of the arteries, and
if he find anything disturbed and inordinate there, he tells the
man that his case is a bad one. That wealthy patient is for-
bidden food, and that day he gets no food in his opulent house,
though, meanwhile, all his domestics feast and make good cheer
In that respect his fortune avails him nothing.

XXIII.

You who wished me to speak extempore, hear now a rude attempt after a finished specimen. For, as I think, I shall venture with a fair chance, when I am to speak improviso, after having made premeditated speeches which have been approved; nor am I afraid that I shall displease in trivial things, since I have given satisfaction in more serious matters. But that you may test and know me in every way, try me in this rough and unfinished sketch, as Lucilius says, whether I am the same on a sudden as when prepared; if, indeed, there are any among you who have not heard any of these off-hand efforts of mine, which you will listen to with the same attention as you hearken to those discourses which we write and recite, and with more indulgence. For so it is usual with wise men to exercise more accurate judgment with elaborate works, and more indulgence towards those that are unprepared. For you weigh and examine what is written, and you hear at once impromptu discourses, and pardon what is amiss in them, and with good reason. For those things which we recite when written, will be such as they were composed, even though you be silent; but those which are to be produced on the spot, and, as it were, in combination with you, will be such as you shall have made them by your favour. The more I sink in my discourse, the more it will be lifted up by you. I perceive that you hear me willingly. So it is in your power to spread my sail, and inflate it, that it may not hang flaccid, or be furled and brailed. Now, I will venture to do that which Aristippus said. That Aristippus was the founder of the Cyrenaic sect, and what he himself most desired, a disciple of Socrates. A certain tyrant asked him, What good had he got by his intent and long-continued pursuit of philosophy? "To be able to speak at my ease and intrepidly with all men," replied Aristippus. This saying was impromptu, for the occasion was sudden; just as in rubble masonry it is necessary that stones should be laid down as they come to hand, no grouting being interposed within, nor their position made even in front, nor their faces arranged by line. I, myself, the builder of this oration, will not bring to it from my quarry a stone cut fair, well squared, and accurately smoothed on all its faces; but I will fit to every part of the work rough and uneven stones, or smooth and slippery, or round and rolling, without correcting them by the rule, or equalizing them on measuring, or adjusting them by the plumb-line. For nothing can be at the same time hurried and deliberate; nor can anything possess at once the merit of elaboration and the grace of despatch. I have yielded to the wish of some who greatly desired that I should speak extempore what was expected of me; and, by Hercules! there is some fear lest that befal me which is narrated by Æsop of his crow: that is, that whilst I catch at this new glory, I shall lose that little glory which I have already acquired. If you call upon me for the apologue, I shall have no objection to deliver a fable.

A Crow and a Fox simultaneously espied a gobbet, and hastened to seize it with equal greed but unequal speed—the Fox running, the Crow flying. The bird outstripped the beast, gliding before him with both wings outspread to the favouring gale; and then exulting at once in the booty and the victory, soared aloft, and perched securely on the top of an oak. Nevertheless, even there the Fox hit the victor with a trick, because he could not hit him with a stone; for he went up to the same tree, and stopping when he saw the spoiler aloft, exulting over his booty, began cunningly to flatter him. "Truly I was foolish to contend in vain with the bird of Apollo, whose body is so elegant, neither very small, nor too large, but just of the size sufficient for use and beauty, with soft plumage, a delicate head, and strong beak. It is a bird of keen eye and tenacious talons. But what shall I say of its colour? For, whereas two colours were superior to all others, black and white, which mark the difference between day and night, Apollo bestowed both on his birds—white on the swan, black on the crow. I wish that, as he granted song to the swan, he had also given voice to this bird, that so beautiful a bird, far the first of the whole feathered creation, the pet of the eloquent god, might not live mute and tongueless." When the Crow heard that this alone was wanting to him that he should surpass the rest of the birds, he resolved to croak as loud as he could, to show that in that respect he was not inferior to the swan; and forgetting the gobbet he held in his beak, he opened it as wide as he could gape; and thus he lost by his song what he had won by his flight; but the Fox recovered by his craft what he had lost in running.

Let us epitomise this fable as compactly as possible. The Crow, to prove itself a vocalist, the only thing which the Fox had pretended was wanting to its great beauty, began to croak, and made the wheedling Fox possessor of the booty it held in its beak.

XXIV

I know well what you desire by this token, namely, that I should proceed with the rest of the Latin matter. For in the beginning, when you asked for different things, I remember to have promised that neither portion of you, neither those who called for Latin nor those who called for Greek, should go away disappointed. Wherefore, if you please, let us conclude that I have talked Greek long enough. It is now time to migrate from Greece to Latium. For we have now come nearly to the middle of this discourse; and, as I think, this latter part, compared with the Greek portion which preceded it, is neither less copious in arguments, nor less abundant in maxims, nor more scant of examples, nor more brief in matter.

END OF THE FLORIDA.

CUPID AND PSYCHE

A MYTHOLOGICAL TALE,

FROM THE

GOLDEN ASS OF APULEIUS.

RENDERED INTO ENGLISH VERSE.

———

I.

O STAY those tears ! the beldam cries,
   Ill dreams good fortunes oft forerun,
Like clouds which skirt the morning skies,
   But melt before the noon-day sun.

Chase from thy soul this idle grief,
   And let my words thine ear engage ;
Thy fears perchance may find relief,
   E'en from the garrulous tales of age.

II.

Once stately reign'd a king and queen,
   As bards of other times have told,
The happiest that were ever seen
   To flourish in the days of old.

Three daughters bless'd their nuptial bed·
   Two daughters exquisitely fair,
Who many a fond youth captive led,
   Made many a hapless youth despair.

The youngest—but no tongue so warm,
   Though matchless eloquence be given,
May dare pourtray her finish'd form,
   The 'prodigality of heaven !'

Say, to delight the wondering earth,
　Does she amongst us mortals roam,
Who from the blue deep took her birth,
　Her nurture from the sparkling foam?

O'er her warm cheek's vermilion dye,
　Waves, lightly waves, her dark-brown hair;
Bright as the winter star her eye,
　Yet peaceful as the summer air.

No one to Paphos take his way,
　Cnidos, Cythera, charm no more;
No throngs, with votive chaplets gay,
　The *immortal* VENUS now adore.

Her temples all in ruin lie,
　Her altars cold, to dust resign'd,
Her withering garlands flap and fly,
　And rustle in the hollow wind.

Whilst on the mortal maid they shower
　The incense they to *her* should bring,
And offer to this fairer flower
　The fairest flow'rets of the spring.

From isles afar, from distant lands,
　Unnumber'd votaries press around,
And view entranc'd, with folded hands,
　Celestial footsteps print the ground.

To her young girls their wishes breathe,
　Commend the fond youth to her care;
Bind round her brows the rosy wreath,
　And sigh to her the ardent prayer.

III.

Parent of nature, nurse of joy,
　From whom the elements arise;
Thou to whom Ida's shepherd boy
　Rightly adjudg'd the golden prize,

O VENUS! will thy better part,
 Immortal love, incline to spare;
Or female envy taint thy heart,
 And plant the Fiend of Vengeance there?

VENUS has called her winged child,
 And with malignant pleasure laugh'd,
That boy who lawless, wicked wild,
 At random aims the flaming shaft;

Him, who all deeds of darkness owns,
 Who breaks so oft the nuptial tie,
And, whilst his luckless victim groans,
 On careless pinions flutters by.—

The dangerous Power to PSYCHE's bower
 She with vindictive fury led,
And bade him thus his vengeance shower
 On the detested virgin's head :—

  " By a mother's sacred name,
   By thine arrows tipp'd with flame,
   By thy joys which often borrow
   Of despair most bitter sorrow,
   Make thy parent's rival know
   Unimaginable woe!
   May her youth's unequall'd bloom
   Unrequited love consume,
   For some wretch of abject birth,
   Wandering outcast of the earth;
   Be for him her fond heart torn,
   May e'en he her torments scorn,
   That all womankind may see
   What it is to injure me.
   Make thy parent's rival know
   Unimaginable woe!"

Then kiss'd her son, and fleet as wind
 She seeks old Ocean's dark-green caves—
Her ivory feet with roses twin'd,
 Brush lightly o'er the trembling waves.

IV.

Young PSYCHE still more beauteous grows,
   She seems unconscious of her charms;
Yet no one plucks this opening rose,
   She takes no suitor to her arms.

Each sister shines a regal bride,
   In sweet connubial union blest;
Each moves conspicuous in the pride
   Of scepter'd state and ermin'd vest.

But PSYCHE owns no lawful lord,
   She walks a goddess from above;
All saw, all prais'd, and all ador'd,
   But no one ever dar'd to love.

Yet half-form'd wishes still will ply
   With feverish dreams the unpractis'd mind,
When ' the clos'd eye, unknowing why,'
   Its wonted slumbers fails to find.

Though the blank heart no passion owns,
   Some soft ideas will intrude,
And the sick girl in silence moans
   Her dull unvaried solitude!

V.

Her father sees his darling's grief,
   Suspects the jealous wrath of heaven,
Hopes from the Oracle relief,
   And asks the fate the Gods had given.

     " On the mountain summit laid
      In her grave-clothes be the maid.
      Never shall thine eyes behold
      Son-in-law of mortal mould;
      But a monster girt with wings,
      Fiercest of created things,
      Scattering flames his hours employing,
      Heaven alike and earth annoying:
      Him the dread decrees of fate
      Destine for thy daughter's mate."

Graceful his silver tresses flow—
   He does not rend his hoary hair,
He utters not the shriek of woe,
   Nor vents the curses of despair;

He does not wring his aged hands,
   No tear-drop fills his frozen eye;
But as a statue fix'd he stands
   In speechless, senseless agony!

VI.

'Tis hard to force its better part
   From the distracted soul away;
But heaven decrees—man's bursting heart
   In vain repines—he must obey!

Now rose the inauspicious morn,
   Mantling in clouds the low'ring skies,
When from her parents must be torn
   The victim of the Destinies.

Loud wailings fill the troubled air,
   Cold tremors every heart assail,
And the low murmurs of despair
   Ride sullen on the hollow gale.

Onward the sad procession goes:
   Do wedding guests then creep so slow?
Say, is it from the bridemaid flows
   The long and sable stole of woe?

And who are they, who, rob'd in white,
   Their black funereal torches wave,
Which shed around such pale blue light
   As issues from the dead man's grave?

They are the bridal train—yet mark,
   They carol loud with tuneful breath:
'Tis not the song of marriage—hark!
   They slowly chant the dirge of Death.

The mountain's utmost height they gain,
    They pour the agonizing prayer;
For soon the melancholy train
    Must leave the sad devoted fair.

Yet PSYCHE chides the tears that fall,
    E'en in her shroud o'ermasters fear,
Wraps round her beauteous limbs the pall,
    And dauntless mounts the bridal bier.

VII.

O SLEEP! sweet friend of human kind,
    Whose magic chains all joy to wear,
Who, soother of the afflicted mind,
    Strew'st roses on the bed of care;

'Twas thou, o'er PSYCHE's fluttering soul,
    Benignly shedd'st thine opiate charms;
Spell-bound she own'd thy mild control,
    Soft cradled in thy downy arms:

Till wafted on young ZEPHYR's wings
    To a fair vale's sequester'd bowers;
Who the unconscious maiden brings,
    And lays her on a couch of flowers.

VIII.

She wakes—and to her glad survey
    Rise round her, high o'erarching trees,
Whose branches gemm'd with blossoms gay,
    Throw perfumes to the lingering breeze.

And, shaded from the noon-tide beam,
    There slowly, slowly curling roll'd
Its silvery waves a lucent stream
    O'er sands of granulated gold.

And in the centre of the wood,
    Not such as kings inhabit here,
A vast and tower-flank'd palace stood,
    Nor such as mortal hands could rear.

Of ivory was the fretted roof,
 On golden columns proudly rais'd,
And silver carvings massy proof
 The walls of ebony emblaz'd.

Round lustres wreaths of diamonds fix'd,
 Their prismy rays profusely pour,
And amethysts with emeralds mix'd
 Inlay the tesselated floor.

While thus the startled stranger greet,
 Within no earthly form confin'd,
Voices, as distant music sweet,
 That floats upon the evening wind:

  " Lull to rest this causeless fear;
  Psyche ! thou art mistress here.
  Happy beyond human measure,
  Slake thy thirsting soul in pleasure ;
  Slaves to thy majestic lover,
  Air-form'd sprites around thee hover,
  Ever for thy bidding stay,
  Instant thy commands obey."

—And ere the lingering word is said,
 Quick as the lightning glance of thought,
With sumptuous fare the banquet's spread,
 By her aërial servants brought.

And flute, and harp, and voice, to fill
 The choral harmony unite,
And make each raptur'd nerve to thrill
 And vibrate with intense delight.

Swiftly the happy hours are fled !
 For night invites her to repose,
And on the silk-embroider'd bed
 Her wearied frame the virgin throws.

Now Darkness o'er the silent sphere
 Her raven-tinctur'd reign assumes—
She stops her breath, she chills to hear
 The rustling sound of waving plumes.

All hush'd around—no friend beside—
    Her heart beats high with new alarms !
—The dreaded husband claims his bride,
    And folds her in his eager arms!

Yet while thick shades are o'er them spread,
    (How hard that lovely couch to scorn !)
Soft gliding from the nuptial bed,
    He flies before the golden morn.

While viewless harps incessant ring
    To greet her on her bridal day,
And viewless minstrels gaily sing
    The Hymeneal roundelay.

And aye when Eve in grateful hour
    Sheds odours from her dewy wings,
The UNKNOWN seeks his mystic bower,
    And to the expectant fair-one springs:

In frantic passion's giddy whirl
    Past, quickly past, his transient stay,
He still eludes the curious girl,
    And steals unseen, unfelt, away;

Ere from the bosom of the Night
    Young Twilight scents the matin air,
And in her gray vest rises light
    Spangled with gems her musky air.

IX.

Though circling o'er, the laughing hours
    In still-increasing raptures roll'd,
Oft gleams the path besprent with flowers
    With tints too clear, too bright to hold !

Thus speaks the INVISIBLE, and sighs,
    And clasps her in his warm embrace,
While the large tear-drops from his eyes
    Fall frequent on her burning face:

" Life of my beating heart ! o'er thee
    Impending danger scowls : beware !
With anxious soul I shuddering see
   The cruel fates their lures prepare.

Soon shall thy sisters seek thee near,
   With loud lament and piercing wail,
And thou each well-known voice shalt hear
   Borne fitful on the moaning gale.

Then, though thy very soul will yearn
   To bid thy messengers convey
The wish'd-for visitants; O turn !
   Turn from their plaints thine ear away.

If nature's feelings conquer still,
   And thou must wayward tempt thy fate,
Thou know'st, obedient to thy will,
   What mystic menials round thee wait.

Yet, as thou'dst shun eternal bale,
   Or never-ceasing misery dread,
Our dark mysterious union veil
   In the deep silence of the dead.

For these the truths the Fates unfold :
   We in these bowers may ever dwell,
If mortal eye shall ne'er behold
   This form, nor tongue my secrets tell.

While from our glad embrace will rise,
   Pure from all taint of earthly leaven,
An infant inmate of the skies,
   The fairest of the host of heaven.

Then spare thyself, thy husband spare,
   And spare thy child, as yet unborn ;
Dash not the dark clouds of despair
   Upon the ruddy hues of morn."

X.

Gaily we launch our little bark,
　The sun-beams on the waters play,
While close behind the ravenous shark
　Expecting waits his destin'd prey.

We sail along the whirlpool's brink,
　Unheeding join the song of glee,
But ah! too late aghast we shrink,
　When whelm'd beneath the treacherous sea

PSYCHE has heard the warning strain—
　Resistless wishes restless spring,
She slights the strain, and bids her train
　Of swift-wing'd sprites her sisters bring.

Her childhood's friends she joys to meet,
　No shade of danger here can find:
Though mingled in communion sweet,
　They cannot sound the viewless mind.

Lock'd in her ever-faithful breast,
　Her secret all discovery braves,
Safe as the orient pearl, will rest,
　Beneath unfathomable waves.

"And who is he whose natal star
　With such unrivall'd splendour shines,
Whose countless stores exceed so far
　All India's inexhausted mines?"

"O! 'tis a youth whose ruddy cheek
　Vies with the morn's vermilion dye,
Or emulates the clouds that streak
　With crimson tints the evening sky.

And mantled he in lively green
　Up the high mountain joys to go,
Or in the wild-wood chace is seen
　The foremost with his silver bow."

Homeward the sisters now return,
  Their bosoms charg'd with deadly hate,
And with excessive envy burn,
  And curse their own inferior fate.

XI.

Exulting Psyche bids again
  The obedient sprites her sisters bear;
Borne by the ministering train,
  Again arrive the baleful pair.

" And who is he whose natal star
  With such unrivall'd splendour shines,
Whose countless stores exceed so far
  All India's inexhausted mines ? "

" O ! he is one unbroke by care,
  The rose of beauty lingers yet,
Though here and there a hoary hair
  Gleams silvery 'midst his locks of jet."

" Cease, cease those fables," swift replied
  One sister with unfeeling scorn,
And " Cease thy tales," the other cried,
  " Nor strive to hide thy state forlorn."

" Still ever erring from the truth,
  Thy childish tongue deceitful ran—
Thy husband neither glows with youth,
  Nor the gray honours boasts of man;

He wears no human form—we know
  Unerring are the words of heaven;
And of all human kind the foe
  Thee for a mate the Gods have given.

We know him well—then wherefore hide
  From thy dear sisters' love thy care,
Nor to our kindred breasts confide
  The ills that thou art doom'd to bear ? "

Then as they wipe the artful tear,
  Loud on the pitying Gods they call,
Till sooth'd by love, or urg'd by fear,
  The trembling PSYCHE tells them all.

" We knew it well—nay, do not start,"
  The base malignant fury cried,
" We know, unhappy girl! thou art
  A vast and venom'd serpent's bride.

We learnt it from the neighbouring hinds,
  Who every night his form survey,
As through yon crystal stream he winds
  In slimy folds his sinuous way.

Or as at day-break he along
  In many a spiral volume trails.
And vibrates quick his forky tongue,
  And glitters in his burnish'd scales.

Yes! though with heaven's own transports warm
  Thy soul in boundless rapture swims,
Soon, coil'd around thy slender form,
  He'll writhing crush thy mangled limbs!"

Thus the hyæna speaks and weeps—
  Cold damps on PSYCHE's forehead start,
Her tingling flesh with horror creeps,
  The life-blood curdling in her heart.

All ghastly pale her beauteous cheek,
  She throws her moonstruck gaze around,
Utters a feeble, faultering shriek,
  And senseless sinks upon the ground.

Then as some parch'd and withering flower
  Reviving sucks the evening dew,
To bide the insufferable power
  Of the meridian sun anew;

So, when the UNKNOWN's distracted wife
  Recovers her unwelcome breath,
She only hails returning life
  To shudder at approaching death.

XII.

The sisters still their schemes pursue,
   Their vengeance ripens in the bud,
And thus they urge her to embrue
   Her weak and innocent hands in blood.

" Cut thou the knot the Fates have tied,
   Nor let dismay thine efforts damp,
But in the figur'd tapestry hide,
   To guide thy stroke, this faithful lamp.

And take this dagger keen and bright,
   And when his eyes are clos'd in rest,
Directed by the friendly light,
   Deep plunge it in the monster's breast."

Thou who in love's soft dreams hast felt,
   Whilst envying Gods were hovering near,
Thy soul in sweet delirium melt,
   Say, canst thou slay thy lover dear?

And canst thou spread thy murderous toils
   For him thy soul's best joy of late;
Ah me! her sickening heart recoils,
   Disgusted from her viperous mate.

XIII.

Her mantle o'er them Darkness throws,
   On the UNKNOWN soft languors creep,
Who leaves his false one to repose,
   And sinks into the arms of sleep.

Now trembling, now distracted; bold,
   And now irresolute she seems;
The blue lamp glimmers in her hold,
   And in her hand the dagger gleams.

Prepar'd to strike she verges near,
   The blue light glimmering from above,
The HIDEOUS SIGHT expects with fear,
   —And gazes on the GOD OF LOVE!

Not such a young and frolic child
    As poets feign, or sculptors plan ;
No, no, she sees with transport wild,
    Eternal beauty veil'd in man.

His cheeks ingrain'd carnation glow'd
    Like rubies on a bed of pearls,
And down his ivory shoulders flow'd
    In clustering braids his golden curls.

Soft as the cygnet's down his wings ;
    And as the falling snow-flake fair,
Each light elastic feather springs,
    And dances in the balmy air.

The pure and vital stream he breathes,
    Makes e'en the lamp shine doubly bright,
Which its gay flame enamoured wreathes,
    And gleams with scintillating light.

There loosely strung that bow was hung,
    Whose twanging cord Immortals fear,
And on the floor his quiver flung,
    Lay, stor'd with many an arrow, near.

Grasp'd in her sacrilegious hands,
    She with the arrows play'd, and laugh'd—
The crimson on her fingers stands,
    She's wounded by the poison'd shaft !

The red blood riots in her veins,
    Her feverish pulses wildly beat,
Whilst every waken'd fibre strains
    And throbs with palpitating heat.

With eyes, where sparkling rapture swims,
    She contemplates his sleeping grace,
Hangs fondly o'er his well-turn'd limbs,
    And joins to his her fervid face.

But as her views intent to foil,
    Or as that form it long'd to kiss,
Dropt from the lamp the burning oil,
    Arous'd him from his dreams of bliss.

Sudden loud thunders shake the skies,
   The enchanted palace sinks around,
And sanguine-streaming fires arise,
   Meteorous from the trembling ground.

And swift as when in fury hurls
   Jove's red right arm the forky light,
The wounded Godhead eddying whirls
   Into the heaven of heavens his flight.

XIV.

In vapoury twilight damp and chill,
   The languid star fades pale away,
The high peak of the distant hill
   Is gilded by the gleams of day.

And who is that distracted fair
   Reclin'd beneath yon spreading yew?
Swoln are her eyes, her dark-brown hair
   Is pearly with the morning dew.

Her spring of life now seems to flag,
   In wild delirium now she raves—
O, see! from that o'erjutting crag
   She plunges in the foaming waves!

But he who o'er the stream presides
   The frantic girl in pity bore,
Quick darting through his billowy tides,
   In safety to the opposing shore.

There in a bower with wood-moss lin'd,
   With violets blue, and cowslips gay,
Old Pan, by Canna's side reclin'd,
   Sung many a rustic roundelay.

While wandering from his heedless eyes,
   His white goats cropt the neighbouring brake,
The God in this unfashioned guise
   With no ungentle feelings spake:

" Sweet girl ! though rural is the air
 That I the king of shepherds wear,
As assay'd silver, tried, and sage,
And prudent are the words of age.
Then list, O list, sweet girl, to me !
By my divining power I see,
Both from thy often-reeling pace,
And from thy pale and haggard face,
And from thy deep and frequent sigh,
While grief hangs heavy on thine eye,
That all the ills thou art doom'd to prove,
Are judgments of the GOD of LOVE.—
Then list, O list, sweet girl, to me,
Seek not by death thy soul to free,
But cast thy cares, thy griefs away,
To CUPID without ceasing pray,
And soon that soft luxurious boy
Will tune anew thy mind to joy."

XV.

The shipman seeks his native vales,
 He's come afar from o'er the sea,
He longs to tell his wond'rous tales
 Of dangers on the stormy lee.

He'll tell the wonder-stirring tales
 To those dear friends he left behind.—
Ah me ! within his native vales
 His sickening soul no friend can find.

Thus PSYCHE to one sister goes,
 That sister's vital spark is fled :
To meet the other next she rose,
 But she is number'd with the dead.

And she will seek her father's state,
 And there her parents' blessings crave—
Press'd by the heavy hand of fate,
 They too rest peaceful in the grave !

XVI.

And now the milk-white Albatross,
  To VENUS who in Ocean laves
Circled with Sea-nymphs, scuds across
  On oary wings the rippling waves.

"Great queen," the feather'd chatterer said,
  "Know'st thou not what thy hopeful son,
Enamour'd of a worthless maid,
  Has in his amorous folly done?

No Nymph, no Muse thy boy adores,
  No Grace, no Goddess is his flame,
His love he on a mortal pours,
  And PSYCHE is the damsel's name.

And groaning now within thy fane,
  In anguish penitent lies he,
For he too late has felt the bane
  Of female curiosity."

VENUS then calls her doves, and soon
  With quick step mounts her golden car,
Arch'd inwards like the waning moon,
  And brilliant as the morning star.

Around her sparrows chirping play,
  Exulting strain their little throats,
And all the warblers of the spray
  Pour sweetly their mellifluous notes.

She cuts the clouds, she skims the heaven,
  Till, reach'd the palace of the sky,
Her fanciful behest is given
  To the wing'd herald MERCURY.

"Take thou this volume in thy hand,
  With PSYCHE's history mark'd, and name,
And thus in every clime and land,
  And every state aloud proclaim—

If any man shall seize and bring
    The flying daughter of a king,
Handmaid of VENUS, or will tell
    Where PSYCHE now conceal'd may dwell,

Let him to Murtia straight repair,
Make the much wish'd discovery there,
And CYTHEREA, queen of charms,
    Sole sovereign of extatic blisses,
Will clasp him in her grateful arms,
    And greet him with seven fervid kisses!"

XVII.

Now four long tedious moons are spent,
    She hears no tidings of her lord,
Yet still her wandering steps are bent
    In search of him her soul ador'd.

She pray'd at CERES' corn-wreath'd shrine,
    And JUNO's altar deck'd with flowers;
But sternly bound by pact divine,
    No succour lend the pitying Powers.

Till wearied with unnumber'd woes,
    And render'd valiant by despair,
She to the Murtian temple goes—
    Perchance her true love tarries there.

O, turn thee from the perilous way!
    Ah! wherefore work thine own annoy
Yon priestess, CUSTOM, marks her prey,
    And eyes thee with malignant joy.

Instant she on her victim springs,
    She mocks the unavailing prayer,
Furious her withered hand enrings,
    And drags her by her flowing hair.

Then laughing VENUS bids with speed
    Her handmaids on the pavement throw
Of all the flowering plants the seed
    That in the Hesperian gardens blow.

And she must each assort before
   The dewfall shall the damp grass steep,
While sentry at the chamber door
   Solicitude and Sorrow keep.

A little ant the mandate heard,
   The oppressive mandate with disdain;
For e'en the weakest 'tis averr'd
   Will on the oppressor turn again.

And insect myriads never ceas'd
   Their labours till the setting sun,
When Venus, rising from the feast,
   With wonder saw the hard task done.

XVIII.

Now rose, in glory rose, the morn,
   And Venus bids her captive go
To yon fair stream, whose currents, borne
   In circling eddies, babbling flow.

" There grazing the wild flock," she cried,
   " With golden fleeces shalt thou see,
Then from the bright ram's shaggy side
   The precious wool bring back to me."

Trembling she goes—she gazes round,—
   Say whence that heavenly voice proceeds,
That like the soft flute's mellow sound
   Breathes sweetly through the whispering reeds?

   " Fierce while glares the noon-day sun,
     Thou the dread adventure shun,
     While the ram his rival scorns
     Furious with his jutting horns;
     But beneath yon plane-tree's shade,
     In concealment be thou laid,
     Till the eve-star, pale and fair,
     Glimmers through the misty air;
     Then in safety may'st thou pull
     From his fleece the golden wool."

Yet though this labour she performs,
    No grace with VENUS can she find;
Her stony heart no pity warms,
    Another trial waits behind.

XIX.

"Down from that cloud-capt mountain's brow
    A never-ceasing cataract pours,
Whose feathery surges dash below
    In thunder on the Stygian shores;

Thou on the dangerous brink must stand,
    And dip this goblet in the spring;
Descending then with steady hand
    The black transparent crystal bring."

Nimbly the mountain steep she'd climb,
    But thence impervious rocks arise,
Whose awful foreheads frown sublime,
    And lift their bold crags to the skies.

While horrid voices howl around,
    "Fly! swiftly fly!"—"Forbear, forbear!"
Vast stones, with heart-appalling sound,
    Are hurl'd into the groaning air.

And on the right, and on the left,
    Four ever-watchful dragons fly,
Flame-breathing through each dizzy cleft,
    Their long and flexile necks they ply.

Though beauty's queen no pity feels,
    The bold rapacious bird of JOVE
His succour to the afflicted deals,
    In reverence to the God of Love.

He sees her blasted hopes expire,
    He leaves the liquid fields of light,
And whirling round in many a gyre
    Majestic wings his rapid flight.

High o'er the dragons see him tower,
   Up-darting through the azure air!
And high above the stony shower
   The bowl his crooked talons bear.

Now to the grateful maid he brings
   The sparkling waters bright and clear,
Then spreads again his ample wings,
   And soaring quits this nether sphere.

XX.

Can Beauty no compassion know?
   Sure Mercy must her bright beams dart,
And piercing through those hills of snow,
   Melt e'en the adamantine heart!

Ah no! by VENUS' stern command
   PSYCHE to PROSERPINE is sped:
Shivering she seeks the dreary land,
   The sun-less mansions of the dead.

The unopen'd casket she must bring,
   Whose weak and fragile sides entomb
From beauty's uncreated spring
   The essence of eternal bloom.

Fearful and sad she journey'd on,
   While silence roll'd the midnight hour,
To where the unsteady moon-beam shone
   Reflected from a ruin'd tower.

And thence she heard these warning notes,
   Caroll'd as clear as clear might be,
Sweet as the mermaid's lay that floats
   Melodious on the charmed sea.

   " Sunk her spirit, whelm'd in woe,
      Does the royal captive go ?
      Does her heart, oppress'd with dread,
      Shudder to approach the dead ?

Where the cavern yawns around,
Enter there the dark profound :
Soon thy path a crippled ass,
By a cripple led, shall pass,
Fainting they beneath their task—
He assistance oft will ask,
But in these infernal lands,
Touch not with unhallow'd hands,
Cautious thou, without delay
Onward, onward, speed thy way !
In old CHARON's creaking boat
O'er the dead stream thou must float,
There the livid corse thou'lt see
Stretch his blue-swoln hand to thee ;
Frown thou on his suit severe,
Mercy were destruction here !
See those crones that on the left
Weave the many-colour'd weft,
See them, how they this way wend,
Asking thee thy aid to lend,
But in these infernal lands
Touch not with unhallow'd hands ;
Cautious thou, without delay
Onward, onward, speed thy way !
Dipt the sop in Hydromel,
Charm the three-neck'd dog of Hell ;
Then from her imperial seat
Thee the shadowy queen shall greet,
Shall for thee the feast prepare—
Thou that feast refuse to share,
But upon the pavement spread
Take the black and mouldy bread—
By the queen soon set at large,
Back now bear thy precious charge :
Over all, thy curious mind
In the chains of prudence bind,
Nor the strict command infringe,
Move not thou the golden hinge !
Gladsome then without delay
Onward, onward, speed thy way .

XXI.

—She has seen the secrets of the deep,
   And through o'erwhelming horrors past,
How her recovering pulses leap,
   To hail the day-star's gleams at last!

" Do I then bear eternal bloom
   Alone to make my tyrant shine ?
Say, rather let its tints illume
   These wan and woe-worn cheeks of mine;

Whilst I will revel in the rays
   Of beauty in the casket hid ;"—
Alas! no beam of beauty plays
   Delightful from the lifted lid!

But from the empty casket sprang
   Of Stygian fogs the baleful breath,
And heavy o'er her blanch'd frame hang
   The damp unwholesome dews of DEATH.

XXII.

The fields of nature to deform
   Not always drives the furious blast,
And shall misfortune's moral storm
   'Gainst meek endurance ever last ?

No, though unnumber'd ills assail,
   Though man behold no succour nigh,
Though with the frailest of the frail,
   Presumption tempt the prying eye ;

Yet, if the germ of virtue live,
   Let constant faith her sufferings brave ;
Goodness is powerful to forgive,
   And Heaven omnipotent to save

CUPID, with downcast, humbled mien,
   Has to the THUNDERER breath'd his care,
The ALMIGHTY FATHER smil'd serene,
   And granted his adorer's prayer.

Now flies he joyful to her aid,
   He gently rais'd her falling head,
With his bright arrow touch'd the maid,
   And rous'd her from her cheerless bed.

He animates anew her charms,
   Warm o'er her breathes the light of love,
Then bears her in his circling arms,
   And stands before the throne of JOVE.

But on the Sovereign of the skies
   What fleshly optics dare to gaze?
And PSYCHE with averted eyes
   Shrinks trembling from th' excessive blaze:

'Till, HEBE raising to her lips
   The ambrosial Goblet foaming high,
Wrapt in extatic trance she sips
   The fount of IMMORTALITY!

Purpled with roses dance the HOURS,
   The GRACES scattering odours play,
And crown'd with never-fading flowers
   The MUSES hymn the jocund lay.

And onwards up the ethereal arch
   Glad HYMEN leads the festive train,
As o'er the rainbow's hues they march,
   And links them in his golden chain.

While soon to bless the faithful pair;
   With eye of laughter, soul of flame,
Burst into life a daughter fair,
   And PLEASURE was the infant's name.

PSYCHE,

OR THE

LEGEND OF LOVE.

A POEM IN SIX CANTOS.

WRITTEN IN THE SPENSERIAN STANZA.

BY

MRS. HENRY TIGHE.

ARGUMENT.

Proem—Psyche introduced—Her royal origin—Envy of Venus—Her instructions to Cupid—The island of Pleasure—The fountains of Joy and of Sorrow—The appearance of Love - Psyche asleep—Mutually wounded—Psyche reveals her dream to her Mother—The Oracle consulted—Psyche abandoned on the Rock by its decree—Carried by Zephyrs to the island of Pleasure—The Palace of Love—Banquet of Love—Marriage of Cupid and Psyche—Psyche's daily solitude—Her request to her Lover—His reluctant consent.

LET not the rugged brow the rhymes accuse,
Which speak of gentle knights and ladies fair,
Nor scorn the lighter labours of the muse,
Who yet, for cruel battles would not dare
The low-strung chords of her weak lyre prepare;
But loves to court repose in slumbery lay,
To tell of goodly bowers and gardens rare,
Of gentle blandishments and amorous play,
And all the lore of love, in courtly verse essay.

And ye whose gentle hearts in thraldom held
The power of mighty Love already own,
When you the pains and dangers have beheld,
Which erst your lord hath for his Psyche known,
For all your sorrows this may well atone,
That he you serve the same hath suffered;
And sure, your fond applause the tale will crown
In which your own distress is pictured,
And all that weary way which you yourselves must tread

Most sweet would to my soul the hope appear,
That sorrow in my verse a charm might find,
To smooth the brow long bent with bitter cheer,
Some short distraction to the joyless mind
Which grief, with heavy chain, hath fast confined
To sad remembrance of its happier state;
For to myself I ask no boon more kind
Than power another's woes to mitigate,
And that soft soothing art which anguish can abate.

And thou, sweet sprite, whose sway doth far extend
Smile on the mean historian of thy fame!
My heart in each distress and fear befriend,
Nor ever let it feel a fiercer flame
Than innocence may cherish free from blame,
And hope may nurse, and sympathy may own;
For, as thy rights I never would disclaim,
But true allegiance offered to thy throne,
So may I love but one, by one beloved alone.

That anxious torture may I never feel,
Which, doubtful, watches o'er a wandering heart,
Oh! who that bitter torment can reveal,
Or tell the pining anguish of that smart!
In those affections may I ne'er have part,
Which easily transferred can learn to rove:
No, dearest Cupid! when I feel thy dart,
For thy sweet Psyche's sake may no false love
The tenderness I prize lightly from me remove!

CANTO I.

Much wearied with her long and dreary way,
And now with toil and sorrow well nigh spent,
Of sad regret and wasting grief the prey,
Fair Psyche through untrodden forests went,
To lone shades uttering oft a vain lament.
And oft in hopeless silence sighing deep,
As she her fatal error did repent,
While dear remembrance bade her ever weep,
And her pale cheek in ceaseless showers of sorrow steep.

'Mid the thick covert of that woodland shade,
A flowery bank there lay undressed by art,
But of the mossy turf spontaneous made;
Here the young branches shot their arms athwart,
And wove the bower so thick in every part,
That the fierce beams of Phœbus glancing strong
Could never through the leaves their fury dart;
But the sweet creeping shrubs that round it throng,
Their loving fragrance mix, and trail their flowers along.

And close beside a little fountain played,
Which through the trembling leaves all joyous shone,
And with the cheerful birds sweet music made,
Kissing the surface of each polished stone
As it flowed past: sure as her favourite throne
Tranquillity might well esteem the bower,
The fresh and cool retreat have called her own,
A pleasant shelter in the sultry hour,
A refuge from the blast, and angry tempest's power.

Wooed by the soothing silence of the scene,
Here Psyche stood, and looking round, lest aught
Which threatened danger near her might have been,
A while to rest her in that quiet spot
She laid her down, and piteously bethought
Herself on the sad changes of her fate,
Which in so short a space so much had wrought,
And now had raised her to such high estate,
And now had plunged her low in sorrow desolate.

Oh! how refreshing seemed the breathing wind
To her faint limbs! and while her snowy hands
From her fair brow her golden hair unbind,
And of her zone unloose the silken bands,
More passing bright unveiled her beauty stands;
For faultless was her form as beauty's queen,
And every winning grace that Love demands,
With mild attempered dignity was seen
Play o'er each lovely limb, and deck her angel mien.

F F

Though solitary now, dismayed, forlorn,
Without attendant through the forest rude,
The peerless maid, of royal lineage born,
By many a royal youth had oft been wooed;
Low at her feet full many a prince had sued,
And homage paid unto her beauty rare;
But all their blandishments her heart withstood;
And well might mortal suitor sure despair,
Since mortal charms were none which might with hers compare.

Yet nought of insolence or haughty pride
Found ever in her gentle breast a place;
Though men her wondrous beauty deified,
And rashly deeming such celestial grace
Could never spring from any earthly race,
Lo! all forsaking Cytherea's shrine,
Her sacred altars now no more embrace,
But to fair Psyche pay those rites divine,
Which, Goddess! are thy due, and should be only thine.

But envy of her beauty's growing fame
Poisoned her sisters' hearts with secret gall,
And oft with seeming piety they blame
The worship which they justly impious call;
And oft, lest evil should their sire befal,
Besought him to forbid the erring crowd
Which hourly thronged around the regal hall,
With incense, gifts, and invocations loud,
To her whose guiltless breast ne'er felt elation proud.

For she was timid as the wintry flower,
That, whiter than the snow it blooms among,
Droops its fair head submissive to the power
Of every angry blast which sweeps along,
Sparing the lovely trembler, while the strong
Majestic tenants of the leafless wood
It levels low. But, ah! the pitying song
Must tell how, than the tempest's self more rude,
Fierce wrath and cruel hate their suppliant prey pursued.

Indignant quitting her deserted fanes,
Now Cytherea sought her favourite isle,
And there from every eye her secret pains
'Mid her thick myrtle bowers concealed a while;
Practised no more the glance, or witching smile,
But nursed the pang she never felt before,
Of mortified disdain; then to beguile
The hours which mortal flattery soothed no more,
She various plans revolved her influence to restore.

She called her son with unaccustomed voice;
Not with those thrilling accents of delight
Which bade so oft enchanted Love rejoice,
Soft as the breezes of a summer's night:
Now choked with rage its change could Love affright;
As all to sudden discontent a prey,
Shunning the cheerful day's enlivening light,
She felt the angry power's malignant sway,
And bade her favourite boy her vengeful will obey.

Bathed in those tears which vanquish human hearts,
" Oh, son beloved!" (the supplaint goddess cried,)
" If e'er thy too indulgent mother's arts
Subdued for thee the potent deities
Who rule my native deep, or haunt the skies;
Or if to me the grateful praise be due,
That to thy sceptre bow the great and wise,
Now let thy fierce revenge my foe pursue,
And let my rival scorned her vain presumption rue.

" For what to me avails my former boast
That, fairer than the wife of Jove confest,
I gained the prize thus basely to be lost?
With me the world's devotion to contest
Behold a mortal dares; though on my breast
Still vainly brilliant shines the magic zone.
Yet, yet I reign: by you my wrongs redrest,
The world with humbled Psyche soon shall own
That Venus, beauty's queen, shall be adored alone.

" Deep let her drink of that dark, bitter spring,
　　Which flows so near thy bright and crystal tide ;
　　Deep let her heart thy sharpest arrow sting,
　　Its tempered barb in that black poison dyed.
　　Let her, for whom contending princes sighed,
　　Feel all the fury of thy fiercest flame
　　For some base wretch to foul disgrace allied,
　　Forgetful of her birth and her fair fame,
Her honours all defiled, and sacrificed to shame."

Then, with sweet pressure of her rosy lip,
　　A kiss she gave bathed in ambrosial dew ;
　　The thrilling joy he would for ever sip,
　　And his moist eyes in ecstasy imbrue.
　　But she whose soul still angry cares pursue,
　　Snatched from the soft caress her glowing charms ;
　　Her vengeful will she then enforced anew,
　　As she in haste dismissed him from her arms,
The cruel draught to seek of anguish and alarms.

'Mid the blue waves by circling seas embraced,
　　A chosen spot of fairest land was seen ;
　　For there with favouring hand had Nature placed
　　All that could lovely make the varied scene :
　　Eternal Spring there spread her mantle green ;
　　There high surrounding hills deep-wooded rose
　　O'er placid lakes ; while marble rocks between
　　The fragrant shrubs their pointed heads disclose,
And balmy breathes each gale which o'er the island blows.

Pleasure had called the fertile lawns her own,
　　And thickly strewed them with her choicest flowers ;
　　Amid the quiet glade her golden throne
　　Bright shone with lustre through o'erarching bowers :
　　There her fair train, the ever-downy Hours,
　　Sport on light wing with the young Joys entwined ;
　　While Hope delighted from her full lap showers
　　Blossoms, whose fragrance can the ravished mind
Inebriate with dreams of rapture unconfined

And in the grassy centre of the isle,
Where the thick verdure spreads a damper shade,
Amid their native rocks concealed a while,
Then o'er the plains in devious streams displayed,
Two gushing fountains rise ; and thence conveyed,
Their waters through the woods and valleys play,
Visit each green recess and secret glade,
With still unmingled, still meandering way,
Nor widely wandering far, can each from other stray.

But of strange contrast are their virtues found,
And oft the lady of that isle has tried
In rocky dens and caverns under ground,
The black deformed stream in vain to hide ;
Bursting all bounds her labours it defied ;
Yet many a flowery sod its course conceals
Through plains where deep its silent waters glide,
Till secret ruin all corroding steals,
And every treacherous arch the hideous gulph reveals.

Forbidding every kindly prosperous growth,
Where'er it ran, a channel bleak it wore ;
The gaping banks receded, as though loth
To touch the poison which disgraced their shore :
There deadly anguish pours unmixed his store
Of all the ills which sting the human breast,
The hopeless tears which past delights deplore,
Heart-gnawing jealousy which knows no rest,
And self-upbraiding shame, by stern remorse opprest.

Oh, how unlike the pure transparent stream,
Which near it bubbles o'er its golden sands !
The impeding stones with pleasant music seem
Its progress to detain from other lands ;
And all its banks, inwreathed with flowery bands,
Ambrosial fragrance shed in grateful dew :
There young Desire enchanted ever stands,
Breathing delight and fragrance ever new,
And bathed in constant joys of fond affection true.

But not to mortals is it e'er allowed
To drink unmingled of that current bright;
Scarce can they taste the pleasurable flood,
Defiled by angry Fortune's envious spite;
Who from the cup of amorous delight
Dashes the sparkling draught of brilliant joy,
Till, with dull sorrow's stream despoiled quite,
No more it cheers the soul nor charms the eye,
But 'mid the poisoned bowl distrust and anguish lie.

Here Cupid tempers his unerring darts,
And in the fount of bliss delights to play;
Here mingles balmy sighs and pleasing smarts,
And here the honied draught will oft allay
With that black poison's all-polluting sway,
For wretched man.   Hither, as Venus willed,
For Psyche's punishment he bent his way :
From either stream his amber vase he filled,
For her were meant the drops which grief alone distilled.

His quiver, sparkling bright with gems and gold,
From his fair plumed shoulder graceful hung,
And from its top in brilliant chords enrolled
Each little vase resplendently was slung :
Still as he flew, around him sportive clung
His frolic train of winged Zephyrs light,
Wafting the fragrance which his tresses flung :
While odours dropped from every ringlet bright,
And from his blue eyes beamed ineffable delight.

Wrapt in a cloud unseen by mortal eye,
He sought the chamber of the royal maid;
There, lulled by careless soft security,
Of the impending mischief nought afraid,
Upon her purple couch was Psyche laid,
Her radiant eyes a downy slumber sealed;
In light transparent veil alone arrayed,
Her bosom's opening charms were half revealed,
And scarce the lucid folds her polished limbs concealed.

A placid smile plays o'er each roseate lip,
Sweet severed lips! while thus your pearls disclose,
That slumbering thus unconscious she may sip
The cruel presage of her future woes!
Lightly, as fall the dews upon the rose,
Upon the coral gates of that sweet cell
The fatal drops he pours; nor yet he knows,
Nor, though a God, can he presaging tell
How he himself shall mourn the ills of that sad spell!

Nor yet content, he from his quiver drew,
Sharpened with skill divine, a shining dart:
No need had he for bow, since thus too true
His hand might wound her all-exposed heart:
Yet her fair side he touched with gentlest art,
And half relenting on her beauties gazed;
Just then awaking with a sudden start,
Her opening eye in humid lustre blazed,
Unseen he still remained, enchanted and amazed.

The dart which in his hand now trembling stood,
As o'er the couch he bent with ravished eye,
Drew with its daring point celestial blood
From his smooth neck's unblemish'd ivory:
Heedless of this, but with a pitying sigh
The evil done now anxious to repair,
He shed in haste the balmy drops of joy
O'er all the silky ringlets of her hair;
Then stretched his plumes divine, and breathed celestial air.

Unhappy Psyche! soon the latent wound
The fading roses of her cheek confess,
Her eyes' bright beams, in swimming sorrows drowned,
Sparkle no more with life and happiness,
Her parents' fond exulting heart to bless;
She shuns adoring crowds, and seeks to hide
The pining sorrows which her soul oppress,
Till to her mother's tears no more denied,
The secret grief she owns, for which she lingering sighed.

A dream of mingled terror and delight
Still heavy hangs upon her troubled soul,
An angry form still swims before her sight,
And still the vengeful thunders seem to roll;
Still crushed to earth she feels the stern control
Of Venus unrelenting, unappeased:
The dream returns, she feels the fancied dole;
Once more the furies on her heart have seized,
But still she views the youth who all her sufferings eased.

Of wondrous beauty did the vision seem,
And in the freshest prime of youthful years;
Such at the close of her distressful dream
A graceful champion to her eyes appears;
Her loved deliverer from her foes and fears
She seems in grateful transport still to press;
Still his soft voice sounds in her ravished ears;
Dissolved in fondest tears of tenderness,
His form she oft invokes her waking eyes to bless.

Nor was it quite a dream, for as she woke,
Ere heavenly mists concealed him from her eye,
One sudden transitory view she took
Of Love's most radiant bright divinity;
From the fair image never can she fly,
As still consumed with vain desire she pines;
While her fond parents heave the anxious sigh,
And to avert her fate seek holy shrines
The threatened ills to learn by auguries and signs.

And now, the royal sacrifice prepared,
The milk-white bull they to the altar lead,
Whose youth the galling yoke as yet had spared,
Now destined by the sacred knife to bleed:
When lo! with sudden spring his horns he freed,
And head-long rushed amid the frighted throng:
While from the smoke-veiled shrine such sounds proceed
As well might strike with awe the soul most strong;
And thus divinely spoke the heaven-inspired tongue.

" On nuptial couch, in nuptial vest arrayed,
  On a tall rock's high summit Psyche place :
  Let all depart, and leave the fated maid
  Who never must a mortal Hymen grace :
  A winged monster of no earthly race
  Thence soon shall bear his trembling bride away ;
  His power extends o'er all the bounds of space,
  And Jove himself has owned his dreaded sway,
Whose flaming breath sheds fire, whom earth and heaven obey."

  With terror, anguish, and astonishment
  The oracle her wretched father hears ;
  Now from his brow the regal honours rent,
  And now in frantic sorrow wild appears,
  Nor threatened plagues, nor punishment he fears,
  Refusing long the sentence to obey,
  Till Psyche, trembling with submissive tears,
  Bids them the sacrifice no more delay,
Prepare the funeral couch, and leave the destined prey.

  Pleased by the ambiguous doom the Fates promulge,
  The angry Goddess and enamoured Boy
  Alike content their various hopes indulge ;
  He, still exploring with an anxious eye
  The future prospect of uncertain joy,
  Plans how the tender object of his care
  He may protect from threatened misery ;
  Ah, sanguine Love ! so oft deceived, forbear
With flattering tints to paint illusive hope so fair.

  But now what lamentations rend the skies !
  In amaracine wreaths the virgin choir
  With Io Hymen mingle funeral cries :
  Lost in the sorrows of the Lydian lyre
  The breathing flutes' melodious notes expire ;
  In sad procession pass the mournful throng,
  Extinguishing with tears the torches' fire,
  While the mute victim weeping crowds among,
By unknown fears oppressed, moves silently along.

But on such scenes of terror and dismay
The mournful Muse delights not long to dwell;
She quits well pleased the melancholy lay,
Nor vainly seeks the parents' woes to tell:
But what to wondering Psyche then befel
When thus abandoned, let her rather say,
Who shuddering looks to see some monster fell
Approach the desert rock to seize his prey,
With cruel fangs devour, or tear her thence away.

When lo! a gentle breeze began to rise,
Breathed by obedient Zephyrs round the maid,
Fanning her bosom with its softest sighs,
A while among her fluttering robes it strayed,
And boldly sportive latent charms displayed:
And then, as Cupid willed, with tenderest care
From the tall rock, where weeping she was laid,
With gliding motion through the yielding air
To Pleasure's blooming isle their lovely charge they bear.

On the green bosom of the turf reclined,
They lightly now the astonished virgin lay,
To placid rest they soothe her troubled mind;
Around her still with watchful care they stay,
Around her still in quiet whispers play:
Till lulling slumbers bid her eyelids close,
Veiling with silky fringe each brilliant ray,
While soft tranquillity divinely flows
O'er all her soul serene, in visions of repose.

Refreshed she rose, and all enchanted gazed
On the rare beauties of the pleasant scene.
Conspicuous far a lofty palace blazed
Upon a sloping bank of softest green;
A fairer edifice was never seen;
The high-ranged columns own no mortal hand,
But seem a temple meet for Beauty's queen.
Like polished snow the marble pillars stand
In grace-attempered majesty sublimely grand.

Gently ascending from a silvery flood,
Above the palace rose the shaded hill,
The lofty eminence was crowned with wood,
And the rich lawns, adorn'd by Nature's skill,
The passing breezes with their odours fill;
Here ever-blooming groves of orange glow,
And here all flowers which from their leaves distil
Ambrosial dew in sweet succession blow,
And trees of matchless size a fragrant shade bestow.

The sun looks glorious 'mid a sky serene,
And bids bright lustre sparkle o'er the tide;
The clear blue ocean at a distance seen
Bounds the gay landscape on the western side,
While closing round it with majestic pride,
The lofty rocks 'mid citron groves arise;
" Sure some divinity must here reside,"
As tranced in some bright vision, Psyche cries,
And scarce believes the bliss, or trusts her charmed eyes.

When lo! a voice divinely sweet she hears,
From unseen lips proceeds the heavenly sound;
" Psyche, approach, dismiss thy timid fears,
At length his bride thy longing spouse has found,
And bids for thee immortal joys abound;
For thee the palace rose at his command,
For thee his love a bridal banquet crowned;
He bids attendant nymphs around thee stand,
Prompt every wish to serve, a fond obedient band."

Increasing wonder filled her ravished soul,
For now the pompous portals opened wide,
There, pausing oft, with timid foot she stole
Through halls high domed, enriched with sculptured pride,
While gay saloons appeared on either side,
In splendid vista opening to her sight;
And all with precious gems so beautified,
And furnished with such exquisite delight,
That scarce the beams of heaven emit such lustre bright.

The amethyst was there of violet hue,
And there the topaz shed its golden ray,
The chrysoberyl, and the sapphire blue
As the clear azure of a sunny day,
Or the mild eyes where amorous glances play;
The snow-white jasper, and the opal's flame,
The blushing ruby, and the agate grey,
And there the gem which bears his luckless name
Whose death by Phœbus mourned ensured him deathless **fame.**

There the green emerald, there cornelians glow,
And rich carbuncles pour eternal light,
With all that India and Peru can shew,
Or Labrador can give so flaming bright
To the charmed mariner's half-dazzled sight:
The coral-paved baths with diamonds blaze:
And all that can the female heart delight
Of fair attire, the last recess displays,
And all that Luxury can ask, her eye surveys.

Now through the hall melodious music stole,
And self-prepared the splendid banquet stands,
Self-poured the nectar sparkles in the bowl,
The lute and viol touched by unseen hands
Aid the soft voices of the choral bands;
O'er the full board a brighter lustre beams
Than Persia's monarch at his feast commands:
For sweet refreshment all inviting seems
To taste celestial food, and pure ambrosial streams

But when meek Eve hung out her dewy star,
And gently veiled with gradual hand the sky,
Lo! the bright folding doors retiring far,
Display to Psyche's captivated eye
All that voluptuous ease could e'er supply
To soothe the spirits in serene repose:
Beneath the velvet's purple canopy
Divinely formed a downy couch arose,
While alabaster lamps a milky light disclose

Once more she hears the hymeneal strain;
Far other voices now attune the lay;
The swelling sounds approach, a while remain,
And then retiring faint dissolved away:
The expiring lamps emit a feebler ray,
And soon in fragrant death extinguished lie:
Then virgin terrors Psyche's soul dismay,
When through the obscuring gloom she nought can spy,
But softly rustling sounds declare some Being nigh.

Oh, you for whom I write! whose hearts can melt
At the soft thrilling voice whose power you prove,
You know what charm, unutterably felt,
Attends the unexpected voice of Love:
Above the lyre, the lute's soft notes above,
With sweet enchantment to the soul it steals,
And bears it to Elysium's happy grove;
You best can tell the rapture Psyche feels
When Love's ambrosial lip the vows of Hymen seals.

" 'Tis he, 'tis my deliverer! deep imprest
Upon my heart those sounds I well recal,"
The blushing maid exclaimed, and on his breast
A tear of trembling ecstasy let fall.
But, ere the breezes of the morning call
Aurora from her purple, humid bed,
Psyche in vain explores the vacant hall,
Her tender lover from her arms is fled,
While sleep his downy wings had o'er her eye-lids spread.

Again the band invisible attend,
And female voices soothe the mournful bride;
Light hands to braid her hair assistance lend,
By some she sees the glowing bracelet tied,
Others officious hover at her side,
And each bright gem for her acceptance bring,
While some, the balmy air diffusing wide,
Fan softer perfumes from each odorous wing
Than the fresh bosom sheds of earliest, sweetest spring.

With songs divine her anxious soul they cheer,
And woo her footsteps to delicious bowers,
They bid the fruit more exquisite appear
Which at her feet its bright profusion showers:
For her they cull unknown, celestial flowers;
The gilded car they bid her fearless guide,
Which at her wish self-moved with wondrous powers
The rapid bird's velocity defied,
While round the blooming isle it rolled with circuit wide.

Again they spread the feast, they strike the lyre,
But to her frequent questions nought reply,
Her lips in vain her lover's name require,
Or wherefore thus concealed he shuns her eye.
But when reluctant twilight veils the sky,
And each pale lamp successively expires;
Again she trembling hears the voice of joy,
Her spouse a tender confidence inspires,
But with a fond embrace ere dawn again retires.

To charm the languid hours of solitude
He oft invites her to the Muse's lore,
For none have vainly e'er the Muse pursued,
And those whom she delights, regret no more
The social, joyous hours, while rapt they soar
To worlds unknown, and live in fancy's dream;
Oh, Muse divine! thee only I implore,
Shed on my soul thy sweet inspiring beams,
And pleasure's gayest scene insipid folly seems!

Silence and solitude the Muses love,
And whom they charm they can alone suffice;
Nor ever tedious hour their votaries prove:
This solace now the lonely Psyche tries,
Or, while her hand the curious needle plies,
She learns from lips unseen celestial strains;
Responsive now with their soft voice she vies,
Or bids her plaintive harp express the pains
Which absence sore inflicts where Love all potent reigns.

But melancholy poisons all her joys,
And secret sorrows all her hopes depress,
Consuming languor every bliss destroys,
And sad she droops repining, comfortless.
Her tender lover well the cause can guess,
And sees too plain inevitable fate
Pursue her to the bowers of happiness.
  "Oh, Psyche! most beloved, ere yet too late,
Dread the impending ills and prize thy tranquil state."

In vain his weeping love he thus advised;
She longs to meet a parent's sweet embrace,
"Oh, were their sorrowinig hearts at least apprised
How Psyche's wondrous lot all fears may chase;
For whom thy love prepared so fair a place!
Let but my bliss their fond complaints repress,
Let me but once behold a mother's face,
Oh, spouse adored! and in full happiness
This love-contented heart its solitude shall bless.

Oh, by those beauties I must ne'er behold!
The spicy-scented ringlets of thine hair:
By that soft neck my loving arms enfold,
Crown with a kind consent thy Psyche's prayer!
Their dear embrace, their blessing let me share;
So shall I stain our couch with tears no more:
But, blest in thee, resign each other care,
Nor seek again thy secret to explore,
Which yet, denied thy sight, I ever must deplore."

Unable to resist her fond request,
Reluctant Cupid thus at last complied,
And sighing clasped her closer to his breast.
"Go then, my Psyche! go, my lovely bride!
But let me in thy faith at least confide,
That by no subtle, impious arts betrayed,
Which, ah! too well I know will all be tried,
Thy simply trusting heart shall e'er be swayed
The secret veil to rend which fate thy screen hath made.

For danger hovers o'er thy smiling days,
One only way to shield thee yet I know ;
Unseen, I may securely guard thy ways,
And save thee from the threatened storm of woe ;
But forced, if known, my Psyche to forego,
Thou never, never must again be mine !
What mutual sorrows hence must ceaseless flow !
Compelled thy dear embraces to resign,
While thou to anguish doomed for lost delights shalt pine.

Solace thy mind with hopes of future joy !
In a dear infant thou shalt see my face ;
Blest mother soon of an immortal boy,
In him his father's features thou shalt trace !
Yet go ! for thou art free, the bounds of space
Are none for thee : attendant Zephyrs stay,
Speak but thy will, and to the wished-for place
Their lovely mistress swift they shall convey :
Yet hither, ah ! return, ere fades the festive day."

"Light of my soul, far dearer than the day !"
(Exulting Psyche cries in grateful joy)
"Me all the bliss of earth could ill repay
For thy most sweet, divine society ;
To thee again with rapture will I fly,
Nor with less pleasure hail the star of eve
Than when in tedious solitude I sigh ;
My vows of silent confidence believe,
Nor think thy Psyche's faith will e'er thy love deceive.

Her suit obtained, in full contentment blest,
Her eyes at length in placid slumbers close.
Sleep, hapless fair ! sleep on thy lover's breast ;
Ah, not again to taste such pure repose !
Till thy sad heart by long experience knows
How much they err, who, to their interest blind,
Slight the calm peace which from retirement flows !
And while they think their fleeting joys to bind,
Banish the tranquil bliss which heaven for man designed

CANTO II.

ARGUMENT.

Introduction — Dangers of the World — Psyche, conveyed by Zephyrs, awakes once more in the paternal mansion—Envy of her Sisters— They plot her ruin—Inspire her with suspicion and terror—Psyche's return to the Palace of Love — Her disobedience — Love asleep— Psyche's amazement — The flight of Love — Sudden banishment of Psyche from the island of Pleasure—Her lamentations—Comforted by Love—Temple of Venus—Task imposed on Psyche conditional to her reconciliation with Venus—Psyche soothed and attended by Inno- cence—Psyche wandering as described in the opening of the first Canto.

Oh happy you! who, blest with present bliss,
See not with fatal prescience future tears,
Nor the dear moment of enjoyment miss
Through gloomy discontent, or sullen fears
Foreboding many a storm for coming years;
Change is the lot of all. Ourselves with scorn
Perhaps shall view what now so fair appears;
And wonder whence the fancied charm was born
Which now with vain despair from our fond grasp is torn!

·Vain schemer, think not to prolong thy joy!
But cherish while it lasts the heavenly boon:
Expand thy sails! thy little bark shall fly
With the full tide of pleasure! though it soon
May feel the influence of the changeful moon,
It yet is thine! then let not doubts obscure
With cloudy vapours veil thy brilliant noon,
Nor let suspicion's tainted breath impure
Poison the favouring gale which speeds thy course secure!

Oh, Psyche, happy in thine ignorance!
Couldst thou but shun this heart-tormenting bane;
Be but content, nor daringly advance
To meet the bitter hour of threatened pain;
Pure spotless dove! seek thy safe nest again;
Let true affection shun the public eye,
And quit the busy circle of the vain,
For there the treacherous snares concealed lie;
Oh timely warned escape! to safe retirement fly!

G G

Bright shone the morn! and now its golden ray
Dispelled the slumbers from her radiant eyes,
Yet still in dreams her fancy seems to play,
For lo! she sees with rapture and surprise
Full in her view the well-known mansion rise,
And each loved scene of first endearment hails;
The air that first received her infant sighs
With wond'ring ecstasy she now inhales,
While every trembling nerve soft tenderness assails.

See from the dear pavilion, where she lay,
Breathless she flies with scarce assured feet,
Swift through the garden wings her eager way,
Her mourning parents' ravished eyes to greet
With loveliest apparition strange and sweet:
Their days of anguish all o'erpaid they deem
By one blest hour of ecstasy so great:
Yet doubtingly they gaze, and anxious seem
To ask their raptured souls, " Oh, is this all a dream?"

The wondrous tale attentively they hear,
Repeated oft in broken words of joy,
She in their arms embraced, while every ear
Hangs on their Psyche's lips, and earnestly
On her is fixed each wonder-speaking eye;
Till the sad hour arrives which bids them part,
And twilight darkens o'er the ruddy sky;
Divinely urged they let their child depart,
Pressed with a fond embrace to each adoring heart.

Trusting that wedded to a spouse divine,
Secure is now their daughter's happiness,
They half contentedly their child resign,
Check the complaint, the rising sigh suppress,
And wipe the silent drops of bitterness.
Nor must she her departure more delay,
But bids them now their weeping Psyche bless;
Then back to the pavilion bends her way,
Ere in the fading west quite sinks expiring day.

But, while her parents listen with delight,
Her sisters' hearts the Furies agitate :
They look with envy on a lot so bright,
And all the honours of her splendid fate,
Scorning the meanness of their humbler state ;
And how they best her ruin may devise
With hidden rancour much they meditate,
Yet still they bear themselves in artful guise,
While 'mid the feigned caress, concealed the venom lies.

By malice urged, by ruthless envy stung,
With secret haste to seize their prey they flew,
Around her neck as in despair they clung ;
Her soft complying nature well they knew,
And trusted by delaying to undo ;
But when they found her resolute to go,
Their well-laid stratagem they then pursue,
And, while they bid their treacherous sorrows flow,
Thus fright her simple heart with images of woe.

" Oh, hapless Psyche ! thoughtless of thy doom !
Yet hear thy sisters who have wept for thee,
Since first a victim to thy living tomb,
Obedient to the oracle's decree,
Constrained we left thee to thy destiny.
Since then no comfort could our woes abate ;
While thou wert lulled in false security
We learned the secret horrors of thy fate,
And heard prophetic lips thy future ills relate.

Yet fearing never to behold thee more,
Our filial care would fain the truth conceal ;
But from the sages' cell this ring we bore,
With power each latent magic to reveal ;
Some hope from hence our anxious bosoms feel
That we from ruin may our Psyche save,
Since Heaven, propitious to our pious zeal,
Thee to our frequent prayers in pity gave,
That warned thou yet mayst shun thy sad untimely grave.

Oh! how shall we declare the fatal truth?
How wound thy tender bosom with alarms?
Tell how the graces of thy blooming youth,
Thy more than mortal, all-adored charms
Have lain enamoured in a sorcerer's arms?
Oh, Psyche! seize on this decisive hour,
Escape the mischief of impending harms!
Return no more to that enchanted bower,
Fly the magician's arts, and dread his cruel power.

If, yet reluctant to forego thy love,
Thy furtive joys and solitary state,
Our fond officious care thy doubts reprove,
At least let some precaution guard thy fate,
Nor may our warning love be prized too late;
This night thyself thou mayst convince thine eyes,
Hide but a lamp, and cautiously await
Till in deep slumber thy magician lies,
This ring shall then disclose his foul deformities.

That monster by the oracle foretold,
Whose cursed spells both gods and men must fear,
In his own image thou shalt then behold,
And shuddering hate what now is prized so dear;
Yet fly not then, though loathsome he appear,
But let this dagger to his breast strike deep;
Thy coward terrors then thou must not hear,
For if with life he rouses from that sleep
Nought then for thee remains, and we must hopeless weep."

Oh! have you seen, when in the northern sky
The transient flame of lambent lightning plays,
In quick succession lucid streamers fly,
Now flashing roseate, and now milky rays,
While struck with awe the astonished rustics gaze?
Thus o'er her cheek the fleeting signals move,
Now pale with fear, now glowing with the blaze
Of much indignant, still confiding love,
Now horror's lurid hue with shame's deep blushes strove.

On her cold, passive hand the ring they place,
And hide the dagger in her folding vest;
Pleased the effects of their dire arts to trace
In the mute agony that swells her breast,
Already in her future ruin blest:
Conscious that now their poor deluded prey
Should never taste again delight or rest,
But sickening in suspicion's gloom decay,
Or urged by terrors rash their treacherous will obey.

While yet irresolute with sad surprise,
'Mid doubt and love she stands in strange suspense,
Lo! gliding from her sisters' wondering eyes
Returning Zephyrs gently bear her thence;
Lost all her hopes, her joys, her confidence,
Back to the earth her mournful eyes she threw,
As if imploring pity and defence;
While bathed in tears her golden tresses flew,
As in the breeze dispersed they caught the precious dew.

Illumined bright now shines the splendid dome,
Melodious accents her arrival hail:
But not the torches' blaze can chase the gloom,
And all the soothing powers of music fail;
Trembling she seeks her couch with horror pale,
But first a lamp conceals in secret shade,
While unknown terrors all her soul assail.
Thus half their treacherous counsel is obeyed,
For still her gentle soul abhors the murderous blade.

And now, with softest whispers of delight,
Love welcomes Psyche still more fondly dear;
Not unobserved, though hid in deepest night,
The silent anguish of her secret fear.
He thinks that tenderness excites the tear
By the late image of her parents' grief,
And half offended seeks in vain to cheer,
Yet, while he speaks, her sorrows feel relief,
Too soon more keen to sting from this suspension brief!

Allowed to settle on celestial eyes
Soft Sleep exulting now exerts his sway,
From Psyche's anxious pillow gladly flies
To veil those orbs, whose pure and lambent ray
The powers of heaven submissively obey.
Trembling and breathless then she softly rose,
And seized the lamp, where it obscurely lay,
With hand too rashly daring to disclose
The sacred veil which hung mysterious o'er her woes.

Twice, as with agitated step she went,
The lamp expiring shone with doubtful gleam,
As though it warned her from her rash intent:
And twice she paused, and on its trembling beam
Gazed with suspended breath, while voices seem
With murmuring sound along the roof to sigh;
As one just waking from a troublous dream,
With palpitating heart and straining eye,
Still fixed with fear remains, still thinks the danger nigh.

Oh, daring Muse! wilt thou indeed essay
To paint the wonders which that lamp could shew?
And canst thou hope in living words to say
The dazzling glories of that heavenly view?
Ah! well I ween, that if with pencil true
That splendid vision could be well exprest,
The fearful awe imprudent Psyche knew
Would seize with rapture every wondering breast,
When Love's all-potent charms divinely stood confest.

All imperceptible to human touch,
His wings display celestial essence light,
The clear effulgence of the blaze is such,
The brilliant plumage shines so heavenly bright
That mortal eyes turn dazzled from the sight;
A youth he seems in manhood's freshest years;
Round his fair neck, as clinging with delight,
Each golden curl resplendently appears,
Or shades his darker brow, which grace majestic wears.

Or o'er his guileless front the ringlets bright
Their rays of sunny lustre seem to throw,
That front than polished ivory more white!
His blooming cheeks with deeper blushes glow
Than roses scattered o'er a bed of snow:
While on his lips, distilled in balmy dews,
(Those lips divine that even in silence know
The heart to touch) persuasion to infuse
Still hangs a rosy charm that never vainly sues.

The friendly curtain of indulgent sleep
Disclosed not yet his eyes' resistless sway,
But from their silky veil there seemed to peep
Some brilliant glances with a softened ray,
Which o'er his features exquisitely play,
And all his polished limbs suffuse with light.
Thus through some narrow space the azure day
Sudden its cheerful rays diffusing bright,
Wide darts its lucid beams, to gild the brow of night

His fatal arrows and celestial bow
Beside the couch were negligently thrown,
Nor needs the god his dazzling arms, to show
His glorious birth, such beauty round him shone
As sure could spring from Beauty's self alone;
The gloom which glowed o'er all of soft desire,
Could well proclaim him Beauty's cherished son:
And beauty's self will oft these charms admire,
And steal his witching smile, his glance's living free.

Speechless with awe, in transport strangely lost,
Long Psyche stood with fixed adoring eye;
Her limbs immoveable, her senses tost
Between amazement, fear, and ecstasy,
She hangs enamoured o'er the Deity.
Till from her trembling hand extinguished falls
The fatal lamp—He starts—and suddenly
Tremendous thunders echo through the halls,
While ruin's hideous crash bursts o'er the affrighted walls.

Dread horror seizes on her sinking heart,
A mortal chillness shudders at her breast,
Her soul shrinks fainting from death's icy dart,
The groan scarce uttered dies but half exprest,
And down she sinks in deadly swoon opprest:
But when at length, awaking from her trance,
The terrors of her fate stand all confessed,
In vain she casts around her timid glance,
The rudely frowning scenes her former joys enhance.

No traces of those joys, alas, remain!
A desert solitude alone appears.
No verdant shade relieves the sandy plain,
The wide-spread waste no gentle fountain cheers,
One barren face the dreary prospect wears;
Nought through the vast horizon meets her eye
To calm the dismal tumult of her fears,
No trace of human habitation nigh,
A sandy wild beneath, above a threatening sky.

The mists of morn yet chill the gloomy air,
And heavily obscure the clouded skies;
In the mute anguish of a fixed despair
Still on the ground immoveable she lies;
At length, with lifted hands and streaming eyes,
Her mournful prayers invoke offended Love,
" Oh, let me hear thy voice once more," she cries,
" In death at least thy pity let me move,
And death, if but forgiven, a kind relief will prove.

" For what can life to thy lost Psyche give,
What can it offer but a gloomy void?
Why thus abandoned should I wish to live?
To mourn the pleasure which I once enjoyed,
The bliss my own rash folly hath destroyed;
Of all my soul most prized, or held most dear,
Nought but the sad remembrance doth abide,
And late repentance of my impious fear;
Remorse and vain regret what living soul can bear!

Oh, art thou then indeed for ever gone!
And art thou heedless of thy Psyche's woe!
From these fond arms for ever art thou flown,
And unregarded must my sorrows flow!
Ah! why too happy did I ever know
The rapturous charms thy tenderness inspires?
Ah! why did thy affections stoop so low?
Why kindle in a mortal breast such fires,
Or with celestial love inflame such rash desires?

"Abandoned thus for ever by thy love,
No greater punishment I now can bear,
From fate no farther malice can I prove;
Not all the horrors of this desert drear,
Nor death itself can now excite a fear;
The peopled earth a solitude as vast
To this despairing heart would now appear;
Here, then, my transient joys for ever past,
Let thine expiring bride thy pardon gain at last!"

Now prostrate on the bare unfriendly ground,
She waits her doom in silent agony;
When lo! the well-known soft celestial sound
She hears once more with breathless ecstasy,
"Oh! yet too dearly loved! Lost Psyche! Why
With cruel fate wouldst thou unite thy power,
And force me thus thine arms adored to fly?
Yet cheer thy drooping soul, some happier hour
Thy banished steps may lead back to thy lover's bower.

"'Though angry Venus we no more can shun,
Appease that anger and I yet am thine!
Lo! where her temple glitters to the sun;
With humble penitence approach her shrine,
Perhaps to pity she may yet incline;
But should her cruel wrath these hopes deceive,
And thou, alas! must never more be mine,
Yet shall thy lover ne'er his Psyche leave,
But, if the fates allow, unseen thy woes relieve.

" Stronger than I, they now forbid my stay;
  Psyche beloved, adieu !"   Scarce can she hear
The last faint words, which gently melt away;
And now more faint the dying sounds appear,
Borne to a distance from her longing ear;
Yet still attentively she stands unmoved,
To catch those accents which her soul could cheer,
That soothing voice which had so sweetly proved
That still his tender heart offending Psyche loved!

    And now the joyous sun had cleared the sky,
    The mist dispelled revealed the splendid fane;
    A palmy grove majestically high
    Screens the fair building from the desert plain;
    Of alabaster white and free from stain
    'Mid the tall trees the tapering columns rose;
    Thither, with fainting steps, and weary pain,
    Obedient to the voice at length she goes,
And at the threshold seeks protection and repose.

    Round the soft scene immortal roses bloom,
    While lucid myrtles in the breezes play;
    No savage beast did ever yet presume
    With foot impure within the grove to stray,
    And far from hence flies every bird of prey;
    Thus, 'mid the sandy Garamantian wild,
    When Macedonia's lord pursued his way,
    The sacred temple of great Ammon smiled,
And green encircling shades the long fatigue beguiled:

    With awe that fearfully her doom awaits
    Still at the portal Psyche timid lies,
    When lo! advancing from the hallowed gates
    Trembling she views with reverential eyes
    An aged priest.   A myrtle bough supplies
    A wand, and roses bind his snowy brows:
    " Bear hence thy feet profane, (he sternly cries,)
    Thy longer stay the goddess disallows,
Fly, nor her fiercer wrath too daringly arouse!"

His pure white robe imploringly she held,
And, bathed in tears, embraced his sacred knees;
Her mournful charms relenting he beheld,
And melting pity in his eye she sees;
" Hope not (he cries) the goddess to appease,
Retire at awful distance from her shrine,
But seek the refuge of those sheltering trees,
And now thy soul with humble awe incline
To hear her sacred will, and mark the words divine.

" Presumptuous Psyche! whose aspiring soul
The God of Love has dared to arrogate;
Rival of Venus! whose supreme control
Is now asserted by all-ruling fate,
No suppliant tears her vengeance shall abate
Till thou hast raised an altar to her power,
Where perfect happiness, in lonely state,
Has fixed her temple in secluded bower,
By foot impure of man untrodden to this hour!

" And on the altar must thou place an urn
Filled from immortal Beauty's sacred spring,
Which foul deformity to grace can turn,
And back to fond affection's eyes can bring
The charms which fleeting fled on transient wing;
Snatched from the rugged steep where first they rise,
Dark rocks their crystal source o'ershadowing,
Let their clear water sparkle to the skies
Where cloudless lustre beams which happiness supplies!

" To Venus thus for ever reconciled,
(This one atonement all her wrath disarms),
From thy loved Cupid then no more exiled
There shalt thou, free from sorrow and alarms,
Enjoy for ever his celestial charms.
But never shalt thou taste a pure repose,
Nor ever meet thy lover's circling arms,
Till, all subdued that shall thy steps oppose,
Thy perils there shall end, escaped from all thy foes."

With meek submissive woe she heard her doom,
Nor to the holy minister replied;
But in the myrtle grove's mysterious gloom
She silently retired her grief to hide.
Hopeless to tread the waste without a guide,
All unrefreshed and faint from toil she lies:
When lo! her present wants are all supplied,
Sent by the hand of Love a turtle flies,
And sets delicious food before her wondering eyes.

Cheered by the favouring omen, softer tears
Relieve her bosom from its cruel weight:
She blames the sad despondence of her fears,
When still protected by a power so great,
His tenderness her toils will mitigate.
Then with renewed strength at length she goes,
Hoping to find some skilled in secret fate,
Some learned sage, who haply might disclose
Where lay that blissful bower, the end of all her woes.

And as she went, behold, with hovering flight
The dove preceded still her doubtful way;
Its spotless plumage of the purest white,
Which shone resplendent in the blaze of day,
Could even in darkest gloom a light display;
Of heavenly birth, when first to mortals given
Named Innocence.   But ah! too short its stay;
By ravenous birds it fearfully was driven
Back to reside with Love, a denizen of heaven.

Now through the trackless wild, o'er many a mile
The messenger of Cupid led the fair,
And cheered with hope her solitary toil,
Till now a brighter face the prospects wear.
Past are the sandy wastes and deserts bare,
And many a verdant hill, and grassy dale,
And trace, that mortal culture might declare,
And many a wild wood dark, and joyous vale
Appeared her soul to soothe, could soothing scenes avail.

But other fears her timid soul distress,
'Mid strangers unprotected and alone,
The desert wilderness alarmed her less
Than cities, thus unfriended and unknown ;
But where the path was all by moss o'ergrown,
There still she chose her solitary way,
Where'er her faithful Dove before had flown
Fearful of nought she might securely stray,
For still his care supplied the wants of every day.

And still she entered every sacred grove
And homage paid to each divinity,
But chief the altar of almighty Love
Weeping embraced with fond imploring eye;
To every oracle her hopes apply,
Instructions for her dangerous path to gain :
Exclaiming oft, with a desponding sigh,
" Ah! how through all such dangers, toil, and pain,
Shall Psyche's helpless steps their object e'er attain !"

And now, remote from every peopled town,
One sultry day a cooling bower she found :
There, as I whilom sung, she laid her down,
Where rich profusion of gay flowers around
Had decked with artless shew the sloping ground;
There the wild rose and modest violet grow,
There all thy charms, Narcissus ! still abound :
There wrapt in verdure fragrant lilies blow,
Lilies that love the vale, and hide their bells of snow.

Thy flowers, Adonis ! bright vermilion shew ;
Still for his love the yellow Crocus pines ;
There, while indignant blushes seem to glow,
Beloved by Phœbus his Acanthus shines ;
Reseda still her drooping head reclines
With faithful homage to his golden rays,
And, though 'mid clouds their lustre he resigns,
An image of the constant heart displays,
While silent still she turns her fond pursuing gaze.

And every sweet that Spring with fairy hands
Scatters in thy green path, enchanting May!
And every flowering shrub there clustering stands
As though they wooed her to a short delay,
Yielding a charm to sooth here weary way;
Soft was the tufted moss, and sweet the breeze,
With lulling sound the murmuring waters play,
With lulling sound from all the rustling trees
The fragrant gale invites to cool refreshing ease.

There as she sought repose, her sorrowing heart
Recalled her absent love with bitter sighs;
Regret had deeply fixed the poisoned dart,
Which ever rankling in her bosom lies ;
In vain she seeks to close her weary eyes,
Those eyes still swim incessantly in tears,
Hope in her cheerless bosom fading dies,
Distracted by a thousand cruel fears,
While banished from his love for ever she appears.

Oh! thou best comforter of that sad heart
Whom fortune's spite assails; come, gentle Sleep,
The weary mourner soothe! for well the art
Thou knowest in soft forgetfulness to steep
The eyes which sorrow taught to watch and weep;
Let blissful visions now her spirits cheer,
Or lull her cares to peace in slumbers deep,
Till, from fatigue refreshed and anxious fear,
Hope, like the morning star, once more shall re-appear.

CANTO III.

ARGUMENT.

PRAISE of Love—Psyche's Champion, with his attendant Constance, described—The Knight assumes the command of Passion, who appears as a Lion—Psyche proceeds under the protection of the Knight—Persuaded to repose in the Bower of loose Delight—Her escape from thence—Led by Innocence to Retirement—Psyche meets Vanity and Flattery—Betrayed by them into the power of Ambition—Rescued by her Knight.

Oh, who art thou who darest of Love complain?
He is a gentle spirit and injures none!
His foes are ours; from them the bitter pain,
The keen, deep anguish, the heart-rending groan,
Which in his milder reign are never known.
His tears are softer than the April showers,
White-handed Innocence supports his throne,
His sighs are sweet as breath of earliest flowers,
Affection guides his steps, and peace protects his bowers.

But scarce admittance he on earth can find,
Opposed by vanity, by fraud ensnared,
Suspicion frights him from the gloomy mind,
And jealousy in vain his smiles has shared,
Whose sullen frown the gentle godhead scared;
From passion's rapid blaze in haste he flies,
His wings alone the fiercer flame has spared;
From him ambition turns his scornful eyes,
And avarice, slave to gold, a generous lord denies.

But chief Inconstancy his power destroys;
To mock his lovely form, an idle train
With magic skill she dressed in transient toys,
By these the selfish votaries she can gain
Whom Love's more simple bands could ne'er detain.
Ah! how shall Psyche through such mortal foes
The fated end of all her toils attain?
Sadly she ponders o'er her hopeless woes,
Till on the pillowy turf she sinks to short repose.

But, as the careless lamb, whom playful chance,
Thoughtless of danger, has enticed to rove,
Amidst her gambols casts a sudden glance
Where lurks her wily foe within the grove,
Anxious to fly, but still afraid to move,
All hopeless of escape—so looks the maid,
Such dread her half-awakened senses prove,
When roused from sleep before her eyes dismayed
A knight all armed appears close 'mid the embowering shade.

Trembling she gazed, until the stranger knight,
Tempering with mildest courtesy the awe
Which majesty inspired, low in her sight
Obeisance made ; nor would he nearer draw,
Till, half subdued surprise and fear, he saw
Pale terror yielding to the rosy grace,
The pure congealed blood begin to thaw,
And flowing through her crystal veins apace
Suffuse with mantling blush her mild celestial face.

Gently approaching then with fairest speech
He proffered service to the lonely dame,
And prayed her that she might not so impeach
The honour of his youth's yet spotless fame,
As aught to fear which might his knighthood shame ;
But if her unprotected steps to guard,
The glory of her champion he might claim,
He asked no other guerdon or reward,
Than what bright honour's self might to his deeds award.

Doubting, and musing much within her mind,
With half-suspicious, half-confiding eye,
A while she stood ; her thoughts bewildered find
No utterance, unwilling to deny
Such proffered aid, yet bashful to reply
With quick assent, since though concealed his face
Beneath his helm, yet might she well espy
And in each fair proportion plainly trace
The symmetry of form, and perfect youthful grace.

Hard were it to describe the nameless charm
That o'er each limb, in every action played,
The softness of that voice, which could disarm
The hand of fury of its deadly blade;
In shining armour was the youth arrayed,
And on his shield a bleeding heart he bore,
His lofty crest light plumes of azure shade,
There shone a wounded dragon bathed in gore,
And bright with silver beamed the silken scarf he wore.

His milk-white steed with glittering trappings blazed,
Whose reins a beauteous boy attendant held,
On the fair squire with wonder Psyche gazed,
For scarce he seemed of age to bear the shield,
Far less a ponderous lance, or sword to wield;
Yet well this little page his lord had served,
His youthful arm had many a foe repelled,
His watchful eye from many a snare preserved,
Nor ever from his steps in any danger swerved.

Graced with the gift of a perpetual youth,
No lapse of years had power his form to change;
Constance was named the boy, whose matchless truth,
Though oft enticed with other lords to range,
Nor fraud, nor force could from that knight estrange;
His mantle of celestial blue was made,
And its bright texture wrought with art so strange
That the fresh brilliant gloss could never fade,
And lustre yet unknown to Psyche's eyes displayed.

Thus while she gazed, behold with horrid roar
A lion from the neighbouring forest rushed,
A golden chain around his neck he bore,
Which richly glowing with carbuncles blushed,
While his fierce eye-balls fiery rage had flushed:
Forth steps the youth before the affrighted fair,
Who in his mighty paw already crushed
Seems in the terrors of her wild despair,
And her mute quivering lips a death-like paleness wear.

But scarce the kingly beast the knight beheld,
When crouching low, submissive at his feet,
His wrath extinguished, and his valour quelled,
He seemed with reverence and obedience sweet
Him as his long-acknowledged lord to greet.
While, in acceptance of the new command,
Well pleased the youth received the homage meet,
Then seized the splendid chain with steady hand,
Full confident to rule, and every foe withstand.

And, when at length recovered from her fear,
The timid Psyche mounts his docile steed,
Much prayed, she tells to his attentive ear
(As on her purposed journey they proceed)
The doubtful course the oracle decreed: .
And how, observant of her friendly guide,
She still pursued its flight, with all the speed
Her fainting strength had hitherto supplied:
What pathless wilds she crossed! What forests darkling wide!

Which having heard, the courteous knight began.
With counsel sweet to soothe her wounded heart;
Divinely eloquent, persuasion ran
The herald of his words ere they depart
His lips, which well might confidence impart
As he revealed how he himself was bound
By solemn vow, that neither force nor art
His helmet should unloose, till he had found
The bower of happiness, that long-sought fairy ground.

" I too (he said) divided from my love,
The offended power of Venus deprecate,
Like thee, through paths untrodden, sadly rove
In search of that fair spot prescribed by fate,
The blessed term of my afflicted state,
Where I the mistress of my soul shall find,
For whose dear sake no toil to me seems great,
Nor any dangers to my search assigned
Can from its purpose fright my ardent longing mind.

" Psyche ! thy soft and sympathising heart
Shall share.the rapture cf thy loyal knight;
He too, in thy content shall bear a part,
Blest witness of thy new-restored delight;
My vows of true allegiance here I plight,
Ne'er to forsake thee till thy perils end,
Thy steps to guard, in thy protection fight,
By counsel aid, and by my arm defend,
And prove myself in all, thy champion and thy friend."

So on they went, her cheerless heart revived
By promised succour in her doubtful way ;
And much of hope she to herself derived,
From the warm eagerness his lips display
In their pursuit to suffer no delay:
" And sure, (she softly sighed) my dearest Lord,
Thy watchful love still guides me as I stray,
Not chance alone could such an aid afford,
Lo ! beasts of prey confess the heaven-assisted sword."

Now from his crystal urn, with chilling hand,
Vesper had sprinkled all the earth with dew,
A misty veil obscured the neighbouring land,
And shut the fading landscape from their view ;
A beaten path they eagerly pursue,
(For now refreshment and repose they need,
As Psyche weary of long travel grew,)
Where by a river's bank it seemed to lead,
Along its sinuous course they heedlessly proceed.

At length the lordly beast that bore the knight
Explored the river's depth with sudden bound :
Psyche, who heard the plunge with strange affright,
Her champion re-assured with welcome sound,
That he the other bank had safely found ;
And, while he spoke, emerging from the shade,
A joyous goodly train appear around,
Of many a gallant youth and white-robed maid,
Who grateful welcome gave, and courteous greeting paid

Quick through the trees a thousand torches blazed
The gloom to banish, and the scene disclose
To Psyche, all irresolute, amazed:
A bridge with stately arch at distance rose,
Thither at once the gay assembly goes,
Not unattended by the charmed knight,
Inviting Psyche to partake repose,
Pointing where shone their bower illumined bright,
Their bower so passing fair, the bower of loose Delight.

At length with timid foot the bridge she past,
And to her guardian knight clung fearfully,
While many a doubting glance around she cast,
If still her watchful dove she might espy;
Feebly it seemed on labouring wing to fly,
Till, dazzled by the sudden glare around,
In painful trance it closed its dizzy eye,
And had it not fair Psyche's bosom found,
Its drooping pinion soon had touched the unhallowed ground.

Hence there arose within her heart sore dread
Which no alluring pleasure could dispel;
The splendid hall with luscious banquet spread,
The soft-breathed flutes which in sweet concert swell,
With melody of song unspeakable;
Nor the light dancing troop in roses drest,
Could chase the terrors which she dared not tell,
While, fondly cherished in her anxious breast,
She strove in vain to soothe the fluttering bird to rest.

On a soft downy couch the guests are placed,
And close behind them stands their watchful page,
But much his strict attendance there disgraced,
And much was scorned his green and tender age,
His calm fixed eye, and steady aspect sage:
But him nor rude disdain, nor mockery,
Nor soothing blandishments could e'er engage
The wanton mazes of their sports to try,
Or from his lord to turn his firm adhering eye.

White-bosomed nymphs around with loosened zones
All on the guests obsequiously tend,
Some sing of love with soft expiring tones,
While Psyche's melting eyes the strain commend;
Some o'er their heads the canopy suspend,
Some hold the sparkling bowl, while some with skill
Ambrosial showers and balmy juices blend,
Or the gay lamps with liquid odours fill,
Whose many-coloured fires divinest sweets distil.

And now a softer light they seemed to shed,
And sweetest music ushered in their queen:
Her languid steps by winged boys are led,
Who in their semblance might have Cupids been;
Close wrapt in veils her following train was seen;
Herself looked lovely in her loose attire,
Her smiling eyes gave lustre to the scene,
And still, where'er they turned their wanton fire,
Each thrilling nerve confessed the rapture they inspire.

The stranger guests she viewed with welcome glad,
And crowned the banquet with reception sweet,
To fill the glowing bowl her nymphs she bad,
And graceful rising from her splendid seat,
She would herself present the sparkling treat;
When lo! the dove, alarmed, with sudden start,
Spurned the bright cup, and dashed it at her feet,
For well he knew 'twas mixed with treacherous art
To sting his Psyche's breast with agonizing smart.

Regardless of her supplicating tears,
Each eye with vengeful rage the insult sees,
Her knight's protection now in vain appears;
The offended sovereign anxious to appease,
A thousand hands prepare the dove to seize;
Nor was this all, for as the tumult rose,
Sudden more thick than swarm of summer bees,
The secret dens their venomed hoards disclose,
And horror at the sight her vital spirits froze.

Hissing aloud with undulations dire,
Their forked tongues unnumbered serpents show,
Their tainted breath emitting poisonous fire,
All turn on Psyche as their mortal foe;
But he, whose arm was never weak or slow,
Now rushed before her with resistless spring,
On either side the oft-repeated blow
Repulsed the malice of their deadly sting,
While sparks of wrathful fire from their fierce jaws they fling.

" Fly, Psyche! these are slander's hellish brood!
Contest I know is vain," her champion cried.
Her passage now the opposing train withstood;
Struck with disgust their hideous forms she spied,
For lo! each silken veil is thrown aside,
And foul deformity, and filth obscene,
With monstrous shapes appear on every side;
But vanished is their fair and treacherous queen,
And with her every charm that decked the enchanted scene

Meanwhile the dove had soared above their reach,
But hovered still in anxious Psyche's sight;
Precursor of escape, it seemed to teach
Whither she safest might direct her flight,
And find a passport in her foes despight;
One rugged path there lay with briars o'ergrown,
Then dark and dismal with the shades of night,
Thither the dove on rapid wing had flown,
Conspicuous 'mid the gloom its silver plumage shone.

Yet she delayed, o'ercome by terror's power,
And scarce her fainting form the knight could shield,
When lo! still active in the trying hour,
Constance rushed fearless through the dreadful field,
With breast-plate firm invulnerably steeled,
He heeded not the storms which round him press,
To any perils he disdained to yield,
Endued with prudence as with hardiness,
And ever skilled to bring due succour in distress.

Lo! swift returning on his master's steed,
In his right hand he held the lion's chain,
The mighty beast his gentleness could lead,
Though little used to bear the curb or rein,
And 'mid those groves accustomed to remain,
Yet now prepared, with sweet submissive grace,
He ready stands the knight to bear again,
While trembling Psyche on the steed they place,
Which swift as lightning flies far from the dreadful chase.

Rough was the rude wild way, and many a thorn
Tore her loose garments in their rapid flight·
O'er many a league the panting fair is borne,
Till now, emerging from the shades of night,
The grey-eyed morn stole forth her pallid light.
Then first she paused, unable to proceed,
Exhausted with fatigue, and pain, and fright.
"Turn, Psyche," cried the youth, "relax thy speed,
And see thyself at length from thy pursuers freed."

'Mid the thick forest was a lonely dell,
Where foot of man was seldom known to tread,
The sloping hills all round in graceful swell
The little green with woods environed;
Hither the dove their passive course had led:
Here the thin smoke blue rising 'mid the trees,
Where broad and brown the deepest umbrage spread
Spoke the abode of safe retired ease,
And Psyche gladly there her dove descending sees.

In lowly cottage, walled with mossy sod,
Close by a little spring's perpetual rill,
A hermit dwelt, who many a year had trod
With sacred solitude that pine-clad hill,
And loved with holy images to fill
His soul enrapt; yet courteous then besought
A while secluded here to rest; and still
Replete with kind and hospitable thought,
To a sequestered bower the weary Psyche brought.

Skilled in the virtue of each healing flower,
And the wild fruit's restoring juice to blend,
He spreads the frugal fare of wholesome power,
And heedfully his cares their wants attend;
A docile ear to his advice they lend,
And sage instruction from his precepts take,
Which much their future journey may befriend;
Wisdom with soothing eloquence he spake,
Pleased to resolve their doubts, and all their cares partake.

In those sweet placid scenes a while they rest,
Till Psyche finds her fainting strength revive;
And here her dove, as in a quiet nest,
Delighted seems to sportive joy alive;
And hence they surest confidence derive.
He plumes his wings, and through his swelling throat
(No more a ruffled, fearful fugitive)
In gentle murmurs pours his dulcet note,
While Psyche listening sits in some still vale remote.

Oh! have you never known the silent charm
That undisturbed retirement yields the soul,
Where no intruder might your peace alarm,
And tenderness hath wept without control,
While melting fondness o'er the bosom stole?
Did fancy never, in some lonely grove,
Abridge the hours which must in absence roll?
Those pensive pleasures did you never prove,
Oh, you have never loved! you know not what is love!

They do not love who can to these prefer
The tumult of the gay, or folly's roar;
The Muse they know not; nor delight in her
Who can the troubled soul to rest restore,
Calm Contemplation: Yes, I must deplore
Their joyless state, even more than his who mourns
His love for ever lost; delight no more
Unto his widowed heart indeed returns,
Yet, while he weeps, his soul their cold indifference spurns.

But if soft hope illumines fancy's dream,
Assuring him of love and constancy,
How exquisite do then the moments seem,
When he may hide himself from every eye,
And cherish the dear thought in secrecy !
While sweet remembrance soothes his thrilling heart,
And brings once more past hours of kindness nigh,
Recals the look of love when forced to part,
And turns to drops of joy the tears that sadly start.

Forgetful of the dangers of her way,
Imagination oft would Psyche bear
To her long travel's end, and that blest day
When Love unveiled should to her eyes appear ;
When she might view his charms exempt from fear,
Taste his pure kisses, feel his balmy sighs,
Rest in the fond embrace of arms so dear,
Gaze with soft rapture on his melting eyes,
And hear his voice divine, the music of the skies !

Their destined course impatient to achieve,
The knight is urgent onward to proceed :
Cheered with recruited strength, they take their leave
Of their kind host, and pay their grateful meed
Of warmest thanks sincere ; onward they speed
Their sunless journey long through forests green,
And tangled thickets rank with many a weed ;
And when at closing day a hut is seen,
They seek the humble roof, nor scorn its welcome mean.

It happened once that, early roused from sleep,
(Ere her damp veil the virgin Morn had cast
From her pale face, not yet with blushes deep
Lovely suffused, as when approaching fast
His herald star proclaims her spouse at last)
Psyche, forsaking soon her homely bed,
Alone had fearless the low threshold past,
And, to beguile the hours which lingering fled,
Light o'er the dewy plain walked forth with nimble tread.

Yet though the knight close wrapped in slumber lay,
Her steps, at distance, still the page pursued,
Fearful that danger might befal her way,
Or lest, entangled in the mazy wood,
Returning she should miss the pathway rude.
The lark now hails the sun with rapturous song,
The cheerful earth resounds with gratitude,
O'er the gay scene as Psyche tript along,
She felt her spirits rise, her lightened heart grow strong.

And hark, soft music steals upon the ear !
'Tis woman's voice most exquisitely sweet !
Behold two female forms approaching near
Arrest with wonder Psyche's timid feet ;
On a gay car, by speckled panthers fleet
Is drawn in gallant state a seeming queen,
And at her foot, on low but graceful seat,
A gentle nymph of lovely form is seen,
In robe of fairest white, with scarf of pleasant green.

In strains of most bewitching harmony,
And still adapted to her sovereign's praise,
She filled the groves with such sweet melody,
That, quite o'ercome with rapture and amaze,
Psyche stood listening to the warbled lays;
Yet with a sullen, scarce approving ear
Her mistress sits, but with attentive gaze
Her eyes she fixes on a mirror clear,
Where still by fancy's spell unrivalled charms appear.

And, as she looked with aspect ever new,
She seemed on change and novel grace intent,
Her robe was formed of ever-varying hue,
And whimsically placed each ornament ;
On her attire, with rich luxuriance spent,
The treasures of the earth, the sea, the air,
Are vainly heaped her wishes to content ;
Yet were her arms and snowy bosom bare,
And both in painted pride shone exquisitely fair.

Her braided tresses in profusion drest,
Circled with diadem, and nodding plumes,
Sported their artful ringlets o'er her breast,
And to the breezes gave their rich perfumes;
Her cheek with tint of borrowed roses blooms:
Used to receive from all rich offerings,
She quaffs with conscious right the fragrant fumes
Which her attendant from a censer flings,
Who graceful feeds the flame with incense while she sings.

Soon as her glance fair Psyche's form had caught,
Her soft attendant smiling she addressed :
"Behold, Lusinga! couldst thou e'er have thought
That these wild woods were so in beauty blest?
Let but that nymph in my attire be drest,
And scarce her loveliness will yield to mine!
At least invite her in our bower to rest,
Before her eyes let all my splendour shine,
Perhaps to dwell with us her heart we may incline."

With softest smile applauding all she heard,
٬Lusinga bowing left her golden seat,
And Psyche, who at first in doubt had feared
While listening to the lay so silver sweet,
Now passive followed with unconscious feet;
Till Constance, all alarmed, impatient flew,
And soft his whispers of the maid entreat
To fly the Syren's song, for well he knew
What lurking dangers hence would to his Lord ensue.

"Oh, do not trust her treacherous lips," he cried,
"She is the subtle slave of Vanity,
Her queen, the child of folly, and of pride,
To lure thee to her power each art will try,
Nor ever will release thee peaceably."
He spoke, but spoke in vain, for lo! from far,
Of giant port they fast approaching spy
A knight, high mounted on a glittering car,
From whose conspicuous crest flames wide a dazzling star

"Psyche escape! Ambition is at hand!"
The page exclaims: while swift as thought he flies;
She would have followed, but with parley bland
Lusinga soon her terrors pacifies.
"Fair nymph, ascend my car," the sovereign cries,
"I will convey thee where thy wishes lead,
Haply the safest course I may advise
How thou thy journey mayst perform with speed;
For ne'er in woods to dwell such beauty was decreed."

So gently urgent her consent they wooed
With much persuasion of the stranger knight,
That yielding Psyche now no more withstood,
But, pointing out to her observant sight
The humble cot where she had passed the night,
She prayed her kind conductress there to turn,
And promised to herself what vast delight
Her wondering knight would feel at her return,
And with what blushing shame the timid page would burn.

But scarcely had she climbed the fatal car,
When swifter than the wind the panthers flew,
The traversed plains and woods, receding far,
Soon shut from trembling Psyche's anxious view
The spot where she had left her guardian true;
With desperate efforts, all in vain she tries
To escape the ills which now too sure she knew
Must from her ill-placed confidence arise;
Betrayed—Ah! self-betrayed, a wretched sacrifice.

She strove to quit the car with sudden bound,
Ah, vain attempt! she now perceived too late
A thousand silken trammels, subtly wound
O'er her fair form, detained her as she sate:
Lost in despair she yields to her sad fate,
And silent hears, but with augmented fright,
The queen describe her brother's splendid state,
Who now outstripped them by his rapid flight,
And prest his foaming steeds to gain the arduous height.

High o'er the spacious plain a mountain rose,
A stately castle on its summit stood:
Huge craggy cliffs behind their strength oppose
To the rough surges of the dashing flood;
The rocky shores a boldly rising wood
On either side conceals; bright shine the towers,
And seem to smile upon the billows rude.
In front the eye, with comprehensive powers,
Sees wide-extended plains enriched with splendid bowers.

Hither they bore the sad reluctant fair,
Who mounts with dizzy eye the awful steep;
The blazing structure seems high poised in air,
And its light pillars tremble o'er the deep:
As yet the heavens are calm, the tempests sleep,
She knows not half the horrors of her fate:
Nor feels the approaching ruin's whirlwind sweep:
Yet with ill-boding fears she past the gate,
And turned with sickening dread from scenes of gorgeous state.

In vain the haughty master of the hall
Invites her to partake his regal throne,
With cold indifference she looks on all
The gilded trophies, and the well-wrought stone
Which in triumphal arches proudly shone:
And as she casts around her timid eye,
Back to her knight her trembling heart is flown,
And many an anxious wish, and many a sigh,
Invokes his gallant arm protection to supply.

Sudden the lurid heavens obscurely frown,
And sweeping gusts the coming storm proclaim;
Flattery's soft voice the howling tempests drown,
While the roofs catch the greedy lightning's flame.
Loud in their fears, the attendant train exclaim
The light-built fabric ne'er can stand the blast,
And all its insecure foundations blame:
Tumultuously they rush: the chief aghast
Beholds his throne o'erturned, his train dispersing fast.

Psyche dismayed, yet thoughtful of escape,
In anxious silence to the portal prest;
And freedom would have hailed in any shape,
Though seen in death's tremendous colours drest:
But ah! she feels the knight's strong grasp arrest
Her trembling steps. "Think not," he cries, " to fly
With yon false crowd, who, by my favours blest,
Can now desert me, when with changeful eye
Inclement fortune frowns from yon dark angry sky."

While yet he spoke loud bursts the groaning hall,
With frightful peal the thundering domes resound,
Disjointed columns in wild ruin fall,
While the huge arches tremble to the ground.
Yet unappalled amid the crash is found
The daring chief: his hold he firm maintains
Though hideous devastation roars around;
Plunged headlong down his prey he still sustains,
Who in his powerful grasp in death-like swoon remains.

Down sinks the palace with its mighty lord,
Hurled from the awful steep with vehemence
Even to the floods below, which angry roared
And gaping wide received the weight immense:
Indignant still, with fearless confidence
He rose, high mounting o'er the heaving waves;
Against their rage one arm is his defence,
The other still his lovely burden saves,
Though strong the billows beat, and fierce the tempest raves.

The blazing star yet shone upon his brow,
And flamed triumphant o'er the dashing main;
He rides secure the watery waste, and now
The sheltering shore he might in safety gain;
The sheltering shore he shuns with proud disdain,
And breasts the adverse tide.   Ah, rash resource!
Yon vessel, Prince, thou never shalt attain!
For plunging 'mid the deep, with generous force,
See where the lion's lord pursues thy hardy course!

Psyche a well-known voice to life restores,
Once more her eyes unclosing view the light,
But not the waters, nor receding shores,
One only object can arrest her sight,
High o'er the flood she sees her valiant knight,
And sudden joy, and hopes scarce trusted cheer
Even in that awful moment's dread affright;
Her feeble cry indeed he cannot hear,
But sees her out-stretched arms, and seems already near.

In vain the giant knight exerts his strength;
Urged by the impetuous youth the lion prest,
And gaining fast upon his flight, at length
Prepared his daring progress to arrest,
And seized with furious jaw his struggling breast;
Gasping he loosed his hold—and Psyche lost
The overwhelming wave with ruin had opprest,
But Constance, ever near when needed most,
The sinking beauty caught, and bore her to the coast.

Stung with the shame of the relinquished prey,
Mad with revenge, and hate, and conscious pride,
The knight, recovered from his short dismay,
Dashes resistless through the foaming tide;
The billows yielding to his arm divide,
As rushing on the youth he seeks the shore;
But now a combat strange on either side
Amid the waves begins; each hopes no more
The engulphing deep his foe shall e'er to light restore.

Beside the cold inhospitable lands,
Where suns long absent dawn with lustre pale,
Thus on his bark the bold Biscayan stands,
And bids his javelin rouse the parent whale:
Fear, pain, and rage at once her breast assail,
The agitated ocean foams around,
Lashed by the sounding fury of her tail,
Or as she mounts the surge with frightful bound,
Wide echoing to her cries the bellowing shores resound.

Fierce was the contest, but at length subdued,
The youth exulting sees his giant foe.
With wonder still the enormous limbs he viewed,
Which lifeless now the waves supporting show.
His starred helm, that now was first laid low,
He seized as trophy of the wonderous fight,
And bade the sparkling gem on Constance glow,
While Psyche's eyes, soft beaming with delight,
Through tears of grateful praise applaud her gallant knight.

CANTO IV.

THE ARGUMENT.

Introduction—Sympathy—Suspicion—Psyche benighted—Credulity re-
presented, according to a Picture by Apelles, as an old Woman, the de-
voted prey of Slander, or the Blatant Beast—Contest between the Knight
and Slander—The Knight wounded—Slander flies—Credulity leads
Psyche to the Castle of Suspicion—Psyche deluded, laments the desertion
of her Knight to the train of Inconstancy—Psyche betrayed by Suspicion
into the power of Jealousy—Persuaded by him that her Knight, by
whom she was then abandoned, was indeed Love—Psyche delivered by
her Knight—Reconciliation.

FULL gladsome was my heart ere while to tell
How proud Ambition owned superior Love;
For ah! too oft his sterner power could quell
The mild affections which more gently move,
And rather silent fled than with him strove:
For Love content and tranquil saw with dread
The busy scenes Ambition's schemes approve,
And, by the hand of Peace obscurely led,
From pride of public life disgusted ever fled.

There are who know not the delicious charm
Of sympathising hearts; let such employ
Their active minds; the trumpet's loud alarm
Shall yield them hope of honourable joy,
And courts may lure them with each splendid toy:
But ne'er may vanity or thirst of fame
The dearer bliss of loving life destroy;
Oh! blind to man's chief good who Love disclaim,
And barter pure delight for glory's empty name!

Blest Psyche! thou hast 'scaped the tyrant's power!
Thy gentle heart shall never know the pain
Which tortures Pride in his most prosperous hour:
Yet dangers still unsung for thee remain;
Nor must thou unmolested hope to gain
Immortal beauty's never-failing spring;
Oh! no—nor yet tranquillity attain:
But though thy heart the pangs of doubt may sting,
Thy faithful knight shall yet thy steps in safety bring.

Warned by late peril now she scarcely dares
Quit for one moment his protecting eye:
Sure in his sight, her soul of nought despairs,
And nought looks dreadful when that arm is nigh
On which her hopes with confidence rely;
By his advice their constant course they bend,
He points where hidden danger they should fly,
On him securely, as her heaven-sent friend,
She bids her grateful heart contentedly depend.

Oh! who the exquisite delight can tell,
The joy which mutual confidence imparts?
Or who can paint the charm unspeakable
Which links in tender bands two faithful hearts?
In vain assailed by fortune's envious darts,
Their mitigated woes are sweetly shared,
And doubled joy reluctantly departs:
Let but the sympathising heart be spared,
What sorrow seems not light, what peril is not dared?

Oh! never may suspicion's gloomy sky
Chill the sweet glow of fondly trusting love!
Nor ever may he feel the scowling eye
Of dark distrust his confidence reprove!
In pleasing error may I rather rove,
With blind reliance on the hand so dear,
Than let cold prudence from my eyes remove
Those sweet delusions, where nor doubt nor fear
Nor foul disloyalty nor cruel change appear.

The noble mind is ever prone to trust;
Yet love with fond anxiety is joined;
And timid tenderness is oft unjust;
The coldness which it dreads too prompt to find,
And torture the too susceptible mind.
Hence rose the gloom which oft o'er Psyche stole
Lest he she loved, unmindful or unkind,
Should careless slight affection's soft control,
Or she long absent lose her influence o'er his soul.

'Twas evening, and the shades which sudden fell
Seemed to forebode a dark unlovely night;
The sighing wood-nymphs from their caves foretel
The storm which soon their quiet shall affright;
Nor cheering star nor moon appears in sight,
Nor taper twinkles through the rustling leaves,
And sheds afar its hospitable light:
But hark! a dismal sound the ear receives,   [ceives.
And through the obscuring gloom the eye strange forms per-

It was a helpless female who exclaimed,
Whose blind and aged form an ass sustained:
Misshaped and timorous, of light ashamed,
In darksome woods her hard-earned food she gained,
And her voracious appetite maintained,
Though all-devouring, yet unsatisfied;
Nor aught of hard digestion she disdained,
Whate'er was offered greedily she tried,
And meanly served, as slave, whoever food supplied.

A cruel monster now her steps pursued,
Well known of yore, and named the Blatant Beast,
And soon he seized his prey with grasp so rude,
So fiercely on her feeble body prest,
That had the courteous knight not soon released
Her unresisting limbs from violence,
She must have sunk by his rough jaws opprest:
The spiteful beast, enraged at the defence,
Now turned upon the knight with foaming vehemence.

But, when his fury felt the couched spear,
On Psyche's unarmed form he bellowing flew ;
'Twas there alone the knight his rage could fear;
Swifter than thought his flaming sword he drew,
And from his hand the doubtful javelin threw,
Lest erring it might wound the trembling fair :
Eager the cruel monster to subdue,
He scorned to use his shield's protecting care,
And rashly left his side in part exposed and bare.

Sharp were the wounds of his avenging steel,
Which forced the roaring beast to quit the field :
Yet ere he fled, the knight unused to feel
The power of any foe, or e'er to yield
To any arm which sword or spear could wield,
Perceived the venom of his tooth impure ;
But, with indignant silence, unrevealed
The pain he bore, while through the gloom obscure
The beast, in vain pursued, urged on his flight secure.

And now the hag, delivered from her fear,
Her grateful thanks upon the knight bestowed,
And, as they onward went, in Psyche's ear
Her tongue with many a horrid tale o'erflowed,
Which warned her to forsake that venturous road,
And seek protection in the neighbouring grove ;
Where dwelt a prudent dame, who oft bestowed
Her sage advice, when pilgrims doomed to rove,
Benighted there, had else with lurking dangers strove.

The knight now softly bade his charge beware,
Nor trust Credulity, whom well he knew ;
Yet he himself, harassed with pain and care,
And heedful of the storm which fiercer grew,
Yielded, a path more sheltered to pursue :
Now soon entangled in a gloomy maze,
Psyche no longer has her knight in view,
Nor sees his page's star-crowned helmet blaze ;
Close at her side alone the hag loquacious strays.

Fearful she stops, and calls aloud in vain,
The storm-roused woods roar only in reply;
Anxious her loved protector to regain,
She trembling listens to Credulity,
Who points where they a glimmering light may spy;
Which, through the shade of intervening trees,
And all the misty blackness of the sky,
Casting a weak and dubious ray she sees,
And fain by this would seek her terrors to appease.

Yet hoping that, allured by that same light
Which singly seemed through all the gloom to shine,
She there at last might meet her wandering knight,
Thither her footsteps doubtingly incline,
As best the uncertain path they could divine,
All tangled as it wound through brake and briar:
While to affright her soul at once combine
A thousand shapeless forms of terror dire—
Here shrieks the ill-omened bird, there glares the meteor's fire.

In the deep centre of the mazy wood,
With matted ivy and wild vine o'ergrown,
A Gothic castle solitary stood,
With massive walls built firm of murky stone;
Long had Credulity its mistress known,
Meagre her form and tawny was her hue,
Unsociably she lived, unloved, alone,
No cheerful prospects gladdened e'er her view,
And her pale hollow eyes oblique their glances threw.

Now had they reached the sad and dreary bower
Where dark Disfida held her gloomy state:
The grated casements strong with iron power,
The huge port-cullis creaking o'er the gate,
The surly guards that round the draw-bridge wait,
Chill Psyche's heart with sad foreboding fears;
Nor ever had she felt so desolate
As when at length her guide the porter hears,
And at the well-known call reluctantly appears.

In hall half lighted with uncertain rays,
Such as expiring tapers transient shed,
The gloomy princess sat, no social blaze
The unkindled hearth supplied, no table spread
Cheered the lone guest who weetless wandered,
But melancholy silence reigned around,
While on her arm she leaned her pensive head,
And anxious watched, as sullenly she frowned,
Of distant whispers low to catch the doubtful sound.

Startled to hear an unaccustomed noise,
Sudden she rose, and on the intruders bent
Her prying eye askance ; but soon the voice
Of her old slave appeased her discontent,
And a half-welcome to her guests she lent :
Her frequent questions satisfied at last,
Through all the neighbouring woods her scouts she sent
To seek the knight, while Psyche's tears flowed fast,
And all the live-long night in anxious woe she past.

The sullen bell had told the midnight hour,
And sleep had laid the busy world to rest,
All but the watchful lady of that bower
And wretched Psyche . her distracted breast
The agony of sad suspense opprest,
Now to the casement eagerly she flies,
And now the wished-for voice her fancy blest :
Alas! the screaming night-bird only cries ;
Only the drear obscure there meets her straining eyes.

Has thy heart sickened with deferred hope ?
Or felt the impatient anguish of suspense ?
Or hast thou tasted of the bitter cup
Which disappointment's withered hands dispense ?
Thou knowest the poison which o'erflowed from hence
O'er Psyche's tedious, miserable hours.
The unheeded notes of plaintive Innocence
No longer soothe her soul with wonted powers,
While false Disfida's tales her listening ear devours.

Of rapid torrents and deep marshy fens,
Of ambushed foes and unseen pits they tell,
Of ruffians rushing from their secret dens,
Of foul magicians and of wizard spell,
The poisoned lance and net invisible ;
While Psyche shuddering sees her knight betrayed
Into the snares of some enchanter fell,
Beholds him bleeding in the treacherous shade,
Or hears his dying voice implore in vain for aid.

At length the cruel messengers return,
Their trampling steeds sound welcome in her ear ;
Her rapid feet the ground impatient spurn,
As eagerly she flies their news to hear.
Alas ! they bring no tidings which may cheer
Her sorrowing soul opprest, disconsolate !
" Dismiss," they cry, " each idly timid fear !
No dangers now thy faithless knight await,
Lured by a wanton fair to bowers of peaceful state.

" We saw him blithely follow where she led,
And urged him to return to thee in vain :
Some other knight, insultingly he said,
Thy charms might soon for thy protection gain,
If still resolved to tread with weary pain
The tedious road to that uncertain land ;
But he should there contentedly remain ;
No other bliss could now his heart demand
Than that new lady's love and kindly proffered hand.

A while she stood in silent wonder lost,
And scarce believes the strange abandonment ;
No fears like this her heart had ever crost,
Nor could she think his mind so lightly bent,
Could swerve so quickly from its first intent ;
Till sudden bursting forth in angry mood
Disfida gave her indignation vent.
" Ah, well I know," she cried, " that wicked brood
Whose cursed ensnaring arts in vain my cares withstood.

"Vile Varia's fickle and inconstant train,
  Perpetual torments of my harassed days :
  Their nightly thefts my fruits, my flowers sustain,
  Their wanton goats o'er all my vineyards graze,
  My corn lies scattered, and my fences blaze,
  My friends, my followers they basely lure ;
  I know their mischievous detested ways!
  My castle vainly have I built so sure,
While from their treacherous wiles my life is insecure.

" But I will lead thee to the glittering sands,
  Where shines their hollow many-coloured fane :
  There, as the circling group fantastic stands,
  Thy truant knight perhaps thou mayst regain
 .From the light arts of that seductive train."
  She paused—but Psyche spoke not in reply ;
  Her noble heart, which swelled with deep disdain,
  Forbad the utterance of a single sigh,
And shamed the indignant tear which started to her eye.

At length with firm, but gentle dignity,
  And cold averted eye, she thus replies :
  "No! let him go : nor power nor wish have I
  His conduct to control.   Let this suffice ;
  Before my path a surer guardian flies,
  By whose direction onward I proceed
  Soon as the morn's first light shall clear the skies."
  She ceased, then languishing her griefs to feed,
Her cold dark chamber sought, from observation freed.

'Twas there regret indulged the bitter tear ;
  She feels herself forsaken and alone :
  "Behold," she cries, " fulfilled is every fear,
  Oh! wretched Psyche, now indeed undone !
  Thy love's protecting care no more is shown,
  He bids his servant leave thee to thy fate,
  Nor longer will the hopeless wanderer own :
  Some fairer, nobler spouse, some worthier mate,
At length by Venus given, shall share his heavenly state.

" Oh ! most adored ! Oh ! most regretted love !
  Oh ! joys that never must again be mine,
  And thou, lost hope, farewell !—vainly I rove,
  For never shall I reach that land divine,
  Nor ever shall thy beams celestial shine
  Again upon my sad unheeded way !
  Oh ! let me here with life my woes resign,
  Or in this gloomy den for ever stay,
And shun the scornful world, nor see detested day.

" But no ! those scenes are hateful to mine eyes,
  And all who spoke or witnessed my disgrace ;
  My soul with horror from this dwelling flies,
  And seeks some tranquil, solitary place,
  Where grief may finish life's unhappy race !"
  So past she the long night, and soon as Morn
  Had first begun to show his cheerful face,
  Her couch, which care had strewn with every thorn,
With heavy heart she left, disquieted, forlorn.

  Not thus Disfida suffered her to part,
  But urged her there in safety to remain,
  Repeating oft to her foreboding heart,
  That fairy land she never could attain :
  But when she saw dissuasion was in vain,
  And Psyche bent her journey to pursue,
  With angry brow she called a trusty train,
  And bade them keep the imprudent fair in view,
And guard her dangerous path with strict observance true.

  In vain their proffered service she declines,
  And dreads the convoy of the scowling band ;
  Their hateful presence with her loss combines,
  She feels betrayed to the destroyer's hand,
  And trembling wanders o'er the dreary land ;
  While as she seeks to escape Disfida's power,
  Her efforts still the officious guards withstand,
  Led in vain circles many a tedious hour,
Undistanced still she sees the gloomy turrets lower.

Till, wearied with her fruitless way, at length
Upon the ground her fainting limbs she threw;
No wish remained to aid exhausted strength,
The mazy path she cared not to pursue,
Since unavailing was the task she knew :
Her murmuring guards to seek for food prepare,
Yet mindful of their charge, still keep in view
The drooping victim of their cruel care,
Who sees the day decline in terror and despair.

Hark ! a low hollow groan she seems to hear
Repeated oft; wondering she looks around :
It seems to issue from some cavern near,
Or low hut hidden by the rising ground ;
For, though it seemed the melancholy sound
Of human voice, no human form was nigh ;
Her eye no human habitation found,
But as she listening gazed attentively,
Her shuddering ears received the deep and long-drawn sigh.

The guard who nearest stood now whispering said,
"If aught of doubt remain within thy mind,
Or wish to know why thus thou wert betrayed,
Or what strange cause thy faithless knight inclined
To leave the charge he with such scorn resigned,
Each curious thought thou now mayst satisfy,
Since here the entrance of a cave we find,
Where dwells, deep hid from day's too garish eye,
A sage whose magic skill can solve each mystery."

He staid not her reply, but urged her on
Reluctant to the dark and dreary cave ;
No beam of cheerful Heaven had ever shone
In the recesses of that gloomy grave,
Where screaming owls their daily dwelling crave.
One sickly lamp the wretched Master shewed;
Devouring fiend ! Who now the prey shall save
From his fell gripe, whose hands in blood imbrued,
In his own bosom seek his lacerated food ?

On the damp ground he sits in sullen woe,
But wildly rolls around his frenzied eye,
And gnaws his withered lips, which still o'erflow
With bitter gall; in foul disorder lie
His black and matted locks; anxiety
Sits on his wrinkled brow and sallow cheek;
The wasted form, the deep-drawn, frequent sigh,
Some slow-consuming malady bespeak,
But medicinal skill the cause in vain shall seek.

"Behold," the treacherous guard exclaimed, "behold,
At length Disfida sends thy promised bride!
Let her, deserted by her knight, be told
What peerless lady lured him from her side;
Thy cares her future safety must provide."
Smiling maliciously as thus he spoke,
He seemed her helpless anguish to deride;
Then swiftly rushing from the den he broke,
Ere from the sudden shock astonished she awoke.

She too had fled; but when the wretch escaped
He closed the cavern's mouth with cruel care;
And now the monster placed his form mis-shaped
To bar the passage of the affrighted fair:
Her spirits die, she breathes polluted air,
And vaporous visions swim before her sight:
His magic skill the sorcerer bids her share,
And lo! as in a glass, she sees her knight
In bower remembered well, the bower of loose Delight.

But oh! what words her feelings can impart!
Feelings to hateful envy near allied!
While on her knight her anxious glances dart:
His plumed helmet, lo! he lays aside;
His face with torturing agony she spied,
Yet cannot from the sight her eyes remove;
No mortal knight she sees had aid supplied,
No mortal knight in her defence had strove;
'Twas Love! 'twas Love himself, her own adored Love.

Poured in soft dalliance at a lady's feet,
In fondest rapture he appeared to lie,
While her fair neck with inclination sweet
Bent o'er his graceful form her melting eye,
Which his looked up to meet in ecstasy.
Their words she heard not; words had ne'er exprest
What well her sickening fancy could supply,
All that their silent eloquence confest,
As breathed the sigh of fire from each impassioned breast.

While thus she gazed, her quivering lips turn pale;
Contending passions rage within her breast,
Nor ever had she known such bitter bale,
Or felt by such fierce agony opprest.
Oft had her gentle heart been sore distrest,
But meekness ever has a lenient power
From anguish half his keenest darts to wrest;
Meekness for her had softened Sorrow's hour,
Those furious fiends subdued which boisterous souls devour.

For there are hearts that, like some sheltered lake,
Ne'er swell with rage, nor foam with violence;
Though its sweet placid calm the tempests shake,
Yet will it ne'er with furious impotence
Dash its rude waves against the rocky fence,
Which nature placed the limits of its reign:
Thrice blest! who feel the peace which flows from hence,
Whom meek-eyed Gentleness can thus restrain;
Whate'er the storms of fate, with her let none complain!

That mild associate Psyche now deserts,
Unlovely passions agitate her soul,
The vile magician all his art exerts,
And triumphs to behold his proud control:
Changed to a serpent's hideous form, he stole
O'er her fair breast to suck her vital blood;
His poisonous involutions round her roll:
Already is his forked tongue imbrued
Warm in the stream of life, her heart's pure purple flood.

Thus wretchedly shè falls Geloso's prey!
But her, once more, unhoped-for aid shall save!
Admitted shines the clear blue light of day
Upon the horrors of that gloomy grave;
Her night's soft voice resounds through all the cave,
The affrighted serpent quits his deadly hold,
Nor dares the vengeance of his arm to brave,
Shrunk to a spider's form, while many a fold
Of self-spun web obscene the sorcerer vile enrolled.

Scarce had the star of his attendant youth
Blazed through the cavern and proclaimed the knight,
When all those spells and visions of untruth,
Bred in dark Erebus and nursed in night,
Dissolving vanished into vapour light;
While Psyche, quite exhausted by her pains,
And hardly trusting her astonished sight,
Now faint and speechless in his arms remains,
Nor memory of the past, nor present sense retains.

Borne from the cavern, and to life restored,
Her opening eyes behold her knight once more,
She sees whom lost with anguish she deplored;
Yet a half-feigned resentment still she bore,
Nor sign of joy her face averted wore,
Though joy unuttered panted at her heart;
In sullen silence much she pondered o'er
What from her side induced him to depart,
And all she since had seen by aid of magic art.

Was it then all a false deluding dream
That wore the semblance of celestial Love?
On this her wavering thoughts bewildered seem
At length to rest; yet onward as they move,
Though much his tender cares her doubts reprove,
And though she longs to hear, and pardon all,
Silence she still preserves: a while he strove
Her free and cheerful spirits to recall,
But found the task was vain; his words unnoticed fail.

Now in his turn offended and surprised,
The knight in silence from her side withdrew;
With pain she marked it, but her pain disguised,
And heedless seemed her journey to pursue,
Nor backward deigned to turn one anxious view
As oft she wished; till mindful of his lord,
Constance alarmed affectionately flew,
Eager to see their mutual peace restored,
And blamed her cold reserve in many a soft-breathed word.

" O Psyche! would not thus thy faithful knight,
Who fondly sought thee many an anxious hour,
Though bleeding yet from that inglorious fight,
Where thou wert rescued from the savage power
Of that fell beast who would thy charms devour:
Still faint with wounds, he ceased not to pursue
Thy heedless course: let not displeasure lower
Thus on thy brow: think not his heart untrue!
Think not that e'er from thee he willingly withdrew."

With self-reproach and sweet returning trust,
While yet he spoke, her generous heart replies,
Soft melting pity bids her now be just,
And own the error which deceived her eyes;
Her little pride she longs to sacrifice,
And ask forgiveness of her suffering knight;
Her suffering knight, alas! no more she spies,
He has withdrawn offended from her sight,
Nor can that gentle voice now hope to stay his flight.

Struggling no more her sorrows to restrain,
Her streaming eyes look round with anxious fear;
Nor are those tender showers now shed in vain,
Her soft lamenting voice has reached his ear,
Where latent he had marked each precious tear;
Sudden as thought behold him at her feet!
Oh! reconciling moment! charm most dear!
What feeling heart thy pleasures would repeat,
Or wish thy dearly purchased bliss, however sweet?

The smiles of joy which swell her glowing cheek,
And o'er her parting lips divinely play,
Returning pleasure eloquently speak,
Forgetful of the tears which lingering stay,
(Like sparkling dew-drops in a sunny day,)
Unheeded tenants of rejoicing eyes;
His wounds her tender care can well repay:
There grateful kindness breathes her balmy sighs,
Beneath her lenient hand how swiftly suffering flies!

Freed from the mazes of Disfida's groves,
The opening landscape brightens to their view;
Psyche, with strength revived, now onward moves
In cheerful hope, with courage to renew
Repeated toils, and perils to pursue:
Thus when some tender plant neglected pines,
Shed o'er its pendent head the kindly dew,
How soon refreshed its vivid lustre shines!
Once more the leaf expands, the drooping tendril twines.

Thus cheered, the knight intreats her to impart
The dangers which her way had since befel,
Her timid lips refuse to speak the art
Which clothed him in a form she loved so well:
That she had thought him Love, she blushed to tell!
Confused she stopt; a gentle pause ensued;
What chance had brought him to the demon's cell
She then enquires; what course he had pursued,
And who his steps had led throughout the mazy wood.

Sooth he had much to say, though modest shame
His gallant deeds forbade him to declare;
For while through those bewildering woods he came,
Assisted by his page's active care,
He had detected Varia's wily snare,
And forced her wanton retinue to flee.
With like disgrace, malignant in despair,
Disfida's slaves their plots defeated see,
Their feeble malice scorned, their destined victims free.

But he had marked the traces of their feet,
And found the path which to the cavern led :
Whence now, rejoicing in reunion sweet,
Their way together cheerfully they tread,
Exempt a while from danger and from dread ;
While Psyche's heart, with confidence more bold,
Full oft the hour of rapture pictured,
When those celestial charms she should behold,
And feel the arms of Love once more his bride enfold.

CANTO V.

ARGUMENT.

INTRODUCTION—Charm of Poetry—Psyche beholds the palace of Chastity—Pleads for the admission of her Knight—Obtains it through the intervention of Hymen—Hymn celebrating the triumphs of Chastity—Psyche, enraptured, desires to devote herself solely to the service of Chastity—Entrusted by her to the protection of the Knight—Psyche's Voyage—Tempest—Coast of Spleen—Psyche received and sheltered by Patience.

DELIGHTFUL visions of my lonely hours !
Charm of my life and solace of my care !
Oh ! would the muse but lend proportioned powers,
And give me language, equal to declare
The wonders which she bids my fancy share,
When rapt in her to other worlds I fly,
See angel forms unutterably fair,
And hear the inexpressive harmony
That seems to float on air, and warble through the sky

Might I the swiftly glancing scenes recal !
Bright as the roseate clouds of summer's eve,
The dreams which hold my soul in willing thrall,
And half my visionary days deceive,
Communicable shape might then receive,
And other hearts be ravished with the strain :
But scarce I seek the airy threads to weave,
When quick confusion mocks the fruitless pain,
And all the fairy forms are vanished from my brain.

Fond dreamer ! meditate thine idle song !
But let thine idle song remain unknown :
The verse, which cheers thy solitude, prolong ;
What, though it charm no moments but thine own,
Though thy loved Psyche smile for thee alone,
Still shall it yield thee pleasure, if not fame,
And when, escaped from tumult, thou hast flown
To thy dear silent hearth's enlivening flame,
There shall the tranquil muse her happy votary claim !

My Psyche's wanderings then she loves to trace ;
Unrols the glowing canvas to my sight ;
Her chaste calm eye, her soft attractive grace,
The lightning of her heavenly smile so bright,
All yield me strange and unconceived delight :
Even now entranced her journey I pursue,
And gaze enraptured on her matchless knight ;
Visions of love, pure, innocent, and true !
Oh ! may your graceful forms for ever bless my view !

See as they tread the green, soft-levelled plain,
Where never weed, nor noxious plant was found !
Psyche enchanted, bids her knight explain
Who rules that lovely and well-cultured ground,
Where fairest flowers and purest springs abound.
" Oh ! object of my anxious cares," (he cried,
As with a half-breathed sigh he gazed around,)
. " A stranger here, full oft I vainly tried
Admittance to obtain, and soothe the sovereign's pride.

" Here Castabella reigns, whose brow severe
Oft chilled my sanguine spirit by its frown ;
Yet have I served her with adoring fear,
Though her ungrateful scorn will oft disown
The faithful homage by her servant shown ;
Me she hath banished from her fair domain,
For crimes my loyal heart had never known ;
While thus excluded vainly I complain,
And feel another's guilt my injured honour stain.

With false assumption of my arms and name,
Knight of the Bleeding Heart miscalled too long,
A vile impostor has disgraced my fame,
And much usurped by violence and wrong,
Which to the virgin queen by right belong;
On me her irritated vengeance falls,
On me, repulsed by force of arms so strong,
That, never suffered to approach her walls,
Unheard, indignant Truth in vain for justice calls

Yet she alone our progress can assist,
And thou, Oh Psyche! must her favour gain;
Nor from thy soft entreaties e'er desist
Till thou free entrance for thy knight obtain;
Here let his faithful services remain
Fixed on thy grateful heart! nor thou consent,
Nor let their force thy gentleness constrain
To leave him, thus disgraced, yet innocent,
Thine undeserved neglect forsaken to lament."

While yet he speaks, before her ravished eyes
The brilliant towers of Castabella shine:
The sun that views them from unclouded skies
Sheds not through heaven a radiance more divine;
The adamantine walls with strength combine
Inimitable lustre ever clear;
Celestial temple! 'tis not lips like mine
Thy glories can reveal to mortal ear,
Or paint the unsullied beams which blaze for ever here

Approaching now the well-defended gates,
Which placed at distance guard the sacred fane,
Their lowly suit a stern repulse awaits;
The timid voice of Psyche pleads in vain,
Nor entrance there together can they gain:
While yet they stay, unwilling to retreat,
The dove, swift-sailing through the ethereal plain,
Has reached already Castabella's seat,
And in her spotless breast has found a welcome sweet.

Caressing oft her well-remembered guest,
Serener smiles illumed her softened brow;
The heaven-sent messenger her soul confest,
And mildly listened to his murmurs low,
Which seemed in pleading eloquence to flow;
His snowy pinions then he wide displayed,
And gently lured her from her throne to go
Even to the gates, where Psyche blushing stayed
Beside her awe-struck knight half doubtingly afraid.

That form majestic might the bravest awe:
Yet Psyche gazed with love unmixed with fear,
And felt those charms her soul attracted draw
As to maternal tenderness most dear;
Congenial souls! they at one glance appear
Linked to each other by a mutual tie:
Her courteous voice invites her to draw near,
And lo! obedient to their sovereign's eye,
To Psyche's willing steps the barriers open fly.

But to the lion, and his gallant lord,
Sudden the affrighted guards the portals close.
Psyche looks back, and mindful of her word,
Mindful of him who saved her from her foes,
Guide of her course and soother of her woes,
The tear that started to her downcast eye,
The deepening blush which eloquently rose,
Silent assistant of the pleading sigh,
To speed the unuttered suit their powers persuasive try.

And now the knight, encouraged to approach.
Asserts his injured fame, and justice claims,
Confutes each charge, repels each foul reproach,
And each accusing falsehood boldly shames,
While conscious Innocence his tongue inflames:
A firm attachment to her reign he vows,
The base impostor's guilty madness blames,
And, while the imputed crimes his spirit rouse,
No intercourse with him his nobler soul allows.

Meantime his faithful page had not been mute,
And he had found a ready warm ally;
For (while his master urged the eager suit)
As through the goodly train he cast his eye,
He chanced exulting 'mid the group to spy
A joyous youth, his fondly-cherished friend;
Hymen, the festive, love-attending boy,
Delighted his assistance hastes to lend,
Laughing unbars the gates, and bids the parley end.

Around their queen the timid virgins crowd,
Who half-consentingly receives the knight,
And checks her sportive boy, whose welcome loud
Speaks his gay triumph and his proud delight:
Yet graceful smiles her happy guests invite
To share the feast with sacred honours blest;
The palace opens to their dazzled sight;
Still as they gazed, the adoring eye confest
That wondering awe which filled each consecrated breast.

All was divine, yet still the fairest queen
Like Dian 'mid her circling nymphs appeared,
Or as Minerva on Parnassus seen,
When condescendingly with smiles she cheered
The silent Muses who her presence feared:
A starry crown its heavenly radiance threw
O'er her pale cheek; for there the rose revered
The purer lilies of her saint-like hue,
Yet oft the mantling blush its transient visits knew.

The hand of Fate, which wove of spotless white
Her wondrous robe, bade it unchangeable
Preserve unsullied its first lustre bright,
Nor e'er might be renewed that sacred spell
If once destroyed; wherefore to guard it well
Two hand-maids she entrusts with special care,
Prudence and Purity, who both excel,
The first in matron dignity of air,
The last in blooming youth unalterably fair.

Favourite of heaven! she at her birth received
With it the brilliant zone that bound her waist,
Which, were the earth of sun and stars bereaved,
By its own light beneficently cast
Could cheer the innocent, and guide the chaste:
Nor armour ever had the virgin bore,
Though oft in warlike scenes her youth she past,
For while her breast this dazzling cestus wore,
The foe who dared to gaze beheld the light no more.

But when her placid hours in peace are spent,
Concealed she bids its latent terrors lie,
Sheathed in a silken scarf, with kind intent
Wove by the gentle hand of Modesty;
And see, the blushing maid with downcast eye
Behind her mistress hides her charms retired!
While, foremost of the group, of stature high,
Firm Courage lifts her brow by Truth inspired,
Who holds a crystal lamp in flames celestial fired.

See, fresh as Hebe, blooming Temperance stand,
Present the nectared fruits, and crown the bowl!
While bright-eyed Honour leads the choral band,
Whose songs divine can animate the soul,
Led willing captive to their high control:
They sing the triumphs of their spotless queen,
And proudly bid immortal fame enrol
Upon her fairest page such as had been
The champions of her cause, the favourites of her reign.

From Pallas first begins the lofty song,
And Cynthia, brightest goddess of the skies;
To her the virgin deities belong,
And each beholds her with a sister's eyes;
The mystic honours next of Fauna* rise;
Her solemn rites which purest hands require;
And Vesta, who her virgins taught to prize,
And guard the sacred symbols of the fire
Which earth could ne'er revive if suffered to expire.

* *The mystic honours next of Fauna.*]—Fauna, called also the Bona
Dea, was celebrated for the exemplary purity of her manners, and after
death was worshipped only by women.

Emblem divine of female purity!
Whose trust betrayed to like sad fate shall doom;
Pursued by scorn, consigned to infamy,
The hapless victims perish in their bloom
'Mid the dark horrors of a living tomb;
Effulgent queen! thou wilt the pure defend
From the dark night of this opprobrious gloom;
Nor even with life thy favouring smiles shall end,
They bid illustrious fame beyond the grave extend.

First of the noble youths whose virtue shone
Conspicuous chief in Castabella's train,
They sing the firm unmoved Bellerophon;
And Peleus flying the Magnesian plain,
Pursued by all a wanton's fierce disdain.
You too, Hippolytus, their songs employ!
Beloved by Phædra, but beloved in vain;
With the chaste honours of the Hebrew boy,
Which time shall ne'er obscure, nor idle scorn destroy.

Nor was unsung whom on Hymettus' brow
The bright Aurora wooed with amorous care;
He, mindful of his sacred nuptial vow,
Refused the goddess though celestial fair,
Breathing pure perfumes and ambrosial air:
Of wanton Circe's baffled arts they tell,
And him, too wise her treacherous cup to share,
Who scorned the enchantress, and her mystic spell,
And all the Syrens' arts could gloriously repel.

The long-tried virtue of his faithful spouse
Now sweetly animates the tuneful string,
Unsullied guardian of her virgin vows!
Who twice ten years had wept her wandering king.
Acastus' mourning daughter* next they sing;
The chaste embrace which clasped her husband's shade:
And thee, Dictynna !† who, with daring spring,
Called from the Cretan rock on Dian's aid:
And still the goddess loves her favourite luckless maid.

---

* *Acastus' mourning daughter.*]—Laodamia.

† *And thee, Dictynna !*]—A virgin of Crete, who threw herself from
a rock into the sea, when pursued by Minos. The Cretans gave her

Pleased to assume herself a name so dear,
She bids her altars to Dictynna rise,
Thus called, she ever turns, with willing ear,
To aid each nymph who for her succour cries.
See how the trembling Arethusa flies
Through pathless woods, o'er rocks and open plains;
In vain to escape the ravisher she tries,
Fast on her rapid flight Alpheus gains,
And scarce her fainting strength the unequal course sustains

And now more near his dreaded steps she hears,
His lengthened shadow flies before her feet,
Now o'er her neck his panting breath appears
To part her locks, which, in disorder sweet,
Ambitious seemed to fan the fervid heat
That flushed her glowing cheek and heightened charms:
Hear how her gasping sighs for aid entreat!
"Dictynna! pitying see my just alarms,
And snatch thy fainting maid from those polluting arms."

The goddess hears, and in a favouring cloud
Conceals her suppliant from Alpheus' sight;
In vain he looks around, and calls aloud,
And wondering seeks the traces of her flight:
Enveloped, still she views him with affright,
An icy coldness creeps o'er all her frame,
And soon, dissolving in a current bright,
The silver stream retains her honoured name,
And still unmingled flows, and guards its virgin fame.

'Twas thus Castalia's sacred fountain sprung,
Once a fair nymph by bright Apollo loved:
To Daphne too his amorous strain he sung,
But sung in vain: her heart remained unmoved,
No vain delight her modest virtue proved
To be the theme of all his wanton lays:
To shun the god the silvan scene she roved;
Nor prized the flattery of his tuneful praise,
Nor one relenting smile his splendid gifts could raise.

name to the rock thus consecrated, and were accustomed to worship
Diana by the name of her unfortunate votary.

Yet were his lips with eloquence endued,
And melting passion warbled o'er his lyre,
And had she yielding listened as he wooed,
The virgin sure had caught the kindling fire,
And fallen a victim to impure desire;
For safety cautious flight alone remained,
While tears of trembling innocence require
Her parents' aid: and lo! that aid obtained,
How suddenly her charms immortal laurels gained!

Dear to the Muses still her honours live:
And they too glory in their virgin name;
To pure delights their tranquil hours they give,
And fear to mingle with a grosser flame
The chaster fires which heaven hath bid them claim:
They smiled when Pan, on Ladon's banks deceived,
The fair Syringa clasped, who, snatched from shame,
Already had her tuneful form received,
And to the breathing winds in airy music grieved.

Still in that tuneful form* to Dian dear
She bids it injured innocence befriend;
Commands her train the sentence to revere,
And in her grove the vocal reeds suspend
Which virtue may from calumny defend:
Self-breathed, when virgin purity appears,
What notes melodious they spontaneous send!
While the rash guilty nymph with horror hears
Deep groans declare her shame to awe-struck wondering ears.

The spotless virgins shall unhurt approach
The stream's rude ordeal,† and the sacred fire.
See the pure maid, indignant of reproach,
The dreadful test of innocence require

* *That tuneful form.*]—In a grove, sacred to Diana, was suspended a syrinx (the pipe into which the nymph Syringa had been metamorphosed), which was said to possess the miraculous power of thus justifying the calumniated.

† *The stream's rude ordeal.*]—The trial of the Stygian fountain, by which the innocent were acquitted, and the guilty disgraced; the waters rising in a wonderful manner, so as to cover the laurel wreath of the unchaste female who dared the examination.

Amid the holy priests and virgin choir!
See her leap fearless on the blazing shrine!
The lambent flames, bright-circling, all aspire
Innoxious wreaths around her form to twine,
And crown with lustrous beams the virgin's brow divine.

Nor was the daring Clusia* then unsung,
Who plunged illustrious from the lofty tower;
The favouring winds around the virgin clung,
And bore her harmless from the tyrant's power:
Nor those, whom Vesta in the trying hour†
Protects from Slander, and restores to fame;
Nor Clelia, shielded from the arrowy shower;
Nor thou! whose purest hands‡ the Sibyls claim,
And bid the modest fane revere Sulpicia's name.

O'er her soft cheek how arch the dimples play,
While pleased the goddess hears Sinope's wiles!§
How oft she mocked the changeful lord of day,
And many a silvan god who sought her smiles:
But chief when Jove her innocence beguiles;
"Grant me a boon," the blushing maid replies,
Urged by his suit: hope o'er his amorous toils
Exulting dawns:—"Thine oath is past," she cries;
"Unalterably pure thy spotless virgin dies!"

* *The daring Clusia*]—Who, to avoid the violence of Torquatus, cast herself from a tower, and was preserved by the winds, which, swelling her garments, supported her as she gently descended to the earth.

† *Vesta in the trying hour.*]—Claudia, a vestal, who having been accused of violating her vow, attested her innocence by drawing up the Tiber, a ship bearing a statue of the goddess, which many thousand men had not been able to remove. Æmilia, who was suspected of unchastity from having inadvertently suffered the sacred flame to expire, by entrusting it to the care of a novice, but, imploring Vesta to justify her innocence, she tore her linen garment, and threw it upon the extinguished ashes of the cold altar; when, in the sight of priests and virgins, a sudden and pure fire was thus enkindled. Tucia, who being falsely accused, carried water from the Tiber to the forum in a sieve, her accuser miraculously disappearing at the same time.

‡ *Whose purest hands.*]—Sulpicia, a Roman lady of remarkable chastity; chosen by the Sibyls to dedicate a temple to Venus Verticordia, in order to obtain greater purity for her contemporary countrywomen.

§ *Sinope's wiles!*]—The nymph Sinope, being persecuted by the addresses of Jupiter, at length stipulated for his promise to grant her whatever she might ask, and having obtained this promise, claimed the gift of perpetual chastity.

Rome shall for ages boast Lucretia's name !
And while its temples moulder into dust
Still triumph in Virginia's rescued fame,
And Scipio's victory over baffled lust :—
Even now the strain prophetically just,
In unborn servants bids their queen rejoice,
And in her British beauties firmly trust;
Thrice happy fair ! who still adore her voice,
The blushing virgin's law, the modest matron's choice '

Psyche with ravished ear the strain attends,
Enraptured hangs upon the heaven-strung lyre ;
Her kindling soul from sensual earth ascends ;
To joys divine her purer thoughts aspire ;
She longs to join the white-robed spotless choir,
And there for ever dwell a hallowed guest :
Even Love himself no longer can inspire
The wishes of the soft enthusiast's breast,
Who, filled with sacred zeal, would there for ever rest;

Despising every meaner low pursuit,
And quite forgetful of her amorous care,
All heedless of her knight, who sad and mute
With wonder hears the strange ungrateful fair,
A prostrate suppliant, pour the fervent prayer
To be received in Castabella's train,
And that in tranquil bliss secluded there,
Her happy votary still she might remain,
Free from each worldly care, and each polluting stain.

With gracious smile the Queen her favourite heard,
And fondly raised, and clasped her to her breast ;
A beam of triumph in her eye appeared,
While ardent Psyche offered her request,
Which to the indignant knight her pride confest:
" Farewell, mistaken Psyche !" he exclaims,
Rising at length with grief and shame opprest,
" Since thy false heart a spouse divine disclaims,
I leave thee to the pomp which here thy pride inflames.

"Yet stay, impetuous youth," the Queen replies,
Abashed, irresolute as Psyche stands,
"My favourite's happiness too dear I prize,
Far other services my soul demands
Than those which here in these sequestered lands
Her zeal would pay: no, let her bear my fame
Even to the bowers where Love himself commands :
There shall my votary reign secure from blame,
And teach his myrtle groves to echo to my name.

"My lovely servant still defend from harms,
And stem with her yon strong opposing tide :
Haste, bear her safely to her lover's arms !
Be it thy care with steady course to guide
The light-winged bark I will myself provide.
Depart in peace ! thou chosen of my heart !
Leave not thy faithful knight's protecting side.
Dear to me both, oh may no treacherous art
Your kindred souls divide, your fair alliance part !

"Here rest to-night; to-morrow shall prepare
The vessel which your destined course shall speed.
Lo ! I consign my Psyche to thy care,
O gallant youth ! for so hath Fate decreed,
And Love himself shall pay the generous meed."
She said, and joined their unreluctant hands.
The grateful knight, from fear and sorrow freed,
Receives with hope revived the dear commands,
And Psyche's modest eye no other law demands.

Now Peace, with downy step and silent hand,
Prepares for each the couch of soft repose :
Fairest attendant ! she with whispers bland
Bids the obedient eye in slumbers close ;
She too the first at early morning goes
With light-foot Cheerfulness the guests to greet,
Who, soothed by quiet dreams refreshed arose.
Ready the labours of the day to meet ;
But first due homage pay at Castabella's feet.

Bright was the prospect which before them shone;
Gay danced the sun-beams o'er the trembling waves:
Who that the faithless ocean had not known,
Which now the strand in placid whispers laves,
Could e'er believe the rage with which it raves,
When angry Boreas bids the storm arise,
And calls his wild winds from their wintry caves?
Now soft Favonius breathes his gentlest sighs,
Auspicious omens wait, serenely smile the skies.

The eager mariners now seize the oar,
The streamers flutter in the favouring gale.
Nor unattended did they leave the shore:
Hymen, whose smiles shall o'er mischance prevail,
Sits at the helm, or spreads the swelling sail:
Swift through the parting waves the vessel flies.
And now at distance scarce can Psyche hail
The shore, so fast receding from her eyes,
Or bless the snowy cliffs which o'er the coast arise.

Pleased with her voyage and the novel scene,
Hope's vivid ray her cheerful heart expands:
Delighted now she eyes the blue serene,
The purple hills, and distant rising lands,
Or, when the sky the silver queen commands,
In pleasing silence listens to the oar
Dashed by the frequent stroke of equal hands;
Or asks her knight if yet the promised shore
May bless her longing eyes when morn shall light restore?

The impatient question oft repeated thus
He smiling hears, and still with many a tale,
Or song of heavenly lore unknown to us
Beguiles the live-long night, or flagging sail,
When the fresh breeze begins their bark to fail.
Strong ran the tide against the vessel's course,
And much they need the kind propitious gale
Steady to bear against its rapid force,
And aid the labouring oars, their tedious last resource.

But lo! the blackening surface of the deep
With sullen murmurs now begins to swell,
On ruffled wing the screaming sea-fowl sweep
The unlovely surge, and piteous seem to tell
How from the low-hung clouds with fury fell
The demons of the tempest threatening rage;
There, brooding future terrors, yet they dwell,
Till with collected force dread war they wage,
And in convulsive gusts the adverse winds engage.

The trembling Psyche, supplicating Heaven,
Lifts to the storm her fate-deploring eye,
Sees o'er her head the livid lightnings driven:
Then, turned in horror from the blazing sky,
Clings to her knight in speechless agony:
He all his force exerts the bark to steer,
And bids the mariners each effort try
To escape the rocky coast which threatens near,
For Hymen taught the youth that dangerous shore to

Who has not listened to his tuneful lay,
That sings so well the hateful cave of Spleen?
Those lands, submitted to her gloomy sway,
Now open to their view a dreary scene,
As the sad subjects of the sullen queen
Hang o'er the cliffs, and blacken all the strand;
And where the entrance of the cave is seen
A peevish, fretful, melancholy band.
Her ever wrangling slaves, in jarring concert stand.

Driven by the hurricane they touch the shore,
The frowning guards prepare to seize their prey,
The knight (attentive to the helm no more)
Resumes his arms, and bids his shield display
Its brilliant orb: "Psyche let no dismay
Possess thy gentle breast," he cheerly cries,
"Behind thy knight in fearless safety stay
Smile at the dart which o'er thee vainly flies,
Secure from each attack their powerless rage despise

" Soon shall the fury of the winds be past,
Serener skies shall brighten to our view,
Let us not yield to the imperious blast
Which now forbids our vessel to pursue
Its purposed course; soon shall the heavens renew
Their calm clear smile; and soon our coward foes,
Despairing thus our courage to subdue,
Shall cease their idle weapons to oppose,
And unmolested Peace restore our lost repose."

Still as he spoke, where'er he turned his shield
The darts drop quivering from each slackened bow,
Unnerved each arm, no force remains to wield
The weighty falchion, or the javelin throw;
Each voice half choked expires in murmurs low,
A dizzy mist obscures their wondering sight,
Their eyes no more their wonted fury know,
With stupid awe they gaze upon the knight,
Or, as his voice they hear, trembling disperse in flight.

Yet raged the storm with unabated power;
A little creek the labouring vessel gains;
There they resolve to endure the blustering hour,
The dashing billows, and the beating rains
Soon as the bark the sheltering bay attains,
And in the shallows moored securely rides,
 . Attentive still to soften all her pains,
The watchful knight for Psyche's ease provides;
Some fisher's hut perchance the shelving harbour hides.

Deep in the sterile bank a grotto stood,
Whose winding caves repel the inclement air,
Worn in the hollowed rock by many a flood
And sounding surge that dashed its white foam there,
The refuge now of a defenceless fair,
Who issuing thence, with courteous kind intent
Approached the knight, and kindly bade him share
Whatever good indulgent heaven had lent
To cheer her hapless years in lonely suffering spent.

More sweet than Health's fresh bloom the wan hue seemed
Which sat upon her pallid cheek ; her eye,
Her placid eye, with dove-like softness beamed ;
Her head unshielded from the pitiless sky,
Loose to the rude wild blast her tresses fly,
Bare were her feet which pressed the shelly shore
With firm unshrinking step ; while smilingly
She eyes the dashing billows as they roar,
And braves the boisterous storms so oft endured before.

Long had she there in silent sorrow dwelt,
And many a year resigned to grief had known ;
Spleen's cruel insolence she oft had felt,
But never would the haughty tyrant own,
Nor heed the darts which, from a distance thrown,
Screened by her cavern she could safely shun ;
The thorny brakes she trod for food alone,
Drank the cold stream which near the grotto run,
And bore the winter's frosts and scorching summer's sun.

In early youth, exchanging mutual vows,
Courage had wooed and won his lovely bride ;
Tossed on those stormy seas, her daring spouse
From her fond arms the cruel waves divide,
And dashed her fainting on that rock's rough side.
Still hope she keeps, and still her constant heart
Expects to hail with each returning tide
His dear remembered bark ; hence can no art
From those unlovely scenes induce her to depart.

When the vexed seas their stormy mountains roll,
She loves the shipwrecked mariner to cheer ;
The trembling wretch escaped from Spleen's control,
Deep in her silent cell conceals his fear,
And panting finds repose and refuge here ;
Benevolently skilled each wound to heal,
To her the sufferer flies, with willing ear
She wooes them all their anguish to reveal,
And while she speaks, they half forget the woes they feel.

Now to her cave has Patience gently brought
Psyche, yet shuddering at the fearful blast,
Largely she heaped with hospitable thought
The blazing pile, and spread the pure repast;
O'er her chilled form her own soft mantle cast,
And soothed her wearied spirits to repose,
Till all the fury of the storm is past,
Till swift-receding clouds the heavens disclose,
And o'er subsiding waves pacific sunshine glows.

CANTO VI.

ARGUMENT.

Introduction—The power of Love to soften adversity—Exhortation to guard Love from the attacks of Ill-temper, which conduct to Indifference and Disgust—Psyche becalmed—Psyche surprised and carried to the Island of Indifference—Pursued and rescued by her Knight—The Voyage concluded—Psyche brought home beholds again the Temple of Love—Is reunited to her Lover, and invited by Venus to receive in Heaven her Apotheosis—Conclusion.

WHEN pleasure sparkles in the cup of youth,
And the gay hours on downy wing advance,
Oh! then 'tis sweet to hear the lip of Truth
Breathe the soft vows of love, sweet to entrance
The raptured soul by intermingling glance
Of mutual bliss; sweet amid roseate bowers,
Led by the hand of Love, to weave the dance,
Or unmolested crop life's fairy flowers,
Or bask in joy's bright sun through calm unclouded hours.

Yet they, who light of heart in May-day pride
Meet love with smiles and gaily amorous song,
(Though he their softest pleasures may provide,
Even then when pleasures in full concert throng,)
They cannot know with what enchantment strong
He steals upon the tender suffering soul,
What gently soothing charms to him belong,
How melting sorrow owns his soft control,
Subsiding passions hushed in milder waves to roll

When vexed by cares and harassed by distress,
The storms of fortune chill thy soul with dread,
Let Love, consoling Love ! still sweetly bless,
And his assuasive balm benignly shed :
His downy plumage o'er thy pillow spread,
Shall lull thy weeping sorrows to repose ;
To Love the tender heart hath ever fled,
As on its mother's breast the infant throws
Its sobbing face, and there in sleep forgets its woes.

Oh ! fondly cherish then the lovely plant,
Which lenient Heaven hath given thy pains to ease;
Its lustre shall thy summer hours enchant,
And load with fragrance every prosperous breeze,
And when rude Winter shall thy roses seize,
When nought through all thy bowers but thorns remain,
This still with undeciduous charms shall please,
Screen from the blast and shelter from the rain,
And still with verdure cheer the desolated plain.

Through the hard season Love with plaintive note
Like the kind red-breast tenderly shall sing,
Which swells 'mid dreary snows its tuneful throat,
Brushing the cold dews from its shivering wing,
With cheerful promise of returning spring
To the mute tenants of the leafless grove.
Guard thy best treasure from the venomed sting
Of baneful peevishness; oh ! never prove
How soon ill-temper's power can banish gentle Love !

Repentance may the storms of passion chase,
And Love, who shrunk affrighted from the blast,
May hush his just complaints in soft embrace,
And smiling wipe his tearful eye at last :
Yet when the wind's rude violence is past,
Look what a wreck the scattered fields display !
See on the ground the withering blossoms cast !
And hear sad Philomel with piteous lay
Deplore the tempest's rage that swept her young away.

The tears capricious Beauty loves to shed,
The pouting lip, the sullen silent tongue,
May wake the impassioned lover's tender dread,
And touch the spring that clasps his soul so strong;
But ah, beware! the gentle power too long
Will not endure the frown of angry strife;
He shuns contention, and the gloomy throng
Who blast the joys of calm domestic life,
And flies when Discord shakes her brand with quarrels rife.

Oh! he will tell you that these quarrels bring
The ruin, not renewal of his flame:
If oft repeated, lo! on rapid wing
He flies to hide his fair but tender frame;
From violence, reproach, or peevish blame
Irrevocably flies.   Lament in vain!
Indifference comes the abandoned heart to claim,
Asserts for ever her repulsive reign,
Close followed by Disgust and all her chilling train.

Indifference, dreaded power! what art shall save
The good so cherished from thy grasping hand?
How shall young Love escape the untimely grave
Thy treacherous arts prepare? or how withstand
The insidious foe, who with her leaden band
Enchains the thoughtless, slumbering deity?
Ah, never more to wake! or e'er expand
His golden pinions to the breezy sky,
Or open to the sun his dim and languid eye.

Who can describe the hopeless, silent pang
With which the gentle heart first marks her sway?
Eyes the sure progress of her icy fang
Resistless, slowly fastening on her prey;
Sees rapture's brilliant colours fade away,
And all the glow of beaming sympathy;
Anxious to watch the cold averted ray
That speaks no more to the fond meeting eye
Enchanting tales of love, and tenderness, and joy.

Too faithful heart! thou never canst retrieve
Thy withered hopes: conceal the cruel pain!
O'er thy lost treasure still in silence grieve;
But never to the unfeeling ear complain:
From fruitless struggles dearly bought refrain!
Submit at once—the bitter task resign,
Nor watch and fan the expiring flame in vain;
Patience, consoling maid, may yet be thine,
Go seek her quiet cell, and hear her voice divine!

But lo! the joyous sun, the soft-breathed gales
By zephyrs sent to kiss the placid seas,
Curl the green wave, and fill the swelling sails;
The seamen's shouts, which jocund hail the breeze,
Call the glad knight the favouring hour to seize.
Her gentle hostess Psyche oft embraced,
Who still solicitous her guest to please,
On her fair breast a talisman had placed,
And with the valued gem her parting blessing graced.

How gaily now the bark pursues its way,   .
Urged by the steady gale! while round the keel
The bubbling currents in sweet whispers play,
Their force repulsive now no more they feel;
No clouds the unsullied face of heaven conceal,
But the clear azure one pure dome displays,
Whether it bids the star of day reveal
His potent beams, or Cynthia's milder rays
On deep cerulean skies invite the eye to gaze.

Almost unconscious they their course pursue,
So smooth the vessel cuts the watery plain;
The wide horizon to their boundless view
Gives but the sky, and Neptune's ample reign:
Still the unruffled bosom of the main
Smiles undiversified by varying wind;
No toil the idle mariners sustain,
While, listless, slumbering o'er his charge reclined,
The pilot cares no more the unerring helm to mind.

With light exulting heart glad Psyche sees
Their rapid progress as they quit the shore:
Yet weary languor steals by slow degrees
Upon her tranquil mind; she joys no more
The never-changing scene to wander o'er
With still admiring eye; the enchanting song
Yields not that lively charm it knew before,
When first enraptured by his tuneful tongue
She bade her vocal knight the heavenly strain prolong.

A damp chill mist now deadens all the air,
A drowsy dullness seems o'er all to creep,
No more the heavens their smile of brightness wear,
The winds are hushed, while the dim glassy deep
Oppressed by sluggish vapours seems to sleep;
See his light scarf the knight o'er Psyche throws,
Solicitous his lovely charge to keep
From still increasing cold; while deep repose
Benumbs each torpid sense, and bids her eye-lids close.

Now as with languid stroke they ply the oars,
While the dense fog obscures their gloomy way;
Hymen, well used to coast these dangerous shores,
Roused from the dreaming trance in which he lay,
Cries to the knight in voice of dread dismay,
"Steer hence thy bark, oh! yet in time beware;
Here lies Petrea, which with baneful sway
Glacella rules, I feel the dank cold air,
I hear her chilling voice, methinks it speaks despair!"

Even while he speaks, behold the vessel stands
Immoveable! in vain the pilot tries
The helm to turn; fixed in the shallow strands,
No more obedient to his hand, it lies,
The disappointed oar no aid supplies
While sweeping o'er the sand it mocks their force.
The anxious knight to Constance now applies,
To his oft-tried assistance has recourse,
And bids his active mind design some swift resource.

Debating doubtfully awhile they stood,
At length on their united strength rely,
To force the bark on the supporting flood;
They rouse the seamen, who half slumbering lie,
Subdued and loaded by the oppressive sky.
Then wading 'mid the fog, with care explore
What side the deepest waters may supply,
And where the shallows least protect the shore,
While through their darksome search the star sheds light before

Mean time deep slumbers of the vaporous mist
Hang on the heavy eye-lids of the fair;
And Hymen too, unable to resist
The drowsy force of the o'erwhelming air,
Laid at her feet at length forgets his care.
When lo! Glacella's treacherous slaves advance,
Deep wrapt in thickest gloom; the sleeping fair
They seize, and bear away in heedless trance,
Long ere her guardian knight suspects the bitter chance.

Thus the lorn traveller imprudent sleeps
Where his high glaciers proud Locendro shews;
Thus o'er his limbs resistless torpor creeps,
As yielding to the fatal deep repose
He sinks benumbed upon the Alpine snows,
And sleeps no more to wake; no more to view
The blooming scenes his native vales disclose.
Or ever more the craggy path pursue,
Or o'er the lichened steep the chamois chase renew.

Lo! to their queen they bear their sleeping prey.
Deep in her ice-built castle's gloomy state,
There on a pompous couch they gently lay
Psyche, as yet unconscious of her fate,
And when her heavy eyes half opening late
Dimly observe the strange and unknown scenes,
As in a dream she views her changed estate,
Gazing around with doubtful, troubled mien
Now on the stupid crowd, now on their dull proud queen.

With vacant smile, and words but half exprest,
In one ungracious, never-varying tone,
Glacella welcomes her bewildered guest,
And bids the chief supporter of her throne
Approach and make their mighty mistress known,
Proud Selfishness, her dark ill-favoured lord!
Her gorgeous seat, which still he shared alone,
He slowly leaves obedient to her word,
And ever as he moved the cringing train adored.

Nought of his shapeless form to sight appears,
Impenetrable furs conceal each part;
Harsh and unpleasing sounds in Psyche's ears
That voice which had subdued full many a heart;
While he, exerting every specious art,
Persuades her to adore their queen's control;
Yet would he not Glacella's name impart,
But with false title, which she artful stole
From fair Philosophy, deludes the erring soul.

"Rest, happy fair!" he cries, "who here hast found
From all the storms of life a safe retreat,
Sorrow thy breast henceforth no more shall wound,
Nor Care invade thee in this quiet seat;
The voice of the distressed no more shall meet
The sympathising ear; another's woes
Shall never interrupt the stillness sweet
Which here shall hush thee to serene repose,
Nor damp the constant joys these scenes for thee disclose.

"Fatigue no more thy soft and lovely frame
With vain benevolence and fruitless care;
No deep-heaved sigh shall here thy pity claim,
Nor hateful Want demand thy wealth to share;
For thee shall Independence still prepare
Pleasures unmingled, and for ever sure;
His lips our sovereign's peaceful laws declare,
Centre existence in thyself secure,
Nor let an alien shade thy sunshine e'er obscure."

He spoke, and lo ! unnumbered doors unfold,
And various scenes of revelry display ;
Here Grandeur sunk beneath the massive gold ;
Here discontented Beauty pined away,
And vainly conscious asked her promised sway ;
Here Luxury prepared his sumptuous feast,
While lurking Apathy behind him lay
To poison all the insipid food he drest,
And shake his poppy crown o'er every sated guest.

The hireling minstrels strke their weary lyre,
And slumber o'er the oft-repeated strain ;
No listless youth to active grace they fire :
Here Eloquence herself might plead in vain,
Nor one of all the heartless crowd could gain :
And thou, oh ! sweeter than the Muses' song,
Affection's voice divine ! with cold disdain
Even thou art heard, while 'mid the insulting throng
Thy daunted, shivering form moves timidly along !

Thus o'er the oiled surface softly slides
The unadmitted stream, rapid it flows,
And from the impervious plain pellucid glides ;
Repulsed with gentle murmurs thus it goes,
Till in the porous earth it finds repose,
Concealed and sheltered in its parent's breast :—
Oh ! man's best treasure in this vale of woes !
Still cheer the sad, and comfort the distrest,
Nor ever be thy voice by selfishness opprest .

Psyche with languid step he leads around,
And bids her all the castle's splendour see.
Here Dissipation's constant sports abound,
While her loose hand in seeming bounty free,
Her scentless roses, painted mimicry,
Profusely sheds ; here Pride unheeded tells
To nodding crowds his ancient pedigree ;
And Folly with reiterated spells
To count her spotted cards the yawning group compels.

"See how, attentive to her subjects' ease,"
To their reluctant prey exclaims her guide,
"Each fleeting joy of life she bids them seize,
Anxious for each gay pastime to provide ;
See her fast-spreading power increasing wide,
Adored and worshipped in each splendid dome :
Lo ! Beauty glows for ever at her side,
She bids her cheek the unvarying rose assume;
And Bacchus sees for her his votive ivy bloom.

"Is aught then wanting in this fairy bower?
Or is there aught which yet thy heart can move?"
That heart, unyielding to their sovereign's power,
In gentle whispers sighing answers, "Love !"
While scornful smiles the fond reply reprove,
"Lo !" he exclaims, "thy vanquished Cupid view;
He oft with powerful arms had vainly strove
Our sovereign's rocky fortress to subdue,
Now, subject to her reign, he yields obedience due."

Wondering she gazed around, and where he points,
An idiot child in golden chains she spies,
Rich cumbrous gems load all his feeble joints,
A gaudy bandage seals his stupid eyes,
And foul Desire his short-lived torch supplies :
By the capricious hand of Fashion led,
Her sudden starts with tottering step he tries
Submissive to attend : him had she bred,
And Selfishness himself the nursling ever fed.

With lustre false his tinsel arms to deck
Ungraceful ornaments around him shone,
Gifts of his sportive guide ; she round his neck
A glittering cord insultingly had thrown,
Loading its pendent purse with many a stone
And worthless dross, and ever as he went,
His leaden darts, with wanton aim unknown,
Now here, now there, in careless chance she sent,
That oft their blunted force in empty air was spent.

Shocked, from the gross imposture Psyche turned
With horror and disgust her fearful eye;
Her fate forlorn in silent anguish mourned,
And called her knight with many a hopeless sigh.
But see, the crowds in sudden tumult fly!
The doors, fast closing to exclude some foe,
Proclaim to Psyche's hopes her hero nigh:
Escaping from her guard she flies, when lo!
His form the bursting gates in awful beauty shew.

"Fly from these dangerous walls," his page exclaims;
"Swift let us haste our floating bark to gain!
See thy knight's wondrous dart in terror flames;
Soon shall these ice-built walls no shape retain!
Nor can their Queen his dreaded sight sustain."
Scarcely she heard while rapidly she fled,
Even as a bird, escaped the wily train
The fowler with destructive art had spread,
Nor panting stays its flight, nor yet foregoes its dread.

See how astonished now the crowd supine,
Roused by his potent voice, confused arise;
In tottering masses o'er their heads decline
Dissolving walls; they gaze with wild surprise,
And each affrighted from the ruin flies:—
Pitying he views the vain unfeeling band
Beneath his care, a vile and worthless prize,
Their Queen alone his vengeful arms demand,
But unknown force was hers his terrors to withstand.

A shield she had of more than Gorgon power,
And whom she would she could transform to stone,
Nor ever had it failed her till that hour:
She proves his form invincible alone,
And calls its force petrific on her own.
Amazed he sees the indurated train,
The callous tenants of the silent throne,
And all the marble subjects of their reign,
Inviolably hard, their breathless shape retain.

The magic shield he thence in triumph bore,
Resolved, in pity to the human race,
Her noxious hands its might should guide no more,
And bade the seas conceal its Hydra face:
Oh! kindly meant, though much defeated grace!
For though the o'erwhelming weight of sounding waves
Conceal its rugged orb a little space,
Snatched by Glacella from the dark deep caves,
Once more the arm of Love with potent spell it braves.

But Psyche, rescued from their cruel scorn,
Urges her knight to hasten from the shore:
The buoyant vessel on the billows borne
Rides proudly o'er the mountain surge once more;
Again they spread the sails, the feathered oar
Skims with impatient stroke the sparkling tide;
The blushing Hymen now their smiles restore
Again to frolic gaily at their side,
Though still their playful taunts reproach their slumbering guide.

Psyche looks back with horror on the coast;
Black, drear, and desolate is all the scene:
The rocky cliffs still human shape may boast;
There the sad victims of the cruel Queen,
Memorials of her baneful power, are seen:
No vine-crowned hills, no glowing vales appear,
Nor the white cottage laughs upon the green;
The black and leafless thorn alone is there,
And the chill mountains lift their summits wild and bare.

Her spirits lighten as they leave behind
The dreary prospect of Glacella's isle;
She blest with gladdened heart the light-winged wind
That bears her swiftly from a scene so vile;
With glistening eye, and hope's prophetic smile,
She hears her knight foretel their dangers o'er,
That sure success shall crown their fated toil,
And soon arriving at that happy shore,
Love shall again be found, and leave his bride no more.

Now, from light slumbers and delicious dreams,
The jocund cry of joy aroused the fair ;
The morn that kissed her eyes with golden beams,
Bade her the universal transport share ;
Divinely breathed the aromatic air,
And Psyche's heart, half fainting with delight,
In the peculiar odour wafted there
Recalled the breezes which, o'er scenes most bright,
Their wings of perfume shook, and lingering stayed their flight.

The lovely shore the mariners descry,
And many a gladsome cheer the prospect hails ;
Its graceful hills rise full before the eye,
While eagerly expanding all their sails
They woo the freshness of the morning gales,
The approaching scenes new-opening charms display,
And Psyche's palpitating courage fails,
She sees arrived at length the important day,
Uncertain yet of power the mandate to obey.

But one dear object every wish confines, .
Her spouse is promised in that bower of rest :
And shall the sun, that now so cheerful shines,
Indeed behold her to his bosom prest,
And in his heavenly smiles of fondness blest?
Oh ! 'tis too much !—exhausted life she fears
Will struggling leave her agitated breast,
Ere to her longing eyes his form appears,
Or the soft hand of Love shall wipe away her tears.

Oh ! how impatience gains upon the soul
When the long-promised hour of joy draws near !
How slow the tardy moments seem to roll !
What spectres rise of inconsistent fear !
To the fond doubting heart its hopes appear
Too brightly fair, too sweet to realize ;
All seem but day-dreams of delight too dear !
Strange hopes and fears in painful contest rise,
While the scarce-trusted bliss seems but to cheat the eyes.

But safely anchored in the happy port,
Led by her knight the golden sands she prest:
His heart beat high, his panting breath heaved short,
And sighs proclaim his agitated breast,
By some important secret thought opprest:
"At length," he cries, "behold the fated spring!
Yon rugged cliff conceals the fountain blest,
(Dark rocks its crystal source o'ershadowing,)
And Constance swift for thee the destined urn shall bring.

He speaks, but scarce she hears, her soul intent
Surveys as in a dream each well-known scene :
Now from the pointed hills her eye she bent
Inquisitive o'er all the sloping green ;
The graceful temple meet for Beauty's queen,
The orange groves that ever blooming glow,
The silvery flood, the ambrosial air serene,
The matchless trees that fragrant shade bestow,
All speak to Psyche's soul, all seem their queen to know.

Let the vain rover, who his youth has past
Misled in idle search of happiness,
Declare, by late experience taught at last,
In all his toils he gained but weariness,
Wooed the coy goddess but to find that less
She ever grants where dearest she is bought;
She loves the sheltering bowers of home to bless,
Marks with her peaceful hand the favourite spot,
And smiles to see that Love has home his Psyche brought.

On the dear earth she kneels the turf to press,
With grateful lips and fondly streaming eyes,
"Are these the unknown bowers of Happiness?
Oh! justly called, and gained at last!" she cries,
As eagerly to seize the urn she flies.
But lo! while yet she gazed with wondering eye,
Constance ascends the steep to gain the prize ;
The eagle's eyry is not built so high
As soon she sees his star bright blazing to the sky.

With light and nimble foot the boy descends,
And lifts the urn triumphant in his hand;
Low at the turf-raised altar Psyche bends,
While her fond eyes her promised Love demand;
Close at her side her faithful guardians stand,
As thus with timid voice she pays her vows,
"Venus, fulfilled is thine adored command,
Thy voice divine the suppliant's claim allows,
The smile of favour grant, restore her heavenly spouse."

Scarce on the altar had she placed the urn,
When lo! in whispers to the ravished ear
Speaks the soft voice of Love! "Turn, Psyche, turn!
And see at last, released from every fear,
Thy spouse, thy faithful knight, thy lover here!"
From his celestial brow the helmet fell,
In joy's full glow, unveiled his charms appear,
Beaming delight and love unspeakable,
While in one rapturous glance their mingling souls they tell

Two tapers thus, with pure converging rays,
In momentary flash their beams unite,
Shedding but one inseparable blaze
Of blended radiance and effulgence bright,
Self-lost in mutual intermingling light;
Thus, in her lover's circling arms embraced,
The fainting Psyche's soul, by sudden flight,
With his its subtlest essence interlaced;
Oh! bliss too vast for thought! by words how poorly traced!

Fond youth! whom Fate hath summoned to depart,
And quit the object of thy tenderest love,
How oft in absence shall thy pensive heart
Count the sad hours which must in exile move,
And still their irksome weariness reprove;
Distance with cruel weight but loads thy chain
With every step which bids thee farther rove,
While thy reverted eye, with fruitless pain,
Shall seek the trodden path its treasure to regain.

For thee what rapturous moments are prepared !
For thee shall dawn the long-expected day !
And he who ne'er thy tender woes hath shared,
Hath never known the transport they shall pay,
To wash the memory of those woes away :
The bitter tears of absence thou must shed,
To know the bliss which tears of joy convey,
When the long hours of sad regret are fled,
And in one dear embrace thy pains compensated !

Even from afar beheld, how eagerly
With rapture thou shalt hail the loved abode !
Perhaps already, with impatient eye,
From the dear casement she hath marked thy road,
And many a sigh for thy return bestowed !
Even there she meets thy fond enamoured glance :
Thy soul with grateful tenderness o'erflowed,
Which firmly bore the hand of hard mischance,
Faints in the stronger power of joy's o'erwhelming trance.

With Psyche thou alone canst sympathise,
Thy heart benevolently shares her joy !
See her unclose her rapture-beaming eyes,
And catch that softly pleasureable sigh,
That tells unutterable ecstasy !
While hark melodious numbers through the air,
On clouds of fragrance wafted from the sky,
Their ravished souls to pious awe prepare,
And lo! the herald doves the Queen of Love declare.

With fond embrace she clasped her long-lost son,
And gracefully received his lovely bride,
"Psyche ! thou hardly hast my favour won !"
With roseate smile her heavenly parent cried,
" Yet hence thy charms immortal, deified,
With the young Joys, thy future offspring fair,
Shall bloom for ever at thy lover's side ;
All-ruling Jove's high mandate I declare,
Blest denizen of Heaven ! arise, its joys to share."

She ceased, and lo! a thousand voices, joined
In sweetest chorus, Love's high triumph sing;
There, with the Graces and the Hours entwined,
His fairy train their rosy garlands bring,
Or round their mistress sport on halcyon wing;
While she enraptured lives in his dear eye,
And drinks immortal love from that pure spring
Of never-failing full felicity,
Bathed in ambrosial showers of bliss eternally!

Dreams of delight, farewell! your charms no more
Shall gild the hours of solitary gloom!
The page remains—but can the page restore
The vanished bowers which Fancy taught to bloom?
Ah, no! her smiles no longer can illume
The path my Psyche treads no more for me:
Consigned to dark oblivion's silent tomb,
The visionary scenes no more I see,
Fast from the fading lines the vivid colours flee!

END OF PSYCHE.

INDEX.

528

INDEX.

Baker's wife, story of the, 175, 176, 180—185

Barbarus, a jealous husband, story of, 177

Bathyllus, the statue of, at Samos, 387

Brahmins, the, 388

Brundusium, 286

Byrrhæna, friend of Lucius, 24, 199

Cæcilius Statius, quoted, 251

Calchas, 368

Calpurnianus, lines to, 252

Calvus, 341

Camœna, 402

Canna, the goddess, 105

Capitolina, 310

Cappadocia, famous for slaves, 162

Carbo, 264, 314

Carthage, praises of, 389, 402

Cassandra, 368

Cassius Longinus, 346

Cato, anecdote of, 264

Catullus, quoted, 252, 257. See Lesbia.

Cenchreæ, 219

Ceres meets Psyche in her temple, 111

Chaldæan Soothsayer, a, 32

Chaldæans, the, 388

Charinus and Critias, lines to, 255

Charite, captive among the robbers, 81—83; attempts to escape with Lucius, 128; rescued by Tlepolemus, 140; her death, 149

Christianity, supposed mockeries of, 140

Chryseros, a cunning miser, 72

Cicero, 341

Circe, 27, n.

Clairvoyance, examples and theory of, 290

Clarus Sicinius, 316

Claudius Maximus, proconsul, 247, seq.

Clemens, a poet, contemporary with Apuleius, 379

Clodia, otherwise Lesbia, 256

Clypeæ, 286

Clytius, 368

Coptic enclosures, 44

Corinth, Lucius at, 208

Cornelian law, the, 163

Cornelius,

Corvinus Celer, 347

Corydon, Virgil's, 256

Crassus, Junius, a witness against Apuleius, 306

Crates, the cynic, 268, 386; lines by, 269

Creophylus, the friend of Homer, 389

Critias, lines to, 255

Crocodile, the, and its dentist, 254

Cupid and Psyche, the story of, 84—123; remarks on, 90, n., 123, n.

Curius, Manius, 264, 265

Cynics, the, 269

Cynthia, the mistress of Propertius, 256

Cyrenaic sect, 404

Cyrus, the elder, 270

Dæmons, theory of, 363, 365

Damigeron, a magician, 336

Dardanus, a magician, 336

Dedication of a ship to Isis, 234

Delia, the mistress of Tibullus, 256

Demeas, 19

Demochares, robbery of the house of, 74—79

Democritus, 274

Demosthenes, 261

Dentifrices, apology for, 252

Deucalion's flood, 289

Diana, statue of, 25

Diogenes, the cynic, 255, 269

Diomede, King of Thrace, 143

Dion, Plato's lines on, 257

Diophanes, a soothsayer, 32

Dirce, legend of, 129

Divination, 290, 356

Divorce, Roman form of, 107

Dramatic exhibition, a, 215

Dragon, adventure with a, 159

Empedocles, 274, 402

Ennius, Q., quoted, 252, 286, 352, 356

Philesietærus, a gallant, story of, 177
Philodespotus, a slave, 42
Philosophy, poverty the handmaid of, 265
Phlius, famous for vegetables, 270
Phrynondas, a magician, 336
Plania, otherwise Delia, 256
Plato, verses by, 257; theory of diseases, 297; his Basileus or king, 312; his rules respecting temples, statues, &c., 312; sundry doctrines, see God of Socrates, *passim*
Plautus quoted, 360, 369, 374, 397
Plutarch, 3
Polycletus, 379
Polycrates, tyrant of Samos, 387
Pontianus, son-in-law of Apuleius, 248, *seq.*
Portius, an amatory poet, 255
Portunus, a sea-god, 87
Poverty, praise of, 265
Proclus, quoted, 222, *n.*
Propertius the poet, 256
Prose, first written by Pherecydes, 389
Protagoras and Euathlus, their reciprocal dilemma, 399
Protaonius, 372
Psyche and Cupid, story of, 84—123; remarks on, 90, *n.*, 123, *n*; versified by Gurney, 407; Mrs. Tighe's Psyche, 431; Psyche proclaimed as a fugitive by the crier Mercury, 241
Pudens Sicinius, stepson of Apuleius, 248
—— Tannonius, advocate against Apuleius, 250, *seq.*
Pudentilla, wife of Apuleius, 247, 274; her history, 315; her letter, 329
Punic language, 344
Punishment, singular, 161; proposed to be inflicted on Charite and Lucius by the robbers, 131
Pyrgoteles, 379
Pyrrhic dance, 215

Pythagoras, 250, 278, 291; sketch of his biography, 388
Pytheas, ædile of Hypata, 20

Regulus, Attilius, 266
Robber's tales, 71; another, 136
Robbers' cave, 69: banquet, 139
—— dame, 70, 82; her death, 131
Rufinus, one of the enemies of Apuleius, 309, *seq.*

Salacia, a sea-goddess, 87
Samos, the island described, 387
Scipio Orfitus, proconsul, 395
Sea-gull, the, bottle-bearer to Venus, 107
Severianus, eulogy on, 382
Sistrum, the, described, 224, *n.*
Socrates, and the witch Meroe, story of, 5
Socrates, the philosopher, dissertation on the demon, or god of, 350, *seq.*: reflections on his undeserved fate, 218, his advice to use a mirror, 261; a saying of, 374
Solon, a voluptuous verse by, 255
Sophocles, anecdote of, 284
Statius, Cæcilius, quoted, 251
Stepmother, the wicked, 196
Syrian goddess, priests of the, 163—173

Tannonius Pudens, advocate against Apuleius, 250, *seq.*
Telephron, his tale of witchcraft, 38
Terence quoted, 369
Thales, the sage, anecdote of, 399
Theseus, father of Lucius, 20
Thrasyleon, a robber, 76
Thrasyllus, Charite, and Tlepolemus, story of, 149
Thyasus, master of Lucius, 204, 206

THE END.

LONDON: PRINTED BY WILLIAM CLOWES AND SONS, STAMFORD STREET.

1575006R0

Printed in Great Britain by Amazon.co.uk, Ltd., Marston Gate.